Memories of an Unremarkable Man

Memories of an Unremarkable Man

Neil Robins

Memories of an Unremarkable Man

Spiderwize
Office 404, 4th Floor
Albany House
324/326 Regent Street
London
W1B 3HH
UK

www.spiderwize.com

ISBN: 978-1-907294-95-2

This book is for Helena and Caroline

Helena, on the right and Caroline, Xmas 2010.

Acknowledgements

At this point in many books, the author thanks those who have helped him or her; researchers, personal assistants, legal teams, publishers, all get their due thanks. I don't have an assistant, I published the book myself and I don't have a legal team. However, grateful thanks go to Mr. Kieron Griffin as Trustee of the Mrs. H.M. Davies Will Trust, for his kind permission to reproduce the poem "Leisure" by W.H. Davies and to Joanne Moore at Spiderwize Publishing for her help and support.

There are however, certain other people that I want to mention. I have agonised for weeks about whether or not to include anyone in this section. If I mention someone in particular but not another person, would that other person be put out that he or she is not mentioned? I toyed with the idea of covering the subject by personal inscriptions inside books that I would give away, but then some people are no longer with us and I want people to know of their contribution to my life. Everybody I know whom I count as a friend is important to me, and if I could mention you all, I would, but in the end, I have decided to bite the bullet and simply get on with it.

In no particular order, thanks to members of Susie's family, notably Jane and David, Nick and Ruth, Jill and Mike (Jill sadly passed away as I came to write this section), Fiona and Carl, Christine and Kevin, for not letting me go: Bob and Helen (Helen is also now sadly deceased), who helped to pick up the pieces: Ray and Sue, who have always seen a Christian in me: Chris, Karen, Matthew, Emily, Stephen and Samantha for treating me as family, Annette and Bill, for nearly 50 years of friendship: my many friends and colleagues at the Parklangley Raquets Club, for putting up with me: Barbara and Geof, simply for being my neighbours: Christina Willis and her family, for laughing with me: Catherine and Lance, Kim, Malcolm and Elaine for trusting me and last but not least, Steve Maidment at Drifters Safaris and Heiko Genzmer at Bush Ways, for believing in me.

None of you and the many others whom I count as friends and family, will have any idea of the depth of love and gratitude I feel for you all.

Foreword

This is my book, it's about me. When I started it, I decided that it would be entirely my effort and should reflect my failings in using the English language. I have written it, read it, edited it, re-written it, re-read it, re-edited it, checked it again and again. If any are left, the spelling mistakes are mine, the grammatical mistakes are mine, the syntax errors are mine and, although I don't think I have split any infinitives, if I have, they are mine also. Legal constraints and fairness prevent me from recounting some events in detail and in these cases, the reader must draw his or her own conclusions. Some of the names have been changed in order to protect the guilty, as well as the innocent!

I am an ordinary man!

By some of today's standards of success measurement, for example, achievements in our careers, making vast sums of money, attaining celebrity status, my life could at best be described as unremarkable. When one reads in the media or sees on television, accounts of how people have suffered major illnesses all their lives, or gone through horrific and traumatic experiences such as The Holocaust, you realise just how insignificant your life can seem. In our modern world, we idolise figures for example, from the television and the sporting world, especially football. Their fame seems to be out of all proportion to what they have achieved when one compares them to someone else who has selflessly devoted their entire lives to the furtherance of, say, medical excellence, or social justice. I often wonder how a football "wunderkind" who has barely turned twenty, or celebrity 'wannabees' with an I.Q. roughly equivalent to their age, whose only discernable talent is to get themselves photographed for the media, have amassed such a wealth of life experience and memories that enables them to write their memoirs.

In my case, three major periods in my unremarkable life come immediately to mind, my scholastic achievements, my marriage and my career. In the first, five years of Grammar School education at one of the best schools in the county, ended with my achieving one GCE pass at 'O' Level, grade six Metalwork (the lowest pass possible) and one CSE Grade 1 pass in Mathematics, which actually counted as an 'O' Level pass, although I did later achieve an 'O' Level pass at English language during a day release college course. My marriage ended in divorce and my career in the Police service came to a shuddering halt upon reaching the second rung of the ladder, sergeant.

All this does not mean however, that I have been unhappy or unfulfilled; I have simply achieved other things in different areas, all of which have produced memories. Some of these memories are good, some bad, some traumatic. It is not my intention in this narrative to amuse the reader, although some incidents are just that, or to encourage a sense of sorrow; or indeed, any other emotion. Nor is it my intention to record every single memory that comes to mind, as well as making the story monumentally dull and boring, it would be quite impossible. No, I wish only to record those memories and events in my life, which for whatever reason, have remained with me all these years and some of which have helped to mould, shape, create or transform the helpless child into the capable man.

Lots of people have talked of life as a "journey" and being at the "crossroads". I honestly have no idea how long this is going to take to write and to be frank, I don't care. I am really relishing the thought of remembering my "journey" so far, and finding out whether I can rise to this self-imposed challenge and document my unremarkable life.

Chapter 1

I was born on the 9th of March 1951 at 6, Hazeldene Road, Weston-Super-Mare, Somerset: an unremarkable event, except for me and my parents of course. My sister Lynne had been born 2 years earlier at the same address on 17th March. Before we were born, both mum and dad lived in Cardiff, and dad had courted mum before the war, but, as in so many cases, they were split apart by the hostilities. When the war was nearly over, he went looking for mum and found her at her parents in Weston, where she had been waiting, hoping he would come for her. They rekindled their relationship, finding that their love for each other was as strong as it ever had been and they married in February 1945. Their love neither died nor diminished for the next 56 years.

My father's name was Ivor Vivian Robins and he was the second eldest of five children born to my grandmother, Elsie and my grandfather, William Robins. I have no knowledge of my grandfather Robins as he died before I was born. Nana Robins however, I do remember very well. Her maiden name was Lawrence and her family owned, (and still does I believe), a stately home somewhere in the Forest of Dean on the Welsh border, around Chepstow. She had at least two brothers, Cyril and Hubert, both of whom, along with her father, traded in cattle and pigs. Apparently, my great grandfather was very clever with figures, and could run his finger up a column of pounds, shillings and pence and have the exact total when he reached the top. The family was extremely adept and shrewd when it came to buying and selling livestock and my great grandfather made several fortunes in his life. Unfortunately, he was a drinking man and he lost all the family money to alcohol. For the rest of her life, and with good reason I suppose, my grandmother had an almost pathological hatred of all things connected with drink.

When she married William Robins, her family thought she had married beneath her as my grandfather was, and remained, a labourer. I really don't know if there was any real love between them; she was a very hard woman, and I think not. However, my grandmother was of the generation that simply accepted their lot in life and she got on with the job of being a dutiful wife and mother.

I don't remember much about either Cyril or Hubert, but I do remember accompanying my father on a visit to Hubert one day and being fascinated by him. He wore rough farmer's clothes, thick heavy trousers with an even thicker waistcoat, hob-nail boots and a grubby neckerchief. Hubert and my father sat and chatted in what I suppose would be the parlour where a fire was burning in the grate. Suddenly, Hubert hawked up some phlegm and spat it in the general direction of the fire, except that it didn't land in the fire. It landed on one of the bars to the fire-grate with a huge hiss. Fascinated, I decided on a closer inspection and I could see that this was a regular occurrence as there was a thick build-up of burnt spittle on just one of the bars. Evidently, he didn't miss very often.

For as long as I can remember, Nana Robins lived alone in a small terraced house at 46 Halsbury Road in the Victoria Park area of Cardiff. When we visited her, my sister and I would play all day in the sitting room or go to the park, Dad would do odd jobs for Nana or tend her small back garden and in particular, her green beans, which were legendary and grew to gigantic proportions. Mum would help Nana around the house and in the evenings, we would all gather around the radio and listen to whatever dad managed to tune it in to. Television for the masses was at least a decade away.

One of the highlights of a visit to Nana Robins was going along to the corner shop, just two doors away. It was owned and run by Mr. Moss, ably assisted by a lady named Cassie. I never knew her last name. The shop was one of the old fashioned grocers and Mr. Moss was an old fashioned gentleman. He always wore a collar and tie and always had on one of those white aprons which seemed to go all the way to the floor; always crisply starched with slight food staining. To this day, I can remember the delicious aroma of the hams and other meats he would have hanging up in the shop, or the cheeses that would be on the counter. Mr. Moss and Cassie were lovely people and both of them adored my parents and my grandmother. Whenever we went into his shop, he would make a huge fuss of us and would have something delicious to give Lynne and I.

Whilst on the subject of Cassie, I must just relate a little story about her, as I won't be mentioning her again in this narrative. My mother died in 2001. My sister had travelled over from Australia and we were sorting out mother's affairs. I had found her address book and was busy informing my mother's friends. One of the people in her book was Cassie, and when I told her about mum, Cassie asked how she had died. I said, "basically, her heart just gave out so I suppose heart failure". Cassie replied "ah! love her, bless her heart!" I'm sure she didn't really realise what she had said and I certainly didn't let on, but it did lighten my mood for a time!

My father had served in World War 2 in the Royal Navy, reaching the rank of Chief Petty Officer. He served on quite a number of ships, the most famous being the cruiser HMS Exeter. He was serving on Exeter when they were ordered, along with other ships, to seek out and engage in battle, the German Pocket Battleship Admiral Graf Spee. This culminated in the now famous Battle of the River Plate off South America. During many actions in the Second World War, it was often the men serving below decks, the enginemen, the stokers, the cooks etc, who didn't survive as the ship was often hit below the water line and sank before they could get off. In the Exeter's case, the opposite was true.

At this time dad was a Petty Officer in charge of the forward gun turret, somebody the Navy referred to as a "topman" because he served on deck. During the action, he was ordered to the rear to take charge of the "aft" gun turret and as he was making his way, the forward turret was blown to pieces by a direct hit from a Graf Spee shell.

The Graf Spee turned her mighty firing power almost fully onto Exeter's decks and gave her such a mauling that there was very little left of her above the water line. Many of dad's colleagues and friends were killed in the action, 61 in total, but dad miraculously survived and sailed with the ship down to the Falkland Islands for emergency repairs and some well earned "r and r". A couple of years before he died, the Imperial War Museum in London contacted him and asked if he would make a tape recording of his personal memories of The Battle of the River Plate. By this time, many other survivors of the action had passed away, and so dad agreed. With his wonderful lilting Welsh accent, he produced a very emotive account of an epic sea battle, a battle which has been firmly cemented into the annals of Naval History; something the British nation seem naturally to empathise with. The tape is still there to this day.

Although he was happy to talk generally about the war and life at sea, like many of his wartime contemporaries, dad never spoke much about what he did during the war. However, years later when I was living in London, he and mum came up for a visit and he asked if my wife and I would take him to the cruiser HMS Belfast, moored permanently in the Pool of London. I didn't realise it at the time, but the Belfast is a sister ship to the Exeter and would be configured in the same way as regards her gunnery. We went on board and as with other tourists, were left simply to wander around inspecting the ship. Ship's gunnery was dad's forte and he began to become immersed in his wartime duties. He had been a teacher for many years by this time and the two activities seemed to merge. As we made our way around the ship, as well as other things, he was explaining how each gun emplacement worked; its calibre, the rate of fire, how it altered its angle of fire etc. Even after all those years, his knowledge was encyclopaedic. After a little while, I noticed that a few other people seemed to be following us around. This number began to swell as we progressed and then I realised what was happening.

There was no official guide to ask, and nobody on board that ship that day could explain the workings of the guns as dad could and these people had simply latched on to someone who had actually fought a Naval action, someone who could describe the terror he felt, the noise, the smell, the sheer helplessness of an ocean sprat being gobbled up by a shark. Eventually, quite a little crowd had formed around dad. They were asking him questions about the action and the guns, he was replying with gusto and of course, he was teaching. He loved it, and I remember being immensely proud of him.

After the Exeter, he was posted to other ships, one of which was HMS Belvoir. On board this ship, dad was engaged in the Sicily Landings, during which he was awarded the Distinguished Service Medal for Gallantry. Occasionally, I would ask how he won the medal, and all he would say was that "loads of people got it", or that, "I was just doing my job". It is one of my most sincere regrets in my life that, before he died, I didn't find out just why he was decorated. I would have loved to have talked with him about it. Since his death in 1991, I have tried to go through the old War Office, now the Ministry of Defence to inspect his citation. I was told that unfortunately, there had been a fire some years earlier, and dad's personal record, along with many others had been destroyed. No copies were kept.

My mother's name was Esther Lilian Lewis, and she was the eldest of two children born to my grandparents Alexander and Lily Lewis. In almost complete contrast to my other set of grandparents, I did know and adore my grandpa Alex. (as he was known) and absolutely hated my grandmother. She was an awful woman and apparently, she treated my grandfather appallingly.

Most of the contact I had with her was when I was still very young and the family was still living in and around Weston-Super-Mare. Being that young, I didn't really understand my intense dislike of her. All I knew really was that, although she was my mother's mother, I never looked forward to seeing her and was really scared to be in her presence. She was a bullying and domineering woman who never showed me any familial love whatsoever. I always got the impression that she would far rather not have me around and I suppose this is the reason I spent most of my time with my grandfather.

Just to give an impression of what she was capable of, my mother told me once that before I had been born, she was out walking in Weston with my sister Lynne in her push-chair. There had been some sort of argument between my mother and her mother. As she was walking along the pavement, my mother saw Nana Lewis on the same pavement coming towards her. My mother smiled at Nana in an effort of reconciliation, but she, upon seeing my mother, immediately crossed the road to the other pavement and carried on walking, completely ignoring my mother and her first grandchild. They were reconciled later of course, but my mother never forgot this and I suspect, never forgave her for it.

When she married my grandfather, her name changed to Lewis. Her maiden name however, was Meakin and she was apparently descended from the Meakin pottery family. Meakin Pottery never achieved the prominence of Royal Doulton or other famous names, but used to produce pottery for more general use. It was eventually swallowed up by one of the larger conglomerates and no longer exists.

My grandparents lived at 29 Ashcombe Road in Weston, a large mid-terraced house on, if I remember correctly, about four levels excluding the half-landings. There were two sitting rooms, one at the rear and the other at the front. Granddad always used to sit in the front room in an old red leather armchair. As my grandmother spent most of her time in the kitchen at the very back of the house, this was probably the spot which was furthest away from her, which suited me admirably. Granddad and I would play games in the front room or he would read to me or we would go out for a walk to the seafront. Looking back on it, I'm sure he realised at a very early stage, the dislike that existed between my grandmother and me and went out of his way to try and protect me from it. If I was not with him at the house, I would pester my mother to take me to see him at his work. He operated the petrol pumps at a local garage called Jack Pruen's.

Compared to the modern and high-tech. petrol pumps of today, these pumps were very old fashioned and odd looking. There was a huge length of red coloured hosepiping, which had to be supported by a metal framework capable of swinging around in an arc of about 180 degrees. From the delivery nozzle, the hose would go up and back over the forecourt to the wall and then down to the pump itself, which stood about six feet high and had a glass bowl on top with the word "SHELL" etched into it. Today of course, petrol stations are everywhere, but back in those days when cars were few and far between and petrol stations even more scarce, this was fascinating territory for a small boy. It didn't matter how many times I went to Pruen's garage to see granddad, he always took me on a tour to show me the workshops and the one or two cars that were for sale in the tiny showroom.

For all my grandmother's faults, she really was a marvellous host at Christmas time. It was the one time of the year when I really didn't mind being in her company, probably because there were so many other family members around. Being as the house in Ashcombe Road was large with many bedrooms, several members of the family descended on her and my grandfather for the festive period. My sister and I used to look forward to this holiday, not only for all the presents we used to receive, but also because we could get together with my four female cousins, all daughters of my mother's only sister, Irene. Auntie Rene had married a man named Frank Whalen, who at that time was still serving in the Royal Air Force as a Flight Sergeant. We didn't get to see too much of them as Uncle Frank was often serving abroad, his last posting being in Singapore. They had four daughters, Ginnie, Catherine, Julie and Jackie. Jackie was actually one of twins, but the other sadly died shortly after birth due to heart problems, and Jackie had been born quite a few years after her sisters. Consequently, she was much younger that the rest of us, and didn't really join in the fun we used to have. All my granddad's sisters used to come and stay and, of course, all their respective husbands.

Out of all of them, only my Auntie Nan was not married and never had been. She was what was called in those days, a Ladies Maid, and she worked for the Beaverbrook family (owners of The Daily Express) in London, looking after Lady Beaverbrook. Auntie Nan was the character of the bunch, always joking that the only thing she really wanted, was a man! As far as any of us was ever aware, this had never happened and I was never ever sure, even years later, whether she really meant it; but she did tell the most wonderful and funny stories of her life in service. It turned out that she had even been invited by The Queen Mother to work in her royal household. Auntie Nan turned the offer down as she thought the Queen Mother needed somebody younger.

Amongst all the other relatives were a strange couple, Uncle Reg and Auntie Eve. In complete contrast to Auntie Nan, these two beauties were very serious in outlook, intensely religious and formed the butt of many a joke between us children. Very regrettable I know, but we were just kids! One of the annual activities of the adults was to go along to the local pub, The Ashcombe, just down the road, on Christmas Eve, never accompanied, of course by Eve and Reg, who were absolute tee-totallers; they hated the demon drink. They would be tucked up in bed by about 10pm as Reg had a very important job to perform every morning at around 6am.

All of us children were much too excited to sleep of course on Christmas Eve, and I remember hearing the adults return at about midnight, all trying desperately hard, and failing quite spectacularly, to be quiet lest they disturb us, or Eve and Reg. They would all be whispering to each other, and then one would say something funny, usually Auntie Nan, and there would be a burst of laughter, followed by frenzied attempts to shut each other up. They would then probably play cards for an hour or two before deciding that the children were all completely asleep, and creeping upstairs to place our presents in our pillowcases. It was a ritual, which occurred every year, and every year we never were asleep when they came in. Eventually, they would all go to bed. Enter, Uncle Reg! He would get up at around 5am every morning, including Christmas Day just to make all the adults a delicious cup of tea. Just why he thought that everyone else should be up and about and drinking tea at the same time he was, remained a complete mystery. All the others had only been in bed for a few hours before that dreaded knock on the door. Lynne and I slept in the room next to mum and dad and I used to hear Uncle Reg coming up the stairs, and knock softly on the door to my parents' room. He would say in his broad Dorset accent, " 'mornin' Ivor, Esther. Your tea's outside here on the landing." I could never make out my dad's reply, probably because it was just a grunt from under the covers. Out of loyalty, one of them would get up, take the tray inside and make out as though this was going to be the highlight of their day. When Reg had finished the tea round, he would go downstairs and start to wash all the dishes in the sink and clear up the glasses left strewn around the living room. However, for all their seemingly strange ways, there was not an ounce of badness or malice in either of them and had only love in their hearts for everyone. They were good people and I shall remember them as such.

One of the highlights at Christmas for me, my sister Lynne and our three older cousins, Ginnie, Catherine and Julie, was the production of our annual tape recorded concert. Dad always borrowed his school's reel-to-reel tape recorder. I don't remember seeing one of these old fashioned machines in recent times, but for us of course, it was the latest in technology. Personal computers hadn't been invented, much less DVD players or personal stereos. We would spend around a week at Nana Lewis' house and for much of that time, we hid ourselves away in various bedrooms, working on our production.

In those days, radio was the most popular medium for the masses, in fact, apart from newspapers, it was the only medium. Radio programmes like Round the Horn, The Navy Lark, The Clitheroe Kid and The Al Read Show were all favourites in many families, and it was from programmes such as these that we obtained most of our ideas. It would start off with one of us having an idea for a sketch, progress with choosing who should play the characters, having endless rehearsals and finally, recording the finished sketch onto the tape. We invented so many different characters, voices and situations, making up the dialogue as we went along. When the recording was finally finished, we would get all the adults into one room and play the tape, which probably didn't last more than about 30 minutes, but which had taken us all week to produce. We tried really hard to make our parents and the other adults laugh, but whether they did or not, it was our production and the fun we had doing it was priceless in those austere days. Lynne and I only used to do these plays with these three cousins, we never did anything like it with any of our relatives on dad's side. Maybe this has something to do with the fact that, even today, I am in close contact with Auntie Rene, Ginnie, Catherine and Julie, but only one of my eight cousins on dad's side, Geofrey, Uncle Mostyn's second son. We deemed my youngest cousin Jackie to be too young to engage in our thespian activities, we were far too mature for her!!

After the war, my father had ended his service as a gunnery instructor, a subject he absolutely adored. He would have stayed on active service, but his eyesight had deteriorated, and he was de-mobbed in May 1946. He had discovered a talent for teaching, and so went on a one year emergency crash course for teachers, finally qualifying, following a two year probationary period in 1950. My father's choice of post-war career was to have a profound effect on my future development.

Chapter 2

My very earliest memory is at the age of around three. My parents had enrolled me in some sort of play school in Weston Super Mare. I remember there were quite a few other children there, and one day I remember all of us skipping gaily around the hall in an endless stream, all chattering and laughing. I was partnered up with some girl, whose name and features totally escape me. We were having so much fun, I inadvertently strayed too far into a corner and collided full tilt with a large table. My momentum seemed to carry me onto the table and then, just as quickly, off it and onto the floor. I didn't really have a clue what was happening and I landed on the other side of the table, on my chin, which split open in a very neat, straight little cut. I was of course, taken straight to the local hospital, where after a little stitching but not much screaming, I was awarded a box of Cadburys Chocolate Fingers for my trouble, a rare treat for those days.

In 1954, my father obtained a new teaching post at Winscombe Primary School in Somerset, and the family moved to the village and into what I remember as a large flat on the ground floor of a large house. The actual layout of the flat, I don't remember, except that it had a trap door to a cellar, which my sister managed to fall into one day. My days were taken up with all those things that any three year old does, shopping with mum, playing in the garden, getting under her feet in the flat. There were obviously very few cars on the road in those days, and I would very happily ride my three-wheeled tricycle endlessly around the village streets. The highlight of my day though, was to go and wait outside the school for dad to finish lessons and then we would go home together. On many occasions I used to see the pupils sitting on the windowsills of one the classrooms. Of course, I had no idea what was going on, and it was years later that I learned from mum that dad used to get all the pupils into his class and tell them stories about life at sea. My father had one of those wonderfully resonant voices, which it was impossible not to listen to. My memories of Winscombe are very few, and two years later, I started school at Bourneville Primary School in Weston.

In 1956, we moved from the rented flat in Winscombe into our own house at 79 Sunnyside Road in Weston-Super-Mare. It was a semi-detached house built of that wonderful grey/white stone, which was and still is, quarried locally. I remember it had a ground, first and second floor, an outside toilet at the back as well as one indoors, a workshop attached to the rear of the house and a garden which stretched down to a lane running along the back and up the side of our neighbour's house.

At around the same time, I had my first experience of actually staying in a hospital. I can't remember the actual illness I had, although I fancy it was Scarlet Fever. No matter, having described the following event to a dear friend of mine in the medical field, she wonders how it didn't scar me for life. Maybe it did! I was on a children's ward and my abiding memory of the nursing staff is being scared to death of them! They wore those big full length white uniforms with massive white hats which fell down their backs, almost to the waist. Very prim, very proper and very scary, they stood for no messing about. The part I had come to hate, and which I remember the most, was when the nurse appeared with *the enamel jug and funnel*!! I knew what she was about to do. And she did it about three times a day! Of course, I had no inkling what she was doing it for, only that I had to adopt a certain position and that it was about to cause a deal of discomfort. I knew the position well and can remember it to this day. I had to strip off my pyjama bottoms and kneel on my bed on all fours with my bottom angled upwards. She then proceeded to insert the funnel deep into my anus and pour some kind of liquid into my bottom. It seemed to last an eternity, and I was so confused and embarrassed about it, for years I never spoke of it to anyone. I was of course, being given an enema. I suppose it worked, I don't remember. What I do remember though quite vividly, is that I suddenly gained the curious ability to suck air into my bottom and break wind at will, an engaging talent for a five year old boy!

Along with our neighbours, the Parker family, the two houses were the first, and also I suppose the last houses on our side of the road. Next to the Parker's house was an open piece of land, which was adjacent to the main road to the seafront. The house fronted onto a very quiet residential road and along the back of the house, ran the main railway line down to the South West of England.

I was never totally absorbed or fascinated by the steam trains which ran up and down the railway all day long. To many a small boy, this would be probably be a dream come true, but for me, it seemed to be only a passing interest, literally, something which caused great excitement for me when an express thundered past the bottom of the house, but when it had gone, so had the interest.

I was much more interested in crossing the fence onto the railway embankment, from which my father had strictly forbidden me. There was another family in the road with young sons around my age, Bernard and Christopher Chapel, and the three of us were often to be found on the forbidden territory playing something like cowboys and indians, although not anywhere near where dad might see us, far too risky. We would be somewhere on the embankment or at the train station all day long. One of our favourite games was at the end of one of the platforms at Weston's station. We would each have a penny coin and we would place it on the railway line. We then waited for a train to run over the penny with its massive drive wheels and the game was to see whose penny had been flattened and stretched out the most. Dull by today's standards I know, but that was what we had in those days.

I was only caught once on the railway line and then it was only because my sister snitched on me to dad. Myself and the Chappel boys were dangerously close to my house, having made our way up the railway line from the station. We concealed ourselves under the bridge, which carried the seafront road and which was adjacent to the open land next to the Parker house, checking to see if the coast was clear. We were intending to go past my house and on to the Chappel boys' house, where we could cross back over the fence into safe territory. All we really had to do was climb back through the fence onto the "safe" side, but that was far too easy! We were small boys looking for any type of adventure. Having established that there seemed to be no movement coming from the vicinity of my house or garden, we began to creep along the very edge of the railway line, just where the bedding stones spill out onto the ground. We were on the far side of the line when suddenly, my sister came down the lane on her bicycle. All three of us immediately hit the deck and we stayed there for what seemed like an eternity. Eventually, I looked up to see Lynne just going through the gate into the back garden. She seemed not to have seen us, but looking around, I saw a massive passenger express train approaching us fast from behind. We had been so absorbed by not letting Lynne see us, I hadn't heard the clatter of the train approaching. The whistle was blowing out an urgent warning to us to stay exactly where we were. The train driver must have been terrified we would suddenly panic and try to cross in front of the train with unthinkable consequences. However, I was only thinking of not being seen. If we moved, Lynne would see us for sure and I would be reported to dad. There was no alternative but to lay flat on the ground, which shook and trembled as the train thundered deafeningly past where we were lying, not three feet away from the massive undercarriage. When the train had gone past, I looked up and saw that Lynne had gone indoors. We quickly got to our feet and carried on alongside the track to opposite the Chapel's house, crossed back over the lines, climbed over the fence and began to play some game in Sunnyside Road.

A few minutes later, I saw my sister approaching from a long way away and I just knew what she was going to say. She never joined in our games, and I began to get a distinct sinking feeling. "Neil" she sneered, "daddy wants you in the house right now." There was no doubt in my mind what would happen when I got indoors and faced him. "Have you been on the railway line?" he demanded. When I said I had, he literally put me across his knee and gave me a thrashing on my buttocks with his leather belt.

I had never received punishment like that before. The most it had ever been was a clip around the ear, (like the time he clipped me at Sunday lunch and my face went into my gravy.) This was different, it really hurt and I was confused. When he finished strapping me, he waited till I had all but stopped crying and then told me why he had done it. Partly, he said because the railway line was a dangerous place for carefree kids like us, but mostly he said, because I had disobeyed him. My parents were not violent by any means, although I appreciate that any form of physical punishment constitutes violence. They used the smack punitively and on this occasion, I think my father reacted out of sheer fear for what might have happened to me. Lynne had obviously told him how close it had been with the train and it scared him. I never went back through the fence.

On a lighter note, I think this would be a good place to introduce the Davies family from Wales. Harold Davies had been dad's boyhood friend from Cardiff. They grew up together and had been best-man at each other's wedding. Uncle Harold, as I called him was a builder by trade with a special talent for working with wood. Although I don't remember the occasion, one of dad's favourite tales about Harold was when mum and dad mentioned to him that they needed a new bannister rail for the house in Sunnyside Road. This was no ordinary banister. The rail went up three flights of stairs and snaked around two landings and dad asked Harold how he should do it. Harold of course, would have none of it. He crossed the Severn Estuary by the White Funnel Steamer and came to the house. He only brought a rule, a plumb-line, pencil and paper with him. Harold stood at the top landing and dropped the plumb-line from the ceiling, all the way to the floor through the gap between the flights of stairs. From the plumb-line, he took various measurements, made a few sketches and then went home to Cardiff. A few weeks later, dad met him off the steamer with the new bannister rail in various lengths, some of which were around 15 feet. The rail was too heavy to carry all the way to the house which was about three miles away from the steamer pier and too long to fit into any car.

They solved the problem by approaching the conductor of one of the open top buses operating in Weston. Dad bought a ticket for every seat on the top deck and then Harold passed all the sections of bannister up to him from the side of the bus. The route for this particular bus took it to within a very short distance from the house. When it arrived at the nearest stop, Harold enlisted the help of the conductor and most of the other passengers to get the bannister off the bus and onto the ground, from where they managed to get it to the house themselves. Harold had constructed the bannister so that the various sections would simply slot together once in position around the stairs. It all fitted absolutely perfectly. From a few simple sketches and some accurate measuring, Harold had made this bannister without the benefit of being able to constantly check the fit or the accuracy of his measurements; he had made it about 50 miles away from where it was intended to be, and it fitted.

Uncle Harold was an old fashioned craftsmen and this was definitely one of the reasons why he and my father loved each other so much. They both had the same perfectionist ideas. All my life, dad had drummed various sayings into me; "if a job's worth doing, it's worth doing well", or "if it's perfect, then it's OK", and I have to say that if I'm glad he taught me one thing, it would be, to do a job to the best of my ability.

Harold and Winnie had four daughters, Julie, Pauline, Margaret and Barbara and one son, Victor. Like my father and Harold, Victor and I remain firm friends to this day, although not perhaps to the intensity of the friendship between our fathers. I'm quite sure that the Davies family will pop up again in this story.

Dad was a great believer in at least trying to do things for oneself, so when I approached him to make me a cart, he replied naturally that I should try and do it myself. I did and, naturally, I failed. I was only about seven years old and didn't have too much in the way of engineering experience. However, my father had insisted that I give it a go. I nailed two large pram wheels I had purloined off a rubbish tip onto the edge of a plank of wood, intending these to be the back wheels and then nailed the two front wheels onto a separate piece of wood, which was then in turn, nailed through the centre of the main plank. This was supposed to be the steering bogey; simple! I had used fairly large nails and the edge of the plank was about ¾" thick. It had the appearance of a modern-day drag racer!

The first time I got onto it, it all held together. It was still holding together when I set off down the hill our house was situated on. It was still holding together as I rapidly picked up speed and tore into the turn into the lane alongside the house, then nothing was holding together. It all collapsed in a spectacular heap. The nails had of course, simply ripped out of the edge of the wood. Crestfallen, I went into dad, who had been waiting for it all to collapse and who then patiently explained why. He explained about weight distribution, about the need for some kind of chassis. He explained turning moments and leverage, and then I understood why he had made me do it myself. Unless I was an absolute mechanical genius, he knew that whatever I constructed wasn't going to work. He also knew that relating my efforts to his explanations would make me understand better. It was a good lesson and to this day, I will at least try and do something myself before admitting defeat and calling in an expert.

Dad then set about making me a cart, and what a cart it was! It had proper axles instead of 6" nails, the front axle was attached to a framework which was in turn bolted through the centre of the chassis. It had a steering rope attached to either end of the front bogey enabling me to turn it whilst sitting down. However, my preferred option was to kneel on the centre plank and hold the two ends of the bogey in my hands. That way, I got a better 'feel' for making turns. It never occurred to me just how dangerous this method was for me; it just felt better. I remember being so proud of my cart, I would turn it upside down at the drop of a hat to show anyone who was interested, the quality of the construction. I had many a happy hour careering down the hill from the railway bridge, round the corner into Sunnyside Road and eventually tearing into the lane. The goal I always set myself was to complete the trip without putting either foot down to slow the cart down and to get as far down the lane as possible before coming to a natural halt, or falling off.

At the end of summer 1956, I started school properly. At this time, Dad had gained a promotion and was deputy headmaster at the local primary school, Bourneville. The school was situated right in the middle of a massive council housing estate, and is still there to this day. I spent my first day in tears. Dad had taken me of course, and then, in my mind simply abandoned me. I have one or two memories of Bourneville; one of them being known as the deputy heads' son and having to withstand some pretty nasty jibes from the other kids, and another, falling head over heels in love with Pamela Bath. She was older than I was, heaven only knows by how many years and I thought she was just beautiful. During assembly, she used to sing in the choir at the front, and wherever I was standing during assembly, I would always try and look at her, and one day, joy of joys, I actually saw her looking at me. During the break-times I would go and try and find her and join in the games she would be playing with her friends. However, I remember on one occasion getting involved in some rough and tumble with Pamela and her friends, being held down on the ground by one of her male friends and a girl snarling at me to go away as I was not welcome. Our relationship was never the same after that! I suppose it was my first dumping!

It was whilst we were living in Weston, that mum and dad bought our first car. It was an Austin 10, registration number EJ6379 and black in colour, as that was all that was available in those days. The seats were crinkly old brown leather and the front passenger and driver's doors opened from front to back instead of the modern way. I don't really know why the system changed with more modern cars, but it seemed to me to be much easier to get in and out of the car with the doors opening as they did on the Austin; you sort of slid into the seat rather than manouvering yourself into the space. The one major drawback with the car was that it lacked a heater. Coming back from a trip to Cardiff, I distinctly remember having to bounce up and down on the back seats to stay even remotely warm, despite being wrapped up in a blanket. By today's high-tech. standards, it was a dinosaur of a car, but we were proud of it and of course lucky to even have a car in those austere post-war years

An event which I shall certainly never forget was when my mother accidentally scolded me with boiling water. It happened on a Sunday, and I used to love Sundays, although not for any religious reasons. I don't remember attending church on a regular or even frequent basis until a few years later. No! I loved Sundays because that's when mum used to serve the tea at around 4pm with boiled egg sandwiches. Sunday afternoon tea was a ritual in our house and almost constituted a meal in itself. My mother was a great cook and made some wonderful cakes, but for me, her boiled egg sandwiches were simply out of this world. Along with the rest of the tea, she used to time boiling the eggs to perfection, taking them out of the water just when the yolk turns from runny to slightly thick and then spreading them over fresh bread with lots of butter and salt. They were always served up warm and were absolutely delicious! However, I digress.

This particular Sunday, it had been a hot day and we were experiencing a terrific rain storm with lightning and thunder directly overhead. The rain seemed to be coming down in almost solid sheets and mum had opened the back door a little to watch the rain. (I often wonder why we humans are so fascinated by water and fire. I can sit for hours and watch a fire burning or waves coming on to a sea-shore.) She was watching the storm outside as she was boiling the kettle for the tea, and she then poured the water into a large jug, which would be placed on the table in order to replenish the teapot. She was at the door, looking outside when, unbeknown to her, I had come up behind her and was looking out at the rain around the side of her skirt. She turned to come back into the room and stumbled over me, pouring the entire contents of the jug of boiling water over my left shoulder and down my back. As it had been so hot, I had not yet put a shirt on for tea, so my flesh was bare. Boy, did I hop around! I was in so much pain, I was bouncing around the room like a ball in a pin-ball machine, I was screaming with pain. My scalded flesh turned a vivid red and blistered almost immediately.

Later, I had extensive scabbing over my left shoulder blade and back, which I proudly showed to anyone who happened to ask what had happened. The scabbing eventually turned to a livid white scar. It has faded over time, but the memory of the pain is still as fresh as those egg sandwiches.

I spent three years at Bourneville School, up till the age of eight, when dad once again gained promotion and was appointed as headmaster of a small Church of England school in Mark, a farming village about 10 miles outside Weston. As a leaving present, Mrs. Parker from next door gave Lynne and I a china mug each. Lynne's was red on the inside and mine was yellow. I think Lynne still has hers and although repaired a few times, mine survived right up to 2001, 42 years, when, after the death of my mother, it was accidentally thrown in the bin.

In 1959, we moved out to Mark.

animals. Today, although I enjoy eating meat, I am totally opposed to blood sports, or killing animals for sport or killing simply for the sake of it. That is not to say that I don't understand the need for animal-number control in certain places such as Africa, but just killing an animal to be able to boast about the fact to friends is abhorrent.

My mother demonstrated a fairly ruthless streak with animals. At the far end of the wood yard, dad had cleared a small area and built a rabbit-run. We had two rabbits, and later on, we added a couple of guinea pigs. They seemed to live together quite happily, until one day, the female guinea pig produced a litter of young. Lynne and I were very excited and paid regular visits to see them. They were absolutely tiny, about 5cms long. One day, I noticed that one of them was not walking properly and was dragging its back legs behind it. I took it to mum and she thought that one of rabbits had inadvertently trodden on it and broken its legs. It was clearly in distress. She took it from me telling me that she would "look after it" and sent me back down to the run to check on the others. A little while later, I went back up to the house and found a bucket with a piece of wood sitting on the top. Not realising what was happening and being naturally curious, I lifted the piece of wood off the bucket and saw the baby guinea pig floating in the water; mum had drowned it. I remember being quite shocked at the sight of the poor little thing, and not a little angry with mum. I realise now of course, she was putting it out of its misery, but I still have to wonder whether drowning it was the best way. Of course, if I had still had my gun, I could have shot it and buried it alongside the swallow!

Mr. Gregory's wood yard also witnessed the maiden, and at the same time, final voyage of the first and probably only land-yacht ever to be constructed and sailed in Mark. It was of course, my old soap cart, modified with a crude sail. Having become bored, and not a little weary of continually pushing myself along with one leg in order to get anywhere, I mentioned to dad how great it would be to have a land-yacht, such as the one I had seen in a boy's magazine. What I had seen was the real thing with a proper mast, sail and "sheets", (sailing term for ropes). Dad however, thought he could do something with the old cart, and together we set about converting it. All we did really, was to fix a long piece of wood vertically at the front, which acted as a mast, attach a second length of wood horizontally at the top of the mast to act as a boom, and then tie on an old bed sheet to the boom to act as a sail. Everything was rigid and the sail was square on to the cart. At the bottom corners of the sail, dad had attached the ropes, which were secured to the rear of the cart to keep the sail from flapping around too much. Soon, everything was ready and all we needed was a windy day.

The wood yard was roughly square in shape. Just behind the house, between it and where the wood was stored, was a clear track where the lorries came and went. It stretched from one side of the yard to the other, was about 50 metres in length and made up entirely of stones, both large and small. It was free from obstructions though, with the exception that the far end of the track, was where the lorry for delivering the paraffin was always parked.

"Cometh the hour, cometh the man"!!!

The great day dawned and everyone, including Mr. and Mrs. Gregory was on hand to watch. I remember it really was quite windy, and dad had forbidden the use of the yacht on the road outside; an eminently sensible though highly frustrating attitude! It wasn't as if cars were streaming past the house. It was busy if one car every five or ten minutes went past! However, I was to use the lorry track from one side to the other, which would take me past the watching crowd, all eagerly waiting for the action. In order to prevent the cart from careering off on its own, dad had loosened the ropes to allow the sail to flap free and weighted the whole thing down with a massive piece of timber on the board where I would sit. I heaved off the piece of timber, sat on the cart and looked around the sail to make sure I would be going in the right direction. I then pulled the sail ropes taught, allowing the wind to fill the sail, knowing full well that from that moment on, there would be no turning back, or indeed, as I was to find out very quickly, no turning of any kind. The wind instantly rammed into the sail when I pulled the ropes and the cart simply shot off across the yard, with me holding on for grim death. I sped past the howling crowd like a rocket! I had expected to be able to wave cheerily at my admirers. Instead, everything was rushing past me and with the solid wheels of the cart rattling madly over the stoney track, my eyes were bouncing in their sockets, practically blinding me!

Now, I knew that the paraffin lorry was parked in its normal bay and I also knew that I was heading for it at a great rate of knots, far faster than I had ever anticipated. Even so, I figured that I could simply turn the front wheels so that I would avoid the lorry and stop at the far end where there was a natural ditch in the ground.

I suppose you could say that having the sail square-on to the cart was a fairly basic design fault as it totally prevented me from having any forward vision. Consequently, although I knew I was heading for the lorry, covering the ground at such a huge speed meant I had no idea just how close I was to it until it was too late. I crashed into the very solid steel front bumper of the Thames Trader lorry. The mast snapped in two like a toothpick, which in turn snapped the boom. The sail, mast, boom and ropes came down in a heap and because I was still going forward, simply enshrouded me completely. The cart carried on going and I ended up lying along the length of the cart with my head hanging over the rear end, my legs and body, along with practically the entire cart under the front of the lorry and the mast, boom and sail in bits all around me.

When I was finally dragged out from underneath the front bumper, which of course didn't even have a scratch on it, the yacht including its intrepid driver, was in a very sorry state. I say "finally", because all the adults watching were unable to move initially owing to them holding their sides with laughter. Eventually, one of them, kindly decided that I should be extricated from the mess. The cart was irreparably damaged, which was just as well really, as I think by that stage, I had practically outgrown it and besides, mum had bought me a bicycle which would have consigned the cart to the scrap-heap anyway. In the event though, it had gone out in a blaze of glory!

When I did play with other kids from the village, we used to have an awful lot of fun. There is much reporting in the media of today about the dangers faced by youngsters out playing and unsupervised by adults. Comparisons are always being made between now and 30 to 40 years ago, when we seemed to live in a more innocent age. I don't know whether there was less danger then or more media coverage now, but we would go off all day long on our bicycles, across the moors, or walking for miles across fields, playing at imaginary soldiers having to ford raging torrents (actually an irrigation channel with almost stagnant water called a "rhyne"). Our parents knew we had gone, but probably not where. I won't say they never used to worry about us, but they never stopped us, or made us play within their sight and hearing. We did seem to live in a society where children developed their skills and knowledge base from experiences and free from intrusive adult supervision.

It was in Mark that I first learned how scared I am of heights. Having climbed up a trellis on the outside of a local farmer's barn, I suddenly became absolutely terrified, and couldn't go up or down. Eventually, one of the older kids had to come up and rescue me. In Mark, I learned how to kill trees by ring-barking them. Dad had given us a lesson at school on the way early man had made dug-out canoes from tree trunks. I had found myself such a trunk in a nearby apple orchard and set about hollowing it out, just as they had done, using only an axe and fire, (helped along by a bit of paraffin from Mr. Gregory). At one stage, I got a little bored and took the axe to four apple trees in the orchard where I was working. I completely stripped the bark around the circumference of the trees, effectively killing them. The owner of the trees however, was very understanding, realising that I had absolutely no idea what I was doing. I found out how rope burns when passed quickly over human skin. I got myself caught in a rope trapeze we had set up in a friend's open barn. I was swinging on a separate length of rope around a corner of stacked hay bales, and my neck caught the trapeze about half way up. I then slid down to the crook in the rope, where my neck was suddenly flicked back and I fell about 15 feet into the hay beneath. I had a nice rope burn around my neck for weeks, and very proud of it I was as well! I found out just how much brambles hurt when I was trying to ride my bike "no-hands", lost control and pitched headlong into a ditch, empty of water, but overgrown with brambles. Luckily, a farmer trundling along on his tractor had seen me go in, and pulled me out, bruised and bloodied. In the lambing season, I helped out on a local farm and watched lambs being born and how the ewe cared for them immediately.

At one stage, about four of us boys each had a pet rook. The toughest boy in the village, Graham Fisher scaled a tree right up to the top-most branches where the nests were, and threw down four fledglings, which we picked up and took to Jack Phippen's barn. Jack's parents owned the manor house and had numerous outbuildings where we built nests for these birds, and tried to raise them with worms and warm milk. Three of them, unsurprisingly, died very quickly, but the fourth survived for weeks. This was David's rook and he'd named it Willoughby. Somehow, Willoughby survived long enough to be almost fully grown. David was heartbroken when it was eventually claimed by dozens of rooks besieging the barn one day and making an almighty racket. Up to that point, David could actually call Willoughby and have it sit on his hand.

I had my first fist fight in Mark, with a boy called Paddy Carey. He lived at the western end of Mark, in fact just inside the next village, Watchett. I have no idea what we fought about, but I remember meeting him at a pre-arranged time in a field. There were three or four other youths around, although none were with me. We got started with Paddy doing a little bit of boxing dancing, trying to put the odd jab in here and there, moving smartly out of the way of a counter attack. I remember looking at him and thinking, "what *is* he doing?" I got fed up then and simply launched myself at him and took him to the ground, where we had a good old fashioned roll around with head locks and fists flailing. I remember none of the other youths got involved in any way, other than to shout encouragement at Paddy. No-one shouted for me, and I distinctly remember wondering why. I hadn't done anything to any of them; I hadn't said anything to them or hurt them in any way. It seemed so unfair for none of them to be on my side when I hadn't done anything wrong. The following Sunday, I couldn't resist a little smirk to myself. Although I hated it, my dad made me sing in the church choir every Sunday morning and evening. On the Sunday following the Big Fight, I came out of the Vestry, in the usual procession to the altar and looked across to where Paddy usually sat with his parents. I saw him sitting there and at the same moment, he looked around at me. I say "looked"; it was more of a malevolent stare, and then only with the one eye which wasn't completely blacked and closed. As I had absolutely no injuries at all, I silently claimed my victory and then got on with singing praises to God! Good old God!

I had numerous fights when I was a boy, some of them simply because I was my father's son. I remember having one fight at Mark school with a boy called Francis Burns, which started during the morning break in the play-ground, halted for lunch, recommenced after lunch, halted for afternoon school, recommenced during the afternoon break, and finally halted for the day at the end of school, with a promise from both of us to re-start in the morning. We didn't, because Mr. Burns came to the school and complained to dad, who sorted out the issue by making us shake hands in front of the whole class. The point I am making here is that no-one else ever got involved. It was only ever between the two antagonists, unlike today, where it would not be unusual to see several youths attacking a solitary person. Fighting seemed more honest then, and I have to wonder why, when I had more fights than the average boy, I was never very good at it, especially later in my youth. I like to think that I used to spare my opponent; "it's a good job I didn't lose my temper, you'd have been for it then!"

There were numerous other incidents, too numerous to list on these pages However, they were experiences from which we learned about life's ups and downs, and how to deal with situations, such as getting locked in a barn by a farmers wife for trying to scrump apples, and getting out by using a penknife to slide the bolt back. Funnily enough, I went back to this same farm sometime around 1995, when I was showing a girlfriend where I used to live and play. The farmer's son Christopher, a very fat boy in the early sixties and still a very fat man in the 90's when I went back, was still living and working the farm, which had been turned into a very successful cider museum. When I saw him, I recognised him instantly. When I told him who I was, he exclaimed, "well, bugger me!," not something which made me tingle with anticipation, but we had a good chat and laugh about old times.

Phippen, Gordon's daughter They were walking along the left side of the road, with their backs to oncoming traffic, which in those days, was about one car or tractor every few minutes. Susan was walking on the grass verge and Lynne was alongside her, just on the very edge of the road. A car came up from behind them and crashed into Lynne, knocking her into the air, past Susan and forward about 10 yards into a thick bramble hedge. The car driver, although he later claimed not to have known what had happened, finally stopped about 150 yards up the road. He wasn't able to say what speed he was doing, but claimed that he had only just turned onto the Causeway at the junction with Fearns Farm, and therefore could not have been travelling fast. The injuries she received and the distance that Lynne was knocked forward belied his claim, but he was never prosecuted for lack of witnesses and evidence of careless driving.

Lynne spent weeks in hospital with several broken bones, initially in intensive care, and made, what was described then as a full recovery apart from numbness to her right hip.

Mark VC County Primary school was tiny. (I never did find out what VC stood for) There were about 90 pupils and only three teachers, including dad, who was also headmaster; Mrs. Downs and Miss Turner, (who was about 70 years of age) being the other two. As I have previously mentioned in this chapter, Mark school was administered by the church authorities, who also employed dad. When he took over the school, he discovered that none of the text books was dated later than about 1890. He tried several times to persuade the governors to buy new books, without success. I remember one day being very excited at having a large bonfire in the field next door to the school, which doubled as our sports field. It wasn't until a number of years later that dad told me after all his failed attempts to get us new books, he had told the authorities that if he didn't get them, he would burn the old ones and force their hand. They, of course, didn't believe him and still refused; hence the bonfire. This was quite a risky strategy really, as he was gambling with his future, but dad's only concern was the effective education of the children at his school, and as such, he was prepared to go out on a limb for us. The new books arrived very shortly after.

Having only three teachers, the school was naturally divided into the three available classrooms. Miss Turner taught the very youngest infants, Mrs. Downs, the middle class and dad taught the older children, up to the age of 11 when they took the 11+ exam to determine which type of education they would go on to, either grammar or secondary modern. Both Lynne and I were put straight into dad's class. I don't really remember what subjects we covered, but they were all general in nature, giving us a basic enough education to enable us to pass the 11+, or fail as the case may be!

It was a very old school, with smelly outside toilets, which emptied straight into the ditch at the back. Consequently, the undergrowth at the back of the school was always lush and green! The school was constructed from red brick and dressed stone and the rooms had the most wonderful parquet flooring with solid pine doors to the rooms.

To the rear of the infants class, which doubled as the dining room at lunch-time, was the kitchen, where Mrs. Bishop and some other ladies cooked the most wonderful meals for us from fresh produce bought from the local farms. In all my subsequent schooling, I never had as good food as Mrs. Bishop cooked. Her speciality was puddings, mostly fruit pies with warm, crusty pastry and fresh custard.

On some days, the local vicar, Mr. Morris would come to the school and talk to us about religion and its importance in our lives. One day, he had been talking about Jesus, when a boy called Richard Bowyer suddenly declared in a loud voice, with his strong Somerset accent, "Jesus?, I ain't never 'eard of ee afore" Mr. Morris was so taken aback that someone hadn't heard of Jesus, he threw him out of the class! Mind you, Richard Bowyer was a little odd to say the least. There was a little grassy patch alongside the playground, and Richard would spend his play-times digging for worms with his fingers and then putting them in his mouth and sucking off the slime! I often wonder whether he ever did manage to find a girlfriend!

All the kids in the school adored my father. Looking back on those years at Mark, the key was probably the fact that he genuinely cared for us, and our education; someone had to, as it certainly wasn't the church. This was farming country, and for generations, the way of things was that the boys would end up working as labourers on local farms, and the girls would marry the local boys and have lots of children. Therefore, what was the point in educating either sex beyond the most rudimentary level. The system was evident from the number of people bearing the same surname. In and around Mark, there were literally hundreds of "Puddys", "Fearns", "Phippens", "Coombs", and others I can't remember. Somerset was reknowned for being a sleepy county educationally, but times were changing, and dad was at the front, waving the education flag for all to see.

Lunchtime in summer was always a favourite time, especially for us boys. Dad was sport mad, and especially liked his tennis and cricket. He couldn't really do much for us in the way of tennis, but with his clever hands, he constructed a set of cricket stumps, which were free standing, and would fall over at the slightest touch of a ball. He had placed three "stumps" into a block of wood, which was slightly rounded on the bottom.

The block would sit on the ground and then rock backwards when touched by the ball. There were no bails of course, there was no point! Straight after his lunch, dad would come out into the playground, where most of the boys and girls would be waiting for him. There were no teams really, it was dad bowling a ball versus everyone else taking turns with a bat and fielding in the play-ground. He would pace out a distance, something far short of a cricket pitch length and put a mark on the ground. All the children would then take it in turns to be at the crease and face dad's ace bowling. He would bowl slow ones mainly, but would add a little spin sometimes, just for the fun. The fielders dotted around the play-ground would shriek with excitement if the ball came their way, race after it and throw it back to dad, who would then throw it at the stumps, accurately or inaccurately, depending on how long the batsman had been "in". This would go on for about two hours!, mainly because dad would be having as much, if not more fun than we were; jacket off, sleeves rolled up and sweat pouring off him. We absolutely loved it, they were fabulous days. Miss Turner had usually gone home by then and Mrs. Downs just sat on the step to the front door of the school, her white, hairy legs slightly parted to allow some draught up her voluminous skirt and looking her usual grumpy self.

In1962, I took and failed the 11+ exam. Lynne had taken the exam 2 years earlier, passed and went to a local grammar school in Burnham, with the unlikely name of "Sexeys". In Somerset at this time, the 11+ consisted of a written examination followed by an interview. I never have been able to understand just why the interview took place, but it was that which I failed. Being as you had to pass both parts, I failed my 11+, and went to Cheddar Secondary Modern School. This upset my father greatly and was probably partly the reason why the family moved to Stoke-on-Trent later that year.

The school was about eight miles away from Mark and we would be taken there and back on a coach, which was owned and driven by a very large and strict man, whose name completely escapes me, if I ever knew it! The toughest boy in the village, Graham Fisher, who I mentioned earlier, was regularly thrown off the bus by the owner, usually for smoking at the back, and would walk home the rest of the way. Graham was usually thrown off about half way home, so he would walk about four miles to his house, nothing for a kid like Graham, but even so, he was only twelve!

I absolutely hated Cheddar school. Even though some of my class-mates in Mark were at the same school, it was vastly different. The kids were even rougher than they were at Mark and it was a lot more unfriendly. However, I did achieve a certain fame whilst there. In a small play area at the back of the school was one of those roundabouts you find in a children's park. At the end of the day, a large group of boys would gather at the roundabout and then eight boys would each grab one of the eight bars around the circumference. All eight boys would then start to rotate the roundabout by pushing the bars around with all their strength. When it was going round as fast as we could make it go, the competition was to see who had the guts to get on first. This was done by grabbing hold of a bar as it sped past and letting the speed of the roundabout pull you onto the platform. Once on, you then had to get to the centre before the centrifugal force threw you back off, such was the speed at which it was turning. It was quite dangerous really as it would only take a slight mis-judgement in timing and you would either collide painfully with one of the metal bars, or worse, be thrown out backwards onto the concrete apron, as happened to me on one occasion. However, I was always the first to get on, was never defeated and for the short time I was at Cheddar, was regarded as the champion "roundabout getter onerer".

I remember absolutely nothing else about Cheddar school, such was its impact on my life.

In the winter of 1962, dad obtained another headmaster post; this time in Kidsgrove, Stoke-on-Trent, Staffordshire, and in the winter of 1962, we moved away from Mark and Somerset.

Chapter 4

The winter of 1962 was one of the worst on record. Snow and ice still covered the entire country as far into the following year as late April. Services ground to a halt, roads were virtually impassable and people died from the prolonged cold. It was against this backdrop, that my family moved to the Potteries area in Stoke-on-Trent, an area not renowned for its balmy climes!

I remember that we arrived at our new house, but our furniture didn't. Motorways were still years away, and apparently, the removal lorry had had to negotiate ice ruts in the road about a foot deep. It got so far, then broke one of its springs and had to be temporarily abandoned. It was eventually repaired, and arrived at the house two or three days later. This was early 1963, and central heating was not yet a major feature of many households, including ours. The cold was intense and all we had were the clothes we had managed to bring with us in our car. For Lynne and I of course, this was a bit of an adventure, albeit a cold one and the four of us spent most of the two days exploring the new area, eating in cafes and sleeping in borrowed blankets on the floor.

The house we moved in to, was in a small cul-de-sac called Maryhill Close. Maryhill was also the name of this particular area of Kidsgrove, and dad's new school was called Maryhill County Primary School. The house was very conveniently situated for dad, as it was not only the first in the row, but also literally across the road from the school gates. It was nothing special; a modern three bedroomed semi-detached house, made from red brick. It had a very small garden at the front and a slightly larger one at the rear. Compared to Portland House in Mark, it was completely characterless and I can think of no redeeming features about it, which would make it stand out in my memory, except one; it was situated on the top of a hill! After three years of complete flatness in Mark, I was once again living on a hill. I was of course, without my trusty cart, but about a month later, I was to be introduced to the joys of sledging down a very steep hill not far from where I lived, but more of that later.

I had also arrived in Kidsgrove without my old bicycle, which had taken me miles around the Somerset country-side. Shortly before we left Mark, and completely unbeknown to me, mum had given it away to a genuinely snotty-nosed kid in the village called Jimmy Clark. It was, and remains a complete mystery to me why she did that. It was a perfectly good bike, and now Lynne had a bike, Jimmy Clark had a bike, and I didn't! I remember feeling quite piqued by this, and took every opportunity to steal Lynne's bike just so that she couldn't ride it!

Generally speaking, a hill would be called just that, a hill, and maybe with a name attached to the front. In the area where I live now, we have Hosey Hill, Titsey Hill, Ide Hill and I live in Biggin Hill. In Stoke-on -Trent however, and I don't have

27

the faintest idea why, a hill was called a "bank", uphill was "up-bank" and downhill was "down-bank." Referring to a hill as a "bank" was the probably the very first stage of my conversion from a deep Somerset accent, to Stokese, and from then on, I called hills, "banks."

Apart from the intense cold, my only other abiding memory of that winter, was being taught how to sledge by some boys I had teamed up with at school. Not far from me was a small lake called Bathpool Lake. Years later, it was converted to a local beauty spot called Bathpool Park. It was an old mining ventilation shaft directly beneath the park, which achieved notoriety as the location where Donald Neilson, otherwise known as the Black Panther had imprisoned and eventually hanged the heiress, Leslie Whittle. At this time however, it was still a lake with a horse riding path all the way around, and situated at the bottom of what to us, was a very steep-sided slope. The water in the lake had frozen to a depth of about 6" to 9" and although, no-one was ice-skating, (you can't play football on ice skates, so no-one did it!), adults and children alike played on the ice.

The way I was taught to sledge, which incidentally seems to be contrary to the way everyone else does it, was to lie on my chest on the sledge so that my head was at the front, and I could hold onto the tops of the runners. The main reason for doing it this way however, was so that the feet would drag along the ground and be used as a crude, but effective form of steering and braking. To go to the left, I stuck my left leg out at an angle to the sledge and scraped my shoe along the ground, effectively creating a slight braking action. The same principle applied to go to the right. In addition to using the feet, and at the same time, throwing the body weight from side to side on the sledge also assisted in steering. Sledging this way has always been more exciting than lying backwards along the sledge and sticking your feet out to the front. I still enjoy sledging today and partake whenever I can. I once won a sledging competition at a ski resort, purely because of the method I adopted. Anyway, back to Bathpool!

Having mastered the rudiments of sledging, myself and my new found friends used to have a competition where we started at the very top of the slope, sledged straight down the slope, onto and across the horse-track, which was about three feet above the water line, take-off from the edge of the horse-track and land as far out onto the lake as possible; the winner of course, being the idiot who could get out the furthest. There were no plastic moulded sledges in those days, they were all made of wood and very sturdy. Even so, I am amazed that no serious injuries ever occurred, or that no-one went straight through the ice, not to be found until April!

I started at Kidsgrove Secondary Modern school in January 1963. This was in the days before comprehensive schools and you either went to a Grammar school, like Lynne, or to a Secondary Modern school, like me. The education was of a far higher standard at Grammar school, and it was a form of elitism, which was largely done away with years later, but which now seems to be making something of a comeback.

Whereas Cheddar school had around 150 pupils, Kidsgrove had something like 1500 in two separate buildings, Upper School and Lower School. The culture shock was brutal! It was a much rougher and tougher school than I had ever experienced, and of course, I was the new kid with a strange accent the locals hadn't ever heard before. My deep Somerset accent was the subject of much hilarity in my new class and it wasn't long before I trained myself to speak like them.

Whereas, I had spent much of my time around farms and in fields, roaming at will over the countryside and playing in hayricks and barns, these kids, the sons and daughters of factory workers, heavy industry workers and miners, played on the streets, hung around outside pubs waiting for their parents and generally got up to no good. I remember one boy in our class called Robert Crizans, ("Pansy" to his friends). He was the first boy to befriend me at Kidsgrove, and he will forever remain in my memory. He turned up at school one day looking totally disheveled and tired out. He explained to me that because he hadn't got home the previous evening before 11pm, his mother had locked the door on him and he had simply roamed the streets all night. He was a tough lad, but he was only 11 years old for goodness sake! Shortly after I left Kidsgrove school, someone broke into a brand new chemistry laboratory in the upper school, had lit a taper, or something and accidentally started a fire in the classroom, which spread and eventually gutted the whole building, causing thousands of pounds worth of damage. I remember that Pansy was absolutely hooked on chemistry and apparently he was suspected of breaking in. Things went from bad to worse for Pansy, and the last I heard of him, he had died after crashing a stolen car he was driving. With a home life like he described, he never really had a chance.

The school was divided physically into two parts, the younger children in the lower part of the school, and the older children in the upper building. I remember being taken to the school by dad on my first day, and being utterly overwhelmed by the sheer number of children milling about. I was shown into my new class, and introduced first to my new teacher, Miss Frew, and secondly of course, to the children, who immediately made fun of my accent. I distinctly remember feeling very alone and very vulnerable on my first day at my new school. All I wanted was to belong and to be accepted into my new society. The mickey-taking didn't last long really, and I was very soon mixing it with my new buddies, although, I cannot say I was ever really happy at Kidsgrove school. There always seemed to be somebody getting on my case!

On one occasion, myself and a couple of friends were out collecting wild-birds eggs! In Mark, I had amassed quite a collection of eggs, (until our cat lay on the tray holding them and crushed the majority) and continued this rather dubious past-time in Kidsgrove. It had been made a criminal offence to collect wild-birds eggs in 1954, but it wasn't really adhered to, especially in rural areas such as Mark in Somerset. I would hazard an opinion that in those days, the vast majority of people wouldn't even have known it was an offence and probably cared less.

I don't really remember how it happened, but we were accosted by three or four older boys, who decided to frog march us to the local policeman's house. I will never believe they did it out of a sense of outrage at us taking common or garden birds eggs, more like, they were simply bullies out for trouble.

The constable wasn't at home, and so they let us go, with a dire warning to me that I would be "got" at school. Why me!?! There were other kids there, why was I singled out for God's sake? Well, nothing happened for a day or two, until one lunch time when I was eating at a table on my own, I was surrounded by a dozen or so youths and told to be at the bike-shed pretty smart. Oh dear, another fight coming up! I remember I was very calm about the whole thing and finished eating my lunch. I then casually made my way down to the bike-shed, to find about 50 or 60 pupils all waiting for me to turn up and eager for the contest to begin.

My opponent was the leader of the bullies from the birds nesting episode. I really didn't want to fight him, but I had no choice and so we got started. He hit me, I hit him, he was on top of me, I got him off and was on top of him, the usual crap! All the while the audience was screaming for blood, as they usually do in those situations. At one point, we were toe to toe and I swung a punch at him. He went down like a sack of potatos and didn't get up. The crowd completely ignored him lying inert on the ground, and I was carried shoulder high from the "field of battle", revelling in my glorious victory. I could already hear some of them saying "did you see that punch, wow!" and could see them faithfully re-enacting the scene. Word of my victory spread very quickly and I was at once, the hero!

The only thing was, I knew I had not connected with the punch, and yet he had gone down. A little while later, I saw an ambulance at the school, and wondered idly for whom it had been called. I found out very soon when Miss Dykes, the headmistress, called me into her office. She was a fearsome woman, around 5'10" tall with a huge bosom and iron grey hair set in a bun at the back of her head. She told me that the other youth in the fight was a severe asthmatic, and had had an attack at the very moment I had swung the punch, which was why he had collapsed and been taken to hospital in a poorly state. Although I tried to explain to her that it was he who had picked on me, she gave me a huge bollocking about fighting, followed by the phrase, which was to haunt me for the rest of my school days, "what would your father say?" That was probably the beginning of my not really caring what my father would say, apart from one serious incident which I describe later!

I was very indifferent to school, especially Kidsgrove. I remember struggling along with French, preferring instead to stare out of the window at the girls doing games in those awful blue knickers, and being a total disaster at arts and crafts. The other subjects have faded into the mists of time.

When I joined the school, for art, my class had been set the task of creating a model of a lion made from papier mache over a wire frame. Several children in the class were quite well advanced with their lion, others were not so advanced, and then there was me. For the life of me, I couldn't get the papier mache to stick to the wire to form a foundation. I tried several times and each time the stuff simply revolved around the smooth wire. There were bits of newspaper everywhere, the glue was spattered all over me and the desk was an absolute mess. I tried sticking small bits onto the wire, large bits onto the wire, wrapping it around and squeezing it together, and nothing seemed to work. Mind you, even if I had finished it, heaven only knows what it would have looked like; nothing resembling a lion, that's for sure! The teacher, an oldish man as I remember, was very patient with me, but in the end, we both just gave up.

My journey to school was a walk of about a mile and a half, and took me through a large sprawling council estate, which is where most of the children at the school lived. Two events on my travels to and from school have remained with me. On one occasion when walking home, I saw a black man for the first time. This was the early sixties remember, and there weren't very many in the country at that time, and certainly none in Somerset. I walked around a corner and he came running towards me from the opposite direction. I remember stopping in my tracks and staring at him in fascination. He was tall, well built and was wearing one of those American baseball type jackets made from a shiny, vivid blue material. Just as he was about to run past me, and without breaking his stride, he pinched the top of his nose and blew a load of snot into someone's hedge. He evidently got some on his fingers because he then casually flicked the remainder into the same hedge and carried on running past me. I watched him run on and then looked back to where he had flicked his load into the hedge; there it was in all its glory, dangling precariously from a twig. I watched in fascination as it slowly elongated, until finally, it parted and fell off.

The second event happened much nearer to the school. My journey took me through the open space in front of the train station, down some steps to the canal tow path and then up another set of steps to the school. The top of the steps from the tow path met with the end of a bridge over the canal, from which I could see the old Harecastle Tunnel. One morning, as I neared the top of the steps, I saw an old man coming over the bridge from the other side of the canal. He must have been in his seventies at least, and was dressed in the ubiquitous thick heavy trousers and waistcoat of the potteries working man. He was walking very slowly, hands in his pockets and head bowed. As we both got nearer to the point where our paths would cross, I could see that he had two huge and ugly growths on his nose, one on each side. These growths were so grotesque and large that they covered almost his entire face and with every step he was taking, they wobbled and shook. Once again, this was a first for me; I had never seen someone with a deformity.

When I look back on this man, it's not the deformity that I see, it's the desperate sadness of his existence that was obvious to me even then. It showed in the way he was walking, or should I say shuffling along and in his whole demeanour. The poor man must have suffered abuse and fear all his life; fear of venturing out in public and having people stare at his deformity, have them make fun of him and humiliate him. Even now, it hurts me to think about what he must have been through, and I am thankful that I only ever saw him that one time. The thought of my being mixed up in a group of kids abusing him because of his deformity is just too horrible to contemplate.

Now, at my age, I have of course seen others with deformities. We grow up, we see these things and we harden ourselves to it, but it's a fact that I could never, and will never be able to watch the film of the life of John Merricks, "The Elephant Man", simply because of the memory of the man in Kidsgrove, and the interminable sadness and suffering that he must have endured.

Besides Pansy, there were one or two odd characters at Kidsgrove school, such as the boy I found openly trying to masturbate in a corner of the boys cloakroom. Another such odd character was a girl in our class, who was to be the catalyst to one of the best lessons, (non-scholastic) I have ever learned. The entire incident has remained with me all these years and went a long way to forming the basis of my knowing what is right and what is wrong. I certainly don't remember her name, if I ever knew it, and most probably, no-one else in the class knew it either. This was because she spent virtually the entire two terms I was at Kidsgrove school, off sick. She would come in for perhaps one or two days and then disappear for the rest of the term. I have described her as "odd" because one of the days she chose to come to school was on the very last day of the summer term, before we broke up for the holiday. Having been off for practically the entire term, who on earth comes to school for the last day, when absolutely no work is done and we're all champing at the bit to get out of the place!

Let me back-track a little. A few weeks before the end of the term, dad had used his influence and arranged for me to re-take the 11+ exam. Remember I have said that Somerset had a ridiculous system of having to pass the written exam and an interview in order to pass the 11+. Staffordshire Education Authority didn't have the interview stage, so presumably, the thinking was that if I could pass the exam again, I might qualify to go to grammar school. One of the best schools in the area, besides Lynne's school for girls, was in a nearby mining town called Biddulph, and it was here that dad arranged for me to take the exam. I was 12 years old at this time and rather confused about what was happening. In transferring from Somerset to Kidsgrove, I had survived a very brutal culture shock, and now dad was trying his level best to give me another! The Potteries was, and still is, an industrial working class area, where the kids, especially the boys, are normally expected to get a rudimentary education and then leave school to find work in a local factory or pottery. The girls were simply expected to leave school, find a man, marry him and raise a family at home, sending their sons into the same industry as their fathers.

There was a huge stigma about going to a grammar school rather than a secondary modern, and grammar school pupils were often the target for ridicule and physical assault. Most boys from a working class area didn't go to grammar school, and they certainly didn't transfer from one to the other, it was as simple as that. All I really wanted, was to belong, to blend in and be accepted into the social structure. I had made friends at Kidsgrove school; they were accepting me as their friend and now I was in danger of once again being uprooted and having to start the process all over again, in an environment which my new found friends had taught me to despise.

In any event, dad took me to Biddulph Grammar School one day and I sat the examination, spending the entire day at the school. It was virtually a brand new school with clean floors, clean toilets, light and airy classrooms, and a massive sports field. All the children seemed perfectly normal and looked very smart in a school uniform with a badge on the blazer and red neck-ties. I found myself beginning to doubt what I had been taught by my secondary school friends, and the more I thought about it, the more I actually wanted to come to this school. The problem was of course, that I was still at secondary modern school and mixing with my friends there.

Not wanting to be the subject of any vitriolic abuse, I kept very quiet about taking the examination, and even went to the lengths of ridiculing a certain girl in the class called Cheryl Gallimore for having a boyfriend at the same grammar school I was trying to enter! (I remember her name because I fancied her!)

So, back to the last day at school. We were all very excited at breaking up for the summer holidays. There had been lots of fooling around all morning, and after lunch, we all trooped back into Miss Frew's classroom for the last hour or so. I used to sit near the back of the class with Pansy, another lad called Chris Grant and a few others whose names I no longer recall. The sickly girl sat right at the front. There was nothing unusual about the classroom; the desks were in rows, Miss Frew sat at the front and alongside her was a cupboard where the class supplies of pens and ink etc. were kept. We had been in class for a few minutes and Miss Frew was late coming in. One of us, and it wasn't me, thought it would be a good laugh if we raided the stores cupboard and stole some of the contents, notebooks, rubbers and the like. Four of us helped ourselves to a good portion of what was in there, and returned to our desks, laughing at our derring-do.

Our form teacher, Miss Frew was a bit of a shrew of a woman, and we used to make fun of her, saying "who frew frew frew the window?" When she came into the class, we conspirators at the back of the class were giggling and generally fooling about, not taking the slightest bit of notice of anyone else. As she got to her desk, "sickly" immediately put her hand up and said in a loud voice, "please miss, those boys at the back have stolen all the jotters from your cupboard". She then pointed to where we were all sitting. The room went silent! Miss Frew told all the guilty parties to stand up and we all remained resolutely sitting down, scowling at the sneak at the front of the class, who in turn, was smirking back at us. When none of us stood up, Miss Frew asked "sickly" to point out who were the guilty ones, and of course, she pointed to all of us in turn. Had we stood up when she told us to, Miss Frew would probably have made us simply put the stuff back and treated the episode for what it was, high spirits. But we had defied her, and this clearly made her very angry. She made us open our desk-lids, and there of course was all the booty. Pansy, me, Chris and the other lad, were marched out of the class and taken direct to Miss Dykes' office.

Corporal punishment in the form of caning was still regularly used in those days, and I was the only one of the four who had never received any strokes of the cane. The worst I had received was a rap across the knuckles with the edge of a ruler, and that was painful enough. The other three were old hands at this sort of thing, and immediately started to take steps to reduce the stinging effects of the caning that was sure to follow Miss Frew's report to Miss Dykes. This was the era of the "teddy boys" and all youths of our age, slicked their hair with brylcreem. According to the other three, rubbing both hands vigorously with brylcreem from the hair reduced the pain of the cane. We were all hard at it, rubbing the hair cream into our hands, when Miss Frew emerged from the office, followed by the nightmarish headmistress, Miss Dykes.

She didn't say anything to us, simply pointed to the first one and marched him into the office. After a few seconds of deafening silence, I heard the swish of the cane and the smack of it landing on an outstretched hand. There were four strokes, presumably two on each hand, probably because both hands had been used in the crime. The lad cried out in pain at each stroke, and it became obvious to me that the old brylcreem ploy was seriously flawed. He came out in tears and she pointed to her next victim, unfortunately, not me. The second lad received the same four strokes and also emerged in tears. I was now beginning to sweat a little with fear, and hoping wildly that I would be next, simply to get it over and done with. No, the third lad was taken in and he received exactly the same as the other two. I distinctly remember thinking that my fate has to be the same as the other three and that four strokes wouldn't be so bad. My turn!

She simply stood in the doorway and glared at me. I tried to hold the stare, but eventually I withered and studied my feet. Having won the battle, she took me into her office, where I confidently expected to receive my four strokes. Once again she simply looked at me, and then uttered the old chestnut, "what would your father say?" I don't think she was inviting any sort of reply and I certainly didn't give her one. She then went on to explain why I was not going to receive the caning the others had. "You are a thief", she said, "and a disgrace to your father." She told me that she was well aware of the fact that I had sat the entrance exam to Biddulph Grammar School and that, despite my behaviour, she believed I really wanted to go to that school. It has always amazed me just how she actually figured that one out, bearing in mind that absolutely nobody else even knew that I had taken the exam, let alone discuss the fact with anyone. I was convinced I had given nothing away, including emotions; but then again, she was the formidable Miss Dykes, the leader of a school of 1500 tough working class kids. I found out just how formidable and ruthless she was when she dropped the bombshell, my punishment.

"You are a thief", she reiterated, "and in my opinion, not fit to attend a grammar school. I shall be writing to the education authority today to inform them of this incident, and recommending that they reject your application. In the meantime, you will tell your father what you have done. I shall say nothing to him, but the education authority will no doubt be in touch with him. Now get out!" It was actually only some years later that I was able to recall the words she used on that day, such was the impact of what she had said to me!

As I left her office, it occurred to me that there was not a shadow of doubt that she would carry out her threat to inform the education authority. I was in serious trouble! But first, I had to deal with my fellow "thieves". They would naturally want to know how I had got on. I walked back into the classroom and simply sat at my desk with my head bowed until the end of class, when everyone leapt out of their chairs and raced for the door and freedom for the next six weeks, everyone that is except me! I was just hoping against hope that they wouldn't ask any questions, so I dithered about getting my books etc into my satchel whilst everyone else was heading for the door. "See you tonight at the flicks", called out Chris as he was leaving with the other conspirators. Thankfully, they had left me alone to deal with the "pain" of my caning.

It had become an established part of the weekend break that four or five of us would go to the local cinema on Friday to catch the early evening film. Chris Grant is the only other boy I really remember being in the group, and sometimes, we met up with some of the girls from the school at the same film. On these occasions, Chris would generally sit apart from us, trying to get Helena Zrobok to snog him and the rest of us mere mortals would divide our time between watching the film, being generally rowdy and looking to see how Chris and Helena were getting on! I always looked forward to the Friday evening outing as it was yet another indicator into how I was being accepted into the Kidsgrove society.

On this particular Friday, although I desperately wanted to go out with my friends, I was so sick with worry about the classroom episode and Miss Dykes' threat, I had to almost drag myself to the cinema. It never really mattered what film was showing, being there was the most important thing to me. I remember this particular film was about Roman times and involved lots of fighting and battle scenes. I can see the lead character in my mind, but for the life of me, cannot recall his name; it'll probably come to me later. It was just the sort of film that our group loved to watch, plenty of action and blood, and everyone was laughing and having a good time, except of course, little old me! I tried desperately hard to put events out of my mind and have a good time, but it simply didn't work. As the film wore on, I became almost paralysed with worry, so much so, that I couldn't stand it any longer. The good time being had by my friends seemed to add to my anguish, and in the end, I simply got up and left the cinema, something I would never ordinarily dream of doing.

Part of the reason I was so worried, or perhaps a better word would be terrified, was that I had made a conscious decision not to tell my father what had happened, in direct disobedience to Miss Dykes. I didn't not tell him out of any rebelliousness, I was simply too scared! It was silly really, because it merely added fuel to the inferno of worry I was experiencing. There was no doubt that he would eventually find out, and not telling him merely meant that I would have to deal with that aspect, in addition to the act itself.

The first few days of the holiday were a blur, but as the days turned into a week, and then two, then three, still with no word from the education authority, the fear gradually subsided, and I became more relaxed and hopeful that I had got away with it. The routine of our house was as normal, dad would do jobs around the house or go over to the school, mum would do the house work and Lynne and I would do our own thing, whatever that was.

About four weeks into the holiday, everything was normal and I had all but forgotten about the incident at school. I remember I was upstairs cleaning my teeth when I heard the postman deliver our letters, at around the same time he did every morning. I paid no attention, until dad bellowed from downstairs, "Neil, get down here now". I just froze on the spot! This could mean only one thing, a letter from the education authority telling my father that his son was a "thief" and not "fit" to attend grammar school.

My terror returned in kind and my mind went into freefall at what was about to happen. Miss Dykes had been true to her promise after all, she had informed the authority, and now I was about to be identified as a thief and receive my inevitable punishment.

I went downstairs to the lounge, where I found dad with the letter in his hand. He did not look amused! He thrust it into my hand and told me to read it out loud. "Dear Mr. Robins" it said, "we are pleased to inform you that your son Neil has passed the entrance examination to Biddulph Grammar School and may take up his studies at that school in September this year." It went on about other stuff I don't remember, and at that time couldn't have cared less. I almost collapsed with relief, especially when I looked up at dad and saw him grinning at me, feeling very pleased with his little joke! Poor old dad, he genuinely thought my reaction was solely at passing the entrance examination, whereas, it was rather more like a condemned man having the noose removed from around his neck.

It was to be over twenty years before I actually related the story to him, and this in part, was the legacy of Miss Dykes' lesson to me. Dad told me that he knew absolutely nothing about what had happened, so it was clear that Miss Dykes had not informed the authority after all. Instead, she had devised a much more cunning form of punishment. Her whole strategy revolved around my telling dad what had happened. She must have guessed that I wouldn't say anything to him, but either way, she was in a win-win situation. If I did tell dad, I would receive punishment from him, and if I didn't, my having to wait for the non-existent letter from the education authority would be my punishment. I often wonder if she ever knew just how effective her strategy had been. Chris and the other lads had probably forgotten the whole incident by the end of the film about the Roman Empire, which incidentally starred Steve Reeves. I had an overwhelming sense of shame, which was one of the reasons I didn't tell dad, and she used this to turn me inside out. In effect, she was making me punish myself, and the longer I had to wait for the letter, the worse it was for me. It would never have worked on Chris and the others, but for me of course, it was different. I had taken the exam, and this was the lever she used.

It was a stunning success; beautifully crafted and ruthlessly delivered. The most important aspect though, is that it has remained with me all these years. I still did some pretty stupid and dishonest things in my youth, as you will see, but it did eventually form the basis of my ability to decide what is right and what is wrong; more than that, it enabled me to associate actions which I know to be wrong with a very personal sense of shame. If I see someone in the street drop a £5 note, there is no way I could keep it rather than give it back to the person who dropped it, even if that person has no knowledge of dropping it. That would be dishonest, and I just know I would suffer inside. Don't get me wrong, I was no angel in my youth and teens. I got into trouble on several occasions after this incident, nothing really serious, but whenever I did something, no punishment was ever so effective and long-lasting as that of Miss Dykes. It just took a few years for the message to finally sink in.

In truth, I owe her a great deal, and I am using these pages to say a very belated, probably posthumous, heartfelt thank you to a very terrifying, but very caring person.

When I left the school that Friday afternoon, and when I left the cinema that Friday evening, it was the last time I ever saw any of my friends from Kidsgrove, and I often wonder if they ever villifed me for becoming a "grammar grub".

In the September of 1963, I started at Biddulph Grammar School, where I forged new friendships, some of which have lasted and indeed flourished to this day.

Chapter 5

Y ou could be forgiven for thinking that, for all the anguish I had suffered over that summer holiday, I would not allow anything else to come between me and my studies at this school, which I very much wanted to attend. You would be wrong!

I actually started at Biddulph Grammar School when the family was still living in Kidsgrove. Every morning my mother would have to drive me to school, a distance of about 7 miles and then pick me up again at the end of the day. During our stay at Kidsgrove, dad had been working on the plans for a bungalow, which my parents wanted to have built on the outskirts of Biddulph. Eventually, the plans were passed, and work started on our own house. Every morning and afternoon, mum and I used to drive past the site and comment on how much the builders had done. It wasn't until the walls started to go up, that mum mentioned to dad that she thought something was wrong with the construction. Dad paid a visit to the site, and immediately realised the builders were building the house the wrong way round! Dad had planned the house to have the front door, path and garage facing Newpool Road, making us number 79 Newpool Road. Instead, the builders had looked at the plans wrongly and we would now be number 1 Birch Avenue. The garage was initially going to be attached to the side of the house, but because of the mistake, it had to be erected at the bottom of the garden, with the drive facing Birch Avenue.

It didn't really bother my parents, although it gave my dad an awful lot more garden to dig. He used to try and get me to help him with the garden, but I always had to go fishing or play football, anything but gardening. (My aversion to gardening still exists today). In the end, dad had spent so much time and effort on making the front lawn, it was the envy of all who passed by. Mum and dad received some sort of compensation from the builders, although I never really knew what, and at that time cared even less. The company were building a mini housing estate around the area at the time, and went bust in the end, due to the "generosity" of the site foreman to other families who had moved into the area, and to those not in receipt of his "gifts", who merely took what they wanted off the site after the workmen had gone home.

My family got on really well with all our neighbours, especially Malcolm and Norma Chadwick next door at 3 Birch Avenue. Malcolm was a "deputy" (quite a senior rank within the coal industry) at the Victoria Colliery where I later went to work and Norma was a housewife. However, the relationship with the neighbours came under a little strain one weekend, when my parents went away for a weekend, leaving me in the house on my own. I had decided that I would have a few friends around for some drinks and to listen to records. Needless to say, my parents knew nothing of my plans. I carefully selected who I was going to invite and gave them the date and time. I didn't want all and sundry to turn up at the house, so told everyone to keep it quiet. Unfortunately, I had made the mistake of telling one particular girl.

She wasn't really a friend, but she did have a magnificent pair of breasts, and had to be invited on that premise alone. She decided to spread the "party" word around at the local dancehall. As a result, I was invaded by around forty or fifty youths and girls, leaving their cars and scooters abandoned everywhere. My heart sank when I saw them arriving en masse. Although I recognized some faces from the Golden Torch dancehall, I was powerless to prevent them coming in to the house.

Chaos ensued, and there was nothing I could do to prevent it. All I could do was limit the damage, which I knew would occur. I had to stuff the cat into the airing cupboard to keep him safe, try and hide other valuables and breakables. All the bedrooms were invaded, one guy vomited all over the lawn, someone else fell into the fishpond, killing all the fish and of course, the music was whacked up to full volume. Eventually, one of the neighbours got fed up with all the row and loud music, and called the police. Thankfully, by the time they arrived, most of the gatecrashers had left, they were like some giant herd of locusts, descending on a patch of vegetation, stripping it bare and moving right along! I had some explaining to do to the police officers who arrived, but it was as nothing compared to what I was going to have to say to my parents.

The following morning, I surveyed the damage. There were beer stains all up the walls, the carpets were stained, furniture was all over the place and the beds were soiled; generally, everything you would expect from a party. Luckily for me, the original people, (except of course, her!) I had invited were still at the house and we set to, tidying up and cleaning everything before my parents arrived home that Sunday evening. We worked our backsides off and eventually, things seemed normal. I took one last look around the house and was satisfied that mum and dad would never know what had happened.

When they returned, my mum walked straight into the kitchen and innocently asked, 'have you been doing some washing?' I was devastated! We had a twin-tub washing machine and mum always kept the pair of tongs inside the washer drum. Having retrieved the articles I had stuffed into the drum for safekeeping, I'd left the tongs outside on the top. I was undone! And they hadn't been in the house barely a minute! I realised immediately I was never going to get away with this, and so, I confessed all. It took about an hour for them and my sister to go all over the house and examine everything, with the mood getting blacker by the minute. In the end, dad came back into the kitchen, where I thought I would receive a verbal thrashing. Instead, he just looked at me and said, 'have you apologised to our neighbours?' When I said I hadn't, I was despatched immediately to every house within earshot of ours to say sorry. 'And,' he said, 'I will be checking!' I think I visited about twenty houses all told, and bless their hearts, they all said they appreciated me coming around and that they "understood." Only one old goat across the road was annoyed. When I visited John, the neighbour on the opposite side to Malcolm and Norma, he gave me a wink and said, "who was in your sister's room?" "Haven't got a clue, why?" I asked, "because all we could hear," he said, "was, get off me, get off me, you dirty bastard!" My friends and I later worked out that this must have been the gobby girl with the big tits! My parents didn't actually speak to me for three days.

My sister ignored me for much longer, (not that that bothered me) and I was grounded for what seemed an eternity.

Moral, beware the woman with large breasts and mouth to match!

Biddulph Grammar School was only about 3 years old when I started there. Apart from being a grammar school in an industrial, working class town, the actual concept of the school was very radical. Most of the teachers were young, in fact, some were only just into their twenties. One or two, including the headmaster, Mr. Kelly and his deputy, Mr. Dean, were relatively ancient at around 40-45 years of age.

We were taught English Literature; what good was that going to be for boys destined for the iron foundry or working down the coal mine. Instead of French, which was the normal language to learn, we were taught German and Russian. This was only fifteen years after World War 2 and relationships with Russia were not too good, especially after The Bay of Pigs episode, but education was obviously changing and with it, the social structures of our communities. It was no longer acceptable that boys simply went into industry and girls had children. The thinking was that we should have a choice and in order to make that choice, we should have a proper education, no matter what our social background.

Our school was the first in England to have a language laboratory. This was a classroom equipped with separate booths with tape recorders where the students could listen to the spoken language and repeat the sentences into the recorders. The teacher would sit at his or her desk on a raised dias in front of the class, and could see into every booth, as well as plug in, talk to us over the headphones and listen to us murdering two of the most wonderfully sounding languages in the world.

The teacher being able to see into the booths was a distinct disadvantage for one boy in the class, John Bath. He had a disgusting habit. I suppose all little boys pick their noses, inspect the "booty" stuck on the end of the index finger and then roll it into a ball and flick it at some unsuspecting classmate. John Bath did all that, apart from flicking it. Instead, after careful examination, and with obvious relish, he ate his pickings. He was always doing it in class, and I expect he thought he could do it with impunity in the language laboratory, thinking that he was hidden from view. The German teacher we had at that time, a lovely lady from Germany, had obviously seen him rooting up his nose and then devouring the contents. She simply pressed the button to speak to all the pupils simultaneously through the headsets, and said in a very patient and understanding manner, 'John dear, stop eating your nose!'

Mr. Kelly, our old headmaster amply demonstrated just how radical the school was. In the summer of 2002, we had reunion. Initially, it was to be just the pupils from our class, many of whom still live and work in the area around Biddulph. There was never any suggestion that the reunion should be expanded to include all pupils until someone visited the "Friends Reunited" website. As a result, the reunion went from just a handful of ex-pupils, to around 150, including many of the teachers, Mr. Kelly and the other headmaster, Mr. Jones. At the end of the evening, which was a resounding success, Mr. Kelly gave an absolutely marvellous speech. He was then in his eighties, but it was clear he had lost none of his old sparkle and wit. We used to call him the "flycatcher" as he had the most odd habit of opening his mouth wide and then shutting it again with a snap of his lower jaw, although this trait had disappeared when we saw him at the reunion.

He related the story of the beginnings of the school, when public meetings were held to discuss its catchment area and pupil mix. At that time, in Biddulph, or indeed in any working class area of England, it was practically unheard of to have a grammar school of boys and girls together. Even in Somerset, the sexes had been separated at grammar school. This was obviously a hot topic amongst the potential parents, and apparently, one man stood up and asked Mr. Kelly whether, in his opinion, he thought that having girls at the school would hold up the progress of the boys!? Being the visionary that he was, Mr. Kelly simply addressed the audience and asked whether any man there, thought that his wife was less intelligent than himself. Apparently, only one brave soul put his hand up, and Mr. Kelly sat down.

I started at the school in September of 1963, in "yellow house". As all pupils were supposedly of roughly equal ability, there was no streaming as such and everybody was either in "yellow" or "red" house. On that first day at school, I was to meet three or four fellow pupils, with whom I would forge friendships that have lasted to this day.

I seem to remember that I did quite well in my first year, finishing top in at least English language. From that point on, my scholastic career took a drastic downturn; so much so in fact, that I fear this will be a chapter, very short on what I actually achieved academically at school. We'll have to see!

One of my favourite entertainers of all time was the wit and raconteur, Peter Ustinov, and I can best sum up my achievements at school by quoting from one of his "one man" shows. He was describing a report on him by one of his senior officers in the Army. It stated, "He sets himself appallingly low standards, which he consistently fails to achieve" A well worn phrase I know, but it does accurately reflect my achievements at school. And to this day, for the life of me, I cannot seem to find a definite reason why. I am an intelligent man and was an intelligent boy; easily the equal of most of my class mates. Yet, unlike me, most of them left the school with at least four or five "O" levels, even if they didn't go on to the sixth form and eventually, university.

It just didn't seem important to me, and I think as I got older, it became even less so. Even dad's position had no effect on me whatsoever. Instead of concentrating on homework, there always seemed to be other and better things to do like playing football or going fishing or going out to the local dancehall. (Discos hadn't been invented then!) I suppose a common thread that runs through all this is that whatever I did, it was always something that gave me pleasure; doing something that was fun and that I and my friends could laugh about. I simply didn't care about school, and being at school for most of the day was even worse.

Writing about all this now has given me small clues to explain my behaviour, one of which involves that much used phrase, "what would your father say." Whilst I cannot be definitive as to the reasons, I do feel that the very fact that dad was who he was, contributed to my lack of achievement. Don't misunderstand me, I am in no way placing the blame at dad's door, or mum's for that matter, although I have to say that I can remember no occasion when either of them actually made me stay in at home to do my homework or sit me down and drill into me the importance of my years at school, especially this school. I like to think that they did, but I simply don't remember it. No, I think it had more to do with my rebelling against dad's position, and cocking a snook at whomever used that phrase to try and get me to work. I think the more they used it, the more I rebelled. I remember saying to an acquaintance, years later that I was "rebel" at school. He replied with the cutting remark that he thought I was simply trying to "boost my own ego". This little exchange has remained with me all these years, and has always caused me to wonder about my rebellious tendencies theory. Was he right? At that time, I really did think he was wrong. Now I'm not so sure, he may have been right! Although I wanted to be thought of as rebellious, and probably was to a certain degree, it's more probable that another reason lay behind the lack of success. Being careless of dad's position would however, appear to at least form part of the reason for my under-achievements.

It was certainly the case that I didn't like some of the teachers, most notably, Mr. Walmsley, the chemistry teacher. He was a short, squat man who was not opposed to using physical violence on us boys. Apart from getting the odd slap for misbehaving in class, I well remember one such episode. This was probably when I was in the second year, and since the first day at school, I had been plagued by the attentions of a female classmate, not blessed shall we say, with good looks! (The mother of one of my best friends once said that everyone had a right to be ugly, but this girl "abused the privilege!") She used to stare at me incessantly in class, and always seemed to be around where I was in the playground at break times. I suppose I got used to it in the end and ignored it, but on one particular day, we were sitting at the same table for lunch, along with six others. The dining tables were arranged in a square and she was sitting adjacent to me. She had been staring at me for the entire meal, which wasn't a problem, but she had also been kicking my leg under the table for about five minutes continuously. Just like the staring, I had ignored it initially, but then I got fed up with it and eventually gave her an almighty kick back, just when Walmsley was looking in my direction. The next thing I knew, I was yanked out of my chair by Walmsley, not by my collar or arm, but by my hair. Still gripping me by the hair, he dragged me across the floor to the door and literally kicked me out of the dining hall with a boot to my backside. He refused to listen to my protestations, and I ended up in front of Mr. Kelly, who did listen to me, but still gave me a lecture about being nice to girls, no matter what!

Where Mr. Walmsley was a brute of a man and a bully, Mr. Dean, the deputy headmaster, was a gentle giant. He was much larger than Walmsley, both in height and girth, but he never used his size to intimidate or punish. He was the woodwork teacher, and I absolutely adored him and woodwork. It was probably the only subject at which I excelled for the three years we were taught it, and it was only three years, as woodwork was not an "O" level subject, unfortunately.

After the third year, woodwork was replaced by metalwork up to GCE level and, along with engineering drawing, this was the only other subject which I enjoyed, eventually achieving the stunning result of a grade six "O" level pass. (Grade six was the absolute lowest pass possible). However, it was woodwork, which I enjoyed the most and was probably the best at in the class.

Maybe here, I have another clue to my under-achievement at school. Woodwork, metalwork and engineering drawing are all technical subjects, as opposed to others such as English, maths or science, which are academic subjects. Although absolutely hopeless at art, (remember the papier mache lion!), creating something out of wood or metal gave me a huge thrill, and I was always prepared to work hard in those lessons, especially when given the right encouragement. Unfortunately, Mr. Dean retired after my second year but he was replaced by an equally capable man. He inspected my woodwork one day and then referred to me as a "craftsman" in front of the rest of the class. My chest swelled with pride.

I have never been good at academia, physics and biology etc. Those subjects at school never held my interest like woodwork and metalwork. Unfortunately, woodwork and metalwork were the only subjects, apart from physical education, in which we were not given homework. I can't help wondering just how different things might have been had I been able to do more practical subjects. I remember once asking the woodwork teacher if I could make myself a fishing box as a project in my spare time. He agreed, provided that I designed it and built it completely alone, but with his guidance. The box was planned out in detail, including the interior, showing the type of wood to be used and the joints for the various parts of the carcass. I was so engrossed in my project, I worked on it during lunch times and after school whenever I could. It became a matter of pride to me that this fishing box would be constructed as well as I could possibly manage, and really did work to the best of my ability. When I finished it, it was shown to other classes as a model of good work before I took it away to use. I think what I am trying to say here is that where I found a subject that really interested me, I was more than willing to get down to work and learn about it. The same was true many years later when I joined the Police Force. The subjects at Training School interested me greatly, and I passed out top of my intake.

Having examined various options to explain my lack of achievement, I think the main reason would have to be my lack of ability in academia, coupled with a fair dose of indifference!

One of my earliest memories at Biddulph grammar school was the day I met Anne Stoddard. It could only have been the second or third day I had been there and during one of the break-times, some kid came up to me and said, 'Anne Stoddard fancies you' and then, typical of an eleven year old, ran off, giggling.

I had no idea who this girl was and so asked one of the local lads to point her out to me. I remember the first time I saw her, she was leaning against the wire netting of the playground, chatting to her friend Jean Wilcox. I was astounded! She was quite the prettiest girl I had ever seen; high cheek bones (which have always attracted me), a miniature ski-jump for a nose, dark wavy hair, slim, and a fantastic pair of legs. I had never seen the like of her before and I was smitten. The trouble was that I was too immature to realise it. Our relationship went on and off the boil like a kettle over the 5 years we spent at school. Most of the "off" periods were my fault, trying to give the impression that I could take or leave our relationship.

It all finally ended when we left school, she went off to teacher training college, and I went down the pit! That is, until we met up again after a chance remark by one of my other friends, Annette. I was married at the time, but the marriage was struggling, and if I'm perfectly honest, was probably doomed. Anne was living in Evesham at that time, separated from her TV weatherman husband, and when we met again, it was obvious that the old spark was still there. However, I was still married and did not betray my wife. When my marriage finally failed, then we had a wonderful and torrid relationship. She had two children by her marriage, Peter and Alison. I think Alison quite liked me but Peter was very cold towards me, why, I don't know. He seemed more sensitive than Alison, and perhaps he saw me as a threat to his father's position, whatever that was. The relationship between Anne and I carried on for a little while, but having just had one very traumatic time, where I had committed myself wholly to one woman and had it thrown back in my face, I wasn't too keen on doing it again. Neither did I see myself being a father to someone else's children, one of whom I was not going to get on with!

We finally broke up when she announced, rather surprisingly that she had accepted a proposal of marriage from some guy she had met skiing, (a sport which I introduced her to). Strangely enough, I was invited to the wedding, although I think the fact she wanted to turn up at the church in my rather knobby sports car had something to do with it. We had some great times in that car, at one stage hurtling along a dual-carriageway towards a roundabout. At about 90mph, she leaned across and shouted, "It's left to Evesham and right to Kent!" Although I knew exactly what she meant, we turned left.

On the day of her wedding, I pitched up with my gleaming sports car, a replica AC Cobra. We had a private chat before we left but then I managed to stuff her and her massive wedding dress into the front seat and we roared off to the church.

I last saw Anne with her husband Roger in 2002 at the school reunion. She seemed very happy with her life, but I can't help wondering how different it might have been had my circumstances not been as they were.

As far as I remember, every other pupil in the class was born and brought up in the area of Biddulph, or at least in the Stoke-on-Trent locale. I, on the other hand, was an outsider! Not only was I originally from Somerset, but I had also moved to Biddulph from Kidsgrove. The distance between the two towns was only around 5 miles, but that was enough to enable Biddulph to have a totally unique way of speaking. It was essentially a Stoke dialect, but with heavily accented and altered words. A question such as, 'are you going home?' would be pronounced, 'aat tha guin wom?' The phrase 'you know' would be pronounced, 'tha knowst' and the actual name of Biddulph would be pronounced 'Biddle', so, 'are you going to Biddulph?' would be 'aat tha guin Biddle?' Very confusing at first, but I soon dropped into it, and after a while, although people could probably tell I wasn't a native, I was very much accepted as a "local", which was exactly the result I was looking for.

Over the following five years, I met and cemented friendships with many local boys and girls. Remarkably, for these days, some of those friendships have lasted to this day, and will carry on lasting. Annette is one of my very best friends. Highly intelligent, intuitive and not afraid to speak her mind; she's put me right on a few occasions! Annette's father was called Harry Kendall. He was Polish and came to fight for the allies during World War 2. His surname then was Kostkowski, but changed it to Kendall when he decided to stay in England. He was a lovely man, very stern looking but with a great sense of humour. He used to work at the same colliery I went to work at. Harry was an "Overman", like a supervisor, and I very often used to bump into him, quite literally, on the coal face as I was struggling to drag all the surveying equipment up the face,

One of the favourite tricks of the face workers down the pit was, whenever they saw a young lad crawling up the coal-face, they would lie in wait for him. We didn't have the overalls the miners have these days and everyone wore their old clothes. Trousers seemed to suffer the most and crotches in them were almost non-existent. The height of the face would vary from about ten feet to only about three feet, and you invariably had to crawl along over the pneumatic "chocks" supporting the face. The only light you had was from the cap lamp, which you held in your hand, consequently, you were always looking downwards and couldn't see someone squatting down in front of you, especially when they had turned off their lamps. You sensed rather than saw someone in front of you and when you looked up, your face was about two inches away from a pair of coal blackened testicles and a penis being swung from side to side. The miner would be wearing a lascivious grin as he greeted you, "'eh-yup youth". "Fuck off" was the general reply and the miner would crawl off chuckling at his latest victim.

Another friendship, which has endured all these years, is between myself and Alan Sherratt. Alan and I were in the same class, and in our younger years, spent practically all our spare time together. We would go fishing, or bike riding or some other pastime. Alan was the first person other than my parents, with whom I went on holiday.

What an adventure! We were only about 12 then, and Mr. and Mrs. Sherratt took their two sons and me to Butlins at Pwllelli, North Wales. Believe me, "Hi De Hi" was not too far from the truth. I remember the cabins we slept in; cold draughty places and drab as ditchwater. The food hall was just chaos! When I think of the food that we were given on that holiday and compare it to what is available today, it's a wonder people ate it. But then, this was the early sixties; the type and quality of food did not seem to be a major priority, and the influence of the Continent had not yet been felt. I remember it was bland and tasteless, but of no matter to me whatsoever, I was on holiday with my best friend and loving it!

Alan was a fantastic sportsman! After we left school, he went on a scholarship to Lillishall Cricket Academy, but ended up playing semi-professional football for Macclesfield Town. Being an industrial area, all schools played football, and all boys were expected to take part. I don't think any school in the area played rugby. There were seven "years" at our school, starting with the First Years and ending with the Upper Sixth, and each "year" had a football side.

Most Saturday mornings during the season, us boys were expected to turn out for the school, and do battle on the football pitch against some other school from the district. Every other "year" at school had a moderately good team, but for some reason, ours was absolute rubbish! Despite the number of hours we would just kick a ball around between us, we lost the vast majority of our matches, and by massive margins. The only shining light in our team was Alan. I remember watching him, and being mesmerised by his ball skills; nothing of course, compared to the players of today, but to us boys, he had magic feet. He was totally self-effacing; a product I think, of his strict upbringing by his parents. His mother was a wonderfully warm and friendly woman. The family had very little money as was the norm on the Miners' Estate and most of the children were expected to help around the house with all the jobs. Alan was no exception. He often wasn't able to come and play football as he had "the pots to do" or "shopping to get". When he did play, it was great. There was none of the posing that one sees on television these days, we simply got on with it. I remember once, about four of us were messing about with a football, and Alan was dribbling around all of us. It became a mission for us to get the ball off him and a mission for him to keep it. This was the only time I can remember Alan actually laughing at other peoples' efforts, and the more we tried to get the ball off him, the more he laughed. It wasn't an arrogant laugh, just someone enjoying his talent.

I think my most abiding memory of Alan was during one of those awful saturday morning matches. It was raining as usual and the ball was sodden. In those days we didn't have the lightweight balls of today; we had those thick brown leather balls which doubled in weight on a wet day. The goalkeeper had booted the ball out from a goal-kick and it was heading in my direction, all of about 20 yards away. He'd got some height on it and it was descending towards me and my opposite number, who was probably feeling the same as me; if I didn't get it right, it was going to hurt! It looked like a small brown comet, with the water streaming away behind the ball as it hurtled towards me. Suddenly, as the ball was just about at head height, Alan came from nowhere, in between the two of us and headed the ball back, almost as far as the goalie had kicked it! My opposite number looked at me and said, 'fuckin' 'ell! 'e must 'ave 'ead like fuckin' concrete!'

Everyone in the team came to dread the end of the term in July, because the results from all the school sports teams for the year were read out to the entire school. When Mr. Kelly came to our football team, there was a general buzz around the hall, with much shuffling about. Some of it was us trying to make ourselves smaller in our seats, but mostly it came from others eagerly awaiting our results and making sure they were in a good position to hear.

It generally went something like, "Now, 3rd year football", (this was where most of the shuffling took place), "matches played 15, matches won, nil, matches drawn, one, matches lost, 14. Goals for 3, goals against 78". Mr. Kelly, bless his heart would always add a "well done" at the end, but people rarely heard it over the hooting and derision which always accompanied our results.

If anyone ever says to me, "where are your roots?" I always reply, "Stoke-on-Trent." This was where I really started to grow up, and where I forged most of my friendships. Some people, younger than myself, with whom I now come into contact, cannot understand the depth of feeling between a bunch of friends, or just how a friendship can last for nearly fifty years. I have mentioned Annette, Anne and Alan, but there's also Geofrey Crowley. I recently went to his wedding in Stoke and our friendship is as strong as ever. But it's not just me and my friends from Biddulph, it's others as well. Another girl in our class was Jeanette Jenion, and she has been best-friends with Annette for longer than I have known either. They were at primary school together, and were inseparable then! Anne is still friendly with her school-friend, Jean Wilcox. Steven Brown and Jennifer Hill, both from our class, were boyfriend and girlfriend right through the five years we were at school. A few years after we all left, Steve and Jennifer got married and today, they are still in love with each other as much as they ever were. They still live in Biddulph, as do some of their grandchildren, and I still see them, although not very much. Our friendships have stood the test of time and I'm grateful for them.

In my early teens, I joined the ranks of the part-time Saturday and Sunday workers. I got myself a job with a local lad cleaning windows. I can't remember how I got the job, although I fancy it was through a mutual friend, and it certainly didn't last very long. The thing I remember most about it though, was that the boss, David Meakin turned out to be a cousin of mine on my mother's side. He was related to the Meakin pottery family, as was my mother's mother. The 'family tie' however, was not strong enough to prevent me leaving the window cleaning business when another school pal invited me to join him and the other boys serving petrol at a local garage. In its own small way, being a petrol boy at Mill Hayes Garage seemed to have some sort of magic about it. The job was much sought after by other lads, and anyone who did work there, achieved minor celebrity status, although for the life of me I can't think why! It was dirty and smelly all the time, cold and wet some of the time and well paid none of the time. But it was huge fun!

The garage comprised a car sales showroom, a mechanical workshop, a paint shop and the petrol sales. It was owned by a man called Donald Ratcliffe, a miserable man who rarely had a good word for anyone. He was assisted by his brother-in-law Brian, who worshipped Don, and a guy called Doug Lithgow. Quite what each was supposed to do, I never really knew, but Brian certainly used to like being the only one there after Don and Doug had gone off to watch Port Vale on a Saturday afternoon. I seem to remember Don was a director.

Although there were usually some comings and goings amongst us petrol boys, there were always four of us working a shift rota over the week-end. When I joined, the unofficial boss was Mick. It was he who had invited me to join and he was best friends with the owner's son, Ian. I last saw Ian not so long ago in a pub in Biddulph. He had married his child-hood sweetheart and become a drunk! He was embarrassing to be around.

When Mick left, I became the boss-boy. When his replacement joined, there was me, Jeff Perry, "Tich" Lawton (so-called because of his obvious lack of height) and Edmund Hak. There was no extra money for the boss-boy position, but it carried a certain amount of kudos. Boy, we used to have some fun! Jeff and I would turn up on a Saturday morning, usually still stoned from the previous nights alcohol intake or pill popping at the local dancehall, the "Golden Torch", Tich hounded and took the piss mercilessly out of Brian, and Ed, well, Ed was Ed, he just got on with things.

I remember once when Tich pinched Brian's hat for a laugh. For some unfathomable reason, this cloth cap was Brian's favourite, and he chased Tich all over the garage premises. Being much older and less fit than Tich, Brian would stop every few yards, draw breath and get even more angry at Tich. He knew Tich was doing it just to wind him up and all he had to do really was ignore it. But no, Brian had to get the upper hand and so he chased Tich, threatening him with all sorts of punishment when he caught him. At one point even Don was laughing at Tich tormenting Brian by waving his hat at him from the top of the car sales park. Eventually Brian's spirit broke, he gave up the chase and shouted at Tich, "you're fired Lawton!" Tich was still trotting along the top of the car park as he simply shouted back, "you can't fire me Brian, you're not the boss" Brian went straight over to Don, who was standing just outside our little booth, to plead his case. I don't think Don had too much time for Brian. He just shouted at Tich to "give him his "stupid fuckin' 'at back." "OK, boss," shouted Tich, emphasizing the "boss" bit and Brian slunk away with his tail between his legs.

Tich was undoubtedly the character amongst us boys. Our weekly pay at this time was 3 shillings an hour, about 15p in today's money. Tich thought this should be a little higher and as I was the boss-boy, was pressed into approaching Don for a rise of sixpence an hour, about two and a half pence today. Don's response was swift and predictable! It had something to do with going away and finding other jobs! I think the rest of us were quite happy with our little number and didn't really want a confrontation with the boss, but Tich argued his case with us at school over the following days. Once again, I approached Don and asked for the rise, (I actually felt like begging him to give in, just so that the whole nasty business could go away) only this time, I carried an ultimatum from "all" the boys. In actual fact, it was from Tich; if Don didn't agree to the rise, we would withdraw our labour! Withdraw our labour, we were petrol boys, we worked on weekends and now we were about to go on strike!! When I delivered the ultimatum, Don didn't flinch, he just kept on polishing one of his cars. "ahh, raight" he said. There was nothing else from him, so I slunk back to the booth where Tich was waiting. He was enjoying this, but he wasn't the one who had to confront Don. It was about two hours later, when Tich had finished his shift and gone home, that Don shouted for me to see him in his little sales office. "Here we go," I thought. I went in and stood in front of Don. "Withdraw your labour, will you?" he said. I was shaking with fear as I stood there and manfully said nothing. "Well", he said "no need, you can have thrupence an hour more" and grinned at me. He was enjoying it more than Tich, who was obviously very pleased at the outcome. Me? I was just glad the whole business had gone away. Petrol boys on strike, I ask you?

One night in winter, the snow had fallen and was lying quite thick on the ground. It was late on Sunday evening and no cars were calling at the garage for petrol because of the snow. Tich and I decided to have a snowball fight around the pumps. When we weren't serving petrol, we used to sit in a small glass encased booth, which seemed to have been attached to the showroom as something of an afterthought. It was where we kept the oil and other accessories and where we kept warm in winter. We started the snowball fight, running in and out of the pumps and around the car sales. In the heat of battle, I had been squeezing this snowball, waiting for the right moment to unleash it at Tich. Unwittingly, I had turned the snow-ball into an ice-ball. As he ran in front of the booth, I threw it and immediately knew what was about to happen. It seemed to take forever to get to where Tich was running. If it had hit him, it would have been a cracking shot, and probably would have killed him into the bargain, but as it turned out, Tich unsportingly ducked at the last second, and of course, it went straight through the glass window. We both knew Don was out and Brian was looking after the place, sitting in the flat at the back of the garage. He was bound to have heard the glass breaking and would be down instantly. Tich saw the problem immediately, the broken glass was on the inside of the booth, along with the melting remains of the ice-ball. In order for us not to get into trouble, everything had to be on the outside.

He galvanised both of us into action before Brian could appear on the scene. We quickly brushed the glass onto a piece of cardboard box and scattered it outside the booth, underneath the hole in the window, being careful, on Tich's insistence to leave a small amount on the floor inside, just to add a little more realism! We had about a minute and a half before Brian would come storming down. Sure enough, down he came, right on time, demanding to know what us "little bastards" had been up to. Tich carefully explained to Brian how he had walked into the booth, slipped on the wet floor, and fallen against an oil can display, which was a freestanding unit. Unfortunately, the unit was against the window; well it had to be didn't it, otherwise how would people see the oil for sale!? Brian was definitely suspicious, as no doubt you or I would be in the same circumstances, but Tich had added a stroke of genius. He had placed the oil display, not only against the window, but actually with one corner through the hole. The ice-ball had mercifully smashed the glass fairly low down. When Brian arrived, it appeared we were outside, "clearing" the glass up; whereas actually, we were still in the act of putting it down! Faced with our abject apologies and Tich's brilliant explanation, delivered with a poker face, the scene he was confronted with and the sheer likelihood of it all happening owing to the weather, Brian had no choice but to accept the inevitable, Tich had won again. Of course, all the footprints and hollow channels in the snow where we had scooped it up to make the snowballs, would have given the game away, had Brian had the wit to look around him!

I think Mill Hayes was my introduction to the world of organised crime! I consider myself pretty lucky to have grown up in an iconic era; that of the "Mods" and the "Rockers", or "greasers" as we used to call them. I was a Mod, and as such, had the obligatory scooter. Mine was a Lambretta SX 150, adorned with copious mirrors, a back rest for the passenger, a fly screen etc etc, all the bits and pieces necessary for a young "Mod". The music of this period was great; all those wonderful Soul artistes such as The Four Tops, The Isley Brothers, Roberta Flack, The Supremes, The Beatles and Rolling Stones of course and many more were the centre of our existence. I remember my friend Jeff Perry and I would go to a record shop in Burslem during our lunch break from college, and Jeff would buy at least two or three records, usually by some obscure recording artist, who then rose to great fame and fortune. If he still possesses his record collection, it's probably worth a fortune these days. He had an almost encyclopeadic knowledge of the music greats of the time. And of course, our clothes; Parkas with fur lined hoods were a must, as were the blue serge suits, and neat, well cut hair. In those days, my hair was so spikey, I had to surreptitiously use a hair net to plaster it onto my scalp. I don't why I bothered, I later found out that my efforts at secrecy had been useless and everyone knew that I did it, laughing at me behind my back.

In total contrast, the "greasers" wore dirty old clothes, had long, greasy hair, generally looked a mess and rode around on huge motor bikes. The two groups didn't get on to say the least!

The one shining moment in my memories of the "mods" and "greasers" was when one of the more infamous "greasers" in Biddulph, a lad called Vickers, accepted a lift back home from college on the back of my scooter. His motor bike had broken down, and I just said to him, "I'll give you a lift home if you want." To my surprise, he accepted, and seemed totally not to care whether he was seen on the back of a mere scooter. The differences of opinion between the two groups, which often ended in huge punch-ups at seaside resorts such as Rhyl or Brighton, were well known in those days, so it must have looked an extraordinary sight, this well known "greaser" on the back of an enemy scooter, his long hair flowing out behind him in the wind, (no obligatory crash helmets in those days), him dressed in dirty old leathers and me in my regulation Parka. I dropped him off at his house, and afterwards, although we were never friends, we always spoke in a friendly manner.

In the Potteries at that time, there were only two major dancing venues, "The Place" and "The Golden Torch". Each was good in its way, but "The Place" was a little more sedate than the "Torch." If I was to tell the absolute truth, I really wanted to go to "The Place" rather than the "Torch", but all my friends went to the latter, and I didn't have the courage to go on my own. Every Friday or Saturday night at "The Torch", there would be a fight, sometimes involving a dozen or more youths. The toilets were a disgrace, continually awash with urine and water, the bar floor was permanently spongey from spilt beer; the seats were always sticky with, whatever! It was an awful place, yet I went there week in, week out.

"Organised crime?" OK! We used to get our wages from Mill Hayes on a Friday night, and I would pick up mine and Jeff's on my way to the "Torch." Somehow, the doorman at the "Torch" got to know that I worked at Mill Hayes and said to me once, 'any chance of some Green Shield Stamps'. We used to give a certain amount of stamps with petrol sales and you could surrender them for goods, much the same as "loyalty cards" today. "What's in it for me?" I asked. He replied, "well I'm the doorman here" Enough said! Every Friday night after that, I would pay my way into the "Torch" with Green Shield Stamps I had pinched, OK stolen, from Mill Hayes. And how did I get to the "Torch", on my scooter, of course. And how did I get the petrol? From Mill Hayes, of course! On a Saturday night, the pump numbers would be taken to show how much petrol had been sold in the week. Don only ever wanted whole numbers, so the tenths were ignored. Sometimes I would do it and sometimes Don himself took them. The numbers would be taken about 30 minutes before we locked up for the night and then Don would disappear up to the flat. When he'd gone, I used to roll my scooter onto the pumps and examine the display to see what the tenths figure was showing. If there was say, two tenths showing on one of the pumps, I would switch it on and take the petrol up to the nine tenths figure, so that a whole gallon wouldn't record. I'd do this on another pump and, having paid only for my two-stroke oil, would end up with a full tank of fuel! Pretty petty stuff I know, but it was organised and it was theft. I'm not proud of either of these tales!

There were several events during my teen years, which have remained with me, and which have served, not only to develop my character, but also to provide a sort of pool of experience, into which I can occasionally dip. Some of these events took place over a few years, and others were short, one-off little gems. The reader may have guessed that I didn't help my dad around the house too much. It wasn't that I was lazy, simply that there always seemed to be better things to do. It was something I regretted later in life, as I think I could probably have had a better relationship with dad much earlier. I always loved and respected him, but couldn't connect with him until I was much older; possibly due to his being a headmaster, I don't know; maybe it was just me!

There was one summer when I did help him to paint the garage, and he said something to me then which has almost become a template for anything I do or attempt. The garage had a skirting just underneath the edge of the roof, and between the skirting and the wall, was a soffit, which ran horizontally around all sides of the garage. Now, owing to the builders' mistake of building the house the wrong way around, the garage was at lower level than the house, and so if you looked out of the kitchen window towards the garage, all you would see would be the roof, the wall and the skirting. The only way you could see the soffit was if you were down at the garage level, looking up under the edge of the roof. I was painting the skirting nearest the house when dad came along to check on my progress. I had deliberately not done the soffit as you couldn't see it and consequently, there was no point. I was on a ladder, and dad was looking up at me and of course, the soffit. "How's it going?" he said. "Fine," I said. There was a small pause before he said, "Are you going to do the soffit?" 'No,' I replied, "there's no point, you can't see it," emphasising the phrase "can't see it"! He just carried on looking up and said, "I can" and walked away.

It wasn't so much the implied instruction to paint the damn soffit, it was the sheer logicality of what he'd said. Having declined to paint it on the grounds of its supposed invisibility, the fact that he could see it, dictated that it should be painted, which after a short wrestle with my conscience, it duly was. The lesson here was that if you are going to do something, do it to the best of your ability. As I've got older and presumably wiser, this little episode returns to me often when I'm working at anything, and guides me towards doing precisely that, the best I can.

One of my hobbies at this time was canoeing. There were no fast flowing rivers in the area for white water kayaking, so I had to content myself by paddling up and down some of the dozens of local canals. I was given my first canoe by a neighbour. It was a single-seater, and quite old, but perfectly serviceable. A couple of pals at school used to come along, and we would take it in turns to paddle around. One of them later obtained a canoe, and so we could go for longer trips.

It wasn't long before I outgrew the single-seater and persuaded dad to buy me a double-seater, which came in kit form. He only agreed to buy it if I paid something towards it and promised to construct it myself, which I did. (yet another lesson)

Whilst waiting for the kit to arrive, four of us decided that we would take our canoes and tents and go on a long trip up the canal towards Manchester. We planned to be away for about a week, and the four comprised me, Alan Sherratt, Michael Lowe and a boy called Stuart Machin. Stuart had his own two-seater canoe, so with my double-seater, we could all paddle and stow the camping gear and food.

The construction of my two-seater was only finished the night before we were due to set off, and then only after hasty repairs had been completed to the covering around the bow. Dad piled both canoes onto the top of his car, stuffed all the gear in and off we went. We had of course, looked on a map and so knew the direction we were heading in, but had no idea of how far we would get in one day, or indeed, over the following five or six days. The other thing we hadn't taken into consideration was all the locks we would encounter, and just what an effort it was to get around them. You had to have a licence to enter the locks on the water, and so, we were left with lugging both canoes, filled to brim with gear, around each lock. I think in the first day and a half, we negotiated something like a dozen locks. It doesn't sound much I know, but remember that each canoe took two of us to manhandle. We had to lift each canoe about three feet out of the water, drag it up onto the canal bank, lift it and then carry it fully loaded for about 75 yards to the other side of the lock, and lower it carefully back into water. It was tiring work and not a little frustrating.

In the afternoon of the second day, after the umpteenth lock, Stuart decided he'd had enough. I have to say that we were all pretty cheesed off with having to do so much carrying, but none of the rest of us had contemplated going home. We spent about an hour trying to persuade Stuart to stay with us, but he wouldn't have it. In the end, we gave up. Stuart phoned his father from a phone box, and we sat down to wait for him. At that point, we all thought Stuart would naturally leave his canoe with us so that we could all be on the water, but then he told us he would be taking his canoe home with him. We tried to reason with him, saying that if he took his canoe away, at any one time one of us would have to walk along the tow-path, and as this was supposed to be a canoeing trip, it sort of defeated the object. He wouldn't have it though, so in exasperation, we took what we could into the one remaining canoe and left him to wait on his own. Prick!!

As it turned out, we only had to negotiate probably two more locks and then we were clear. On the third day, we found a smashing camp site right on the canal bank at the edge of a field, with a farmhouse not too far away. We spoke to the farmer, who was happy to let us camp.

Owing to our change in circumstances, we decided to stay here for the rest of the trip, generally messing about in the canoe and taking walks into the local town. I can't remember the name of the town, but on our way back to the camp site one afternoon, we walked over the crest of a hump-back bridge spanning the canal, and I saw a car driving away in the distance. It was a long way off, but I saw a large white object on the roof. For a fleeting moment, I thought it was dad bringing my spare canoe for us, but then it couldn't have been, how would he know we were there?

When we got back to the camp, there was a message pinned to the flap of the tent to go and speak to the farmer. He told us that a man had come to the farm asking about a group of three lads. The farmer didn't know our names, but he thought it was obviously us the man was looking for. He said he had a white canoe on the top of his car and from this, I knew it was dad. The farmer told us the man would return in the morning. That evening, we had a chat amongst ourselves and decided that when dad came in the morning, we would pack up and go home. We'd had our holiday and thoroughly enjoyed ourselves, apart from Stuart letting us down, but now would be a good note to end on.

Dad arrived bright and early the next morning, and we loaded up the gear into his car. We thanked the farmer for his kindness; he hadn't charged us anything for camping on his field and had even supplied us with fresh milk every day, what a lovely man. On the way home dad told us what had happened and how he had found us. Apparently, Stuart's father had come to see him, and told him what Stuart had done. He was pretty angry with Stuart and embarrassed about his son's selfishness. He told dad where Stuart had left us, and bless his heart, dad immediately loaded up the second canoe and set off in search of us. He figured that we hadn't got very far with only one canoe and just kept stopping at various houses along the canal-side, asking the occupants if they had seen us. Eventually, someone said they thought three lads were camping at so-and-so's farm, and hey presto, there he was.

I remember being very proud of my dad on this day, and he told us just how proud of us he was that we had decided to carry on even when the going got, relatively difficult for us. It would have been very easy to have gone home with Stuart, but we had all decided sub-consciously, that we were made of sterner stuff.

I mentioned earlier on this chapter that I consider myself fortunate to have been a teenager in an iconic era. I also have to say that I scraped through this period by the skin of my teeth. Why? Because when we used to go out on a Friday, Saturday or Sunday night, I would "pop" maybe a dozen or so pills before getting to the venue, usually the "Torch." Essentially, I was, and still am really, a shy person. Dancing, even in a massive crowd, makes me very nervous. I seem to get the impression that everyone is looking at me attempting to move to the beat, and laughing at me. Taking pills was a way of overcoming this shyness and enjoying myself. I had no real idea of the danger I was placing myself in from addiction or from the crime aspect.

The effect the pills had was quite remarkable, and it is easy to see why they were popular amongst the youth of that time. All inhibitions disappeared and the taker was sent off on a "high." Unlike LSD, which was also popular at the time, you didn't get hallucinations with the "high," just a great sense of 'who cares!' Depending on the number you took, the effects would last for some time, at least for the entire evening, and sometimes well into the night. I remember lying in bed on a Sunday night after going out to the Crystal Rooms dance hall in Newcastle. The pills I had taken would keep me awake all night long, quietly humming music to myself, clicking my fingers and generally moving my whole body in time to the tune in my head. However, I was never so far out of it that I wasn't aware of what was happening. I would watch the time on the clock, and at the right time, would listen for my father to get out of bed on the Monday morning, go to the toilet and then begin the process of getting me and my sister out of bed for school. I listened for him to come down the hall to my room. I would then physically stop myself moving and humming and pretend to be asleep. When he called 'Neil!' to wake me up, I would answer in a groggy voice and reply 'yeah yeah' or something like that. Fortunately, he never came right into the room, only shouted at me from the doorway, and so the deception was that much easier. When he closed the door, I would immediately start the humming and moving again, eventually springing out of bed to get dressed, but still having the presence of mind to act sleepy when I greeted mum or dad in the kitchen.

The pills themselves were nothing more that slimming tablets, usually prescribed to women who were depressed after child-birth or who were attempting to lose weight. They had various common names such as "blueys," "green and clears" and "bombers". The problem was of course, that they were, and still are addictive. I never really thought about the consequences of taking these pills, I just knew that they enabled me to lose my inhibitions, and enjoy myself. Practically everyone in my circle at that time used to pop pills at one time or another, but there were some people, for whom it became a nightmare. Thankfully, I never got too near to these people, I was always on the periphery of this inner circle of mods. What scares me most, is thinking about how I would have reacted had I had the opportunity to join this group, or at least be seen with them. The people I'm talking about usually went from the "Golden Torch" on a Saturday night up to a venue in Manchester called "The Twisted Wheel." This was an all-night club, and most of those from the "in crowd" would go along. Whilst I, and many other youths at this time were mods, there were some youths who were far more prominent, and achieved almost celebrity status. Two in particular spring to mind, "Tombo" and "Sparky". I didn't know either of them personally or their real names, but you couldn't go to the "Torch" without either seeing them or hearing about them in some way. They were certainly high profile in the mod fraternity, and people used to revere them. I shudder to think what may have happened if I had been able to go along to the "'Wheel" on one of these nights.

Many of the guys who ran with Sparky and Tombo, with some of whom I had a passing aquaintance, ended up in prison, having been convicted of burgling some chemist or surgery in order to steal the pills and sell them on. I was so keen to be liked and accepted, I'm not sure I would have had the strength of character to say "no," and that's what scares me now when I think of this period in my life.

And so, I came to the final chapter of my school life, my G.C.E. exams. I seem to remember I took eight exams all told, English Language, German, Geography, History, Engineering Drawing, Metalwork and two Mathematics exams, both G.C.E. and C.S.E The latter was a lower standard exam and I had been put in for this because I was so bad at the higher level. Why I wasn't put in for all C.S.E.s, I don't know. The day my exams started was an awful reckoning for me. I had suddenly realised just what an absolute idiot I had been. I had done practically no revision or studying, kidding myself that I was going to be alright; after all, the pass mark was only 45%! How difficult could they be? At the time I walked into the exam hall, I seemed to sense that I was doomed. Panic set in, and of course, I made a complete hash of everything, but at the same time, trying desperately to keep up my "couldn't care less" attitude. When it was all over, I breathed a huge sigh of relief, content to wait for the results. Even then I thought some miracle may occur, but as I talked over the exams with others in my class, I knew what those results would be.

At that time, I was going out with a school friend, Jill. We were practically inseparable, right up to the time I went to visit some other girl I had met on a field trip somewhere. Nothing happened between us, but of course Jill got to hear about it, and promptly dumped me. I had heard through the grapevine that she wasn't best pleased with me, so I went up to her house to explain myself, and got the door slammed in my face! She said she never wanted to see me again. The old "couldn't care less" attitude took over and I tried to put a brave face on it all, but I was devastated. I was desperate to see her again and get back with her, but she wouldn't have it. A few weeks later, I saw her brother and he was very excited about the fact that he was going to have a brother! I didn't understand what he meant until he told me that Jill was going to marry a man she had met at "The Place." I next saw her a few years later at Annette's wedding. She was still married and had a beautiful daughter. She seemed happy, and I thought it had probably turned out for the best.

It was to be many years before I saw Jill again. It was at some party or other back in Biddulph, and Jill was there with her second husband, Clive. Annette had kept me up to date with Jill's life and I knew that she had had another daughter. I was divorced at that time, and Annette told me that everyone, including Jill and Clive would be meeting at her house prior to the party. I have to admit to being a little nervous at meeting her again, and of course Clive. How would he react to me?

I needn't have worried, the evening went with a bang, and Jill and I seemed reconciled. The day after the party, we spent some time alone together, and she told me that her relationship with Clive wasn't that good. We spoke about how our lives had taken such different paths, but here we were again, together.

It wasn't long before a passionate and beautiful relationship began between us. Jill would travel down from Yorkshire to come and stay with me. On occasions, she even brought both of her daughters with her. We went on holiday to Kenya together, we went for weekends away and generally enjoyed each other. We laughed all the time, and both of us seemed completely at ease in each other's company; but all the time, I had this little niggle that she was married to another man and that what we were doing was wrong. I know she felt it too and at last wrote to me to say that she couldn't carry on deceiving Clive, and that she couldn't see me any more. I was very saddened by this, but at the same time, relieved that the burden of guilt had been removed. I couldn't undo what had been done, but felt that at least, if I saw her with Clive again, I wouldn't feel quite so bad. He was no angel, but the fact remained, he was Jill's husband.

Clive died a few years ago after a long battle with a brain tumour. Their relationship had grown stronger over the years that Jill and I had not seen each other, and when he died, she was devastated. I so wanted to contact her again, but felt that she needed to be left alone and that if she wanted me, she would contact me.

We did get back in touch eventually, and the relationship started all over again. It was different this time though. There didn't seem to be the same intensity on my part. I seemed to be afraid of her and of committing myself to her. The prospect of commitment hadn't been important before as she was still married to Clive. Now, it was different, there were no barriers to Jill and I being together permanently. But somehow, I couldn't take that extra step. (It was to be repeating pattern.) I had been hurt badly over my marriage break-up, and had closed all doors to my inner self. I tried desperately hard to regain the old feelings, but it simply wasn't happening. In the end, she again called it off and today, Jill is very happy in her relationship. I will always feel a deep love for Jill; she infects everyone she encounters with her sparkle and zest for life. I'm just sad that when it mattered, I wasn't able to be the person she deserves.

Back to the exam results! When they came out, I was so convinced that I had failed everything, I couldn't face going to the school to pick them up. Jill got them for me, and they were as bad as I feared. I had failed everything, apart from Metalwork, in which I had barely scraped a pass and C.S.E. maths. The maths result was actually grade 1, which constituted a G.C.E. pass, so after five years education at one of the top grammar schools in the county, I had the grand total of two G.C.E. passes, both at grade 6, the lowest possible grade. My father was, shall we say, disappointed! Deep down, I felt rather ashamed, I knew that more was expected of me. I also knew that sacrifices had been made to get me into Biddulph Grammar School, including Lynne having to travel from Biddulph back to Kidsgrove to attend her school. And what had I done to repay them, absolutely nothing! Being hopeless at academia was not an excuse, I knew it had been a waste.

The last weeks and months at school were spent trying to sort out what career I was going to have. Mum and dad were determined that I would have a "career" and not just a job. I had always wanted to follow dad into the Royal Navy, but he wouldn't let me do it unless I went in as an officer. This meant going to Dartmouth Naval College for some years, and to me, that was another school! No thanks, not a chance! So what was I going to do? Someone at school suggested that I had a look at a company called English Electric. They manufactured mainly washing machines and other kitchen appliances, but they were also getting involved with some new technology, something called a computer!

This was 1968, and computers were largely unheard of, at least amongst ordinary people. I had nothing else to do, so I went along to the company for a look. I spoke to one of the white-coated boffins there, who tried to explain to me that programming a computer was a highly skilled job, that one day, computers would dominate our world, and that computer programmers would command a huge salary. He proudly showed me into this massive room, which contained rows and rows of cabinets with tape spools spinning erratically backwards and forwards. "This," he said proudly, "is our computer!" "What, the whole thing, one computer?" I said. "Yes," he replied, "one day, everything will be controlled by one of these" I tried to act interested, ask some intelligent questions, but I had already made up my mind and said to myself that this "computer" thing would never take off!!

So what was I going to do? I don't really remember how it came about, desperation probably, but eventually, I signed indenture forms with the National Coal Board to be an apprentice mining surveyor. This was a good move for me, only one day a week at college, and the rest at work, earning some money. The only down-side was just that, the practical work was down in the bowels of the earth, on the coal faces.

And so, I left school in the summer of 1968, to begin my seven year apprenticeship as a Mining Surveyor. Seven years!!

Chapter 6

The coal mine, more commonly known simply as, The Pit! There can hardly ever have been a worse environment for man to work in; hot, airless, dirty, dusty, dark, highly dangerous and nearly 500 yards below the surface. Yet, amongst the men who worked down the pit, there was such camaraderie as one would be unlikely to encounter almost anywhere else, except maybe the armed forces. The very conditions in which these men toiled, cemented friendships and commanded loyalty.

Biddulph is situated on the outskirts of the manufacturing heartland of England, about 35 miles north of Birmingham. In 1968, when I started down the pit, there were two collieries in Biddulph, Victoria (known locally as "The Bull") and Chatterley Whitfield. I know nothing about Chatterley Whitfield except that it was used as a training pit for other collieries in the area. It was where I did my basic training before starting at "The Bull." Even though I was joining the surveying staff, every man working below had to have a degree of mining knowledge and competence to avoid any serious accidents. Chief amongst the more deadly dangers, was gas. Over the centuries, it has been responsible for countless deaths in coal mines the world over. It alone was responsible for the invention of probably the most important piece of safety equipment ever, the "Davy Lamp."

Wherever one encounters coal beneath the surface, gas is omnipresent. The two most common types we encountered were "black-damp", which causes death by suffocation owing to the lack of oxygen in the mix and is therefore non-flammable, and "fire-damp", otherwise known as methane or marsh-gas which was very definitely inflammable. During my training, I remember watching a demonstration of what methane gas can do. It's lighter than air, and so floats to the roof, where it gathers in pockets created by the unevenness of the roof strata. Without proper and adequate ventilation, igniting methane will have devastating effects. The instructors set up a long glass tube with a bulbous bit on the end, much like a "yard of ale" tube, only two or three times as long. A small amount of Methane was introduced at the open end and allowed to gather at the top of the tube and travel down to the bulbous end. It was then ignited and a blue flame shot along the length of the tube. When the flame reached the bulbous end, the gas that had accumulated, exploded. There wasn't enough gas in the tube to cause the end of the tube to shatter, but it showed quite clearly just how dangerous methane can be, and how seriously we should treat the danger. With all the countless millions of tons of coal beneath the surface, imagine the amount of methane gas present!

Before the "Davy Lamp" there was no safe means of testing for gas, apart from the Canary bird. (Victoria colliery still had a Canary when I went there in 1968.) Miners had no artificial lighting in those days, and so had to light their way and their work with naked flames from candles. The naked flame would often ignite the gas and cause an explosion. Countless lives were lost in this way. Around 1815, Sir Humphrey Davy, a renowned scientist invented the lamp which still bears his name.

He constructed a glass tube with a lighted candle inside, around which, was sufficient wire gauze to "mask" the heat of the naked flame. With this lamp, there was not enough heat to ignite the gas, but the miner could still see what he was doing. In later years, the lamp was modified and improved. Electric lighting was installed in the pit, but the "Davy Lamp" was still used to test for gas. Using the same principle, the lamp is held up into the roof of the tunnel. If methane is present, a dull blue hue hangs over the flame in the lamp, indicating the presence of the gas. Steps would then be taken to disperse the gas harmlessly, as only a large build-up of methane causes explosions. It always seemed odd to me that countless men have died from igniting gas with a flame, yet that very flame in a controlled environment has probably saved as many lives, if not more.

When my basic training was finished, I started in the surveying office at Victoria Colliery. There were five others in the office besides me, and I hated them all, except the boss Robert Scott, whom I remember as a decent man. The second-in-command, Arthur Clowes was a man who hated Bob Scott simply because he was in charge. Arthur thought he should be the boss. He was a weasel of a man, bitter, sarcastic and cruel. The next down the line was Geof, I don't recall his surname, but he was very friendly with one of the other apprentices in the office, Alan Addams. Alan was a good-looking lad and seemed to have a lot of success with women. Much of the time in the office seemed to be taken with Alan relating the details of his latest conquest, much to the delight of Arthur and Geof, who seemed to idolise him for his sexual prowess. I, on the other hand, was still a virgin at this time, and today, I thank my lucky stars that I wasn't tempted to start making up stories about sexual encounters simply to keep up with the likes of Alan.

Arthur, Alan and Geof were very friendly with each other and between them made many a joke at the expense of myself or the third apprentice. Arthur had this nasty little habit of whispering to Alan or Geof whilst looking in your direction. Both would then burst out laughing. I think Geof was probably a decent man when on his own or with his family, but as I only ever saw him at work with the others, I only saw this side of him. The other person in the office was another apprentice, more senior than Alan or I, but I don't recall either of his names. He was just arrogant and condescending about his position over Alan and myself. However, senior as he was, even he didn't escape the mockery of the others. I grew to dislike going to work in the office intensely, as I felt I was becoming ever more withdrawn and isolated. The less I had to do with the others, the better I liked it, and only felt normal when I had finished work for the day or the week-end and could get away from them. I suppose it was all part of growing up and so-called "character building". Compared to Alan, I was pretty immature for my age, but it was still unnecessarily nasty.

Let me take you through a typical day at work. We'd start at 9am and my first job would be to make tea for the office. We'd all sit in the little ante-room where we had an old fashioned machine for reproducing the colliery plans. Alan would then regale us with his exploits of the previous night, and then we would go into the drawing office, where Bob Scott informed Arthur or Geof where they would be surveying that day. Both Arthur and Geof were qualified Mining Surveyors, Arthur having the higher qualification entitling him to have the letters F.R.I.C.S. after his name. I don't think Geof cared a great deal, as long as he was able to earn money.

Bob Scott was a finickity man, very precise and proper, earning him the nickname of "Bobbity" from Arthur; another example of his mocking, sneering sense of humour, if indeed it was humour.

Let us assume that Geof is going to lead the party. He would get out the plans of the area we would be going to, and then all of us would pore over them, Geof explaining what we were going to survey, along with any difficulties we may encounter such as recent rock falls or flooding. It sounds a little exciting, it wasn't! The run-of-the-mill daily surveys were to keep the new headings being dug on their precise bearing in order to reach the new coal seam. A "heading" was another name for a tunnel, but it was so-called because essentially, the headings were the tunnels leading to and from the coal-faces. They themselves were given names, some of them wonderful sounding, such as "Bellringer" or "Ten Foot" or "Havelock".

It was a very major undertaking to open up a new seam. Hundreds of thousands of tons of rock would have to be blasted away with explosives in order to dig the headings, massive coal extraction machinery known as "shearers" would be taken down the pit in parts and re-assembled in situ, rail lines would have to be laid, conveyor belts constructed, dozens of huge hydraulic supports known as "chocks" transported to the face etc etc. And when the seam had been worked out, all the machinery would then have to be dismantled and taken back out of the pit and so the decision on how best to get the coal out was crucial.

Geologists had conducted their surveys prior to this and established exactly where the seams of coal were located. Between them, the surveyors and the management, a decision would be reached as to how best to access the seams and whether or not the amount of coal that could be extracted made the effort financially viable.

Having decided where we were going, the surveying party would head over to the shower complex to change into pit clothes. Each miner and surface worker had two lockers, one for clean clothes and the other for his pit clothes. This was in the days before miners were allocated working overalls and old trousers and jackets were the norm. We'd strip naked in the "clean" side, walk through the shower area into the "dirty" side, get our pit clothes on and then go to the canteen for a lovely, greasy sausage sandwich and a cup of tea before going down.

The canteen ladies were great! They were always laughing and joking with the men, lots of innuendo and sauciness from both sides, and all the ladies had those great big "bee-hive" hair-dos, formed into a rock solid shape by massive amounts of hairspray that used to pervade the airspace around them and make your nose itch. Tea was served in giant mugs, strong and sweet, the sandwiches were the size of door-steps and you went down the pit, a happy man.

From the canteen, we'd go to the lamp-room. Each employee at the colliery had a cap-lamp allocated to him, along with two "checks". One of the checks was brass and round in shape, and the other was aluminium and square in shape. These two seemingly innocuous little objects were probably the most important items a miner possessed. In the lamp-room, one of us would draw out a "Davy Safety Lamp". We would then make our way to the shaft.

Every colliery has two working shafts; there may be other redundant shafts in the area, but there always has to be two in operation at the same time. These are known as "upcast" and "downcast". The "downcast" shaft is where the clean surface air is drawn down through the colliery by massive ventilation fans. These fans suck the air through all the workings in the pit, and eventually out to the surface via the "upcast" shaft. Consequently, the air coming up the "upcast" shaft is foul and dusty. For some God forsaken reason I know not, the coal travelled out of the pit in the "downcast" shaft and the men travelled up and down in the foul air of the "upcast" shaft.

I was always fascinated by the "winding gear"; massive great steel wheels around which a steel cable, about 6inches in diameter would travel, bringing the "cages" up and down. The cable was drawn by a huge electric engine and controlled by one man, the "winchman". This was in the days before computers could control everything, and the winchman had to rely on his skill and knowledge to assess when the "cage" was reaching pit-bottom. The cage would contain anything up to twenty men at a time, and each and every one was reliant on the winchman not to get it wrong and crash the cage into the pit-bottom floor. There was the occasional parting of the winch cable, sending the cage and any occupants to certain and gruesome death at the pit-bottom, but thankfully, these events were extremely rare.

The part that particularly fascinated me was that to assist the winchman, there was a simple system of markers on a board to tell him when the cage was at pit-bottom. It must have worked on a gear system and consisted of three white painted marks, two static and one which moved up and down a steel rod, between the two static markers and in time with the movement up and down of the cage. The moving marks would line up with the static ones when the cage was at the bottom or the top. The winchman would watch the two marks coming together and slow the cage down, finally stopping the winch when they were together.

Compared to today's electronic and computerised standards, this was stone-age technology. The shaft was around 500 yards deep, the cable would stretch and contract with weight and yet, the winchman, acting blindly, could stop the cage within inches of the pit-bottom, allowing the men to walk straight out of the cage onto the pit floor simply by watching two white marks coming together. And he never failed!

The two shafts were not far away from each other and sometimes at the end of a shift, when we were waiting for the cage to descend, I would wander over to the coal-riding shaft and just watch the operation. When coal was being loaded, it was a hive and a buzz of activity, but I was always more fascinated by the sheer drama of the arrival of the coal truck cage. It was a three tier cage, each of which could hold about three trucks. If any man rode to the surface in one of these cages, he would be dead before he got to the surface, such was the speed at which the cages were drawn up. The change in pressure was far too much for the human body to adjust to in so short a time.

A bell would ring when the cage was about to descend from the surface, at which time miners gravitated away from the edge of the shaft. You could hear nothing at first, but gradually, a rumbling sound could be heard above you. The sound got louder and louder and was then accompanied by a whistling noise as the wind screeched through the cables. Eventually, the noise became deafeningly loud, the blast of air being pushed down in front of the cage was strong enough to blow your coat-tails up and your helmet clean off. When the cage arrived, it did so with a mighty crash, which if you were at pit-bottom, blindfolded and unaware of what to expect, would scare you half to death.

Here again, the "winchman" did his bit. When the cage reached the bottom, it was travelling so fast, that the steel cable would stretch something like a foot or more, so much so that it always ended up below the railway tracks, but only ever by a few inches. Obviously, the cage and the tracks had to be exactly level or the trucks wouldn't go in, and the man at "pit-bottom" simply clicked a buzzer to the "winchman" to go up or down those precious few inches. I saw this operation many times, but I never ceased to be enthralled by the skill of the "winchman."

To go into the "downcast" shaft, you had to go through an airlock, and then to the cage area itself. Here, you were met by the all-powerful "cage-man". He would subject you to a body search before allowing you to descend. The purpose of this was to look for "contraband". This was always in the form of cigarettes, lighters and matches, even dead ones. With all the explosive gases around, I can't imagine anyone being so stupid as to take a lighter down the pit, but I suppose it had happened in the past. If this man found any contraband at all, especially a live match anywhere on your person, you were not allowed down the mine. He would report you to the manager, and the punishment was instant, on-the-spot dismissal, such was the importance placed on contraband, quite rightly so too.

Most miners smoked, and they got around the tobacco habit by taking "twist" with them down the pit. This was a length of pure tobacco, with the consistency of liquorice. A miner would bite off a length and chew it, spitting out the juice onto the floor. I can't think of a more disgusting habit. I remember trying it once and making the mistake of swallowing some of the juice. It was almost pure nicotine, and as such, almost pure poison! I vomited on the spot, much to the amusement of my so-called colleagues and fellow pit dwellers.

Having conducted his search, the "cage man" would collect one of the two "checks" every miner collected with his cap-lamp. You gave the brass one to the cage-man when you went down and the aluminium one when you came up to the surface, effectively exiting the mine. The "checks" were stamped with the same number as your personal cap-lamp, and when both "checks" had been received by the "cage-man", he would replace them on the peg in the lamp-room. If only one "check" was present, it meant that man was still down the pit. This was the only way that the authorities had of telling exactly who was down the pit at any one given time, and was obviously, especially important in cases of explosion or cave-ins, when every miner or underground worker had to be accounted for. It was a very simple system, which relied on the common sense of the worker and which, worked. To my knowledge, the system was never abused, it was thought to be sacrosanct.

The journey down the shaft would take around 10 minutes. As we got lower, I could feel my ears popping with the pressure difference and water dripped continuously. At one stage, we passed old workings where the shaft had previously been sunk to. Peering into the blackness of the abandoned roadway as we trundled on down always struck me as eerie.

Once we reached the pit bottom, we started our long trudge to whichever heading or face we were going to survey. It was a long trek to the nearest workings, along a roadway called the "main crut." I have no idea of the origins of the name. Alongside where we were walking was the only man-riding conveyor belt in the mine. It allowed tired men to get a lift from their workings to the cage area. Riding it was governed by a set of strict rules, but more about that later.

Walking along the "main crut" was a hazardous journey in itself. The ground was very uneven, and in places, went down slopes, or "banks". There was a rail system running throughout the pit for coal trucks and when these trucks needed to negotiate a slope, a miner operated a winch at the top to lower or pull the trucks along the slope. It was always dangerous to walk down the slopes for fear of banging your head on an "acker". These were part of the safety system for these trucks, to prevent them running down the slope out of control if they broke free, and killing or maiming men at the bottom. They were massive steel girders, which were attached to the roof at one end and which could swing down to the ground at the pull of a lever by the winchman at the top of the slope to form a sort of ramp, up which the runaway trucks would travel and crash into the roof and then to the floor, so preventing them careering to the bottom of the slope. If it ever happened, it was usually a mess, but preferable by far, to the destruction they would cause if they ran away unchecked. When they were not deployed, the "ackers" would lie close to and parallel to the roof. However, over time, the free end would hang down a little from the roof, just enough to catch the unwary miner, who would probably have chosen just that moment to take his helmet off and wipe his forehead. The slopes were always slippery with water and negotiating them meant watching for your footing rather than what was up above. Collisions with "ackers" were commonplace.

Having negotiated all the "ackers" and heavy steel air-lock doors and abandoned machinery and flooded roadways and miners relieving themselves, squatting in a "scrape", we would arrive at our destination. For the first few occasions down the pit, this was all very strange, and not a little daunting to me. For instance, I had never seen a man with his trousers around his ankles, defecating in public before. Being down the pit was a fascinating experience to begin with, a bit like an adventure, but eventually, I got used to seeing and experiencing these things. It's like most things you do every day, you eventually pay no attention and the fascination is lost. In the end, I just wanted to get down the pit, do the job and get out as quickly as I could.

Our destination was usually a new heading being driven in to a new coal-face. The surveyor's job was to ensure that the heading was not only going in the right direction, but was also straight. Some miners used to think they were so good, they could keep the heading going in the right direction, without any assistance from us, almost as if they could "smell" the coal. There was always a reason, usually a rubbish one why they were several feet away from the bearing when we put the theodolite in.

Keeping the roadways straight and level was easy really, and like other things, very simply done. The surveyor would place the theodolite over an established benchmark at the beginning of the heading. He would then turn the instrument around to the required bearing. Meanwhile, the trainee, or lackey, me! would be mixing up a solution of limedust and water in a little pot to create a sort of paint. Part of my equipment was a ball of string, a paint brush and a pot, which I never went down the pit without. The limedust was used to cover the walls of the heading to keep gas down, and was everywhere. The paint I would make up in the pot was white and when prepared, I would have to walk all the way down to the end of the heading, where the men were working and hang the lamp from one of the roof girders. Moving his cap-lamp either left or right, Geof would then indicate to me which way to move the lamp until it was directly on line with the bearing, at which point, I slapped a daub of paint onto the roof girder. I then ran the string from my new mark to the last mark and painted the girders where the string ran. The miners then knew by how much they had to correct their heading simply by looking along the roof marks. If the line was dead centre, they were fine, if the line was 2 feet to the right of centre, they knew they had to correct the next stage by 2 feet to the left. After painting the bearing, I would hold a measuring staff for Geof to sight through the theodolite. This was to determine whether the heading was staying level, or creeping up or down.

Once a year, we would have to survey the whole pit, both current and old workings. When a coal seam has been worked-out, all the headings and roadways remain there but are not maintained. Over a period of time, the workings begin to collapse. I remember having to crawl along roadways that would have been around 10 feet high when they were first constructed, but were then only maybe 2-3 feet high. The weight of strata above the roadways, countless millions of tons, would push solid steel girders through the rocky floor. The roadways and headings were shaped in an arch. The girders placed along the sides and under the roof were called "rings" and had to be one yard apart. They were immensely strong but eventually had to give-way under the enormous downward pressure.

One man I encountered several times down the pit was known to me only as "sheep-shagger Bates". I don't think I ever knew his real name, and didn't care too much anyway. He had a really bad habit of spitting into my paint pot. It wasn't your normal, everyday spit, like when you clean your teeth and spit into the sink; no, this was a stream of disgusting, brown tobacco juice, which he used to save up just for me. He would creep up behind me, or just to the side, and then spit this stream of foul liquid from around five feet away, straight into the centre of the pot. He never missed, but he did get a full pot thrown over him once. Didn't stop him spitting in my can though!

Occasionally, I would get down to the roadway working end just when the "shotfirer" was about to blast the rock away. He was the man who set off the explosives drilled into the rock. His was a highly responsible job, but it was usually quite relaxed. When he was ready to fire, he would shout just that, "fire", at which point you took cover behind heavy steel shields and covered your ears. In reality, you had just seconds to find cover as the "shot-firer" assumed everyone knew he was about to blast, and shouting "fire" was a mere formality. There was a very heavy, dull thud and then the steel shields would be bombarded with thousands of little rocks, most the size of peanuts. If you didn't cover your ears, the pressure wave could burst your eardrums, and if you didn't get behind the shields fully enough, you got hurt.

Having completed the surveying task for the day, we would make our way back to the start of the "main crut" and the man-riding belt. The strictest rule about riding this belt was that you were not allowed to lie down on it. Having done a full shift down a hot and airless pit, the last thing you wanted to do was sit upright and stay alert. The belt itself ran over a series of rollers, and so had a gentle undulating movement, a soporific effect. Even doing the short spells we did down the pit, I would very often succumb to the motion and lie back on the coal. As soon as you did this, you fell asleep, or I did anyway. This was the second strictest rule. It was bad if you broke the first rule, but if you did, you were absolutely not to break the second and fall asleep. Death could easily follow, as I very nearly found out one day. I broke the first rule and then almost immediately the second. As assistant, I had to carry the tripod legs and these I placed on the belt with me, usually just at my side. At the far end of the belt, was a landing stage about 20 feet in length where you jumped off and ran just a few steps to slow your momentum down. The only warning you got that the landing stage was approaching were signs on the roof, not much good if you're asleep! The belt continued for about ten yards beyond the landing stage, and then went over a huge drum. The coal, which was on the belt, was hurled down onto a metal plate and was then scraped backwards into a large hopper. The pieces of coal were often the size of an armchair, so if they fell on you, goodnight!

The first I knew that I had arrived at the landing stage was a frienzied shout from Geof. I was awake instantly, and instinctively knew I was in trouble. I had the space of about ten yards in which to get up, grab the tripod legs and stumble back fast enough over huge lumps of coal, against the speed of the belt, back to the nearest point that I could grab onto the landing stage. I reckon I had about 2 or 3 seconds before I was going to get crushed.

There was an emergency-stop pull-wire, which ran along the length of the belt, but my colleagues were never going to get to that in time, they just watched in amusement as I got nearer to the edge and oblivion. Some survival instinct inside me kicked in and I was stumbling back along the belt with the tripod almost as soon as I had woken up. I gradually got nearer and nearer to the stage and eventually made a huge lunge and grabbed on to one of the posts with my free hand and dragged myself over the coal onto the stage. When I eventually stood on the landing, battered and bruised, Geof looked at me and said, without one ounce of sympathy, "Yuh daft bugger!" I have to admit, he was right. This was the closest I have ever come to death, and ever want to come.

At the end of a trip down the mine, we always went back in to the canteen for a lovely hot cup of tea and a freshly made meat pie. There was always terrific banter in the canteen between the ladies behind the counter and the miners, much of it being sexual innuendo. In those days and in that sort of society, men were hugely dominant over women. Miners were, and still are, tough men engaged in a dangerous occupation; there was no political correctness in those days and women were expected simply to support their men. A few women though, such as our canteen ladies, gave back as good as they got. At the start and end of a shift, the canteen was always an amusing place to be.

After the tea, we would go for a shower. Remember, the shower block was split into three parts; the clean side lockers, through to the showers and then out to the dirty side lockers, going in reverse when coming out of the pit. The area was generally known as the "pit-head baths" This was where I had my one and only introduction to colliery homosexuality. Every pit had its fair share of homosexuals, although in those days, it was kept very quiet, and certainly nobody ever "came out".

Even as a rather naïve seventeen year old, I had always had my doubts about a man named Alfie. He was a short, ugly man of about 60, and unfortunately, he changed his clean clothes in the same locker bay as me. One day, I had come out of the pit early, on my own and had gone for a shower. I noticed there was only one other shower being used in the baths, but paid no attention. It was an accepted practice amongst miners that, because the dirt and coal dust got just about everywhere over your body, another person using the showers would come to you and say "wash your back, bud?" ("Bud" was a common name for anyone, much like "mate" or "pal") There was nothing sinister about it, nothing remotely sexual, it was just something that every miner did for every one else, simply to get clean. Incidentally, it was a practice that came back to haunt me many years later. After a rugby match one Saturday, I was taking a shower along with all the other players. I must have been in something of a dream world, because I suddenly heard myself saying to the guy showering next to me, "wash your back?" As they were coming out of my mouth, I desperately wanted to take the words back, especially after the look he gave me, but I braved it out and tried to look as manly as possible! I'm sure he wouldn't have accepted my explanation anyway, that I wasn't gay and wasn't being, shall we say, over friendly!

Anyway, it was Alfie using the other shower and we both washed each other's back as normal. I hung around in the shower for a while, but eventually went to the "clean" bay. Alfie followed me. I glanced over to him at one stage and saw he was hunched over, with his hands down in front of him, although at that stage, I paid no attention. The lockers were arranged on two levels, and mine was on the upper tier and so I had to stand on a small ledge to get to my clothes. I was standing on the ledge drying myself off, when Alfie suddenly turned around and looked up at me. He had a massive erection and was leering at my body, as he played with his penis, bouncing it up and down in his hand, grinning with horrible, tobacco stained teeth. I think that day, I broke all records for getting clothes on in some form of order, any order, just to get the hell away from him. Nasty little man!

Having had tea and showers, we would head back to the office to let Bob Scott know what we had done and any problems. The actual surveyor, Geof would then update the plans for the area we had been in with the progress the heading had made. And that was a typical day.

At the time I was there, I neither liked nor really disliked working down the pit. Looking back though, I see my time there as a real experience. It was a tough environment and I feel I'm all the better for the experience. Many of my friends and colleagues express surprise when I tell them my first job was down the pit. It's not a place any of them would like to work, but each and every one is always interested to know what it was like.

Today, absolutely nothing remains of Victoria Colliery, "The Bull", except the memories. It has been completely razed to the ground. The shafts have all been filled in, the unmistakable colliery winding-gear broken up for scrap, the rail sidings paved over, the slag-heap landscaped and the land used to create another industrial estate. Financial and environmental considerations contributed to the death of "The Bull." It is fitting that the land is still being used for manufacturing purposes, but somehow, it doesn't seem right that a thoroughly modern, but characterless brick and steel industrial estate now occupies the site where there was once a crucial part of British manufacturing; where men literally tore a living out of rock rather than press a few buttons; men who depended on each other and whose lives and families over generations, were inextricably linked to mining for their survival, but who are now largely forgotten. It will be their grandchildren who will be employed in these new units. I wonder if they spare a thought for the men who worked and died beneath their feet.

I continued to work in the pit until 1970, when a couple of events altered my life and shaped my future.

Chapter 7

The first event was nothing to do with me, but all the same, it had its effect as it was the precursor to the fragmentation of my family.

My sister Lynne had been going out with a man named David Archer from Burslem, one of the pottery towns. He was a qualified draughtsman, and in 1970, they got married and announced that they would be emigrating to Australia on the "assisted passage" scheme. This was a scheme instigated by the Australian government whereby suitably qualified people, mostly from England, could go and live and work in that country. Instead of paying the normal air fare to Australia, chosen people could travel there for £10 each. They had to make a commitment to stay there for a certain length of time, otherwise, they would be liable to repay to the government, the balance of their air fares and costs. This was a really gutsy decision on their part, as David would have to re-qualify to Australian standards before he could get proper work. I have often wondered whether those "standards" were actually higher in Australia, or whether they were just doing the usual thing of dumbing-down anything British.

The second event had a far greater impact on me directly. Not long after Lynne and Dave had married and left for Australia, my father had, unbeknown to me, travelled down to Dorset for an interview with the local education authority. I remember sitting in the lounge of our bungalow the evening he arrived home, and my mother being very excited about something. After a brief conversation between them in the kitchen, my mother came into the lounge and announced that she and my father would be moving to Bournemouth in Dorset as he had been accepted as headmaster of the biggest primary school in the area, at a place called Ferndown.

I remember feeling rather detached at the time about what my parents were about to do Nothing was mentioned about me. Neither mum nor dad ever sat me down at this stage or any other for that matter, and discussed my future with me; I was left very much to sort out my own life. Looking back on it, I suppose it was odd that neither of them discussed this with me, but then, that was how our family was, and it was certainly in character with my mother's outlook on life.

It was only about two years before my mother died and about eight years after dad had passed away, that I asked mum what plans they had for me at this time. "None," she replied. I pointed out the fact that I was engaged on an apprenticeship scheme, living at home and had just turned 18. "So?" she replied, "we knew that you would either lodge at Malcolm and Norma's next door and finish your apprenticeship, or you would spread your wings and go elsewhere. Either way, we knew you would survive!" "Survive!" I thought, what an odd way to describe your only son's future.

Many years later, when I received some counselling about the break-up of my marriage, the counsellor isolated this incident as being one of the single most important events to shape my character and life; I was effectively being abandoned by my parents. I suppose some may think that at the age of 18, a young man should be spreading his wings and learning how to cope with life. I don't disagree with this, but one usually accomplishes this with the aid and succour of one's parents. Don't mis-understand me, I bear absolutely no grudge against either of my parents for doing what they did. Largely as a result of their leaving me behind, I am a very independent person and perfectly happy with the way I am. It was just that neither of them made any provision for me. They didn't talk to me about it, they made no suggestions, they didn't relate the difficulties I would face or the challenges I would have to meet. I was being forced to face the realities of life in an abrupt and fairly brutal way, they simply assumed that I would get on with it and, "survive!"

When the realisation that I would be on my own finally sank in, I determined that I would indeed spread my wings, and eventually left the National Coal Board to go and lodge with Uncle Harold and Auntie Winnie Davies who lived in a lovely little village called Wenvoe, just outside Cardiff. (Harold was the man who made the banister.) They weren't actually related to me, but Harold and Winnie were mum and dad's best, and lifelong friends; calling them "aunt" and "uncle" was natural. They had a son Victor, and it was Victor who seduced me with stories of how much money he was making in the world of selling. I mean, he had to be successful, he drove a company car, a brand new Ford Cortina!! This was what I was going to do, this life was for me, sharp suits, company car, expense account, money coming out of my ears. The only problem with this master-plan was that Victor was, and still is, a natural salesman who could sell snow to Eskimos, and although I didn't know it at that time, I was to learn that I wouldn't be able to sell them a heater to save my life!

And so, in the summer of 1970, I left Biddulph to go and make my fortune in the exciting world of selling.

My first job was as a bread and cake salesman for the Co-operative Wholesale Society in Bridgend, about 30 miles outside Cardiff. I was replacing a lady named Gladys. I knew that one day, I would break into the top echelon of selling, just like my hero and mentor, Victor and took this job merely to fill the gap whilst I watched and waited for the perfect opportunity to unleash my talents on an unsuspecting selling world.

I think to describe myself as a "salesman" for the Co-op was a bit far fetched as all I did was deliver the bread on an established round and, "oh, and by the way, see if you can sell a few cakes whilst you're at it!" I remember the cakes were priced at 3d each (old money), and I ate far more than I ever sold, although as I had to pay for all the ones I did eat, I suppose in some odd way I was selling them, to myself. The co-op depot manager was always pleased with my selling performance but never knew that it was actually me buying all the cakes I supposedly "sold."

The best part about this job was the little electric van the Coop supplied for me. The round itself comprised mostly rural farmland, with open fields and thousands of sheep grazing alongside the roads. Being mostly farmland, there was hardly any traffic around, and the roads themselves were little more than tarmac tracks, many of them quite narrow. There was a particular part of the round where I had to drive up a steep hill and then down the equally steep other side. The electric van would struggle up the hill, seemingly about to run out of power just as she reached the brow. I used to stop the van here, admire the view for a few seconds and take in the scene below me, checking whether any sheep were grazing a little too near the roadside or whether I would encounter other vehicles. When the coast was clear, I used to take off the handbrake and career down the hill as fast as the little van would go. I could hear all the loaves of bread jumping around in the trays behind me and the van itself would be rattling along, bouncing and weaving all over the road until finally, I reached the end of the hill where I had to negotiate a tight right hand bend. Fortunately, I could see everything ahead of me and never encountered another vehicle as I yanked the wheel over and hung myself out of the right hand side to act as a counter-weight. The van lurched over to the left and then to the right as she eventually came back to the normal position. Quite how it never went all the way over was a miracle, but then, I never thought about it at the time, it was always such good fun to do it, the highlight of an otherwise very dull day.

If I really put my mind to it and made a big effort, I could have finished the round and been back at the depot by midday. However, I never seemed to be able to refuse any of the dozen or so cups of tea offered by the customers. I really should have collected money from them for their bread-bills, but I usually left empty handed or with a promise of "next week, baker" As pleased as he was with my "selling", my depot manager was not impressed with my money collection, especially when he discovered that there was a shortfall of about £20 in the returns I did make. We went through my books with a fine-tooth comb, including the time when Gladys was doing the round. We concluded that, although I wasn't the best at recording sales and deliveries, the money was missing from Gladys' time on the round. What a nice person! She nicks £20 and then leaves the firm to allow some poor schmuck to get the blame. The manager knew what had gone on but even so, I still had to repay half the outstanding amount, the other half was paid by the firm.

As it was, I used to get home from the bread round in the mid afternoon, and then have virtually nothing to do for the rest of the day or evening. I didn't have any friends other than Victor in the area, and he was always away on sales trips or out with his girlfriend, Irene. Time to do something about it! I looked in the local paper one evening and saw a large advert for the Top Rank Suite in Queen Street, Cardiff. This was a night spot for dancing, drinking and eating. I went straight down and asked the manager for a part-time job doing anything. I was immediately set on as a barman and started that Saturday night.

The Top Rank, or "The Rank" as it was known locally, fast became the centre of my existence. I made friends there, it was where I had fun and most important of all, it was where I came to be accepted. Just as I had been an outsider from Somerset arriving in Stoke-on-Trent, so I was an outsider from Stoke arriving in Cardiff. When I look back on those days in Cardiff and "The Rank", it never ceases to amaze me just how quickly the other workers at the Rank accepted me into their circle. They were all, without exception from the local neighbourhoods and most of them knew each other. When I arrived, I think they sensed that it had taken a deal of courage to approach the Rank in the first place and actually make attempts to find and make new friends. Coming from the area, they wouldn't have had to do what I did, but I think they appreciated just how hard it must have been and respected me for it. For my part, I knew I had to do it, or just sit at home getting more and more frustrated.

I eventually transferred from the bar-staff to the door supervisory staff (better known as "bouncers") to which I was manifestly unsuited. The fights I had had at school were nothing compared to the viciousness of the fights at the Top Rank, most of which were alcohol fuelled. I was completely unprepared, and as a result, lost a few teeth. There was however, one event whilst I was still working behind the bar, which must count as a milestone in my life. I lost my "cherry" to a local girl who had certain obvious charms and who wasn't particularly fussy about using them.

I had noticed her quite a few times hanging around the bar as we were closing up. She would chat and we would share a joke or two. One evening, I was wiping glasses and she marched up to where I was working and placed her folded arms on the bar. She then literally heaved her massive breasts up and over her arms and spread them in front of her. It was impossible not to notice them or overlook the obvious invitation, so I offered her a lift home in my Ford Anglia motor car. She lived in a suburb of Cardiff called Gabalfa and to get there we had to go past a derelict industrial estate, and it was behind an old factory, in the back of my Anglia with a girl who could at best be described as "loose", that I lost my virginity.

I was still doing the bread round at this stage, and when I transferred to the door supervisors, we often wouldn't finish until around 3am or even later. We sometimes had to lay out tables for a function the following day and couldn't go off until we had finished. I then went home to Wenvoe, slept for about two hours, and then drove the thirty miles to Bridgend. I distinctly remember falling asleep at the wheel of my car on at least one occasion and falling asleep at the wheel of the electric cart several times. It was stupid really, but then I'm saying that with the benefit of experience and age. At the time, I felt it was necessary in order for me to stay with my new friends.

I became particularly friendly with three guys at the Rank, Dave Giles, John Rees and Geoffrey Britton. These three more than any of the others seemed to look after me. They always included me if they were going out for the evening to another club called "Tito's," or if they were just going to chill out watching football or rugby at home, then I would be invited.

Dave's mum and John's mum both treated me as if I was another son. I never met Geof's parents much, as he didn't live at home. Oddly enough though, it was Geof with whom I was most friendly. I was best-man at his wedding to Valerie, another worker at the Rank and became God-father to his first daughter. I had moved away by this time, but still remained in contact, making visits down to Cardiff to see them. Geof had become a coach driver at this time and would travel all over the country, spending long periods away. He earned good money, but it probably contributed to his marriage break-up. Sadly, I eventually lost contact with the family. I think I got a little fed up with always being the one to have to travel to see them or to make contact in the first place.

I seem to remember Geof was going off the rails a little at this time. I think he had a girlfriend somewhere and I remember he was very upset when his brother was sent to prison for something or other. He came to my wedding in 1979, but our friendship seemed to be suffering.

Eventually, he left Val and the two girls and I never saw him again. I had never been terribly friendly with Val and I took this opportunity to break my contact with the family. I didn't see them for several years and had no contact from Val. I did once get a pang of conscience and went back to visit Val and the girls at their old house. When I got there, I found that they had moved away with no forwarding address. I walked away with little or no regret, but I do sometimes wonder what happened to the girls, whose names you have probably guessed, I can't remember. Isn't that sad?

I had two girlfriends whilst I was in Cardiff, Janet Rapson and Carol Hughes although I hasten to add, never at the same time. They both worked at the Rank and both knew each other. As I remember, my relationship with both of them was on/off all the time and when I wasn't going out with Janet, I was seeing Carol and vice-versa. The odd thing about the entire situation was that whilst I spent most of my time with Janet, I really wanted to be with Carol, but she didn't return the depth of my feelings, and Janet wanted to be with me but I didn't really return her feelings.

Carol was the girl I took to Bournemouth to meet my parents and they just adored her. But she didn't want me. I lost touch with both Janet and Carol when I left Cardiff, but did hear through the grapevine that Carol had married a production manager with Marks and Spencer, where she worked as a supervisor. I never heard from Janet after she moved to Guernsey.

Living with Uncle Harold and Auntie Winnie at this time was just a joy. They both adored each other, but Harold was forever larking around and joking with her. If they had a mild argument, he would end it by saying, "you bloody old thing you!" At this stage, Winnie knew she had won the day and just carried on what she had been doing.

They had this wonderful dog called "Rags". Harold had gone to the local dog pound to replace their old spaniel which had recently died. Harold used to relate the story of just how he came to pick Rags, which was a perfect name for him owing to his really shaggy and unkempt coat. He had walked down the row of kennels containing dogs and had been tempted by a lot, but then he came across this really scruffy looking animal, which was standing on its hind legs with its front paws on the netting. It barked at Harold and he just fell for it, telling the staff there and then that he would take it home.

They brought the dog out and Harold put it into the car. When he got home, he noticed that Rags had a limp, and investigating further, he found an ugly scar just under one of his back legs, near to his groin. More than that, it was obvious that the wound hadn't healed fully, or should I say properly, and was actually suppurating. Harold hadn't noticed this limp or wound when he was at the pound because Rags had been standing on his back legs and Harold hadn't seen him moving. Undeterred, Harold took the dog to a vet who told him that the wound might smell a bit from time to time, would never heal fully but wouldn't cause Rags any pain or suffering.

This suited Harold down to the ground as he and Rags had instantly formed this wonderful relationship.

I remember Harold and Rags had a game where he would be at one end of the lounge and Rags at the other. Harold would start growling, which would start Rags growling. Harold's growls would grow louder, along with Rags'. Harold would then start to pretend to attack Rags, which just sent the dog mad with excitement. He would howl and bark and jump around the place, and eventually the two would meet in the middle of the room, "barking" at each other. I'm not at all sure Harold wasn't doing it simply to wind up Auntie Winnie, who would eventually charge into the room shouting at the top of her voice to shut the pair of them up, and then throwing them out of the house. Laughing and muttering under his breath, Harold would take Rags into the garden. Poor Auntie Winnie did suffer a little with Harold's antics.

Although causing Rags no discomfort, the suppuration from the wound, which had apparently been caused by a hit and run car accident started to smell, badly! It got so bad at times, that poor old Rags would be confined to the garage. Eventually, because there were now several grandchildren around, Winnie persuaded Harold that Rags had to go, it just wasn't hygienic.

Harold had previously noticed a change in Rags and taken him to the vet. Unfortunately, the vet had now told Harold that the wound was probably causing a deal of discomfort to Rags and that he was suffering and would continue to suffer. With the intervention of Auntie Winnie, there was now only one solution.

On the day Harold was to take Rags to the vet, he didn't talk to anyone. The mood in the house was awful and Harold was clearly suffering. Victor, and some of the other relatives had offered to take Rags to the vet, knowing just how much this was affecting him, but Harold had steadfastly refused. He knew that it was the right thing to do by his family, and would allow no-one else to carry out the task. I think it was through some sense of loyalty to Rags that Harold insisted on doing this himself. Harold's face and manner when he returned without Rags remain with me to this day. I can't remember anyone looking so distraught and I'm sure that tears had been spilt from this strong and wonderful man.

He was silent and very down for many days, and the house seemed empty for a long time after Rags, we all missed him terribly, he was such a character. Even Auntie Winnie, who had suffered the most from Harold and Rag's antics, was missing him. But then the house was filled with the laughter of his grandchildren, and gradually Harold came back to the family.

I eventually left the bread round and started work as a car salesman at a local dealership called Evan Williams. It was here that I began to have suspicions that I was not cut out for selling. The commission in those days for selling a car was £2. I only worked there for about four months and can remember selling about three cars. When I say "selling" it would be more accurate to say that I showed the customer the cars and then let them make up their own minds. I simply couldn't think of anything to say to these people which would induce them to buy any particular car.

As a contrast, the disc-jockey at the Top Rank, whose stage-name was Ray Marand, (a.k.a. Raymond Lovegrove!) joined the sales staff, and in one day sold four cars, probably doubling his salary! Most car sales people these days drive around in "company" cars, usually chosen from the sales stock. No such luck with Evan Williams; I was driving around in my old Ford Anglia.

The best thing I remember about this car was the air horn that I had fitted; La Cucaracha (or some such spelling!) Working late on a Saturday evening at the car showroom meant I really had to get my skates on to get to the Top Rank in time for work. I rarely made it, but had to travel past the front entrance to the suite on my way in. As I got near to the Rank, I sounded the horn, which was pretty unmistakable and the boys on the door would send the message down to the office that "Neil's here"! One of the girls in the office would then book me in, and I would arrive all dressed and ready to go about 15 minutes later after parking the Anglia. The management were aware of my little system I'm sure, but even if they were, they said and did nothing; they were pretty relaxed people really.

So, back to selling cars; I was eventually sacked from this interesting and challenging position after telling the sales manager that the reason I was late back from lunch one day was because I had been for an interview for another job. Discreet, don't you think? Unfortunately, I wasn't offered the other job at the time I was being sacked, and faced the prospect of being on the dole. Then the other company contacted me to say that the person they wanted was no longer interested in the position and was I still available? Only second best eh! Hmmmm! let me think about this!! Pride, what pride??!! I needed a job, and so I started my third job in Cardiff within 12 months, as a Trainee Negotiator with an estate agency called Harold Greene.

I hated it, they hated me and I left after one month!

My selling career was in tatters! I realised at last that I was not going to make a fortune, or even get to drive a Ford Cortina! After leaving Harold Greene, I did go on the dole, but not in Cardiff. By this time, I had left Harold and Winnie's house and had set up in a flat with two other guys from the Top Rank. We had a great time whilst there, but after the debacle of the estate agency, I left Cardiff to go and live with mum and dad for a while in Bournemouth.

Chapter 8

I remember that dad left Biddulph to go down to Bournemouth before mum, who was left behind to complete the sale of the bungalow, and lived in a caravan until he'd found a suitable home for them both. I think he was there for about 6 months before he finally found a lovely two bedroomed flat, set in beautiful gardens alongside the River Bourne. The gardens themselves were known as Branksome Gardens and stretched away from the seafront for about a mile towards Poole. The "river" was little more than a stream really, but the gardens as a whole were lovely, very relaxing to stroll through with beautifully cut and prepared lawns, weeping willow trees along the banks of the river and glorious flower-beds which were just fabulous in the spring and summer. I'm no gardener, but nobody with a pulse could fail to appreciate the beauty of these gardens. And mum and dad had chosen to live right in the middle of them!

Their flat was on the fifth floor and was quite spacious with a lounge/dining room, kitchen, bathroom and two bedrooms. My room was pretty small really, but adequate for me, and the few possessions I owned. I arrived in Bournemouth in the summer of 1971, and immediately signed on the dole. I remember this upset dad hugely. He was of the generation that believed in the work ethic. To go on the dole and receive money for sitting at home was anathema to him, and I have to say, I felt very uncomfortable with it myself.

I was saved from spending most of my days at "Chalkie White's" snooker hall by an unlikely source. I had run out of cigarettes one evening at home and decided to take a walk into town to get some. For some unknown reason, I decided to walk up to The Roundhouse Hotel, a distance of about 2 miles from mum and dad's flat. In order to get to the hotel, I had to walk past, or at least near to any number of pubs etc where I could have purchased cigarettes. When I got to the hotel, which was at the top of a hill known as The Lansdowne, I decided to stay and have a quick drink. As I was leaving the hotel bar, I heard a voice call "Neil??" I turned round and recognised a guy called Mel Gravesner, who had been the catering manager at The Top Rank in Cardiff. He had left the suite suddenly and of course, the rumours had begun immediately about his departure being under some pretty major cloud. Needless to say, I was very surprised to see him in Bournemouth and although, I never really had that much to do with him in Cardiff, we chatted over a drink as if we were long lost buddies. He explained to me that he had come directly to Bournemouth from Cardiff, and was now the deputy manager of the hotel. Eventually, I left and his parting words to me were, "if you need anything, come and see me." I was in his office the next day saying that my "need" was for a job! Much to the dismay and pleasure of my parents, I began work as a waiter at the hotel; dismay at doing such a menial task and pleasure at not claiming benefit any more!

Most of the other waiters in the restaurant were either Spanish or Italian and apart from me, the only other English guy there was oddly enough, the wine waiter. His name was Brian and he was a weedy, obsequious little chap who was relentlessly bullied by the restaurant manager, a Spaniard named Mr. Pillau. He was a tall, stout man with a very ruddy drinkers' complexion and greasy hair, who used to continually adjust his crotch. He didn't really have too many kind words for anybody, but I think Mr. Pillau quite liked me really. He used to call me "Robin" although I think this was more from his inability to pronounce my surname correctly than through any form of affection!

My duties in the restaurant consisted almost entirely of clearing away the diners' plates after they had finished their meals and then re-laying the tables for the next diners. That was all there was for me to do, but I still managed to upset Mr. Pillau one evening by tripping over a chair leg and distributing the contents of six or eight sugar bowls I was carrying, under three or four tables of diners. Luckily for me, the sugar was in lump form and the diners were very understanding as I crawled in and out of the tables picking up the lumps. Mr. Pillau's face just got redder and redder as he bellowed at me from the doorway, "you peeeck up every seeengle luuump!"

I had been working at the hotel for about a month when Mel asked me to help out one of the other waiters, a guy called Giovanni, who did the floor service. Giovanni had the nickname of "the singing waiter" because of his tendency to burst into Italian love songs at the drop of a hat. I was later to learn that this was more due to his being almost constantly drunk than through any romantic notions of being a natural singer!

Giovanni was always very busy in the afternoons and had asked for help. And so I started to help him out two or three afternoons a week. I learned how to prepare and present a tea tray, how to carry it, loaded with goodies, perched on one hand above my right shoulder, opening swing doors and manoeuvring seamlessly through them without dropping or spilling the contents. And I learned how to spin a tray on the end of one finger, all useful stuff really!

On my first shift, Giovanni took me down to the farthest part of the kitchen, a pantry in the pastry chef's department. Here, he explained to me how the system worked. If the guests paid for their room service on their bill, the money went to the hotel, but if they paid cash, well then, that was ours. "A leetle perk" was how he described it. He went on to say that the hotel knew about this "leetle perk." I was so naïve in those days, I actually believed him! I didn't think that the management wouldn't condone such blatant corruption and certainly couldn't see that we were actually stealing the hotel's money. Giovanni had been there for years, the thought that he may have been a little bent never entered my head. I thought it was a wonderful arrangement, and helped Giovanni out whenever I could.

A few weeks later, I arrived for work in the morning and was told by Mr Tennerini, the head waiter that Giovanni had been sacked the day before for being just a little too drunk at work, and that I was to take over the floor service.

I thought all my Christmases had come at once, and immediately set about being an efficient floor waiter, preparing and selling as many afternoon teas as I could. If the guests ever asked how they should pay, the answer was always that "cash would be best" as they wouldn't get a larger bill at the end of their stay. After all, they wouldn't care less, they had paid and that was that!

Everything went swimmingly well for the next few months. I served breakfast and tea to a honeymoon couple, whom I didn't once catch out of bed for ten days and even served afternoon tea to my old boss Harold Greene, who had come to Bournemouth for a holiday. I made so much money, relatively speaking, that I was able to go out and buy myself another car, another Ford Anglia, my second.

One afternoon, Mr. Pillau called me over to where he was standing by a strange new machine. He explained that this was a new way of accounting for the teas and breakfasts I served on the floors. Whenever I made a sale, I was to record the details into the machine, which would then produce a slip. After this, I was to take the money I had collected for the service and the slips over to reception and "pay in as normal!" "Pay in as normal", his words hit me like a thunderbolt!! Suddenly, everything became clear. Why had I been so stupid as to think that the hotel knew about and condoned the "leetle perk." I remember experiencing two distinct emotions, shame that I would be thought of as a thief and anger at my own stupidity. There was nothing I could do, but to start using the new system that very day. I wasn't about to admit all to Mr. Pillau, and so, at the end of my shift, I took all the money I had collected, along with the slips over to reception. The girl on reception that afternoon looked at me quizzically when I gave her a load of cash, as if to say "how come they're paying cash all of a sudden?"

I was mortified at my stupidity! I genuinely believed that what I had been doing was accepted by the hotel management, and it was the reality of my stupidity which probably bugged me the most. I hadn't been intentionally dishonest, unlike my antics at Mill Hayes Garage, but I was in danger here of losing my job because I had been keeping the money. No-one was likely to believe my story. This, in my view, was serious.

There was only one thing for it, I had to admit everything to Mel and offer to pay all the money back, even if it meant selling my car. After a sleepness night, I went to the hotel early the next day and caught Mel as he was about to go into a meeting with the manager. I explained everything to him, leaving nothing out. I remember thinking his expression was very strange, almost benign. "Don't worry," he said, "I'll talk it over with the boss." I waited outside the managers' office for about two hours before Mel finally emerged. He was about to walk straight past me when I asked him how it had gone. "What?" he said. "The money," I almost shouted. "Oh that," he said, "huhhh! don't worry, just start paying in from now" And that was that, I wasn't going to go to prison or lose my job for stealing, I wasn't even being required to pay the money back, I could carry on as normal, just not pocketing the money.

Mel probably didn't even mention it to the manager. Looking back now, it's likely that there was a "leetle perk" aspect to the whole affair. Catering wages were notoriously low and scams like this would have been normal, wrong, but normal.

I quite enjoyed my time at the hotel, but after a while, I knew that I would have to start thinking about a proper career. I liked the catering trade and so applied for and got a job as Trainee Catering Manager with Mecca, the leisure company. Having worked at the Top Rank Suite, I rather fancied doing my training at one of the many Mecca Ballrooms dotted around the country, eventually to become some highly paid catering manager enjoying music, bands, dancing and girls at some glitzy venue; what a combination for a young buck! Where did I end up? Working under a dragon-lady named Iris McCord at the Mecca Bingo Hall in Portswood, Southampton, that's where!

The main thing I remember about training as a catering manager with Mecca is that I don't remember much training occurring. I learned how to make thousands of sandwiches using the least amount of margarine possible and how to scoop hundreds of ice creams for the interval, all with a hole in the middle; the bigger the hole, the more profit there was in the sale of the ice cream. This was Iris McCord's ethos, profit, profit, profit! Never mind whether the customers were happy with just sandwiches, tea and ice-cream with holes, this was what they got or they went without.

In the evenings, there was a bar upstairs where the customers could get a drink. Knowing about my time as a barman in Cardiff, Iris had placed me in charge of the bar. On a Saturday night, the hall would be filled to capacity, about 2000 people and dozens of them would crowd into the tiny little bar area where I would be working my rocks off just to get everyone served in time for the second session to begin. In order to cope, I would pull around twenty pints of beer and have them lined up on the counter ready for the onslaught. Fortunately, everyone knew that this was what I had to do to get everyone served and they knew that the drinks would only have been pulled minutes earlier. Occasionally, I had someone to help me, a lovely Irish girl called Philomena McDonald. Unfortunately, it was Philomena who very nearly got me lynched by the manager, Gary Bean.

I had asked Philomena to go to the switch control room and turn on the bank of nine light switches, not realising that she hadn't done this before. All the lights went off momentarily, but then came back on. She returned about two minutes later stating that she had done it. A few hours later, the resident engineer was running about the place panicking over something I knew nothing about. It all became clear however, when Bean called me into his office, ordered me to sit down and no sooner had I done so than he suddenly jumped out of his seat and started berating me. He was shouting and screaming obscenities at me, he was apoplectic with rage! I was still unaware of my latest misdemeanour, (there had been others!) when he eventually calmed down and explained that the boiler had been temporarily shut down and immediately restarted. I can't remember the exact details, but the gist was that the boiler had been restarted too soon. The oil wasn't being pumped in and therefore the boiler was heating up nothing but air. It was reaching a critical stage with an electrical circuit shorting out when the engineer, Chris, suddenly realised what was happening and had shut it down. Apparently, about another five minutes would have seen the boiler explode, and as it was right under the stage, it would have taken the whole hall and most of the people with it!

I was getting the blame, quite rightly, because the main switches in the switch room had been switched OFF and then back ON. This was my job and so I was to blame. When I asked Philomena what she had done, she took me to the room and showed me. The switches I needed her to use were ordinary light switches set on a single panel. Coincidentally, there were nine main power switches, set in a line in the same room. These were all set to ON, including the boiler switch. Philomena thought these were the switches I meant and simply turned the switch handles, not realizing she was changing them from ON to OFF. She hadn't seen that the main lights had gone out as the bar area was in darkness. She realised her mistake when she saw the small bank of nine switches. Of course, she then simply threw all the main switches back to ON, including the boiler, which had then shorted out.

Nobody had taken any notice of the slight interruption in the hall lighting, including the engineer, probably thinking it was just a blip. Eventually, Chris realized the boiler wasn't operating as it should have been, proving he at least was on the ball, otherwise the Mecca Bingo Hall in Portswood would have been just a hole in the ground! That wouldn't have done much for Iris' profit margins!

In the early 70's, Portswood was a fairly run down area of Southampton, with bingo as one of the main leisure attractions. When I first moved there, I think I had one of the worst bed-sitting rooms anyone can imagine. It was a dark, small, grubby room situated over a café and so was also quite smelly. However, the worst aspect was that it was also the habitat of a certain cat, which couldn't understand that I, as a human paying rent, took precedence, and didn't particularly want it squatting in my room. I came home one evening from the bingo hall to find that the cat had deposited a neat pile of excreta smack in the middle of my bed! The owners of the café were less than impressed when I woke them up after midnight to demand more bedding and more control over the blasted cat. They were however apologetic and promised to keep the cat out of my room. The next night I came home to find that the cat had done exactly the same thing, only this time, it had obviously had the runs, as the deposit lay in a fetid little pool, again in the middle of the bed and which had soaked through to the mattress. I slept on the floor that night! The next day, the deputy manager took pity on me and offered me a room in his house, which I jumped at. I went straight back to the bed-sit room, packed my meagre supply of clothes and left without paying the balance of the rent. They never chased me for it and if they had, I think my reply would have been something along the lines of "take it out of the cat, most other things seem to come out of it!"

One of the brighter aspects of bingo-hall life was watching the customers, especially the regulars. They were mostly middle-aged women who would come to the afternoon sessions, spend vast amounts of money they probably couldn't afford on a leisure activity which at its most active, required them to circle some numbers with a marker pen. However, the dexterity and skill, which they demonstrated was a sight to behold. Some of the more experienced women bought an additional book of numbers and so had to look for some of the numbers being repeated on the second card.

They often pre-marked them prior to the game commencing, but nevertheless, the speed at which they checked these cards during the game, was fantastic, and they never seemed to miss a number. The best time though was watching these same women's reactions when someone called out "BINGO!" They ranged from mild curiosity to glowering hatred, especially if they had spent more money doubling their chances with the extra book and the winner only had the one book!

In the interval, the regulars would get their tea and sandwiches and immediately go out to the entrance hall to start queuing for the gaming machines. The country had not long gone decimal, and these one-arm bandit machines took the equivalent of one shilling, 5 new pence, both coins being the same size in those days. These machines were so popular that the customers would form queues to play them. It was quite definitely a gambling addiction, an almost incessant need to spend hard earned money on something where the odds were so heavily stacked against them. The manager, Gary Bean had had to instigate a rule to prevent people from hogging them. The rule was that any one person could put a maximum of twenty coins into the machine in any one session, namely £1. If this person wanted to play more, he or she would have to leave the machine and go to the back of the queue and wait for their turn to come round again. I would watch in fascination as these women pumped coin after coin after coin into these machines and then queued up at the back to spend even more money. And of course. the best bit was when someone had just pumped in their pound, left the machine and the very next punter took the jackpot! They would mumble and grumble about that for days!

Another bright spot in an otherwise very dull environment was Larry, the bingo caller. He was without doubt the first real "character" I encountered. He used to manage a Mecca betting shop before falling foul of the organisation, and ending up calling the bingo numbers. Every year, Mecca had a manager's ball at some venue. Every manager in the country would be invited, along with husbands, wives, girlfriends and boyfriends. Larry told me that he had turned up at one of the functions with a stunning black girl on his arm, which seemingly upset some senior manager present. Larry was summoned to the head office in London the following Monday and sacked as a manager. Allegedly, she was "not the sort of girl" he should have taken to the ball! There wasn't any right of appeal in those days and Larry had to accept his "punishment". He did however, ask for a job somewhere, and was told he could call the bingo numbers in Portswood, a job way below his talents and potential, even I could see that! Things were different in those days, "political correctness" did not exist and apparently amongst the Mecca hierarchy, neither did morality.

Larry was a born entertainer! He would stand up on the stage and be the absolute epicentre of the game of Bingo. He always made it funny and entertaining, especially if the machine broke down for any reason, which it occasionally did. Larry was always ready with his repertoire of jokes, making sure that the attention of the customers, his "audience," was diverted away from the repairs to the machine. He never panicked or dried up whilst he was on stage, and was a great favourite amongst staff and customers alike.

On one occasion, he told me that he had entered a competition to be the "pub entertainer of the year" for a particular chain of pubs. He wanted me to go over to his flat and help him work out a script. For some reason I never really fathomed but admired, he stipulated that his "act" had to be clean, no dirty or rude jokes. Larry was very intelligent and I think he really enjoyed a "clever" joke over one, which relied on smut to be funny. When he told jokes at the bingo hall, they were generally smutty, funny but smutty, because he knew that was what they enjoyed and he was paid to entertain. I think on this occasion, he was trying to get away from the usual smut and send some form of message to his pub audience that "clever" can be funny.

We sat in his lounge until four or five o'clock in the morning simply telling each other jokes. I don't remember ever laughing so much for so long a period, we had a wonderful time! Every now and then, he would make a note of some joke for inclusion into his act, and eventually, Larry worked out a script of clean jokes, which would last about 10 minutes.

Both myself and his girlfriend went along to the pub on the night of his act, convinced that he would win hands down. We had pushed our way to the front in order to get the best view of his act, and were treated to the spectacle of someone dying an absolute death by silence! His "act" bombed, nobody laughed at any of his jokes. The best was a titter or a chuckle, there was definitely no laughing! He carried on bravely and professionally, never letting it slip that he was twisting inside with embarrassment. When it was finally over, he was given a polite clap as he exited the stage at speed! There was no post-mortem on his performance, he knew exactly what had happened, the audience simply did not respond to his "clean" jokes. Needless to say, he did not become "pub entertainer" of that year!

The following week however, as a direct result of his appearance at the pub, he was invited to do another session at a different place. This time, he succumbed to the old smutty routine and ended up going back week after week, he was so popular.

One particular day, I was absent-mindedly wiping glasses in the bar when I suddenly thought, "what the hell am I doing here?" I looked around me and suddenly realised that I hated my job, disliked the people around me, (except Philomena), disliked my living environment and was never going anywhere in the catering business. The thoughts of a glamorous lifestyle were fading quickly, and were being replaced by a sudden desire to get a working trade behind me. I began to realise that perhaps I shouldn't have been so quick to get out of my apprenticeship, and that it really was best to have something to fall back on. Maybe, at the age of 21, I was growing up at last! So, how am I going to get a trade behind me at this age? Aha! thinks me, the Army!! Dad will go absolutely potty I thought, but then, it's my life.

I thought long and hard over the next few days and decided that as I had been pretty good at engineering drawing at school, I would try to become some sort of draughtsman. I went to the Army recruiting office in Southampton and was told that I could become a design draughtsman, there were 13 vacancies on the next course and all I had to do was take a short exam and sign up!

I went a little further and worked out that if I joined up for 6 years instead of three, I could do the design draughtsman's course and then transfer to the Army Air Corps to learn how to fly helicopters. I talked all this over with the sergeant in the recruiting office and he assured me that my plan was sound and would work providing I was prepared to commit myself.

A day was arranged for me to attend the recruiting office and take this monster exam! To say that the exam was very easy would not be exaggerating, but then, I do understand that "easy" is a relative word. If you know the answer to any question, it's easy. If you don't know the answer, it's hard. I did pass the exam, or should I say test, and subsequently handed my notice in to Mecca, an event which didn't exactly ring alarm bells amongst the managerial hierarchy. Dad though, was very upset. He was really against my entering the Army. He tended to think of all soldiers as "cannon fodder".

I was given a date on which I was to attend the Army office in Southampton. On this day, the 11th October 1972, I was sworn in to Her Majesty's Armed Forces, given the "Queen's Shilling", a bible and a week's leave! I was told to report to Sutton Coldfield Army Barracks the following week.

Sutton Coldfield, what a depressing place! On the 18th of October, myself and the other recruits were picked up at the train station and taken to the barracks, where we would be spending the next three days taking tests and interviews. At the end of the three days, we were expected to come up with three choices of career in the Army, and they would decide whether we were suitable for one of those choices or not. I was quite safe as I had already been assured of a place on the next draughtsman's course anyway! The barracks themselves were drab and lifeless; long low buildings as I remember with unsmiling Army personnel marching about, crashing to attention everywhere and generally being very Army-like.

The food was nothing if not plentiful. My first meal in the canteen proved something of a nightmare though. Not realising that the several trays of different meats such as sausages and chops were meant to be a choice, I selected something from every tray. The food was all free, and so I was going to have my fill! When I got to the end of the line, I came up against a crusty old sergeant who took one look at the food heaped up on my plate, pointed to a few items and then barked "put that, that and that BACK!" I then had to work my way back along the queue saying "excuse me," "sorry," "do you mind if I just squeeze in here….." I think someone even pinched a sausage off my plate as I was negotiating my way back along the disgruntled queue!

There was nothing to do in the evenings except mingle and chat with the other recruits. I don't remember anything about my fellow barrack buddies, but I do remember we all got on well, which was just as well, because on the second night, there was a massive fight at the other end of our barracks, which began to spread down to where we were billeted. There were dozens of youths involved. It all happened very quickly and I don't think the MPs were in too much of a rush to get there and stop it. Rooms were being trashed and kit thrown all over the place. We didn't want anything to do with this and decided to barricade ourselves in the room and pushed beds and cupboards up against the door. We could hear the melee outside and there were a couple of thumps on our door, just before the MPs did finally arrive and break it up. The following morning, the camp commander arrived at the barracks and surveyed the scene. A lot of the mess had already been cleared up, but he decided to punish everyone in the place, including us in our barricaded room by telling us to pick up every cigarette dog-end over the entire camp. Army discipline, you can't beat it!

After taking all the tests I, like everyone else, had to make my three choices of career. My first was obviously design draughtsmanship, after all I had been told that there were 13 vacancies and my test results had all but secured me a place on this course. Many of the other recruits were so sure of their chosen careers, that they put down choices like The Light Infantry, or The Royal Greenjackets as their second and third choices. At the end of the process, everyone had an interview with the Senior Personnel Selection Officer, Major somebody or other. As my second choice I had put down seaman navigator on the Army ships and for my third choice Intelligence Corps. Thankfully, I had not gone for the usual "cannon fodder" choices.

During my interview, this major told me that I couldn't have my third choice as I had two endorsements on my driving licence. As part of the Intelligence Corps training, I would have to be attached to The Royal Corps of Transport to learn to drive the Army vehicles, something deemed impossible with driving endorsements. After telling me this, he left the room for a short period. When he returned, he dropped the bomb-shell! I couldn't have my first choice, design draughtsman. "Why not?" I asked. "Because you're not already an apprentice with the Army," he said, "there is no direct entry onto this scheme." "Well, can't I become an apprentice," I asked. "No," he said, "you're too old." And that was that! I was beginning to wonder whether I had made yet another mistake over my choice of career, when I heard him telling me that I could have my second choice, seaman navigator. My maths would have to be brushed up, he told me, but that wasn't a problem. "What does that involve?" I asked. "You'll be posted to The Royal Corps of Transport," he said. I stared at him in disbelief for a moment, and then said, "but you've just told me I can't be in the Intelligence Corps because I would have to be attached to the Royal Corps of Transport, which can't happen, because I have two endorsements on my driving licence, and now you are actually posting me to The Royal Corps of Transport!" He huffed and puffed for a few seconds, stared down at his papers and then said, "well, there it is Robins, take it or leave it." "Thank you very much sir," I said, "I'll leave it" and walked out of the office, and the Army.

It had become obvious to me that I had been conned at the recruiting office. They had deliberately mis-represented the position to me in order simply, to get my signature on the piece of paper, to join The Army! It became even more clear when I learned that out of all the recruits on the base at that time, only one guy had been given his first choice. All the others had been refused their first choice, but given their second or third, the "cannon fodder" choices! When I told my Company Sergeant Major, a wonderful man named Alfred Ogden, what I had not been told at the recruiting office, he went ballistic! I think he was genuinely ashamed of his Army colleagues on that day.

The final twist of the knife occurred when I was given my 'Certificate of Service'. The dates of service read "11ᵗʰ October 1972" to "21ˢᵗ October 1972" and under "reason for leaving," some clerk had typed, "not finally approved for Army service." This time, I went ballistic, and showed sergeant Ogden the certificate. Good old Alfie came to the rescue and marched into the office with me in tow. "This man has chosen to leave the Army of his own accord," he thundered, "he hasn't even begun basic training. How can he be 'not finally approved'." The clerk grumpily took the Certificate off me and replaced it in the type-writer. When I got it back, it read, "not finally approved for Army service, (left of own accord.)"

I remember feeling quite cheated by this experience. I had been very excited by the prospect of qualifying in a job I knew I would enjoy, and being encouraged by the staff at the Army recruiting office simply added to my enthusiasm. Finding out later that I had been virtually tricked into joining, and the way I had been treated at Sutton Coldfield, left a bitter taste about the Army. I just couldn't understand why they felt they had to behave like that. The reputation of the Army had never been particularly high, and this sort of behaviour was never going to help to improve it. After leaving the Army, I did look at other ways of obtaining professional training through various courses etc, and for a short time, even thought about joining the R.A.F. (my parents would have died early if I done this to them), none of which were successful.

My parents, especially dad, were overjoyed to see me back at the flat in Bournemouth. I had telephoned dad from Sutton Coldfield and told him I would be coming home. I remember he said nothing at the time, and there was an element of 'I told you so', but dad would never have said that, even if he was thinking it. So, I settled back into life at my parents flat, signed back on the dole and played more snooker at Chalkie Whites.

I remember I used to take quite long walks, especially in the evenings. Mum and dad's flat could become rather claustrophobic and I just liked to get away on my own, (something which remains with me today). When I had arrived in Cardiff, I had gone straight out and made attempts to meet new people. Bournemouth wasn't that sort of place. The people in Cardiff had been warm and welcoming, whereas in Bournemouth, there was a different atmosphere, much colder and much more cliquey. It was a much richer place than Cardiff and consequently, people had a lot more money to spend.

I went out to a few places and quickly realised that unless you had a decent amount of cash behind you, drove something akin to an E Type Jaguar and spoke with no accent, you were not 'accepted'. It was a very cosmopolitan town as there were several language schools situated there. This meant of course, that the students' parents were wealthy and so, naturally, were the students themselves. Everything surrounding Bournemouth's social society revolved around money. If you had it, you were in, if not, you were out. Simple and straightforward, I suppose, but I found the place very unfriendly and so took to taking walks in the evenings, if only to observe the evening people of Bournemouth and rue the fact I didn't have enough money to join them.

During this period, whilst contemplating my future, I made several trips back to Cardiff to see my friends and at least have some company. On one of these trips, I was driving my old Ford Anglia estate, my third by this time, across the Severn Bridge. This was an engineering marvel at the time.

When I was boy in Weston-Super-Mare, we used to travel over to Cardiff by road. There was no bridge spanning the River Severn in those days and in order to avoid a long detour around Gloucester to cross the Severn, it was necessary to take the Beachley-Aust river ferry. For a young boy, this was an adventure, for the driver of a car, it could be a nightmare! There are now two Severn Bridges and if you go across the older of the two, you can still see the old wooden ramp leading down to the ferry on the English side. It still looks as rickety as it was then. Cars would have to drive down the ramp, wet and slippery from the algae left by the tide or rain, execute a ninety degree turn onto the ferry and then get parked by the ferry-men. Sometimes, in executing the turn onto the ferry, cars would slide down the ramp sideways for a few feet, making the back end of the car lower than the ramp entrance. The ferry-men would then have to come out and assist the car back up the ramp by pushing, until it eventually lined up with the gate and could drive onto the ferry.

Cars were parked by means of a turntable in order to get as many cars as possible onto the deck, leaving very little room for passengers. Fully loaded, the ferries would ride dangerously low in the water, the gunwhale being a matter of maybe 18" to 2 feet above the water line. The skipper of the ferry had to take a wide sweep across the current in the river and at times, the current would be so vicious that the ferry would heel over at a really alarming angle. The River Severn at this point, has some of the most dangerous currents in the world; just looking out over the bridge, one can see the eddies and whirlpools forming. If one of these ferries crashed or sank, the loss of life would have been catastrophic, but they never did. I don't remember ever hearing of an accident involving a Severn ferry, but now the traffic flows across either one of two magnificent bridges. Remembering these ferry trips now, my thoughts are a mixture of nostalgia and memories of what was essentially, a very scary trip. Nothing like it would be allowed to operate these days.

I remember watching the first bridge being constructed. It was being built out from both sides of the river at the same time, eventually to meet in the middle. Every time we took the Severn ferry, we had to go underneath the bridge, and every time, the two ends were closer to meeting in the middle. The two halves finally met to within half an inch! Considering the entire length of the bridge is around a mile and a half, over one of the most dangerous rivers in the world, this was an amazing feat of engineering. Compared to the precarious ferry trips, driving across the bridge was an absolute joy, except one time when I was driving my old Ford Anglia.

I was on my way back to Cardiff to visit my friends and was in the nearside lane, when suddenly and with no warning whatsoever, the car veered across the road into the next lane and beyond, then back to the nearside. The whole car was shaking and vibrating and the steering wheel was just turning in my hands with no response from the car, it seemed to be going just where it wanted to go! I had visions of crashing through the safety barriers and plunging into the vicious, muddy water of the Severn, never to be seen again!

I slammed on the brakes, such as they were and eventually limped off the bridge, having scared dozens of other drivers half to death, to find that the metal around the steering box had rotted away, completely detaching it from the bulkhead, effectively removing control through the steering wheel. I did however discover that if I drove at 10mph or less, I did have marginal control. In those days, I had no breakdown cover and couldn't afford a call-out fee from a rescue company. I crept along the hard shoulder and finally arrived at John's house about 4 hours later. I abandoned the car there and caught the bus home. For all I know, it's still there! And that was the end of Anglia number three!

One of the shortest jobs I had in my less than illustrious working life, apart from the Army was selling life insurance coupled with Unit Trusts investments for a company called Brookdale Hutton. I have no recollection of how or even why I started with this company, probably wooed with the usual promise of rich rewards for very little effort. Once again, dad was mortified at my choice of employment and did his level best to persuade me not to do it, especially when I told him I would not be getting a salary but relying on commission.

I was sent off on a weeks' training course, to learn how to approach people in the street with a spurious street survey, how to select them in the first place, how to ask questions concerning their savings and financial habits and then, how to get the all important foot in the door. "Once in," they said, "they're all yours!" I remember one guy who called door-to-door spoke to us, and said his method of getting through the door was to show the housewife a wind-up mouse and then set it off into her house. He would immediately go after it to get it back, giving her no time to object, and hey presto, he was in! Apparently, he never came out without a sale.

After the course was finished, I was to be let loose on an unsuspecting public, but if truth be told, I was less than enthusiastic about approaching ordinary hard-working people and asking impertinent questions about their finances. As a final part of the training, I went out one evening with one of the top salesmen to an appointment he had with a prospective customer. The customer was very sceptical, but I listened to this guy smooth-talk him into putting his signature on a piece of paper he had had no intention of signing. It was almost a work of art to watch him in action.

He sweet-talked, he cajoled, he explained patiently, he listened, he watched the body language and reacted accordingly. He bullied in the nicest possible way and in the end, the customer was left with absolutely no doubt in his mind that he should sign up to this agreement immediately or risk not reaping substantial financial rewards.

I was finally let loose on the streets with my little clip-board and a series of questions I was to ask people I selected as prospective customers. The majority of the questions were rubbish and had nothing to do with my "survey," but there was one question about their saving habits, which was the cruncher. Their answer to this question would enable me to make appointments with these people to go around to their houses and, ultimately, sell them a policy. I was supposed to make probably half a dozen appointments for any one day. That first day, I made one, a nice elderly couple as I remember. I went round to their house later that evening, made an abortive, half-hearted attempt to sell them a policy in something I had very little faith in myself, and spent the rest of the evening chatting and drinking coffee.

I didn't go back to the office the next day or ever, but the name Brookdale Hutton popped up a few years later during a TV programme highlighting, shall we say, dubious selling methods.

So, back on the dole and back to more snooker at 'Chalkie Whites'!

This latest period on the dole didn't last long, (thankfully, none of them did) as I soon secured yet another position, Trainee Manager with British Home Stores. My dad had been badgering me for quite some time to at least get some training behind me, which I had been trying to achieve, and to stick at one job for long enough to get that training, which I definitely was not achieving. I wasn't overly worried about my lack of staying power concerning careers, (or should I say jobs!), but dad's concern was beginning to niggle a little. I suppose I knew he was right, but simply wasn't going to admit it to myself, and certainly didn't admit it to him until many years later. I keep mentioning my father in this respect simply because he was the "worrier." I knew my mother was sympathetic to my father's concerns, but she was always a much freer spirit than he was and I think she knew better than he, that I would eventually find my place. Dad thought this latest position would be the one for me, a management post in a go-ahead, exciting retail company.

To be fair, I was quite excited about it too. It seemed to offer much of what I thought I was looking for, decent salary, prestige etc, but at that time, I had had a major shift in my outlook. I no longer really wanted to be a top-notch salesman like Victor, I had begun to feel that I wanted to work with people, in personnel and a firm such as B.H.S., with its thousands of workers, would be the ideal vehicle for me to achieve this. The problem was that the position for which I had been accepted was trainee store manager, and which meant I had to go through the retail training. At that time, the company had no idea of my aspirations. They thought of me as a prospective store manager, just as they thought of all their trainee managers who had gone through the correct process of training for managing a retail department. The thought that somebody, more accurately a man, would actually want to do something else within the company, simply didn't occur to them. I was leaning more towards personnel work, but in those days, it was generally women who performed this role. It was rare to find a man doing it.

I started my training with British Home Stores in Southampton in January 1973. I had found myself a decent little flat in a house owned by a woman with the wonderful name of Mrs Mott, and lived there with three other tenants in the other flats. One of these tenants, Pam Dyer would remain a close friend to this day. It was a bed-sitter really, but was big enough for me and my meager possessions. I only had one suit and two or three shirts in those days so the dire lack of wardrobe space wasn't really a problem.

The store was managed by a man called Barry Gamble. He was essentially a nice guy, friendly, a firm manager and very committed to the company and his job. His deputy manager was a guy called Nigel Calladine, and he was more committed than Gamble! They worked well together and the store was one of the more successful ones, bearing in mind that at this time our rivals, Marks and Spencer were thought to be the benchmark for departmental stores. Shops such as B.H.S., C&A etc. were thought of as much more down-market than M&S; it was certainly true that in those days, one needed a university degree in order to be taken on as a trainee manager with M&S.

I can't say I remember too much about my actual training. I very quickly lost interest in how many pairs of this or that my department had sold. I got really bored with the whole business and only stayed really, to finish the training and give my father something to smile about. The possibility of working in personnel seemed to be getting more and more remote. I remember talking to him about the way I was feeling and he persuaded me to at least stay the course for the training, which I did. It would be fair to say however, that B.H.S. did at least have a structure to their training programme, unlike Mecca. I remember having to work in various departments in the store other than the sales floor, such as the restaurant, the food department, the office and the stock-room. This latter department was run by a wonderful man named Mr. Smith. He was very short and dumpy, loved his job and had a fantastic sense of humour. Unfortunately, he liked a drink and would often arrive for work reeking of the previous nights' boozing, but for all that, he was great to work with and he liked to train people. It was all very dull really, but I do remember one member of staff, who would brighten my day, Ken Greatorex, the food-hall manager.

We used to have a manager's meeting first thing in the morning, and every so often, Ken would tell us about his journey to work on the local ferry across a well-known stretch of water. He lived somewhere outside Southampton and had to catch this ferry really early in the morning.

It all started with an apology for being late one morning, and by him just making a casual remark about the ferry being fog-bound, and how he had been sent "for'ard" by the captain, to keep a "sharp eye!" His colourful local accent seemed to make it all the more believable. After this, his "tales" of seafaring derring-do, got better and bolder every time, and more funny. They would always start off with him saying, "what a journey I had this morning!" That was the signal for someone to say, "go on then, what happened this time!" "Well!" he would say, and then just launch into some wonderful tale of adventure, which might have included cutlass duels with marauding pirates, being threatened with "keel-hauling" for some trivial misdemeanour on board, collisions at sea, 'U' Boats, raging storms, ghost ships gliding out of the mirk, all manner of scenarios. Ken himself, would act out various parts, such as being sent up to the "crow's nest" to look out for the local pirates, or "swinging the lead" and calling out the depth of water, "by the mark, two fathoms, me lover!!" or making the noise of a fog-horn through a rolled up newspaper! Whatever, he was fantastically inventive with his stories and of course, we just encouraged him, he was fun to listen to, even Calladine laughed, occasionally!

And the reason we all loved these stories was because we all knew that this particular ferry trip was only about 10 minutes from one side of the river to the other, including docking and casting off! It would have been practically impossible for anything remotely like an adventure to occur in the time it took to cross the water, but Ken made it sound as though it was a romantic, high-sea adventure. He certainly had a talent for story-telling, and was probably like me, a round peg in a square hole.

It was a different story however, once the meeting was over. Ken was only marginally better at his job than I was, and was continually getting hassle from the managers, especially Calladine, who really disliked him. It was almost as though he was getting even with Ken for daring to make people laugh during a meeting, I thought he was great fun though, and so did most of the other members of staff. Even when he was on the sales floor, he was always laughing with his staff, and was generally, just nice to be around. Calladine was too serious, he thought only about the store's performance and how it would reflect on him. He did have a sense of humour as I remember, but it seemed forced, as if he felt he should laugh, rather want to.

On one occasion, Barry Gamble called a meeting of the various departmental managers to announce that head office had decided to have a major staff morale-boosting campaign coupled with a performance drive. It would be centred around pictures of two faces, one smiling and the other not, "Miss Happy" and "Miss Glum" and we were asked to come up with suitable ideas.

They would represent good and bad performance by having an actual happy or glum face painted on a piece of card, and during this meeting I rattled off at least half a dozen ideas on how each of the faces could be used. One idea was where all the "Miss Glums" were being swept up into a heap by "Miss Happy", and in another, B.H.S. commandeered the use of one lane in a ten-pin bowling alley where a B.H.S. in-house newspaper photographer would photograph staged shots of a "Miss Happy" face on a bowling ball scattering "Miss Glum" pins. Each of the pins had been suspended with fishing gut at various angles to simulate the ball travelling through them. There were other ideas which I can't now recall, but at the end of the meeting, Gamble said to me "if only you could be this creative on the sales floor", fat chance!! Maybe he could see that my talents lay elsewhere.

At various points during my training, I had meetings with the personnel manageress, Mrs Tannhauser to discuss my performance. She was a fearsome woman who ruled her department with a rod of iron. Every time we met, she would ask where I thought I was in my training, and I would say that I could probably do better, but that it was because I really wanted to be in personnel rather than retail. I tried to tell her that that was where I thought my talents lay, not in figuring out which article sells better on a particular point of the counter! She would then explain just how impossible that would be and that I should be more interested in what I was doing, what I was training for! She never really listened to me, simply patronised me.

I got more and more frustrated with what I was doing, but I had promised dad and so I determined that I would stay, at least for the training. I really don't know why they didn't just sack me, I was pretty useless on the sales-floor, and it must have been obvious that I had no interest. Instead, they extended my training period by three months. I was no better after this extension, but they still made me a full Departmental Manager with a three hundred pounds a year pay increase. I distinctly remember Barry Gamble handing me the pay-rise with the words, "here, they seem to think you're worth this."

I have always wondered whether he was being sarcastic, or whether he was just trying to jolly me along a little, trying to get me to perform well. As nice a guy that he was, I do think it was the former.

Having this promotion and pay rise meant very little to me really, as I had by then, secretly applied for the Metropolitan Police Force, (it was a "force" in those days). I had learned my lesson from my days at Evan Williams Car Sales in Cardiff and had told no-one about my application, not even my parents. It came as quite a shock to them to have a burly police sergeant from Bournemouth on their door-step one day, asking all sorts of questions about me. They immediately thought I was in trouble with the law, of course, but in actual fact, he was doing the normal application background checks.

My letter of acceptance for the police had come in summer, 1974. Why the police? Looking back on it, I think I was always destined to be a man in uniform, it simply wasn't going to be the Army, Navy or Air Force. I had really examined my desire to work with people and having looked through the Met's brochure, had come to the conclusion that here was the opportunity to do just that and whole lot more if I wanted to. The choice of career path within the police was, (and still is) very broad and varied, but more of this later.

I resigned on a morning which Barry Gamble had set aside for a long management meeting to discuss a forthcoming sales promotion. It was naughty really, but I waited until he got to the part which I was to play in this venture, and then simply told him and the other members of the team that I wouldn't be taking part, as I was would be resigning that day and leaving before the promotion took place. I got my punishment for this needless bit of theatricals merely by looking at Gamble's face. He was hurt, not by the fact that I was leaving, but just by the way I had chosen to tell him; he didn't deserve it and I would apologise to him today if I could.

I did not, however anticipate the flurry of activity, which followed my formal resignation. I knew how bad I was at my job. I also knew that everyone else knew, including managers more senior than Gamble, and I certainly wasn't expecting a fuss. Barry Gamble had, of course had a chat with me as to why, and I told him straight, that I had said all along that I wanted to work with people rather than items of merchandise. I told him that I realised just how ineffective I was at my job and had made no secret of the fact that I realised it, we had discussed it on many occasions. It was a shame, I said, that nobody was listening to me, and then went to get on with my work, determined to show that I was leaving for a valid reason and not just out of spite at the company.

During that day, I think I must have received at least four or five phone calls from head office, each one from a more senior member of staff. At one stage, I was asked what it would take to get me to stay on? This was confusing, why on earth were they asking me to stay? In any event, I replied that I wouldn't be staying, that I had made up my mind to join the police but also that it might have been different, had someone (Tannhauser!) listened to me about working with personnel. The next phone call was from the senior personnel manager (a man, I hasten to add!) offering me a position within the personnel department in head office in London. This was a bolt straight out of the blue! I was at last being offered a job more suitable to me, someone was, at last, listening to me! But too late! I thanked him for the offer and explained that it was too late, I had made up my mind to go. I don't remember having a smirk of satisfaction on my face, but I can't really imagine that there wasn't one.

And so I left British Home Stores and Southampton in October 1974. I missed nothing! I left behind a grotty little flat, which I had swapped with Pam Dyer, my co-tenant because she needed more room; I left behind a company whose managers were incapable of thinking 'outside the box'; I left behind a girl at B.H.S. with whom I had been having an on-off relationship and who had the best and longest legs I had ever seen, but to whom I could never really get close. (Incidentally, her brother was one of the Army sergeants I had spoken to in the recruiting office in Southampton.) It had been the worst kept secret at the store. Fraternising with the staff was taboo for the managers, which made me dislike one certain manager even more, because for all his posturing about managers' performance, and despite being married, he was always trying to get one particular member of staff, a supervisor, to go out with him, which she steadfastly refused to do.

For all that, I enjoyed my time in Southampton. I had met and worked with some great people, Barry Gamble, Mr. Smith, Ken Greatorex, Philip Kitchen, (now there was a man with a bright future in the retail trade) Roger Hillman, with whose family I am still friendly, and who went on to do great things in the world of credit control. All these people had an influence on me in some way shape or form and I think, due to them, I matured a little, and I was at least at peace with myself over my father's anxieties about me. I had really started to beat myself up about the way I had let him and my mother down, and I was absolutely certain that joining the police was the way to set things straight between us. He was overjoyed at my joining, but he was to have an even greater influence on my police career than he had on my other ventures.

My retail training at BHS was quite useless to me but one thing I did take away was that I couldn't ask someone to do a job that I couldn't do myself; something I have always tried to adhere to since. Barry Gamble gave me a specific piece of advice about management, which I have also continued to use up to this day. He told me to look closely at all the managers I would ever work with or for. "When you leave that person," he said, "take with you all the best bits and leave behind all the bad. That way, you'll incorporate all the good practice into your own management style." Good advice, which I have always tried to pass on to aspiring, younger police officers.

Chapter 9

I joined the Metropolitan Police Force on 21st October 1974, coincidentally, two years to the day after leaving the Army. I had gone through the selection process without a hitch, including the most stringent medical test imaginable. It was held at Paddington Green police station and consisted of standing naked on a mat with printed feet marks, answering some minor questions about previous medical history and finally, turning round on the mat and bending over. Precisely what this was meant to show, (apart from the obvious) neither I, nor anyone else was able work out, but from this, we were all declared medically fit!

After swearing more allegiance to the Queen, I, along my fellow probationary officers, was taken to the training school at Hendon. Looking back on it, I do sometimes wonder just how I got through the selection process. Today, they wouldn't look at me with an employment record like the one I had at that time. I can only surmise that times were difficult for recruiting police officers then. As long as you didn't have a criminal record, or a nasty, communicable disease, there wasn't much that they would refuse you on. I do remember that only a very short time prior to my joining, there had been severe unrest amongst the police due to the low pay and bad conditions of service. The government had reacted positively and raised the salary substantially, but it would be several more years before a proper pay review system would be in place.

Hendon training establishment was built in the late sixties and reflected the thinking on housing of that era. The accommodation blocks were drab, concrete, high-rise towers, consisting of twenty or more floors. The rooms were sparse, but clean and bright, and I do remember that the beds were extremely comfortable. None of the rooms were en-suite, (heaven forbid!), the toilets and showers being set in the middle of the floor and again, were clean and fresh.

The teaching block was quite modern, with light, airy class-rooms and escalators serving the first floor. The entire block was set out in pleasant surroundings with flower-beds and a large fountain in the centre of the complex.

Running down one side of the school was a train line from Hendon Central to Colindale and on the other side, a series of run-down buildings, which were obviously going to be developed over time. One of these buildings contained the swimming pool, a rather nasty, grubby little place where the instructors made us jump off the high board. We weren't taught any swimming, this place was just for recreational swimming, but as part of our training, we had to make this high jump, why, I have no idea. I remember most of us had completed our jumps and were seated at the far end, enjoying the terror on the faces of our colleagues, forgetting that we had probably looked just like that only minutes before.

One lad jumped off and as he was heading for the water, his legs suddenly came apart, and he hit the surface in a star formation. The collective intake of breath from our end of the pool was sharp enough to be heard outside the building. Poor lad, he was sore for a long time! The infant Police National Computer complex, the driving school and the Cadet School made up the remaining buildings on that side.

Directly in front of the class-room block was the large statue of Sir Robert Peel, the founder of the modern police force, and the origin of the old words for police, "peelers" and "bobbies". All the classes used to line up in front of this statue for morning parade, which was always conducted by Sergeant Sidney Butcher, "old Sid" to us, although absolutely never to his face!. He'd been in the police for a number of years even then, and rumour had it that he had been moved to training school under a cloud. We were later to find out just how thick that cloud had been.

Sid Butcher used to take classes for drill practice, marching us aimlessly up and down the tarmac roadways of the complex, shouting and screaming at us to keep in step and swing our arms correctly. The Metropolitan is still probably the only police force in the country that never marches anywhere when the officers are on public duty, but I used to quite enjoy the discipline of marching in time and step, and Sid was always on hand to make us laugh with his little sayings. For some reason, he absolutely hated ex-cadets and would halt the drill practice if a train went by, so that the ex-cadets could "get the number!"

My abiding memory of Sid though, was the first parade after the 12-day Christmas break, January 1975. We all lined up in our classes and Sid shouted the usual order, "class captains, take the roll." At this time, each class captain had to take one pace forward and shout out the number of officers who were absent from the class that day and the reason, and the number of officers present. One class-captain stepped forward and shouted the number of officers present, but then added "one PC late, Sergeant!" Old Sid looked up from his clip-board and eyed the class captain from under his helmet. "Late," he shouted, "fuckin' late! He's 'ad twelve fuckin' days to get here, how can 'e be fuckin' late? You send the little twat to my office when 'e gets 'ere!" "Yes, Sergeant," whimpered the class captain. However, Sid was a gem really, a true character; an old fashioned policeman, who probably wouldn't have fitted in anyway to the modern policing methods, which were developing in those days. I think he was at training school for want of a better place to hide him away.

The intake on that Monday 21st October 1974, numbered about twenty men and women, all from vastly different backgrounds and walks of life, including a farmer, a bus conductor and JCB digger driver. I can't remember any more, apart from the two guys from Oxford University. They were both graduate entrants and destined to go a long way in a relatively short space of time, which they have. Ian Blair was knighted, and became Commissioner of the Metropolitan Police and the other, Tom Lloyd, became the Chief Constable of Cambridgeshire Constabulary. It is interesting to note however, that they both started at the bottom, with everyone else. They had to learn their policing craft first, before they took on high office. It would have been very easy for them both to have spent as little time as possible doing actual police work, hiding away in some discreet office, but they both loved being coppers, especially

Ian. He went along the CID route and became a "force expert" on rape, researching it in America and eventually writing a book on the subject. He was also responsible for putting some pretty corrupt police officers behind bars in a well-publicised anti-corruption drive.

Having two guys from the same university in the same class was unusual in those days. What was not unusual however, was that there were no black or Asian officers in our intake for that week, it was wholly white and mostly male. We were split into two classes, Red and Yellow, and in our class, we only had three female officers that I can remember. The police service had treated women officers very much as ancillary workers up to around the 1960s. They had been used predominantly to look after children who had somehow found their way into the justice system, or were given duties as office staff and were certainly not thought clever enough or tough enough to take on the rigours of police patrolling. When I joined however, the women officers were being given the respect they deserved, and were being treated on a basis equal to their male counterparts. It still didn't sit right with a lot of male officers though. I remember one incident at training school when a senior officer was inspecting the morning parade. As he walked along the line of officers, he stopped at an attractive young female recruit and pressed his hands into her breasts. Apparently, he was testing out her reactions! In reality, he was being a bully and was trying to demonstrate just how superior male officers were thought at the time to be over female officers. Thank God, those days are gone!

Race relations around the country were not good at this time and relations between the police and the black community especially, were pretty dire. However, that is not to say that no black or Asian men and women had joined the police, they had, but they were very, very few in number.

The first black officer in the Met. was a man called Norwell Roberts, or "Noz," who served on the same division as me for my first few years. I didn't know him at all well, but he was a lovely guy, who reputedly suffered massive abuse from his relatives and so-called friends for joining the police.

At that time, the country was moving inexorably into a period of intense activity by organisations on the extremes of the political spectrum, all operating under the guise of effecting change through peaceful persuasion, but in reality, some of them used tactics of mayhem and unrest in an effort to achieve their aims; The Socialist Workers Party, The National Front, Campaign for Nuclear Disarmament, The Communist Party, Trade Unions, Arthur Scargill (president of the miners union), skinheads, militant car workers, the Greenham Common women, along with others, they all played a massive role in creating the political and social shape of Britain for decades to come.

One thing common to all these organizations and individuals, was that they were all anti-police. I went on numerous so-called "peaceful" demonstrations, which invariably ended in a huge punch-up with the police. I'm sure that many persons on the rallies or demonstrations were there for a genuine cause, but there always seemed to be an extreme element, hidden within their ranks, that was intent on violence. As a body, we the police, although fairly fed up with being constantly targeted and pilloried as "right wing fascists" nearly always won the physical battles. The political ones, we had to leave to the likes of our senior officers or the Home Secretary of the day. Although the political extremes are less obvious today, we still see rallies and marches for genuine causes being hi-jacked by rogue elements.

Our first instructor was a Sergeant called Donald Dymer. As seriously as we took our training, it was always possible to have a laugh with Sergeant Dymer. I well remember two incidents with him, which not only caused a huge laugh in the class, but also went some way towards creating a particular reputation for me, which I wasn't at all certain I liked.

The first incident occurred on the first morning we were all in our new surroundings, the first time we were all together in the classroom. In those days, it was traditional where possible, for ex-servicemen to perform the roles of class-captain and deputy. They were thought to be better at marching and discipline etc. Sergeant Dymer asked all the ex-servicemen in the class to raise their hands. As I had actually taken the "Queen's shilling", I put up my hand. It had more to do with my not wanting to make any mistake at that stage, than trying to impress Sergeant Dymer. Rightly or wrongly, I didn't want the powers-that-be to find out later that I had been in the Army and didn't volunteer the information when asked. I had no idea at that stage why we were being asked this question, so I put up my hand. However, it soon became obvious that this was going to be embarrassing for me.

The first two guys Sergeant Dymer asked proudly replied that they had been in established and recognizable units such as The Marines or The Parachute Regiment for a number of years. Then it was my turn! "And you?" he said to me. I had no choice at this stage, I had to plough on. "The General Service Corps, sergeant", I said truthfully if a little timidly. After a few seconds of looking puzzled, Sergeant Dymer said, "Oh, right, how long were you in?" Here we go, I thought. "Well sergeant" I said, "I joined on the 11th October 1972, and I left on the 21st October 1972". I was being deadly serious, but of course it sounded as though I was having a joke. Expecting to receive an answer amounting to several years, Dymer had this blank expression on his face, and seemed shocked when he finally realised the exact number of days I had been in the Army. "10 days", he thundered, "10 fuckin' days! I've had longer fuckin' 'olidays!" By now, the rest of the class were laughing as much at me as Sergeant Dymer's outburst. And then, I seemed to sense rather than figure a way out of this embarrassment, so when the laughter died down and before Sergeant Dymer could say anything else, I spluttered, "yes Sergeant, and for a week of that I was on leave!" Absolute uproar! I was made deputy class captain, Rod Brown being appointed as captain on the strength of his having been in the police before. I think Sergeant Dymer liked me really!

The second incident took place some weeks later. Some of the classrooms had large glass windows which faced out onto the escalators. We were in such a classroom one day when Sergeant Dymer came up the escalator and saw us all laughing at something. In actual fact, as he was coming up the escalator, I had remarked that Sergeant Dymer looked a little like Fred Flintstone, which he most definitely did, and that was all that was said at that stage. Sergeant Dymer came into the class and we all stood up as he entered, as we had been taught. Sergeant Dymer stood at the front and motioned for us to sit down. "Not you, Robins", he said, without preamble. "Now, tell me what you were all laughing at." Why he picked on me. I have no idea. Even though I had made the remark, he didn't know that and I was no more guilty than anyone else in the class. I think it was just that, he picked on me! "Nothing Sergeant", I said, very unconvincingly. "One more time Robins, what were you laughing at?" This now sounded as though it was going to get serious! The class had hushed, sensing that I was about to receive a mauling. Now, bearing in mind that I was a lowly police recruit, standing in front of a demi-God, a Metropolitan Police Sergeant Instructor, I can only imagine that, somewhere deep inside me, is a self-destructive streak. Sergeant Dymer was not smiling, he was not laughing, he did not have any expression which might indicate fun or frivolity. To this day, I have no idea why, but I then said, "Nothing really Sergeant, but we were just wondering whether your wife's name happens to be Wilma?" That was it, pandemonium! The other students were almost on the floor with laughter, relieved that they could give voice to their emotions. Me, I had to stand there and face Dymer, who was glaring at me. However, I got the distinct impression his heart was not in any punishment. Slowly, his face creased into a grin and he told me to sit down. I don't think it was the first time the likeness had been alluded to!

On another occasion, we were having a lesson on summonses. The Commandant of the school, Chief Superintendent Howlett, or "Zoom" to everyone else, because he was forever zooming all over the place at full speed, was sitting at the back. The lecturer asked if anyone had ever received a summons and how long it had taken to arrive. A few put up their hands, including me. The answers ranged around 2-3 months and then he asked me. "Well," I said "on average......" The Chief Superintendent laughed but I hadn't meant it as a joke, I was being serious.

I never set out to establish myself as the class joker, but it seemed that I had unwittingly earned myself the reputation as just that. I remember being secretly quite worried about this. This was not me, I didn't do this sort of thing, I'm not inventive enough. However, it didn't interfere with my studies and I continued to pass my weekly exams with the top marks in the class earning several expressions of praise for my efforts from Sergeant Dymer.

Not being naturally bright, I really had to work at studying, unlike Messrs Blair and Lloyd, who seemed to spend most of their time in the evenings in the Greyhound pub whilst I had to study the books. I remember that I used to go into Tom's room in the morning just to make sure he was up. I often found him reading the work that I had spent most of the last evening trying to get to grips with and learn as an "A" report (a passage which had to be recited word perfect). As if this wasn't enough, he was reading it whilst applying the polish to "bull" up the toe-caps on his boots. Tom would pass the daily test having done the smallest amount of work possible, which was infuriating to say the least; but then, both Ian Blair and Tom Lloyd were exceptionally gifted students.

At Training School, we had sixteen weeks of legislation instruction, role plays for various scenarios, physical fitness, exams, parades and drilling. There were three distinct periods in the sixteen weeks, junior, intermediate and senior. At each stage, there were exams to pass. Failure was not an option for me, as I had to prove to myself that I was not a complete dunce. My scholastic achievements still weighed heavily on my mind and I was determined to do well here, for me and my parents. I wanted them to be proud of me at last. At the end of the course, there was one big exam to take, and I passed top of the class. It was totally meaningless to anyone else, but I had actually achieved higher marks than both Ian Blair and Tom Lloyd. They had both become something approaching icons at the school because of their sheer intellect, and the fact that I had beaten them made me realise that I could achieve at least, small victories. During the latter stages of the training, it seemed that Ian and I were destined to share some kind of friendship.

Our initial training finished in February 1975 and immediately, I experienced another first. I flew out of the country on holiday for the first time in my life. To my surprise, Ian had asked if I was interested in taking a short break with him somewhere at the end of the course, just to relax and celebrate finishing. If anyone had asked me who Ian would invite to go with him, I would have said Tom, just as anyone else would have. However, I agreed and we settled on Majorca. It didn't really matter to me where I went, any place would have been an adventure for me.

I don't remember too much about the holiday in Majorca, except that we were at a hotel in Palma called the Hotel Timor. The travel company had laid on the usual sight-seeing trips and evening functions. The only one of the latter aspect I remember is the good old favourite, the medieval banquet. It was the first time I had ever experienced anything like this, and looking back on it now, am horrified to remember just how drunk and stupid I got. It was one of those drink and eat as much as you can events, and I took it to the limit. I remember being very ill, but at some stage, I had made some sort of contact with a woman at the next table.

She was married, but when we got home, she and I had quite a torrid little affair. She was the first woman to introduce me to the joys of oral sex. I remember she worked in a squalid little office near London Bridge, and whenever I went to her office to meet her, we would end up having sex in the office toilet of all places, lying full length on the grubby floor! I think her husband eventually became suspicious, and that was the end of that! All in all though, it was a great week away on holiday with Ian. He was vastly more experienced than me at travelling and looked after me the whole time.

I had arrived at training school the proud owner of a white convertible MG "A" sports car. It was a real classic even in those days, but it was always breaking down on me. I remember trying to get home to Bournemouth on three separate week-ends, and on each occasion, being towed back to the training school by the same AA breakdown man; very embarrassing!

One day, I saw an advert for a scrapped MGA in the local paper and mentioned to Ian that I was going to have a look at it. He asked to come along and when we got to the garage, he ended up buying a decent, complete MGA and I bought the scrap car for the engine and other bits. All three cars were stored in the car park at Hendon, until that is, I was ordered to get rid of the scrapped car as it was a bit of an eyesore and they didn't want the place looking like a scrap-yard, understandable I suppose.

At the end of the intermediate period in the training, we were allocated our divisions where we would serve. The plum posting for any twenty-something officer would be anywhere in the centre of London, a "licence to print money", Dymer had said. Both Ian and I were posted to "C Division", in the very heart of the West End, Ian going to West End Central, the busiest part and myself going to historic Bow Street Police station, which now sadly, no longer exists. Not only that, we both lived at the same Section House, (lodging for single male and female officers) on the same floor, and we both parked our MGAs in the same garage. We saw a lot of each other over the next couple of years, but then Ian's career went into the expected over-drive and over the following 28 years, we've seen very little of each other. We are still friends though, and have the occasional chat over coffee.

I started at Bow Street police station in February of 1975, a young, raw, desperately keen probationary constable. In those days, probationers were the lowest of the low, right at the bottom of the pecking order. It had been like that since the police had been formed back in 1839.

When I joined, there was a system called the "parent constable" where the probationer was teamed up with an older, much more experienced officer for the first two weeks at the station. It was the "parent's" job to teach the probationer the "ropes", explain how things worked and teach him or her, the rudiments of working on the streets. Fine system, you might think, wrong!

Parent constables never volunteered for the job, they were always told to do it, and one of the ways the parent expressed his displeasure (women constables didn't do "parent") was to make the probationer feel right at home by making him walk at least one full pace behind. That way, the supposed superiority of the parent was maintained, and the probationer was reminded that he was at the bottom of the pile. Wherever the parent went, the probationer followed, and that included regular visits to the public houses on the ground for a few pints in the back. More constables have fallen foul of senior officers over drink than anything else. The galling thing is that these same senior officers had more than likely partaken of the free beer supplied by "friendly" landlords themselves and had got away with it!

Another way to make the probationer feel wanted and appreciated was to make him or her sit at a different table than the established constables for their meal, more commonly called their "grub break". If you tried to even speak to an experienced constable at one of the other tables, the chances were that you would at best be ignored, at worst, verbally abused.

So, life for a probationer in those days was pretty grim. You got the worst jobs in the worst conditions. If anybody had to stand on insecure premises in the pouring rain, it was the probationer, if vomit had to be cleaned up in a cell, it was the probationer, nobody spoke to you and after the "parent" period, nobody wanted to patrol with you because they didn't trust you. The trust aspect had nothing to do with being able to do the job, it had everything to do with being able to keep your mouth shut. Lots of things used to go on which shouldn't have happened, things which simply wouldn't happen today, and as part of the "relief", (a police term for the team of officers you were posted to) you were expected to say nothing.

It was very much an "us and them" situation, the "them" being sergeants and above. They knew what the constables got up to and the constables knew they knew. The trick for us constables, was always to stay one step ahead. Once the rest of the relief felt they could trust you, you were accepted, gradually, but they could make life hell if you betrayed that trust. Fortunately for me, I was never placed in the position where I had to choose between what I knew was wrong, and I mean legally wrong and the "trust" of my colleagues. I'm not talking about having the odd beer on duty, there were much more serious things going on. For instance, a whole relief at a station in south London was once arrested for burglary. They would sort out a prospective target premises, and then, whilst on duty, burgle the place, use police transport to take the goods away and then sell the stolen items in markets. This was an isolated incident and was certainly not part of the norm, as it were, but it is true to say that, in those days, far more officers were closer to criminality and criminals than they should have been.

I remember the day I was "accepted". It was an early turn and I had just walked into the canteen for my refreshments, or "grub" as it was known. I had been at Bow Street for about 6 months and in the whole of that period, I had been the only probationer at the station. As such, I had been the butt of all the jokes, done all the nasty little jobs, kept my mouth shut and my ears open and generally, just got on with my job. It would be another three months before another probationer arrived and I could move off the bottom of the pile. I had just placed my food order at the counter, when one of my colleagues shouted across the canteen at me demanding to know if I was any good at cards? I wasn't, but then again I wasn't about to tell them that. This was the holy of holies, the card school! The experienced officers always played contract whist every grub-break, and to be invited to join this elite club meant the end of my initiation period and my acceptance onto the relief. I was delighted! I couldn't play cards to save my life, and still can't, but they enjoyed taking my money and I didn't begrudge it. Finally, I felt I belonged and then I really started to enjoy the work.

I enjoyed every waking moment at work, all the patrolling, the contact with people, making arrests and prosecuting at court. Nothing gave me more pleasure than simply walking along a street in uniform, occasionally chatting to shopkeepers and always feeling part of the community. Strangers used to say "hello" or "good morning" and from me, they always received an acknowledgement. It was difficult at first to get used to people looking at me, but then I figured it wasn't me they were looking at but the uniform. I knew I had made the right choice of career at last and I wore my uniform with immense personal pride.

I particularly enjoyed Saturday night duty when I could act as passenger on the station van, because the van got involved in most things, from taking calls to dealing with drunken fights and transporting prisoners. Part of our ground covered Leicester Square, when you could drive around it. There were lots of discos, clubs and restaurants in the area and action was guaranteed until well into the early hours. When everything had died down, we would find ourselves a little hideaway and play cards for the rest of the night. Sometimes we even went into the Lyceum Ballroom at the bottom of Wellington Street and played cards whilst the cleaners hoovered around us.

When the time came to get back to the station, we would leave at intervals and arrive back at the nick as if we'd all been out on patrol. There used to be problems if it was raining during the night, because then you had to walk around to get wet enough to convince the section sergeant you had been walking the streets all night, or get a colleague to put a hose on you in the back yard! Seriously!

As part of the two year training programme, I had to attend monthly classes called "CTC". It actually stood for Continuation Training Centre and was held at West End Central police station. The two days consisted of tutorials and then an exam at the end. The centre was run by an Inspector, who had a bad foot and couldn't walk properly. It didn't however, stop him playing squash for the police and very good he was too, as I found out one day when he challenged me to a game. I think he gave me a seven point start in every game and I lost them all!

The other instructor was a sergeant named Bert Black. He was a hugely popular Scot, whose favourite pastime was reminiscing about old times. It was quite easy for us to side-track him and he would talk for ages and have us in fits of laughter at his stories.

There were a number of set exercises we had to complete and the largest of these was a project that had to be researched, written up and then presented to the class over about 10 minutes. For the life of me I don't know why, but I got really excited about this, especially when I saw the list of subjects we could choose from. I had read some fictional books about high finance and found them fascinating.

On the list of subjects was Property Speculation and Development. This obviously had nothing whatsoever to do with policing, but it was on the list and I chose it. I think I made some sort of connection between the high finance fiction I had read and this subject. The officers who had been through the probation period and experienced the project, all said that all we had to do really, was to go to the library, find a book on the subject, photocopy some pages, read them a few times and then regurgitate the information to the class. This however, was not good enough for me. I threw myself into the project and went at it like a man possessed of some sort of devil.

I chose to show the comparison between two buildings in central London, how much each had cost, how much rent each building generated and how much each building was worth at that time. Part of my research led me to a man called Richard Seifert. He was an architect and had designed one of the buildings. Unfortunately, he also had connections to man named Harry Hyams, who had the reputation of being, shall we say, a bit of a rogue. When I explained my research plan to the Inspector, he went very quiet and told me to wait whilst he made a phone call. He came back and told me I had to go and see the Divisional Commander to explain why I wanted to interview Richard Seifert. Clearly, I had set off a few alarm bells, but after I explained why I needed to speak to Mr. Seifert, the Commander allowed me to make the appointment. I think he was more than a little amazed that somebody was actually putting some effort into one of the projects. I became absolutely engrossed in this project and conducted a large amount of research in my own time.

Eventually, it was finished and my presentation took up the whole of one afternoon at CTC. Not only that, I had got my dad to get his secretary to type up the whole thing and bind it into a booklet amounting to around twenty pages, which I still have. The Inspector was very impressed with my work, and my colleagues all thought I was a shit for showing them up!

What good did it do me? Nothing whatsoever, maybe a line on my personal file, but the point was that I had enjoyed it immensely and alongside my success at Training School, I had proved to myself that I could apply myself to something I enjoyed. This was partly the reason why I concluded earlier that my poor scholastic results had more to do with the fact that I didn't enjoy the academic subjects than anything else.

The remainder of my probationary period went very smoothly. I was, and still am really, one of those people who will never set the world alight with ideas or sheer dynamism. I am a plodder, I get on with my work and whatever I achieve comes from application and hard work. So it was with my CTC studies. I passed every one with flying colours, but what was more important to me was the fact that I had been completely accepted onto the relief at Bow Street. I had become an integral part of the team and was respected for my efforts. As I had become older, I had developed a sense of integrity and was not afraid to challenge something I thought was entirely wrong, as I shall explain later. It was not until the very end of my probationary period that I experienced the nastier side of policing, the Notting Hill Carnival riot of 1976, and the start of the Grunwicks trade dispute in the same month.

Lynne and I aged around 5 and 3 respectively.

Me, aged around 16 proudly wearing my first suit.

A super picture of Lynne in Australia.

Mum and dad at his retirement from teaching, a typical photo of mum.

Me and my replica AC Cobra sports car, circa 1991.

Myself and Press at the end of one of the Botswana safaris, circa 1995.

Myself and Chris enjoying a beer in Zambia, circa 2001.

Dad and his best friend Harold on an activity holiday!

Dad trying his best to mount a camel in Morocco. Silly old bugger!

Mum, on the left and her sister Rene at the end of Clevedon pier. This is where mum's ashes were spread.

**Possibly my favourite photograph, dad aged around 23 serving
on H.M.S. Exeter.**

Mum and dad walking on Weston seafront. What a handsome couple!

Myself and one of my best friends, Annette.

Myself, Susie (foreground), Jane, David and their two children, the night before starting our world trip.

The photograph of Livingstone for which I was arrested in Zambia.

Susie and I near the end of our trip, happier times.

Jane's son Benjamin, sartorially challenged aged 2!

Chapter 10

In August 1976, a photo-processing company in West London called "Grunwicks" sacked an Asian male. His mother walked out of her job in protest, and in doing so, started a bitter two year dispute over Union recognition at the plant. The workers had no union representation and consequently, were allegedly exploited by management. In those days, the practises of "secondary picketing" (the picketing of premises having business connections with a separate company in dispute) and "flying pickets" (workers from other companies picketing premises) were legal.

At the height of the dispute, something like 8000 pickets were massed outside the gates of Grunwicks, policed by ill-equipped officers who bore the brunt of the pickets' anger, because they couldn't get into the premises. The dispute was nothing to do with us, but as a police force, it was, and still is, our duty to protect property from wrong-doers. Some of the pickets had such twisted logic, that because we were lawfully protecting the plant and its occupants, we were viewed very much on the side of Grunwicks and as such, the enemy. There were genuine protesters there with genuine grievances against Grunwicks. However, the extremists in their midst, managed to whip a lawful protest into a howling mob, hell-bent on violence, mostly against the police.

This was a public order situation and the training we received in those days for dealing with this type of situation was paltry compared to today's modern methods. We had no protective equipment and wore our usual uniforms and cork beat-duty helmets.

The manoeuvre I remember most because of its sheer stupidity, was called the "Trudge and Wedge". Officers had to form themselves into an inverted 'V' shape, lock arms and face outwards. This was the "wedge". We then had to move forward as a unit, stamping our feet in rhythm and forcing our way into the crowd, effectively splitting them up. This was the "trudge". The main thing wrong with this manoeuvre was that we had to face outwards into the crowd, and the people we faced were none too fussy about giving the officers a good kick in the groin area. Once that happened and a few officers had gone down, the formation broke down immediately and completely, and we were left to fight the pickets back with some pretty brutal hand-to-hand fighting.

The pickets armed themselves with lengths of wood from placards, stones and anything else that came to hand, and we had our truncheons, lengths of wood, about a foot long which were about as much good in that environment as lollipop sticks! We had to get so close to the pickets to have any chance and they could just poke us with their longer bits of wood.

The violence was appalling! I had never encountered anything like it. The sheer viciousness of the attacks mounted on the police lines defied belief in those days. I am not trying to say that the police were angels, we weren't, we gave as good as we got most of the time. The pickets always massively out-numbered us, but I don't think they figured on us getting so angry and wound up. It was always the pickets who began any trouble, but we had had so much of it, that most of us were just up for a good fight and couldn't wait for the order to clear them away. It was like setting loose hunting dogs. En-masse, we would surge forward and just rip into the crowd, lashing out indiscriminately at pickets. Anybody who stood in front of us got "sticked". Then both sides would withdraw and lick their wounds.

And so it went on, day after day for almost two years. Eventually, the pickets gave up, the unions were not recognised and very little changed. Very little that is, apart from the police. We had entered a new era of political activity accompanied by mindless and numbing violence.

Over the following decade or so, there were some pretty awful industrial disputes and political rallies, which were fuelled by hatred and which ended in pure violence. The chief protagonists in those days were the ultra-left Anti-Nazi League and the ultra-right National Front. Many of these battle grounds started as legitimate disputes, as Grunwicks had, but then they simply got high-jacked by the political extremists with even more extreme agendas. The Wapping dispute was another good case in point.

News International had decided to move its operation from Fleet Street to a brand new facility in Wapping. Much of the old technology, such as type-setting by hand with blocks would be swept away and new working practices invoked. The workers were told that there were jobs for all of them, but they had to accept the new practices and move with the company to Wapping. Some of the work-force did accept the News International offer, but many of them didn't accept and went on strike. Consequently, we had another Grunwicks type dispute to police, workers to protect and premises to secure.

It started peacefully enough, but was eventually taken over by political extremists on the left of the spectrum, and again, the violence was appalling. Lorries were attacked as they delivered newsprint, cars were attacked and stoned as they came and went from the premises, and the police were attacked, merely because we were there to try and keep the peace and protect people going about their legitimate business.

The media were present from the outset and some of the reporting was dubious to say the least. Prominent media personnel, such as Kate Adie reported nightly from the scene and seemed to relish being in the thick of the violence. Ms. Adie received a well publicized blow to her head from a police truncheon for her trouble.

The mob were constantly trying to get into the premises but were always rebuffed by the police. If they had succeeded, the consequences for the safety of the non-striking workers would have been dire. There were nightly battles between the pickets and the police, both sides claiming the violence was started by the other.

In the end, the dispute simply dissolved away. The News International company did, and still does, produce its newspapers from Wapping and the new practices at the heart of the dispute are now fully accepted in the printing industry. What on earth was it all for?

Immigration by Afro-Caribbean people had been growing steadily since the Second World War. The vast majority of the so-called "first generation" of black people had settled well into the country, partly because they occupied areas where other Afro-Caribbean people had already settled. It was almost like a self-imposed "apartheid", which of course means separateness. It was understandable though, that they felt much more at home with their own culture surrounding them.

Although the Afro-Caribbeans could already speak English, many Indian immigrants never learned our language and never assimilated into our society, preferring instead to keep to the security of their own communities. Consequently, the jobs they obtained were the low paid menial jobs without responsibility or prospects for advancement. This had a polarising effect on our society. The immigrants were seen by some sections of the white community as second-class citizens and this, in turn, helped to found some of the more prominent political parties and highlight the existence of other groups with extreme political views and aspirations. Chief amongst these, were the right-wing National Front and their nemesis, the equally ultra but left-wing Anti-Nazi League. Whenever either of these two groups held a rally or march, it was certain that the other party would arrive mob-handed at some stage. Each would later claim that they had simply wanted to have discourse with their counterparts and persuade them to their way of thinking. The reality however, was that violence always ensued and the police were always in the middle, as we still are today.

The Afro-Caribbean immigrants had brought with them the culture of carnival. I well remember having carnival parades through Biddulph when I was younger and these ended in a fair-ground. All they consisted of were a few lorries decked out with bunting, and one of them carried the "Carnival Queen" for that year. These however, were nothing compared to the carnivals which were brought over by the Afro-Caribbeans. Dozens of lorries and vans would parade through the streets, many of them carrying steel-bands and playing reggae music at the top of the volume, hundreds of people walked in procession, decked out in fantastic costumes. Drugs and crime were endemic.

The cultivation, supply, use and possession of marijuana, or cannabis is controlled by the Misuse of Drugs Act 1971. Before that, the UK had relatively little legislation to control the use of illegal drugs. However, in those days, Britain didn't have the drug related problems it has today. Most of the present illegal drugs were available, but heroin was not that common, and cocaine was exhorbitantly expensive and was almost exclusively the preserve of the rich and famous. Cannabis however, was different in that it was and still is a major part of the religion and movement known as Rastafarianism. The vast majority of the followers of this religion are black and many of the new settlers in the UK brought its practises with them from the West Indies. Rastafarians believe it has its roots in certain passages of the Bible, which encourages people to eat "the herb of the earth." The use of cannabis in the West Indies was widespread amongst its inhabitants, but when they came to the United Kingdom, they came up against the laws governing its use and possession. As the vast majority of the revellers at the Notting Hill Carnival were, and still are Afro-Caribbeans, the smoking of cannabis "joints" was seen by them to be perfectly normal. As police officers however, we had a duty to arrest those we found with the drug. Although this was not the cause of the clash in 1976, it certainly didn't help.

As in all subsequent years, the area of Notting Hill in west London hosted the annual two day event with many thousands of people attending from all around the UK and Europe. There had been sporadic violence at previous carnivals in Notting Hill, which seemed to be where the carnival had found its English home, but not on a scale which would mar the 1976 event, and for 4 or 5 successive years after. The vast majority of those attending the carnival, both black and white, simply wanted to enjoy the music and soak up the atmosphere. However, because of the vast numbers attending, many youths, mainly black it has to be said although some white youths were involved, had come intent on causing trouble and committing crime. The relationship between the black community and police had been under strain for several years prior to this carnival and the actions of this small minority were to sour relations even further for years to come. That is not to say the police were blameless in this breakdown of relations. I knew of several officers who were very biased against the black community and took every opportunity to arrest them for something. I was not one of those officers.

I was still in my probation at this time, and still pretty green around the edges. In 1976, there had been a lot of talk about possible violence at the carnival, but we dismissed it as pure rumour. Everybody seemed to be having a really good time, however, there was an edge to the whole affair. Tension was evident all around, and got worse as the day wore on. Eventually, it all boiled over, and violence flared. Apparently, police officers had tried to arrest a black youth they had seen trying to steal from someone's pocket. Other black youths went to his assistance and to stop his arrest, sparking off the violence, which had been simmering just below the fragile surface. Word spread rapidly and violence flared in many parts of the carnival.

I remember sitting on an old police coach and being driven at speed in response to a call for assistance from other officers on the ground around Portobello Road. We got off the bus in a relatively quiet road, just around the corner. We were obviously near the heart of the carnival as the music was blaring from what seemed like hundreds of speakers, sited under the A4 Westway. Apart from the main parade, many youths congregated around massive speaker systems blaring out reggae music almost non-stop. It was these groups, which swelled in size during the day that caused most of the trouble. We received instructions from a senior officer that we were to walk down Portobello Road and clear some trouble-makers from the area. Simple!

When we walked around the corner, there were thousands of black youths milling about, music was blaring from loud-speakers under the motor-way and the tension was almost tangible. I remember looking down Portobello Road and feeling distinctly uneasy. It was just a sea of black faces and Rastafarian hats, (commonly known as "tea-cosy hats"). The sergeants with us formed us up into a sort of column two abreast, and we set off down the right hand side of the road, close to the building line. As we went, the crowd was parting in front of us to allow us to make our way, but as I looked behind at one stage, it was also closing back up after us, hemming us in. We had walked about a hundred yards or so down the road, when it started. A bottle came flying over and smashed against the wall above us. Then another, and another. It became obvious that we had been ordered into a very hostile environment.

Very soon, bricks and bottles were flying all around us. The bottles were smashing against the walls and showering us with glass and the bricks and stones were thumping into our bodies. Suddenly, the crowd parted. We took the opportunity, and split into two lines across the road, each facing in the opposite direction. We had our truncheons drawn at this stage. In the police at this time, an officer was not allowed to draw his truncheon in a public order situation unless the order had been given. In this particular instance, it hadn't, but I think the attitude "fuck you, Jack" prevailed and we just drew them anyway. We were facing imminent attack from a hostile crowd, which outnumbered us probably, fifty to one. Not drawing our truncheons would have been very stupid.

It was an extremely scary scene, and I think we just reacted naturally and went on the offensive. Both lines charged into the crowd and dispersed them to some degree, but we were of course, isolated and very vulnerable. As we were fighting with the crowds, the bottles and other missiles were raining down on us. The sergeants were screaming into their radios for urgent assistance, which eventually arrived, but not before several officers had been struck by flying bricks and bottles. We were eventually able to fight our way back up Portobello Road through some fairly fierce hand-to-hand fighting, and this was where the infamous dustbin lids legend was born. Ask any officer who was there at this time and he will tell you, almost fondly, that officers scoured the front gardens of the surrounding houses for dustbin lids to act as shields. Those officers who didn't find a lid, like me, found empty milk crates, not as good as a lid, but at least it was something. Those without a lid or crate, used whatever came to hand.

The violence continued well into the night. The youths were running us ragged as they knew all the little alleys and passages. They would duck down these and re-emerge at another spot to throw more missiles at us, and then duck away again. I don't think it was orchestrated, but at the time, all we were interested in, was not getting injured and going home!

At about two in the morning, I remember sitting in the front garden of a house in Oxford Gardens with about four other officers from my station. We were exhausted and bloodied and were having a rest, waiting wearily for our next order to go back to the fray. Suddenly, the door to the house opened and we all jumped up and turned to face this new threat. A black woman appeared in the door-way holding a large bowl. "Here you are, boys", she said, and placed the bowl on the step. It was full of hard-boiled eggs, which she had prepared for us. We all thanked her profusely for her kindness, apologised for sitting in her garden and tucked into the still warm eggs.

This was to be another lesson the Metropolitan Police learned on this night, keep the officers on the ground well-fed and watered. We had had no food or drink for hours on end and this was adding to our exhaustion. In later years and at other similar events, the catering branch made huge strides towards keeping everybody fed and today, it would be pretty difficult to find criticism of the quality or quantity of food presented to us on demonstrations and the like. An off-shoot of all this was the birth of "tea-pot 1", a mobile canteen, capable of being deployed very quickly to scenes where officers are engaged in any activity and where they have no access to food or water.

About an hour later, we were back at the top of Portobello Road. Most of the trouble-makers had disappeared or been arrested or taken to hospital, but a small, but violent group of youths were stubbornly refusing to disperse. The odd bottle kept coming over, and the constables lined up to face them, including me, were getting ever more angry at having to stand there and listen to the youths taunting us and dodging the silent missiles. Our mood was getting uglier by the minute, not only with the youths, but also with our senior officers, who seemed reluctant to let us go. Constables were openly shouting abuse at them, swearing at them and generally making their feelings pretty well understood. It was amazing to me then, and still is now as I remember that night, that we all remained disciplined and didn't just break ranks and go for the crowd.

Eventually, a superintendent stepped in front of us and pointed towards the crowd of youths. He started to tell us to disperse them, and got about as far as, "Right, I want you to....". He was then trampled in the stampede that was us going to finish the job.

We raced down towards the youths and they turned and started to run away. Unfortunately for them, our adrenelin was pumping, and we pretty soon raced them down. What happened then was not pretty. I remember at one stage running down the road towards the youths and finding myself momentarily alongside a black lady, who was running in the same direction as me, towards the group! I lashed out to my right and struck her with my truncheon. She fell, and I raced on without looking back. As a unit, we fell on the youths, males and females, and they received a fearful beating.

For once in the day, we were not outnumbered or under attack with bricks and bottles. Anger and frustration took over from restraint and reason. We were like a pack of hunting dogs on prey, and we had cornered our prey under one of the fly-overs. Fists, boots, truncheons, dust-bin lids were all being liberally applied to whoever got in the way. Arrest was not an option for us at this time, we wanted some vengeance for the violence and abuse we had endured for much of the day, and we were going to get it.

Order was restored when senior officers began to arrive and pull us off the crowd, but by this time, it was practically over anyway. I think they maybe took their time getting to us! I saw the lady I had struck, in with the youths. She was covered in blood, as were most of them and us. At that time, I didn't care one jot for her condition; not an episode I remember with pride, but there again, why was she running towards the fighting and not away from it? The only explanation I had at that time was that she intended to join in.

Valuable lessons were learned from the 1976 Notting Hill Riot. Serious disorder marred the carnival for several years following 1976, and it would be just as long before any trust at all, was restored by either side.

Today, the Notting Hill Carnival is generally peaceful, although criminals are still attracted to the area by the vast numbers. Gangs of black youths still "steam" their way through the crowds, snatching jewellery and purses and unfortunately, a few years ago, two murders were committed. However, the degree of cooperation between the carnival organisers and the police is now at a level which would have been considered inconceivable in 1976. The residents of Notting Hill must have breathed a sigh of relief when, at a subsequent carnival, a photograph was published in the daily newspapers of a uniformed police officer dancing in the street with a black female dressed in a colourful carnival outfit. Better times were ahead!

Police officers are now officially told to ignore the smoking of cannabis in public. Although still a criminal offence, it is thought to be of minor importance compared to the safe running of the carnival. Unfortunately, some black youths like to goad police officers at the Notting Hill carnival by speaking to the officers whilst smoking "reefers" and blowing the smoke into their faces. This sort of behaviour is almost bound to cause more trouble.

In October 1976, I finished my probationary period and was confirmed in the rank of Constable. Almost immediately, I came under pressure from two sources. The first was my relief Inspector, a hugely capable and intelligent man named David Stockley, who had not only taught himself Polish because his wife was from that country, but who had also been "called to the Bar" having passed his barristers' exams. The second source was my father. He had become immensely proud of me and both he and Inspector Stockley were urging me to carry on my studies and take the Sergeants exam. In those days, it was practically unheard of to take the promotion exam with less than five years experience, but Inspector Stockley told me in no uncertain terms that, unless I took and passed the exam quickly, I would very soon be left behind on the promotion ladder, and Dad was of the same opinion. However, I was not keen as they were. I was having lots of fun as a constable and I wanted to join Special Branch, which investigated people rather than crimes. It was one of the reasons I had joined the police in the first place.

Chapter 11

The next three years or so became a whirlwind of events and activity, some of which served to shape my life to this day.

I had really settled into life as a constable at Bow Street. I got on well with my colleagues, I think I was well thought of by the senior officers and I was very happy with my life. I was living in single officers' accommodation at the infamous Trenchard Section House in Broadwick Street, smack in the middle of Soho, supervised by the feared and hated Sergeant Perryman. I think the only reason he was hated was because he was so focused on keeping us young bucks out of trouble in one of the most notorious vice areas of Europe, he was seen as a bar to us having fun.

He ran Trenchard by a very strict, but simple set of rules. If you broke the rules, you paid, if you lived by the rules, you kept Perryman at bay. For us young officers, it was a real game to try and outwit Perryman, especially where young women were involved. There was only one door into the building and then you had to pass the wardens office. He was Perryman's "snout" and would report the fact that an officer had taken a young lady to his room. Perryman's rule was that all visiting women had to leave the section house by midnight and I remember one evening, when I was "entertaining" in my room, there was a thunderous rap on the door. Perryman's voice boomed out, "PC Robins, I know you have a woman in there. It's midnight, get her out, get her out". He waited outside the door until we emerged, sort of dressed, at which time he escorted us both to the front door and saw her off the premises. He was a real "killjoy" at times, but later on, he really surprised me by allowing my fiancée to sleep at Trenchard after her night duties. I had come to realize that Sgt. Perryman had only the best interests and safety of the officers at heart and I began to treat him with the respect he deserved, and I think he responded in kind.

To many officers living in Trenchard House at that time, Soho was a massive magnet. All the local establishments, such as clubs and pubs could distinguish a police officer when he or she entered the premises. Generally, the officers were well looked after by the staff, although there were one or two incidents where some officers had made a nuisance of themselves. On one such occasion, several of us were in the canteen fairly late at night when suddenly, there was an almighty ruckus at the front door. We rushed out to find two or three constables trying to hold the door closed against several youths who were intent on getting in. Apparently, the officers had been to a Turkish club and somehow upset some of the youths inside. It was probably over a woman, it usually was. The Turks had chased the officers through the Soho streets and had very nearly caught up with them before the officers managed to get into Trenchard. When the rest of us arrived, the Turks thought better of it and went away shouting dire threats of revenge and violence on the "pigs." I myself rarely went out in Soho. I don't really know why, it just never appealed to, me. I had always been more than happy to go on a night out when I was younger, living in Biddulph, but for some reason, the night-spots of Soho held no fascination for me whatsoever. Consequently, I didn't make too many friends within the walls of Trenchard House.

I am coming now to a most influential event in my life; the day I met my future wife. When I met her, her name was Susan Bing and she was a student nurse at St. Thomas' Hospital in London. She always preferred to be called Susie. For some reason, I always had a problem with this. Having spent most of my teenage years trying to identify with my working-class friends in Stoke, hearing the name Susie just sounded rather pretentious to me. In any event, I compromised and called her "Soos". I don't think she ever liked it too much and it was definitely wrong of me not to call her how she wished. The reason I mention all this now is because after we were separated and before we were even divorced, she changed her name by deed poll from Susan to Susie and changed her surname from Robins to Stephens, this being her grandfather's surname.

I remember it was a warm spring day in 1977. I was on early turn and due to finish my shift at 2pm. I had been posted to Leicester Square beat, part of which included the National Gallery in Trafalgar Square. It was about 1pm, and I was walking down Charing Cross Road towards the back of the Gallery, when somebody stopped me and told me there were two people collapsed by the statue to Henry Irving.

When I got there, sure enough, two people, a man and a woman were lying on the pavement, seemingly unconscious. Having been in the West End for a few years, I knew that these two were either drunk, in which case, I could take them to the station under arrest for being drunk in a public place, or had taken a drug overdose, in which case, I should call an ambulance and take them to hospital. The former course of action was preferable as it would enable me to get off duty on time. The latter course would mean extra duty. I looked at my watch, and then at them. Fatefully, I decided that I should call an ambulance, which duly arrived and they were carted off to St. Thomas' Hospital. As they were only semi-conscious and they had no identification on them, it was my duty to accompany them to hospital. (If either of them had died, I would have had to provide continuity of identification at the inquest and to state that nothing had happened to them en route, just a bit of procedure really.) At St. Thomas', they were taken straight into the special room, the "resus room", set aside for drug addicts, followed dutifully by me.

When I walked into the room, I saw the most beautiful woman I had ever seen. She was sitting on a stool, laughing with some of her nursing colleagues. I remember her smile struck me like a thunderbolt. It was broad daylight and the room well lit, but her smile seemed to light the entire space around her, as if everything else was in darkness. I was absolutely captivated! I know we spoke, but about what, I don't remember, probably about the two "druggies".

I hung around the "resus. room" for much longer than I needed to, hoping just to talk to her some more, which I didn't. Eventually, I had to leave and walked the whole way back to Bow Street, not because there was no transport, but because I was wrestling with my shyness, trying to figure out whether I had the courage to phone the hospital and ask her out. I distinctly remember asking myself "why on earth would she want to go out with me? She probably has dozens of boyfriends, most of them doctors, most of them wealthy and not one of them a penniless clod like me".

When I got back to the station, I had worked myself into such a lather, I went straight into an unused office. I knew if I didn't do it straight away, I would never do it. I phoned the hospital, asked for the "resus. room" and suddenly remembered, I didn't even know her name. Shit!! I was stuck, and this was going to be embarrassing. Someone answered the phone and I just asked to speak to the fair haired nurse who had dealt with the policeman and the two "druggies". "That was me", she said. Well, I shut my eyes, and asked her out. "okay", she said. I walked back to Trenchard with a very big grin on my face.

We agreed to meet on the embankment a few days later and go for a drink. The appointed time came and went, and then a further five minutes came and went, then another, and another. I looked at my watch and saw it was half an hour past the meeting time. I remember feeling totally dejected, but not surprised. "What on earth would a beautiful woman like her be doing out with the likes of me?" was the question running over and over in my head. I had been walking up and down the pavement and turned for the last time before heading home, when suddenly, there she was, just getting off the bus. She told me later that she very nearly didn't go on the date and it was only her flat-mate who had persuaded her to go.

That made me feel special! When I asked her out, Susie was actually in a relationship with a guy called Chris. Had I known that at the time, it wouldn't have made the slightest difference, I would still have asked her! Apparently, he was a bit distraught at first to learn that Susie had been out with me, but later started an intense relationship with the flat-mate, Susie's best friend at the time, who, incidentally hated me with a passion. I've always wondered about her and Chris, whether or not she persuaded Susie to go on our first date, hoping it would split up Susie and Chris leaving the field clear for her, but I seem to remember, they did eventually marry.

Anyway, we went for a drink on one of those restaurant/bar ships moored alongside the Embankment. I remained totally smitten by her and, it seemed, I made an impression on her. At the end of the evening, I was a little more relaxed and was able to ask her out again with a degree of confidence. Her reply took me by surprise. She seemed enthusiastic about seeing me again.. And that was how I met and started my relationship with my future ex-wife.

Later in the year, myself, mum and dad went to Canada to visit Lynne and David in Toronto, Canada. They were still living permanently in Australia, but David had taken a contract to work in Toronto for two years. During the arrangements, it became obvious there wasn't going to be enough room for me in their flat, so I got in touch with the International Police Association and asked them to put me in touch with a policeman in Toronto who would give me a bed for five days and maybe show me a little of the city. The I.P.A. is a sort of club for police around the globe. There are reciprocal arrangements in place for officers visiting other countries. The organization will arrange accommodation and visits to various places and is an excellent way for officers to get around and see other countries. The down-side is that the majority of the members are totally absorbed with their work and talk about little else. And of course, I might have to provide the same level of courtesy to a visiting officer. It didn't happen because as soon as I returned to the UK, I left the organization.

I wasn't crazy about the idea of staying the entire time with Lynne and Dave anyway and not being able to stay there was a nice little excuse. However, I spent five of the most boring days of my life with one of the most boring people I have ever met. He talked about nothing other than police work, and when he wasn't talking about that, he was pointing out planes to me flying high over the city. "Hey, there's one" he'd say, pointing skywards. I had made the mistake of telling him that I liked planes and found them fascinating. He was only trying to be friendly and he wasn't nasty or anything, but boy! was he boring.

After enduring him for five days, I travelled down to New York by bus and spent the following five days in a total whirl. The I.P.A. had booked me into a room on the 23rd floor of a hotel on West 42nd Street in Times Square, overlooking the bus station and most of the area, right in the centre of the action. Although I wasn't looking forward to doing it, I intended to make contact with some local cops who could perhaps show me a little of the city or at least point me to some areas of interest. I walked out of the hotel on the first morning and saw a "black and white" police car parked against the kerb. The two officers were out of the vehicle dealing with something on the pavement, so I hung around and waited for them to finish. It was all getting a little heated on the pavement and eventually, after a lot of shouting and good earthy New York swearing, the two officers went back to their car. Nervously, I approached one of the officers and produced my warrant card. I was just about to introduce myself, when he looked at my card and snapped in that wonderful Bronx accent, "get in the car." I was a little taken aback at first, and didn't actually move. It was only when he shouted "get in the fuckin' car" that I actually dived onto the back seat and the car roared off. The two officers then spent the next ten minutes venting a lot of anger, shouting and swearing as only Americans can. They were obviously very wound up from the incident on the street. They eventually calmed down, and then they seemed to remember that I was sitting in the back. The passenger turned to face me and introduced himself as Freddie Horn, Detective Freddie Horn. I'm ashamed to say I don't remember the drivers' name or the names of any of the many other New York police officers to whom I was introduced over the following days.

Fred Horn just had one of those names that sticks in the memory, and he was a bit of a character. They all were really I suppose. I was picked up at my hotel every morning in the police car and taken on patrol with them everywhere. We went to armed incidents, reports of burglaries, robberies on "HeShe Street" (a local name for a street frequented by transvestites), everything. I joined in their off-duty time playing softball and went to their drinking parties. If Freddie or his partner couldn't make it for some reason, someone else was there to take me for a typical New York "eggs over-easy" breakfast, and then out onto the patrol.

On one evening, they were off on some sort of operation, which they couldn't take me on. Fred turned to me and said, "you seen Star Wars?" I hadn't even heard of it let alone seen it, so I was taken to the cinema, or should I say, movies. We pulled up in the "black and white" at the side of the moviehouse, and Fred had a hurried conversation with some guy by the side-door, which at that time was shut. Suddenly, I was ushered into the cinema through this door and plonked into a seat adjacent to the door. As I sat down, I heard lots of shuffling and coughing. I looked at the door, which was still open and saw that Fred was nicely silhouetted against the street lighting, his policeman's cap being unmistakeable. It was only after I had sat down that I realised all the shuffling I had heard was the drugs being dropped onto the floor. The drug-using population of New York were not best friends with the local police, and there I was, obviously connected somehow to the police, sitting amongst them all, if not a stooge, then at the least, someone not to be trusted. I spent a nervous few minutes expecting a light tap on my shoulder, but thankfully, nothing happened, and then that fantastic sound of trumpets at the start of Star Wars blasted through the sound system. It certainly made me jump, and I was then treated to a New York style movie viewing. I don't think there was any time, when there wasn't somebody talking or moving around. It would annoy the hell out of me here in England, but it didn't seem to matter there. I was enthralled by the movie, and when the part came on where Harrison Ford takes the Millenium Falcon into "hyper-space" and the screen just explodes into dots, the entire cinema hooted, clapped, whistled, stamped their feet, shouted and whooped. It was amazing. In England, there may have been a small gasp of appreciation and quiet murmuring. There, they really went for it and it was fun, as were the entire five days I spent there.

In November 1977, I applied for, and was accepted into Special Branch. I was immediately posted out to Heathrow Airport on S.B. duties and worked out of Terminal One. Believe me, in those days, Terminal One was nothing more than a shell. It was used for internal flights and had only one or two check-in desks. In fact, it had more bars than check-in desks, as we Special Branch officers knew only too well!

I remember one evening I had arranged to meet Susie at Charing Cross Railway Station, but I stayed in the bar too long. I couldn't get a staff bus back to the staff car-park and had to run through the tunnel, which is about 1/2 mile long, and then on to the car parks, about another 1/2 mile. Not far, you might think, but with 7 or 8 Gin and Tonics sloshing around inside me, my legs weren't working too well. I was then left to get into the centre of London, a journey which would normally take about an hour.

I was already late before I even left the car park. I had a pretty quick car in those days, a Lancia Fulvia, and I made the journey in twenty minutes flat. How on earth I didn't have an accident or wasn't done for speeding or drink/drive I don't know, I was absolutely pissed. When I got to the station, I fell out of the car and staggered off to find Susie. She was pacing up and down and when she saw the state I was in, she was not best pleased to say the least, and quite rightly so too. It didn't occur to me that she might have been worried I had had an accident or something.

By this time, I had succumbed to the pressure exerted by dad and Inspector Stockley and had begun studying for the sergeants' exam, which would be held in the following April, 1978. The Special Branch work out at the airport was pretty boring, and during the long lulls between flights to and from the Irish Republic or Belfast, I could spend the time studying. Christmas and New Year 1977 came and went. The studying became ever more intense, as did my relationship with Susie.

When I had met her, I had two other girlfriends whom I was seeing, unbeknown to each other, or Susie. One was a girl from New Scotland Yard and the other, a married woman I had met through a friend at British Home Stores. Both were gorgeous and extremely sexy. However, it was Susie I didn't want to lose, and so, I finished seeing the other two in favour of her. I put up with the boredom at the airport because I knew it was only a prelude to becoming a confirmed Detective Constable, engaged on real Special Branch work at New Scotland Yard.

I took the promotion examination in April 1978, and passed. I came in the top 100, in fact, I seem to remember, I came about 55th. This enabled me to apply for an "accelerated promotion" scheme, whereby, I would attend Bramshill Police College for an intensive course and thereafter, shoot up the promotion ladder. Susie wasn't at all keen to see me go as it meant I would be away for weeks on end, but she did appreciate the opportunity. Needless to say, I failed the interview and when I phoned Susie with the result, I said, "I have good news and bad news, which do you want first." "The bad", she said. "Okay, I'm not going to Bramshill!" Silence!! "And the good news?" "I'm not going to Bramshill!" She laughed, as I hoped she would, and our relationship deepened.

And then I made probably one of the worst decisions I can remember. The Commissioner of the Metropolitan Police, Sir David McNee, withdrew Metropolitan Special Branch officers from all the major provincial ports around the country such as Dover, Felixstowe or even Gatwick Airport. All the ports around the country were staffed by Metropolitan Police Special Branch officers, and withdrawing them meant that they would have to be staffed by Special Branch officers from that force area, and the Metropolitan officers would return to duties in London, at New Scotland Yard. This, in effect, meant that there would be no room for the officers recently inducted into Special Branch, me amongst them. It took most of us by surprise, and for a while, no-one really knew what would happen.

Senior management then sent out a memo, which stated that the officers most recently accepted for Special Branch, and who were waiting to become Detective Constables on probation, could either remain at Heathrow Airport, and wait for vacancies to occur naturally, or return to their stations and continue with uniform duties until such time as they could transfer to the Yard. The memo went on to say that it might be as long as two years before all the newly recruited S.B. officers were inducted into New Scotland Yard. Those officers still at their stations would have to stay there in any event.

This placed me into a dilemma. I had passed the promotion examination, and would be promoted in October 1979 with five years service. This date would be within the projected two years waiting time for Special Branch. It seemed to me that on this basis, I was wasting my time at Heathrow, as I would become a sergeant before I could become a Detective Constable at the Yard. Had McNee not scrapped the scheme, I could have become a probationary D.C., gone through the training period and then been confirmed as a D.C., returned to uniform duties as a sergeant for the obligatory one year and then returned to Special Branch as a substantive Detective Sergeant, incidentally, the best rank in the force. I made the fateful decision to return to uniform duties in order to gain as much experience as possible before my promotion. Had I sought advice on the subject, I might have found out that I could in fact, have delayed my promotion until such time as I had completed my probationary period as a D.C. and then taken up the promotion. But I didn't, and as a consequence, I never returned to what I really wanted to do in the Police, work in the Special Branch. It is one of the decisions I have real regrets about. However, as I said in the introduction, my life went off in other directions, but I can't help wondering just how different my career would have been had it not been for this disastrous decision. I did make attempts to go back to Special Branch later in my career, but by then, for one reason or another, it was too late.

The following 18 months or so made a complete mockery of my decision. Bearing in mind I had returned to uniform to gain experience and perform the role of acting sergeant, if I spent more than three months back in uniform, I would probably be exaggerating.

1978 was memorable for me for another reason, Susie and I visited Rome. It was the second time I had been abroad, the first being with Ian from training school. We went to all the usual tourist spots like The Trevi Fountain, the various art galleries and of course, Pompeii. I marvelled at just how dedicated the archaeologists must have been to dig the entire village out from the centuries old volcanic dust that had buried it. We met two Canadian tourists here who made us laugh by referring to the plaster-cast models of the stricken Pompeiian citizens as "crispy critters." However, more memorable for me, was the visit we made to St Peter's Basilica, and specifically, the carved marble statue of The Pieta by Michaelangelo. I hadn't even heard of it before this trip but I remember standing in front of the statue, absolutely mesmerised by the exquisite carving. It was the first time any piece of artwork had had such an effect on me. The look on the Madonna's face, the way Christ was laid across her lap, the folds in her gown all held my rapt attention but the most beautiful and intriguing aspect to the work was the way the fingers on her left hand had been carved. I know now that they had been restored following damage a few centuries earlier, but that didn't matter. Someone had carved them in the most intricate and lifelike manner. Various scholars have attempted to interpret the whole work of The Pieta and in particular, her left hand. But for me, her left hand seems to symbolize the question, "Why?" I was captivated and stood before the statue for what seemed like an age. To this day, I have a love of finely carved objects, full of character and have collected various examples, mainly studies of heads and faces.

I returned to Bow Street from Heathrow around May 1978. Within a short time, I was seconded onto the West End Central Crime Squad. I really didn't want to go on this unit, but was ordered to go, and that was that. Some of it was quite exciting, but mostly, I wandered around the West End with my partner, who also wasn't keen, looking for "three card trick" gamers or hanging around the tube stations, watching for pickpockets. There was one incident though, which remains firmly in my memory.

The Crime Squad was run by a Detective Inspector, supported by a Detective Sergeant. The whole unit was overseen by the Detective Chief Superintendent and consequently, there was a distinct C.I.D. flavour to the whole squad. In those days, we received our expenses, or "incidentals" in a small brown envelope, collected from the administration office.

I collected mine one day, and found that £1-50p had been deducted. (Bear in mind this was 1978, £1-50 was £1-50!) I went to the admin. officer and asked why it had been deducted, and he told me it was on the instructions of my boss, Detective Inspector Batt, in charge of the Crime Squad. 50p was for "Pete the Feet" who was retiring, and the other £1 was for Detective Chief Superintendent Walters, who was leaving the division. This money was deducted without my permission, and although I wasn't happy about it, I decided to say nothing about the 50p for Pete as I knew him and wished him well. I was not however, going to involuntarily subscribe money for a man I didn't even know.

In those days, the C.I.D. was pretty corrupt in many ways. There had been a series of high-profile anti-corruption initiatives, driven by the Commissioner. They had been started by the previous Commissioner, Sir Robert Mark. This man hated the C.I.D. and was determined to clean up the corruption, rife within its ranks. The initiatives ended the careers of some very high-ranking officers, who had enjoyed the best of both worlds for a long time; not only earning a very decent salary with lots of perks attached, but also accepting vast amounts of money from the criminal underworld for heavens knows what "services". The crime squad was seen as a jumping off point into the C.I.D. and if you wanted in, you had to put up with the sort of bullying attitude that would never be acceptable today. Most of the constables in the office were intent on joining the C.I.D. and so, put up with it. I had no intentions of going into that department, and had no compunction in challenging the Detective Inspector about the deduction, in the office, in front of other members of the squad.

He was sitting at his desk when I entered the main office. Most of the rest of the squad were working in there as well, all typing up reports of one sort or another. The frank exchange of views went something like this, "Did you take a pound out of my expenses?" I asked. "It's for the Detective Chief Superintendent", he said. "That's not what I asked" I said, "did you take a pound out of my expenses?" He said, "Yes, it's for the boss' leaving present." "Who gave you permission to do that?" I asked. "No-one, look, it's for your boss, the Detective Chief Superintendent". "I don't care who it's for," I said, "I don't even know the D.C.S., I wouldn't know him if I passed him in the street, why should I donate to a present for him? You didn't ask, I'd like my pound back please!" "What?" the D.I. thundered. "I'd like my pound back please!" I can remember the stare he gave me, pure malevolence. I can also remember that the clacking of the typewriters had gradually dwindled to nothing, the silence was deafening! All eyes and ears were on the two protagonists at the front of the office, one, a highly experienced detective in the exalted rank of D.I., the other, a spratt, barely out of his probation. Batt tried one more time, "This is for your boss, the head of the C.I.D. on this division." "Exactly", I said. "I don't know him, I don't want to donate any money to anyone in the C.I.D., you didn't ask my permission to donate my money, I'd like my pound back please." With that, he reached into his drawer, slammed a one pound note onto the desk and shouted, "There's your fuckin' pound, now get out!"

Many years after this little exchange, a phrase was coined in the Metropolitan Police, "Integrity is not negotiable!" Some of the constables in the office that day approached me after and said how they wished they had done the same. Well, it wasn't that difficult! Batt and his sidekick, Detective Sergeant Mann employed bully-boy tactics, exploiting officers' desires to join C.I.D. They tried to get their own back on me by trying to remove me from the money-spinning Christmas duties, but they were too late; I earned a fortune and they hated me even more.

Having spent about four miserable months on the Crime Squad, much of the latter part of it watching my back, looking for the knife-wielding Batt or Mann, I returned to Bow Street early in the new year 1979, intent on getting some acting-sergeant experience. I was there for about two weeks, when I was posted back to West End Central, only this time, I was attached to the Clubs Office, and more properly, Clubs Clubs. I had made it known earlier that I was interested in working on the Clubs section, but the powers-that-be had posted me to the Crime Squad instead.

Clubs Office was the generic name for the department that dealt with the various types of vice in the West End. Within the office were several small sub-departments, each specialising in one type of activity, and each being prefixed with the term "Clubs", for example, Clubs Books (pornography), Clubs Toms (prostitutes), Clubs Juveniles and Clubs Clubs. We dealt with the night-club scene. I was partnered with a very experienced Clubs officer named Mick. I hadn't asked for the "clubs" sub-section, it just happened.

Night-clubs in those days were not as they are today, discos. Then, a club was just that. A place where bona-fide members could go for the evening, maybe have dinner, watch a top-class cabaret, dance a little and then retire home or to the hotel in the early hours. These were the good, reputable clubs. We however, tended to concentrate on the not-so-good ones; where one could buy illegal membership on the door for a tenner into the doorman's pocket, where the "food" was probably a sandwich, where champagne was at least £50 for a rubbish bottle and where "hostesses" constantly harangued you for attention and to get you to spend your money in the club. The "hostesses" were nothing more than prostitutes really, who charged even more for their services.

Before I relate a few memories from the Clubs office, the following was a typical day for myself and Mick. I had moved from Trenchard by this time and was living with Susie in a flat in Streatham. I would get up in the morning at about 11am, get showered and dressed and leave for the West End at about midday. I would meet Mick in a pub around the corner from Trenchard House at about 1pm, for a "livener", a salt-beef sandwich and a gin & tonic. From here, we would go to a pub called "The Green Man" in Wardour Street and meet two guys from the film industry, who usually had some interesting little titbits of information on which clubs were being "naughty". Having plied them with copious amounts of alcohol. Mick and I would head back to the office around 4pm to do our research. Each club had a licence in one form or another, which often had attachments or terms of operating. Having selected the club or clubs we would concentrate on for that night, we read up on the licence conditions, wrote up our duty "diaries", put in our expenses for the previous day and went home.

After having dinner at home, I would return to the West End at about 11pm and meet Mick at a pre-arranged venue. We would then go drinking, posing as whatever was called for, doing whatever was necessary to get into the target clubs in order to gain sufficient evidence to obtain a warrant to raid the place and shut it down.

We didn't usually finish until around 3am, when we would go to our local "friendly" club for a wind-down drink and discussion before heading home, both having had way too much to drink. I would bounce off the walls in the flat on my way to the bedroom, collapse into bed and snore my way round to 11am, when I would get up and head back for my "livener".

An officer on "Clubs Clubs" was only allowed to do one 90 day attachment per year. This was to prevent an individual officer turning alcoholic, courtesy of the police. In my case, I can say with certainty that after my 90 days, I was as close to alcohol dependency as I ever wish to be. According to Susie, I reeked of the stuff 24 hours a day.

As well as "investigating" clubs, the odd unusual job would come into the office. On one particular day, Mick and I were asked by our boss to meet a woman named "Tina". She turned out to be an ex-prostitute who had a grudge against a certain individual running an illegal poker game in premises just off Piccadilly Circus. Ordinarily, we wouldn't get involved with people's personal battles, but the Clubs Office knew of this game and the individual concerned. Other officers had tried to run surveillance on the game previously, but the location of the gaming room had always thwarted them. The main problem was that no-one could get inside the gaming room, which was locked from the inside by a very substantial door which could not easily be beaten down. Any attempt at forced entry would immediately see the gaming table cleared of all money and chips, and if entry was gained, all that would be found would be a bunch of friends having a friendly poker game. (Playing poker was, and still is, not illegal. It only becomes illegal when the "house" takes a slice of the "pot", usually 5 or 10 per cent. This "slice" gets put into a container underneath the table from a slot cut into the table-top.) As if this wasn't enough, the individual concerned was an ex-policeman who had been sacked for some sort of serious offence. He evidently still had contacts within the force, who would give him the nod if his premises were being looked at. For this reason, our meeting with "Tina" was kept very hush-hush. She regularly played in this game and offered to get one of us inside in order that an entry could be effected. Apparently, she had been ripped off by the owner to the tune of a few thousand pounds, and wanted revenge. Whatever her motivation, we didn't much care, we had an opportunity to take this game down and close him for good. After several meetings, we formulated a plan. "Tina" would take me into the game as her "toy-boy" boyfriend with a seemingly unending source of funds for her, and I had to act the part of a bored rich-boy looking for any sort of "action".

Tina and I attended the game several times over the following weeks, just to get me known at the club. We would only leave after Tina felt she had either won or lost enough for that night. I never took part in the game, Tina always did that. I just had to sit there, be nice to her, watch the game for hours on end and overtly, pass her money every now and then. The others in the game looked on me as a rich idiot, their contempt for me was almost tangible!

There were some big villains attending this game, and the talk around the table would often revolve around criminality. I remember them once talking about some un-named guy who had kidnapped someone for a ransom, but generally, the talk was of armed robberies, East-end gang-fights and the like. It was difficult to continuously look bored and uninterested, so I took a book with me and sat there reading whilst she gambled away the state's money. I always kept an ear on what was being said around the table and reported back anything of interest.

Back at the office, we decided to launch the raid on a particular night, keeping the venue a close secret, and the raiding party would be let in to the club by me at a very precise time, something like 28 and a half minutes past the hour. I had practised how long it took me to get to the door, silently counting the seconds and had left on my own a few times previously, hoping it wouldn't arouse suspicion when I would do it for real.

On the night of the raid, Tina and I were there as normal. At a precise moment, I started a blazing row with her. I obviously couldn't look at my watch whilst having this "row", so had to judge how long it lasted and time my "flouncing" exit to coincide with the raiding party waiting on the other side of the door.

It worked perfectly, and as I opened the door, I was deliberately knocked over, trodden on and eventually slammed up against a wall by an officer. The raiding party would usually take around an hour to complete all the necessary documentation and then they would leave. Ordinarily, Mick and I would both be in a club when it was raided and would remain there after to maintain our anonymity. In the case of this gaming club, we had Tina to think of, and so it was agreed that I would have to remain there with her and brazen out any attempt to point fingers. Clearly, if I left the club with the raiding party, Tina would be in serious trouble. Any hope I had of convincing the clientele that I was nothing other than Tina's "bit of stuff" was useless.

After the raid, they rumbled me straight away. They may have been crooks and thieves etc, but they were all intelligent and street-wise men. Strangely, nothing was said to me, but I do remember one regular player coming over to the table where I had remained seated, and staring at me intently as he ground out a cigarette in the ashtray. It must have taken him at least a minute to practically grind it into dust, and all the time, he just stared at me. I have to say, this man scared me. They had obviously been suspicious of me from the start, that would have been natural, but they had no reason to doubt my cover story. When the raid happened, they simply put two and two together. But if that was scary, what happened next almost scarred me for life.

Tina and I eventually left the club, very relieved but unharmed. It was my intention to drive her back to her flat in Westbourne Terrace. As we walked along the street away from the club, I looked behind and saw one of the gamers also coming out from the club. He looked first one way and then saw us and started to walk after us. As soon as we got around the corner, I practically lifted Tina off her feet in my haste to get to my car, which I had left conveniently close-by. We managed to drive away without being seen, or so I thought. Tina lived in one of those huge houses on Westbourne Terrace with an in-and-out drive. I had parked the car in a space and seen her into the flat. As I walked out a few minutes later, I heard an engine to my right. I looked round and immediately a pair of headlights blinded me and the engine was gunned.

As I crossed the drive to my car, this other vehicle shot forward and was aiming straight for me. It was only about 10 yards away and was on me in a flash. I jumped straight through the hedge and out onto the pavement. As I started running down Westbourne Terrace, the car turned out of the drive and came after me with squealing tyres. I didn't have much of a start on it and it was catching me up rapidly. I came to a junction and turned sharp right. The car was obviously going too fast and mercifully, missed the junction. As it was reversing, I was running down the street for all I was worth. I turned into another street and immediately dived through a hedge into someone's front garden. The car screeched around the corner and shot past. As soon as it had gone, I ran out of the garden, doubled back along the first street and dived through another hedge. In this garden I hid right under the hedge and held my breath as I heard the car cruising by, very slowly, obviously looking for me. I must have laid there for about 30-40 minutes, before I figured the coast was clear and I could retrieve my car and drive home.

We didn't have our usual routine the following day, as we had to debrief on the raid. When I got to the office, one of the other guys on Clubs, Paul, an absolutely lovely man asked me if the local police had picked me up? "What?" I said. Paul then told me that they realized I would be in the company of some very dangerous and suspicious characters after the raid. He had arranged for a local plain-clothes police car to wait for me at Tina's to make sure I was OK!! The car that was chasing me was a police car. When I recounted the story, and had everybody in fits of laughter at my little escapade, we figured out that when I suddenly ran off, they probably thought I was not the person they were sent to check on. When I dived through the hedge, their suspicions were definitely aroused and started to chase me as a potential burglar.

There were a couple of other little incidents on Clubs, like the time an American friend of mine, Robert Hoppenstedt, or Hopper to his friends and family, asked if he could come on a raid. He was studying business at Regents Park College and his wife Peggie was studying nursing with Susie. We were due to raid a club called "The 19th Hole" and I arranged for Hopper to be with me in the club. Mick would also be there of course, but in a different part. Unbeknown to Hopper, I had briefed Paul and we decided to have a little fun with him.

When the club was raided, I had said to Hopper to just go along with what the officer said to him and answer the questions. Hopper and I were sitting on a long couch along with several other drinkers when the raid happened. We could hear Paul asking very perfunctory questions of these others, such as name and address and date of birth.

When Paul got to Hopper, he gave him a really rough ride. All the others had remained seated, but with Hopper, Paul demanded he stand up. Paul was a big man and towered over Hopper. In an overly loud voice he was asking all manner of questions like what was he doing in UK, where did he get his money, who supported him, was he aware that he was in an illegal drinking club, was he aware that he would be reported to the Foreign Office for violation of his visa and did he have someone who could pack his bag for him as he wouldn't be returning home before being booted out of the country for breaking the law. Hopper started to look around for me, but I had disappeared and was watching Hopper wilting from a distance.

Paul left Hopper with the promise not to arrest him then and there, but he was to hold himself in readiness for a call from the Immigration Service about the revocation of his student visa. As a parting shot, Paul told him he had "dealt with freeloaders like you before".

Poor old Hopper, he went ashen and I have to say that even I would have believed Paul, he was that good. I am still friends with Hopper today, and he still reminds me, and berates me about this little joke every time I see him. He also reminds me about the time I arranged for him to go on patrol in a fast-patrol car, and how he nearly had a heart attack when the crew responded to an emergency, traveling at speeds of around 90 mph on traffic-laden roads.

All in all, I had a great time on Clubs Clubs and was even working until 4am on the day of my wedding, on 19th May 1979 in Broadstairs, Susie's home town. I remember it absolutely poured down with rain the day before and during most of the night, and it poured with rain the day after, the 20th May. Saturday 19th May however, was a spectacularly bright and sunny spring day, perfect for getting married.

Chapter 12

My feelings for Susie had deepened to an extent I had never experienced before. I was totally smitten by her and loved her to distraction. As well as being affectionate, tactile and very intelligent, she was stunningly beautiful. She was about 5'7" tall, slim with thick, silky fair hair which hung below her shoulders, a beautiful smile and bright blue eyes.

The fact she was so stunning however, made me feel very insecure, especially at the beginning of our relationship. I'm neither the best looking guy in the world, nor the smartest, nor someone who had huge prospects. Her mother Pam, disliked me intensely at this time and made no secret of the fact that, instead of me, Susie should find herself a doctor to marry, someone who would have social status and prospects, not some poor copper who didn't possess many social skills. I remember I used to live in fear of Susie telling me that it was all over as she had found some gorgeous brain-surgeon or gynaecologist. As regards her family, the bright spots on my horizon were Susie's brothers, aunts and uncles and especially her grandmother, Nanny Green, who all accepted me for what I was and who were not afraid to show it. Above all these however, was Susie's twin sister Jane. She was and remains one of my closest friends. Along with her husband David, and their two children Ben and Bethany, they have always showed me unstinting love and support, even in the dark hours after my divorce. When that happened, I had begun to prepare myself for Susie's family to distance themselves from me, but they never let me go. They never allowed me to drift away, and having them as friends and confidantes has enriched my life no end.

I remember once Susie and I were visiting Pam and her partner Mac in Broadstairs. For reasons known only to Mac, he had bought a sailing boat, which he neither knew how to sail nor had any intentions of learning. Mac had said to me that he and I should go and look at his boat, which we did. It was nothing special, just an ordinary, small sailing boat. "Come on" he said, "let's take it for a motor down the channel." Now, at that time, I knew nothing about sailing, but I did know that tides came in and went out, including tidal channels like the Sandwich Channel. The tide was obviously ebbing and I was a little dubious. However, Mac said we'd only be gone for a short while, and then we'd come back. So we cast off from the quayside and set off down the channel at a huge rate of knots. The speed of the tide combined with the engine meant we went much further than either of us realized at first. When we eventually turned around, the little engine made absolutely no headway at all back up the channel, the speed of the ebbing tide was just too great for it to cope. Even at full throttle and revving its little heart out, it was no match for the relentless run of the tide.

Eventually of course, we grounded in the soft mud. Then I did something which sometimes returns to me in nightmares! To stop the boat drifting back out into the channel when the tide came back in, I jumped overboard into the shallow water with the anchor. My intention was to attach the anchor securely to the bank-side. It was a completely stupid thing to do because I had no way of knowing whether the mud into which I was jumping was the clinging, sinking mud, which was common in that area and which would have sucked me inexorably under. Mac would never have been able to pull me clear and any rescue would never have reached me in time. I just became focused on stopping the boat from drifting. Throwing the anchor at the bank would have been useless, one of us had to get off to secure it. When I did jump overboard, I landed with a soft splosh and immediately sank in the mud. It was at that moment, I realized what a fool I was. The boat was actually aground at that stage and wasn't going anywhere. There was ample time to test the mud before I jumped in, but neither of us thought of that.

Anyway, thankfully, but unbeknown to Mac, the boat had a twin keel and so simply settled upright into the mud. Although it had been a bright spring day, the water was still damn cold and, after struggling through the mud to the bank, I was covered up to my waist in awful, stinking mud.

All we had to do was wait for the tide to turn and then simply motor back to the harbour, but the turn of the tide was hours away. We were a fair distance away from the mooring and Mac didn't fancy leaving the boat unattended in so isolated a spot, so I volunteered to stay with the boat while Mac walked back to the car to go home and collect dry clothes for me and some hot drinks.

He was gone for about five, freezing cold, shivering hours. There was absolutely nothing on board I could cover myself with to stay or even get warm. When he eventually got back, he told me it was further back to the harbour than we thought and that he had had to cross fields, climb gates, scramble through hedges etc in order to reach the car. Mac had a very highly developed sense of theatre and could make any story sound like a true "Boys-own" adventure.

However, he announced with great ceremony that he had brought sandwiches and hot soup in Thermos flasks for us both and clothes for me. Apparently, he rather over-dramatised my situation to Pam and Susie, telling them how I had nearly drowned saving his boat and that I was now in danger of perishing from the cold, which actually wasn't far from the truth. Apparently, Susie was in tears as Pam had prepared the food and drink whilst at the same time berating Mac and me for being complete idiots; again, not far from the truth! Unfortunately, rather than hot coffee in the flasks, Pam had prepared both with mushroom soup, the only soup I couldn't eat or drink as mushrooms make me nauseous. I often wonder about that mushroom soup!

The tide came back in of course, and by this time, both Mac and I had fallen into a deep sleep. I was woken by the sound of water lapping against the side of the boat and once Mac was awake, we started the engine and raced as quickly back to the mooring as we had raced away from it.

We eventually got back to the flat in the early hours of the morning. Later in the day when Pam and I met, neither of us spoke to the other, but Susie told me later that

Pam had, once again, spent all that evening we were in the channel, trying to persuade her not to marry me, saying how irresponsible I was nearly making a widow of her before we were even married. Apparently, she did the same the night before the wedding. It was really quite upsetting for me, not only because Pam obviously disliked me, but also because, out of all the mothers of my previous girlfriends I had met, she was the only one I couldn't get on with, and here I was, about to marry her daughter and become part of her family.

To be fair, I did take great delight in winding Pam up! If we were visiting and Pam had prepared spaghetti Bolognese containing finely chopped mushrooms, I would sit for ages carefully picking out each mushroom morsel and arranging them neatly around the outside of my plate before starting to eat. This really used to get her angry!

The 19th May 1979 was a beautiful day! I had a massive hang-over from being out in the clubs until 4am, but still managed, somehow to drive down to Broadstairs. Myself and my best-man Roger had been fitted with the best grey mohair suits that Moss Bros. in Covent Garden had in the shop. They were brand new and had been altered specially for me. I had become friendly at that stage with one of the Moss Bros. family and he pulled out all the stops for me for this special day. The journey down went without a hitch, everyone we had invited had arrived and when I walked into the church, my heart nearly burst with pride. Everyone looked so happy and glad to be a part of this day!

The colours and outfits were fantastic but I think the thing I remember most was that, seemingly timed just for this occasion, all the flowers in the church garden had blossomed due to the heavy overnight rain.

The garden was simply a riot of yellow flowers and the grass was almost impossibly green. Looking up, the sky was cloudless and endlessly blue. It was going to be a lovely day! And indeed it was! I had married a woman I both loved and adored, my family was there to see me, as were my most of my intimate and close friends.

We had deliberately chosen hymns that most people would know, and the singing was lusty and tuneful. The photographs were taken in the garden amongst all the wonderful flowers, and all of our families and friends mingled and laughed with each other as though they had known each other for ever.

At the reception, my father gave a touching and warm speech, and everyone on Uncle Harold's table fell in love with him as he regaled them with funny stories about him and dad. Later in the evening, some would-be party gatecrashers were politely shown the door by a couple of my larger police colleagues and the entire evening went off without a hitch. Everyone danced and enjoyed themselves. Looking back on it, it was a most marvellous day.

Then Susie and I were alone in our room, and for no apparent reason, she burst into tears and couldn't stop crying. My head was filled with the sound of her racking sobs and I felt completely helpless. She could neither tell me nor show me what was wrong. Maybe I thought, she didn't want to ruin my day, but she never did tell me what she was crying over. Years later however, it all became apparent what the problem had been, but at that time, I think I persuaded myself that she was simply overcome with the emotion of the day. If I'm honest, I probably half guessed that she thought she had made a mistake, but I wasn't going to allow the demons of despair to ruin my day, our day! It was however, but a prelude to the bad times to come.

1979 was also the year that my career came to a standstill. Paradoxically, it was my promotion to sergeant, which signalled the halt.

I was due to be promoted in October 1979, and so, after my honeymoon, had four months in which to get up to speed with sergeanty-type things. The postings were controlled by the all-powerful duties office, and more nearly, its 'supremo', PC Johnnie Walters. He was a lovely man, and when I joined, he had about 25 years service. He would wander around the station with his little wooden duties board and when he spotted a likely candidate, he would sidle up to him and murmer, "wanna work Sunday son? Double time!" You always felt Johnnie was doing you a favour, as though he had sought you out to offer you the overtime first. In reality, it was probably because somebody else had been pencilled in to do it and had "persuaded" Johnnie that he couldn't do it. We all loved him though, he was a true and genuine character.

In those days, Sergeants spent much of their time in the station office, making entries in various ledgers and books and dealing with persons at the front counter. In order to do the latter, a sergeant had to know what he or she was doing. It had been my intention to spend as much time in the office as possible learning what to do.

However, the first thing the duties office did for me on my return, was to send me to Hendon for three weeks on a driving course. After a little more annual leave, I eventually spent about two months on the relief acting as Sergeant, and most of this time was spent out on the ground and not in the office.

When I eventually made Sergeant and went back to Hendon for the initial course, I had a very rude awakening. Practically the entire four week course was geared around a sergeant's duties inside the station, as Station Officer.

It was expected that each officer would have a good knowledge of station duties, which was essential in order to fulfil the role of sergeant. I had spent practically no time in the station office, and so had almost no knowledge or experience, and it showed me up in the classroom with my colleagues. On one occasion, the instructor came into the room after a break and placed a gun on my desk. He said, "I've just found this in my loft, sergeant. My father got it in the First World War. Can you deal with it please?" There were lots of little clues in this scenario, but I simply didn't know what to do. I gazed blankly at the instructor and then passed the gun to my neighbour, saying, "Here you go constable, deal with this please!" It raised a bit of a laugh, but more importantly, it emphasised my lack of knowledge to the entire class, which to say the least, was embarrassing. I tried to hide my lack of knowledge behind a façade of bravado and flippant comments. Unfortunately, this did not fool the instructors. At the end of the course, the head of the course made it very plain to me that he had been persuaded to pass me against his better judgement and that he doubted I would "make it as a sergeant." (He was wrong about this, as "make it as a sergeant" is all I have ever done!)

I was posted to Carter Street police station as a sergeant in November 1979, and received a very large culture shock. Bow Street had been a nice, pleasant little West End station where generally, everyone was polite and respectful. Bow Street itself, had only an historical reputation. Carter Street police station however, had an entirely different reputation. For a start, it was in a really tough area, where resident criminals probably outnumbered law-abiding citizens, and the majority of the population absolutely hated the police, sometimes for good reason. On many occasions, people who had been arrested had begged the officers not to take them to Carter Street station, as they knew they could well be in for a beating at some stage during their incarceration. It was part of the process at Carter Street, and if they had been arrested for anything resembling violence towards an officer, the "punishment" was swift and severe. Having the population hate and despise you as police officers created a garrison-type environment. The police officers at Carter Street, rightly or wrongly, truly believed that it was an urban war with the population, and they, the police, would win by sheer force of domination. I never allowed myself to become involved in this "domination" and by the time I went to Carter Street, times were changing, but the reputation stayed.

At this time, there were very few black people living in Southwark, and more especially around the Elephant and Castle area, which is where I was posted. The mainly white population hated black people almost as much as they hated the police. There was a standing joke at Carter Street at this time that if a policeman was fighting with a black man and a white man wanted to intervene, he would be hard pushed to know whose side to come in on!

Whilst the police officers at Bow Street were by no means angels, the officers at Carter Street made them look like pussy-cats. It was nothing to walk into a cell at Carter Street and find a police officer washing fresh blood off the walls, or to find a prisoner who had been there for maybe four days and had not even been spoken to. "Soften him up a bit!" Whatever happened inside the station, the rule was that it never left there; the garrison mentality, where each officer depended on the next, was all encompassing. If we officers at Bow Street had thought of ourselves as "switched on", the officers at Carter Street were simply leagues ahead. There wasn't a trick in the book they didn't know, especially out on the streets and their mistrust of the local population was matched only by their mistrust of sergeants and above.

It was into this cauldron, that I was despatched in November 1979, as a newly promoted sergeant with barely 5 years experience. It meant that I was up against constables with something like four or five times my level of experience. To supervise effectively, I had to know all their little dodges and tricks in order to remain one step ahead. It was an absolute baptism of fire, and I got severely burned. Put simply, I wasn't up to the job. Not only did I not have the experience or knowledge to supervise and lead effectively, I didn't possess the maturity or authority to even bluff my way through, although I did give this a good go. I didn't fool anyone, especially my senior officers.

For the next three years, my annual reports were appalling and consisted mainly of how dismayed they were at my performance. The potential I had shown as a constable was matched only by my incompetence as a sergeant.

The turning point for me came in the shape of one of my duty officers, Inspector Stuart Boud. When he arrived on the relief, he was so appalled at my performance, he decided that I should be Station Officer for six months solid. The S.O. dealt with all the callers at the front counter, dealt with the prisoners and had to keep the station registers up to date for the Superintendent to check on a daily basis. He or she never went out onto the streets. It was like a life sentence. The post of Station Officer was the worst job for a sergeant, and at the time, I absolutely loathed Inspector Boud for doing it. I still hadn't really admitted to myself that I was useless, and consequently blamed him for my shortcomings.

However, the superintendent, who was a real brute of a man himself, thought it a bit severe, and after a few months, I was relieved of the posting. By this time however, I had undergone something of a transformation. The "punishment" posting had opened my eyes, not only to my failings as a sergeant but also to the hugely flippant attitude I had adopted in order to try and bluff my way through. From that moment on, my performance improved, and the following three years saw me getting increasingly better reports. I was at last, beginning to live up to my potential, which I knew I possessed.

I have long since thanked Inspector Boud secretly to myself. Without him, I don't think I would have made it. He left Carter Street station before I did, and I didn't see him for years. It was only a few weeks before retiring from the police service myself, that I ran into him again. I made a special point of saying thank you!

Susie and I spent our honeymoon in Devon, at some big old manor house, which had been mentioned in the Domesday Book. I seem to remember, we were both happy, but nothing else about the honeymoon, comes to mind. That wouldn't be true about the first year of our marriage, especially the end of the first year.

We were still living in our flat at Streatham, and after the euphoria of our courtship, the relationship seemed to suffer under the additional responsibility of marriage. I had heard it said that marriages often suffered in their first year. Couples who had been perfectly happy just living or being together, suddenly witnessed the breakdown of their relationship within that first year of marriage. I think, like most people would, I simply pooh-poohed the idea, but it certainly happened to us.

For my part, even marriage had not totally allayed my insecurity about Susie. Trivial and inconsequential events and remarks would heighten my fears irrationally. I was nervous when she went out with her friends, would some handsome man step in and take her feelings? Sometimes, I felt she was simply resigned to her marriage to me. All through the first year, there were little arguments and niggles, which weren't there before we married. These culminated in an incident in a little Welsh fishing village called Solva, on the west coast of Wales.

During our courtship, we had met many of each other's friends, and on one occasion, we had all gone as a large group to the rowing regatta at Henley. There were friends of friends there whom we didn't know, and of course, vice versa. Our friends Maggie and Peter were there with their friends, one of whom was a police officer from Weymouth. Maggie was one of Susie's nursing colleagues, and she and

Maggie had become firm friends. Not long after the day at Henley, Susie went down to Weymouth to stay with Maggie at her home.

Solva was, and still is a delightful little fishing village, situated on a remote part of the Welsh coastline, very near to the cathedral city of St. Davids, which isn't that much bigger than Solva. Pam's family was from this part of Wales, and Solva in particular. Her father, Tom Stevens was born in the village, as was her mother and after a whirlwind romance, they married. Tom unfortunately, died very young after getting an ear infection from swimming in Solva bay, and of course both Pam and her mother were devastated. For many years after, Susie's family held almost a pilgrimage to Solva every year for an annual holiday. However, even without the family connection, it was a beautiful place to go and relax.

The village itself nestles in a very narrow little valley with really steep hillsides on both sides. A snaking inlet from the sea leads one right up, into the village, which, until a road was pushed through from Haverfordwest, was only accessible from the sea. Ships used to call there with food supplies and fishing gear, which of course, was the life-blood of the community. In more modern times, the fishing fleets have gone, and the village earns its money from tourism. The rows of tiny fishing cottages along the main street have largely been given over to 'holiday lets' and the locals have moved to more modern housing on the hillsides.

Two of the older residents of the village, still living in the house in which they were born, were two ladies, lovingly called "the aunties", Nellie and Polly. Each of them was only around 5'0" or so, which was just as well as no room in their house was above 5'6" high. Nellie and Polly, along with their sister Agnes who lived in another house, were Pam's father's sisters, hence "the aunties", and more friendly, kind, happy and contented people you would be hard pushed to find. It was worth going to Solva just to spend time in their company, sit by the Aga cooker, savouring freshly cooked Welsh Cakes and listen to their stories of life in Solva in the early part of the century.

Susie and I, along with several other family members including Jane, had made the trip sometime in the summer of 1980, probably around July or August. Our marriage had been bumping along a fairly rocky road for some time, somewhere near the "bottom". However, despite my persistent insecurity, we were still together.

We were all staying in one house on the main street, Susie and I occupying an upstairs bedroom. Our days were mostly taken up with trips to the aunties or walks to the little harbour and up and around the hillsides. One day, Susie had gone out with Jane to the harbour and I was left alone in the house. At this stage, I beg the readers' indulgence to believe that what I did next was not planned or even thought of by me until it happened. I was in our bedroom, when suddenly, I seemed to be consumed with an overpowering urge to look in Susie's handbag, which was lying open on the dressing table. I could see the top of a letter nestling just inside the bag in handwriting I didn't recognise. This same force seemed to be telling me that I should read this letter, and to my eternal shame, I retrieved it from her bag and read it! It was what I had dreaded. It was a very personal letter from the policeman in Weymouth, written after her visit to Maggie. My emotions took off! I was stunned, hurt, devastated and almost consumed with anger, all at the same time. I can't even begin to recollect the thoughts I had at that time, I simply stormed out of the house. As I left the front door and turned onto the street, through eyes misty with tears and rage, I saw Susie and the others walking towards the house. They took up all the pavement and without a word, I simply barged through them, scattering them like skittles. It has always been a trait of mine that when I am really angry, words do not come to me, and so it was on this occasion. I had no idea where to go, I simply knew that I had to be alone. Someone called out, "Neil?!?" but I ignored them and continued my somewhat blind charge along the street.

There weren't that many places I could go to be alone, but one of them was a particular rock, which looked out over the sea. Whether anybody came looking for me, I don't know, but I spent about four terribly lonely hours on this rock, just thinking and mulling over what I had found. Was my marriage finished? Had I lost her? Did she return this other man's feelings? Why? I hasten to add that the letter had been written to Susie, there was nothing to suggest that it was in reply to one from her. But why had she kept it? All these thoughts and many others whizzed around my head endlessly. Eventually, I came off the rock and went to find Susie.

I had come to a conclusion, which although alien to me at the time, I was convinced was the way forward. I had to change! This little episode had forced me to think through my entire being, the way I was, the way I treated Susie. I examined everything about me and came to the conclusion that, whatever had happened, had happened because of me and how I treated her. I didn't have the complete answer at this stage, which was why I had to find Susie.

We went to one of the little dining rooms, occupied a table and just talked. We talked like I had never talked before. We talked for more hours and Susie gave me the answer. I loved her to distraction, but I didn't know how to show it. All my life, our family had never really demonstrated love and affection. We never gave each other a hug or a kiss on the cheek, except perhaps when we children went off to bed. We never simply told each other that we loved them no matter what. We never cuddled each other when we were afraid or had hurt ourselves. Susie's family did, and from me, she had never received it. She missed it sorely. The question now was whether I could give it. Her explaining all this to me was like a heavy blanket being lifted off me, everything became so clear, change or lose her!

My life changed inexorably at that precise moment. There is a line in a Jack Nicholson film where he says, "you make me want to be a better man". I can't put it any clearer than this, Susie made me see the light, and from that moment on, I determined that whatever else happened to us, it would not be for want of demonstrable love from me! What had happened in Weymouth? I don't know, I never really asked, but it was pretty obvious something bad had happened. A letter like that is not written on a whim. It still took me a while to get over this incident and part of the process was learning how to trust her.

I still looked for little tell-tale signs and I struggled with the whole thing for some time. Still insecure, I even once looked in her handbag again for another letter. After a while though, it became easier for me and my relationship with this woman I still adored and loved, took off to another plane, a level I had not previously even dreamt of.

1981 saw the worst Inner City riots since the race riots of the 1950s in Notting Hill. One of the areas which had been settled by black people was Brixton in south London, a neighbouring area to Southwark where I was still based as a sergeant. Racial tension had been simmering between the police and the black community in Brixton for a number of years, and violence eventually erupted in the spring of 1981. Most commentators will have the reader believe that the fault lay entirely with the police's treatment of black people, but whilst the police were not completely blameless, we were not completely to blame either.

Having lived and worked in this arena, my honest opinion would be that each side was as much to blame as the other. On the one hand, the police did "stop and search" a large number of black youths. On the other hand, a large number of black youths were committing crime in an area populated largely by black people. Whether this was due to the social deprivation of the area at that time or to simple criminal tendencies, I don't know. There was a very definite culture difference between the two sides and it would be fair to say that the police were very uneasy about the black culture, probably because we didn't understand the significance of loud reggae music and cannabis consumption. However, it would also be fair to say that the average police officer wanted nothing more than to uphold the law and have a peaceful day.

I think black people to a certain extent, became scapegoats for all that was ailing in Britain at that time, and the police became caught up in the process. There were of course, certain officers who revelled in this way of thinking and acting. They did arrest black youths because they were an easy target, but it was not true of all police officers. It was equally true that political activists saw the black community as a means of challenging the authorities. Sadly, relations between the police and the community of Brixton reached an all time low when, in the spring of 1981, The Special Patrol Group launched an operation of "stop and search" in the area.

The Special Patrol Group, more commonly referred to as the SPG, was a group of officers who would be called in to a designated area to try and solve particular problems, or to enact initiatives such as the one in Brixton. They were very good at what they did, and had a fearsome reputation. This operation however, provided the catalyst to three days of rioting, looting, burning and destruction not seen before in Britain. It was not a race riot as such. The violence was aimed primarily at the police, but various individuals took the opportunity to ransack damaged and insecure shops and houses. And to a certain extent, the violence was orchestrated. They had simply been waiting for the right opportunity.

I have no idea how or where the violence began, probably some innocuous little incident, which spiralled out of control. Remember that this period was witness to some intense political activity by some pretty extreme bodies and individuals. Some of these bodies and individuals were very publicly anti-police, anti-establishment, anti anything really that wasn't anarchic. The black community in Brixton, whilst having very definite reasons to distrust the police, was to a certain extent in my opinion, manipulated into violence by some of the more extreme elements, who used them almost as a private army.

I was on duty in the Station Office at Carter Street, when the call came through that officers in Brixton were under attack in several streets, by youths hurling bricks and bottles. We were told that we would not be going home that afternoon, but would be sent to assist colleagues in Brixton. I made a quick phone call to Susie to tell her not to wait for me but to go out to our pre-arranged dinner with Jane and her then boyfriend Nick.

When I got to Brixton, only about 30 minutes later, I was appalled by what I saw. In a matter of only around two hours, the streets were littered with burnt out cars, barricades had been erected in some streets, shops were on fire and property was being looted. I found myself with other Carter Street officers in a side street off the infamous "Front Line", Railton Road. This was the road which housed most of the more extreme elements and which the black youths liked to boast about the police not daring to patrol it.

We were being confronted by a large group of black youths at the top of the road, who would make sporadic forays down towards our lines and hurl stones and bottles. We had absolutely no protection with us at that time and simply had to dodge the missiles or get hurt. The one thing we didn't do, was retreat.

After the riots in Notting Hill a few years previously, the police had tested and bought a number of plastic riot shields. We had been shown how to use them to the greatest effect, but had had no practise with them. After about an hour or so of being pinned down by all the missiles, a white woman suddenly appeared around the corner and shouted that she wanted to talk to the senior officer present in our group. She was alone and an Inspector met her in the road, halfway between the two sides.

After a brief conversation, he came back and told us that the woman had said if we withdrew, she would guarantee that the youths with her would disperse and that we would be safe. He apparently had replied that neither he nor us had any intention of withdrawing and he told her that if they didn't disperse immediately, we would do it for them. One could suggest that if we had withdrawn, the youths would have had no reason to throw the bricks and bottles. Experience told us however, that they would simply move on to another target for their violence. And in any event, the police never withdrew from a scenario such as the one we were confronted with on that day.

Just then a large green truck arrived behind us and the driver began to unload a batch of riot shields. Now we had protection, we could make our way up the street to where the youths were sheltering behind the wall of a pub and disperse them. I grabbed a shield and with two others, formed up into a "shield unit", a line of three interlinked shields. We began to make our way up the road. Suddenly, from around the corner, flaming missiles were being hurled at us. None of us had ever faced a petrol bomb before and it would probably be fair to say initially, in the two or three seconds they were in the air, we didn't click as to what they were. There must have been at least a dozen or so winging their way towards us. During our introduction to the shields, they hadn't told us about petrol bombs, only bricks and empty bottles.

The flaming bottles began smashing all around us, but gamely, we made our way up the street, dodging the flames, when all of a sudden, a huge flash of flame came up inside my shield and for a brief second, I was completely engulfed in a fire-ball. The petrol bomb, which I hadn't seen, had smashed and burst right at the foot of my shield, just as I was lifting it fractionally off the ground to move it. I was in the act of taking a step forward and so, unavoidably, I stepped right into the flames. The flaming petrol splashed onto me and up my trousers, which immediately caught fire. My hair and beard were singed and smoking, but it was my legs, which were burning. I was on fire! Most of the petrol had been prevented from going onto my bare skin by a stout pair of boots, but nevertheless, I could smell my flesh burning.

I remember dropping the shield and immediately being dragged away by my colleagues, who were frantically trying to put out the flames with their hands. They got me to a safe area and finally patted out the flames. I was taken to Kings College Hospital, where I was treated for burns and lacerations to my legs from the smashing bottles.

Strangely enough, Susie had steadfastly refused to go out to dinner with Jane and Nick. She told me later that when she heard that the rioting had become very serious, she "knew" that I would be injured and that she had to be either at the hospital or at home. Unfortunately, it was the hospital.

After the rioting, people recollected seeing bottles with rags in the tops, waiting to be ignited and hurled as petrol bombs, in several locations where the youths had congregated. There is no way that these could have been collected on the spot. They had to have been prepared earlier for use in the event of violence erupting. The operation by the S.P.G. provided the perfect excuse. Sadly, it lasted three days and nights. Many people were injured on both sides and many people lost property and cars etc, some even lost their livelihoods. Does it seem right that people, demonstrating their grievances against the police should loot shops and destroy property belonging to innocent members of the public? This aspect seemed to get a bit lost after the riot.

It did however, spark a major enquiry headed by an eminent judge at the time, Lord Scarman who, although placing the blame for igniting the riot firmly at the door of the police, did make certain recommendations to both sides which, having been acted upon, have made Brixton a much safer and more pleasant place to live. The road where I was petrol-bombed, no longer exists, and in an effort to encourage better relationships in the community, the old "Front Line" has been demolished and the area completely re-developed with new housing. The community and the police now have a far greater understanding of each other's needs and consequently, generally live in peace with each other. There is always going to be the odd bust-up between those who wish to break the law and those who seek to prevent it, but it will never be on the scale of the 1981 disturbances. The communities of Brixton and its surrounding neighbours are much more aware of hard-line politics and seem to be more resistant to manipulation. There is still racial tension in the area, but now there are safeguards operating within the Social Services and the police to monitor these tensions, and if they are seen to be escalating, there are contingency plans in force to take the necessary steps to reduce them, peacefully.

Before I move on, I just want to relate a little story about a guy called Dennis. Part of the area covered by Carter Street police station was Camberwell SE5. It had its own little police station in the High Street and as sergeants, we would often have to go and perform station duty. This meant just sitting in a cramped office, waiting for callers at the front counter.

One of the "characters" of Camberwell at this time was Dennis, who was invariably accompanied by at least one of his pack of dogs. He lived in what could only be described as a hovel of a flat, just along the road from the police station. He had lived in Camberwell all his life and, apart from his mangy dogs, was easily recognisable because, no matter what the weather, Dennis always wore a pair of shorts, grubby and stained with God knows what. His legs were also grubby and stained with God knows what and it was difficult to see where his shorts ended and his legs began! The standing joke at Carter Street about Dennis was that nobody wanted to have to break into his flat if ever he wasn't seen on the streets for a few days, as it probably meant he was dead in his flat and one of his dogs had eaten him for lunch.

One evening in winter, I was on duty in the station office, when I heard a commotion outside. As I was about to investigate, Dennis stumbled in through the narrow doors, cradling one of his dogs in his arms. He had difficulty getting through the doors as this dog was obviously not just dead, but stiff throughout its entire body due to rigor-mortice. It was a fairly large dog with disgusting, matted fur, made all the worse because of the smell it was giving off. Once inside, Dennis began wailing about his "sick" dog and begging me to help. I patiently pointed out to him that the dog was in fact, dead, and probably had been so for days, if not weeks.

It was obviously a bit of a hazard to health, mine, and so I told him that he should take it out and dispose of it properly. He wouldn't stop wailing and crying and so eventually, I almost pushed him and the dog out of the station back onto the road. The station at Camberwell fronted onto the busy main road between Peckham and the Oval, and of course, this was rush-hour. When I thought I had got rid of him, I heard him shouting outside and looked out of the window. Dennis had hold of the dog's back legs like two sticks of wood and was swinging the corpse around his head. Suddenly, he smashed the dog's body onto the front steps of the station in full view of the horrified passing motorists. Pedestrians were desperately trying to avoid being thumped by Dennis' dead dog and were jumping into the roadway, creating even more havoc! The onlookers of course, only saw this poor, obviously distressed little man in shorts, swinging what must have looked like a live dog around by the back legs and smashing its head on the police station steps.

As I bolted out onto the road, I could hear the corpse making contact with the concrete steps. Neither Dennis nor the dog touched the ground as he and the corpse were swiftly dragged back into the station. I frog-marched Dennis, who was dragging the dead dog by its tail, down to the back door, where I kicked him out into the yard and out through the back gates with a dire warning not to return.

I called for the police van to meet me at the back gates and they took the dog away somewhere and disposed of it. They probably left it under a car on Brixton's section. If it was the other way around, they would have done the same to us.

Dennis was, shall we say, not quite all there. He was harmless really, but after this little incident, I always kept the inner doors tightly shut, so that anyone wanting to come in would have to knock. Years later, officers did find Dennis dead in his flat. Fortunately, there was evidence of dog-food in bowls, so supplementing their diet had not been necessary.

Chapter 13

For my part, the years between 1981 and 1985 were a golden mix of an ever deepening and loving relationship between Susie and I, and a career, which seemed to be emerging from the depths of incompetence. Following my "punishment posting" from Inspector Boud, I had really started to become an efficient sergeant, capable of doing the job for which I was being paid, i.e. to supervise. I had made a disastrous start and had three bad reports to my name by 1982. My target for the following three years was to get three good reports, after which, I could apply for other postings.

Part of any selection process within the Metropolitan Police was the inclusion of annual reports, known then as A.Q.R.s, Annual Qualifying Reports. It was impossible to go anywhere else within the organisation without at least three good reports. I had been shown the error of my ways by Mr. Boud and had become determined to show my senior officers what I was capable of. By 1985, I had reached my target and had achieved those elusive good reports.

Up to that point, any officer could stay put at whatever station they were at for the duration of their service. Many officers at Carter Street at that time had been there for 25 years or more and would never move to another station. Unfortunately, some high-flying senior officers thought this was wrong and that officers should be encouraged to transfer stations for their own development. Those who chose not to transfer voluntarily could be posted against their will. Many officers refused to go willingly and the latter came into force as policy under the title, Inter-District Development Transfer, or I.D.T. It was meant to ensure that officers gained experience policing in different conditions and demographic areas. In effect of course, it meant that as officers were transferred in, so others had to be transferred out, against their wishes. Five years was the cut-off point and anyone with that amount of service at the one station, provided they had not served more than 25 years in total, was transferred to another station, for their "development". In late 1985, I was transferred from Carter Street to Croydon Police station. The system worked for a few years. Officers were initially transferred to stations to further their experience, but then it fell into disrepute as officers began to be transferred to other areas simply to make up the numbers. One officer from Carter Street was transferred to the next-door station, for his "development".

I went with good reports but it also meant that I couldn't apply for other units, such as a return to Special Branch until I had served at least one year at my new station. It was my intention to do just this, but as it turned out, other events would overtake me and ultimately thwart my plans.

In 1982, we had sold our flat in Streatham after an agonising wait of 18 months for a buyer and had bought a house in Biggin Hill, Kent, from where I am writing these words. When we first had the idea of moving, I had wanted to move more to the South West of London, around Sutton or Cheam. Housing over there was plentiful and cheap, transport links were good and a lot of my colleagues lived in the area.

One day, back at Streatham after a fruitless house search, Susie suddenly burst into tears. Through the sobs, she told me she desperately didn't want to go to the South West, she wanted to be nearer her twin sister Jane, who was living over in Chislehurst with her then boyfriend, Nick. Chislehurst is South East of London, but it really didn't matter that much to me where we went. Susie wanted to go there and so we started our search in the Kent area, eventually finding this house.

We moved in February 1982. About a year later, Jane split up with her boyfriend, met another man named David, married him and moved over to South West London!

As the months and years rolled by, I fell ever more in love with Susie. The demons of doubt had deserted me, and I trusted her beyond description. To me at that time, it was inconceivable that anything could happen to us, which would cause us to split up. Even my relationship with my mother-in-law Pam, had grown into one of mutual friendship and respect.

Susie and I were very much together in all aspects bar one, we never really shared a common interest. Most other couples I know these days have at least one mutual interest, which occupies them and means they do at least spend some time together. It would be true to say that for us, this would probably have been a luxury, as we both worked shifts and often didn't see each other for days, but it never crossed my mind that as a couple, we should try and spend time together doing something which interested us both.

Susie was always far more interested in the arts than I was and she was a very enthusiastic follower of the local Christian Fellowship, headed by a man who became one of my closest friends, Ray Lowe. Susie continually tried to get me to attend their services, and on the odd occasion I did. What I saw actually scared me a little. It was almost as though some of the congregation, including Susie had entered some sort of trance. People would be swaying from side to side, holding their hands in the air. Those nearest the aisles would be dancing up and down, clapping and skipping, but what really scared me was the sight of someone on the floor of the aisle, moaning and writhing around as if in some great pain. This was explained by Susie as the Holy Spirit entering this person, and "saving" them.

I was always rather sceptical about this but I don't see these people as fakes. Something was happening to them, something I can't explain and if it was the Holy Spirit, then all I can say is that, maybe they are the lucky ones. I never experienced anything approaching a spiritual encounter, but I always said to Susie and to Ray, that if ever I felt that "God was knocking on my door, I would answer it". I genuinely felt this then, and still do today. If the Spirit is going to call me, then it will let me know. It never has, but I think all my Christian friends would agree that I practise Christian values such as honesty and integrity, friendship and forgiveness. I think this is about as close as I will get to being a "born again Christian" without being called, and that sits well with me.

The closest Susie and I came to sharing an interest, was when I bought a speed boat, and took up water-skiing. At some stage, Susie told me that she wasn't going to ski as her knees wouldn't take the strain, (she had trained as a dancer with the result that her knees were very weak), but that she was happy to drive the boat. We had some great fun times with our boat, especially with friends who would be invited along down to the Kent coast for a week-end of skiing, eating and drinking. It never seemed to me that Susie was doing all this under sufferance, but looking back on it now, I think that was probably the case. It would be very easy for me to say here, "if only she had said something" or "if only I had been more aware", but neither of us did or said anything, and anyway, life was good at this time. Thoughts like these would certainly not have occurred to me

Susie and I were very different in our make-up. I had thought about this, and was satisfied that this was probably why our relationship was working so well. From a very early age, I had been fiercely independent. Spending time alone was (and still is) important to me, which conversely made the time I was with Susie even more special. Spending time apart, pursuing separate hobbies and interests meant that we didn't live in each others' pocket, or get in each others' way. It meant we didn't have any arguments or experience each others' annoying little habits which, when spending almost all one's time in another's company, can easily become very large annoying habits. (All this was to happen in a few years time.)

Although I relished my independence, I missed Susie terribly when I was away from her and looked forward immensely to being at her side. What made it even more special, was that she seemed to miss me, and coming back together was always a magic time, for me at least.

Whereas I was very happy with my own company, Susie was far more gregarious and outgoing. She would often be off with her friends, or down to her family in Broadstairs. She revelled in company and was superb as a hostess, always trying to be the centre of attention, which invariably, she was. Being a beautiful, intelligent, determined, fun-loving person, it seemed that nothing would be impossible to her, and that she could achieve anything she put her mind to.

In 1984, we decided that, instead of going to Solva in West Wales for a summer holiday, we would take advantage of the fact that my mother-in-law, Pam and her husband Mac owned a flat on the east coast of Spain. Pam had always told us that we would be welcome to go anytime, and so Susie, Jane, David, myself and another friend called Jane Emmanuel, all went to the flat in Gandia in August of that year.

The holiday very nearly didn't get off the ground at all. Living only about 30 minutes from Gatwick Airport, everybody came to our house first and then we all went to the airport in Susie's Ford Escort. I had arranged for the car to be stored in the police compound at the airport. When we were about 10 minutes away from the airport, Susie jokingly said, "Now Neil, you have got the key to the flat, haven't you?" "No", I said, "you have." "No", she said, "I told you it was on table and to pick it up." I looked at her and she looked me, and everybody else was looking out the windows. It was obviously still on the table. We couldn't get in to the flat without the key as there was no caretaker on site. I dropped them all off at the terminal, turned around and raced back to the house. It would be at least an hour's travelling time to and from the house and then I had to park the car and get back to the check-in before they closed the flight on me. I skidded to a stop at the house, bolted up the steps, grabbed the key and raced off back to the airport. I smiled at a very bemused looking neighbour on the way out.

I got the car into the car pound and raced into the terminal, where I found all the others alone at the check-in. The airline staff, bless them, had held the flight open for me to get there. I was only about 15 minutes late, but they could easily have closed it on me. We were all very grateful and thanked them profusely.

It was a wonderful holiday. For the entire two weeks, we did practically nothing else but lie in the sun, swim in the pool or go driving in the mountains. The weather was of course, hot and sunny which was a bit of a blow to Jane E. (as we called her) as she suffered some sort of allergy to the sun.

I coined the phrase of the holiday when David and I went to play tennis and had to chuck off some local kids. I said to David, "I'll bet they're saying Sheety Gringos". The sad thing was that they were probably better than us!

One day, I decided that I would walk to the next town along the beach. From our balcony, I could see it in the distance, sometimes clearly, sometimes through the haze, but had no real idea of how far away it was. It must have been in the second week of the holiday as Pam and Mac had joined us. I never realised it at the time, but this was probably one of those times I had to get away from the crowd.

I set off mid-morning, walking along the surf line, the water just lapping over my bare feet. I look back on some of these times now and wonder to myself just how much more stupid I could get. Blazing sun, coarse sand and bare feet, very intelligent!

The leisurely stroll to the next town and back turned into an 8 kilometre barefoot hike. When I reached the next village, I did contemplate taking a taxi back to Gandia, but bravely, or should I say stubbornly, decided against it and set off back along the beach. At the end, when I got back to where the others were sunning themselves in the late afternoon, I had become so determined to finish the walk and so focussed on reaching the breakwater at the far end of the beach, which I had set as my target, I totally ignored them as I strode gamely on.

I did see Pam and Susie looking in my direction. Pam had a very quizzical look on her face and was saying something to Susie and pointing towards me. Susie was shaking her head in a very resigned fashion and simply shrugged her shoulders, obviously saying something like "I don't have the faintest idea where he's been or what he's doing". My feet were so swollen and burnt, I couldn't walk or put any weight on them for three days. Secretly though, I was very proud of myself. I had set myself a target and, despite knowing I was going to suffer for it, never gave up.

I think there was also an element of wishing to impress Susie. I was no match for her intellectually, and so I had to make use of my strength and guts to make that impression. To this day, I have no idea just how much of an impression this stupid little jaunt had made, although I would venture to guess, not much!

The beach at Gandia was fabulous and was swept and raked early every morning. One day, just before breakfast, I looked over the balcony and had a great idea. Susie was still in bed, so I told Jane to make sure she didn't come to the kitchen or to a window overlooking the beach. I grabbed a tennis raquet and ran down to the beach. In giant letters about 12 feet high, I wrote "GOOD MORNING SUSIE" in the sand. As I was writing, I heard people laughing from other flats overlooking the beach and when I had finished, I turned round to see several people waving and clapping. Susie appeared then and burst out laughing. For days after, people we met in the lifts and outside on the concourse, greeted us with "good morning Susie".

Jane and David had not been married long at this stage, but Jane was already pregnant with their first child, Benjamin. For a holiday, they had planned to repeat their honeymoon trip and go skiing, but Jane had worked out that she would not be allowed to fly as she would be too near her time of birth. Having been severely bitten by the skiing bug, David suggested that I take Jane's place. And that was my introduction to skiing, which probably bit me even harder than it had bitten David. However, this conversation around the dinner table about skiing, sparked off another topic. We started talking about adventure type holidays and how much fun they would be. At one point, I fatefully turned to Susie and said, "Why don't we do it?" We talked about it a little more, laughed and joked about the cost and the logistics of saving enough money and organising the whole thing. I think the rest of the group treated it quite light-heartedly, but I think Susie guessed that with me, the idea had very quickly taken hold.

We didn't talk about it further until we got home, when I broached the subject again. It didn't take us long to decide that the "holiday to end holidays" would be a 10 day white –water rafting trip down through the entire length of the Grand Canyon in Arizona, U.S.A. It would be an expensive trip, but we were determined to do it and set about saving our pennies. Seeing one of the great natural wonders of the world whilst white-water rafting, seemed to tick all the boxes for both Susie and myself.

We would fly first to Dallas, Texas and then connect to Las Vegas where we would stay in one of the big hotels on "the strip". From there, we and the rest of the rafters would be collected and taken by bus to the embarkation point called Lee's Ferry, way above the main part of the Grand Canyon, where the Colorado River was reasonably quiet and slow-running. Here we would meet the raft-guides, get briefed on the trip, formally meet our co-rafters and get on that river! Finally, we would return to the hotel, spend one night in Las Vegas and then return home via Los Angeles.

Why did I say "fateful" when Susie and I first discussed it? This "holiday to end holidays" would be the start of the inexorable downturn in my marriage to Susie. The events, which occurred during this trip and over the next few years, took me completely by surprise and brought me to the edge of despair.

On 17th July 1986, we arrived in Dallas to begin our adventure. We had deliberately chosen to go in July as that would be the height of the summer with almost guaranteed sunshine. The rafting trip was run by a company called Grand

Canyon Expeditions, and they used large pontoon-type inflatable rafts, capable of carrying massive amounts of equipment as well as the passengers.

There were two rafts, each with a raft guide and an assistant known quaintly as a "swamper." The trip leader was a young, fair haired health fanatic named Chris Andersen. His "swamper" was an older man, a veterinary surgeon who lived in Seattle, Washington named Dick Hazen. Dick was a lovely, gentle guy who just exuded calmness and serenity. The other raft guide went only by the name "Goldie". He was one of those people who did raft guiding in the summer and ski-patrolling at Jackson Hole in the winter. His "swamper" was a female, who had clearly been chosen for her, shall we say, rather obvious charms and very little else!

Chris and Goldie were very different physically. Goldie was short, thick-set and very muscular, whereas Chris was tall, lean and obviously very fit. They were both however, equally passionate about the ecology of the Canyon, and between them, possessed a vast amount of knowledge about the history of the canyon, the fauna and flora, and the various Indian tribes who had settled in the region over the centuries. During the trip, Susie would become completely infatuated with Chris.

There were about 16 passengers on the trip, including us, but Susie and I were the only non-Americans. From my trip to New York, almost nine years previously, I knew that Americans were warm-hearted and generous to a fault. I was not disappointed by our company on this holiday. I don't remember them all, but some do stand out in my memory, and I am still in touch with some of them today.

We seemed to get closest to two married couples, Del and Hannah, and Sam and Pattie. Del was definitely the joker of the pack. He was a raucous plumber from Chicago, who loved his beer and dirty jokes and his long-suffering, demure wife Hannah, was a school teacher. They were as different as chalk and cheese, but the bond between them was obvious. Sam was a doctor from Indianapolis and his wife, Pattie was a nurse at the same hospital. The rest were a mixed bunch of people from all over the States, including a high-flying banking executive from Portland, Oregon, her friend who looked like Barbie's mum, a carpet sales executive from the heart of Georgia and his wife who ran a small farm, a married couple from inner Los Angeles and others I don't now remember. Whoever they were, they took Susie and I to their hearts. They wanted to know all about us, what we did, what England was like, did we know the Queen, was it actually that cold and damp in England? They really went out of their way, to make us feel welcome and part of their country.

After the introductions, we set off down the river. I remember it was a glorious day and everybody was in very high spirits. Although he knew no-one else on the trip either, Del had already made his presence felt with his humour and everyone seemed to take to him immediately. Every day, everybody was encouraged to change rafts and be with different people. Eventually of course, we all got to know one another and swapping over rafts became the norm.

Many years later, I became a qualified raft–guide myself and when I now look back on the rafts that were used on our trip down the Colorado, I realise that they were actually quite boring. They were about 20-25 feet long, with large inflatable tubes attached to the sides, hence the name "pontoon rafts". Whereas the rafts I used later were powered purely by either paddles or oars, these "pontoon" had engines on the back, they were simply much too large to power by paddle or oar. Occasionally, the guides would cut the engines on the rafts and allow them to drift along with the current. This was always a magical time and, as if by telepathy, nobody spoke for long periods, preferring to lie prone somewhere on the raft and stare up at the sheer canyon walls or marvel at the weird shapes the river had cut into the rocks.

The sheer size of the Colorado river rafts meant that, when running through even the biggest rapids on the river, Lava Falls, excitement was generally limited to the amount of water that cascaded over the raft. The length of the raft meant that it simply rode over most of the rapids instead of occasionally going through them. The weight of the equipment stored below the water-line meant that the centre of gravity was extremely low and the likelihood of the raft flipping over was practically zero. I think we need to remember that this is America, the litigation capital of the world. Grand Canyon Expeditions simply couldn't take the risk that multiple law-suits would be issued should the raft flip and send clients into the maelstrom of the rapid. However, rafting is an "extreme" sport! On the Zambezi in Africa, rafts flipping over, or powering through monstrous rapids in an almost vertical position is normal; clients feel cheated otherwise!

There are two main differences between a trip down the Zambezi and a trip down through the Grand Canyon. First, the clientele on the Colorado river will probably be mainly American, middle age and middle class, who enjoy their comforts, as opposed to the young, care-free "travellers" who go down the Zambezi and don't give comfort a second thought; for them, the rougher the better. Secondly, the Colorado clients are there as much to see the Canyon in all its glory and learn about its history and evolution as to raft the Colorado River, as opposed to the Zambezi rafters, who are generally adrenelin junkies unable to get enough excitement out of anything, no matter how "extreme." For them, the Zambezi and its canyons are merely the tool for their excitement satisfaction.

Having motored on a little way from Lee's Ferry, we eventually came into the Canyon itself and encountered the first rapids. Susie and I were on the second raft, along with Del and Hannah. The first raft was quite a way ahead of us and dropped down through the first rapid out of our sight. We could hear the faint screams in the distance, at which point, Del turned to everyone on the raft and exclaimed, "better watch out girls, sounds like they're sacrificing virgins again!" Everyone was in high spirits when we reached this first rapid. We all got our first soaking and the raft simply glided over the top of the rapid, bending only slightly in the middle. I remember feeling rather deflated by the lack of excitement in this first rapid, but the sheer majesty of the scenery certainly made up for it.

The rafts carried absolutely everything that we would need on this trip. Bearing in mind that most of us had never experienced, shall we say, the rougher side of living, some of the equipment we carried was designed not only to give the "feel" of the outdoors, but also to allow some degree of comfort, certainly for the ladies amongst us.

All the staff on the trip were highly ecologically conscious, and to this end, the strictest instruction we were given was that no-one was to defecate on the ground or, heaven forbid, in the river. Chris explained to us that urine contained no infections and so, it was permissible to relieve oneself in the river, but solids were a big no-no. Anyone who simply had "to go" was provided with a portable canister which was so uncomfortable that after the first few occasions, everyone held on!

When we set up our first camp, the staff carried ashore two very large, plate steel containers, a tent pack and a couple of boxes. We then watched in mild amusement and curiosity as the tent was erected, one of the steel containers placed inside and a complete toilet fitted to the top. It even had a fold-up seat and a loo-roll holder, and was affectionately known as "the porta-potty". This of course, provided at least a degree of comfort and privacy, provided that no-one forgot to tap the side of the tent before entering, but then we began to wonder about the other container.

As if reading our minds, we were all bade to follow Chris and Dick some way away from the camp-site, where, nestling in amongst some rocks and looking out onto the spectacular scenery, we found the other container with another complete toilet fixed to the top, but without a tent. Chris told us this was the "loo with a view", for people who preferred to sit and contemplate the surroundings whilst performing the necessary function. The "loo with a view" became Del's second home. Every morning after we first saw it, he could be found sitting on the loo, gazing out over the river. As the holiday progressed, some clients would take a short stroll along the river bank before breakfast, me included. It was quite a shock to see him sitting there for the first time, but then it became the norm and completely acceptable. "g'morning Del" would be the greeting as he sat there with his shorts around his ankles and a look of serenity and satisfaction on his face. For the stroller, it was a case of determinedly looking away. Some of the others may have tried it, but I think eventually, he was probably the only person who used it, the rest of us being rather too shy to allow others to actually witness the event.

You may have noticed, I used the singular word "function" earlier. This was due to the other part of Chris' briefing about the use of the toilets, and with which I always had the greatest difficulty. As well as promising painful mutilation if any faeces found their way into the river, we were told that we should try at all costs not to urinate whilst defecating into the containers. The reason was quite simple, the staff had to carry these containers on and off the rafts twice a day. As the days went by, they would naturally get much heavier and if they contained gallons of urine as well, they would become almost impossible to lift. Now, my natural rhythm, as I suspect it would be for most people, is to perform both functions at the same time. One seems to go quite naturally with the other. We were told that we should pee into the river before entering the tent, or worse, vice-versa! I tried my best to conform to these wishes, but whenever I stood peeing at the waters edge after having just got up, the urge to use the tent became overwhelming, and turned into a dash for the loo.

The first time I did this, I found the tent occupied and spent the next few minutes stumbling desperately over the rocks to get to the "loo with a view." Fortunately, Dell hadn't beaten me to it, but as I wasn't too keen on the others seeing me at my toilet, I was on and off that loo seat in lightning quick time. Sitting on the "porta-potty" first and trying not to pee into the container at the same time, was simply impossible, and judging by the sloshing sound which eventually came from each container as the holiday progressed, most other people agreed.

As we journeyed deeper into the canyon, the scenery became ever more spectacular and the water of the river, ever more green. It didn't matter which raft we were on, Chris, Dick and Goldie constantly educated us with their extensive knowledge of the region. Facts and figures, geological formations, tribal history, historical stories about the first man to traverse the river in a boat, a man called Powell and stories of their previous trips down through this magnificent scar in the landscape, we listened to all of it in rapt concentration. The other "swamper" said virtually nothing, I think because she knew nothing.

Being the middle of July, the heat of the sun was almost unbearable, made even worse when a slight breeze blew up the river into our faces. It was like a hair dryer on the hottest setting. It caught in the back of your throat and we had to screw up our eyes against the searing heat. The Grand Canyon and its surrounding desert is one of the hottest regions in the world, and this was one of the reasons we had chosen to do the trip in July, it was part of the experience. However, it wasn't to last.

On about the third day of the trip, none of us had noticed the huge clouds, which had been building up on the horizon, none of us except that is Chris, of course. He remarked on the "big old thunderheads" up there, and we all looked up in dismay, not believing it could actually rain in July.

Even Chris doubted it, until the next day that is. The sun disappeared and the heavens opened. I had never experienced rain like it. It came down in torrents and thunder crashed all around us. The relative narrowness of the gorge seemed to amplify the tremendous noise of the thunder-claps. Whereas before, the searing heat blinded our eyes, now it was the stinging rain drops, and of course some of the others didn't have sufficient rain gear. Being British however, and ever conscious of weather changes, it was normal for Susie and I to pack rain wear for any holiday and on this trip, thank goodness we did. The temperature dropped dramatically and instead of protecting ourselves from the sun, we shivered in the cold and wet conditions, which would have been infinitely worse without rain-gear.

That evening's camp was not much fun, but the next morning was an even bigger surprise. We were treated to the Colorado River living up to its name. The colour of the water had changed from a startling green to a deep red/orange. "Colorado" means the colour red in Spanish. Chris tried to buoy our spirits by telling us all we were priveleged to witness the change in colour, but in truth, we were all rather disappointed by it. It rained for the next few days and the weather never returned to the heat at the beginning of the trip, and the Colorado river never regained its beautiful green.

It was about halfway through the trip, that I noticed Susie had become a little withdrawn. I remember thinking it was probably the experience of the Canyon and the river. She was always rather spiritual and had already exclaimed just how in awe she was of the entire place. She had however, begun to talk incessantly about Chris and his attributes. I wasn't really concerned. He was an exceptional man, fit and good looking with an almost encyclopaedic knowledge of the region. Susie was a voracious reader and learner, and her spirituality meant that for her, the trip was as much about the emotion of the place as learning of its history.

Very often, the rafts would pull into the shore and we would all hike up small side-canyons to spectacularly beautiful waterfalls and pools where we could swim. Susie would ensure that she walked as near to Chris as was possible. At the time, I put it down to her seemingly never ending thirst for knowledge, but as the days went by, I did become a little concerned. A few of the others had remarked on Susie's behaviour to me and it became obvious that they were seeing something different to me. And so I watched her on a few occasions when Chris was explaining some feature of the canyon or relating some little story about a different trip. She never took her eyes off him for a moment, and her expression was of a little school-girl besotted with her teacher.

I remember one occasion when we were returning from one of these little side-hikes. Susie and I were walking down the track together, slightly behind all the others. Chris came running down the path in his sandals and passed us with a cheery greeting. Susie simply gazed after him and murmured, "just look at him, so fit". It wasn't so much the words as the way she said them. I was now beginning to sense that something was wrong, and rather than soak up the atmosphere and experience of the canyon, I began to trawl my memory for some little snippet of information, which might give a clue as to what I had done to cause her to behave and treat me this way. It had to be my fault.

Our relationship leading up to the trip had been wonderful, loving and deep. I simply couldn't believe that she would be so fickle and shallow as to fall for the inadvertent charms of our tour guide. Admiration I could understand and accept, I felt the same way, but this was almost puppy-dog behaviour. She followed him everywhere, hanging around him, trying to talk to him. As hard as I tried, I could not put my finger on why Susie had begun to act in this way.

The worse point came however, on the evening of the day she remarked on Chris' fitness. Some of the clients had brought small tents, but the rest of us slept in our bags in the open. (On rainy nights, we sheltered under some overhang, or just got wet) The camps we made were always on a sandy stretch, big enough to give everybody enough private space when sleeping. Susie and I were no exception. This one evening, we had made camp and after dinner and a chat around the fire, I started to roll out our sleeping bags and prepare our space. I had chosen one little spot and was in the process of smoothing the sand out to a flatter surface when Susie appeared and gathered up her sleeping bag. Without a word, she removed herself from the spot I had chosen and walked to another spot about 10-15 metres away. She didn't make any claim to it being a better spot, she was completely alone, but she didn't say anything about my joining her. She didn't even look at me. She simply got into her bag and went to sleep.

The demons began to swarm in my head. What on earth was going on! What had I done? Why was she doing this, for everybody to see? Why was she embarrassing me like this? And embarrassing it was! We never slept together in the same spot for the rest of the trip. We had become friendly with everyone on the trip and more than one of them remarked about Susie's behaviour. Del came to me once and said simply with a benign expression, "Wow fella, you're really suffering." I tried to enjoy the rest of the trip, but my mind was too taken up with trying to sort out this problem.

She wouldn't speak with me about it, saying that nothing was wrong and that I was imagining things.

Whatever else she thought was happening, it was me who had to contend with her infatuation with Chris and her very public rejection of me. These are painful memories for me, but as wispy clouds signal bad weather, they were simply the harbinger of worse times to come.

I carried on trying to enjoy the trip, but Susie's behaviour was foremost in my mind. Near the end of the trip, we hiked up a side canyon for most of the morning. We followed the path of a small stream, occasionally stopping at pools with exquisitely clear water. Our route took us across this stream many times and occasionally, we had to wade across waist deep, but the water was always crystal clear and luke-warm We eventually reached our destination, which was a waterfall, with the stream cascading over a rocky ledge into a deep pool, where the depth made it look the colour of an emerald. We had lunch here and spent an hilarious couple of hours jumping off the rocky ledge into the deliciously cool water, seeing who could make the most outrageous jump.

Behind the main fall of water, you could walk along a path and stand under the less violent cascades. I well remember Sam doing this. He was of rather a stout build, and when he stood under the water and arched his back, the only thing you could see was his ample stomach sticking out beyond the falling water. Susie, of course, hung around wherever Chris was.

The trip ended at Lake Mead with a celebration in the form of ice-cream, which astoundingly had been with us all the time. It had been kept nearly frozen by being in the bottom of the raft storage, in constant contact with the cold river water. The rafts were de-flated and the equipment packed up in remarkably quick time. We all then got onto our buses and headed back to Las Vegas, dropping some passengers off along the way with the usual promises of never-ending friendship and "keeping in touch."

Despite the problems I had experienced with Susie, I looked at the positive aspects of the trip. I had met some wonderful people, made new friends from the other side of the world and felt a deep contentment that I had experienced one of the most spectacular places on earth. There were places in the canyon where the walls towered above us for hundreds of metres. There were places in these walls where ancient Havasupai Indians had made crude shelters and we could see the harshness of their existence. We could see where the raging flood waters of the Colorado River had carved weird, but wonderful sweeping shapes into the rocks. The biggest set of rapids, Lava Falls existed simply because of ancient rock falls where the water struck these massive obstacles in the river and had been forced around them, creating separate channels and dangerous swirling whirlpools.

By contrast, we had experienced the stillness and silence of the canyon where the river simply meandered silently and gracefully through narrow gorges. You could close your eyes and be instantly transported back to this same silence, millions of years ago. It was impossible not to look aesthetically at this place, it was impossible for it not to touch your soul. And then, as if God switched off the beauty light, we found ourselves back in the glitz of Las Vegas.

At the start and end of our adventure, we were booked into a large hotel right at the end of the "strip." Driving along the "strip" it was quite literally, the last building before you hit the desert. I don't remember its name and am quite certain, it's now been re-developed into something even larger and gaudier. Like every other hotel in Las Vegas, the entire ground floor was given over to the gaming machines and tables of the casino. It was impossible to ignore the gambling as you had to walk right through it to get to reception.

If you remember, I had experienced a little of gaming machines when I worked at Mecca Bingo, but walking through the ground floor of this relatively small hotel, it was obvious that the Mecca gamblers were very small-time compared to those in Las Vegas. I saw rows and rows and rows of slot machines. At every machine, a man or woman was actually sitting down on a stool, as if they would be there for so long, their legs would give way. Beside every one of them was a large bucket and every now and then, he or she would dip into this bucket and bring up a handful of coins. Their pockets were obviously not big enough to carry all the cash they needed.

On the other side of them would be the remains of a dinner or lunch they had had served to them sitting at their machine, clearly reluctant to allow the next punter the opportunity to win any of the money they had put in. Lights were flashing everywhere and uniformed waiters scuttled about with huge drinks on trays.

Beyond the slot-machines were the actual gaming tables. There were tables for blackjack, craps, poker, roulette and others I had never seen before. Above all this was the steady hum and din of money crashing out of a machine, or the whoop of delight from some lucky punter, or the sudden ringing of jackpot-bells, and just the general hubbub of the conversation of hundreds of people.

Susie and I would spend just the one night here at this hotel before setting off for Los Angeles and the flight home the next day. After dinner, I suggested to Susie that we should spend our last $50 in the casino and see how far it took us. She would have $25 and I would have the same to gamble away any way we liked; it would be fun. I viewed it as part of our holiday. We had been to, and experienced one of the most spectacular places on earth and now, we were in an American casino. We should experience this as well, I explained to her. She refused point blank to gamble any money, and no amount of persuasion would change her mind. It was only $50, I pleaded, but no, she steadfastly refused to go and gamble. In the end, we compromised. I managed to persuade her to at least come down onto the casino floor with me and just watch. All I wanted was for us to enjoy ourselves. I had no illusions that the $50 would not get swallowed up, but it would be fun for a couple of hours just to see how far we could make it go. She trailed reluctantly after me as we got onto the ground floor and I headed for a blackjack table.

I can play cards, but not very well and I'm certainly no gambler and have never understood the intricacies of any card game. This game of blackjack was no exception, but at one stage, I was doing quite well, more by luck than judgement. Susie had taken up station behind me, watching what was happening, or so I thought. I had noticed that the blackjack dealer occasionally looked beyond me and had seen others a few tables away doing the same thing. There was so much going on at the same time, I had simply ignored it. Then, when the dealer paid me out yet again, I turned round to make some remark to Susie, and there she was, standing about 3 yards behind me, with me but not with me if you understand, reading a book! This was what the others had been looking at.

Of all the hundreds of thousands of people in the hundreds of casinos, bars and theatres in Las Vegas, Susie had to be the only person standing there reading a book! She was holding it up as one would hold a songbook in church, making the point that she was only in the casino under sufferance and that no matter what was going on around her, she would read her book. I just stared at her in disbelief for a few moments.

It wasn't the fact she was reading the book, it was just that, even for that short space of time, she couldn't be "with me." People were pointing at her and so I suggested she went back upstairs. She turned on her heels and walked away without a word. I felt relieved she had gone but angry and sad that she had chosen to make her point in so theatrical a fashion. All she had to say was that she wasn't enjoying it, but that I could. She could have read her book somewhere else.

At that moment, I felt very alone and genuinely feared for our future.

Chapter 14

W hatever I thought about my experience with Susie in the Grand Canyon, it did not prepare me for what was to come.

We returned from our trip in August 1985. I tried very hard not to think about all that had happened with Susie and tried to concentrate on the positive aspects. As we returned to our normal life-styles, I felt that maybe what had happened was just a blip in our relationship and that we would now return to what we had before and make it even better. However, as I sit here and remember these times, it was obvious that things weren't right, and in September 1985, Susie announced that she wanted to leave me. "Just for a while", she said, "a couple of weeks, just to have some independence."

I remember sitting in an armchair listening to her telling me how she felt. To be perfectly honest, most of what she said remains a blur in my memory. The sheer force of what she was saying to me blocked out rational and reasonable thought by me. I do remember her saying that she regretted not having experienced 'life'. She felt that as she had married me when she was 21, she had missed out on a large chunk of living. Her brother Paul was a bit of a "wild-child" at this time, and she felt that if she went and stayed with him for the two weeks, she could purge this desire to savour another side of life, the side she felt she had missed out on. She said she felt there was a big wide world out there, which she needed to see, obviously without me.

My response was to turn fear into attack. "If you go" I said, "you go for good", desperately trying to shock her into not going. I regretted my little outburst immediately, fearing that she would indeed go for good! I was however, desperate! She simply shrugged her shoulders in resignation, but then repeated she wanted to go only for two weeks. Her expression was completely bland. Those "two weeks" turned into six months and as I feared, a full-blown separation.

Looking back on it now, there can be no doubt that the "two weeks" was just an excuse and that her plan was indeed, to leave the marriage full-stop. In just a few short months, I had journeyed from contentment and fulfillment to uncertainty and despair. Members of Susie's family, notably Jane and David were horrified at her actions. Jane and I had become extremely close and, platonically, we probably loved each other as much as our spouses. Susie had phoned her with the news of our separation, and she then phoned me. She broke down and sobbed uncontrollably. David, along with most of her family also phoned with messages of support, but, ironically, it was a letter from Pam, Susie's mother, which had the most impact on me. In it, she apologised for the way she had treated me earlier in my marriage to Susie and that she hadn't appreciated the man I was. I was very touched by this and the other messages of support.

In a way, I can sympathise with Susie's feelings. She had gone straight into nursing from school, which meant she hadn't had a break from studying since she was 5 years old, and as such, she had concentrated on her career rather than have a good time whilst she was young. On top of this of course, was the fact that she was a married woman at the age of 21; an age when many men and women are finding out about the big wide world by travelling, or staying out all night at wild parties, or simply taking off for weekends. It became clear to me that she obviously felt constrained by her marriage and was now struggling with coming to terms with what, in her mind, she felt she had missed out on. I, of course, was going to be the casualty of her missing out and deep down, I think I realised this without ever articulating it.

Paul lived with some of his friends in a flat on Brixton Road. He has matured into a really nice guy, but in those days, he was a bit of a hell-raiser and I think this was what Susie wanted to experience. She quit her job with the local Health Authority as a District Nurse and went to work for some outfit selling advertising space over the phone. This really was a huge departure from what she had been doing. She was going from a very caring profession into the dark, dog-eat-dog world of cold-call selling. It was like the creation of a beautiful butterfly going back to a chrysalis.

As a nurse, she was kind, caring and deeply involved in her work. As an anonymous person selling advertising space, she seemed to adopt a coarse and vulgar attitude to life. I remember one conversation I was having with her over the phone one evening. She suddenly cut me short, saying she had to go and "have a dump." This was not the Susie I knew, and at that point she scared me. The almost total commitment to her Christian faith seemed to evaporate into thin air. She no longer attended any services and appeared to be determined to live her life in direct contradiction to her faith, turning her back on things and people I thought she valued.

For my part, paradoxically, I turned to the leader of Susie's Baptist Church for help in understanding what was happening, Ray Lowe. He was as bemused as me and promised to write to Susie. She and Ray had always appeared to be good friends, but later, when she returned, she was scathing about "those damn letters from Ray". He was never a man to hold back on his thoughts and I think he told her exactly what he thought of her and her actions. Many people gave me fantastic support in those dark days, not least Ray and his lovely wife Sue, but also many of her fellow Christians, some of whom I hardly knew. I will never forget the kindness these people showed me, a person they knew was not of their belief but someone whom they saw as a human being, suffering.

Time went by and the weeks turned into months. Susie and I would speak on the phone occasionally and the conversation would always end with her saying she was not ready to return home. As the months went by, our conversations became ever fewer and I reverted to the life of a single man. This was not intentional on my part, I simply fell back into it. However, I was never unfaithful to Susie. Since committing myself to Susie, I had neither looked at nor wanted any other woman. I knew next to nothing about what she was doing or with whom she was doing it, I could only hope. Thoughts about her being with someone else tormented me for many months, probably years.

By "single life" I mean that everything I did was solely for me. I had no other person to take into consideration and I did exactly what I wanted. It was strange at first, but I remember it didn't take long to settle back into that way of life. The pain never went away however, and I missed her sorely. To alleviate that pain, I started to think about leaving the police and going away for a couple of years, travelling the world. I became more and more excited by this idea and a yearning to travel really started to grow within me.

In the latter part of 1986, I had made up my mind to go and started to make elementary plans. I told no-one of my idea initially except one person, Jane, my sister-in-law. I remember her reaction when I told her over the phone, she burst into tears, fearful that she was now going to lose me. I tried to re-assure her that she would always be a part of my life no matter what happened between Susie and I, and eventually she accepted that I simply had to go.

By the early part of 1987, I had accepted that Susie would not be returning home. We hardly spoke on the phone and I rarely got to see her. I remember going around to the flat on Brixton Road one evening and ringing the door-bell. Paul answered and after exchanging pleasantries, Susie came down and we sat in my car, another MG "A" I had bought to try and purge my pain. We talked for ages, but at the end, she remained determined to stay away saying she was enjoying herself too much to return. After that meeting, I remember thinking that that was the end, I would never get to see her again. She went back inside the flat without a backward glance and in my mind I said goodbye. She clearly felt that life with me was far too dull and that the only way she could ever be herself, was away from me. I was sad about this, but by this time, I had told myself that this was how it was going to be. She was going to have her life and I must prepare for my life without her. I still loved and adored her, but it wasn't being returned.

I had settled into life as a uniformed sergeant at Croydon police station. When Susie left, I had given up all thoughts of doing something different with my career and simply concentrated on what I knew. When I arrived at Croydon, my Inspector was a man with whom I had served at Carter Street, Alan Strong. He was a lovely man and a good Inspector to work for. We got on famously and I was now, at last beginning to feel that I was respected for my abilities as a sergeant.

One day, Mr. Strong asked me if I would meet him for lunch. This was unusual, as although we got on very well at work, we didn't socialise, both of us preferring to keep our private lives separate from work. I agreed to meet him and we had lunch at some pub or other near to where he lived. I immediately felt that he had something specific he wanted to talk about and I was not wrong!

Although it was not mentioned during our little chat, he knew that I had applied to join the Royalty Protection Department as he would have had to minute my application. This was the department which looked after the security for the Royal Household, personal bodyguards and the like. After our lunch, he turned to me and asked quite simply whether I would be interested in joining the Freemasons. I was completely taken aback by this question, I didn't even realise he was a member of the organisation. (It was very much treated with suspicion in those days, by those who didn't belong.) Freemasonry had interested me for years and for all that time, I had harboured a quiet desire to be a part of it, although looking back on it now, I think my interest was borne solely of the fact that it was a "secret" organisation. However, here I was being invited to join by a man I respected enormously. If he had chosen me, then surely I must be a worthy person. He explained that he was a member of a "lodge" which, throughout its history, had always had police officers as members.

For some reason, he had become the last police officer at the lodge and he wanted me to carry on the tradition, to carry the flag for the police. I remember thinking how honoured I was, but I immediately knew that I would not join. To this day, I cannot explain the reason for feeling the way I did, but something inside me was telling me to say no. I couldn't tell Alan just how I was feeling, so I told him how honoured I was at the invitation but that I wanted time to think about it. He accepted that, but then said something, which didn't connect with me until years later. "Okay", he said, "but let me tell you that it will be to your personal benefit for you to join *now*" I heard him saying it, but didn't get *what* he was saying, dismissing it as just something to persuade me to join. I was still shocked at the invitation.

I told him later that I wouldn't join and that was the end of that, but I recounted this story to a friend many years later, including what Alan had said to me. She got the implication immediately. Many other senior officers belonged to the Freemasons and if I had elected to join Mr. Strong's lodge, my entry to the Royalty Protection Department would have been guaranteed; my "personal benefit". I never did get into the Royalty Protection Department and if that would have been the only reason for my acceptance, I'm glad I turned down Alan's offer.

As the weeks and months rolled by, I became ever more used to my enforced separation, although never really accepting it. My colleagues at work figured that something had gone very wrong at home. I was always terribly proud of Susie and from our almost daily conversations on the phone prior to her departure, they could tell that ours was a special relationship. Now, suddenly, the phone calls had stopped and my behaviour became somewhat erratic. The word slowly leaked out and some of my more close colleagues did their best to support me and give me encouragement. Looking back on it, I must have been suffering more than I knew.

On one occasion, the Mayor of Croydon paid a visit to the station and was given the grand tour. I was working in the custody office at the time, and he spoke to me about my duties. The Chief Superintendent sent for me immediately after the visit and gave me a dressing down for the way I had spoken to him. I honestly can't remember now what it was I was supposed to have said, but it was apparently very rude and off-hand. I seemed to be living my life in a blur.

Christmas and New Year came and went, and then one day in February 1987, I was the custody officer on early turn. I remember I was polishing my shoes when one of the gaolers on duty called me to the phone saying that it was a woman who wanted to speak to me. I picked up the phone and heard a very quiet, almost tremulous voice on the other end. It was Susie telling me she wanted to come home.

I remember feeling distinctly ambivalent at this news. I suppose I should have been ecstatic, but instead, I seemed to act very nonchalantly. "OK", I said, "when?"

She moved back into the house a few days later, and I have to say, this was a brave thing to do. She must have been terrified of the reaction from some of our neighbours. They all knew that she had gone, and now she was coming home and would have to meet them at some stage and speak to them.

After she moved back however, it was never the same and I think I realised that it would never be as it was before, no matter how hard we tried. The one thing I had always impressed on Susie was that once I had committed myself to the person I married, that would be it, I would never betray that commitment. Although it was never mentioned by me, what that actually meant of course, was whilst I was still married. I had always said to her that, even though I was not a religious person, the vows I would take at church during the marriage ceremony meant a lot to me and I would live my married life according to them. Now I felt betrayed and let down by someone who purported to be a "christian," espousing christian values and beliefs. I suppose in some ways, I wanted her back with me. She was my wife and I loved her, but the speed with which she had cast me and her values aside, made me very fearful for our future together. Having said all that, feeling the way I did about her, I was determined to try my hardest to get our relationship back on track. That the relationship would be different to before she left, was never in doubt, and the one thing I never considered, was whether she still loved me?

At some stage over the next few weeks, I mentioned the fact that I had been planning to take my trip around the world. I don't remember being at all surprised when she said that it was a great idea.

And so we settled back into some degree of normality, Susie went back into agency nursing and I continued as a sergeant at Croydon. To the outside world, things would seem pretty normal, only Susie and I knew that it wasn't the same as before she left. There seemed to be an edge to our relationship, as if something major was always about to happen. I never asked her about her time away, preferring to be safe in the knowledge that what I didn't know wasn't going to hurt me, and she didn't volunteer any information. I think I convinced myself that as she hadn't said anything, nothing bad could have happened. I was probably deluding myself, but at that time, I didn't want anything to interfere with our getting back together. I wanted to give both of us every chance. Consequently, when she suggested that we do the trip together, I readily agreed.

As time went by, we plotted and planned our way around the world. We would talk late into the night about all the places we wanted to visit, poring over atlases and maps. We read travel books galore, and from these, a plan and a route emerged. Obviously, we couldn't go absolutely everywhere, and a lot of our discussions were about the places we would have to leave out of our itinerary, most notably, South America. From the books we read, I calculated how much money we would need for each day, taking into account the standard of living in that country. From the outset, we both agreed that we didn't want to work our way around the world, we would save our money and spend it as we went. There are really only two ways to do a trip like this, either you go to a country and get work to earn money to travel on to the next destination, or you save all your money to begin with. The problem with the first method is that you won't be able to move on unless you find sufficient work to earn enough money to buy your next ticket. If there is no work available, you could be stuck in one place for quite some time. Great if you like the place, a nightmare if you don't. And it's time-intensive. It could take weeks or months before you have enough money left after living expenses to buy your next ticket, and most countries won't let you in without a return ticket anyway. If you have an unlimited amount of time to complete the trip, then this is a good way of doing it, but Susie and I had agreed that we would be away for just one year, and so we decided that we had to see as much as possible in that time.

When we had decided which countries we wanted to visit, when and in which order, we had long chats with Lawrence, our local travel agent. His knowledge and expertise helped us enormously with tickets, visas, innoculations etc. From our conversations with Lawrence, the plan of our route began to take shape. We arranged our flights so that we would always be travelling westwards. There were two main reasons for this; firstly the cost, much cheaper to keep going in one general direction, and secondly, always moving on in that same direction gives an added feeling of travelling towards a destination, in our case, back home.

We decided that we would fly first to the U.S.A. and spend around ten weeks travelling all over. From the States, we would fly to Fiji via Hawaii and from there on to Australia. (New Zealand was one of the casualties on the destinations list). From Darwin in the north of Australia, we would go to Bali and then overland through Indonesia, on up through Malaysia, Burma and Thailand to Hong Kong. From Hong Kong we would travel overland into and around China, eventually ending back at Hong Kong. From there we would go on to Nepal and down through to India. The sheer vastness of this sub-continent precluded us from seeing anywhere near all of it, so we decided to concentrate on the Rajhastan area, and from there to Bombay where we would fly to Kenya. From Kenya, we would head south through Tanzania, Zimbabwe, and Botswana to South Africa. The last leg of the trip would be to fly from Johannesburg to Amsterdam for a few days to sort out our bags and tidy ourselves up before flying into Heathrow for what was bound to be an emotional reunion with friends and relatives.

Planning the route was only one aspect of this undertaking. We also had to arrange visas, innoculations, equipment, clothes etc. We had to decide on what to do with the house whilst we were away, and of course, our possessions. We had to write to friends abroad and ask them for accommodation, and alter the plans slightly if we were unable to stay with them. We had to arrange for the banks, building society and various credit card companies to be aware of our trip and make arrangements through power-of-attorney to make scheduled payments on time. There was insurance to arrange, medical supplies and last but not least, we had to save enough money to pay for the whole thing. (I keep saying "we". I think I'm being kind here, as I don't remember Susie doing much of the arranging at all.)

I calculated the cost of the entire trip would be in the region of around £15,000. I double and triple-checked my figures and always came up around this sum, and so, this is what we started to aim for. This £15,000 however, was only the money we needed for the trip. We would need money for when we returned, and so I added a further £5000 to the total, making £20,000 in all. A daunting figure! We decided that a few possessions would need to be sold, amongst them, Susie's car and my speedboat and water-ski equipment. I wasn't too sad about this, as I had begun to get a bit bored with the whole thing anyway. This was never going to give us the money we needed, and so we decided on a radical plan of action.

Our projected start date was in April 1988, and this gave us around 15 months in which to plan the trip and save enough money to pay for it. At this time, I was friendly with a guy named Graham Pankhurst, (sadly, we are no longer in touch). Graham was the ex-husband of a close friend of ours, Ann Davis, and he was working in the financial world, specialising in Unit Trusts. I arranged to meet Graham for lunch one day to tell him of our plans and ask his advice about some of the more risky funds.

As a general rule, the riskier the fund, the greater the return. I told him I had a certain amount of money to invest in some stable Unit Trusts but was also interested in taking a little more risk with other funds. Graham was very enthusiastic about my plan. He loved what he did and I think he saw it as much of a challenge for himself as it was for me. We ended the lunch with Graham promising to do some research and to be in touch. I didn't have long to wait. A few days later, Graham came up with a number of very high-risk investment funds. They were untried and losing my investment was a good possibility. However, if the funds performed well, the returns could be astronomical. I decided to go for it, and Graham arranged for me to invest about £10,000 in various funds. This meant that I would have to double my money after tax in less than 15 months. With the savings aspect under way, both Susie and I relaxed a little and simply got on with the myriad of necessary little tasks. It seemed that from that moment on, we were forever doing something towards our trip. Once we had solved one little problem, two or three others would pop up in their place. However, we just got on with it, and in truth, I really enjoyed planning the whole thing. I found it all very challenging and solving the various problems along the way just added to my sense of achievement. I began to look forward to 2nd May 1988, our departure date, with ever increasing excitement.

During the five or six years golden years of my marriage to Susie, a friend of mine Nick and myself had taken sailing lessons on a large reservoir, Bewl Water. We learnt in small dinghies called Wayfarers and soon yearned to be in larger boats, sailing on the sea. We got in touch with some sailing outfits on the south coast and eventually ended up taking numerous weekend sailing trips with a company named Britannia Sailing. We went in all weathers and on one occasion, there was only Nick and I on the boat with the instructor. This was probably due to the fact that every morning we would have to scrape the ice off the winches and decks and ropes etc. Nobody else was stupid enough to go sailing for fun in such appalling weather.

Both Nick and I learned an awful lot about big-boat sailing during these trips, Nick probably more than me, and we always had lots of laughs and good fun. However, the one thing I learned to my cost was that as soon as the sea became anywhere near rough, I would be laid low with sea-sickness. It didn't matter what I tried, I always suffered from it. These days, I can't believe just how much I persevered with sailing in the face of such debilitating sickness. I remember once paying £90 for a berth on a yacht taking part in a race across the English Channel from Cowes to Cherbourg. We set off in a gale and as soon as the yacht got into the English Channel, I was ill and spent the rest of the crossing down below in my bunk being massively sick. I didn't manage to get out of my bunk until we were half-way back to Cowes, when the weather had calmed so much, we were having to use the engine to make progress. I mention all this now as my sailing was to have a disastrous effect on our savings.

By October 1987, the investments I had made were all performing much better than I, or even Graham had expected. They had done so well that some of the more risky funds had actually increased in value by more than 100%. I read the financial pages of the daily newspapers regularly and all were predicting that the "Bull-market" would continue for some time yet. Accordingly, when I calculated that with our savings and the proceeds of the sales of some of our possessions, we had achieved our £20,000 target at the start of that October, I had no inclination to take the money out of the market. There was no point, leaving the money in would only increase the holding and provide an even softer cushion for when we returned.

Some time within the first few days of October, I was contacted by a firm, which specialised in recruiting crews for yacht deliveries. I had joined the register some months before and this was the first time they had contacted me. They wanted to know if I was available to crew a 60 feet 'Ocean' yacht from Poole to Lanzarote in the Canary Islands. The boat was to leave Poole on Sunday 18th October and arrive some ten days later in Lanzarote. It would be skippered by the owner and his wife and have three other crew members. I thought this was going to be a great adventure, sailing on the high-seas out of sight of land for most of the trip. Susie didn't mind my going and so I agreed. For such an adventure, I would put up with my sea-sickness.

On 16th October, the south of England was hit by the worst storms in living memory, the Hurricane of 1987. I remember I was night duty when the storm struck. The winds had been building all day, but the weatherman Michael Fish famously refuted the idea that we were to suffer a Hurricane.

The storm reached its peak around 3am that night. Trees were being uprooted, roofs were being ripped off houses and debris was being flung around everywhere. For those of us who had to be out in it, it was extremely scary. At one point, the little panda-car I was driving was actually being blown sideways by the force of the wind. When daylight came, we could see the devastation caused by the 100m.p.h. winds. However, my duty was not to end that day at 0600 as usual.

At about 0530, a call came in that a car had been struck by a falling tree on Brighton Road in Purley, injuring the driver and passengers. As the supervising officer, I made my way to the call and found a roadside tree had been blown over and one of the branches had gone through the windscreen, pinning the driver to his seat. He was dead, his chest crushed by the weight of the branch. As the first supervisor at the scene, it was my responsibility to deal with the immediate accident and make any other further enquiries. I would then have to compile a report for the Coroner.

Having spoken later to the deceased man's wife, it appeared that he was taking his sister, her husband and a friend to Gatwick airport so that they could catch a flight to Spain. Apparently, they were on their way to buy a bar out there and start a new life. They had gone first to the train station at East Croydon for the Gatwick Express but were turned away due to trees on the line. They then tried to get to The Purley Way, which would take them to the airport, but found the road blocked at the far end, again by fallen trees. Undaunted, the driver turned around and started to make his way down Brighton Road towards Purley. Their progress was agonisingly slow, as the driver had to snake around several trees lying across the road.

As he was manouvering around one tree, his car was heading towards the offside pavement, when a tree directly in front was suddenly uprooted and fell onto the car. The passengers all suffered minor cuts and bruises, but a branch shaped like a bent arm had gone through the windscreen and struck the driver square in the chest. The only point of contact with this branch was the 'elbow' shaped bend and it was this, which struck him and killed him instantly.

My report concluded that no-one could possibly be to blame for this tragic "act of God". The circumstances still remain with me to this day. It seemed that this poor man was almost being guided to his death by an unseen hand. The number of times he had to try other routes to get to the airport and the precise moment he arrived opposite that tree all indicated that maybe, this was his time. A total of 19 people were killed in that storm and almost a billion pounds worth of damage was caused.

Recently, the city of New Orleans in the U.S.A. was struck by Hurricane Katrina. Even though I experienced first hand, the storm of 1987, I can't even begin to imagine what it must have been like in that city.

Two days after the great storm, we set sail on the yacht delivery to Lanzarote. One of the three crew pulled out at the last minute, leaving myself and one other crew member, plus the owner and his wife. The owner's intention was to sail the yacht down to the Canaries, where he would take part in the Round-the-Island race, and then head off to the Bahamas for the summer, chartering his yacht to the rich and famous.

It was a beautiful boat, fitted out with all the mod-cons including "George", the auto-pilot, roller-furled main-sail and gib and up-to-the-minute navigation systems.

It was "George" that nearly got me into severe trouble on our first evening. It was about 6pm when we left the marina at Poole and set off on a south-westerly course for the western tip of France. The weather was not particularly good and there was a big swell running. This was the first trip I had undertaken where we would be sailing 24 hours and not putting into port every night. Consequently, we had to arrange ourselves into "watches". The skipper's wife was not going to take part in the sailing, and so there were three of us to divide into day and night, each of us taking four hourly watches. My first shift was from midnight to 4am. And right up to the time my watch started, I was being sick. This time however, I was not able to disappear down below, I had to stand my watch and put up with the sickness. About half way through the watch, I was hunkered down behind the cockpit canopy with "George" doing the navigation. Everyone else was asleep in their bunks.

The engine was running and the night was black. I remember it was raining, but not at all windy, hence the engine. Having been sea-sick for most of the evening, I was feeling very sorry for myself and was trying to keep as warm as possible. The rule was that at night, the "watch" had to keep a sharp look-out for other boats or ships, even from behind the canopy. I had popped my head up for a look around and seeing no lights anywhere, had hunkered back down into my jacket. A short while later, I popped up for another look and saw a huge trawler with nets down about a quarter of a mile away, approaching us from our starboard (right) side.

She was lit up like a Christmas tree, and even in my foggy, sick-induced state, I calculated immediately that we were on a collision course. I jumped up and immediately switched off "George". I then grabbed the wheel and yanked it over to starboard, intending to steer around the back of the trawler. We had some sail set and thankfully, the wind was off the port side, so swinging the yacht to starboard meant I was taking her off the wind and running before it. As with all boats and ships, they take precious few seconds to respond, and this yacht was no different. She came round agonisingly slowly, the back of the trawler getting closer and closer. I knew I didn't just have to skirt the stern of the ship to avoid her nets and I could see that we would disect her course at an angle. I just had to hope and pray the keel on our yacht didn't snag the nets. I kept on veering away all the time and after much praying and holding of breath, I cleared the trawler's stern cleanly, but it must have been very, very close.

When I was clear of the trawler, I put her back onto the original heading, reset "George" and hunkered down again. I can only think I lost track of time a bit with my sea-sickness and left it a little too late to have a look around. The old adage of the sea, "steam must give way to sail" does not apply to trawlers with nets down, however, the skipper of the trawler should have sounded her horn, giving the collision warning, but she was a trawler. Trawlermen hate yachtsmen. If I hadn't seen the trawler and collided with her, there is no doubt, we would have sunk, a glass-fibre hull does not compete with a steel one! The skipper of the trawler obviously wasn't bothered. If I had snagged his nets, he would have been able to claim massive damages. He was probably watching our yacht getting closer to his ship, but if he did see us, it was very bad seaman-ship not to sound the warning, worse than my little error! I never told the skipper how close we had come to being sunk that night, I didn't want to worry him.

The second big scare on this trip came about a week later. I had been sick almost constantly for the first three days, but had then settled into a state of permanent nausea and was actually enjoying the trip.

On this particular day, I had drawn the early morning watch, from 4am to 8am. We were crossing the Bay of Biscay, and after the storms in England the previous week, the weather was remarkably calm with hardly any wind, unusual for the Bay of Biscay, which has a stormy reputation. Once again, we had the engine on. At daybreak, about 6am, I decided to have a little fun and switched off the engine and "George" and sailed the yacht with what little wind we had. There was quite a swell running and she was rising and falling with the waves beautifully. As the wind and our heading were constant, I had no need to tack or jibe, I only had to keep the sails trimmed nicely, which I could do from the cockpit. The skipper came to relieve me at 8am, but I told him I didn't need relieving, everything was fine. He checked our heading and went back to bed. I was having a lot of fun.

At about 9am, everyone was up and about. The auto-pilot was on, along with the engine and we were all in the galley having coffee when suddenly, and with no warning whatsoever, the yacht heeled right over onto her port (left) side. I had been sitting on a sofa opposite the cooker when I was pitched headlong into the Galley space. I remember seeing a wall of green water cascading down through the open hatch as I passed it in mid-air, along with other bits of tackle and gear. Anything, which wasn't secured to a bulkhead or the floor, was flung around the cabin, including us.

The chaos seemed to go on forever, but slowly, she righted herself and we all sent a prayer of thanks to the person who had invented the self-righting keel. After we had picked ourselves up and checked out the injuries and damage, we began to wonder just what had happened. In the end, we discounted the obvious answer, a collision with a whale or other ship, as there had been no collision sound.

The skipper eventually decided that we had been hit by a rogue wave, which had hit us broadside and was so big, it simply knocked us over. In the absence of anything else, there seemed to be no other answer. However, for me, this was not the scary bit. The rule on board was that when moving around the deck, you had to "clip-on" to a safety wire running all around the side of the yacht, but this was not necessary when in the cockpit. Had that wave hit us a few hours earlier, in the darkness, whoever had been in the cockpit would most likely have been pitched out into the sea. After righting herself, the yacht would have carried on sailing for at least half a mile before the rest of the crew had got themselves together and realised a crewmember was missing. By this time, the chances of being picked up would have been rapidly reducing. The temperature of the water in the Bay would have meant that someone would only survive immersion without proper survival clothing for a short period of time, too short for the rescuers to come about and return on the reciprocal course. The tidal drift would have taken the stricken sailor inexorably away from the yacht's course. There is a set procedure for returning to pick up a sailor overboard, but in the darkness and confusion of the knock-down, it would have been nigh impossible. That sailor would have been me.

We eventually made Arecife Harbour fourteen days after setting sail from Poole and picked up a mooring amongst the disgusting raw sewerage floating around. My fellow crew member was going on to the Bahamas with the yacht and so I was the only one who would be leaving. I said my farewells the next day and headed for the bars of Gran Canaria. However, my mission was not to get absolutely slaughtered, it was to try and find someone with a return ticket to the U.K. which they wanted to sell, (you could do that in those days).

I tried all day without success and eventually had to give in to buying a scheduled flight from the main airport to Heathrow on the only airline flying in or out of the island, Iberia Airways. I was really grumpy when I boarded the plane, as I knew that all my fellow passengers had flown from England, had two weeks in the sun at a decent hotel, probably on half-board and were now flying home, all at around half the cost of my one-way ticket, which cost me £350. I was not amused!

All in all, I think it was this trip, which eventually made up my mind that big-boat sailing was not for me. I remember asking myself whether all the sickness that I endured, the damp sleeping conditions, cramped into a berth designed for a midget was worth it. I decided it wasn't, and to this day, I haven't set foot on a big sailing boat, apart from a short sail later, in Hong Kong harbour.

I arrived home late that Sunday evening, tired and pretty exhausted. Having been away from home for the two weeks, I was totally out of touch with any major news events. Susie never mentioned anything to me when I did get home, so naturally, I thought everything was rosy in the garden, so to speak.

After dinner that evening, Susie mentioned to me that a friend was having severe money problems. I immediately responded by offering to make a gift to her of £1000. "Can we afford it?" Susie asked. "Of course," I said, knowing that all our investments in the Unit Trusts were well ahead of schedule. With the market as it was, even the loss of £1000 would quickly be made up.

Susie still didn't say anything to me, and the next morning, I went back to work. It had become my habit to pick up a daily newspaper and check the current value of our investments. As I turned to the financial pages, I started to read about the after effects of the most spectacular crash of the U.K. Stock Market ever recorded, on Monday 19th October 1987, two days after had I set sail.

I remember my hands began to shake as I read on. The reports were referring to the crash as "Black Monday," when millions and millions had been wiped off the value of shares, including Unit Trusts. I began to feel decidedly ill as I checked out the value of our investments. "No," I said to myself, "this can't be right," and checked the values over and over again. The certainty of the situation began to sink into me and I calculated that we had lost thousands up to that point. As I still had the stocks, our losses may have been even more, depending on whether I could sell. Our losses were small compared to the losses some other people had suffered, but for us, it was devastating, and my first thought was whether we would ever be able to recover enough to cover the cost of our trip. My second thought was how on earth my friend in the Unit Trust business hadn't been able to steer us clear of this disaster.

When I spoke to Susie later that evening, she told me that she thought it was odd that I had so readily offered to make the gift of the £1000 and that she thought I would have known of the crash, assuming we listened to the BBC World Service, which we didn't! Neither had I picked up any news on my way home. In any event, I asked her whether Graham had phoned her with the news of the crash and she said he hadn't. I spoke to Graham myself later that day and he explained that, quite reasonably I suppose, that particular Monday, the phones were ringing off the hook and most calls were from clients wanting to get out of the market and salvage what they could. The "crash" became so severe that eventually, the decision was made to ignore the phones in order to try and stem the flow of money out of the market. This course of action would have been undertaken by numerous other brokerage firms, all trying to steady the market. He admitted he hadn't phoned Susie with the news, partly because he knew I was abroad and that all the stocks were in my name, but mainly because he was simply too wrapped up in the whole debacle.

I can't say I blame him for not phoning Susie during the first chaotic days of the crash, but I must admit, I do find it strange he didn't phone as soon as he knew just how severe it was going to be. He must have had some sort of information that something big was happening and I think he could have phoned Susie to ask what I would have wanted. If we were just clients to him, then I could understand his reluctance, but we were also his friends and he knew that the investments were to finance our trip abroad. The fact that the stocks were in my name would have been a factor, but I'm sure he could have made some sort of sale agreement. Maybe I'm being a little selfish here, but the fact of the matter is that we lost over a third of the money we needed to make the trip. I think Graham felt a little guilty about his lack of contact as he promised to see what he could do about salvaging the rest of our investments. He pulled in some favours and managed to sell the remaining stock at over the quoted price, and we came out of the market with £13000. When it was all over and we could examine our position carefully, we had to decide whether to call off the trip altogether, postpone it until we had recovered our losses or just go with what we had.

By this time, much of the planning had been completed, all the flights had been booked, arrangements made for accommodation in other countries and, of course, everyone knew we were going. To cancel or even postpone the trip was not the solution, and so we decided to go, no matter what money we had at the time. And it was at this point, my colleagues and senior officers at work played a massive role in enabling us to make the trip.

There had been a prison dispute going on for some time in late 1987 and instead of going to prison as normal, many prisoners on remand had been housed at police stations. They were looked after and guarded by police officers on overtime, which was paid for by Central Government, it did not come from the Metropolitan Police budget. Consequently, many officers performed this task on overtime by working their leave days. The unwritten rule used to be that during a working month, officers had to have at least four days off, allowing them to work a maximum of four weekly leaves. This "rule" was designed to alleviate welfare issues. Although some officers had no desire to work any of their leaves for the prison dispute, commonly referred to as the "B11 prisoners" some others would have happily worked every single day available for the extra money. Senior officers, quite rightly, foresaw problems with this in that officers' health could be affected and family life disrupted to the point of separation or even divorce. However, my situation was wholly unique. All my colleagues knew that I was financing the trip with the investments and consequently, knew that I must have suffered relatively large losses in the crash. Working my weekly leaves for the "B11" dispute was a possible way of recovering some of the lost money.

Other sergeants began to approach me and offered to stand down for their duties on "B11" in favour of myself. My Inspector told me that the "unwritten rule" would be waived especially for me so that I could work more than the four weekly leaves, but that he would still have to keep a close eye on my welfare. As a result, I would work something like six or even seven leaves in a month on overtime, and gradually, as the months went by, the losses reduced. By the time we actually left, I had recovered all the money we had lost and had a little spare!

Nobody, not even me, was quite sure whether I would be able to recoup my losses in this way, but the fact that all my colleagues and senior officers, especially my Inspector had rallied around me at this time, meant far more to me than mere money. I felt that the only way I was going to be able to thank them enough was simply to go on the trip and do everything their generosity had enabled me to do. Their actions will always have a special place in my memory.

Christmas and New Year came and went, the money crisis was easing with every month that went by, but one problem persisted, what to do with our house here in Biggin Hill. It was mortgaged and we couldn't afford to put a lump sum of money aside to pay the mortgage monthly. The answer came right out of the blue when one of Jane's friends, Wendy phoned and asked whether she and her friend Lillie could rent our house for the entire year we would be away.

This was manna from heaven! Not only would we be able to pay the mortgage, but we would have somebody we knew and trusted living in the house. We knew that we could leave all our possessions in their care and not worry at all about their safety. I remember that interest rates at that time were running at 9%, and rather stupidly, I didn't make any enquiries about fixed-rate mortgages. I think I was too relieved that at least somebody would be looking after the house.

I arranged with the two girls that they would pay a rent of £350 per month, which was just enough to pay the monthly mortgage. Unfortunately, whilst we were away, the interest rate shot up to 15%. The £350 rent didn't cover the re-payments for many of the months we were away, and so, when we returned, there were letters from the Building Society demanding that we repay our arrears immediately or suffer re-possession. It didn't really amount to that much, and the Building Society was very good about the whole thing. They explained it was a standard letter they sent out and that there were people on their books with arrears amounting in some cases to around £10,000. My arrears of about £600 was rather small beer in comparison, but it still gave me a bit of a fright.

The months went rolling by and the date of our departure, May 2nd 1988, grew ever nearer. Gradually, everything came together, and the time was approaching when I would host a leaving drink for my colleagues at some pub or other around Croydon. Various reports had been submitted on my behalf by my Chief Superintendent asking that I be granted "special leave of absence" for my trip as it was always my intention to return to the police. He argued it on the basis that I didn't want to leave permanently, that I simply wanted to go away for a longer holiday than most people. I would return to the police with a much greater understanding of the cultural differences between the various groups of people in the country at that time and that this greater understanding would undoubtedly help in police/population relations. The blinkered bureaucrats of New Scotland Yard, unsurprisingly refused all requests, and I resigned from the police on 1st April 1988. (The twist in the tail here for me was that when I did return to the police 18 months later, a system of "career breaks" had been introduced whereby officers could go on extended leave, without pay of course, but still employed by the police. This system was to come in very useful, about 6 years later.) I had been warned that if I left, I may not be re-recruited, they may be up to establishment strength. Fat chance!!

Although I planned to hold a leaving drink, I hadn't made any firm arrangements, so I was rather surprised when an officer named Vince Fuller came to me one day and apologised that he would not be able to attend my function. I looked at him quizzically, and he blustered on about something I couldn't understand and walked off. I thought at the time, he was just anticipating that I would host a leaving drink at some stage and he was confused about when. All was to become clear a short while later, and once again my colleagues astounded me with their generosity.

I was very friendly at this time with a fellow sergeant named Alan Goddard. He said to me one day that he wanted to take Susie and I out to a posh Chinese restaurant over in Kenley for a farewell dinner. He would pick us up in his car so that at least Susie and I could have a drink with him. On the evening we were to go, Susie and I were ready and waiting when he arrived at the front door. When we walked out to the road, there was a gleaming Rolls Royce waiting for us, with the nice little touch about the registration number, "ROB 1". He had borrowed the car from a friend of his named "Rob" he explained, and we set off for the restaurant.

It was a glorious car with sumptuous leather seats and an aroma inside that only expensive luxury cars seem to have. I was humbled by the fact that Alan had thought enough of Susie and I to have arranged this for us and very grateful to Alan's friend for the loan of his car.

On the way to the restaurant Alan explained that we would have to cut across the airfield at Kenley as there was something he needed to pick up. I remember thinking this was a little unusual as we could drive to the other side of the airfield just as quickly, but I was so enamoured with the gesture of the Rolls, I didn't give it a second thought.

We turned onto the airfield at one of the gates and started to drive along one of the tarmac tracks. In the distance I could see the colourful lights of a party and remarked to Alan that someone must be having a large barbecue. Suddenly, Alan turned off the track and started to drive across the field itself, towards these coloured lights. As we approached, I said to Alan, "Hey look, there's Harry Gallevan, and there's Roy, and there's……" The penny finally dropped!

Alan had secretly arranged for a massive barbecue party as a farewell to Susie and I. Almost all our team of constables, sergeants, Inspectors, some senior officers, their wives, their girlfriends, their boyfriends, some of our own friends whom Alan had been able to contact; they were all there. It was a complete surprise and I wouldn't be understating it when I say I was absolutely dumbfounded. I was so shocked, I didn't get out of the car, I simply stared at everyone laughing and raising their glasses to us. When I did eventually get out and join them, I remember distinctly having more than a small tear in my eyes and I gave Alan a hug.

When I went into the party area, I was shaking hands with everybody and just enjoying this special moment. The barbecue specialist, Roy had arranged for a whole suckling pig to be on the spit, roasting for our arrival, along with a huge array of salad material and vegetables.

It was a fantastic party, probably the best night out I have ever had, and at the end of it, I made a rather emotional speech, which of course, was right off the cuff.

Whilst I had just the best time, Susie spent practically the entire evening sitting in a corner, chatting with her friend Ann. It was no secret between us that she disliked my police colleagues and friends, but she could at least have made some effort to mingle and thank them for their kindness. I found it inexcusable that Susie, who simply adored being the centre of attention, could treat my friends and colleagues this way. Her attitude was embarrassing to say the least.

Later, I thought about what Vince had said to me about not being able to attend my "do". He was of course referring to the barbecue I knew nothing about and apparently, when he was talking to me, Alan was standing behind me waving his arms, shaking his head and gently drawing a finger across his throat. That's when Vince got the message and walked off.

The last few weeks before our trip was a whirl of visits to relatives and friends, last minute arrangements, dinner parties and of course, packing. We had both bought large rucksacks, which we had practised packing several times. No matter how I packed mine, it always ended up bulging at the sides. Even though we had planned the trip so that we would be in the sun a lot of the time and wearing just "T" shirts and shorts, we still seemed to have an awful lot of gear and equipment including medical stores. I must admit to feeling a little uneasy about having to hump this amount of gear around the world and I was especially uneasy about Susie's rucksack. It wasn't as large as mine, but she was physically strong and I knew her determination would prevent her from giving in.

The final party we attended was a lunch-time get together with close friends, including Jane and David, at our friend's flat belonging to Jane Emmanuel. The two Janes and Susie were all exceptionally close friends and it was all rather emotional at the end. I remember waving Jane and David off at the end of the party and Susie bursting in to tears at the sight of her beloved sister disappearing into the distance. Neither Jane nor David was going to be at the airport when we flew out and this was going to be the first time that the twins had been so far apart from each other for such a long time. David later told me that Jane had sobbed for days afterwards.

My last day at work consisted almost entirely of shaking hands and saying farewell to everyone. My fellow sergeants had all signed a mock-up of a custody record, which is used to record the history of a person detained at the station, with comments such as, "he is off on a journey which most of us would not have the courage to undertake. Good luck!" The officers on my team said farewell and insisted I came back to see them when I returned and tell them all about my adventures; something which I was determined to do.

And so, on May 2nd 1988, Susie and I left England, our families, our jobs, our friends, our security and the relative safety of our environment, for a journey neither of us ever believed we would undertake. Although neither of us thought of it in these terms, it would test our resolve, our marriage, our health and ultimately, our personal courage to keep going in the face of adversity when things went wrong. And some things did go wrong, badly wrong, mostly for Susie.

Chapter 15

I am now faced with the prospect of describing our journey around the world. The one thing I want to avoid is to make it sound like a travel book, which, being as the trip was over 17 years ago, is not likely. I cannot remember all the little places we stayed at or visited, but I do however, have very vivid memories of some of the more notable events and experiences, and it is these I wish to share in more detail.

Planning to stay in America for around ten weeks, was probably our first mistake. It was too long, but as well as seeing something of the States, doing this part of the trip was as much about visiting friends. The fact remains however that we were on a time schedule and looking back on the trip, whilst it was great to see our friends, we could have spent less time with them and more time exploring.

Our first port of call however, was with Peg and "Hopper" (short for his surname Hoppenstedt) in New Haven, Connecticut. You may remember Peg had trained with Susie in nursing whilst her husband Hopper was studying at the business school in Regents Park. We deliberately chose to stay here first as we could get used to carrying our large rucksacks around and if necessary, send stuff home to UK from a friendly country. I don't remember being overly excited whilst we were at Heathrow preparing to fly out, I think I was just glad that all the preparation was now over and we could get on with it. When we landed at J.F.K. airport however, I began to feel as though we really were on our way and started to look forward to whatever life was going to throw at us over the next twelve months.

Peg and Hopper were their usual ebullient selves. They had a nice house in New Haven and from there they took us around some of the more well known locations, such as Cape Cod. From here, we went on down to New York where we stayed for a couple of days visiting the museums and galleries etc. When we were planning the trip, we agreed that when we weren't staying with friends or relatives, we would stay in decent accommodation, neither too expensive nor too cheap. Neither of us fancied the idea of waking up in the morning scratching flea bites, but we were prepared for the less salubrious hotels and hostels. New York however, was very expensive for us and so the visit lasted only a couple of days before we continued south on the overnight train to the capitol, Washington. Here again, we visited more galleries, museums and tourist spots you know, the ones you can't possibly leave out, The Space Centre, Arlington Cemetry, The White House etc etc.

In Washington, we experienced our first taste of Hostel living and had all our food stolen out of the fridge, so much for fellow-travellers' cameraderie! The hostel itself was OK, a bit cramped but clean and generally, the other people there were friendly and helpful. I remember thinking that, (notwithstanding our missing food!) if this was how it was going to be most of the time, then the trip would be just fine!

After about three or four days in Washington, we took another overnight train down to Atlanta, Georgia, where we were due to stay with a couple from the rafting holiday, Lynne and Phil. As nice a couple of people as they were, their surname escapes me; maybe it had something to do with the fact they were living in the most boring place in America, a place called Calhoun, the carpet capitol of the States! Almost everyone in the town, was employed in some way within the carpet manufacturing business, and it was a well known statistic that most of the population of Calhoun had never ventured beyond the Georgia state-line and some had not even gone out of Calhoun. I mean no disrespect to our hosts, but the town was boring beyond description, there simply was nothing to do. And we were due to stay for a week!

I remember that he was a carpet company executive and she was a housewife looking after their three children, who were, as I remember, great fun. They lived on a 10 acre ranch with horses, real wild-west "cutting" ponies, so named for their ability to turn on a sixpence, vital when cowboys are "cutting" out a steer from the herd. They did their best to entertain us, including a trip to meet their town-sheriff, a huge black guy named Willie, who had a matchstick stuck in the side of his mouth the whole time he was talking to us, but in the end, both Susie and I were relieved to be heading off to another place, and I suspect our hosts were pretty relieved to be rid of us too.

Our next stop was Indiana and another couple from the rafting trip, Sam and Pattie Fitzsimmons, the doctor and nurse. They lived in a town called Evansville and in truth, this town was probably as boring as Calhoun, but at least Sam and Pattie got out a bit more and we travelled around. Sam was a pilot and had a part-share in a private plane. One of the places he flew us to was Kings Island, a pleasure park somewhere in the American mid-west, I don't remember the exact location.

We had a great day out, but Susie had a bad time with her back on one of the roller-coasters, reputedly, the longest in the world at that time. I remember her screaming and seeing her face all screwed up in what I thought was pleasure and laughter. Unfortunately, the bumpy ride was jolting her back badly, and she was in fact screaming with pain. She was already having trouble eating food as she had a sharp pain in the back of her mouth whenever she chewed, and this ride just added to her misery.

From Evansville, Sam flew us up to Indianopolis, where we met up with Del and Hannah from the Grand Canyon. The highlight of this part of our trip was to go and see the Indianapolis 500 motor race. Del had secured four seats for us in a grandstand alongside the long bend at one end of the track. From here we could see right into an area they called the "snakepit", which was an enclosure in the middle of the circuit where it seemed that anything went!

It was full of camper vans and Hells Angels with their bikes. I have to admit that watching racing cars go around an oval circuit time after time after time got very boring, except when a collision occurred, which was usually quite spectacular. In the "snakepit" however, there was always something going on, from women dancing naked to vehicles being set on fire.

I remember one unfortunate police officer walking too close to the fence and being pelted with beer cans. Liquid was flying out of the cans as they flew towards the officer. One has to assume that the beer had been drunk and the cans actually contained another kind of liquid, also yellow in colour.

The toilets at the track were an absolute disgrace, but as Del explained, the real die-hard race fans didn't bother to use them. He explained that most of the men attached a condom to their penises. The condom then had a length of tube attached to the end, which was long enough to reach the ground under the seating area. When the men wanted to urinate, they simply peed into the condom and it drained out of the tube and onto the ground. A quick walk past the grandstand on the way to the toilets confirmed what Del had said, it was awash with stale urine. I have no idea what the women did, but I suspect they didn't go to the same lengths as the men.

After the race, Del and Hannah drove us up to their house in Illinois, just outside Chicago. We stayed there for about another week, and then headed south to Denver. From here we wanted to travel up to Seattle on the west coast and to do so, I contacted a firm which then, was called "Auto-Driveaway". When business-people and executives in America re-locate, for example from New York to San Fransisco, they often don't take their cars with them as the distances can sometimes be too great. Auto-Driveaway matched up other people, usually travellers like us, wanting to go to certain places, with cars which needed to be taken to the same location. As it happened, they had a car which needed to go to Seattle and so we drove up through Yellowstone National park, across the Rockies and down to Seattle, arriving on the appointed day and delivering the car as instructed, on time.

In Seattle, we stayed with Dick Hazen, the swamper from the rafting trip. By this time, Susie's toothache had worsened dramatically, to the point where she could only eat yoghurt.

Dick was a vetinary surgeon and he knew a good dentist. He insisted on calling his friend and asking what to do about Susie's tooth. We were a little skeptical because of the price we would have to pay. However, something was going to have to be done, despite what it cost, so we agreed to Dick contacting the dentist. Apparently, Dick did a deal with the dentist for him to fix Susie's teeth free and then Dick would treat the dentist's dog for nothing. I have to say that Dick was typical of most Americans I have ever encountered, generous to a fault.

The dentist found that Susie had a bit of filling sticking into her gum, which had been left by the dentist she visited here in Biggin Hill prior to travelling and which was now causing an infection in the gum. She had a pretty major procedure carried out on her mouth, which took about two hours under an anaesthetic. I remember thinking, "thank God that's been sorted out", but it was only to be the first in a long line of injuries and ailments suffered by Susie on this trip.

After a short spell at Dick's holiday cottage on Prince Edward Island, just off the west coast, we travelled on down to San Fransisco, via Portland, Oregon. After taking in a camping trip to Yosemite National Park, where I think I was bitten by every mosquito in the park, we then went on to Los Angeles by car down the famous Route 66. From L.A., we flew out, via Hawaii, to one of the places I was most keen to visit, Fiji.

We landed in the capitol Suva on Viti Lavu early morning and found ourselves some accommodation. Since an early age, I had been fascinated by the stories my dad had told of the South Sea Islands, Captain Cook, the Bounty mutineers of Pitcairn Island and so forth. I had seen pictures of the inhabitants of these islands and for some reason, Fiji seemed to dominate my imagination.

Maybe it was because it was the best known of the South Sea Islands, or maybe because they had, and still do have a fantastic rugby heritage, I don't know. I simply remember being very excited at the prospect of visiting my boyhood dream place. In many ways I wasn't disappointed, but the deprivation and decay around the island certainly saddened me. I think it was the first time I had been to a "Third World" country and wasn't really prepared for the poverty I encountered. Outside the capital, the villages were rundown and the houses seemed to be made mostly of rusting corrugated iron sheeting. What shops there were, had hardly any goods in them and the roads, although originally tarmaced, were so full of potholes, they resembled a Swiss cheese.

We decided to take a short excursion to one of the smaller islands and stay in a holiday cottage, complete with thatched roof, right on the white-sand beach. It was an idyllic spot, and we were both looking forward to this immensely, but returned to the main island the following day. During our first (and only) night in the cottage, we were up all night trying to protect our food and bags from a mass of marauding mice. They were everywhere, all over the floor, the kitchen surfaces, hundreds of them. When we thought we had done enough to keep everything away from them, they would start again, scurrying over the reed matting on the floors and over the tables. The final straw came when Susie saw one sitting at the end of the bed, almost challenging us to try and defeat them once more. She screamed, shot out of bed and immediately began packing our bags. I'm not really that squeamish, but even I had to admit that sharing a house with hundreds of verminous little creatures intent on eating their way through absolutely everything they could find, was not my idea of fun.

When we there in 1988, there was a lot of conflict between the indigenous Fijians and the largely immigrant Asian community. The Fijians were complaining that the Asians were beginning to dominate the society with shops and restaurants, squeezing out the local population, and beginning to have a large say in the politics of the islands. I have no intention of arguing the case for or against, save to say that maybe the economy of Fiji was ripe for an injection of new ideas and commerce. The entrepreneurial skills and talents of the Asian community are well known, as we have witnessed here in the U.K. and maybe it was time the Fijians embraced this.

Whatever, the main aspect of Fiji that I remember most was the genuine warmth and friendliness of the indigenous population. I remember once walking along the beach, picking up enormous sea-shells out of the sand. A large Fijian man came waddling down the beach from his house on the shore and waded straight into the surf. Instead of swimming, he began to perform his morning ritual of bathing in the sea. He was naked except for a large wrap around his waist. When he had finished, he walked back up the beach and began simply to talk to Susie and I. It seemed it was the most natural thing in the world for him to do. We talked about the islands, where we were from, where we were going, his family, the ritual of bathing, all sorts of subjects. He was such a gentle and genuine man, but the thing that struck me most was that he could have simply ignored us and walked back to his house. This would certainly have been the norm here in Europe. Instead, he engaged with us and we with him. Lovely man!

From Fiji, we flew to Australia and landed at Sydney. I had contacted my sister in Perth but she had told me that they would be away themselves during our visit. I remember she wrote, "You're welcome to come, but we won't be here!"

We had been given the use of a flat overlooking the park in which the Sydney Opera House is situated, and it didn't get much better view-wise. We did all the usual stuff, the Opera House, the bridge, Bondi Beach, (which was very disappointing, small and dirty) etc. For all that, I really didn't like Sydney at all and was looking forward to travelling north up to Cairns and the Barrier reef.

One night, when we were asleep, the phone rang. It was about 1am and both of us wondered whether we should answer it. I eventually picked up the receiver and heard my friend Ray Lowe on the other end. He apologised for the late hour in Sydney but he thought we would want to know that our friend Chris from Biggin Hill, had had a nasty accident where he had lost an eye on a building site. Apparently, Chris had been clearing a site to start landscaping and had pulled a scaffolding pole out of the ground. Unfortunately, the pole was holding back a reinforcing steel rod used in foundations. When Chris had pulled out the pole, the rod had sprung back and struck Chris a glancing blow across his face. This had detached the retina in Chris' left eye, and he would be permanently blind in this eye. 13000 miles away, there was absolutely nothing I or Susie could do about it. We knew that the fellowship community in Biggin Hill would rally around Chris and Karen, but all the same, I felt quite helpless being so far away. It played on my mind for a long time, but Ray had instructed us not to interrupt the trip, everything would be taken care of. This was the first of two major accidents that would befall Chris, the second, and more serious accident coming many years later.

At the end of our stay in Sydney, we contracted with a car hire firm to deliver a car up to Cairns and spent four days driving up the east coast of Australia. During the trip, we had to drive along seemingly endless stretches of deserted back roads, which got pretty boring and induced that awful state of nodding-dog doziness at the wheel.

As I approached a bridge over a dried up river bed, I passed a sign which I saw but took absolutely no notice of whatsoever. In my dozy state, I suddenly realised that coming towards me from the other end of the bridge was one of those massive road-train vehicles. What really woke me up however, was the realisation that he was taking up virtually all the narrow road on the bridge and he wasn't slowing down. I distinctly remember glancing down to my left and seeing the sandy river-bed many feet below, too many feet to survive driving off the bridge. By this time, it was too late for any braking, we were only yards apart. He obviously wasn't going to stop, and probably couldn't anyway. There was nothing for it but to try and squeeze by the side of him. I don't actually remember closing my eyes, but then again. I don't actually remember much of what happened when we passed, but it had to be close, suicidally close! I have a sneaky suspicion, I closed them and just hoped for the best. It didn't help that Susie screamed quite loudly and the lorry driver was continually sounding his bull-horn as he approached us. Goodness knows what the truck driver was saying as we passed but it wouldn't have been complimentary about me. The sound of that bull-horn seemed to go on forever, as the truck sped by.

When we had passed and I had stopped to gather myself back together, I drove back over the bridge to look at the sign. It said "one vehicle at a time". Obviously first come, first served sort of thing. In the whole of the vastness of Australia, I had to miss this crucial sign, drive onto a one-lane bridge at exactly the same time as a monster truck where only one of us was supposed to get through. Even a few seconds earlier or later, I would have been fine. Boy, Susie gave me some grief for that one!

Cairns' growth has been due almost entirely to the proximity of that natural wonder, The Great Barrier Reef. When we arrived in 1988, almost every person we passed on the street was a traveller and almost every other building was a hotel or a back-packers hostel. I would hazard a guess, that at any given time, every nationality in the world would be represented at Cairns. I don't remember too much about the town but our hostel was right on the sea front. It was a massive place, on about three levels with an annexe outside. Susie and I stayed at this hostel twice, as we took an excursion north of Cairns and then returned a few days later.

On our second stay, we had been placed in the annexe, which unfortunately was right alongside the pool. We were only there for one night and were due to leave early the following day for Ayers Rock, and so had gone to bed early. The sleeping arrangements comprised a set of bunk beds. Susie was up top and I was underneath. At around 2am, there was an almighty crash and splash as a group of British tourists, obviously drunk, decided to have an impromptu swimming party. We put up with the noise for around 10-15 minutes and all the time, I could hear Susie tutting and huffing and puffing above me. By this time, I had adopted a fairly laid back approach to these things, but I have to say that it was getting a bit ridiculous. Suddenly, I heard Susie throw back her covers, muttering to herself, and then noisily open the window onto the pool. In her best, cultured English accent, she said, "look, it's past 2 o'clock. Some of us are trying to sleep as we have an early start. Do you mind not making that awful racket and go to bed!" With that, she slammed shut the window, convinced that her little tirade had worked, and indeed, it seemed that it had. I could still hear muted giggles and someone noisily "ssshhhing" everyone at the poolside. It went quiet for a few minutes, and then another huge splash and gales of laughter. It was obviously too much to ask of them. We both lay there for a moment listening to the noise, when there was the sound of a window being crashed open in the room directly above us. A man with a booming American accent shouted at the top his voice, "HEY, SHUT THE FUCK UP!!!" Then it really did go quiet, and after a pause of about three seconds of glorious silence, I heard Susie sigh, and then say, "gosh, I wish I'd said that!" I knew there was no way that she could have said the "F" word, but the fact she had so wanted to, amused me even more.

No trip to Cairns would be complete without a trip to the Barrier Reef, and we were no exception. We had purchased a couple of face masks and snorkelling tubes in Sydney, ready for when we went out to the reef. On the way up to Cairns, we had stopped at a fantastic beach for a swim and to get used to the face masks and tubes. I have never been a keen swimmer and I had certainly never gone diving or snorkelling. So I was very proud of myself when I forced myself to swim around underwater in the shallows with my face mask on, breathing through a plastic tube. The reward of course, was to see the fantastic fish-life, all the colours you can imagine and in some of the most wonderfully clear waters in the world.

We booked ourselves onto one of the many boat tours out to the Reef and took our snorkelling gear with us. Having survived the little training session with the mask and tube, I was really quite looking forward to getting onto the reef and swimming about. The trip out to the reef was about two hours and during the journey, the guy leading the trip asked if anyone on board the boat had not done a dive and for a small fee, would like to do one down to the reef. "That sounds good," I thought and put my hand up. I had barely mastered the snorkel and mask let alone scuba-gear but I thought we would at least get some instruction. I think I was caught up in the magic of seeing the sea-life around the Australian coast. The fact that I was not a strong swimmer never entered my head, but even so, I was determined to have a go

The guy's female assistant helped me and a few others into scuba-diving gear and gave us a one minute lesson on how to breathe through the mouthpiece and how to rise back to the surface by holding up some tube or other above our heads; then it was over the side and under the surface! Then it was immediate panic and an almighty thrash to get back to the surface! Although I had fancied myself as having mastered the knack of breathing through a tube when I was swimming around with only my face under the water, I had a total mental block about the natural rhythm of breathing when completely immersed under the surface. As a result, I simply couldn't persuade myself to breathe in through this metal thing I had clamped in my jaws. Everything was so alien to me, and a mad panic to get back up into the air ensued. Like a missile, I shot up to the surface where, fortunately, one of the assistants had seen me and swam over to help. I was taking in great gulps of air as though there wasn't much left, but she calmed me down and then slowly took me under again, staying with me the whole time. She indicated for me just to try and relax. As we went down, I could feel myself coming under control and mercifully, I started to breathe, a bit panicky at first, then more rhythmically. She stayed with me a while longer until she figured I was OK and then she swam off, leaving me to the joys of the Barrier Reef from underwater.

As I swam deeper, only to a depth of around 10-15 feet, I became aware of a blinding pain right between my eyes and just above my nose. I remember thinking that anyone who endures this sort of pain and does this for a sport, must be crazy. I knew I was only going to be down for a matter of minutes and so, was determined to put up with the searing pain and enjoy the magic of swimming with the wonderful array of fish in and around the reef.

It was only later that I realised just how pre-occupied I had become. I was not a strong swimmer, I had never dived before and had had no lessons in scuba-diving, I was virtually on my own and worst of all, had no insurance cover. The boat owner was hugely irresponsible in not only inviting untrained people to dive but also in not giving proper instruction and ensuring their safety. One of the basic rules of diving is that as you go deeper, the pressure increases and you have to "equalise", much as you would do in an aircraft. The searing pain I had felt was as a result of the pressure build-up on my sinuses through not equalising. Had I ventured any deeper, I may have done permanent damage, but I didn't know any of this, as we hadn't been taught what to do. It was obvious that the only thing the owner was interested in was how much extra money he could get out of the trip. Safety was an irrelevance!

After leaving Cairns, we travelled to Ayers Rock, where I did the usual tourist thing of climbing the rock. Susie stayed firmly on the ground. There has been much in the press over the recent years as to how the Aborigines value Ayers Rock, or Uluruhu as they call it, as their sacred place. Tourists are now discouraged from climbing the rock and encouraged to look more at the religious significance of the area. In those days, there was no such fuss being made and the religious beliefs of the local population were scarcely mentioned. I remember, a white tour guide showing us around the base of the rock, bemoaning the fact that the Aborigines, whilst quietly claiming the rock as theirs, were all lying around, drunk! If this rock was so significant to them, why was he showing the tourists around and not them, he was asking.

The history and current situation of the Aborigines of Australia is not something I intend to discuss here. At the time, I had no regrets about clambering over this "sacred" rock, but would not do it today out of respect to them. If I had a deeply held belief in a rock, I don't think I would want some heathen tourist climbing all over it, completely ignoring its place in my culture. We got the usual photograph of the rock changing colour as the sun went down and then left for Darwin. I have to say that I wasn't that impressed with Ayers Rock and found the nearby Olgas much more interesting to look at. At the end of the day though, they are both lumps of rock sticking out of the ground. I do feel that if the sun didn't have such a startling effect on the colours and hues of Ayers Rock, it certainly wouldn't have the prominence it does today. The Aborigines would not be moaning about the likes of someone like me clambering all over it and they could have it all to themselves. Lucky old them!

We spent four or five days in Darwin, taking in a crocodile safari in Kakadu National Park, where Crocodile Dundee was filmed. The day before we were due to leave, Susie developed a small rash on her chest. As Darwin was extremely hot, we both thought this was just a heat-rash, an opinion confirmed by a pharmicist where we bought some cream to get rid of it.

We left Darwin and flew on to Bali, landing in the capitol Denpasar. Somehow, we had both forgotten to pack the cream we had bought for Susie's little rash and had left it behind in Darwin. This wasn't really a problem as the rash had all but gone, or so we thought!

In those days, Bali was more a resort for boozy Australians, who concentrated around the Kuta Beach area. In reality, the island is beautiful, especially inland where wood-carving is the main occupation. Their labours were everywhere to be seen, from tiny little figures of humans, to gigantic fish, all beautifully carved and polished. Medical facilities, however were not much in evidence.

We stayed at a hostel with the quaint name of "The Two Brothers Hotel". In the room next to us, was a young couple from Holland, travelling the world as we were. We stayed at the hostel for three days and during that entire time, the Dutchman next door never came out of his room. The reason was explained to us on our last evening. On their first day, they were walking back to the hostel, when they witnessed a murder right in front of them. Some local man was stabbed to death and the attackers ran off. Balinese men, like most South East Asians are fairly short in stature, but this Dutchman was huge, nearly 7 feet tall! He figured, quite fairly that if he ventured out, he would be rather distinctive; there couldn't be too many 7 feet tall Europeans in Denpasar at that time. If the attackers saw him on the street, they may have wanted him not to be able to identify them. The poor man was scared out of his wits, and quite rightly so too. He wanted nothing to do with it and so had hidden himself away, hoping the police didn't trace him.

They were staying longer than we were and so I have no idea what eventually happened, whether they actually managed to get out without something unfortunate befalling them, or rather, him!

Over the next few weeks, we travelled by bus and train up through Indonesia taking in Jakarta and Singapore. In Jakarta, we stayed in a small guest house which had paper thin walls. Sometime around midnight, we were woken by the sound of laughing and giggling coming from the next door room. There was obviously a girl in there, and we eventually worked out that two men were with her. The laughing eventually turned into sounds of some very passionate and energetic lovemaking, the squeaking bed-springs were a dead giveaway! The lovemaking finally reached its climax and silence reigned, but only for about two minutes. It was obvious that male number two was now having his turn, and inevitably, he also reached climax and silence reigned for another hour or so.

During this time, we of course dropped off back to sleep, only to be woken again by the same sounds. We had to listen to another round of noisy lovemaking and whilst in the first place, we had giggled about it, it was now getting beyond a joke. Apart from anything, the two men were obviously using the woman like a dartboard! I decided to do something about it and went next door. I knocked quite gently and the door was opened just a fraction, but enough that I could see the woman naked on the bed. I politely asked them to keep the noise down, and the man who had answered the door apologised profusely and we all parted friends.

About 30 minutes later, it started again. I angrily went to the next room and this time, I knocked a little louder. I expected the door to be opened only a little, as before. As the door opened, my hand shot through the narrow opening and I shoved the door aside. I gripped the man firmly round his throat, and thrust him back into the room, where the other two were hard at it on the bed. I warned them all of dire consequences if the noise didn't cease from that moment on and asked the man I was throttling if he understood, shaking him as I emphasized the question. As I had effectively cut off his air-supply, he nodded meekly and I left. No more noise!

By this time, the rash on Susie's chest, which we thought had been cleared up, had spread to almost her entire body. It was violently red and her skin seemed to be flaking off everywhere. We now rued the fact that we had inadvertently left the cream in Darwin, although in retrospect, it probably wouldn't have been of much use anyway. Whatever Susie had, it wasn't a heat rash. Susie was in constant pain 24 hours a day. Her skin was itching like crazy, and if she scratched at all, she created open wounds and sores, making it worse still.

I was tearing my hair out because I could see just how much discomfort she was in and there was nothing I could do. We bought more cream of some sort from a chemist somewhere, but it didn't help at all. The heat of the daytime made it worse and at night, she couldn't sleep because of the intense itching. She was suffering, and I hated it. At one stage, I even suggested she take a flight home to get it seen to and I would meet her somewhere along the way. She steadfastly refused to give up and so we carried on. Gradually, but painfully slowly, Susie's skin began to recover.

From Singapore, after taking tea and drinks in the world famous "Writers Bar" and "The Long Bar" at Raffles hotel, we caught an overnight train to Bangkok, Thailand, where we checked into a fairly seedy hotel right alongside the main station, named The Huahulumphong Hotel. The only positive aspect of this hotel was that the cockroaches were a bit slow and easy to crush. They were all over the place, including in the bedroom and always seemed to occupy the pathetic little shower that we had in the room. By this time however, we had become used to little annoyances like this and we weren't overly bothered.

From Bangkok, we had planned to travel to Rangoon in Burma, but political strife had meant the borders had been shut. Instead, we decided to stay a while longer in Thailand and to travel north to a place called Chiangmai. The main form of transport in this region of the world is the tuk-tuk, a sort of motorised, three wheeler scooter with a canopy. They were made famous by one of the James Bond films. I don't imagine any of the drivers had anything approaching licences to drive and insurance would be a non-starter. They were however, very efficient around the town and great fun to ride in.

We had arranged our train tickets for a particular day and before catching our train north, we had visited a market, where Susie had bought some very attractive silk clothes. We arrived back at the train station in plenty of time to catch our train, but then Susie suddenly exclaimed that she left the clothing on the market stall. Although I didn't think it was that important, I didn't want her to suffer any more anxiety, and so I hired a tuk-tuk back to the market. It wasn't that far and I was sure I would make it back in time for the train. There wasn't too much chance that the items would still be there, but I was willing to try.

The tuk-tuk driver raced off when I told him I was in a hurry. After only a short distance though, he pulled to the side of the road and pulled out a load of photographs of semi-naked women. He tried to show them to me, asking if I would like "a nice girl". I told him no politely at first, and we set off again. He pulled over again a short distance later and again tried to sell me a girl, and again, I refused, a little less politely this time. When he did it a third time, I threatened to punch his lights out if he didn't drive straight to the market! He got the message and didn't bother to try again.

Of course, the clothing wasn't there and after all the stops, I was now running short of time. I managed to get a tuk-tuk and headed off back to the station. There was heavy traffic on the way back and I made sure the driver didn't stop too many times or offer to sell me any girls! We skidded into the train station and Susie and I threw our bags onto the train seconds before it pulled out. I think she realised I didn't have her clothing by the mood I was in.

When the train pulled into Chiangmai, we were met by the usual throng of people waving placards, advertising the names of various hostels in the town. All one had to do was point to a particular person, and you were whisked off to that place. Susie chose a placard with the unlikely name of "The Je'Taime Guest House".

It was a fabulous place and made all the more interesting as it had a resident artist and sculptor on the premises, who didn't mind at all as we watched him at work. The accommodation was in beautiful gardens with separate chalets set around in a semi-circle. They were clean, light and airy with no cockroaches! By this time, the rash on Susie's body was abating and life for her was much more comfortable. It had completely gone by the time we reached Hong Kong and we would never find out exactly what had caused it. The best guess from a doctor we spoke to there was some sort of allergic reaction, which was slightly worrying, as we wouldn't know what to avoid in the future. Thankfully though, it never re-appeared.

In Chiangmai, we did all the usual tourist type things such as an elephant safari into the jungles of Thailand. I wasn't too sure about taking this little excursion as it just seemed rather gimmicky. The area was perfectly accessible by 4x4 vehicles and riding atop a "domestic" elephant just didn't seem right. (Many years later, I would refuse to ride on an ostrich!)

However, I did the trip and it was interesting. We went into hills and visited tribes-people in little villages, slept in their huts, ate their food and one or two of our fellow travellers indulged in a little of the local product, opium. I learned that it was from this region, or rather more to the east of where we were, in an area known as The Golden Triangle, that the word "hippie" was born. Travellers to this area, where opium was practically the only commodity grown, would lie on their sides, their hips, smoking the drug through a special pipe. A lot of them never left, such was the power of the raw opium. Our guide on this trip, who incidentally also owned the guest house, told us that at that time, the Thai government was trying to persuade the farmers to grow cash crops, such as potatoes or other vegetables instead of opium. There would be subsidies from the government to compensate for the drop in revenues that the farmers would suffer from not selling valuable opium. These subsidies however, didn't come close to matching the previous income for the farmers, and a lot simply went back to growing the poppies. It was illegal, but in an area as vast as The Golden Triangle and beyond, detection and prevention was almost impossible.

We also did all the usual markets for beautiful silk clothes and teak carvings. It was in one such market, an antique market in the centre of Chiangmai, that I bought myself an old sword, a South-East Asian Dha with a bamboo scabbard. I remember that it took two or three visits to the market before the owner and I agreed on a price.

Susie took no part in the negotiations whatsoever and I think she thought I was a little mad. I saw it hanging in the shop window and simply fell in love with it. I have no inclination for swords or knives, I just liked the shape and feel of the weapon, and it was an antique, a relic. Anyway, I bought this thing, and that's where my problems started. I planned to post the sword home. We had posted many packages home from our travels, and this sword shouldn't present a problem.

When I got it back to the guest house, I bought a box and packaged it up. Now, the sword itself, is over four feet long, including the hilt. I hired a moped from the guest house owner and took it off to the post office in town. A very nice official there took it from me and disappeared behind the counter. He re-appeared a few minutes later with a tape measure. Together, we both measured the sword, confirming its length and then he told me that it was not possible to post this from Thailand, as it was too long! It being a sword was no problem, but the package itself was simply too long. There was no way I could reduce the length as that was the length of the sword. I argued with the official for ages, pleaded with him, begged him to send it, but he held fast and refused. I left the post office with my prized possession, not sure of what to do next. I think I was also a little afraid of what Susie would say, or rather not say, but think!

We were due to leave the following day, and had booked our tickets on the overnight train down to Bangkok, stopping off along the way to visit various places. What the hell was I going to do with this sword? Taking it to Hong Kong, our next destination was not an option as the government there had banned the import of swords owing to the tendency for Chinese and Asians to use them on each other during fights. I couldn't take it to Bangkok, as I would only have the same problem there. I pondered the problem all night long and eventually came to the conclusion that I would have to leave the sword there and forget about it.

The following morning, we had packed our bags ready for the train journey and I was passing the time watching the resident sculptor making something out of metal. He was using metal working tools including a hacksaw, and it suddenly hit me what I could do with my sword.

I remembered the post office official telling me the package was too long by about 4". I ran off to get the sword from our room and then borrowed a hammer from the artist. He watched with a rather bemused look on his face as I took hold of the sword, took a deep breath and gave the handle, which was about 15 inches in length, a smart tap on the end with the hammer. The ancient wooden and rattan bound handle flicked off, to reveal the end of the metal blade buried into the handle. I took the artist's tape measure and measured the length of the sword without the handle. If it was within the correct boundaries, I could simply lay the handle alongside the sword in the package and re-assemble it later. Excitedly, I looked at the tape measure, and found it was still about an inch over length! If it had been under, it would have been a bonus, but now I did what I had planned anyway. I borrowed the artist's hack-saw and sawed an inch and a half off the end of the metal hilt. Sacrilege really, but at least it would now fit into the package and was under regulation length. Susie had joined me by now, and we both hurriedly packed up the sword into the package, tied it up and rode back to the post office on the moped. Two people on a Honda 50 moped is a bit of a squeeze anyway, but when the passenger is trying to hold onto a four foot long package at the same time, it must have looked positively hilarious.

We raced up to the counter, pushing in front of a lot of rather ticked off people and spoke hurriedly to the official who had measured it before. He got the measure out again, and after a minute examination of the tape, finally declared it to be under the regulation length. "Thank God for that", I muttered. "OK" he said, "can I see your permit?" "Permit, what permit?" I thundered. He then explained that under Thai law, anyone exporting an antique, had to have a permit and a letter of authenticity from the local official, whom in this case, was the curator of the local museum. Having stared at him in disbelief for several seconds, I said, "and where exactly is the museum", not realising that Chiangmai even had one! He explained it was out of town, up on top of a hill. Susie and I raced out of the post office and back to the moped. I looked at my watch, it was around midday, lunch time, the sacred lunch! There was however, nothing else I could do, but go for it. We whined our way back through the town, the little moped's engine working overtime and followed the directions the post official had given us. The hill was very long and winding and I just prayed the Honda had enough guts and petrol to get us up there. We eventually arrived outside the main door to the museum, to find it not only shut, but locked!

Damn, I thought, and then simply started hammering on the door, more out of frustration than anything else. I knew that nothing disturbs the Thai at lunch, but today was my day! The curator answered my incessant and impatient banging with a polite, "yes?" I thanked her for answering the door and apologised for the noise. I explained what I needed and, bless her heart, she agreed to look at it. She immediately exclaimed that it was indeed an antique, and that she would be happy to provide the authentication. "Yes", I thought triumphantly. "May I see the photo please?"

For the second time in less than an hour, I was dumbstruck and simply stared at her! She patiently explained that in order for the authentication certificate to be issued, a photograph must be produced, and no, there was not a camera on the premises. The nearest photographer was back in town, in some back-street or other. God, this was getting hard, but she promised to wait for me to get back. I looked at my watch again, it was now about 1pm, and our train left at 4pm. I didn't even want to see the look on Susie's face!

We re-mounted the old Honda once again and set off as fast we could go, back down to the town. I found the photographer's shop right where she said it was. Shut! Lunchtime! Well, it worked before I thought, so try again. I just started hammering on the door, whilst Susie tried desperately hard not to look as though she was with me. This really was my day, the photographer answered the door and was as polite and accommodating as the curator. He quickly took the photographs I needed, and then we had to wait an agonising 30–40 minutes for them to develop. We eventually got them, I paid the man way over the odds for them, thanked him profusely and raced off again for the museum at about 2pm. That poor moped really had a battering that day, as did Susie. I can only imagine the difficulty she had holding this blessed great parcel being buffeted around by the wind and all time, trying to keep her balance on the back of a very unstable moped being driven by a very unstable driver.

The curator opened the door within seconds, examined the photos, stuck them on the certificate and then, holy of holies, signed the sheet and handed it to me with a lovely smile. I think she must have realised just what a commotion all this was causing. 2-30pm, back on the moped, back down to the town, back into the post office, pushing in again, more grumpy people, back to the same assistant, who examined the photographs and certificate and compared them to the sword. Finally, "yes, this is OK" and glory be, he stamped the parcel and took it behind the counter. 3-15pm, back on the moped, back to the guest house, dump the moped, anywhere, pick up our bags, grab a taxi and off to the station. We got there a full five minutes before the train was due to leave, which considering our timetable for that day was pretty remarkable. I distinctly remember Susie snarling to me when we had boarded, "that thing had better get back home!", and amazingly, it did!

We got back to Bangkok a couple of days before we were due to fly on to Hong Kong, so we took a day excursion to see the infamous Bridge on the River Kwai at Kananchaburie. What an eerie place! Although now largely rebuilt in modern materials, just standing anywhere within sight of the bridge, one could sense the suffering building it caused to those allied soldiers. The cemetery was even more emotive, immaculately kept with gleaming white head-stones; not really a place to linger and we took our leave much saddened by what we had experienced.

These local trains travelled along quite slowly, and due to the oppressive heat, had no windows. On the way back to Bangkok, Susie was sitting next to the open window, when suddenly she cried out in pain as something struck her right in the middle of one of her eyes. I did my best to see what it was, but she could hardly open her eye-lid, the pain was intense. It gradually eased, but she spent yet another very uncomfortable night in The Huahulumphong Hotel, before we caught our flight to Hong Kong, and relief!

Chapter 16

Hong Kong! The first thing I realised about Hong Kong was that, to all intents and purposes, I had just been there!

I found very little difference between Singapore and H.K.; both were full of high-rise office blocks, both were situated on the water-side, both seemed packed to capacity with people and both were full of Chinese food markets and shops. Hong Kong is obviously larger, probably more densely populated, there is more to see than in Singapore, and it is vastly more colourful, but essentially, both places are made up of the same elements. If I had my time over, I would definitely not go to both cities. If I had to choose one, it would be Hong Kong.

Our first port of call when we got there was to get Susie's eye fixed. We already had a pre-arranged appointment with a clinic to have our prophylactic injections topped up, and so we simply asked for a referral. After a thorough examination, Susie had another operation, this time to remove a tiny piece of plastic, which had embedded itself in the eye. There is an awful lot of detritus and dust that blows around in the wind in places such as Thailand and this tiny piece of plastic had struck Susie right in the eye; a rotten piece of luck. If the train in Thailand had had windows, it wouldn't have happened, but there we are, that was the way of it. For the first two or three days of our visit, Susie had to wear patches on both eyes after the operation.

Hong Kong is a very vibrant city, with lots going on day and night. Hotels are plentiful and some are quite cheap, but we were staying with a friend of mine and his wife. Mike Howard had joined the police a week before me, but after two years in the Met, he transferred to The Royal Hong Kong Police as an Inspector in the drugs squad. He really fell on his feet, not ever expecting such a plumb posting on his arrival. He met his wife Belinda a few years later when she came out to visit her family. Between them, Mike and Belinda gave us a marvellous time during our stay.

I would like to be able to say that I remember Hong Kong most for all its fabulous markets and shops selling cheap clothing (which didn't actually work out all that cheap considering the amount of money we spent on "cheap" items!), or the wonderful restaurants and night life, or the fantastic views from the top of the mountains overlooking the bay, or simply the manic bustle of every day life in one of the most crowded cities in the world. Unfortunately, I can't. I remember Hong Kong most because of the furious row Susie and I had one morning in Mike and Belinda's flat. In fact, it wasn't so much a row, more of a screaming tantrum by Susie, sparked off by something I had said to her. Throughout the trip up to that point, Susie had very gradually been losing weight. She didn't have that much to start with and she was vegetarian. She had always claimed to be able to survive on food such as nuts and pulses, but on this trip, she was wasting away before my eyes, and didn't seem to be bothered. I appreciated that she had been ill, but that just seemed all the more reason for her to eat properly and regain her strength, nuts and pulses didn't seem to be cutting it! To this end, I had been chipping away at her, trying to get her to eat, making remarks, which I hoped would find the spot and make her realise how pathetically thin she was.

In retrospect, I should have had more courage and challenged her directly rather than going around the back-door, so to speak. This one particular morning, I made some remark which certainly hit a spot, just not the one I was looking for! She exploded in a temper I had never experienced before. She was screaming at the top of her voice for me to leave her alone, that I didn't understand and simply to "shut up! shut up! SHUT UP!" Her face was contorted with blood and anger and finally, she broke down in tears and sobbed her heart out.

I had no idea what to do! I just stood there, listening to and watching her, totally transfixed. In the end, I simply sat down and waited for her to recover herself. When she was calm, she told me not to keep going on at her about her weight and her health, she said she knew what she was doing and that was that. I tried to tell her that I wasn't saying these things out of spite or nastiness, I wasn't mocking her, I was simply trying to help her in my own stupid, ham-fisted way. I was worried about her and the way she was getting thinner and thinner, was scaring me. She understood that really, but was adamant that my chipping away at her was to stop. So it did!

The ironic thing about this little episode, is that when we met up with Susie's mother much later on in South Africa, she took me aside and gave me a really hard time over a photograph, which had been developed by Jane from a roll we had sent back, This photo showed Susie in her worst emaciated state, a state which had alarmed Pam to the point where she had almost boarded a plane with the intention of intercepting us and "rescuing" her daughter. I felt bad about the incident in Hong Kong, so I didn't mention it. However, Pam would never know that at the time she was speaking to me, I was infinitely more concerned about Susie's health than she was.

From Hong Kong, we travelled by fast train into China, arriving at the nearest Chinese city to the "West", Canton, or as it is now, Guangzhou. For China, the reader must bear in mind that the country had only recently opened its doors to tourists. Up to that point, China had very much been a closed country from the tourism aspect. Individual or independent travellers however, were still discouraged at all times, not turned away, just discouraged in favour of organised groups. The reason for this was that groups of tourists tended to follow guided tours, which invariably ended at some government shop where the tourists were relieved of lots of money for items costing a fraction of that amount in the markets.

Having consulted our "bible", the Lonely Planet Guide to China, we had decided to stay first at a small down-market hotel with the authentic Chinese name of "The White Swan". It was situated on the banks of the Pearl River leading down to Hong Kong and promised clean, airy rooms. When we arrived there, we found it had been demolished and replaced with a sky-scraper hotel with the same name, no doubt preparing for the onslaught of organized groups. It wasn't only the building which had gone up. The prices were way out of our budget range, catering instead for the rich tourists taking a few days excursion into China from Hong Kong. They were learning really fast! However, it was at this hotel, that one of those wonderful, unrehearsed and accidental moments occurred, which remain in your memory forever.

As we arrived in the hotel foyer, so too did six other fellow travellers, travelling as three couples. We had all arrived on the same train out of Hong Kong. None of us knew each other, but as we all stood there in the splendour of the marble foyer, knowing we couldn't possibly afford to stay there, we all eventually graduated to the centre, wondering what to do. The Lonely Planet book was obviously out of date so even if we tried another hotel, there was no guarantee it would be as described or even there at all. Everyone else had been expecting the same as us and were obviously thinking the same as us.

Suddenly, one of the others, a man named Mukesh, addressed all of us and said, "Right, come on, follow me", and marched out of the hotel, followed by his wife Hema. The rest of us all looked at each other, thought "what the hell", and six other lost souls followed Mukesh and Hema, as ordered. We turned right out of the hotel and began to walk in single file along the pavement, snaking in and around bemused Chinese onlookers. We all had big rucksacks and travellers-style clothing, and as a result, people seemed to be getting out of our way. Mukesh eventually marched into the foyer of another, smaller hotel, straight up to the front desk and gave the bell a smart rap for attention. He was obviously a man used to getting things done. The assistant popped out from behind a screen and before she could say anything, Mukesh bellowed, "I want four double rooms for me and my tour group please", turning round to indicate us, "and I'd like to know how much discount you'll be giving me for a block booking?" The rest of us just tried to look as though we knew each other, making polite conversation and smiling! The flustered assistant was taken completely off guard and quoted Mukesh a figure, which was way below what we would have paid at The White Swan. "Oh, and I'd like all the rooms near or adjacent to each other please!" The young desk clerk busied herself with her paperwork and the porters helped us up with our luggage to the four rooms, all set in one corner of the hotel.

When we had all shut our doors and the corridor was silent, somebody poked their head out and called the all clear. We then filed into Mukesh and Hema's room and made the formal introductions. We all just started laughing and shaking hands with each other, but Mukesh was laughing the loudest, clearly a man used to getting his way.

That same night, Mukesh invited us all to dine with him and Hema as it was Hema's birthday. All eight of us trooped into a huge Chinese dining room and were seated at a wonderful table, spread with all kinds of goodies and Chinese wine. After about an hour, when we had all had a good drink and sang Hema happy birthday, she suddenly stood up and exclaimed, "Oh, just look at him", pointing to a rather pathetic looking young man stood in the doorway, staring into the restaurant. He was on his own and clearly a westerner. His expression was a mixture of pure fright, loneliness and hunger. He just had to be on his own, and we couldn't let him drown in the sea of Chinese bodies. Hema tried immediately to get his attention, but he didn't see her. By now, we were all looking over at him and trying to get his attention, but he wasn't looking in our direction. Suddenly, Susie got up onto her chair, and above the awful din of the restaurant, let out one of her ear piercing whistles, which momentarily, stopped all conversation in the dining room. The young man immediately looked over at us, along with every other diner in the place, waving him over to our table. The look on his face was priceless, pure relief at not having to face the prospect of sitting alone in the chaos and without hesitation, he bounded over to our table and was plonked on a chair stolen from another table. We made some attempt at introductions and then simply carried on with our conversations and eating. To all intents and purposes, we all had all known each other forever. Then we were nine!

We all spent the following day together, exploring the city and ate together the following evening, before splitting up the next day to go our separate ways. There were the usual promises to stay in touch etc etc. Two days later, and purely by accident, six of us ended up at the same hostel in the same town, Yangshuo, deep in the Karst mountains and famous for its cormorant fishermen on the river Li, and the fun and laughter carried on for another few days.

The day Susie and I were leaving Canton, a man sidled up to me and whispered, "change money?" The official currency of China is the yuan. However, in those days, tourists had to spend what were called F.E.C. or Foreign Exchange Certificates. One FEC was equivalent to one yuan in value, but the local population couldn't possess FEC and technically, tourists could not possess yuan, but if you wanted to buy something from a market, you had to have yuan and not FEC. Conversely, well connected Chinese citizens who had obtained FEC through some dubious means, could spend them illicitly in FEC shops, buying goods not generally available on the open market. Consequently, a thriving black market was operating in the purchase of FEC in exchange for up to double their value in yuan, i.e. one FEC was worth two yuan, but each would have the same value.

This particular man offered me a rate of 2.2 yuan to one FEC, a very good deal. Currency dealing on the streets was illegal, as one might expect, but everyone was doing it! The man took me to a secluded area under a sort of walkway, still on the street but nice and quiet. I wanted to exchange a thousand FEC, for which he would give me two thousand two hundred yuan. He made a show of counting out the money in front of me and then handing me the bundle. When I counted it, there was only 1600 yuan. Looking surprised, he took it back and realised his mistake, placing a further bundle on top. He insisted I watch him count it and sure enough, there was 2.2 thousand yuan in his hand. I took out my 1000 FEC and just as we were exchanging the money, someone called out "POLICE!!" The exchange however, had taken place. Everyone, including me turned sharply away and walked off before the police arrived. I had my yuan stuffed in my pocket and he had his FEC.

I went straight back to the hotel and went into the toilet on the ground floor to count my money again and congratulate myself on such a good deal. To my bewilderment, I could only count 1300 yuan, 900 short! I had watched him count out the money and had taken the whole bundle from him at the exchange. I had popped the money straight into my pocket on the street and so couldn't understand where it had gone. I looked all round the toilet and then even retraced my steps back to the exchange spot. Nothing! I was totally bemused, but eventually thought I must have dropped it somewhere. Still, I was 300 yuan up on the deal, so went away quite happy.

It wasn't until I spoke to an old China hand in a little village in the foothills of the Himalayas, that I understood what had happened. He had asked me if I had experienced the "exchange trick?" Suddenly, I knew I had been conned in Canton, but was curious to know how.

He explained that when the man took out the second bundle and counted it in front of me, he had surreptitiously slipped a finger in between the bundles at 1300, which was probably a guess. It would have been too obvious for him to keep his finger on the 1600 pile. At the point of exchange, the shout of "police" was bogus, I had hold of the entire bundle, or so I thought and the trader had hold of my FEC. When we dashed away, he simply slid out the 900 yuan from the pile I was holding and I never saw anything remotely suspicious, very clever and very deft! The timing was absolutely perfect. When I heard how he had done it, I was just impressed and didn't begrudge it one bit.

Later on, another man tried the same trick in Beijing. This time I was ready, but he wasn't anywhere near as good as the first guy. I just kept hold of the yuan and when he failed to remove the target amount, we simply smiled at each other and I said to him, "you need to practice a bit more!"

Later on, we were visiting a city called Kunming. From there, we had traveled out to a beautiful lake-side town called Dali, in the Himalayan foothills. On our way back to Kunming, our bus suffered a double blowout. It was a pretty rickety old bus and a puncture was almost inevitable. However, both tyres on one of the rear axles blew out simultaneously as the bus careered around a bend. The driver got all the passengers off the bus and then proceeded to squat alongside the wheel, looking as though he was trying to re-inflate the tyres by sheer willpower. He was there for about twenty minutes, staring at the wheels before he finally gave up and took both wheels off the axle. He stopped a passing van, spoke to the driver and then loaded both wheels into the back and set off for the nearest town. Apparently, he didn't even have one spare wheel, let alone two. Fortunately for Susie and I, one of the passengers could speak a little English and she kept us informed. The driver expected to be about an hour as the town was quite nearby. The rest of us passengers could only pass the time by just sitting around the roadside, there being absolutely nothing else to do!

We were chatting to our friend when, in the distance, I heard the clip-clop of a horse galloping along the tarmac road. There was very little traffic and the area was rural, but even so, the sound seemed strange. It got louder and louder and then suddenly a donkey came around the bend at full gallop, nothing else, just a donkey! There was nobody with it, it wasn't pulling anything, it had no bridle or saddle. It looked for all the world as though it was making a break for freedom! I thought this was quite a funny scene in itself, but then about 30 seconds later, round the bend, also at full speed, came a tiny Chinese man, obviously out of breath and carrying some reins. His stocky little bow-legs were going ten to the dozen! He stopped at one of the passengers and breathlessly gabbled something off in Chinese. The passengers laughed and pointed down the road. The little man thanked them and set off as fast as he could in pursuit of his donkey, which by now was well out of sight. Our friend told us he'd gasped, "has anyone seen a donkey?" as if they passed unnoticed all day long, galloping for their lives! It struck me as quaint that as keen to catch his donkey as this man clearly was, he still had the time and good manners to bow and thank the people he spoke to.

About two hours later, the driver finally arrived back with our tyres, and about 30 minutes later, we were on our way again. Susie and I had to be back in Kunming before the ticket agency closed, to pick up excursion tickets to somewhere else. The trip was leaving early and we wouldn't be able to collect them in the morning. I looked at my watch and figured we should just about make it. The driver had returned with a friend of his and the pair of them sat chatting at the front of the bus as the driver continued his maniac style of driving.

About ten minutes later, we drove into the town where he had had the tyres repaired, and the driver pulled over to the side of the road, switched off the engine and went to get off the bus with his friend. Several people stood up and demanded to know where he was going! "It's dinner time," he explained. We had just spent two hours at the road side with nothing to eat, he had spent the last two hours in the town, and now he was going to have dinner!? Pandemonium broke out! Passengers were screaming at him in Chinese, everyone was shouting abuse at him, one passenger even blocked his way off the bus. When our friend told us what was being said, we joined in the shouting, not that what we were saying would have any impact.

Suddenly, Susie stood up on one of the seats and started to chant, "Kunming now, Kunming now, Kunming now!" The other passengers, bless their hearts obviously didn't have the first clue what she was saying, but it sounded really good and she was passionate about it too! The rest of the passengers very quickly picked up the words and started shouting it with Susie, even I did! Not only that though, they started stamping their feet, and the bus started to rock from side to side. The noise was thunderous. I sneaked a glance outside at one stage and saw quite a crowd of bemused onlookers around the bus, all watching this spectacle. Eventually, the driver had to give in, if he didn't, I think his life would have been in danger! He started the bus and drove us on our way, to whoops of delight and laughter from us passengers.

His friend wandered down the bus and sat in a seat in front of a middle-aged Chinese woman. Still wound up from the driver incident, this woman obviously said something pretty nasty to the man, and he obviously replied with something equally nasty. Both of them then had a blazing and prolonged slanging match, where each in turn would hurl an insult at the other, only to get a worse one back. Our friend was keeping us up to date and we were all laughing at these two having a go at each other. Apparently, the insults really were quite basic and ribald! This carried on till we reached the outskirts of Kunming. By this time, we had missed the ticket office, but we didn't care really. What was happening on the bus was much better, absolutely priceless.

The bus finally stopped and the man got up to leave. As he was making his way down the aisle, the pair of them were still hurling insults at each other. As he was going down the steps onto the pavement, they were still at it. Finally, he popped his head back round the front seat, lashed her with one final, vitriolic insult and hopped off the bus, obviously thinking he'd got the last word in. Unfortunately for him, the woman was sitting next to a window. She watched him walking down alongside the bus to where she was sitting and then suddenly whipped back the window, hawked from the very depths of her throat, and spat fully on to the top his head. Judging by the ferocious bellow that came from outside, she had obviously found her mark. The rest of us were just rolling in the aisles with laughter, it was so funny! We finally got off the bus at the terminus, the driver acknowledging our thanks with a growl. I don't think he realised just how lucky he had been that night!

We spent four, absolutely wonderful weeks in China. We had visited many areas where the local people had never seen anyone not of Chinese appearance. We had so many encounters with the local Chinese, so many adventures, met some truly marvellous people and gazed upon some of the most stunning scenery in the world. In Beijing, I was invited to play a game of roadside pool against a local youth, much to the delight of a crowd of around a hundred spilling out into the road, who had gathered to watch the "Kwai lo" (foreign devil). I used to go to the local market to buy one orange, simply to watch the woman operate her abacus at blinding speed to calculate the cost. On the train from Beijing back to Canton, we travelled with an American couple and their son Django. He was about seven years old and the parents had had absolutely no qualms about taking him out of school for a year to travel the world. In Yangshuo, we had met a remarkable young Chinese man with a club foot. His disability and the Chinese culture prevented him from being employed at anything other than menial tasks, even though he was capable of far more. In order to better his life, he had taught himself to speak, read and write English and was applying for jobs with the tourist board. In Dali, we had taken a boat trip on the crystal clear lake in a hollowed out canoe, about a hundred years old, the snow-capped Himalayas towering above us. In another town, I queued for hours to buy train tickets, only to have the window shut down on me when the teller saw I was a foreigner. I joined the back of the next queue, and the same thing happened, very frustrating! We saw how the Chinese had little regard for the suffering of animals. In China, animals are either for working or eating; pets don't exist! We saw dogs bound for the restaurant, three of them stuffed into cages only big enough to take one, a pedlar sitting in the street slitting the throats of live pigeons and throwing them into a basket for the cooking pot, a fishmonger in the market in Canton demonstrating his skill by filleting a live fish, then holding up the carcass for the crowd, eager to see the heart still beating!

Having had the privilege of undertaking a trip like this, I am firmly of the opinion that little things that happen to you are probably even more memorable than the sights. One evening, Susie was once again ill and had taken to her bed. She didn't want to eat, so I went out to find myself some food. Walking down the street, I decided I would try an authentic Chinese restaurant selling authentic Chinese food, where no tourists were catered for. We hadn't taken on this challenge so far, simply because of the time it would probably take to order and eat. That is, providing we could get the waiter to take an order from us.

I walked into a completely empty restaurant, selected a table and sat down. I could hear chattering coming from behind a curtain, where obviously the waiters were taking a good look at this "Kwai Lo". Eventually, one of them approached me rather timidly and presented me with a menu. I could hear them obviously discussing the fact that I didn't even know whether the menu was the right way up. I struggled to find something that I might recognise from Hong Kong or Guangzhou and was on the verge of giving up and going off to find somewhere easier, when one of the waiters appeared and beckoned to me. I was the only person in there, so he had to be referring to me. I stood up and followed him behind the screen. I found myself in the kitchen with the chef, who then proceeded to show me every single pot and pan containing food that he was cooking. From this I could tell what was meat and what was vegetable. I could tell if it was beef or duck or chicken, I could identify other substances from their smell. The chef was grinning at me the whole time and then indicated to the waiter's pad. I took the hint and simply pointed to whatever dish I wanted on my plate. The chef never stopped smiling the whole time and neither did I.

When my food came, it was brought out by the chef and the waiter together and presented to me with great aplomb. He was still smiling! By this time, other people had come into the restaurant and were fascinated to find this westerner in their midst, eating some of the most delicious Chinese food I have ever had. At the end, I paid for my meal with FEC, which was far more beneficial to them as they could sell them on the black-market, doubling their value in yuan. I gave a tip to everyone and thanked the chef, who was still smiling. Little episodes such as this absolutely make a trip!

I think if I had to name one place on our trip which stood out more than anywhere else, it would have to be China. The cultural contrasts between China and the West were stunning to experience. It having only just opened up to tourism after thousands of years of isolation, the curiosity of the local people was fantastic to experience. Most had never seen a westerner, especially one with hairy arms and a beard! I used to get tiny little Chinese children tugging at the hairs on my arms and my beard, and then running off in terror when they realised they were attached!

Sadly though, it came to an end, and we eventually arrived back at Mike and Belinda's in Hong Kong for another couple of days, before moving on to Nepal. We tried to get into Tibet, but failed miserably at the hands of the Chinese officials. Yet another example of Chinese bureaucracy regarding individual travellers.

In Nepal, we stayed in the Thamel district of Kathmandu for about a week, mixing with hundreds of fellow travellers, all eager for information about various places other people had been to. Susie again, wasn't very well at this stage, and spent most of her time in bed. I went on a three day rafting trip down one of the big rivers in Nepal, The Trisuli, actually feeling quite relieved to be on my own for a while. Our rafting guide was a Scottish guy named Gerry, and he was very good on the raft.

This trip was totally different to the Grand Canyon, the rafts were much smaller and the passengers were up for a little more adventure in the rapids, which were bigger than those on the Colorado. I had a wonderful time on this trip, apart from anything because I could have a little break from Susie, and she from me. Spending 24 hours a day in each others' pockets was beginning to leave its mark, and time away from each other was becoming crucial. This was also the time when I fell in love with rafting. I continually pestered Gerry to let me guide the raft through one of the rapids, and he finally gave in, allowing me to guide the raft through a rapid called "Coffee Pot", a swirling whirlpool on one side and a sheer cliff wall on the other. I neatly avoided the whirlpool and then used the rock-face to bounce off and bring us back onto course. Gerry, and the rest of the crew were impressed with my natural expertise, and I promised myself that I would look into doing more of this back home, if possible!

From Nepal, we travelled overland by bus to India, arriving at a friends house in Delhi. He was a contact arranged for us by Susie's friend Jane E, who had stayed with him on a previous trip. A dapper little man, he was an ex colonel in the Indian Army, who lived with his young son and daughter. He wanted only to be of help to us and to make our stay as memorable as possible. There really was nothing too difficult for this man. Having said that, I really didn't take to India all that well. There were parts that I enjoyed, such as the magnificent palaces and buildings, (although by the time we had visited our fifth "red fort" I was getting rather bored with them), the relaxed pace of life, but then, other parts dismayed me. There were several occasions when we were accosted by local Indian youths. On one such occasion, two lads on a scooter rode their bike directly at us as we were walking along the side of the road. They narrowly missed us as we jumped out of the way. There was no way that this was accidental as I watched them alter course in our direction. On another occasion, the pillion passenger on another scooter grabbed Susie's breast as he rode by. She had to physically stop me from hi-jacking a tuk-tuk and going after them. We had stones thrown at us in one town.

I appreciate India is a poor nation, but it wasn't as if we looked like a million dollars ourselves. However, that is the only reason I can think of to explain their behaviour, jealousy. These lads saw us as rich, white tourists. The money we were spending on this trip would probably feed them for years, but that is no excuse.

On the other side of the coin, I was equally dismayed by the antics of some of our fellow travellers. In a hostel in Bombay, now Mumbai, one such male traveller was boasting how he had bartered the price of an item down to practically nothing. When he told us how much it was to start with, I realised it was about 10pence and he'd bartered it down to around 2p!! What a hero! Don't misunderstand me, I fully agree with the spirit of barter and enjoy it, but when the item starts off so cheap, there's really only need to get it down 1 or 2 pence, then everyone wins; the customer gets a cheaper deal and the seller retains his or her dignity and respect, as well as making a profit.

We spent four weeks in India and from the start, we realised that we were not going to see much if we tried to cover the whole of the country in that time. Instead, we decided to concentrate more over to the Rajasthan area, taking in Agra and the stunningly beautiful Taj Mahal, built by Shah Jahan, on the way. We visited Jaipur, Jodhpur, Udaipur, Ajmer, eventually arriving in Jaisalmer and the desert area in the west of the country.

It's a stunningly beautiful place where time seems to have stood still. The pace of life was incredibly slow in Rajasthan, especially in the desert town of Jaisalmer. We spent most of our time relaxing with fellow travelers amongst the many drinking houses and cafes, watching spectacular sunsets, wandering around the narrow streets, which remained cool even in the heat of the afternoon. We rode on camels, or rather I did and took some wonderful pictures of the local people. The men were absolutely resplendent in their flowing robes and disheveled turbans, and every one of them seemed to have a magnificent handle-bar moustache. The women were just mysterious!

Eventually, we took a slow train ride out of the desert, where the waiters carrying full trays of drinks would hop from one carriage to the next via the steps leading up into the carriage itself and passengers who couldn't get a seat, rode on the roof. The train took us back to Bombay and the flight onwards to Nairobi, Kenya.

Like me, Susie had vomitted and diarrhoeaed her way through China and India, but mercifully, she had not suffered any major incapacity or illness even though she was desperately weak and fragile by this stage. I never really stopped worrying about her, but after the episode at Mike and Belinda's, I didn't dare say anything.

However, her physical condition was about to take a turn for the worse.

Chapter 17

We landed at Nairobi international airport in Kenya, on a rain-sodden Christmas Eve morning 1988. A couple from Susie's fellowship here in Biggin Hill had arranged for us to stay with friends of theirs in Nairobi. However, we had received a message from them that they were out of town for the first week or so and that they had booked us into an hotel near the airport. They had said that another couple, John and Audrey Preece would pick us up from there. Both Susie and I had decided that we wouldn't intrude on their Christmas, and would spend the first couple of days we were there at the hotel. We were both pretty exhausted from India, Susie especially, and we spent most of that day and night, sleeping.

Christmas Day 1988 was just as wet as Christmas Eve 1988. We both groaned when we looked out of the window and saw the rain slashing down in torrents; only to be expected really I suppose, it was after all, the wet season! Neither of us fancied going out in the rain and were debating what to do for food etc, when around mid-morning, there was a knock at our door. The gentleman introduced himself as our replacement host, John Preece and he insisted that Susie and I not only join them for Christmas lunch, but also that we move from the hotel to their house. Things were looking up! We hurriedly got our "best" clothes out, packed the rest and off we went. I remember it was one of those wonderful old colonial type houses, with the verandah that goes all the way around. There was quite a gathering at the table, lots of food and we were made to feel very welcome by one and all. Things were definitely looking up!

It seemed that everyone around the table either worked for, or was associated with an organisation called Missionary Aviation Fellowship, or MAF for short. As the name suggests, they specialised in flying missionaries around that part of Africa, especially into the less accessible areas of Somalia, Sudan and Ethiopia, north and east of Kenya. Two or three of the men around the table were pilots working for MAF and the rest were ground staff and administrators.

We had just finished our main course, when our host, John Preece, took a phone call. He returned, rather ashen faced and told the gathering that one of their pilots was missing. He had been flying a party into Sudan, north of Kenya, and had not been heard of for some hours. He had filed a flight plan, so they did know where he was supposed to be, but he was very overdue and our host feared something had happened to him. Suddenly, all the men got up from the table and prepared to leave. There wasn't a moan or groan from anyone as the gathering broke up. It was like a well-oiled machine being started, everyone seemed to know exactly what was required, except Susie and I of course, we were rather bemused by the whole thing.

Our host explained that this was an emergency and MAF would prepare to launch a rescue mission as soon as possible. He explained that the pilot had flown into a remote desert area, renowned for its lawlessness. If the pilot had had to make a forced landing there, the chances of survival would be slim. If the desert didn't get him, then the free-roaming bandits would. Time was of the essence and a plane would have to be prepared, stripped of seating and extras and long range fuel tanks fitted. He asked me if I would give a hand to prepare the plane, which I of course readily agreed to.

We raced off to the airfield and immediately began to take out the seats etc from a twin engine Beech aircraft. We stripped out everything not absolutely necessary and the engineers fitted the tanks.

After a frantic three or four hours, the plane was ready to go. Our host then approached me and asked if I, as a police officer, was trained in First Aid. I spluttered that yes, I was but hadn't done a refresher course for a while. If I was dying, I wouldn't want me to try and save my life!! No matter, I was the only one who seemed to fit the bill and they wanted me to go on the mission. Susie was far more qualified then I was, but she was terribly weak by this stage anyway and it seemed that only men were to take part in the rescue attempt. Part of me was thrilled to be taking part, and another part was horrified that if we found the plane crashed with survivors, they might be relying on me to patch them up and possibly save their lives! I decided that, given the choice, I would rather not go as I was convinced that my First Aid skills could very well have disastrous results. However, I couldn't just say, "sorry, not going!" I would muddle through, somehow.

In the end though, nobody went. By the time the plane was ready, darkness was approaching and the search party would need good light to fly over the barren landscape. No news had been received, and it seemed the rescue mission would take place, but the take-off was postponed till the next day. However, during that night, word reached MAF that the plane had been found, crashed with no survivors, in a remote desert region. The mood was very sombre in the house over the next few days, and Susie and I were grateful that we could escape the atmosphere and explore Nairobi, including a visit to Kenya's tourist attraction, the farm where Karen Blixen, of the film Out Of Africa fame, grew coffee.

We spent some time up at Lake Nakuru, famous for its flocks of flamingos, where I inadvertently tried to book a night's accommodation in a brothel, and then headed for a small island off the northern coast of Kenya, Lamu. I remember being particularly excited about visiting Lamu as I had read about the island in the Lonely Planet guide book. It formed part of the ancient Omani Arab trading route from the middle-east down to places like Zanzibar, Dar-es-Salaam and Madagascar. The local inhabitants were far removed from what one might expect Africans to look like. They were lighter in skin colour than normal Africans and wore flowing Arab robes and fez hats. Goods were still transported in and out of Lamu by huge wooden dhows and unloaded by gangs of workmen treading precariously along a narrow gang-plank. We decided to go overland to Lamu via Mombasa and set off in one of the oldest looking buses I had ever seen. If this thing ever got to Lamu, it would be a miracle.

About three hours after leaving Mombasa, the driver was negotiating a bend in a remote village, when he collided with a car, which came careering around the bend in the opposite direction. I'm quite sure the driver of the car wasn't expecting to meet a bus anywhere on his route. Damage was done to both bus and car, and dutifully, both parties stopped and inspected the damage.

The Kenyan police and judicial system was, and still is based on the British model. Consequently, there was a set procedure for dealing with accidents. One might assume that being this far from civilisation, both parties would simply put it down to experience and drive on. No! One or other of them decided that the police would have to be called. Called from where, and how, there were no phones or radios!? However, all the passengers dutifully got off the bus, resigned to a long wait for the local constable to appear, which he did after about an hour, laboriously pedalling an ancient "sit-up-and-beg" type bicycle. I still have no idea to this day how he got the message, although I suspect by "bush telegraph" and runners.

I was really curious to see how he dealt with this incident, which was probably the biggest event on his patch for many weeks. It was like watching one of my own constables at work in England, except that this guy took probably four times as long to do anything. He meticulously recorded statements and names of witnesses, and then got out his tape measure and began to measure the scene. He treated it as though someone had been murdered, he was taking it very seriously, as one poor local inhabitant found out. An old man on a bicycle inadvertently pedalled his way round the bend and right into the middle of the accident scene where the constable was taking measurements. I had seen this man come around the bend, he must have been about 70 years old and clearly oblivious to the drama around him. The officer saw him approaching and instead of warning him and asking him to go around, he strode over to the old man and knocked him clean off the bike with a slap to the side of his head. Before he hit the ground, the constable was on him, grabbing him by his jacket lapels and screaming into his terrified face, "What are you doing? Can't you see I am very busy? Can't you see I'm trying to do the sketch-plan." The old man just stared blankly at him, as if to say, "sketch-plan, what the hell is a sketch plan?" I felt rather sorry for the old man, but was more amused by the constable's dogged determination to do the job correctly. A "sketch-plan", out here!?! As I stood there, I imagined what would happen in England if someone inadvertently pedalled into an accident scene where the officer was trying to do the "sketch-plan" and got a slap for his troubles!

We eventually set off again and reached the quayside opposite Lamu without further incident. The island lies off the coast, about a couple of hundred yards distant. We crossed the channel in a small boat and landed at one of the most enchanting and fascinating places I have ever been to. It was like stepping back three or four centuries. Just setting foot on Lamu excited the imagination. Trading dhows, political intrigue, power battles for control of the waterways, slavery, men trading noisily on the shore-line, harems and eunuchs, it was all there and the imagination ran riot!: narrow little alleyways and streets where goods were still transported by ridiculously overloaded donkeys, and made dark by the buildings crowding onto them; light-skinned African men in flowing white Arab robes and fez hats, and women covered from head to foot in the traditional Arab hibabs, with just their eyes visible to the world. As western tourists, we did our best to conform to their traditions and not offend anyone by showing too much flesh, but our way of dressing and carrying ourselves, was put firmly in the shade by these gracious and elegant people.

I had my first brush with African authorities when I accidentally took a photograph of a government building on the quayside. I was actually photographing the unloading of a dhow, it just happened that the Post Office was in the background. I had been seen by some uniformed official or other and was immediately summoned to him. He accepted my explanation and I got away with a ticking off! Not so, on my second, and far more serious brush with the law a few weeks later!

Apart from wandering around the town, savouring the spicey smells and watching a centuries old way of life, there wasn't really that much to do. I seem to remember, there was a museum of sorts, but that was very quickly "done" and the rest of our time was spent lazing around on one of the beaches, watching the dhows entering and leaving port. In a very curious way, time seemed to drift by, completely unnoticed. We would sleep when we were tired, eat when we were hungry. There was no routine at all to our existence at this time. Unfortunately, once again, Susie wasn't very well and spent long periods resting in bed. I was quite used to this by now and wasn't overly concerned. The food on Lamu was quite decent, with plenty of fruit and vegetables for her.

On one particular day, one of the local youths with whom we had become friendly, invited myself and Susie to sail out to a reef on his dhow to do some snorkelling, for a small fee, of course. These guys, as nice as they were, did nothing for nothing! I jumped at the chance, but Susie wasn't feeling up to it and decided she needed to rest more.

We left in the early morning as it was a good couple of hours sailing time to the reef. Having done a little sailing myself in England, I was fascinated to watch how the boys handled the heavy, sluggish boat. To me, it seemed impossible that the awkward lateen sail could be handled with such dexterity and skill on the open sea, but it was as though they were sailing a small, lightweight dinghy on a lake.

We spent most of the late morning and early afternoon on the reef snorkelling and swimming around and eventually got back to Lamu in the early evening. As we were making our way up the channel into port, I could see a friend of ours waving to me from the beach. Susie and I seemed to be able to make friends easily on this trip and this man was staying at the same hostel as us. We had spent many a happy hour talking and reminiscing over a few late evening drinks.

On this occasion however, there seemed to be an urgency about him. He ran along the beach and met me as I was coming off the dhow. He told me that Susie was in a bad way. I raced up to the hostel and found her still in bed, but bathed in sweat and deathly pale. She was so weak, she could hardly turn her head to look at me. I immediately felt a huge hammer-blow of guilt that I had left her alone and gone to enjoy myself whilst she was suffering. I made sure she was OK and then ran off to find a doctor.

As one might imagine, there weren't too many on the island of Lamu, in fact only one, but I did manage to track him down and get him to see Susie in the hotel room. He examined her for a long time and took blood samples. When he had finished, he took me to one side and told me that Susie was very ill and needed immediate hospital treatment, which clearly wasn't available on Lamu. He also said that she was far too weak to make the return journey by road. "What's wrong with her," I asked. He said he wasn't sure, but he would make some tests on her blood samples that evening and I was to see him in his surgery later.

I returned to see him as instructed and the news was even worse. In his opinion he said, because of her general weakness, she was suffering from two separate illnesses. Not only that, the tests he had carried out on her blood samples had shown a desperately low white cell count. White blood cells combat disease and viruses. Her count was so low, she had almost no immunity to illness. This really was ringing alarm bells for me now! During the next day, Susie was no better and I immediately arranged for her to be airlifted back to Nairobi, to be met at the airport by our contacts there and then taken immediately to hospital. Having checked our finances, we couldn't afford for me to fly as well and so I left that same day, having bought a ticket for the bus back to Nairobi. It took Susie 45 minutes to fly there and it took me 2 days.

When I got back to Nairobi, I found Susie waiting for me at the house we had stayed in previously. She had been to hospital, had been kept in overnight and discharged the following day with drugs to take. I suspect that Susie had been none too keen to remain for long in a Kenyan hospital.

They had taken more blood samples for testing, although I don't think either of us really expected to hear the results, Third World hospitals are not renowned for efficiency. Whilst waiting, we stayed with our original hosts for the following week and during that time, we made the decision that we would head straight for Zimbabwe after Nairobi. Our plan initially, was that we would go overland through Tanzania down to Harare, where we would stay with a couple named Evan and Mary Williams. However, having sought advice from our hosts and their friends, I decided that Tanzania was not going to be on our agenda. The privation there was appalling, the water was bad, the transport was bad, disease was rife, the food would be awful and Susie simply wasn't strong enough to make the journey. We would still go to the Williams' but now the whole of that part of our trip would be brought forward by about a week. I made some telephone calls from the house in Nairobi and everything was arranged, bar the flights.

A couple of days later, I went into Nairobi with the intention of buying our flights down to Harare. Buying Susie's evacuation flight from Lamu had dented our finances severely and so I decided to see if I could get a little extra money by exchanging some dollars on the black-market currency exchange. It worked in much the same way as in China and all I had to do really was to wander around long enough and sooner or later, someone would approach me and whisper, "change money?"

Sure enough, an Asian man came up to me and we agreed the price. We wandered around the streets for a while, just to make sure no police were around, and then walked up a narrow alleyway between two streets. The Asian then ducked into a doorway and through it, into the back of a shop. Now, one would imagine that a man who had been a police officer on the streets of London for thirteen years and who had back-packed almost around the world, would have realised that something was not quite right here! On my own, in a seedy part of an African town, in the dimly-lit back of a shop, carrying a day-sack containing travellers' cheques, cash and my passport and conducting a highly illegal money transaction, any normal, rational human being would have alarm bells ringing. Not me! I just carried on regardless, my only defence being that I had done it before.

I only wanted to change a hundred dollars and took it out of my wallet to do the exchange to Kenyan Shillings. At that moment, three other black youths walked into the back-room. The Asian guy grabbed my hundred dollar note and ran out of the shop into the alley. I thought immediately I was in for a beating and the loss of everything in my wallet. Strangely enough though, they never made a move towards me and to this day, I have no idea why! Remembering the incident now after all these years, it still plagues me just how stupid I was.

Still expecting the beating, I calmly popped my wallet back into my day-sack and zipped it up. I then strode towards the door, and they let me go. Odd! As I exited into the alleyway, I just caught sight of the Asian man turning a corner onto the main street. I took off after him, my day-sack bouncing around on my shoulder as I hadn't had time to put it on properly. As I turned the corner after my hundred dollars, I again saw him just ducking behind a rack of dresses on a street vendor's rail. When I got to the rail, I saw him sitting on a stool, trying to look as though he was part of the street scene. Without breaking stride, I ran up to him and kicked him in the head, straight off the stool and onto the pavement, taking a rack of clothes with him, Still trying to hold onto my day-sack with one hand, we then had a fist fight on the mean streets of Nairobi!

I had read in the Lonely Planets guide that there had been instances where thieves had been caught on the streets of Nairobi and literally beaten to death. This man had stolen a hundred dollars from me and, although I didn't wish him beaten to death, I instinctively started to yell at the top of my voice, "Thief, thief, help!!" However, nobody came to help and we carried on battling on the street. At one stage, we fell into a travel agent's shop, scattering the clients, (coincidentally, it was at the back of this shop where it all started). We were fighting furiously, but even with one hand firmly holding my day-sack, I was getting the better of him. As we crashed back out onto the street, I managed to pin him up against a car and was kneeing him in the groin, when he shouted for me to take my money and held out the hundred dollar note. I grabbed it from him and he ran off up the street. I was absolutely exhausted.

Fighting was never my thing and I think it was only sheer adrenaline and anger at being so stupid, that carried me through. A fairly large crowd had gathered around at that time, and I felt distinctly uneasy, especially as I hadn't seen the other three black youths. I found my shoe, which had come off in the melee and went back into the travel agent's and asked for some water and a chair. They willingly obliged and told me to stay there as long as I wished.

As I sat and drank my water, I was mulling over why the crowd hadn't acted to apprehend the thief. I came to the conclusion that as long as the thief and the crowd are all black, then action might be taken by them. Here however, we had an Asian man, probably native to Kenya, fighting with a white man, obviously an old colonial!

There was no chance they would come to the aid of a white man fighting with an Asian, in fact, if they had helped anyone at all, it would have been the Asian. All in all, I think I was pretty lucky to come away from this little episode intact. When I figured it was safe to leave the shop, I went straight to the bank and exchanged my money legally, which of course, was what I should have done in the first place.

I never told Susie what had happened that day, but later on, she heard me telling someone about it in South Africa. When she got me on her own, she slapped me, and then she shouted at me, in that order!

We had been back in Nairobi for around a week, when our hosts told us that they thought it was "time to leave" their house! Susie had been recovering well and was stronger, but by no means at full strength. We were due to leave for Harare two days later anyway, but still they asked us to leave. It all got a bit nasty really and in the end, both Susie and I were relieved to be gone.

A couple of days after arriving back from Lamu, I found I was missing four hundred dollars from my wallet. I hadn't spent it and hadn't left my wallet out anywhere in public. Our hosts employed a black man as a sort of domestic servant, and I asked him if he had seen anything of my money. I had stayed in a pretty dodgy hostel on my way back to Nairobi from Lamu, but I asked this guy anyway simply to eliminate possibilities. He however, took my question to be me accusing him outright of theft and went straight to our hosts. I told them and him I wasn't accusing anyone, I was merely asking if perhaps I had dropped it somewhere in the house and had he found it. However, they weren't having any of it, and I think it was a convenient excuse to ask us to leave.

It seems that it had all been discussed between various members of MAF, because as we were talking to our hosts, the couple from MAF we were originally due to stay with came to the house and invited us to stay with them until we left for Harare. The end of this sad episode came when the original hosts accused me of leaving without paying a puny little telephone bill, which I had run up talking to Evan in Zimbabwe. As it happened, I had left the money for the calls on the table as we left the house, my conscience was clear. Maybe somebody else had removed it.

Whilst at our new hosts, the medical equivalent of an atom-bomb was about to be dropped!

The couple we went to stay with were Christina and Martin Willis and their three children Adele, Sarah and Simeon. Martin was one of the senior pilots at MAF, and as a family, couldn't have been nicer than our original hosts. Despite the invite to Christmas lunch, I had never been comfortable staying with them, they were very cold and distant, something Susie and I had not been used to before.

The night before we were due to leave for Harare, the entire Willis family and us were playing some board game in the lounge. Christina happened to look up and saw their family doctor walking up the path to the house. Martin and Christina had asked him to oversee Susie's case at hospital and the blood test results would be sent to him. However, neither Susie nor I paid any attention to his arrival, people came and went from the house all the time.

Christina answered the knock at the door and then both she and the doctor came into the lounge. He asked if he could speak to Susie and I in private and looked deadly serious. The exact words he said to Susie have long been blotted out, but he told her that her blood sample had been tested for various illnesses and viruses. Everything came back negative, except for one disease, which was usually fatal. The illnesses she had contracted on Lamu were as a result of her low white blood cell count, which in turn, was connected to this disease.

However, neither of us could believe what we were hearing. He went through it again and slowly, it sank in, Susie had been told she had a terminal illness!! As one can imagine, this was pretty devastating news and I cannot begin to imagine how Susie felt inside. My head was reeling, so goodness knows what was happening to Susie. We asked Martin and Christina to come back into the room, where both Susie and I were in tears. The doctor, bless his heart, stayed for quite some time with us as we discussed what to do next. The doctor, Martin and Christina were all in agreement, we should go on and finish the trip. Nothing was going to happen in the immediate future, we simply had to keep Susie as strong as possible. The doctor gave us the number of a colleague down in Harare, where we could get another blood test done to try and confirm the Nairobi result. We of course, just hoped they had got it wrong!

As the disease was not infectious, we decided that we would say nothing to anyone at this stage, including family members. This was a very conscious decision. Susie had a good knowledge at that time about this particular disease and in any event, there was a very real chance that the blood tests in Nairobi would prove to be negative after all.

It was however, a terrible time for Susie, and there was nothing either of us could do, but wait!

All in all, our time in Kenya was nothing, if not memorable.

Chapter 18

W e flew on down to Harare, really glad that we had made the decision to skip over Tanzania, and were met at the airport by our next hosts, Evan and Mary Williams. Both Zimbabwe citizens, a more delightful couple, you couldn't wish to meet; a complete contrast to the Nairobi 2! They were well aware of Susie's health problems, apart from the specifics and allowed us as much use of the telephone as necessary in order to make our doctor's appointments.

We made our appointment and went to see him in his surgery a few days later, where he took more blood from Susie for tests. Whilst we were there, Susie complained to me about a pain in her stomach. I said she should get the doctor to examine her, but she tried to dismiss it as "wind." I nearly blew my top with her and practically ordered her to let the doctor examine her. She reluctantly agreed after much harsh whispering of dissent. The doctor told her she had a liver infection. I distinctly remember thinking, "God, when is this all going to end?" and then immediately pushed the thought from my head. Susie's health was taking a real battering, a person with less will-power and resolve would have given up long ago, but Susie took the news on the chin, so to speak. She was still desperately weak but we took some day trips with Evan and Mary and returned to the doctor a few days later.

He had only bad news, the test results were the same as in Nairobi, positive! Two separate tests, two separate laboratories, two identical results. For me, it seemed pretty conclusive, but Susie and I talked long and hard about how she might have contracted the disease in the first place. She was not convinced that the tests in Nairobi and Harare were conducted under the most stringent of conditions. Gradually, she began to convince us both that maybe the test results were still wrong and as soon as we got home, she would go directly to her old hospital St. Thomas' in London for better and more accurate tests. Having decided on this course, we both felt better and more positive about the whole episode.

In the meantime, we took a trip down to Victoria Falls. It never ceases to amuse me whenever I read about how the explorer, David Livingstone "discovered" the falls, failing to mention the people who had lived in that area for generations. They are of course, a magnificent spectacle and we were there at the right time of year, the rainy season, to see them in full flow, right along the length, from Devil's Cataract to the double rainbow at Rainbow Falls where the Zambezi continues as a river.

In 1989, travellers only went to Victoria Falls to see the falls, but these days, there's a whole industry built up around things to do at the falls. Rafting, bungee jumping, helicopter rides, micro-light flights, gorge swinging, walking safaris, it's all there if you want it, but back in 1989, there was little or nothing of that available.

We had flown down from Harare and were due to leave Victoria Falls at around 4-45pm one particular day. During the trip, I had been saving some of the more interesting coins from the places we had visited and had at least one coin from each country. As we were so close to Zambia, I thought it would be a good idea to pop across the border into the nearest town of Livingstone. I had heard they had a decent museum there with much of it dedicated to David Livingstone. He was after all, a very significant figure in the history of the region, and I wanted to see the display to find out more about the man and the area; and of course, I could get some more coins to add to my collection. I was about to have my second, and far more serious brush with African authority.

One of the main activities for the local population in Victoria Falls, was to trade for souvenirs in the markets and on the roadside. There was a thriving barter economy and I knew where there was a lovely African carving that I could barter for with a pair of running shoes I no longer wanted.

Susie was initially going to come with me to Livingstone, but part of the way towards the border, she said she didn't feel too well and instead of coming along, would wait for me at the Victoria Falls hotel. I had packed the running shoes into my day-sack and would go and see the trader on my way back to the hotel.

The border crossing was routine for Africa, with much examination and scrutinisation by the official, who took his responsibilities extremely seriously. Zambian and Zimbabwean citizens crossing between the two countries had no problem, but nothing would rush these guys as they pored suspiciously over a white man's passport. Remember that Zimbabwe was, and still is governed by Robert Mugabe, no friend of the whites and Zambia was at that time, ruled by Kenneth Kaunda, an out and out marxist whose administration was paranoid about South African spies. Once everything was seen to be in order with my passport, the official took up the stamp he had been caressing lovingly, and with blinding speed, thumped the stamp onto the ink pad two or three times making it jump around on the desk and placed an entry stamp with a resounding crash, onto a page already crowded with other immigration stamps. The fact that there were lots of empty pages where his stamp would not obliterate others, didn't seem to occur to him. Once through the border controls, I took a taxi into Livingstone and got dropped off at the museum. The taxi driver seemed a decent guy, so I arranged for him to pick me up at the museum at 1pm.

It was about 10-30am when I got into the museum, and I left it at about 11-30am. It was obviously too early for the taxi, so I decided to take a walk along the main street and round the back of the town, where I figured there would be a market.

The first thing I noticed, was that the buildings were all old-colonial style, with wide verandahs. The main street itself was very wide and split into a dual-carriageway. The reason for its great width was so that ox-drawn carts of the colonial era, could turn around. However, the main thing I noticed about Livingstone, was that I was the only white person I could see on the streets. I'm sure there were others there, but at that time, I could not see another white face. I wasn't overly concerned about this, but it was noticeable. I of course, stood out like a sore thumb! As I wandered up the main street, I noticed people were looking at me, but didn't pay the slightest attention. I was more than used to this by now, having travelled through China and India.

At the top of the main street, where the buildings petered out, I turned around and looked back down the length of the main street, and decided to take a quick photograph of the street as a momento. I took one photo, but thought the camera hadn't wound on properly, so took another and then popped the camera back into my bag and started to walk back down the main street.

About half way along, I was suddenly approached by an African man in the brightest blue uniform I had ever seen. If it hadn't been made of cloth, it would have been dazzling. He was quite an innocuous little man really, but demanded to see my passport. When I asked him why, he simply repeated that he wanted to see it and held out his hand. I still didn't give it to him, but took a casual look around me and saw very plainly that I had been surrounded by four other males in badly fitting suits. This was probably why the uniformed official had a nasty attitude. I really didn't like the look of these guys, and so, took out my passport and reluctantly, gave it to the official. He examined it and then said that I was to go with him. "Why?" I asked, but didn't get an answer. Instead, the other four began to crowd into me and I was hustled along the street after the security man. Other people on the street were very definitely getting out of the way of these guys and the white man they were escorting. Maybe they knew something, maybe they had seen it all before. I was now a little concerned.

I was taken to a building down a side street, and on the way, I passed a notice, which stated, "No Photography." This sign was in the side road and I hadn't seen one on the main street. However, now I knew what the problem was, I was confident I could sort it out quickly and be on my way. Having talked my way out of trouble in Kenya over the photo on the dockside, I didn't think these guys would take a photo of a street too seriously! That may well have been the case had the security officer not ramped it up a bit.

The security man and the others gabbled away to each other in their own language, not allowing me to say anything. Eventually, one of them took hold of my arm and began to push me out of a gate. I pushed back in protest, but was immediately surrounded again by the pack! Best just to go with the flow for now, I said to myself, and then found I was on my way down to the local police station. I was pushed onto a bench and made to sit. I still had all five of them with me, and my repeated demands to be told what was going on, were met with stoney silence. Only on one occasion, did one of them actually tell me they were waiting for a senior officer. I was now beginning to become very concerned. I looked at my watch and noticed it was about 1230. I asked one of the guards to phone the Victoria Falls Hotel and get a message to Susie, which they point blank refused to do.

When I got up off the bench, I was told to sit down, which I didn't. I had my hands in my pockets, and was told to take them out, which I didn't. One of the men in suits shoved me roughly back onto the bench. We weren't getting along too well, and it was getting worse by the minute. I repeatedly asked what was going on and they repeatedly said nothing!

Eventually, after about half an hour, a black male sauntered down the steps to the foyer. He had a quick conversation with the other men and looked completely unconcerned about anything. I remember he was dressed in blue jeans and black plastic shoes. No introductions were made, and I was then escorted up the stairs and taken into an office, where I sat on one side of a massive desk with a name plate, across from the same man with the plastic shoes. I shall never forget his name, Superintendent Muchimba! Behind me, were ranged the four goons in cheap suits, all seated in a row, but no sign of 'blue uniform'.

Now began my interrogation! Muchimba asked all sorts of questions, including where I lived, who I was with, where was Susie, how much money I had, how much had I paid for the trip, what was I doing in Zambia etc etc. The questions were repeated over and over in a random order, Muchimba hoping that I would trip myself up. I, however had nothing to hide and so answered all his questions politely and firmly.

My camera had been confiscated at the previous building and now sat on the desk between Muchimba and myself. I told him I realised why I had been brought in and apologised for taking a photograph of the street, but emphasised, it was just that, a photo of a street. I explained that I was a serving police officer in England and pointed out that my occupation was written on the front page of my passport. In those days, I still had the old fashioned blue UK passport with the personal details, including occupation, written by hand. I tried to convince Muchimba that as a serving police officer, I was not about to do anything intentionally illegal in a foreign country. What had happened was a mistake, for which, I was extremely sorry. I was praying that he didn't ask to see my warrant card, which of course, I didn't have because I had in fact, resigned from the police and was no longer serving. If he had asked to see it, I would have said that I wasn't allowed to take it with me on such a long trip and that he would have to take my word for it. I wasn't that confident about this strategy, but mercifully, he didn't ask to see it.

All through the interrogation, I had been looking anxiously behind me as my passport was being passed along amongst the goons, any of whom could simply have made it disappear. I began to realise I was in very serious trouble with these guys, and without my passport, I was sunk. It struck me that at no time had my name been written down anywhere, and the only record of my being in Zambia was in my passport, which at that time, I did not have!

Then came the crunch question! "Have you been to South Africa?" asked Muchimba. I had my answer ready as I was expecting the question sooner or later. "No", I answered truthfully, "we are going home to England after Zimbabwe", I lied. Muchimba repeatedly asked the same questions about South Africa and my intentions, changing only the order in which he asked them. He also asked whether I, or any of my or Susie's family had any connection with South Africa. I was now lying to just about every question he was asking; one slip on my part and I would have been caught out, with dire consequences.

The Apartheid regime was still in operation in South Africa at that time, and fortunately, no visa was required for UK citizens. Consequently, nothing of the sort appeared in my passport. There was nothing to indicate our intention to go to South

Africa, he would have to believe me or not. Time was getting on, and I was looking anxiously at my watch, which Muchimba picked up on. I told him I had a flight out of Victoria Falls back to Harare at 1645 that day, and that Susie was waiting for me. I told him she was very ill, and would be desperately worried by now. When I asked him to arrange a phone call to the hotel, he again refused.

Instead, he called in the security guard with the bright blue uniform and asked him what he knew about me. His reply almost knocked me off my chair! He told Muchimba that he had been approached by several members of the public, who had seen me walking around the streets of Livingstone taking pictures of military vehicles! I remembered that I had seen a type of jeep parked on the street when I took the photograph, but hadn't registered its significance. However, what the security man told Muchimba was a bare-faced lie. I jumped up out of my chair and shouted into his face that he was a liar.

I realised that my situation had just become a lot worse. If he could tell such a bald lie, anything was possible with these guys! I was dragged off him and shoved roughly back onto my chair. I picked up the camera off the table, tossed it to Muchimba and told him that he could check the film and see that I was telling the truth and the guard was lying, hell, he could even keep the damn camera, just let me go! Now, I was getting desperate to get out of there!

My interrogation then continued with my views on the apartheid regime in South Africa, which I of course, denounced in no uncertain terms; no, I had no friends there, no, I had no relatives there, no, I had no business there, no, I would definitely not be going, the same questions over and over. I was concentrating very hard on my answers, aware that one slip would be disastrous for me.

Eventually, the questioning stopped, and I was taken into another room, again without my passport. I tried to keep calm, but my nerves were jangling, I was desperate to get my passport back, without it, I was "persona non grata." At that time, my situation seemed to be getting worse by the minute. I knew my fate was being discussed in the other room and there wasn't a thing I could do about it.

The time was now about 3-30pm. Even leaving right now, I was never going to get back to Victoria Falls in time for my flight. About 10 minutes later, I was called back in to see Muchimba. He threw me my passport and simply told me to get out of Zambia. "With pleasure", I said, and then went on, "as you've held me here for so long on the word of a liar, can I get a lift to the border?" Nobody answered me and I took that as a no!

I dashed out of the building, determined to get as far away from Livingstone in as short a time as possible. I had been wearing sandals up to that stage and after leaving the police station, I changed into the running shoes I was carrying, preparing for the 10k run to the border. I had the idea of getting a taxi, but was prepared to run for the border if necessary.

As I got to the top of the road and turned onto the main street, there was an urgent hooting of a car horn. I looked over the road, and saw the taxi driver who was supposed to meet me outside the museum. He turned his car around and stopped alongside me. "Where were you?" he asked. I told him I had been held at the police station on some trumped-up charge or other and had just been released. He asked if I needed to get to the border. "Do I ever?!" I said. He simply told me to get in the back and off we roared. I had to get in the back, as he already had a fare sitting in the front! I can't remember ever being in the back of a car travelling so fast and being so scared the whole thing would disintegrate around me! We rattled and bounced our way to the border in a matter of minutes and with the help of the taxi man, whizzed through the Zambian side and then down to the Zimbabwe end. Here, the taxi driver would have to leave me. I shook his hand and thanked him warmly. After the episode in the police station, I was grateful for any sign of friendliness and help. I pressed all my remaining Zimbabwe dollars into his hand. At that time, Zimbabwe dollars were the currency to have and I had just given him, what he would think was a small fortune.

I ran into the border control and immediately saw it was full! Under ordinary circumstances, I would be ashamed of what I did next but at this time, I figured it was necessary. I ran to the head of the queue and barged my way in, all the while shouting "Sorry, sorry, got a flight to catch, sorry!"

The immigration official was none too impressed, just as the others in the queue were not impressed, but he did process me quickly and wave me through with that curious sideways flick of the head that African immigration officials seem to have. (I often wonder if they get special training in head-flicking!) I zipped through customs and ran into Zimbabwe and safety!

I had about 30 minutes to collect Susie from the hotel, get our bags brought over from our hotel, and get to the airport and check-in. I ran up the path to the Victoria Falls hotel and ran into the lounge where I knew Susie would be waiting. She was there, pacing up and down, her face indicating she was becoming more than mildly panicked! She of course was desperate to know where I had been and I was just desperate to get to the airport. "I'll tell you later," I said. We had packed our bags that morning and Susie had arranged for them to be brought to where she was waiting, but they were late coming over from our hotel and so we jumped into one of the Victoria Falls hotel courtesy cars and sped off to intercept them on their way to us. By this time, the hotel bus had left for the airport with other passengers. Our bus had left much earlier. This was another bus for a later flight.

We saw the car from our hotel coming towards us and managed to stop it and unload our bags. We then sped off again in pursuit of the bus and managed to stop that as well. We threw our bags up onto the bus, got in, drove off, ran into the terminal, just made the desk in time, checked in and flew out.

As the plane took off and climbed steeply, I noisily sucked in a huge lung-full of air and exhaled slowly and deliberately. Susie had realised long before that something was wrong. During the flight, I told her what had happened, and she too let out a huge lung-full of air.

Neither of us however, realised the true potential of what had happened to me until we got back to Harare, and I recounted the tale to Evan and Mary. Up to that point, I hadn't really thought about the "offence" for which I had been detained. I knew it had to do with photographs and I knew the guard had lied about my activities. I knew they took their security seriously, but Evan and Mary shook me to the core by explaining that I had, in effect, been arrested for spying! Being white, my interrogators would have assumed that I was working for the South African government. Being led by a Marxist, Kenneth Kaunda, the Zambian government was a fervent disciple of the regime in place at that time in Soviet Russia. How ever they dealt with their dissidents, Zambia did the same; how ever they dealt with their criminals, Zambia did the same; how ever they made people disappear, Zambia did the same. Evan and Mary told me about a friend of theirs whose son had been arrested in Zambia, under exactly the same circumstances, taking an innocent photograph on a street. They received no news of him at all, they had no idea what had happened to him. After prolonged and difficult enquiries with the Zambian authorities, their son was eventually located a year later, in a mental asylum. This was a favourite method of the Soviet authorities, when wanting to make some person or other disappear.

We talked about it for a long time, and came to the conclusion, that the only reason I had got out was the fact that I had "police officer" written in my passport, and that I had convinced them I was still serving! Had I been to South Africa, I would never have been allowed to leave. Having no written record of my being in Zambia at all, the authorities would have had no difficulty whatsoever in hiding the fact I had been detained and imprisoned there. Thinking back on this episode, I shudder to imagine what would happen under the same circumstances today, with no occupation written into my passport and nothing to support my story. A little bit of creative thinking, lying through my teeth and exaggeration certainly saved me that day.

Whilst we were staying at Victoria Falls, we had seen the wonderful old-style train carriages that were still in use between Zimbabwe and South Africa. Despite what one might have read in the press about the vilification of the apartheid regime in South Africa, the fact remained that several land-locked countries surrounding the republic, most notably Zimbabwe, relied upon the vast road and rail infrastructure of South Africa in order to export and import goods through her ports.

At that time, Zimbabwe was a major producer of wheat for bread, so much so in fact, the country was called the "bread basket of Africa". Unfortunately, not so today. Robert Mugabe was constantly haranguing the apartheid government in South Africa, whilst all the while trading with that same country for transport of its goods to deep-sea ports. These rail links also provided a cheap and easy way to travel to the republic from neighbouring countries, in some degree of comfort.

The carriages were something out of the old colonial days, plush seating, comfortable beds in the sleeper compartments and lots of wood-panelling. We decided to take the train down to Johannesburg, not really caring how long it took. We travelled through Botswana, down to Gabarone, where we changed trains and entered South Africa through Mafeking. One of the first sights I had of South Africa was watching two plain clothed security guys crouching behind a building, with pistols drawn. At that time, the country was fighting a bush-war in what was then, South West Africa (Namibia) and having to contend with severe unrest in local townships, as well as having to protect her borders. The reasons were all the same, freedom and equality for all the nation's non-white population.

At the time, I was not the least bit interested in the politics of South Africa, I simply wanted to see the country described in various travel documentaries as stunning and beautiful. However, as soon as we entered South Africa, I realised that we were not going to be able to escape the impact that apartheid had on its victims. The first time we encountered it was on the train from Mafeking.

I had requested and paid for a compartment to ourselves, which was granted by the train company. Before we left Mafeking, a black man and his wife attempted to seat themselves in our compartment. I blocked his way in and told him that the compartment was reserved for us, which it was. He went off muttering something about getting the guard, and returned a short while later with the conductor, who was Asian. The black man tried to persuade the conductor to allow him and his wife into the compartment, even though they didn't have the right tickets. When the conductor refused, the black male started to accuse me of being racist and that, being white, I thought I was "superior" to him and should have a compartment to myself. The conductor was much more reasonable and jumped to my defence. Eventually, the black male and his wife, were seated in the next door compartment, along with about four others which, according to the conductor, is where he should have been anyway.

I found this little episode, rather unsettling and began to get nervous about what else we would experience in South Africa. No one can be in any doubt as to how much abuse and discrimination the blacks and Asians suffered in the apartheid years, but that did not give this man the right to demand something he was not entitled to, simply because of his colour.

The second time we encountered the "system" was when we arrived at Johannesburg main train station. It would be true to say that blacks and other ethnic workers were the main users of the train system. Hence, when our train pulled into Johannesburg, the vast majority of passengers were black and Asian. Susie and I just naturally followed them to wherever the ticket barrier was going to be. I remember thinking there were an awful lot of them and we seemed to be the only white faces around. (remember Livingstone!) People were staring at us and even then, it didn't dawn on us that we were going to the wrong place.

When we got to the barrier, we were told off by a black ticket collector for using the "Nie Blanc" exit and not the "Nie Schwarz" (No Whites and No Blacks respectively). It seemed a little incongruous to me that, in a society, which forcibly separated blacks and whites to the detriment of blacks, we were being told off for accidentally going against the regime by one of the people suffering most under it!

The most cryptic way we came across of discriminating against the blacks was when we pulled up to an hotel somewhere in the south of the country. There was a sign on the wall, which read, "Non International". We puzzled over this for a while, thinking that it may be just for local people and then I went inside to enquire whether we, as British travellers would be able to stay there. "Oh, yes" the lady said, "that sign just means no blacks!" We thought about not staying at this place, then figured that any hotel or hostel in the area was likely to adopt the same policy, and so, we swallowed a bit of pride and booked in for the night.

Susie and I stayed for seven wonderful weeks, exploring the whole of South Africa, east to west and north to south. Susie's health had improved dramatically over these weeks, mostly due to the fact that we were eating good and wholesome food, were relaxed and getting plenty of exercise, walking on beaches that stretched for miles, swimming in the sea and walking up and down hills, or Kopjes as they are known there. Incredibly, during the entire time we were in South Africa, Susie suffered not one day of illness, a real blessing for her! We had stayed with David's brother Bob, his wife Helen, (now sadly deceased) and their three wonderful daughters, Lisa, Samantha and Phillippa who all lived in a large house in the Randpark Ridge area of Johannesburg.

One of the biggest disappointments for me, was our visit to the legendary site of the battle of Rorke's Drift, made famous by the film "Zulu". When we eventually found the place along an old dirt-track, there was very little to suggest that the battle had even taken place. The old storehouse had been replaced with a new shop, which was predictable I suppose, and the only evidence of the old storehouse was in a tiny corner of the new shop where part of its foundations was visible through a glass screen. A small innocuous notice proclaimed that the half a dozen or so bricks we were looking at, was in fact, part of the old storehouse and garrison. There was nothing else there. I even stood outside and tried to get a feel of what it must have felt like to be a part of the British force facing thousands of Zulu warriors, attacking time after time. There was no notice giving any details, there were no books on the subject, no signposts, nothing to give the place an atmosphere, except the old cemetery. It was overgrown with weeds and in desperate need of some T.L.C. but you could still read some of the headstones.

In complete contrast to this place however, was the site of the preceding battle at Isandhlwana when around 1200 British soldiers were attacked and slain by Zulu warriors. Here, there was a massive slate engraving in a small, but informative museum showing the positions of the British force left behind by Lord Chelmsford when he took his main force to reconnoitre the enemy's positions. Nearby, was a memorial to the fallen Zulu warriors. In addition to the museum, were hundreds of stone cairns on the battlefield itself, depicting where various British units stood and died fighting the Zulu army of around 20,000 men. It is still an imprisonable offence in South Africa, to remove any article from this site, be it a stone, a bullet casing, a piece of rusting iron, anything.

The most remarkable aspect of the site though, was the incredible, emotive atmosphere one experienced by simply standing and looking around. The area is remote and largely silent. With no invasive noise to disturb the imagination, standing there with eyes closed and mind free to wander, the noises of death and battle were all too easily heard.

We also visited the site of the Battle of Blood River, where "voortrekkers" fought with thousands of Zulu warriors. Whilst we were there, I noticed a small African boy beckoning us over to where he was standing on the other side of a wire fence. He was selling models of buffalo he'd made from the mud of the river. I bought two models from him, giving him his asking price of around 3 Rand. He was quite a pathetic sight, dressed only in grubby shorts and shirt, but he had such an engaging smile and although, the models didn't really look like buffalo, his enterprise deserved success. I still have the models.

Eventually, our time in South Africa came to end, and with it, the end of our trip. There was however, to be one more adventure, or should I say, a marvellous stroke of luck.

From Johannesburg, we planned to fly to Amsterdam for a few days in order that we could just sort out last minute bags and prepare ourselves for what was promised to be an emotional reunion with our relatives, especially for Jane and Susie. I don't think those two had ever spent so long apart from one another, and I know Susie missed Jane desperately.

We landed at Schipol airport, just outside Amsterdam at about 6am on a Saturday morning in April 1989. From the airport, we took the train into the city, arriving at about 7-30am. Where accommodation is not pre-booked, the Dutch have a curious system of hotel booking. Each traveller or party has to attend the tourist centre opposite the train station and book accommodation directly through them. It was not possible simply to approach a hotel and ask for a room.

The tourist office is directly opposite the train station. I wandered across to the office when we arrived and found it shut. There was a notice on the door stating that it would open at 9am, and so, coffee and croissants were the order of the day for breakfast. At about 0850, I thought I would go back over and wait by the door, to be one of the first in. The waiting room in the station was unfortunately placed where we had no view of the Tourist Office, and so I was completely unprepared for the hundreds of young tourists crowding into the office and outside around the doors. Unbeknown to us, the office had apparently opened early due to the large number of people waiting outside. Not only were they all young, but they were practically all British and all wearing the fashionable black clothes of the time; from the air, it must have looked like a giant ink-spot! The only thing I could do was get into one of the six queues of tourists snaking out onto the pavement, all waiting to speak to a receptionist on the desk at the end of the queue. I realized that I was going to be in the queue for a very long time. Susie had wandered across with our bags and was now waiting outside in the spring sunshine.

It was our intention to book a double room with an en-suite bathroom somewhere in the centre of Amsterdam, near to or on a canal. Unfortunately, that was also the intention of absolutely everyone else in the place. As I got closer to the desk, I could hear that people were being allotted rooms out at Schipol airport, the supply of rooms in the centre having dried up. It didn't look like we were going to get our wish to stay by the canals.

With nothing else to do but watch the crowds around me, I noticed that, on at least two or three occasions, people had wandered down to the head of the queue I was in, to look at some poster or other, and then surreptitiously slithered into the queue ahead of all the rest of us, effectively pushing in! I was too far down the back of the queue to do anything about it, and anyway, everybody was going out to the airport. So what, if I had to wait just a few minutes longer to get seen to, I'd had to wait far longer in other queues around the world and I simply wasn't bothered. Perhaps the people at the front of the queue should have said something. I was also wondering just why this week-end was so busy, or perhaps it was always like this on a Saturday in Amsterdam. Susie later told me it was Easter week-end!

Anyway, I eventually got to the front; my turn! Like everyone else, I asked for my double room with en-suite in the centre of the city, and, like everyone else was told that the only accommodation left in Amsterdam was out at the airport. The young lady was just about to book my room at the airport, when her phone rang. She politely excused herself and picked up the receiver. She spoke some words in Dutch, thanked the caller and hung up. She then looked at me and said, "A double room has just come free in the city-centre alongside one of the canals, would you like to take that?" I stared at her for a second, then heard myself saying, "But does it have an en-suite bathroom?" She stared back at me for an even longer second and then I remembered where I was, at the head of a queue of people, all trying desperately to get anything in the city centre, with or without a bathroom! Not wanting someone to grab it over my head, I shouted, "I'll take it, I'll take it."

And so, Susie and I ended up at a lovely little hotel, right on the canal side, with the bathroom right next-door to our room. Apparently, what had happened was that a young man had arrived to take up his booking and then promptly fallen down the stairs, breaking his leg. The hotelier had telephoned the tourist office just at the moment I had reached the counter, not only that, he phoned the booking clerk I was dealing with. There were five others he could have chosen. However, the most incredible aspect to me was that, had I been one place back, or one place ahead in the queue, or if all those people hadn't pushed in, or at least one less person had pushed in, or one more, I wouldn't have been in the exactly the right place at exactly the right time.

We left Amsterdam two days later on a Monday, and flew our last leg to Heathrow. At Schipol airport, I bought Susie a small gold bracelet as a momento of our trip and then we girded our loins to face the relatives waiting for us at Heathrow. We knew it would be emotional and we weren't disappointed.

As soon as Susie poked her head around the corner of the arrivals screen, there was shriek and a scream that could only have come from Jane. The two of them fell together and hugged and kissed each other for all their worth. My mum and dad were there, David was there and, bless their hearts, so were Chris and Karen, our friends from Biggin Hill. It was an incredibly emotional time, even for me. The trip was over, we had done it, we were safe, we were back home, and I was being greeted and fussed over by the people I loved most in this world.

Looking back on the trip now, I am not at all amazed at how much I remember of it, it was a fantastic time. What I have written here is but a small portion of those memories. The experience really was "once in a lifetime."

Chapter 19

After the initial euphoria of our arrival home had died down, one of the first things David said to me was, "Enjoy your day off tomorrow, you're working on Wednesday!" I had telephoned David from Bob's house in Johannesburg and explained that I would be applying to re-join the police, but that the application was likely to take a few months. I needed to pay the mortgage and the food bills etc, and so, was in need of a job. I had asked him to look out for a suitable job for me, just until I got back into the police. At that time, David was deputy Treasurer for the UK arm of General Electric, based over in Kingston-upon-Thames. He had approached a lovely guy by the name of Bill Cobb in his office and apparently there was a space for me there doing odd jobs around the office. They had recently "let go" of their maintenance man and needed someone to step in at short notice. David thought this would be ideal for me. He explained that it would only be temporary, a few weeks perhaps, but at least it was work. The next day, I went back to our house in Biggin Hill to collect my tools and on Wednesday morning, I pitched up at David's office.

David was there with Bill and one other man, whom I think was senior to them. They asked me a few questions and then went into a sort of huddle, occasionally looking over at me and whispering among themselves. After a short while, Bill and the other guy approached and told me that the other maintenance man had been "kicked into touch" as unreliable. David had vouched for me and that was good enough for them. The senior man then explained that he had been paid £8-50 an hour and that they couldn't possibly pay me that amount. £8-50 was an hourly fortune in those days. Instead, the man said that they were prepared to pay me £8-00 an hour, was I interested? Was I interested!?! After picking my jaw off the floor, I readily accepted their generous offer, after which David said I should have gone for £8-25 an hour.! "David" I said, "I would have been happy with £4 an hour!"

I started work that very morning, convinced that I would only be there for a couple of weeks. It turned into two years! After the first few months, I was told that I wasn't really needed any more, and so left the company, only to re-join on a part-time basis when Bill phoned me to say that they did in fact need me. I was always swamped with work when I got there and would work till about 10pm trying to get everything done. There were shelves to put up, take down or both, desks to repair, chairs to repair, door handles etc etc. After I re-joined the police, I was even placed on a retainer basis, and they would call me when they needed me, but that I would be paid a certain amount even if I wasn't needed. I should have told the police about this extra work as "a business interest", but somehow, never got round to doing it. Eventually, after helping G.E. move to different offices on two occasions, Bill told me that my services were reluctantly being dispensed with, I was really, really no longer needed. The writing had been on the wall for some time, and I was simply waiting for the news. I'd had a good run and thoroughly enjoyed my time at G.E. especially working for Bill Cobb, a true gentleman!

The other thing that happened as soon as we got back, was that Susie went straight to St. Thomas' hospital for more blood tests. She immediately found work as an agency nurse, and in the meantime, all we could do was wait for the results. European health services are far more advanced than those of Africa and Susie's blood was sent to clinics around Europe. I was working in G.E. one day and phoned Susie from there. She immediately told me she had received the results of her tests in a letter from the hospital. She was negative, she did not have a terminal illness! The relief that flooded my emotions was indescribable. Imagine what was happening in Susie's head! We had agreed that we would meet at Jane's house that evening anyway, and she would explain everything to me then.

I remember we were in the kitchen of Jane's house as Susie explained what had happened abroad. Apparently, in a clinical test, previously run on 1000 people from Fiji, every one of them was apparently reported as having a low white cell count. This was virtually impossible, and so more tests were conducted. As a result, a virus was isolated, one which suppressed the immunity capability of white blood cells. This virus was peculiar to Fiji where Susie had apparently picked it up and from that moment on, her white cell count was decreasing, along with her immunity from illness. The "positive" results we had received from Kenya and Zimbabwe were known as "false positives" insofar as for them, it couldn't have been anything else, they had no knowledge of this Fijian virus.

Jane had not been present when Susie was telling me this, but walked into the kitchen at some point near the end. It was practically impossible for those two not to be able to read each other's faces and Jane knew immediately that something was wrong. Susie then explained to Jane what had happened abroad and back at St. Thomas'. Jane promptly collapsed like a sack of potatos on the floor, closely followed by Susie and me. At that precise moment, David walked into the kitchen and found Jane, Susie and myself in tears with Susie and myself trying to console an inconsolable Jane. He naturally demanded to know what was going on, and when Susie told him, joined us on the floor. I had bought a bottle of champagne for the occasion and when everyone was calm and smiles had returned, I popped the cork for a very special celebration!

During my little break from G.E., I went to work for a stationery delivery company in South Norwood as a driver, again on a temporary basis whilst waiting for my start date back with the police. All I had to do really was to learn where certain premises were on a particular route and deliver their stationery. I went in one day and was asked if I was available to deliver some packages to Warrington in the north of England, the next day and then deliver something in South Wales on the return trip. I jumped at this chance as I could stop off and see my friends Annette and Bill in Biddulph, whom I hadn't seen in a couple of years. I picked up the van and parcels the next day and got to Annette's late that same evening. As we were having dinner, she casually dropped in to the conversation that she had bumped into Anne, my ex-girlfriend from school. I hadn't seen her for years and Annette told me that she was living in Evesham with her two children but had recently split up from her TV weatherman husband. She had been visiting her father, who still lived in Biddulph. I asked how she was etc etc, and that was that, or so I thought!

I rejoined the police in September 1989 and was posted back to Croydon police station, with the same shoulder number (PS12ZD), on the same team and at the same rank. It was almost as though I hadn't been away! So much for the dire warnings I had been given before I resigned!

Over the following year, my relationship with Susie changed. The canyon trip, her departure in 1986, her return in 1987, the world trip, had all had an effect on our marriage. We were still together, but it had changed inexorably. I realised it, but was still trying to make things work. If the marriage was to be on a different basis than before, then so-be-it, as long as Susie stayed committed, something which I had begun to doubt.

Initially, after our return, Susie did agency nursing but later started HIV counselling, something she had wanted to do for some time. During this period, I got the distinct impression that I was being left behind. Her enthusiasm for her work was becoming all consuming, yet again, but this time it was different. There was a remoteness about her; she would spend periods away from home, eventually, during the week, renting a room in a house with two Iraqi girls. She would spend a lot of time in London visiting jazz clubs. She told me she visited one particular club so often, she helped with serving drinks at tables. I couldn't help but be concerned about these latest developments, especially the jazz club. It would be fair to say that my imagination began to run a little wild over what she was doing at these clubs and especially with whom she may have been doing it. When I voiced my concerns over the effect it was having on me and our marriage, she would say that I was welcome to come along and see for myself, but I knew the opposite was true. Still, I hung on to the hope that this was just another of Susie's phases, and that she would eventually see that I was waiting for her on the other side.

It seemed that all my waking time seemed to be spent trying to work out where my marriage was going. When Annette told me she had met Anne again, I began to wonder what she looked like now and began to think about getting back in touch. I suppose if I'm honest, I wanted to see her again, although at that time, not for any reason other than curiosity and for a chance to catch up. There was an awful lot of rubbish in my life at this time and meeting up with an old school friend, albeit an ex-girlfriend seemed a good, distracting idea. With the benefit of hind-sight however, this was probably not a good idea.

Anne and I did meet several weeks later and I have to admit that I found her as attractive then, as I had at school all those years ago. The fact remained however, that I was married to Susie and Anne did not enter into the equation. I think the difference from Susie's perspective would be that, whilst I was with her and trying desperately to hold on, she was rapidly drifting away from me and not making too much effort to hold on. She spent increasing amounts of time away from home, and really only came back on weekends. I remember I tackled her about it once, saying that I was not interested in having a "weekend wife" and that I wanted our marriage back. Susie appeared not to care about my "interests" and carried on regardless.

I had told Susie about Anne, how she was an old school-friend etc, but I think deep down, my ulterior motive was to try and send Susie a message. I wanted to say that this is what would happen if we drifted too far apart; she would find new friends and I would find new friends, each of us ultimately finding a new life without the other. Was this what she wanted? What I should have done of course was to sit down with Susie and talk about the whole situation, but I know now that I didn't because I was too afraid that the outcome would be that Susie would call it a day and leave for ever.

At one stage, Anne mentioned to me that she wanted to learn how to ski and take her children to the Alps. I was planning to go out and visit my ski-guide pal Nick in France anyway, and so told Anne that if she wanted to arrange her holiday around the time I was going, we could travel and ski together and I could help her with her lessons, be a sort of friendly face. We had a great week in Avoriaz, she and her children absolutely adored skiing (and still go regularly to this day), the weather was good and the snow was deep.

Avoriaz is set on a plateau and is accessed mostly by a cable-car. Anne stayed with her children in a hotel at the foot of the cable-car, whereas I was bunking on the Nick's floor in the main resort. She and I met only on the slopes during the day and we met only once for dinner, on the last evening before going home on the train. She came up to the resort from her hotel and we went out to a restaurant somewhere in the town. At the end of the evening, I escorted her down to her hotel in the cable-car. There was an obvious attraction between us. She understood my loyalty to Susie but that didn't stop her making her own feelings known. It was gratifying to know that someone else found me attractive, but she went to the hotel and I caught the cable-car straight back up to the resort and the loneliness of Nick's floor. Looking back now, going skiing with Anne probably wasn't the smartest move I could have made, but it was done in innocence and in the end, it made little difference to my overall situation.

Almost as soon as I had returned to Croydon, I was approached by an officer with the wonderful name of Valentine Murray, with a view to organising an expedition to walk across the three masifs of the Pecos de Europa mountain range in northern Spain. Apparently, nobody had done the entire walk, although I always doubted this, and Val was very excited about us doing it. I too, thought it a cracking idea, and so we set about gathering together a small team, which eventually turned into 12 of us.

We organised it so that there were a group of walkers and a back-up team who would meet us at various stages with supplies such as food, water and medical. Once that was done, we had to choose a charity to which, the money we raised through sponsorship would be donated. I suggested the Terrence Higgins Trust as Susie had become very involved with H.I.V. counselling. However, there was a bit of a crisis within the organisation at that time over funds, and we were told by our Chief Superintendent, that it wasn't suitable. Instead, he told us we would be doing it for the "Wellwoman Clinic" at the local hospital, the Mayday. This decision didn't sit too well with me as I was of the opinion that as we were doing the expedition, we should be the ones to decide which charity to support, and I knew that the staff at

Mayday hospital were very anti-police and took every opportunity to disrupt any enquiries we had at the hospital. However, that was the deal, Mayday Hospital or we couldn't have the special leave the Chief Superintendent was prepared to grant us.

We caught the overnight ferry from Plymouth to Santander, northern Spain in our vehicles loaned to us by one of our sponsors, and spent the first day sorting out gear and swimming in the icy waters of the Atlantic. The tidal currents are fierce along this part of the coast, as one of the back-up team found out when the tide sucked his false teeth clean out of his mouth! We then spent ten exhausting days walking up near vertical slopes carrying huge packs and slipping and sliding down treacherous scree slopes. I remember at least two of the guys dropped out through injuries and exhaustion going down these slopes.

On one of the days, we had to negotiate a narrow ledge, just about wide enough to accommodate one person. There was solid rock with an overhang on one side and a sheer drop for a few hundred feet on the other. This was a nightmare for me with my fear of heights, and the only way I could get across this ledge was by wearing my Beau Brummell style kepi to the side so that the flap shielded my view of the drop to my left. After that, the rest was easy, just hard slogging up the mountain side all day. We were overtaken by a group of young men about half way up and met them again at the top. We camped virtually in the same spot and shared some beers with them that evening. It turned out they were Special Forces soldiers just out for some recreation, walking up mountains for fun!! Actually, they congratulated us for getting to the top not long after them. Praise indeed!

We completed the traverse of all three masifs and eventually headed home to Croydon, fully satisfied with our achievement. When all the sponsorship money came in and expenses had been deducted, the figure totalled £10,000, which was handed over to the hospital by the Chief Superintendent at a small ceremony I didn't attend. There was no publicity, no pictures in the local paper, there wasn't even a mention in the police newspaper, "The Job". The hospital representative said thanks very much and that was that! I did wonder whether it had all been worth the effort, but decided it was, despite the attitude of the hospital towards police.

Since joining the police in 1974, myself and Susie had been friends with a fellow officer, Stuart and his wife Diane. They lived in Surrey, and I have to say, they seemed the ideal couple. They had a lovely house, two super little boys, they were both good-looking people and appeared to love each other to distraction. Unfortunately, it turned out that Diane was the archetypal, long-suffering wife of a philandering husband. Things went from bad to worse for Diane and Stuart, and eventually she called time on their marriage. Stuart went to live with a woman he had been having an affair with in the east end of London, but even she kicked him out in the end.

Susie and I tried to keep in touch with Diane and the boys, but after a number of years, she drifted away and I've not seen or heard from her since. I hope she is well and happy. Stuart, on the other hand, was always the one to try and keep in touch with us. He was a friend and although I disapproved of the way he had treated Diane, he had never done I or Susie any harm. For this reason, he was welcome in our house.

On one occasion, Stuart had asked if he could come down to visit and bring his new girlfriend. Of course, we said, we'd be delighted to meet her. They turned up and Stuart introduced a stunning-looking black girl. I shall call her Monica. We had dinner out on the patio at the back of our house and during the conversation, I asked Monica what she did for a living. She shot a glance at Stuart, who nodded for her to go ahead, and she told us she worked in and around the west-end of London. Not only that, Stuart told us he was living with her in her flat. A sort of loose association had developed between the two of them and when Stuart told Monica he had been kicked out of his flat in the east-end, she offered to put him up at her flat. There was an obvious sexual attraction between the two of them and Stuart jumped at the opportunity; a classic case of thinking with something other than his head!

A few weeks after his visit to us, Stuart's world came tumbling down around him, incidentally, having a devastating effect on my own relationship with Susie. You may remember that earlier in this narrative, I mentioned the vice section at West End Central police station. Stuart told me what had happened. The house he was living at had apparently been under surveillance, and as a result, he found himself suspended from duty and under investigation. As soon as he was relieved from duty, he telephoned me and asked if he could come and stay for a while, just till he got himself sorted out. Susie and I of course agreed. Despite his obvious shortcomings, Stuart was a friend in a bit of need.

At roughly the same time, another friend of mine George, had managed to get himself banned from driving for three months for speeding. He absolutely had to rely on his car to get him to appointments with his clients and without it, he was staring unemployment in the face. I happened to mention to George that Stuart was staying with us for a while and not working. He immediately saw the opportunity and suggested that Stuart might like to do some chauffeuring for him until his ban was finished. George had a Jaguar XJ as a company car and Stuart jumped at the chance, if only to keep active. The insurance for Stuart to drive was sorted out and all went well for almost the entire period, both parties being highly satisfied with the arrangement. His ban was virtually finished when, late one night, George phoned me to tell me that Stuart had crashed the Jaguar on the M6 Motorway on his way to visit Monica in Manchester where she had moved to after her flat was raided and she was arrested again. Stuart had no permission to take the car to Manchester and had, in effect, taken the car without consent, invalidating the insurance. Understandably, George was furious that Stuart had gone behind his back like this and I was embarrassed to say the least. George didn't press any charges against Stuart, although he could easily have done so. If he had, Stuart's career in the police would have been in even greater tatters than it currently was. I let the two of them make their own arrangements about the repair of the Jaguar, but needless to say, George never saw Stuart again!

Stuart was a highly personable and likeable man with a good sense of humour, with which he wooed the ladies. From the start, it was obvious he was highly motivated by sex. At training school, he had taken up with one of the female officers. I met her by chance many years later and she told me just how infatuated she had been with Stuart. He used to come into my room early morning, having just negotiated the underground tunnels between the two tower blocks housing the male and female students. These tunnels were out of bounds to students and were regularly patrolled by the Section House Sergeant. Stuart had spent most nights with this female officer, which I had no problem with, but I didn't understand why he had to come and tell me every time he stayed there. On one occasion he was bragging about how many times he had made love to the female officer that night and, as if in confirmation, took out his penis to inspect it. Unfortunately, he had got too near the radiator, which at that time in the morning was piping hot. He yelped as the tip of his penis touched the red-hot radiator. Apparently, the poor lad had a blister there for days, which put paid to his nocturnal adventures for a while.

I remember coming home from work one evening to find Susie and Stuart in the lounge, huddled around the open fire. Looking back now, there was nothing overtly wrong with how they were situated, he was lying on the floor propped up on one elbow facing her and she was sitting close to him on a pouffe. It just seemed unnatural, rather intimate. Everything appeared to be going wrong at that stage, Susie was drifting away, our marriage was in trouble, deep trouble and I was extremely worried for our future. There was a man living in our house who was no stranger to women. When I saw them together like that, a minor alarm bell rang off in my head. It was irrational really, but I had become so worried about our marriage that any little incident such as this was going to spark concern. However, that alarm rang only for an instant and I dismissed the thought almost as soon as it entered my head. I convinced myself that we were all good friends and why shouldn't they enjoy each other's company.

At some stage around this period, Susie had secured a position at the Charing Cross Hospital in London. In order that she didn't have to travel up there every day from Biggin Hill, she decided to find herself some digs, and started to lodge with two Iraqi girls in their flat during the week. By this stage, our relationship was looking ever more tenuous. I telephoned Susie on occasion at her flat, but I never visited. I felt that she was withdrawing from our marriage and in my own strange little way, I thought if I interfered with her life where she was staying, she would disappear altogether. I desperately wanted her back with me in our house and for our marriage to get back to what it used to be, but at the same time, she had to want to come home. I was not going to go cap-in-hand to her and beg.

Late one evening, my world collapsed. I received a phone call from Monica. By this time, Stuart had resigned from the police, left our house and had joined her in Manchester. At first, I thought something had happened to one of them, but then she related part of a letter which Susie had apparently written to Stuart, and following further conversation with Monica, I felt I had no option but to challenge both Stuart and Susie. I will not relate the specifics. I spoke to Stuart first. His reputation always preceded him and I caught him out in a lie fairly easily. However, it was when I listened to Susie's self-contradictory replies to my questions that I felt the life-blood of our marriage ebb away, but still I clung on.

The final act came a few weeks later, in early November 1990. Susie had come home for the week-end and I just knew that something major was about to happen. She had cooked a meal for us and as we sat eating, I turned to her and said, "You're going again aren't you?" She looked at me and slowly nodded her head. "Is it for good this time?" I asked, and she said it was. She didn't finish her meal, she simply left, and at that point, I knew my marriage was over, lost forever!

I couldn't feel devastated about this as I'd expected as much for a while. All the same, a huge sadness came over me, but no tears fell, I think that particular well was dry. I sat alone in the lounge for the rest of the evening and most of the night, feeling myself slipping into a massive void. This woman whom I adored and loved to distraction, who had forced me to change and declare my love but who had ultimately shunned me had walked out of my life, seemingly for good. I felt drained and exhausted, but when I did finally get to bed, sleep would not come. My mind returned time and again to that night immediately after our wedding when she had burst into tears for seemingly, no reason. Now, it was becoming clear that there had been a reason.

In the middle of the following week, Susie telephoned and asked if we could meet in a restaurant in London to discuss the situation. In my naivety, I thought maybe she wanted to talk about a reconciliation and was consequently looking forward to the meeting. We met in a small restaurant in St. Martins Lane, near Trafalgar Square. It was one of those places where the staff had jammed in as many tables as possible, at the expense of privacy. The table alongside us was only a matter of 18 inches away.

With the pleasantries out of the way, Susie then took me by surprise by starting to explain why she was not going to come home. She was talking in a cold and totally emotionless way. I knew it mattered to her to tell me and I think this was just her way of dealing with what she felt she had to do. There was a lot of noise, as is usual in a west-end restaurant, and Susie almost had to shout to enable me to hear what she was saying. Unfortunately, the couple on the next table could also hear what Susie was shouting. I listened to her, and all the while, was acutely aware that the next-door couple were listening to her as well. I could see the woman opposite me looking in my direction, and then guiltily looking away. Suddenly, a massive heat began to spread all over my body. It started in my lower legs and spread rapidly throughout my entire body. I became increasingly uncomfortable, but more than that, I became increasingly angry. It was becoming embarrassing to sit there and listen to Susie telling me, and the next-door table why she would not be coming home. Why did this have to be done in so public a manner, why couldn't we have met somewhere more private, but then, that was Susie, still going for centre-stage.

The heat became overwhelming and eventually I decided, rightly or wrongly that I simply wasn't going to put up with being treated in this way. I stood up, shoved rather than pushed my chair back, dug into my pocket and threw a £20 note onto the table. I told Susie to "pay the bill and keep the change", I was off! I picked up my coat and walked out of the restaurant, and out of Susie's life forever. As I walked out, I glanced over to her. The couple on the next-door table were both looking at me, along with a few others, but Susie had lit a cigarette and was just staring straight ahead, seemingly completely careless of the situation. She seemed a world away from the woman I had married.

That was the last time I ever saw Susie. I have spoken to her a few times on the phone when she has picked it up at Jane's house, but I have not seen her since I walked out of the restaurant. I suppose I could have simply called the whole tragic train of events to a halt much earlier, after our conversation about the letter. However, this was the woman I adored. I wasn't going to do anything to precipitate her leaving, I didn't want to have to wonder whether our relationship would have improved but for my calling a halt. That thought would have haunted me forever and I remain convinced I did the right thing by allowing her to make the decision.

According to my friends and colleagues at Croydon, my behaviour and attitude over the next few weeks and months became a little erratic, to say the least. A few people had a word with me, and eventually I got permission to take some compassionate leave and fly down to South Africa to stay with Bob and Helen, who were only too happy to have me there at this time. Before I went, I wrote a letter to Susie and gave it to Jane to read and then give to Susie. I had never written a letter like that before and everything just came out. It was directly from my heart. I didn't have to compose it, correct it or read it over and over. The words were simply flowing from my pen. I gave it to Jane, who read it and was sobbing her heart out by the end. Strangely enough, I don't remember one single word of that letter although it was probably the most important one I have ever written.

I flew back to England a week later and so desperately wanted to see Susie waiting for me on the other side of the barrier. She wasn't, Jane was. She told me nothing had changed, that Susie would not be coming home and how she wished that it was Susie waiting for me and not her. During the time I was in South Africa, Susie had attended the house and cleared out all her things. It took me a long time to be able to open her side of the wardrobe in our bedroom, and see the emptiness; it was almost a direct reflection of how I was feeling at that time.

Chapter 20

In August 1990, I had begun to study for my Inspector's exams. I always knew I would study for them and with Susie living with the two Iraqi girls, it seemed the ideal time. There comes a point in the study programme when you feel like giving up, and then having got past that barrier, there comes a time when you feel you have done too much work to give up. When Susie finally left in November, I had reached the second point and was determined to carry on regardless, although it took a monumental amount of willpower and concentration.

Christmas and New Year came and went, and then in January 1991, the first letter from Susie's solicitor arrived, declaring her intention to divorce me on the grounds of an "irretrievable marriage breakdown". I replied to that letter and added that I was trying to study for a major exam to be held in April 1991. I told the solicitor, that I did not wish to be disturbed until after my exam, at which time, I would deal with any and all paperwork. I told him I was not going to contest Susie's petition, but in the meantime, leave me alone! Another letter arrived from the solicitor, prompting the same reply from me. Susie was then on the phone asking why I hadn't supplied the information requested. I repeated to her what I had written to the solicitor and she then begged me not to waste time and not to make her wait the full five years, which was my option. She obviously wanted this divorce settled very quickly, and I began to wonder why. Yet another letter arrived, at which point, I phoned her solicitor and told him that if he sent any more, not only would they go straight into the bin unopened, but I would dig my heels in and make Susie wait, the full five years if need be. I told him to leave me alone until after April, adding that I didn't think that was unreasonable. No more letters arrived until I notified him that I was ready to deal with the divorce.

Not long after the divorce decree nisi had been granted, I came home from work one evening feeling pretty brutal. I sat for a long time on the sofa just staring straight ahead, trying to rid myself of the many thoughts going through my head. Suddenly, I knew what I wanted to do. I lit a fire in the grate in the lounge. Over the years, we had accumulated several albums of photographs and I retrieved all of them from the loft. I opened each one in turn and removed every photograph. When the fire was going nicely, I looked at each photo in turn before tossing each one individually into the flames. I then turned to the pile of photos we had taken during our world trip, over 1200 of them. No, I thought, I rather wanted to keep these and put them to one side. I then took out our wedding album from its box. It was just a plain white album with fancy covers and tissue fly-leaves. These photos I didn't look at, I simply removed them from the album and threw them into the fire. I had seen them so many times, I knew each one by heart. I watched the flames taking away the record of my marriage; I watched till the flames died down and the blackened remains spilled out onto the hearth. I then put the wedding album into the rubbish bin along with all the others. Contrary to what you may think, I have never had any regrets about burning these photos. It was as if I was drawing my line instead of having it drawn for me.

The Decree Absolute was granted in the middle of 1991. My respect for Susie had been sinking very gradually over the months since she left and started pressurising me to settle the divorce. The gradual sinking accelerated one day before it was all finalized. I received a letter from Susie in which she informed me that she had officially changed her name from Susan Robins to Susie Stephens, this being her grandfather's surname. Susie never knew her grandfather on her mother's side, he died early in his life, but Susie's mother Pam doted on his memory and I figured this probably had something to do with Susie's choice. There were a number of aspects about this which upset me. The letter was written in a very formal manner, as if I was some total stranger receiving a business letter. I remember thinking about and mourning the fact that our once loving relationship, had turned into something so sterile and empty. I couldn't understand why she was acting so cold and insensitively about the whole affair. She knew how it was slicing me into ribbons, yet she still insisted on ditching my name as soon as she could when she only had to wait a few more months until after the divorce was finalized. The most upsetting aspect though was thinking how my father would react. He adored Susie and she adored him. He was desperately sad about our divorce and so, knowing how much Susie's actions would have upset him, I never told him or my mother about her ditching the surname "Robins" in so insensitive a fashion. Did she not understand the effect that that would have had on dad? I think at that time, my respect level for Susie was at rock bottom.

That decline in respect turned to cynicism when David later came to visit me on his own. This was unusual because David had never come to visit me without Jane and the children, but I was glad to see him in any event. The reason for the visit became clear however, when he told me he was sorry to have to tell me, but Susie was about to re-marry. I was a little sad at the news, but not because I thought Susie would never get married again.

Since our return from the trip, Susie had seemed to reject her faith as a Christian, or at least large parts of it. She always loved going to her local fellowship meetings, the house-groups in the evenings and various other activities, which she seemed to abandon. Her pastor, Ray Lowe had written letters to her about his concerns for her faith which she also rejected. After her total embrace of the faith in her early years, total rejection seemed quite out of character. I had however, come to accept that Susie's ideals could change very quickly.

Even as a non-Christian, for me, the vows I took in church, were the cement that bound us together in marriage. I believed in them and I never doubted that Susie did too. Gradually, it seemed that Susie's move away from Christianity and then divorcing me, were not wholly unconnected. The only ground for divorce in the bible is marital unfaithfulness or desertion. As far as I knew, neither of us had been unfaithful to the other and I hadn't deserted her, therefore, there would be no grounds for divorce, according to the bible. I couldn't believe that a person who was so devoutly Christian could turn against her faith so suddenly. Now she was to re-marry soon after our divorce. Not only that, her prospective new partner just happened to work at the same hospital and was a Christian. Suddenly, the reason for all the pressure to settle the divorce early, became all too apparent. I learned later from a friend of hers that, following her marriage, she had come back to Christianity in a very "dramatic" fashion, as only Susie could manage. This completed the picture for me.

In my opinion, and I stress it is only my opinion, and maybe a cynical one at that, Susie's move away from Christianity enabled her to divorce me and re-marry with a clearer conscience. With all the divorce rubbish out of the way, Christianity comes back on the menu! If I'm right, and I have no hard evidence to support my theory, only intuition, this was quite simply, breathtaking arrogance and manipulation on her part. I may be completely wrong, but that's how the parts fit in my view.

My cynical views were reinforced about four years later. I was having a wonderful relationship with a German woman I had met in Africa. Her name was Sabine, and she had met with Jane, who obviously communicated the news to Susie. Up to that time, I was pretty unsettled and uncaring about most things but being with Sabine had brought some degree of stability to my life.

One day, a letter arrived on my door-mat and I recognised the writing immediately, Susie's. The letter was asking me to forgive her for the "despicable" way she had treated me, which I didn't "deserve". It was the next sentence though, which really grabbed my attention. She asked my forgiveness and stressed that she was always amazed at how easily God had always forgiven her for the wrongs she had committed! She said it didn't seem to matter what she did, God always forgave her.

I got the distinct impression that not only had she waited until she thought I was settled with a new partner, and therefore would be more, shall we say, accommodating with my "forgiveness", but she was saying that if the Almighty could forgive her, then there was no reason I couldn't. I sat on the letter for about two years. Suddenly, one day, I felt the urge to reply. I simply told her that, yes, she had inflicted severe hurt and pain and that I would be able to forgive in time. "Meanwhile", I said, she had "broken my heart, for which you must answer to me, but you also broke your vows before God, for which, you must answer to Him." I don't know if she ever received the letter, but as Ray said, it didn't matter, my conscience was clear and I could move on.

As I write these words, I'm not sure that "forgiveness" is the right word, and in truth, I think a more accurate substitute would be acceptance. Susie became such a huge part of my life, having a profound influence on me; she altered my way of thinking and acting, forcing me to confront my many shortcomings. That said, I have often wrestled with the question of whether Susie ever really or indeed actually, loved me. I think not. However, I have always held the conviction that whatever Susie did to me, she did not do it from any sense of malice or desire to cause hurt and pain. Certainly, there were many things she could have avoided and she could have been more sensitive, but in ending the marriage, she did what she felt she had to do and unfortunately, I got burned in the process. I have to accept that. Insensitivity does not equate to malice. It would be different if I believed that malice and hurt were her driving forces, then I think "forgiveness" would be necessary, and probably not forthcoming.

One question that nagged me for a number of years after the break-up was, could I have done more to try and save my marriage? Indeed, could Susie and I as a couple, have done more to save it? Looking back on it now, I don't think there was any chance the marriage could have been saved. That doesn't necessarily mean that I think I did all I could. I remember being emotionally tortured at the time and all I could think of was "why was this happening?" I was completely caught up in the maelstrom of my emotions, clear thinking and problem-solving wasn't something I could do at that time. The reason why the question haunted me for years was that I later remembered the subject of the organization called Relate was mentioned, I think by Susie. "Relate" is the organization dedicated to counselling couples whose marriage is in trouble. It was mentioned once and then forgotten. Thinking back on it, it was such an obvious route to try and because I didn't insist on us going, I have to accept that it was perhaps, a lost opportunity. There have been many things in my life that I have beaten myself up about, and not trying "Relate" is one of them. That said, I truly feel now that the inevitable would only have been delayed.

Many questions about my relationship with Susie remain unanswered. I think that says more about me than anything else, my failings to find answers. I could have stayed in the restaurant that evening in St. Martin's Lane and listened to what Susie had to say, it would have provided a few answers, it's just that I didn't want to share those with the next-door table! I could have asked these questions at any time since, but I haven't and that poses one more question, why not? The answer is quite simply that I didn't want to risk hearing something I wouldn't like. I found the whole episode very traumatic and at times, devastating. Hearing something that I feared, would simply have added to the trauma. To this day, I still fear the answers and will not now ask any questions; maybe I will on my death-bed, when it won't matter quite so much. I can't get away from what happened, but it's history, it's gone and I've moved on. Equally, I'm quite sure Susie will not want to dredge up the past. She moved seamlessly into her new marriage, is happy and thriving. I wish them well.

Do I regret making that fateful decision at the statue to Henry Irving all those years before, and which led me to Susie? The answer, in respect to Susie, would have to be, yes! I told Susie from the beginning that I viewed marriage as a total commitment, not something to be cast aside in the event of boredom or with the onset of problems. It didn't seem unreasonable to me to expect the same from my partner. What I was saying to her was, please don't marry me if you feel unable to return my commitment to you. In accepting my proposal of marriage, she was reciprocating my total commitment to her. And that's why I felt betrayed! Had I not made that decision at Henry Irving, I would not have met Susie. Had I made a different decision, I would not have met the people of her family who have become close and life-long friends, but there again, I may well not have had to struggle so hard with my emotions.

Committing myself to another partner since Susie has been very difficult for me, and hasn't happened yet. For a long time, part of me was saying to Susie, "so you think I'm settled do you, well I'll show you I'm not and you're the cause". It was as if I was somehow getting revenge on Susie, showing her that she knew me not at all. This was partly the reason I could never commit myself to other women, beautiful women. I no longer think this way, but the demons of commitment, although much smaller, still lurk in the shadows. I am a work in progress!

Do I think Susie was ever unfaithful to me? It's an easy question to write here, but the consequences of the wrong answer could be devastating. That however, is not the reason I never asked the question. Susie's behaviour was often erratic and at times, disturbing but that does not translate to infidelity. I have always preferred to believe that she was not unfaithful. I am not so naïve as to think there are no doubts, but I no longer torture myself about them. Only Susie knows the real answer, and now, I don't think I want to know.

Having visited and re-visited this subject over the years that I have been writing this, I have come to the conclusion that the break-up of my marriage was as much to do with me as it was Susie, notwithstanding any outside influences, real or imagined. That is not to say I did anything drastically bad to warrant my being divorced. I simply think she married the wrong man. I think she probably figured that out on our wedding night, hence the tears, but struggled on with the marriage in any event. I desperately wanted it to work, but it wasn't going to be. I wish she had turned down my proposal of marriage, and I'm sure she does too.

I've painted a fairly bleak picture of my marriage, especially the last weeks and months, but I do try and remember the good points. After the shaky start in 1979, the years between 1980 and 1986 were wonderful and in fairness, Susie is entirely responsible for the emotional education I received. She not only showed me the joy of demonstrating love and affection, but also how important it is for the other person, something I had never even contemplated before. My family was never demonstrable, I don't remember my mother or father ever hugging me for the sake of hugging. Oh, I knew they loved me, but it was taken for granted. I never realized there was another way of doing it, until I met Susie. Whether or not she was making a supreme effort between 1980 and 1986 to make the marriage work, I will never know, but I will remember those years for the rest of my life. I was happy!

I continued to study for my Inspector's exam right up to the beginning of April. At that time, mum and dad were living in their bungalow in Coychurch, a small village just outside Bridgend in South Wales. Dad had not been well for a few days and had had breathing difficulties, His G.P. had sent him to the hospital for a check-up, and whilst they didn't think anything serious was wrong, they decided to keep him in overnight, just to be sure. I remember I was early-turn the following day at Kenley police station, a satellite of Croydon. At about 9am, I telephoned the ward at the hospital to find out how dad was and to ask if he was coming out that morning. The nurse I spoke to on the ward seemed flustered when I told her who I was, and asked me to hold on whilst she fetched the ward sister. I had had enough experience in dealing with people to recognise that something was wrong. A bad feeling descended on me. The nursing sister came on the phone and told me that my dad had died earlier that morning. It was completely unexpected and she thought it had been a heart attack, but wouldn't be sure until the post-mortem. I could tell that the poor sister hadn't been expecting my call as she asked if I had spoken to my mother, who had been informed immediately. It wasn't the best way to tell anyone that a loved one had passed away, but unfortunately, I hadn't given her a choice.

I was devastated and simply dropped the phone, cradling my head in my arms and sobbing my heart out. The station officer on duty, a female officer, saw my distress and immediately took over. She ushered me into an office and called my Inspector. He called back a few minutes later when I had gathered myself together, and told me to go to my mother. The police are excellent in this regard, everything possible is done to make sure the bereaved officer is looked after. I told him I would be alright to drive to Wales and left immediately. The date was the 6th April 1991, two weeks to the day before my Inspector's exam.

I called in at Jane and David's house on the way over to Wales to let them know. They had met my parents once or twice and thought the world of them, and, I knew that Jane would pass the news to Susie. She adored my father and he adored her, but the same relationship did not exist between Susie and my mother. I also knew that Susie would be very upset, but that was the least of my troubles.

When I got to Wales, mum was surrounded by, and being comforted by friends and relatives. She was obviously distraught and kept saying she couldn't believe he had gone. Mum and dad's best friends, Winnie and Harold Davies, who also lived in the village, were at the house along with all their family who lived nearby. I was especially glad that Victor was there. Not only are we good friends, he is excellent in a crisis and I knew I could rely on him for anything. Although our family and the Davies family are not blood relatives, we may just as well be, such is the bond between us. It was Victor who had telephoned Lynne in Australia and told her dad had died. The next few days were taken up with making all the arrangements for the funeral, collecting Lynne from the airport, revising my studies when and where I could, speaking to the vicar about readings etc etc.

It had always been dad's wish that he be cremated and then buried at sea with a Naval service. Over the last years of his life, he had started going to The Battle of the River Plate reunions and had made a number of friends amongst the old sailors. Mum had telephoned the chairman of the River Plate Association to tell him the sad news and ask how we go about contacting the Navy about a service for dad. He told mum that the Navy no longer conducted that type of service for ex-Royal Navy seamen, they only did it for serving men and women. We were desperately disappointed, but we agreed that we would not make a hasty decision about dad's interment, and thank goodness we didn't. The ashes would remain at the funeral director Mr. Watkins' parlour, until we had made a decision. He was quite happy to do this for us.

Lynne arrived a few days later and, bless her heart, she was visibly upset. Although she didn't see much of dad, she still loved him very much. She later came with me to see dad's body at the funeral parlour and broke down when she saw him. She had to have been very brave to do this as she admitted to me afterwards that it was the first time she had ever seen a dead body, "why did it have to be dad's?" she asked.

Before she arrived, mum and I agreed that neither of us wanted friends and relatives moping about the place after the funeral. We would rather have them celebrate his life than to be dark and miserable about his death. He had gone and that was that, let's remember him with glad hearts and be grateful he had been amongst us, we agreed. Lynne didn't necessarily see it that way however, and one day after returning from shopping, mum came in to the room where I was studying and told me to speak to Lynne about what we wanted for dad after the funeral. Apparently, Lynne thought we were treating it a bit like a "party." When I explained to Lynne how we felt, she was absolutely fine with it, she just didn't see it at first. It wasn't as if we would be dancing in the aisles or anything, we would simply remember him as he would have wanted us to. The usual tea and coffee would be available, but so would sparkling wine with orange-juice and beer and other wine. People would be encouraged to laugh and smile about dad.

The funeral service itself went without a hitch. I had decided, or rather the vicar decided that I should do a reading at the church. He had chosen a suitable passage for me, but I had also given the same passage to Victor with the instructions that he was to sit behind me. If he saw that I wasn't getting out of my seat at the service, he was to step in and deliver the reading. I managed it in the end, although it was a little croaky. The "wake" went as we wanted it to, everyone talking about dad and laughing and smiling. The time for tears could come later.

We finally laid dad to rest following a chance conversation I had with an ex-Naval seaman, who had only recently been discharged and joined the police. By the time I returned to duty at Croydon, most people knew about dad's death and many offered their condolences. This particular officer spoke to me one day, and I happened to mention to him that dad had been ex-Royal Navy, had served on H.M.S. Exeter in the Battle of the River Plate, had been awarded the D.S.M. and how sad mum and I were that we were now not able to give him his last wish, to be buried at sea. "Why's that?" the officer asked. When I told him the Navy no longer carried out these services for ex-seamen, he said "rubbish, here contact this man, he'll sort it all out for you and make the arrangements." He handed me the contact number for a Naval officer down at Portsmouth and I was overjoyed at the news. I telephoned the officer straight away and told him about dad and his service. He told me he could arrange for a burial-at-sea for dad provided I could supply his old service number identification, which I could. When I telephoned mum with the news, she burst into tears.

Over the next few weeks, the arrangements were finalised for the service to take place. We had been given very specific instructions about the casket. The ashes had to be fully encased in lead and the surrounding wooden casket had to have holes drilled into it to allow it to sink immediately. It wouldn't have been seemly to have a deceased's casket floating around like a piece of driftwood for a few minutes before finally going under!

I made one of my regular trips over to Wales and went to see the undertaker, Mr. Watkins. I think the best way I could describe Mr. Watkins and do him justice would be to say that he was one of the truest gentlemen I had ever met. Nothing was too much trouble, he was kind, attentive and respectful without being obsequious. When

I told him how I needed the casket, his eyes lit up as he had never had a request like this before. He simply said in his wonderful, soft Welsh lilt, that he would "do dad proud". He made us a beautiful casket finished in polished wood with the ashes completely sealed in a lead container. When it was all over, I contacted Mr. Watkins to ask for his invoice. He said he wouldn't be sending one, as it had been a pleasure for him to have made dad's casket and to deal with my family. My eyes get moist even now when I recall the generosity of spirit of this man.

Our instructions from the Navy stipulated that myself, mum and a maximum of four other mourners would be met at one of the entrance gates to the Naval Dockyard at Portsmouth. We were asked to be punctual. The other four mourners mum chose were of course, Harold and Winnie Davies, and my cousin Geofrey and his wife Pamela. The reader may remember that Geofrey was one of dad's nephews he had guided when his brother Mostyn died. Of all three of Mostyn's boys, Geofrey was the closest to dad, and mum wanted him there.

Mum travelled to Portsmouth with Harold and Winnie and they brought the casket. I met all five outside the gate and carried the casket through to the dockyard. Just inside the gate, we were approached by a naval security guard, who took our details. At that moment, I became aware of the crunch, crunch, crunch of a squad of marching men. As I looked around, I saw a Naval Officer in full uniform leading a further two ratings, also in full uniform, marching smartly towards us. They all crashed to attention in front of us and the officer saluted. He took one more pace, and came to attention again. He asked if we were the "party Robins?" to which, I replied we were. The officer snapped an order at one of the ratings to step forward, and the casket was immediately taken from me. There was however, nothing rushed or insincere about any of their actions. The officer was deeply respectful and the rating simply but gently, took the casket from me. The officer then bade us to follow him as he and the ratings turned smartly about, and we were escorted to a small dock with a launch tied alongside. Here, the officer introduced us to the Naval Chaplain. He gave a final salute and then he and the escort then turned about and marched away. They were absolutely faultless in their appearance, uniforms and demeanour.

The base chaplain greeted us on the dockside and explained that the boat was the Admiral's Barge and was always used for burial services. Dad's casket was carried on board by a rating and placed on a small platform to one side of the boat. It was then covered with a Union Jack flag.

We set off from the dock immediately and motored out into the harbour basin, and then out through the narrow entrance and exit. Just off Portsmouth, are three circular forts rising directly out from the waters of the Solent. They were built around 1865-1880 as a defence against French warships. The expanse of water in between all three forts is the official Royal Navy burial ground. Our trip out to the forts took about 15 to 20 minutes and on the way out, I noticed the barge was flying a Royal Ensign flag at half-mast, a traditional mark of respect. It struck me then just how seriously and reverently the Navy personnel were treating this. It wouldn't be any different for anyone else accorded the honour of a Naval burial at sea, but at that time, it meant the whole world to me and my mother. When the barge arrived in the middle of the three forts, the rating driving the barge cut the engines to a mere idle, and the chaplain then performed the burial service, ending with those immortal words, "we now commit his body to the deep."

A rating sitting alongside the platform where the casket had been placed, then lifted one end, and dad slid gracefully out from under the Union Jack, into the water and disappeared beneath the waves. The chaplain said a few more words of the service and then the barge driver slowly increased speed and drove the barge in a tight circle three times. Part of the burial service includes the words "smooth the waters" and by turning tight circles, the bulk of the barge created a "lee" in the water, smoothing them just over where dad had been committed to the sea.

With the burial service complete, the Royal Ensign was hoisted to full-mast and we motored back into the harbour and the dock. The chaplain then invited us to have tea with him and to look over the base chapel, whilst a calligrapher entered dad's details into a book of remembrance, which is always on display at the chapel.

And so we were able to give dad his last wish, to go back to the sea, which he had always loved, and for this, I will always be grateful to the Royal Navy. The service they gave to myself and my mother was second to none, simple, plain courteous service. Considering the number of times they must perform this ceremony, they treated us with dignity and respect, and because of dad, made us feel special.

Whenever I think of my dad, my emotions, range between love, sorrow, anger, pride, but overwhelmingly, regret. Regret that I was such a disappointment to him as a student and young man, regret that, having settled myself into the police force as a career, I was not able to realise his hopes and ambitions for me, regret that whatever the outcome of the examination I was about to take when he died, he would never know the result. And we were beginning to do more things together, pottering about and helping him in his garden and going down to the bowls rink with him and Harold for a relaxing game. Now he was gone, and with him went my opportunity to show him just how much I loved him and respected him. I'm sure he never doubted my love, but it had become important to me to demonstrate it to him, to make up for all that he hadn't received from me when he should have.

I took my examination as scheduled on 20th April 1991. In those days, the exam was known as the "competitive" exam, and the one I took in that year, was to be the last of this type. A new, national examination had been devised, and this would replace the current system in 1992. The "competitive" examination, which was unique to the Met. meant that, if the Metropolitan Police stipulated that they needed a certain number of Inspectors immediately, then those sergeants who passed the exam within that number, i.e. "competitively", were promoted to Inspector straight away. Those sergeants who passed the exam, but were below that required number, passed as "qualifiers". In 1991, the magic number was 50. Anyone who passed within 1-50 was made an Inspector immediately, the rest would have to sit a selection board later in the year.

It was an unfair system really as it favoured those officers who were able to study the most and the hardest. Many sergeants were family men and women, and for them, studying whilst trying to maintain a family was really difficult. Often, the most capable officers were not able to study as well as those with no commitments. In other words, officers were chosen as Inspectors immediately, purely on their ability to study, rather than their capabilities.

With everything that had gone on in my life in the months before the exam, I found it very hard to concentrate, but on the day, I simply did my best. When I turned the paper over, I remember saying to myself, "well pop, here goes, this is for you."

The exam was held on a Saturday afternoon, and after it, I spent the week-end with Anne in Evesham. She was well aware of dad's death and that Susie and I were separated and getting divorced. I needed to be with someone whom I knew wanted to be with me. The time I spent with Anne was a wonderful release from all the trauma that I had had to deal with during the previous six months.

The results of the exam were made known in the following June, and I had passed, but at number 84. This was 34 places below that magic 50. Even so, I took great satisfaction from the fact that I had passed in any event. Analysing the results, I figured that as hundreds of sergeants had sat the exam, passing at 84 was no mean feat. It meant however, that I had missed the cut-off point by something like 2 or 3 marks. Many officers said I could apply for a re-mark, bearing in mind all that had happened to me, but I refused, saying that I had done my best, and I would be asking for the re-mark on the back of dad's death, which somehow didn't seem right to me.

The next stage for me was to apply for a selection board, to be held later in the year, around October. Here again, the system was unfair as it meant that officers applying for the board were required to keep studying to maintain the knowledge gained, long after the others had finished. We had already been examined on the theoretical knowledge and thought competent enough to pass. Why did we have to be tested again? The board would consist of two Chief Superintendents and a Commander and each would ask separate questions, some on aspects of personal development and achievement, but mostly on law and procedure, which was why a candidate had to keep studying. It seemed incongruous to me that some officers could be promoted immediately because they got slightly higher marks in an exam, whereas others, who had also achieved the pass mark, would have to do so much more to convince senior officers they could perform the role of Inspector.

I arrived for my interview looking the smartest I had ever been. There was not a speck of dust or dirt anywhere on me and my uniform had creases like razors. I answered all their questions, quoting correctly from the "Bible", a massive volume named "General Orders", the Police and Criminal Evidence Act and the corresponding Codes of Practice. I know I didn't give an incorrect answer. I was most closely questioned on my reasons for going abroad and travelling. Having resigned, my "commitment" to the Metropolitan Police was being put under the microscope. I did my best to explain my reasons, and to convince them that my going did not mean I was any less committed to the police service. I don't think they were convinced! During the interview, the Commander floored me with a request to clarify a remark I had made to a Superintendent, TEN years earlier. I knew exactly what he was talking about, but had no idea it had gone on my record and even less idea it would be raised at this interview. I dealt with it, but coming straight out of "left field" I did struggle a bit. They wouldn't be allowed to get away with that these days. The remark had been dealt with at the time and to raise it in this forum, would be regarded as grossly unfair.

Right at the end of the interview, the Commander thanked me for my time and answers, giving the usual "we'll let you know" speech, and I began to get out of my seat. One of the Chief Superintendents then said, "Sergeant Robins, just before you go, I'd like to say that, despite your beard, you're very well turned out!" "Despite your beard!" It was not uncommon for male officers to have full beards in those days, but some senior officers still harked back to the days when they were not allowed. This Chief Superintendent was obviously one of those, and as soon as he said it, I knew I had failed.

I can never say that I was discriminated against because of my beard, but there would be no other reason for him to say it other than to communicate to me his dislike of any officer having facial growth, be it a moustache or a beard. There were six of us taking our boards that day from Croydon police station, all very capable officers. Only one passed and he was a university graduate who had transferred in from Surrey Constabulary. Talking amongst ourselves, we all came to the conclusion that the board had looked for reasons to fail rather than to pass.

One of the most galling things about failing the board for all of us however, was that, despite the failure, the senior management at the station still posted us as Acting Inspectors, when the substantive Inspector was not available for duty on the team. Apparently, we were not good enough to do the job full time, but were good enough to fill a hole when it suited the senior officers! They won all round really, as they knew we couldn't refuse to perform the role of Acting Inspector, to do so was not only akin to promotional suicide, but also a disciplinary offence. On the other hand, they knew we were capable of doing the job and so were never afraid that teams would be leaderless, and of course, it meant that we got experience of performing the functions of an Inspector. Was I the victim of an unfair system, damn right I was!

The question for me then though, was just how far was I prepared to go to play their game, and was I prepared to jump through the various hoops. The answer turned out to be not very far with not too much jumping!

I have always been convinced of my ability to be an Inspector and above. I've been motivated enough to study and prepare for the various procedures, my problem has been that I haven't really moved along with the way an Inspector performs his or her duty. To me, an Inspector leads his or her team, that's the way I have always viewed an Inspector's duty. To the senior officers though, it's more about figures and towing the party line, neither of which I'm any good at. However, I'm a great believer in destiny and as it's turned out, my destiny was never to move beyond sergeant. I applied twice more to become an Inspector, failing both times, one of them quite spectacularly.

One of the high spots of 1991 for me, was my purchase of an absolutely fantastic sports car, a replica AC Cobra. I had always wanted one and having been advised by my solicitor to spend some cash that was hanging around in various bank accounts prior to the Decree Absolute, I contacted a company in Brighton, Southern Roadcraft and spent the next three months negotiating a deal for them to produce a car for me.

In July 1991, I took possession of my Cobra, in British Racing Green with a broad cream coloured stripe going right over the car, powered by a Rover SD1 3.5 litre engine with a manual gear box, side exhausts and leather interior. Boy, did I have some fun with this car, it was an absolute pleasure to drive, very fast, very noisy and stunning looking. When I went down motorways, I would get police cars cruising alongside me, giving me the thumbs up and if I got stuck in jams, other motorists, usually men, would strike up conversations with me about the car. I even had someone follow me home one evening simply to ask what I had "under the bonnet!?"

My one abiding memory with the Cobra was a few years later when my girlfriend Sabine, and I decided to go down to Canterbury for the day. We initially set out in my ordinary car, but because it was a lovely day, warm with blue skies, we turned back and got the Cobra out, "The Baby" as Sabine called it. As we were going down the A2 towards Kent, I noticed some very threatening looking clouds in the distance. They got steadily darker and darker and seemed to be hovering right where I was heading.

I decided that we would stop under the next bridge and put up the hood, which was a bit of a mission as the frame had to be assembled before the actual hood placed over it. We never made it. It didn't just start with a few spatters, the rain simply fell in torrents with no warning at all. I had to pull over and put the hood up at the side of the road in rain so heavy, I could barely see vehicles passing in the furthest lane.

Within minutes, rain water was running down the gutters in rivers, it wouldn't even run away to the storm drains there was so much. The drivers of the passing vehicles thought it was hugely funny and were tooting their horns as they passed. When the hood finally went up, about three minutes later, there was about two inches of water sloshing around in the footwells of the car. The leather seats were sodden with water and of course, we were both soaked to the skin. Just as we set off again, the rain started to ease off. A mile down the road, it had stopped. Another half a mile further on, the sun came out! About two minutes later, we stopped at a "Little Chef" restaurant for a cup of coffee. We sploshed our way in, much to the amusement of the other diners, leaving wet footprints as we each set off for our respective toilets and blow driers!

I had the car for seven years, during which time I never got tired of driving it. It was however, an expensive luxury and I sold it when I felt I had had my fun and wanted to go back to having a motor-bike.

And that was 1991; an eventful year for me; an awful one, a traumatic one, a disappointing one, a frustrating one and on occasions, an angry one. The next two years, saw me settle down into something of a routine at work. I wasn't really that happy, but was determined to put the past behind me and move ahead. Relationships came and went, some "friends" common to both Susie and I disappeared, but knowing that Jane and David and most of Susie's family had not abandoned me, was a huge comfort. I don't know how it would have been without their support, but whatever, it would have been that bit harder.

Chapter 21

1994, one of the defining periods in my life and a year which saw me succeeding at something which, in my wildest dreams, I never would have expected.

After 1991, life in general, but especially at Croydon police station, was beginning to get a bit dull, to say the least. The world trip, sailing the open oceans, clambering up and down mountains etc, had given me a taste and a yearning for some more adventure. I had applied to do other things within the police force, but kept getting turned down. I think the senior officers were doubting my commitment to the Metropolitan Police. My view was that although I took breaks away, when I was actually doing the job, my commitment to the police was 100%. Unfortunately, the senior officers didn't quite see it that way!

In late 1993, the taste for adventure became acute and I was beginning to think about taking another break from the police force. Just about the only thing of note I had done up to then, was to go up to Scotland in the middle of winter and take a raft-guides course. I had been well and truly bitten by the rafting bug following my excursion down the Trisuli River in Nepal. I knew I wasn't ever going to earn my living at it, but just learning the techniques and intricacies of reading the river would be enough. However, why I did it in winter, I just don't know! I remember, it was so cold on one of the days we were in the water, I wore my dry-suit over my wet-suit, and was still cold!

I hadn't made any plans to go anywhere at that stage, but I knew I was going to have to go again. The opportunity arrived in the shape of one Gordon Suckling O.B.E.

Gordon and his wife Peggy were missionaries in Zambia. They had founded and ran a mission in the North West Province of Zambia, called Sachibondu, right next to the border with what was then Zaire, a very unstable country where banditry was rife. Gordon had been awarded the O.B.E. for his services to mission work and had connections to the Christian Fellowship in Southampton, which was where Chris and Karen were living with their four children, Matthew, Stephen, Emily and Samantha. Since my divorce, I had become extremely close to the family and saw them regularly. Gordon had come to Southampton, not only to visit old friends, but also to try and find someone who was willing to go out to the mission in Zambia, and manage the farm. A succession of bad managers had meant that the farm, which supplied produce for not only the mission, but also to the local community in Mwinilunga was on its knees. Just to give an example, each cow in the dairy herd was yielding only one litre of milk per day when they should have been producing around eight!

240

Chris and Karen heard Gordon speaking at the fellowship about the farm and Chris immediately thought that this was God calling him to Zambia. He had no knowledge or training in farm management whatsoever, and yet he was convinced that this was what he had to do, this was where God was directing him. Karen was not so sure at this stage, she was engaged in a nursing programme, but agreed to go out to the mission with Chris to look things over. If she liked it, she would support Chris in any decision he might make. In the event, she fell in love with Sachibondu. The nearest town to the mission is Mwinilunga, which is just over 250 kilometres west from the Copperbelt and any other town, and the mission itself is around thirty kilometers into the bush from Mwinilunga.

After several long discussions and the visit to the mission, Gordon agreed that Chris and Karen should come out and manage the farm. And so, they prepared to take their children from the relative comfort of Southampton and their friends, to the very real deprivation of living in the bush in Zambia, in one of the poorest and most deprived areas of the country. There would be no parks to play in, no McDonalds restaurants, no cinemas or pubs and bars. There would be no shops just down the road, no supermarkets. The quality of the food is poor, the water comes directly from the local lake and would have to be filtered several times before it could be drunk There is nothing anywhere near the mission, which might come even close to resembling their life in Southampton. And yet, they couldn't wait to get there; Chris and Karen that is; I think the older children had severe reservations (Samantha was too young and didn't have a clue what was going on), but equally, were eager to experience this new way of life. I suspect they never thought that they would never see most of their friends in Southampton ever again. I cannot adequately describe just how much respect I have for Chris and Karen for making this decision, one of the bravest I have ever come across.

Although I had no idea what it would involve, but thought that it would at the least, be an exciting and interesting venture, I asked Chris and Karen about the possibility of my going out to the farm and working with them for a short while, and their response was very positive.

I decided that I would ask my senior managers for a 1 year career break, which was granted, but I wasn't sure I wanted to spend the entire time on the farm. If I was going for a year, there may be other things to do and achieve. An idea popped into my head, a fairly ridiculous one, but an idea!

Having been to Johannesburg on several occasions by that time, I had come across a safari company named "Drifters". They had a shop in one of the shopping malls in Sandton City, an affluent area of Johannesburg. I wrote to the head office and asked about the possibility of working for them as a sort of safari camp skivvy, doing the washing up etc, but at the same time, experiencing life on safari. Their reply was that no, I couldn't do that as they had no such position, and in any event, anyone who did work for Drifters was required to undertake and pass what they called the "Guides' Course". I had no aspirations of being a Safari Guide, but they sent me the prospectus anyway, and after reading it, I decided to do it in any event as it was very cheap for me considering the exchange rate and it looked as though it would be really interesting.

By this time, Chris and Karen had made their arrangements with Gordon for arriving at the farm. They would start in April 1994 and I would arrive in July. I organised my guides' course for November 1994. Having the qualification for raft-guiding, I decided that I would also stop off at Victoria Falls and make contact with a man named Peter who was running a river-rafting operation on the Zambezi.

In those days, adventure companies in this part of Africa were only just starting to flourish, and all were based in Victoria Falls, Zimbabwe. These days, under the despotic and disastrous leadership of Robert Mugabe, many of those companies previously based on the Zimbabwe side of the Falls have transferred their operations to Livingstone in Zambia. By the time I had decided to go to Africa, I had been getting experience as a raft guide in Wales at a centre called Canolfan Tryweryn, but I will cover this more fully in the next chapter.

Something, which I never mentioned before, would now begin to be a bit of a worry for Chris and Karen as they prepared to go abroad. On the day after Susie finally left the house, Chris had made a surprise visit to me. After hearing what he had to say, I could only imagine the anguish he had to go through. Of course, I told him that Susie had finally gone the night before and he realised the hurt and pain I was suffering. He, however, had come to me to ask for a loan of £10,000! I know he was in absolute turmoil as to whether or not to ask me for the loan, but in the end, he had to. If he didn't, his landscaping business would go to the wall due to a disastrous decision he had made over a car!

The early 1990's saw a massive boom in the sale and purchase of classic cars, both here in the U.K. and abroad. The value of an 'E' Type Jaguar for instance, quadrupled in value in probably just as many months during the height of the boom. But for every boom, there is a bust, and poor old Chris had bought himself a classic car with the compensation he received for the loss of his eye, just when the market began to bust. He had bought a Porsche 356 Coupe from some guy in Canada. The guy in Canada had shipped the car over and told Chris he had insured it for the sea crossing. He lied! During the trip, the car was damaged and had to be repaired at Chris' expense. The plan was to put the car straight into an auction here in the U.K. and make a quick profit. The repairs however, took longer than anticipated and when Chris finally did get it into an auction, the bottom was already falling out of the market. In fact, it was in freefall! Chris got nowhere the asking price and decided to hang on to the Porsche to see if the market recovered. It never did, and Chris had to pay out more and more money for the car in the way of welding and engine repairs and simple maintenance. I remember he told me once that having purchased the car for around £12,000, his total spend on the car was something approaching £30,000.

When he came to me that morning, he needed the loan to keep his business afloat as he'd used a lot of his capital on the Porsche. He didn't want to go to the bank because of interest payments and was desperate not to have to go to Karen's parents, her mother hated him with a passion, but he would if I couldn't help him. Chris had always been a stalwart friend to me and I wasn't about to let him down, although I could only manage to give him £9000. In return for the money, I was to receive an official half-share in the damned Porsche! Whoopee!

The upshot was, that when they decided to go to Zambia, the Porsche had to be sold. Chris had a few enquiries, but because he was conscious of my involvement, he turned down all the offers because they weren't high enough. Eventually, he became desperate to sell it, but as the time for their departure to Zambia, came ever closer, the enquiries on the car became fewer and fewer. With everything else they had to arrange, the last thing they wanted to deal with, was the sale of the Porsche. At the end of the day, if push came to shove and all else failed, I would have had to take the car and keep it at my house till it was sold. I really didn't want to do this as I had no room for it, and Chris was very aware of how I felt.

The container they had arranged to transport their belongings was due to arrive on a Saturday morning. At about 6pm, the evening before, a man telephoned Chris asking whether the car was still for sale. Chris hadn't renewed the advertisement as he didn't see the point, they would be gone by the time it came out in the paper. This guy had obviously held off phoning on the off-chance it would still be available and so, could get it at a reduced price. He was in luck, wasn't he! He came round early that Saturday morning, viewed it and offered Chris £4000 cash! He'd hardly got the words out before Chris nearly had his hand off. And so, I duly received £4000 on an investment of £9000. Hardly the business deal of the century, but then, I didn't lend Chris the money to make a profit, but then again, I didn't really expect to lose over half the loan. I was fairly ticked off by the whole affair, and at one stage suggested that they pay back another £1000, just to reduce my arrears. However, I immediately regretted my churlishness and thought again about their position. I have never mentioned it to them since and have been more than happy to call it quits and move on! It meant far more to me that Chris and Karen didn't have this debt hanging over their heads than to get my money back.

Chris was absolutely hopeless at sorting out his equipment ready for shipping. Two days before the container was due to arrive. He called me and asked if I would go down and help him. I was off that day, and so trundled on down to Southampton. "It's the garage that needs sorting", he said. When I looked in there, he hadn't done a damned thing about sorting out his landscaping gear. He had saws, blades, tools, ropes, harnesses, protective gear, electrical tools, drills all over the place. There was no point in shouting at him, Karen had done all that! We just got on with it and eventually finished sorting it all out ready for packing about 2am! When I left the house, it was the last I saw of them until I arrived on the farm a few months later.

Most of their possessions, in fact all of them that were going with them, were packed into the container. This included Chris' old Landrover that he used in his landscaping business, and a box of mine containing stuff that I thought might be useful for me on the farm. I had put a rather large knife which I had had for years in there along with old clothes and other bits and pieces. Although I'd never used the knife, I was very attached to it. When I arrived on the farm in July, Chris told me the story about how most of their belongings and mine had been either stolen or damaged, some beyond repair, en route to Sachibondu Mission.

The container was shipped by P&O to Dar es Salaam, and from there, it was to go by road to Lusaka. The company which was transporting the container by road was called ZamCargo, and was actually run by Gordon Suckling's son, Ken. A nice, neat little arrangement you might think! The goods in the container were to be placed into a bonded warehouse in Lusaka for customs purposes, and once cleared, would be taken by lorry up to Chris and Karen on the mission. They had a really nice big house overlooking the lake and the whole family were eagerly awaiting the arrival of their furniture, children's toys and bikes etc etc.

On the way from Dar es Salaam to Lusaka, the lorry transporting the container, crashed and overturned, tipping the container onto its roof. It stayed like that for a number of days, until the company could get recovery trucks and a crane out to right the vehicle and replace the container onto the truck. Once that was done, the lorry continued on its journey and arrived in Lusaka about ten days late.

The goods were placed into the bonded warehouse, which should have been sealed and not opened by anyone without the presence of Chris or Karen. Those are the rules! However, as so often happens in Africa, the rules were flouted. The warehouse was opened by some official or other, in the absence of Chris or Karen, and most of Chris' tools and equipment simply walked out of the warehouse in some grubby little African official's hands! Clothes were stolen, toys were stolen, kitchen goods were stolen, In fact everything of any value was stolen. Everything in my box went too.

The goods that were left behind in the warehouse had either been smashed to pieces by the crash, or were rendered completely useless due to the diesel oil which had leaked from the Landrover when it was upside down. The children's beds were in pieces, their bikes all had buckled wheels, their clothing was diesel stained, as were all their mattresses. There was nothing of any use left in the warehouse, other than the Landrover, which was so old, the thieves probably didn't want it! All in all, Chris and Karen reckon they lost around £3000-£4000 worth of goods. And so they made an insurance claim! P&O refused to pay out because their insurance only covered the goods in transit on the open sea. Once they arrived in Dar es Salaam, they were no longer their concern. Chris had wrongly assumed that because the container belonged to P&O, it would be insured all the way to Lusaka.

Chris' next move was to approach Ken Suckling and seek compensation from ZamCargo. This of course, was awkward because of the connection to Gordon, for whom Chris was working. Ken Suckling refused to entertain Chris' claim on the grounds that the goods were not insured and ZamCargo would not be held responsible for an accident! Next, Chris approached the Zambian government in Lusaka regarding the opening of the warehouse. They refused all claims for compensation on the grounds they were unable to state whom had opened the warehouse. They accepted that it shouldn't have been opened, but without someone to blame, refused to budge!

I can understand P&O's position. I can even understand the government's position, having dealt with African administrations before. What I cannot accept and never will, is Ken Suckling's refusal to assist Chris and Karen. He had the position and the ability to have addressed their more immediate needs and at least replaced some of their damaged goods. He knew Chris and Karen had shipped out everything they owned and now had lost it all, and yet he refused to help in any way. I thought his lack of compassion disgraceful. Gordon and his wife Peggy refused to intervene on family grounds. There were other missionaries in that area of Zambia, and none of them offered to help in any way, probably because of Gordon and Peggy.

This was my first introduction to the magnanimity of missionaries. Over the coming months, there would be other incidents which reflected the mean-spiritedness of most of the so-called missionaries in the area.

The relationship between Chris and Karen and Gordon and Peggy was strained at the best of times. I think this was because Gordon was very set in his ways and often tried to tell Chris how to run the farm. Chris' view was that if Gordon was right, what the hell was he doing there? Peggy and Karen clashed because of their dominant personalities. At one stage, I had had enough of their bickering and told them all to sit around a table and work out their differences. If they didn't, everything was going to end in tears. Consequently, all four of them sat down one evening and thrashed it all out. After the meeting, the atmosphere was much better, not brilliant by any means, but better. However, from that moment on, it always seemed to me that Gordon would address me rather than Chris whenever we were together. I do think this was the divisive side of Gordon coming to the fore.

Peggy was quite simply white and superior! I remember at lunch one day, she was eulogising just how good to the black people, whites had been, how they were brought to Christianity and taught how to feed themselves and live in the modern world. Once her speech had finished, she picked up a little bell off the table and rang it shrilly to summon Noah, the 'house-boy' and inform him that he may clear all the dishes away! I don't ever remember hearing her say "please" or "thank you".

However, for all that, I really liked Peggy, and Gordon especially. He would invite me to lunch at their house and then we would spend hours talking and debating about the Bible and Christianity. I think he saw me as something of a son, a lost soul he was going to save. Chris and Ray had been trying that for years and failed, Gordon would get no further, but I so enjoyed discussing things with Gordon. He was an eloquent and intelligent man, but was also an ex "white-hunter" who had hunted and shot game for meat for his mission. The walls of their house were adorned with all sorts of hunting "trophies", including record length horns and hippopotamus teeth, and no get-together would be complete without a hunting story from Gordon. As I write this, Gordon has now sadly passed away, but Peggy is still ruling the mission with the rod of iron she picked up from Gordon, bless her!!

The land owned by the mission station, Sachibondu, covered a large area, although the actual mission occupied only a tiny fraction of that. Gordon and Peggy had arrived in the area some twenty years previously and cleared the land, built the houses, built the church, built the schools and workshops, built the clinic and generally ministered to the local people. They built a dam across the river and created a lake for fresh water. An engineer modified an old tractor engine and gearbox and created hydro-electric power from the dam. In the dry season, when the water level was low, the light bulbs would be very dim because of the low power output, but in the rainy season, the bulbs would burn as bright as any western town with modern power stations. The clinic was run by Ruth, who at some stage in her life, had apparently obtained a medical qualification, although some of us jokingly doubted this! What was certain however, was that she rarely updated herself with new practises or drugs. Karen had had some training as a nurse and was horrified at how out of date Ruth actually was. To be fair, this was not intentional on Ruth's part, it was very difficult to obtain information or instruction on new procedures etc being so far into the bush and the internet hadn't arrived in Zambia at that time. It became a lighthearted discussion between Chris, Karen and I just how the population of the mission continued to grow rather than decline under Ruth's medical expertise! All joking aside though, everybody on the mission was grateful to Ruth simply for being there and trying to do her best for the population, despite poor equipment and the lack of drugs. There were also bible schools, and workshops run by local people who had been trained by missionaries away from Sachibondu. It was a veritable little community in the middle of nowhere!

And then of course, there was the farm! It was mainly dairy. In fact, when Chris arrived it was only dairy, just! Later, Chris cleared some land and began a programme of arable farming where the local people grew their own maize and squashes. Peggy had her own orchard of apple trees, but they didn't amount to much because of the poor soil, which in turn couldn't be fertilized with cattle manure owing to the fact that the cattle didn't have enough to eat to create the manure in the first place!

The dairy herd consisted of around 15 pathetic looking cows. They were so emaciated, their ribs showed clearly through their hides. This was partly due to very little good pasture around the farm and partly due to the fact that to get to good pasture, the cows had to walk several kilometers twice a day, after the morning and evening milking. The first thing Chris did when he got there was to extract some money out of the mission benefactors, (some group in Germany) and put the cows on a high yield supplement, which he fed to them while they were being milked. Eventually, the milk yield went up from 1 litre per day per cow, to over 8 litres per day per cow, but the supplement was expensive and often ran out.

Soon after arriving, Chris purchased two pigs, which he named Wilbur and Charlotte, from the adjoining farm run by the Fisher family. Peggy was the sister of the Fisher patriarch, who was a very powerful and influential man in the area. Chris' idea was to breed pigs, slaughter and butcher them and then sell the meat to the local people in Mwinilunga and Sachibondu. As a qualified butcher, he knew what he was talking about. Both pigs were fattened to the correct weight and then mated. The first litter arrived soon after, and the programme got off to a flying start. Chris continued to breed the pigs and then sell the butchered meat right up until they left the farm, two years later. The programme came to a crashing halt however, when Chris and Karen took a short break down to Victoria Falls. In their absence, the mission trustees decided to kill Wilbur the boar as they needed meat for a bible conference to be held on the mission. Wilbur was the only boar Chris had at the correct weight and so, couldn't breed any more pigs for months. This was one of the reasons why Chris and Karen decided that they should leave the farm. Chris was the farm manager, and yet had not even been consulted over the killing of Wilbur. If he had have been, he would obviously have said no, which was probably why it was done whilst they were away.

Whilst Chris was doing his stuff with the cows, pigs and chickens (which he started later), Karen busied herself with the mission administration, making butter and cheese, selling the bulk of the milk from the back of the Landrover down in the "Boma" (which translates to "town"), taking care of the children, filtering water and checking that the cleaner they employed to help with the housework had actually done what she said she had done! Quite how she managed to juggle all her activities around the day, was always a mystery to me. She was never still! They had arrived on the mission during the school summer holidays, and so the four children had a wonderful four or five weeks getting to know the local people, especially the children, wandering over the mission, being taken into the bush, learning the local language, Lunda (Samantha, the youngest was fluent in a matter of months) and generally making their own fun around the farm.

The two boys, Matthew and Stephen would often head off into the bush all day with the local boys who showed them how to trap, skin and roast bush-rats or how to trap small birds. The Lunda people were renowned for their trapping expertise, so much so in fact, they had trapped out all the game. There were no antelope left, no predators large or small, no buffalo, no crocodiles (thank goodness) or hippo. Only birds and snakes remained and the latter were creatures you definitely didn't want around. Chris once shot a Black Mamba, the most dangerous snake in Africa, which was swimming across the lake directly towards them, clean through the head from about twenty metres. The farm boys talked about this shot for weeks after, hailing Chris as a great hunter. They were simple people and these things meant a lot to them. The girls tended to hang around the mission and the farm but all four of them seemed to simply melt into the demograhics of the mission, as if they had been there all their lives.

After Gordon and Peggy, the first person I met on the farm was Jacob, Chris' foreman. He was remarkable for the livid blue scar, which covered most of his ample nose. Apparently, he and his wife had a terrible fight one night when they were both drunk, and she had bitten through most of his nose. When I met her later, I realised why he lost the fight, and was amazed she only managed to get half his nose! She was a good 18 inches taller than him and at least three stones heavier! A powerful woman!

As a foreman, however, Jacob was useless. Unfortunately for Chris, there was no one else who was anywhere near as intelligent as Jacob, and he was pretty thick! Chris would threaten to sack Jacob probably once a week because of his incompetence, but never did. One of Jacob's tasks was simply to tell Chris when the farm was running short of feed for the cows, or was running short of ground mealie-meal. He only had to go into the store and count the sacks that were left. Time after time Chris would tell a farm hand to get some stores, only to be told, "Ah, Bwana, we have not!" Chris would be apoplectic with rage and "JACOB!!" would boom out across the farm. Jacob would then come scurrying up to Chris to ask the problem. He could never understand why Chris wanted to know early about the stores. In the African mind, you had stores until you ran out, planning early replenishment simply didn't occur to them.

There was an abandoned tractor right in the middle of the farm-yard, slowly sinking into the sand. It had apparently been supplied new by the trustees. The battery went flat one day, so they tried to bump start it with a trailer attached. The only problem with this plan was that the tractor was parked on a downhill slope and when they let the brake off, the driver couldn't get it into gear. The tractor sped off down the slope, at which point, the driver thought better of his position. He jumped off and the tractor and trailer went careering down the hill, only stopping when it crashed into the lake, and sank! It was days before it had been recovered back to the yard, where it was dumped and then left to rot!

It's been 13 years since I was on the farm at Sachibondu. I can really only remember some of the other workers. One of them was Webbie, a short dapper little man, who was on the run from Jonas Savimbi's army in Angola. Apparently, one didn't desert from Savimbi's army and if caught, Webbie would be under sentence of death. Rodwill was the worker who milked the cows. He was married, but, as rumour had it, that didn't stop him, along with John who was Ruth's adopted African son from allegedly producing many of the "fatherless" children on the mission.

Having seen him run, I once timed Rodwill running a hundred metres in bare feet along a dirt road. He ran it in 12seconds. No training, no starting blocks, no fancy running shoes, and I was told that Alex in the bible school was even faster than Rodwill! I wondered then just what these guys could achieve with the right training and equipment.

John Morosh was our fearless hunter. He was always to be seen with his hunting axe. John's problem however, was that the hunters who had gone before him had hunted everything out, so there was nothing left for poor old John to go and catch, apart from the odd bird or two. Finally, there was Kafir, Gordon's driver. We had to be careful how we pronounced his name, Kafir, as in "wafer" and not Kaffir, as in the derogatory South African term for a black person!

I well remember the incident when Kafir volunteered to slaughter a cow for a bible conference on the mission. These were held fairly regularly, and the farm was expected to provide the meat. Chris was asked by Gordon to slaughter a suitable cow, and Chris chose an old bovine near the end of her productive life. She was a rather sad old thing and was always the last to arrive from the grazing grounds for milking. Unfortunately, the "slaughter" turned into more of an "execution!"

Having chosen the victim, the next problem, was how we were going to slaughter her. Being the ex white-hunter, Gordon immediately shouted that we should shoot her. (as he was a little hard of hearing, Gordon shouted everything) He produced one of his old guns, but immediately declined to pull the trigger himself on account of his failing eyesight. I think it was more a case of selective myopia! However, Kafir jumped up straight away and volunteered his services as executioner-in-chief!

Both Chris and I had our doubts about this, as Kafir admitted that he'd hardly ever shot any gun, let alone one pointed at an animal. As usual, Gordon overrode Chris' objections and handed Kafir the gun and ammunition. We were even more doubtful when Chris and I saw the weapon, it was a shotgun! Even at close range, the large-bore cartridges probably wouldn't kill the animal unless the shot was directly behind the head and into the brain. Even that was doubtful! However, Chris loaded it up with a cartridge and handed it to Kafir, telling him to get as close to the animal as possible and aim just behind the head. Kafir however, was obviously none too keen on getting in close and dirty and fired from about five yards away.

This first shot missed spectacularly, and succeeded only in blowing off most of the poor animal's snout. She was now careering in what for her, must have been absolute agony around the enclosure we had secured her in, blood and mucous spraying out of the gaping hole where her nose had been. Undeterred, Kafir reloaded the gun and fired a second shot. As the cow obviously wasn't going to stand still for him, he had to fire at the moving target. The second shot missed by even more than the first and this time, removed a huge patch of flesh from her shoulder. At this point, Chris uttered an unutterable oath and snatched the gun from Kafir, only to be told that Gordon didn't have any more shells. We all stood around for a second or two, mesmorised by the pathetic sight of the cow racing blindly around the enclosure, bleeding from the severe flesh wound on her shoulder and snorting pathetically through the void that should have been her snout.

Suddenly, up jumped our fearless hunter, John Morosh. He told Chris he could despatch the poor animal with one blow of his axe. Although doubtful, without any other option, Chris told him to go ahead. We managed to slow the animal down and quieted her sufficiently enough for John to approach from the side and sink his slim-headed axe deep into the base of her skull, killing her instantly. Chris and I heaved a huge sigh of relief, and both of us swore we would never go through that trauma again. As it happened, it didn't quite work out that way!

The carcass was dragged to the "A" frame where Chris butchered her expertly. The funniest part though was watching Stephen, Chris' second son, chasing all the African boys around, holding the severed udder like a set of bagpipes, squirting them with the still warm milk.

The second time we had to slaughter a cow for a conference, Chris decided that we wouldn't get involved and the workers on the farm should do it their way. Chris and I would simply look on as interested spectators. Once the cow had been separated, one of the boys lassoed one of her rear hooves with a length of rope. The cow, of course panicked like crazy and immediately began to career around the farm, with about six of the african workers all in a line, hanging on to part of the rope, and being towed and jerked around with every step this demented cow took. As the lassoed leg shot forward, so all the African boys were catapulted forward at the same time, trying to stay on their feet, which some of them didn't. They just got dragged along the ground till eventually they let go of the rope. It was a bit like a sketch from a Benny Hill programme. Wherever the cow went, the boys just got dragged along with her. If she turned a corner, the man at the end of the rope had to sprint and jump to keep up with the others whilst still trying to hold on for dear life. Chris and I were just in fits of laughter, until she headed directly for me and I had to dive to the side to avoid being trampled on. Eventually, they got the rope turned around a tree and began pulling the cow in towards it. When she was right up against the tree, with nowhere to go, one of the boys pulled her tail and she sat down on her haunches. Enter John Morosh with his axe! He missed with his first swipe, succeeding only in opening up a huge gash at the top of her neck, sending the poor animal almost wild with pain. She was thrashing around at the end of the rope and John did well to get anywhere near her for the second blow. It was aimed a little better and went straight into her skull. She was dead, at last! Thankfully, we weren't treated to any more African style slaughter methods.

Executions notwithstanding, I had just the most wonderful time on the farm! Peggy and Gordon were essentially good people and I enjoyed their company. I got on really well with all the African workers and I think they liked and, more importantly, respected me. My days were generally filled with working on various projects which Chris would set for me.

One of the first, was to set about repairing the main culvert running under the track leading onto the farm. The rains in Zambia come down big-time, and they hadn't long finished when I arrived at Sachibondu. The rain is channeled away via these culverts and the run-off from this one was so severe, it had washed away the culvert completely, resulting in some of the road also going down the rain channel.

Now, I know nothing about culvert construction! I know what they do, but how to support the road above the culvert properly, no! Chris had simply said to me, "Repair that culvert for me please" and walked off. I had one or two of the farm lads with me, and they gently suggested that we go into the bush and cut some new timber to shore up the crumbling road surface.

When I looked at the culvert, it really was of the simplest construction. Large baulks of timber, placed alongside each other to form the sides and thinner poles laid across the top to form the roadway. Other tree trunks were placed at an angle to support the road surface. We muddled our way through, and eventually finished it. By the time I came to leave the farm, it hadn't collapsed, so I was quite proud of that.

Other projects included felling and cutting up trees for firewood, taking the milk, butter and cheese to the Boma in the Landrover, repairing fences, working in the milling shed all sorts of things. Everyday, brought new challenges, and I loved it! And I especially loved working with the African boys. They were essentially a lazy bunch; leave them to their own devices and nothing would get done. You had to be on them all the time, chivvying them along; but as long as they knew what was required and you worked alongside them, getting your hands dirty so to speak, they were great and worked hard. A classic example of this was the pole-bridge across the river below the dam.

After leaving the farm and going to South Africa, I returned for a short period, the reason for which I will explain later. However, before going to South Africa, I had rescued some large blocks from a ruined building and used them to raise the level of the dam wall. This raised the water level in the lake during the rainy season, effectively prolonging the length of time water flowed over the hydro-electric generator vanes. When I returned, I wandered down to the dam to inspect the brick-work. Amazingly, it was still in place and working to good effect. However, just below the dam was a bridge, constructed entirely of poles cut from the bush and tied together with bark-rope. The bridge was the only means of crossing the river, other than actually wading through fairly deep and fast flowing water, or walking about a mile further down-stream to a shallow ford.

When I got to the bridge, it was a mess. During the previous rains, the river was flowing so fast, it had caused the bridge to collapse. Some of the poles had obviously been swept away, but the majority just lay in a tangled heap at both sides of the river. When I asked some of the local people how long it had been like that, they told me "ah, long time bwana Neil", which could mean anything from days to months. They didn't have much concept of time. However long it had been, it was obvious that none of the locals had even thought of repairing it. They would prefer to walk to the ford rather than get stuck in and repair it, or leave it to someone else. I decided there and then that the next day, I would set about clearing away the debris and trying to rebuild the bridge for the local people. Some of the bridge support poles were still intact and from these, I could work out how to re-construct it. I had no idea what I was about to start.

I arrived early the next morning and started to pull the poles from the river and place them along the river bank to re-use. Some of the local women passed by on the other side, on their way to the ford. They watched me for a while, talking about the "chindeli" (white man) and then continued on their journeys. I had been there about an hour with Webbie helping me, when one or two local men turned up from the next village. They watched us for a while, then waded in and started to help us. Then a few more turned up, and a few more, and yet more. After a couple of hours there were about twenty or thirty local men and women all helping. Some of the men cut more poles, whilst others twisted bark into rope. Yet more women turned up with food and water.

All the men were "foremen", each with their own idea of how it should be rebuilt. They would shout and argue with each other over where and how certain poles should be placed. They would discuss long and hard whether this pole or that pole should face or lean this way or that. Everybody seemed to have something to say, but at the same time, everybody was involved. The big thing for me though was that they were actually there, talking and arguing, and rebuilding their own bridge.

I realised the moment and gradually let them take over and do it themselves, however they wanted it. They would gladly have followed my instructions as the "bwana" but I felt this would be wrong. In the end, I just got on with whatever any one of them asked me to do. When it was finished, it was much better than the old bridge, more solid, with handrails along each side, and much better than anything I could have done. However, if I hadn't gone to the bridge and started it, they would never have done it themselves. After an exhausting day in the sun, I went home that night with a huge grin of satisfaction on my face, knowing that I had been instrumental in making something good happen.

The biggest project I undertook on the farm resulted from a casual remark by Chris over lunch one day. I forget what we were talking about now, but Chris mused over how useful it would be to have some sort of sketch plan of the farm and the mission itself. After a while, he asked if I could produce something. I thought about it and came to the conclusion that, yes, I could produce a sketch plan, but I was convinced I could produce something much better, an accurate scale plan of the entire mission showing all the fences, houses and buildings, all the roadways and tracks and the lake and the river. All I would need would be a compass, a pen, a ruler, a notebook, a protractor and several sheets of paper. The only item I would not have would be a long tape measure, but as the roads and fences were hundreds of metres in length, I decided I could do it by pacing out the metres. Not exactly the most accurate method, but with patience and discipline, it would be good enough. I told Chris what I thought. He didn't have to be convinced that I could do it, he has this wonderful attitude that if I say I can do it, that's the end of the discussion.

I made my starting point the intersection of the main roadway with the track leading to Peggy and Gordon's house. I took an accurate compass reading and noted the bearing of the roadway. I then started to walk in measured steps, out towards the mission boundary. I had practised walking at a precise stride, more or less one metre in length. Each stride may have differed by a few inches or so, but over the thousands of metres I was to walk, I figured it wouldn't matter that much.

My plan was to walk each road and fence line around the mission, eventually ending up back at the intersection. With a bit of luck and accuracy, I wouldn't be too far out. When the perimeters had been mapped, I would then start to map the interior roads and buildings. I wasn't going to measure the dimensions of each house or building, merely showing their position would be enough.

When I reached the point in the main road where it turned slightly to the right, I halted and noted the number of strides to that point. I then took another bearing along the next part of the road, relative to the first. I drew a line in my notebook to represent each part of the road, noted the measurement and the angle change where it turned. Luckily for me, the roads were all pretty straight, with not too many bends and turns. I carried on like this till I reached the outer limit of the mission, a fence line, which cut the road left and right at right angles.

When I finished noting the measurements, I saw that I had the beginnings of a plan in my notebook. Although I figured that I would have to concentrate like mad to keep count of the number of strides, I realised that it was very possible to do it this way. From that point on, it became a mission to complete the project properly and accurately. Apart from anything, I had told Chris that I could do it and wasn't prepared to let him down. As I progressed, I became more and more excited about producing my plan.

I carried on like this all the way around the perimeter of the mission. I ignored little jinks in the fence-line left and right, only noting the major turns. Over the next couple of days, I must have walked miles and miles through fairly thick bush, over fallen trees, across streams and marshes, through little villages on the outskirts of the mission. People in the villages seemed slightly bemused at the sight of the "chindeli" walking and counting at the same time. At the end of each day, I would end at a precise point where I could start again easily the following day.

As the main roadway cut the mission in half, much like a line drawn through the middle of a circle, I concentrated on each half of the whole in turn. Having walked the entire length of each side of the perimeter, I eventually ended up back at the intersection where I started. Satisfied that I had included everything on the outside, I started to transfer the measurements onto a preliminary plan. To do this, I would need a fairly large area of paper, which I got by sellotaping several sheets of A4 paper together. I decided on the scale I would use, and then using a ruler and protractor, began to transfer the measurements and bearings. The lines on the map simply retraced my steps around the mission. The biggest question was going to be, had I been accurate enough with my bearings and strides to join up the end of the last line, to the start of the first? To my surprise and absolute delight, the two points married up to within an inch. Making slight adjustments to the angles to get them together wasn't going to be a problem.

The next stage was measuring and plotting all the roads that led off the main road, and all the roads that led off these lesser roads. This took almost as long as the perimeter as there were lots of them, and more twisty. When these were plotted, the buildings positions were noted and then transferred onto the plan.

The preliminary plan was completed, and it all worked. Having shown the plan to Chris, Karen and Gordon, we all decided that it was good enough to make a proper plan with all the buildings such as the church and the clinic named, and the various houses and farm buildings shown. Yet more sheets of A4 were sellotaped together and I reproduced the plan, writing all the titles in a nice calligraphic script. (I had practised calligraphy since working down the pit back in the late 60's).

As it happened, I produced the final version at a time when the mission benefactors from Germany were visiting. I seem to remember the main guy's name was Traulgut. He was mightily impressed with my efforts and actually took the plan back to Germany with him, with the intention of reproducing it again on proper paper, generally making it look far more professional than it did then.

I thoroughly enjoyed the challenge of making this plan. It tested my resolve to keep going, to keep concentrating and to find ways of overcoming annoying little obstacles. In fact, the whole experience of working on the farm, was a series of problems which needed to be solved. Being so far from "civilsation", if something was not available on the farm, it had to be either made, adapted from something else or substituted. Using an old tractor engine and gearbox for the hydro-electric turbine was a classic example of the ingenuity and versatility that one needed to make the farm work.

I remember once working in the workshop on some machine or other. I wandered down to the house and asked Karen if she had any old rags she could give me for hand-wipes. "Look around Neil," she said "they're wearing them!" The clothes that the African workers wore were indeed, almost in complete tatters. It showed me that nothing in this land is wasted, apart from abandoned tractors, but even that was being stripped for mechanical parts to be adapted for other uses. Practically everything was either re-cycled, handed on to the next wearer or adapted for something else.

Theft was a big problem on the farm and the mission in general. Some of the farm-workers were a little, shall we say, light-fingered, but the main problem lay with villagers from outside the mission compound wandering through the farm. At night, everything had to be securely locked away and it was part of Chris' and my responsibilities to make sure that locks were firmly attached. During the day, some parts of the farm were necessarily unattended and items were always at risk of being spirited away. The one part we all thought was pretty inviolate was the farmhouse itself. However, although there was nearly always someone around, it was still possible for someone to sneak onto the house grounds and remove things.

One particular day, Stephen's bicycle was stolen from outside the house. All the farm workers were questioned, and one of them came up with where the bike had been taken, but not the name of the thief. It was apparently to be found in a small village, about two hours walk from the farm. I decided to pay the village a visit. When Karen said she wanted to go as well, Chris and I both groaned inwardly. When she gets going, Karen is one formidable woman, and one of her sons having his bike nicked had lit the "blue-touch paper."

When we got to the village, we were greeted in the usual polite fashion, and then sat down with the headman to discuss the bike. When we left, we didn't have the bike, but the headman promised to look into it, which meant it was there and would be magically produced later. A couple of days after our visit, it was duly returned overnight, and we forgot about the incident as the thief would never be caught.

Dealing with a thief on the compound was always a risky business if the local police became involved. Before Chris and Karen had arrived on the mission, there had been several incidents where thieves had been carted off to the police station in Mwinilunga, and been severely beaten for their trouble. There was even a rumour one had been beaten to death. Consequently, Chris, Karen and I would be very reluctant to involve the local police in any handling of prisoners.

One particular day, just after the farm had finished for the day, we heard a commotion outside on the track leading down to the farmhouse. When we went outside, Jacob and about five others were literally dragging a man down the path. His hands and feet had been securely bound with rope and he was being dragged along the ground feet first, with his head bouncing off the fair-sized rocks on the way. Jacob and the others were all shouting at him in Lunda, and one or two well-aimed kicks found their way into his ribs. It was obvious this man had severely pissed them off!

He was unceremoniously dumped onto the concrete apron just outside the house, and Jacob approached Chris with the explanation. They had caught a thief! Not just any thief though, this was the man who had stolen Stephen's bike, and he had been caught trying to steal something else from the farm. Jacob and the others had delivered him to Chris in order that "justice" might be meted out!

It struck me as an odd situation. Generations before the white rule of the country, the local populations dealt with their own problems. The white man came along, annexed the country and called it Northern Rhodesia. This was at the height of the colonial period. The Government was white, the judiciary was white, the local administrators were white, black soldiers in the army, were supervised by white officers, in fact, anyone with any power or authority was white. The black population was ruled by the whites in their own country, and if the black people had a problem, it was sorted out by the white administrators. Eventually, of course, this was deemed wrong, and countries such as Northern Rhodesia became independent of the colonial power, but not until the middle of the twentieth century. Northern Rhodesia was re-named Zambia, and the infrastructure reverted to black control. Consequently, problems experienced by black people were sorted out by black administrators, as it should be.

However, even after independence, there are still areas where the white people are seen as being in charge, and the mission at Sachibondu is one of those places. It was probably as much to do with the forceful personality of Gordon Suckling as anything else. Everyone on the mission and the farm deferred to Gordon, what he said was generally law! This patriarchal attitude was probably one of the reasons he and Chris didn't really see eye to eye. Chris would not allow himself to be subjected to the sort of bullying tactics usually employed by either Gordon or Peggy.

The situation with this thief was odd because we were in a country governed by black people, where the relatively few white people were tolerated, especially under the rule of the previous president, the ultra left wing Kenneth Kaunda, and yet, this group of black workers, were expecting Chris, a white man, to sort this problem out. They had no concept of doing it themselves. In their eyes, the "bwana" was still the boss, and they were more than happy to defer to Chris or Gordon. The ending of the colonial period seemed to mean very little to these people.

Chris now had to take some form of action about the thief in order, not only to satisfy Jacob and the other workers, but also to maintain the respect for the "bwana" that was so important to Jacob and the others. Without that respect, Gordon's missionary authority would have been severely undermined.

We listened to what Jacob had to say, trying very hard not to laugh at the man wriggling like an eel on the floor. Apparently, the man had been caught red-handed stealing some item or other. There was no room for a defence! Chris did ask the trussed-up prisoner if he had anything to say about his stealing, but the poor man was rambling so much, not even Jacob could decipher what he was saying. We figured he was pleading for his life! Chris then took me to one side to discuss the situation. I told him we couldn't possibly call the authorities, and he agreed. But we had to do something in order not to lose face in front of Jacob and the others. Chris then came up with the master stroke, an ingenious idea that would satisfy everyone concerned, especially him! He turned to me and said, "Well you're the policeman, you sort it out!" With that, he turned away and went back inside the house. I just stared blankly at his receding back.

Eventually, I turned to Jacob, who was staring expectantly at me and asked him what he and the others wanted to happen to this man. They all went into a huddle, and returned with their verdict. It was unanimous, he must be beaten! My heart sank, as Africans took beatings very seriously! Jacob said that he must receive twenty lashes with a particularly whippy type of stick across his bare flesh, and they must be delivered by Jacob. Delivered with the usual enthusiasm that Africans put into meting out a beating, twenty lashes would do some very serious damage to this guy, it might even have killed him. I listened to Jacob and then told him what was going to happen.

I told him I accepted that the thief had to be punished and punished by Africans in the African way. He would be driven deep into the bush to a suitable punishment site. There, in my capacity as the "Bwana", I would pronounce sentence on him and he would be stripped of his trousers. However, he was not to receive twenty lashes, he would receive five lashes across his naked buttocks, and I would see to it that blood was not drawn. After the beating, he would be left in the bush to find his own way home. It would be extremely painful for him, but without blood being drawn, there was no risk of infection. Jacob and the others thought this was a very suitable punishment, and immediately dragged him off to the Landrover. Although I wanted very much to let the man walk to the vehicle, it was important that Jacob and the others delivered their little bit of "justice", after all, they had caught him, he was their prisoner.

We set off for the bush and Jacob directed me to a spot about 20 kilometers away from the farm, deep in virgin bush. All the way, they were taunting the man and taking little digs at him. I knew this because every now and then he let out a little yelp of pain! When we got to the spot, he was unloaded from the back of the Landrover and spilled out onto the ground. Jacob had immediately gone off in search of his stick. He returned a few minutes later, enthusiastically swishing a length of branch, stripped of leaves and bark, about five feet long, and very whippy!

Jacob was smiling broadly; he was about to inflict severe pain on someone, and he was going to enjoy it! The man's trousers were removed and I then, very solemnly, pronounced my sentence on him. He immediately began to squirm, and beg me for mercy. He was screaming and crying in his anguish! I told him to shut up and thank his lucky stars it would only be five lashes. The others held him face down. Jacob looked at me, and I nodded. He took such a massive swing at the man's buttocks, he almost fell over himself, and he connected with a sickening sort of snapping sound. A huge weal came up instantly, and I thought this man will be lucky not to get blood drawn. Jacob delivered the next four with as much gusto as the first and I was relieved to see that, although I could plainly see five livid lash marks on his behind, there was no blood. That didn't really matter to the man on the ground though, he was writhing and screaming in agony. Jacob and the others just laughed at him!

When it was over, I bent down to him and told him that if I ever saw him on the farm again, the punishment would be left to Jacob to decide. I made sure he understood what that meant, and we returned to the farm, with the boys all singing away happily! I thanked Chris very much for his benevolence in allowing me to deal with the thief, but we did laugh about it, and still do!

My time on the farm came to an end in the first week of October. Word had spread around the mission that I was about to leave, precipitating one of the most extraordinary and memorable events in my life.

For the whole of the day before I was due to leave, I was visited by dozens of people who lived on and around the mission. Many of them brought me gifts to take with me and all of them told me how sad they were that I was to leave, and couldn't I stay a little longer? These people barely had the essentials to enable them to live, let alone bestow gifts on some person they had only met a few short months earlier. I was completely unprepared for this outpouring of sorrow at my departure, and was very moved. I cannot explain on these pages just how I felt. Over the relatively short period of time I had spent on the farm, I had always tried hard to help them where I could, respecting them for who they were and not giving the impression I considered myself to be superior because of my colour. I had learned how to greet them in their own style and language, something which is hugely significant to them. It consisted of a small curtsy, with one hand gently beating the heart and then even more gently, clapping two hands together, all the while saying, "Mwane, mwane" which is a respectful way of saying hello. I had obviously made an impact on these people and I was humbled and deeply gratified by their generosity.

The next day, I said a tearful goodbye to Gordon and Peggy. Peggy was the stronger of the two, but when I embraced Gordon, his eyes were mistier than mine and I realised just how much I had come to love him for all his faults and foibles. When Chris drove me off the mission that day, I waved to Gordon until I could no longer see him. As we drove along the track, men, women and especially children were running alongside the Landrover, all trying to shake or hold my hand before I finally left. In the houses that we passed, people were shouting my name and waving. Others were waiting alongside the roadway and stopped the Landrover to say goodbye.

When we had left them all behind, I was silent for a long time, and Chris, bless him, didn't interfere with my thoughts.

I was going on to another adventure in South Africa, but for that moment, my heart and soul were left behind on a remote mission station, deep in the Zambian bush.

Chapter 22

I left the farm and mission station at the beginning of October 1994. My plan was to travel down to South Africa, via Victoria Falls and take up my place on the 'Guides Course' I had arranged with Drifters Safaris. After that, I had no idea, but was fairly sure something would crop up.

A couple of months prior to leaving for Zambia, I had taken a trip to North Wales, to a place called Frongoch, near Lake Bala in the Snowdonia National Park. This is where the National White-water Centre is situated, named Canolfan Tryweryn. As well as international kayaking, the centre also runs guided rafting trips along a 1.5 kilometer course. The river Tryweryn itself occurs naturally, but is a mere babbling brook until the water authority opens the taps to the reservoir, which feeds the Tryweryn and turns it into a veritable torrent with rapids graded at 3 and 4. Every rafting river in the world, even the Zambezi had rapids graded only from 1 to 5. The rapids in the Tryweryn are really quite technical rather than simply massive with huge volumes of water. Boulders have been placed in the water course to create obstructions, groins have been built out into the river to create eddies and in one particular place where a natural waterfall occurs, the authorities have created an artificial slope, known affectionately as "ski-slope" where the water drops into a "hole" and boils out the other side. Rafts dropping this hole sideways will usually flip over, tossing clients and the guide into the river. When the water authority decides that water is needed down in Chester and opens the taps, kayaking and rafting take place. They try to do it most weekends, but not always.

I introduced myself rather nervously to the person running the rafting operation, a very down-to-earth Welsh lady named Sarah. I was nervous about my being at Canolfan Tryweryn for two reasons really. First, when I was on the course in Scotland, I was acutely aware that all the other students were about 25 to 30 years younger than I was. It was obviously a young man's sport, but I balanced this against the fact that everyone else on the course was doing it for future employment, whereas I was there purely for the enjoyment. During the introductions on the course, I remember one guy saying to me after I introduced the fact that I was a serving police officer and simply wanted to learn how to guide a raft, "So, you're only here for the crack!?!" When I told him I was, he looked long and hard at me, and said, "cool"! The second reason was that at some stage, I was going to have to demonstrate the skills and techniques I had learned in Scotland. It wasn't as if I could go to a river somewhere and practise, and I knew that the guys I would be working with were all professional, or at least semi-professional guides, who really knew their business. I knew that as soon as I sat on the back of the raft, I would be guiding for real. How would they treat me? Would they respect me?

Sarah called over a young man called Paul and introduced me as a new guide, albeit "prospective". She told Paul to take me down the river with clients to assess my skill level. It turned out that Paul was a member of the Great Britain Kayaking team and rafted regularly on the Tryweryn. He was also a really pleasant and knowledgeable guy. He knew how nerve-wracking it was for me, he'd been through it himself, as of course, had all the other guides on the river that day. At the end of my assessment, Paul passed me as capable, but I should spend the first few runs on the river with an experienced guide.

Sarah was OK with this, and by the end of the day, both she and Paul were happy that I could return and guide rafts down the Tryweryn alone. It was a great day for me, as I had proved to myself and others that I was just as good as other people in a sport generally regarded as the reserve of the young and carefree.

When I returned from Africa, I contacted the centre at Canolfan Tryweryn and arranged to go up for some rafting week-ends. The management had changed significantly, but my name was remembered, and it was the start of a long association with raft-guiding, which saw me visiting the centre most week-ends I was off duty. I gradually became more expert at placing the raft and clients just where I needed them to be in the river, apart from some notable incidents. On one occasion, I committed the ultimate sin, and got bounced off the back of the raft, right in front of the centre and the watching public. I had a full raft of eight burly rugby players from Liverpool, who were all up for the trip. Having me shouting orders to them from the back of the raft was easy for them and they all paddled in unison, working as a team, but when I got bounced off and they set off alone down the river towards Chester, about a hundred miles away, they suddenly got a bit ragged in their paddling! When I eventually managed to stand up in the torrent, they were already about fifty yards away, running hard with the current. I stood in the middle of the river shouting at the top of my voice to paddle together to try and see them through the next rapid, but it was all to avail. There were paddles going in every known direction. Some were furiously paddling backwards, trying to slow the raft down, others were trying to turn into the river bank, and still others were just bemused by the whole thing and looking around. At one point, another guide saw what was happening and tried to time a jump from the river-bank into the raft to take control. It was one of those classic silent-movie type moments where the hero tries to save the stricken woman by jumping from the rail bridge onto the back of the train carriage, and just missing the end, landing in a heap on the tracks. He missed the back of the raft by inches, and he also stood in the current and watched the raft drifting gaily down the river towards Chester.

Theoretically, if the raft stayed in the centre of the river, the clients would join the River Dee, drift through Chester, past Liverpool and probably some of their houses, and eventually end up in the Irish Sea! Fortunately, this was their last run of the session and they knew that they simply had to get to the bank in order to stop. They got it together eventually where the river current eases off somewhat, paddled the raft to a suitable spot where it could be beached, about a mile further down the river. When they got back to the centre, I expected a bit of a roasting from them, but they all thought it was hugely funny, a bonus for their fee. The centre-manager, John wasn't that impressed, but then, there wasn't a guide there who hadn't been bounced off a raft before. I just happened to do it at the worst possible location.

I returned to the centre on average about twice a month, spending a small fortune on petrol to get there and back. It was a five hour journey up, and an even longer journey back through Sunday evening motorway traffic. I eventually "retired" from rafting around 2000. The management had changed yet again and the emphasis was being placed on younger men and women doing it for their living. Up to that point, many of the guides like me were freelance and part-time. We were paid for the sessions we ran, but things were changing, and the management wanted it to be operated on a far more professional basis, with the guides actually employed by the governing body, the Welsh Canoeing Association. As a result, freelancers like me were being squeezed out and I began to be offered fewer and fewer sessions. To be truthful, the travelling times were beginning to get to me anyway, and rather than be told that I was no longer needed, I thought this was a good time to bow out.

I had had five wonderful and exciting years doing something which thrilled me every time I took to the water. Every run down the river was different, because the clients were always different. Most were excellent and up for an adventure, some were useless and hated the experience. Most wanted to get wet, but some tried everything to stay dry! Whilst I always tried to give them value for money, (as in the case of the Liverpool rugby players!) and give them an exciting time, it was always probably me who enjoyed each run more than them. I earned a degree of respect from all the much younger guides for my ability and enthusiasm, but I was never going to be as good as them. They did it every day, all day for their living. I didn't need to do that, all I wanted to do was have some fun, and I did!

Before going off to Africa, Sarah from the Canolfan Tryweryn centre, gave me the name of a man who was heading-up a rafting operation in Victoria Falls, Zimbabwe. His name was Peter, and the name of his company was Safari Par Excellence. I wrote to him before leaving and he kindly wrote back and invited me to Victoria Falls to check-out his operation and maybe do some guiding on the Zambezi. It struck me as odd that, for all their expertise and knowledge, most, if not all the guides at the Tryweryn centre had not rafted on a river such as the Zambezi. Yet, here was little old me, with hardly any time on any rivers and fresh out of the box of raft-guides, being offered the opportunity to raft-guide on one of the mightiest rivers in the world. The sheer amount of water flowing over the rapids on the Zambezi has to be seen to be appreciated. It's the only river in the world where you have to wait for the water level to drop after the rainy season. It's just too much otherwise.

I arrived in Victoria Falls and immediately introduced myself to my contact. He was delighted to see me and told me to be at the office at 8am the next day for a briefing. I was to go on the river with an experienced guide.

The next day, after all the preparation and briefing, we got onto the river and paddled to the first rapid. Unlike the centre in Wales, "Safpar", as it was known, operated two types of raft, paddle rafts where the clients each have a paddle and help to power the raft along, and oar-rafts, where the guide sits in the middle of the raft and operates two oars like a rowing boat. This particular day, I was in an oar-raft.

The guide rowed us to the first rapid on the river, and having rafted the Tryweryn only a few times up to that point, I was rather unprepared for the fifteen feet drop over the edge, into the maelstrom of water below the rapid. It was a fantastic experience. The raft glided over the edge, hit the water nose-first and flipped over. The canyon was echoing to the screams of the clients as they were all pitched out and under the water, including me! Eventually, thankfully, heads bobbed up all over the place, coughing and spluttering. I remember being amazed at how quickly the guide had regained the raft, righted it and was pulling clients back on board. The experience of being pitched into swirling cold water didn't dampen any spirits and none of us could wait until we got to the next rapid.

As on the Tryweryn, the briefing given by the guides before the trip is absolutely vital for safety reasons, It tells the clients what they can expect at each rapid, and on the Zambezi, there was always a kayaker in attendance to help anyone drifting away from the raft in the current. Each of the rapids had a name, which I forget now, but as we approached one rapid, I remember the guide telling us that it would probably be better if we didn't fall out of the raft as we went through. He explained that after the first drop into the "hole", the river would suck you under and hold you under for around ten seconds. You would then surface for a split second, during which time, it was advisable to take a breath before the river pulled you under again for a second time. You would again surface for a split second before the current grabbed you a third time and held on to you for a further ten to fifteen seconds, spinning you over and over under water, completely disorientating you and generally beating the crap of you! The guide told us it was a scary experience and one not to be sampled deliberately.

As we went through the rapid, only one person fell out of the raft, me! And he was right, the river did grab me three times, it did hold me under three times, and it did beat the crap out of me! I remember it distinctly, as I really did think I wasn't going to survive. Each time I came up and struggled to get a breath, I was sucked under before I could close my mouth. The water entered my lungs and the urge to cough was almost overwhelming. I just about had time to take air in the second time, let alone have a good old cough, before being pitched over and over under the water. I came up the third time to see the raft disappearing in the distance and someone shouting like a maniac at me to grab the back of the kayak. I somehow managed to grab hold of the back and he towed me to the raft about a hundred yards further downstream. I was a sorry sight getting back into the raft, but we set off again, everyone else eager for the next rapid. Me, I was just glad to back in the raft! All in all, I came out of the raft about four times that day. I seemed to be spending as much time under the water, as on top of it.

After rafting through the last rapid, the rafts were drawn into a shallow beach area of the river. The equipment was taken out and the rafts de-flated. Everything was then carried up the incredibly steep Zambezi Gorge via a winding path. The climb out took around 40-45 minutes and at one stage, I was overtaken by a sinewy black youth carrying a massive pack on his back. This same youth then smiled at me as he made his way back down the gorge to pick up another load to carry out. I learned afterwards that the black youths were paid by how many loads they carried up the gorge side to the lorries waiting to take the equipment and the clients back to Victoria Falls, and a very welcome cold beer.

The support kayaks also took video footage of each raft going through the rapids, all the flips, all the dumpings into the river, the scrambles to get back into the rafts, the lunch-time antics and eventually the climb out. The video was shown in one of the local bars, after which, the clients and the raft-guides partied the night away in a disco. The guides however, had to be back up at six in the morning to prepare for the next day's rafting. I know for a fact that some of them didn't even bother going to bed that night.

I had a fantastic day's rafting with "SafPar", but having seen what was expected of the guides before and after the day's rafting, I decided that there was no way I was going to even attempt to become a guide on the Zambezi. I was never going to be able to keep up the pace! Although I felt I could handle the rafting, this really was a young man's position and I was happy to pass. My contact completely understood my position. He told me I was welcome back anytime and wished me well in Johannesburg, to where I was heading after leaving Victoria Falls.I was not to know at that stage, that the "Mighty Zambezi" river would have three more attempts at drowning me before I finally left Africa.

I hung around Victoria Falls for another couple of days, for no reason other than it was a nice place. I had bought a train ticket all the way from Vic. Falls to Johannesburg, via Bulawayo, ("The place of Killing") Zimbabwe.

I had taken the train from Lusaka to Livingstone and then on to Victoria Falls a couple of days earlier, and thoroughly enjoyed the experience. (The reader may remember that Livingstone was where I was arrested for "spying" in 1989. I didn't see too much of Livingstone this time as I arrived after dark and left the following morning before dawn). The Zambian train carriages were old but clean, the seats were comfortable but the plastic material caused you to sweat, the diesel engine was powerful, but oh! so slow. We rumbled rhythmically along through the seemingly never-ending bush, stopping at each remote village on the way to pick up or drop off passengers. There were no stations or platforms in these places and passengers either jumped the few feet from the bottom step onto the ground, or clambered up as best they could. Amidst all this, the food sellers would run up and down the length of the train, trading in samosas and scrawny chicken pieces, which were practically all bone. They were scrupulously honest, always returning with change if they had to get it from someone else, and even amidst what would appear to the casual observer, to be absolute chaos, they never seemed to forget which carriage the customer was in.

There was only one track between Livingstone and Lusaka and trains were scheduled to leave simultaneously from both places to travel to the other. Consequently, half way along the track was a passing place where the track was divided into two. The train from Livingstone to Lusaka was called the "up" train and the one going the other way was the "down" train. Whichever got to the passing place first had to take the side track and stop and wait for the other train to pass. If the other train had broken down or was running very late, there was nothing to do but wait it out, and sweat it out. (This happened to me more than once in later travels around the area.)

The train from Victoria Falls to Bulawayo was a relic from the Victorian era; plush cloth seating, curtains at the windows and wood paneling everywhere, an absolute joy, but just as slow as the Zambian trains. The train from Bulawayo to Johannesburg was a little more modern, completely soulless, but faster. I finally arrived in Johannesburg sometime around the middle of November 1994, spent some time relaxing with Bob and Helen and sorting out my gear for the forthcoming Guides Course with Drifters Safaris.

The course was due to start from Drifters' base in Northcliffe, Johannesburg early one Monday morning. I had been told to report at 8am to meet my fellow students and the instructors. To say that I was extremely nervous about this, would be an understatement! Having thought a lot about what I was about to do, the main aspect that struck me was that here was I, a 43 year old London police officer about to take a fortnight's course on learning about the fauna and flora of South Africa with people half my age, twice as capable and who did at least live on the continent! What the hell was I doing?

I arrived in good time at the base, and reported my arrival. There were, as I expected, about six or seven other people milling around with lots of bags and gear, all brimming with youthful strength and vitality. The one thing that seemed to bind them all together was that they all spoke with the same South African accent. Heavens knows what they initially made of me, standing on my own just watching what was going on. They probably didn't even think I was on the course! Suddenly, my thoughts were interrupted by my name being called out, "Neil Robins, where's Neil Robins?" Having decided not to bolt straight back to Bob and Helen's house and safety, I took a deep breath, and called out, "here". I was approached by a young woman with a fantastic shock of dark, curly hair. Her name was Anne-Marie and she was the course organiser. "Hello", she said, "I just wanted to say Hi and welcome, you must be nervous about this!" We shook hands and suddenly, all my fears and anxieties slipped away. She introduced me personally to the course leader, Steve Maidment, who was a Drifters director and also her fiancee. Between them, they made the introductions to the other guys on the course and I immediately began to feel that I was going to enjoy this after all. True, they were all South African and all bar one as it turned out, was much younger than me, but right from the start, they all took an immense interest in me, my job and my motivation for being there in the first place.

Over the following two weeks, I think they all rather took to me and gave me a good deal of respect for having the courage to get of my box and do something different. I shall certainly never forget how Anne-Marie realised my situation and how she eased it for me. I am still in touch to this day with Steve and Anne-Marie and see them whenever I go back to Johannesburg.

When it was time to leave, we all piled onto the strangest looking vehicle I had ever seen. It was bright yellow, with doors halfway down the side, windows that didn't open and hatches in the roof. The seating was cramped and uncomfortable and when we were travelling along, we had to shout at each other to make ourselves heard above the engine noise. And this was to be our home for the next two weeks, great!!

We were briefed before the vehicle left, that the course would start the moment we turned onto the road from the base. We would have certain points of interest made known to us and we were expected to make copious notes as we went along, difficult in this rattley old bus!

I really don't remember exactly where we went and exactly everything we did over the two weeks, and even if I did, I wouldn't bore the reader with the minutiae. There were however, some defining moments for me over the weeks that came and I shall attempt to recount some of these.

As the course progressed, I became a lot more relaxed and really began to enjoy the company of my fellow students. One guy especially was the course comedian. His name was Van Zeyl Schultz. The Africaans language is derived from Dutch and many of the names adopted by South Africans have Dutch origins. "Van Zeyl" however, is not a fore-name as such, rather a surname. Van Zeyl explained it one day as his mother having had so many children, when he was born she'd ran out of christian names and so started on the surnames she knew! I think having two surnames shaped his future character somehow, because this guy was one of the most naturally funny men I have ever come across. He was a gifted mimic, his impression of Nelson Mandela was demanded every day, as was Murray Walker commentating at an imaginary Formula 1 race. His wit was just the quickest and he never stopped fooling around, which I think, was probably his undoing in the end. He was also a drinker and a long time after, Steve and I were chatting about the course. He told me that Van Zeyl had applied for a job as a guide with Drifters and that he had had no hesitation in turning him down on account that the company could never trust him not to drink or fool around all the time. Nobody could match Van Zeyl for wit and humour, but I did my little bit by insisting that everyone on the course learned the first verse of what became known as the "song of the day." I'm one of these people who knows the first few lines or verses of lots of songs, but never the whole thing. During the long, hot hours we spent driving, Van Zeyl made us laugh and I sang a different song every day.

As we travelled to the various destinations, Steve regaled us with information about the area we were in, the common and latin names of trees, the names of birds and animals, their habitat etc etc. I was always going to be struggling with this information, but in the end, other qualities I displayed would ultimately impress Steve and the other instructor, Douwe, (pronounced "doowa")

Early on in the course, we spent three days hiking in the Drakensberg Mountains, sleeping in caves and out in the open. Steve explained about the mechanics of anabatic and catabatic winds, the geology, where the water and rivers emanated from and at night, we had tutorials on stellar navigation and star recognition. I began to wonder whether Steve had a live feed from some computer source or other, such was his knowledge. In fact, as Van Zeyl was just about the funniest man I had ever come across, so Steve was the most intelligent and knowledgeable. He answered all our questions and explained everything in easy to understand terms, even though his knowledge went much, much deeper.

On one particular day, we hiked up a really steep and long incline. It was made more difficult by the heat and the fact we had to negotiate large rocky outcrops. The climb took us most of the afternoon and by the end of it, our packs seemed to be almost twice as heavy, such was the effort it took. There was one woman on the course, who was about the same age as me, but nowhere near as fit. She really struggled with this climb, and by the time most of us had reached the cabin at the top where we would spend the night, she was a good two to three hundred yards behind us back down the mountain. It was obvious she was having problems, as we could see her stopping every few yards. Steve and Douwe were behind her, trying to chivvy her along but it was clear she was seriously flagging. The climb had exhausted me and I felt completely drained, but when I saw this woman struggling, I went back down the mountain to where she was. I took her pack off and slung it on my back and then walked with her up the mountain. It was obvious she wasn't as strong as the rest of us, but the mere fact that, despite being exhausted, I had gone back for her and relieved her of her burden, seemed to give her renewed energy and she made it to the top. It was a seemingly minor little incident, but apparently, Steve had noted that I was the only one to notice this and take some form of action. He and Douwe were deliberately not helping her to see if any of us would.

I scored another little point the next day, when we had descended to the bottom to meet the transport. We were sitting outside on a hotel verandah having a very welcome cold beer. A flock of small birds landed on the ground near us and began pecking at whatever they could find in the grass. I looked over at them, and just muttered, "Bronze Mannekins." Steve obviously heard what I had said and asked how I, a British police officer would know that. I told him that during my walks around the mission farm, I took a bird book with me to try and identify as many species as I could. Bronze Mannekins were common around the mission, as were other little seed-eaters such as Waxbills, and so recognition of them was easy when I saw them later on the verandah. It wasn't so much the fact that I had identified a species of bird, but more that I had actively tried to learn about the African fauna and flora. Yet another little piece of information to be stored in Steve's considerable memory!

As the course progressed, I began to feel ever more comfortable with my surroundings and my colleagues. Even the discomfort of the truck paled into insignificance. The "song of the day" had become an established feature of the routine and I seemed to be regarded more as a friend than an outsider.

Two of my course colleagues intrigued me more than others, Frikke and Leon. We all had our motives for being on the course; Van Zeyl was looking for work, I was there for the experience and Frikke and Leon were on holiday from the gold mine they both worked at. Neither had any intention of going into the safari or environment business, they were just there for fun. Frikke was the more outgoing of the two, always laughing and appearing to be enjoying himself hugely. Leon was more brooding. I distinctly remember talking to Leon one day and looking directly into his eyes. They had a blankness about them, a vacancy and although I could see he was looking back at me, I just knew that he wasn't seeing me. He was actually, quite scary to talk to.

One night, we had stopped at the house belonging to a friend of the owner of Drifters, Andy Dott. Steve had dictated that we would be sleeping outside on the rough ground, even though dark rain clouds had been gathering overhead all day. I remember it was around midnight when the wind suddenly whipped up, distant thunder began to get louder and the lightning more frequent. A violent storm was imminent. I was watching the sky, when I became aware of someone moving around in the gloom, shaking bodies awake and moving us indoors. Anyone who has experienced an African thunderstorm, will know that outside in it, is not the place to be!

I was peeling my sleeping bag off me and just idly watching the figure shaking people awake, when he approached Leon's sleeping body and touched the feet end of his bag. The next few moments became a blur of action. Leon had come out of his sleeping bag with blinding speed and had taken hold of the guy's throat. He had taken him to the ground and was on top of him, throttling him. The guy was struggling wildly and it was only Frikke coming to his rescue almost immediately that seemed to save him.

The following morning, after the storm had passed, Leon and I were washing dishes. I asked him if he had been in the Special Forces. He looked at me and asked if I had seen what had happened the previous night. When I said I had, he explained that, yes, he had been in the forces, in the Angolan bush-war. He had been trained to survive for weeks in the bush without food, water or equipment of any kind. He had been trained to kill silently and swiftly. His instructors would attack him deliberately when he had fallen asleep and so, he had developed a method of sleeping, just under the surface as it were. He had been trained to attack in an instant and when the poor guy woke him the previous night, Leon was back in the Angolan bush. He went on to say that his Army service had been 10 or 12 years previously, but he simply couldn't shake the training he had been given. He regularly received requests to join some mercenary unit or other, fighting some tin-pot little war somewhere in Africa. He always refused, just wanting to lead a normal life like a normal guy. I got the impression that he was quite bitter about his experiences in the bush, and I can't say I blame him. I later came across other guys working for Drifters who had had similar training and experiences. The owner, Andy liked to employ ex-forces guys as he thought they would be tougher than most and more able to withstand the rigours of safari life. Some of them were, shall we say, a little off-centre.

The course progressed with us learning about such diverse subjects as vehicle mechanics, plant leaf variations and construction, rifle shooting, off-road driving and jumping from a 20 feet high cliff into a river and then swimming 400 yards, fortunately with the current! We even watched while a professional hunter skinned a freshly killed Impala antelope. He hadn't shot it just for us, the animal had a massive abscess on her side and wouldn't have survived much longer in any event.

After nearly two weeks, we arrived at a private game park called "Hope" somewhere in the Eastern Transvaal. The first night we were there, an actual Drifters Safari came in and passed by our camp. Steve told us they would be camping just down the road from us, and some of us thought it would be nice if we popped over there later and introduced ourselves. An idea suddenly occurred to me; "What if," I said to the others, "we sneaked as close to the camp as possible and then, from the darkness of the bush, sang them some songs?" If we did it right, it would seem that the voices would be coming directly out of the night. Steve thought it was a cracking idea and so did the others, Van Zeyl especially.

We decided that the first song would be the first verse of "You've lost that loving feeling" by the Righteous Brothers. The others however, decided that I would sing the verse solo, and they would come in at the end with the chorus, "Dah dum, dah dum, dah dum, dah dum, daaaah dum" The second song was a rather bawdy version of the old classic "Ten green bottles" dramatically shortened to one verse and the third song completely escapes me.

When we had eaten, Steve told us the clients would be chilling out around their fire, so we set off to walk the half-mile to their camp. It was a really dark night with no moon-light and completely still. As we got nearer to them, we could hear their chatter in the distance. We crept to within about 10 or 12 feet of their camp, just on the edge of the bush, trying desperately not to laugh, giggle or snort.

At a suitable lull in the conversation, and not without a considerable effort from me to control my nerves, I started to sing, strong and loud. I have to say, I surprised even myself. I was immediately in tune, not wavering and hitting all the notes. As I was singing, I became aware of the others all turning to look at me, amazement on their faces. We could see the group around the fire, and they all turned around in their chairs to see where the singing was coming from, some were giggling but I have to say that most were just listening and later laughing at our songs. In the end, of course, we came out of the bush and spent a very pleasant few hours chatting with them and drinking coffee. They had really appreciated our little joke and enjoyed being serenaded immensely. Van Zeyl later told me that, whilst he and the others thought I had a good voice, they didn't realise I was that good. I'm not, but they really were surprised and enjoyed the joke all the more for its success.

The second to last night in "Hope" would be spent sleeping out in the game park itself, rather than in the crude shelters we had used up till then. After dinner, we were all briefed as to what was going to happen and what we should do. There was an element of danger to this as hyena were present in the park. There were no other predator animals such as lion, but even so, with hyena around, there was still danger.

After briefing, we all piled onto the old Land-Rover belonging to the owner and were driven blind-fold around the park. We would complete this exercise in pairs, and when our names were called, we took the blind-folds off and jumped down from the vehicle, armed only with our sleeping bags, except me that is! Whilst being driven around, I suddenly remembered I had left my sleeping bag in the camp and was much too embarrassed to admit as much. When Van Zeyl and I arrived at our spot, I told him what I had forgotten and after he stopped laughing, he loaned me his coat. I spent a very uncomfortable night, freezing cold and wondering if a wandering hyena would bite my feet off.

After two weeks of an intensive course, this Sunday was our last day, and the day of the big examination! Anything we had covered over the previous weeks, any place we had visited, anything we had seen or been told about, could be included. The exam was to last around four hours, although the time allowed was fairly flexible. Leon and Frikke were the only two not to take the exam, although I must admit, I had wondered whether it was going to be worth my while to do so. I had only joined the course in the first place because for me, the cost was really cheap and it comprised a lot of what I enjoyed doing anyway. The prospect of my becoming a guide seemed too remote to contemplate. However, I thought as I had come all the way from England to do the course, not to take the exam at the end, seemed pointless.

Having persuaded myself to sit the exam, I began to look forward to testing my own knowledge. I had made copious notes throughout the course, and these did stand me in good stead during some parts, but my enthusiasm began to wane when I read the questions about identifying birds, animals and trees. There were twenty-five pictures of each, and I reckon I got about six or seven in each category of birds and animals. The trees were almost a complete mystery, they all looked the same, apart from the 'Umbrella Thorn', which is quite distinctive. When I read the question, "Name the five towers of Cape Town Fort," my answer was a rather flippant, "Ask me one on sport!!" I knew I hadn't done that well at the end, but there we are. My excuse was, "I'm English, what do you expect?"

That evening, after dinner, I asked Steve what he thought was next for me, if anything. His reply rather took me by surprise. He explained that the boss, Andy Dott, didn't really like anyone who wasn't male, South African and ex-forces. Two out of three wouldn't cut it for him, but he would have a word with Andy about me the following day when we got back to Johannesburg, and that was really all I could hope for.

We arrived back at Drifters' base the following afternoon, and said our goodbyes, and thanked each other for a great trip. We'd had lots of laughs, learned a few things and made new friends, but for me, above everything was the fact that I had had yet another taste of Africa, different from Zambia and Victoria Falls. This time, I had learned a little about Africa which few people tend to bother with. The animals, birds and trees seem to be taken mostly for granted, even by Africans, both black and white. I was given this taste by a man whose passion for African fauna and flora was a joy to behold. I felt privileged that I had spent time with Steve, and even if I went no further than the Drifters base that Monday afternoon, the experience would have been worthwhile.

I went back to Bob and Helen's house in Randpark Ridge that evening, full of what I had learned on the course and eager to share it with them. The next day, I was in the middle of explaining something to them, when I was called to the phone by one of the girls, (Bob and Helen had three daughters, all living at home). It was Steve, telling me that the boss, Andy wanted to see me the following day at 10am.

I arrived shortly before 10, spoke briefly with Anne-Marie, and then went in to see Andy Dott, the owner of Drifters. I remember the conversation we had was short. It was obvious he didn't like me much, but he was gracious enough to tell me that Steve had told him how well I had done on the course! I was slightly puzzled by this, until Andy said that my exam mark was "crap" but that Steve and Douwe had marked me extremely high on leadership and communication, the best on the course! He went on to say that he needed people who could lead a group on safari and communicate with them. If I was interested in becoming a guide, he said, my bird, animal and tree knowledge would grow with each trip, and there were always books I could refer to. I suddenly realised he was offering me a position as Safari Guide, which I accepted with alacrity. "Good" he said, "you start tomorrow!"

After the interview, I went back to Bob and Helen's house to tell them the good news, not only that I had been offered the post of Safari Guide, but also that I will need to stay at their house when not on safari. As I suspected, this posed no problem, but all the same, I was grateful that I could stay there and not have to find temporary digs with someone else. They were both very happy for me, Bob especially, as he liked my attitude to life, go out and sample what it holds!

Chapter 23

I arrived for my first day at Drifters, and was introduced to a man-mountain named Ian Oberholzer, who would be my mentor for my first trip, which was a 16-day camping safari around Botswana. The guide I was replacing, Udo, sold me all his equipment, which I then transported out to the operations base at Lammermoor, on the outskirts of Johannesburg, where the operations director and the man responsible for getting me into Drifters, Steve was waiting to greet me.

The one item of equipment I didn't have however, was a braai (barbecue) grid. "No problem," said Steve, and gave me some lengths of steel and some mesh. "There you go, make one!" This was probably the one and only time, when my one and only "O" level from school, metalwork, might have come in useful. However, the "O" level course didn't include welding and grinding etc, but Ian helped me and together we made a very satisfactory grid, which lasted me all the time I was with Drifters.

The owner of Drifters, Andy Dott had started the business some years previously by placing an advert in a magazine, offering trips into the Drakensburg Mountains in an old VW Camper. The telephone contact he gave was the number of a local phone box, and he would wait around at the phone-box all day, just in case someone called. From this inauspicious beginning, Drifters grew into a major player in the safari business. If not liked, Andy was well respected for his business acumen and his commitment to conservation. Unfortunately, his people skills and personality let him down sadly. He employed only the minimum number of guides he needed, who were often sent off on safaris tired and exhausted from a previous trip. There was no fall-back position. It would however, be remiss of me to dismiss the fact that, despite his prejudices, he was willing to employ me in a position where the reputation of his company rested solely with the guide for two weeks. He wasn't at all bothered by the fact that I would be working illegally and if caught, would be deported. As the employer, he would also run a certain risk of trouble with the Immigration Service. There again, he knew better than I. As it turned out, I entered and left South Africa six times by the same "gate" and dealt with the same officials, who always gave me three months stay.

One point in my favour was that, at this time, the border officials were white. Had they been black, the situation would have been very different. The border crossing between Botswana and Zimbabwe at Kazangula for example, was a nightmare by comparison because the black officials would not allow anyone through with even the slightest mistake on paperwork. I had to check all the clients' paperwork before handing it to the officials for the inevitable stamping.

Whilst working for Drifters, I met a young man, who was to have an influence on my life to this day. His name then, was Heiko Gelaitis. When I went to work for Drifters, Heiko was already regarded as the number 1 guide, even at his tender age of

21. As much as I regard myself as "unremarkable", Heiko was, and remains, the complete opposite. There will be more about Heiko later in the narrative.

I went off on my first safari with nine clients around Botswana and ending at Victoria Falls, sometime in the first week of December 1994. The plan was that, Ian Oberholzer would be the actual guide, but I would be doing all the work, driving, cooking, spotting animals, running the camp, buying food etc. Ian would watch and evaluate everything I did on the trip, reporting back to Steve and Andy when we reached Victoria Falls in Zimbabwe.

I eventually conducted six wild-camp safaris around Botswana, but for the sake of boredom, I intend to take the reader only on the first and describe it in some detail. Where certain events took place on later safaris, I shall describe them at the point at which they occurred.

The clients generally stayed overnight at the Drifters Inn, located next to the office in Northcliffe, ready for a 6am start on Saturday morning. Andy would gather them all together in the lounge of the Inn, greet them and then brief them as to the following 16 days. All the camping gear, luggage, cooking equipment and some food, was loaded into, and onto the roof, of the transfer vehicle, a Toyota Hiace people carrier, and we then set off for Nata in Botswana, a mere twelve hour drive away!

At Nata, we camped at an established site, Nata Camp and the following morning, set off for the game parks of Moremi and Chobe in the safari four-wheel drive truck, which on this occasion was a Mercedes-Benz Unimog, affectionately known as "BJ" (for the first two letters of its registration number). On the way, we diverted onto the Makgadikgadi Salt Pans for the first night.

The pans are situated at the very extreme edge of the Okavango Delta and comprise vast "lakes" of pure white salt crust. Occasionally, during very heavy rains, these "lakes" flood to a depth of around 9 inches, completely altering the landscape. On a later trip, I was fortunate enough to be camping on the pans on a night when the moon was at its fullest. At 2am, I tried to get everyone out of their tents to look at the moonlight reflecting off the salt on the pan, it was so beautiful. No-one could be bothered to even poke their head out of the tent!

From the salt pans, we headed north and on to Maun ("The place of Short Reeds" in the local language, Tswana). Maun was, and still is to some degree, regarded as a bit of a frontier town. It's the place where practically every safari company in the region runs into and out of. Consequently, it's a bit of a wild place. Rules and laws, which apply to everywhere else, are not necessarily abided by in Maun. Over the years, it has developed into a thriving town. Entire companies have based their operations there and these days, it's possible to arrange any kind of safari an individual might desire.

In Maun, we picked up fresh meat and vegetables in preparation for the next three days, which would be spent camping in the depths of the Okavango Delta. Ian knew exactly what he had to buy, but he made me go through the menu for the next days and work out what we needed. This would be excellent training for me and over the following trips, I never underestimated the amount of food we needed.

Drifters had a guide based in Maun, at the Crocodile Camp, who would spend three months there. His job was to look after the safari trucks and get them serviced or repaired as necessary whilst we were in the delta. This was my first meeting with Heiko, a tall, superbly muscled young man who looked rather like a Greek god, but with an ego to match. I was later to discover just what an extraordinary man Heiko is, a brilliant engineer, fine sportsman, sharp businessman and generally, not someone to be trifled with. On this occasion, I remember him telling Ian and I that after we had returned from the Delta and left Maun for the parks, he was going to take his jeep and go and "try to break Victoria Falls!" If ever there was a man who could find a way to do that, it was Heiko.

When everything was ready, we drove "BJ" into the bush for around two hours, towards the Delta, eventually arriving at our destination, a small village on the waters edge called Ditchipi. Heiko drove in with us, as this was where our journey into the Delta would begin and Heiko would drive "BJ" back to Maun for some servicing.

The Okavango Delta is one of the most extraordinary environmental locations in the world. In my opinion, the ancients missed this one off the list of Natural Wonders of the World.

It is a completely landlocked delta, formed when the Earth's crust moved and created a Rift Valley. The water comes from the Okavango River, which rises in Angola and then flows into Botswana. The heavy rains of December to February feed the flood, but the water doesn't actually reach the delta area and Maun, until around six months later. Over a distance of around 250 kilometres, the fall is only about 50 metres, so the progress of the water is slow in the extreme. The slow pace of the current enables the sand and silt in the water to be deposited in the delta, leaving the water exceptionally clear and drinkable.

So much sand has been deposited over the ages, that the original level of the valley, is now some 300 metres below the present delta floor. Around 95% of the delta water evaporates before reaching the main drainage river, the Thamakalane, and some of the rest simply disappears into the sand. In any one spot in the delta, the current flows inexorably south, but then it just disappears. It seems to defy logic, which dictates that any body of water with a current, must eventually empty into the ocean or at least, a large lake. Not so with the Okavango Delta; it's a phenomenon which has to be experienced to be believed. And the beauty of the area in the wet season never ceased to amaze me!

At Ditchipi, we transferred all the camping gear, food and water we would need into rough-hewn, dug-out canoes called "Mokkorros". This is virtually the only way to travel the area, apart from flying in, which is cheating really. The mokkorros were powered by a single person, male or female, standing at the back of the canoe and poling it along, much like one would "punt" a boat on the River Cam in Cambridge. We would then sit on top of the luggage and gear and enjoy the trip. How on earth the polers kept the mokkorros upright was always a mystery to me as, although they had a flat bottom, they had no keel. The passengers, including me, were all under strict instructions not to move around too much. It wasn't so much getting dunked in the water, it was losing the equipment, which was of more concern to me. Clients can swim, tents and food containers can't!

At the waters' edge at Ditchipi, the safari guide and the head-poler from the village enter into prolonged discussions as to how many mokkorros would be needed for a particular trip. As the polers were paid by the number used, the head-poler would always try and make a case for taking far too many mokkorros, ergo, far too many polers! I always enjoyed the interaction between myself and the head-poler, arguing our respective cases back and forth. I have to say though, that I always knew exactly how many polers and mokkorros I would need, but it was important that we negotiated and reach an amicable settlement, in my favour!

We spent the next day and a half, traveling northwards in the delta, to a particular camp opposite Chief's Island. The only sounds which accompanied us, were the eerie cries of the African Fish Eagles, perched high in the trees and the gentle splash of the mokkorro pole being dragged through the water, and that was hardly audible. The mokkorros slid silently over the water and the clients generally snoozed, reclined and gazed the day away.

I eventually went into the Delta on six separate occasions, and each time, we seemed to take a different route through the water channels. To anyone not brought up in the delta, the myriad waterways would seem like a watery maze, there are literally thousands of them, but the polers always knew exactly where they were, which was just as well, because I, as the "guide", didn't have a clue!

The camps we made were always under a group of shady trees. The clients set their tents around in a rough semi-circle, with the table in the middle and the camp-fire just on the edge. Drifter's safaris were always sold as "participative" trips, with the clients helping out setting up the camp, erecting their own tents and helping with the cooking. It was never mandatory, but the way we briefed them on the first night at Nata, we made it plain that they would get far more out of the trip, if they took part in the actual experience. Otherwise, they may as well have stayed at home and gone to a safari park, or a lodge where everything would be done for them and they would just go out on game-drives morning and evening. Our way, they would actually take part in a "safari", smell and taste the African bush, get dirty and gain some small experience of what it was like to live there.

Lunch on the second day in the Delta was always a high point. The polers knew exactly where we would stop for lunch, and pulled into the bank to unload the lunch table, chairs and food. The clients would amuse themselves idly at the waters' edge, taking endless photographs or simply chatting, and then watch bemused, as we carried the table and chairs etc into the water and set the lunch table actually in the water, in the middle of the channel, on a shallow, sand-bank. The food would be laid out on the table and the clients invited to wade out into the current and sit down for lunch. I can think of few more pleasant experiences than sitting under the African sun, in one of the most beautiful places on earth, laughing and eating lunch at a table with clear, cool water flowing over my feet and ankles. The clients loved it, and so did I!

The second and third nights in the delta, were spent at the same camp, under a clump of trees with a vast open plain on one side and the river channel on the other.

Across the other side of the channel, lay Chief's Island, where we would walk on the third morning and just up-channel from our camp, a group of hippopotamus, known most often as a pod, resided. On land, hippos walk to find grazing, but in the water, they fiercely protect their territory from intruders. One bite from an adult hippo could easily kill a human, and hippopotamus account for the most number of human deaths in Africa. They generally didn't bother the mokkorros, although there had been occasions when grumpy hippos had overturned craft and tipped clients, polers, food etc into the water, but swimming anywhere near to their territory was absolutely forbidden by me and any other guide with even a modicum of sense.

After a long hot day, squeezed into a tiny space, the first thing many clients wanted to do was get into the water and cool off. When we got to the camp, they were told there was a "swimming hole" just beyond the camp. It wasn't part of the main channel and was therefore safe from the hippos, they could cool off there.

On one trip, one of the polers came running up to me as I was setting up the kitchen. He pointed excitedly out into the main channel to where two or three male clients had decided to go for a swim, completely ignoring my instructions! The hippo territory was about 100 metres up-stream, and much too close for comfort, which was why they weren't allowed to swim there. I thought this was fairly simple to understand, even for Germans who could speak English! The poler and I ran to the mokkorros, with me shouting at the top of my voice for them to get out of the water immediately. The channel at this point was a good 150 metres wide and they weren't really listening to me. They were having a fine old time, shouting and splashing around in the water, just the thing to attract an angry hippo bull! We poled frantically across the channel to where they were, with me expecting to see the bulk of an adult hippo rise at any moment. We reached them in double quick time and they soon realised I was serious about them getting out of the water. I could see the hippos in the distance, just bobbing around on the surface, snorting and blowing and looking in the direction of the swimmers, but I had no idea of what was happening underwater. Hippos can travel long distances under the surface, certainly a few hundred metres. If one of the adults took exception to the German swimmers being that near to their territory, it could attack from under-water and the victim wouldn't stand a chance!

When I had finally run out of derivations of the word "idiot", we poled the clients back across the channel into the camp. They told me they had understood what I had said to them earlier about not swimming, but didn't think I was that serious about it! After the next tirade and volley of abuse from me, we reached the camp, and they rather sheepishly wandered up to and into their tents, much to the amusement of the other polers who had gathered at the waters edge to "welcome" them back with hoots of derision. Love their hearts!!

Most of the morning of the third day in the delta, was taken up with a walk on Chief's Island. The clients were all fully briefed the previous evening on what to do if we happened to stumble across a dangerous animal, such lion or buffalo. Basically, they were told to do exactly as we told them. The guides never carried guns, we had to rely on knowledge of animal behaviour and some good old-fashioned common sense.

The head poler, normally one of two guys named James or Landy, would lead the walk, the clients would walk behind, always in single file and the guide would bring up the rear. They were warned not to wear bright clothing or chatter out loud, in case an animal became spooked and saw us as a threat. We walked for about four or five hours, until about 11am, when it became extremely hot and then made our way back to camp for breakfast.

On one particular trip, we were on our way back to camp, not having seen too much in the way of game. Concentration levels were obviously low as I could see Landy at the head of the file, swishing the heads off flowers with his "knob-kerrie" as he walked along and I was planning the breakfast. The sun was getting hot, the day was peaceful, with only birdsong to listen to. The path we were on took us into some long grass, about up to our waists, when suddenly, the peace was shattered by the most awful and frightening cacophany of noise. We had inadvertently walked into a pride of lions, chilling out in the long grass after their morning kill and feast. They bomb-burst away from us, snarling, and hissing and crashing through the grass to safer ground. Everyone naturally froze, especially Landy, as he would have been the first for pudding! However, it only took a second or two to realise what was going on, and I hustled all the clients up close together to give the impression of an even bigger animal than the lions first imagined. For all its power and majesty, the lion doesn't possess much of an imagination, and it sees a group of people, not as that, but as an animal bigger and more powerful than it, and something definitely to get away from.

We could see most of the pride when they had run 50 or 60 yards away, staring back at us but even so, we still kept very close together, watching the pride the whole time and crept through the long grass in case any stragglers were lurking around. It would have been especially dangerous had any cubs been around and left behind.

It was a very scary moment, and one I suspect the clients, like me, will not forget in a rush! Back in the camp, I cooked up a huge brunch of bacon, eggs, sausage, tomatoes, fried potatos and beans whilst the clients loudly reflected on their adventure. After brunch, I went to sleep!

The fourth and final day was taken up with returning to Ditchipi, loading the equipment back into "BJ" and heading back to Crocodile Camp for a well earned shower. All the while, Ian was watching and evaluating how I was doing; how I was treating and communicating with the clients, how well I was getting on with the cooking and how well my knowledge was growing. I had decided not to try and kid the clients that I knew the fauna and flora like the back of my hand. Consequently, when they asked a question I couldn't immediately answer, I told them so and looked it up later from the library of books that we carried in the equipment. I always made sure I gave them an answer, even if it was a little late. The clients seemed to appreciate this, after all, they knew I was just training, and I think Ian was impressed by this attitude.

After a night in Crocodile Camp, we set off early the following morning for our journey through the game-parks towards Victoria Falls. Botswana had a rule that every safari going through the parks, had to have a local guide with them. On this trip, and every one after for me, our local man was "Press", a curious name, but did he know his way around! On evening game drives, we could be out for two or three hours, just driving aimlessly around looking for game. At some stage, I would say to Press, "let's go home for dinner" and he would know instantly where he was and where the road back to camp was. He always knew that, when it was getting dark, I would call a halt and had driven the truck to a position, which would get us back to camp within a few minutes.

The following four days were taken up with travelling around and through the game parks of Moremi and Chobe, spotting game and wild-camping at places with wonderful names such as Third Bridge and Xwai River. The "wild-camps" we used were so called because they were not fenced in at all, wild animals could come and go through the camp at will, and some of the time, we had to use the bush as our toilet.

Some of the animal visitations were welcome, and some were not. After dinner at Xwai River, we were often visited in the evening by a hyena, which would come right into the camp, walking past the clients sitting in their chairs with that very particular hunched gait. I must admit to being slightly nervous the first time it happened to me, but Ian was great and told all the clients simply to sit still and watch.

Xwai River was where we cooked a large joint of lamb in the open fire. We would then leave the bone on a plate at the edge of the table, knowing that the hyena, a dirty, ugly old thing, would come in eventually. We didn't tell the clients it would come, but told them that something may happen and if it did, just sit still and don't make a sudden move. When it came in to the camp, it walked right past the clients and gently lifted the bone off the plate, right in front of them. The hyena would then slope off into the night and devour every last sliver of bone in a series of crunches that sounded like someone crushing a bag of crisps.

I suppose we could be criticized for leaving the bone out for the hyena to take. The animal is however, a natural scavenger. Whilst they will hunt if necessary, hyena prefer to take the scraps left by other animals and are known to chase lions away from a kill. Taking the bone off the plate was just a natural thing for the animal to do. If we had buried it, the hyena would have smelt and dug it up, so what would be the difference? There is a human side I suppose, in that the hyena would get too used to human presence, but they already knew that scrap food would be available in and around the camps, so they hung around, even with humans still there. They're not stupid, but they are lazy and they know where the easy meal is to be found!

On another occasion at the same camp, I was making my way back to the camp after taking a shower, when I became aware of a thundering sound in the distance. I looked up and saw a herd of Impala antelope in full flight coming towards the camp. Something had obviously panicked them, and I soon saw what it was, a pack of wild dogs. These are not only the most efficient hunters in Africa, but also one of the most endangered species alive. It was rare even to see one, but to see a pack of them hunting, was even more rare. And this pack was hunting Impala right through my camp. I shouted to everyone to stand perfectly still as the Impala galloped furiously past and around the tents, followed by the eager wild-dogs, panting from the chase.

Wild-dogs hunt in a pack as other predators do, but their intelligence and communication is incredible. They will split their prey into smaller and smaller herds, eventually singling out one animal. The wild-dog pack then splits with some dogs running at a tangent to the quarry in order to cut it off and ambush it. They will hunt and chase that animal, sometimes for miles, until it can go no further and starts to falter. The wild-dogs nip and bite at the ankles of the hunted animal, causing them to bleed, they will bite chunks from the flesh as the animal is running, panic-stricken, and then, when the animal can go no further and is too weak to fight back, the dogs descend and fall on it as a pack, and literally tear it to bits, still alive. The animal suffers a desperate end, but that's how it is in Africa. It really is the survival of the fittest.

I had one or two lion stroll through the camp on occasions, although this was usually at night, but at another camp, I was visited by a huge, old bull elephant. I learned later, it had already eaten several baskets, which some other travellers were carrying on top of their vehicle Their camp was not far from ours and the old bull simply called on us because we were next in line. It wandered in out of the night, silent and massive with its trunk searching out good things to eat.

When you see elephants on the television or the films, you don't get a realistic impression of their size. When an old bull wanders your way to within a few metres, it is incredible just how big they are, and this one was huge! Fortunately, I had seen it coming from behind the clients and got them out of the way before it ambled its way in. This old thing had seen everything and been everywhere and was not the least bit stressed by the presence of humans. The clients were all seated around the camp-fire and when I shouted the warning to them, they all jumped up as one and ran over to where Press and I were. I watched as the elephant began to investigate the tents set at the edge of the camp. If we didn't get the elephant out of the camp, it would trash everything there, tents, food, equipment and could even cause serious injury if it panicked and bolted through the camp. Press and I had to figure a way of getting rid of it safely and quickly. The old trick of clapping hands together loudly and slowly didn't work, it obviously knew that one. Shouting at it didn't work. In the end, I drove the diesel truck at it, not with the intention of ramming it, just to scare it. After two or three attempts, the revving engine seemed to do the trick and he wandered off, back into the night with hardly a sound as he slid into the bush.

On most of my trips to Botswana, I took along a video camera and filmed as much as I could. I knew that I was only there for a short period, (although Andy had told me he wanted me for at least two years) and wanted to bring as many memories back as I could. I didn't see anything wrong with this and neither did Ian. After one trip however, an American woman complained vociferously about me to Andy in a letter, which he showed me. This woman clearly had a major beef against me and amongst other things, she claimed that my knowledge of birds, animals and trees was poor and that "with his video camera, he seems to be on his own personal trip." I had just returned to Johannesburg after picking up a vehicle from the Eastern Transvaal, when Andy called me into the office and showed me the letter. As I was reading it, I had to sit down. She said the most awful things about the trip she had been on and was really bitter about me, for some reason.

It had been a very successful trip from the point of view of game spotting. We had seen cheetah hunting across the veld, lion feasting in the early morning on a zebra. We had even watched as a young leopard stalked, hunted and finally attacked a ram Impala. However, even the leopard attack had apparently failed to impress the American woman. I don't remember exactly what she said in the letter, but it was pretty vitriolic. Andy cross examined me about the trip for around thirty minutes, and all the while, I was getting more and more angry, not with her, with him. He was refusing to back me. He seemed convinced that I must have done something to annoy this woman. It was as if he had been waiting for me to fall and this was going to be his opportunity to bring me down. We ended up having a huge shouting match in his office.

The row calmed after we both read the feedback forms from the clients. There had only been 4 on this particular trip, the American woman, an Australian guy and a South African man and woman. (The Australian was just about the rudest, most disgusting man I had ever come across!) The American woman scored me 1 or 2 out of ten for just about every category, including knowledge. The other three scored me 8 or 9 in every category, including knowledge. Andy eventually had to admit that perhaps this woman had a problem, not of my making. He told me he would reply to her and I told him, I would also write to her. When I told the other guides about the letter of complaint, they all replied with the same question, "Did you bed her?" When I told them I hadn't, they said, "there you go then!" Simple!

The main issue for me in this sorry saga, was that Andy Dott, simply couldn't accept that I was any good at being a guide and representing his company. There was never any word of encouragement from him. By the time I left the company, I felt I was at least the equal of some of the other guides, although not the most experienced ones and had done my best for the company. The clients often asked questions about the company and I was sometimes a little critical about the way things were done, but I never said anything which I hadn't already discussed with Steve. My feed-back sheets from the clients were always positive, saying how good a job I had done. All Andy had to say about this though, was to ask how much I had paid them to make those positive comments!

The issue was finally resolved when I went back to the company about 18 months later for a visit. Andy and I had a laugh about the American woman and he told me that he received another complaint from her through her booking agent in the States, who described her as a "difficult person, probably impossible to please." This time, she was complaining that Andy had shown me her letter, and he had apparently replied to the effect that she should mind her own business, he was owner of the company and he would do what he liked and employ who he liked!

After viewing the game in the parks for four days, we exited from Moremi Game Park through the North Gate and journeyed north towards Victoria Falls. This particular day was especially arduous as we had to travel the very tough "sand road". All the roads in the parks were sand roads, but this one had a particularly bad reputation and had earned its own name. Soft, deep, sand which would run through your fingers like water but which seemed to grip the tyres and reduce progress to a grinding crawl. The area itself is an ancient sand dune desert which, over time, has become marginally fertile but with only the hardiest trees and shrubs being able to survive. It never ceased to amaze me that anything at all could grow there, the soil was simply sand!

The distance we had to travel this day was about 200 kilometres and an early start was essential. It was practically impossible to do more than about 15 or 20 kilometres an hour for most of the trip, which meant a really hard, sweaty day at the wheel. It was especially tough for the clients sitting in the back because, whereas they had nothing to do all day except sit and get thrown around, at least I was busy keeping "BJ" in the track and watching for nasty little surprises like sharp tree roots protruding through the sand. These roots could split tyres and cause hours of delay changing wheels or repairing punctures. I have always been especially proud of the fact that, through all my trips around Botswana, I only ever had two or three punctures and never once suffered a major breakdown. Other guides seemed to be constantly breaking the safari trucks and having to wait for the guide at Maun to reach them. In those days, we didn't have radios or mobile phones and if we broke down, we would have to wait for a vehicle coming in the opposite direction, hope that they would be going on to Maun and ask them to pass a message on to the Drifters guide at Crocodile Lodge. Assuming the message was delivered, it could still be another two days before a replacement vehicle could be brought from Maun. The clients had all been briefed that this was a possibility, but thankfully, I never had to suffer it. (Ian told me later, that part of his report back to Andy on my performance that trip, was the respect I had shown for the vehicle and the terrain.)

Progress towards Victoria Falls was tortuous, BJ's engine would be revving rhythmically as she struggled to pull the weight through the soft, cloying sand. The sun was hot and regular stops were needed to cool the engine and the clients alike. This experience however, was partly what they had paid their money for.

On and on we ground, hour after hour, mile after mile in the African heat, Eventually, after seemingly endless hours of grinding through the sand, the roads became firmer, progress was quicker, the clients' mood lifted and we emerged, quite suddenly, from the bush and drove into a small village, about 50 kilometres from our next camp, Serondela. I say "suddenly" because there were no signs indicating the village, no outlying houses or shelters. The village simply appeared after we had rounded a bend.

I drove into the heart of the village and Ian told me to pull over at a roadside shop. Before the vehicle had stopped however, he and Press were off the truck and racing each other to the shop. As he was sprinting along, Ian shouted back to the rest of us, "Cold drinks!" Apparently, this was the only shop for miles around with anything that resembled a fridge. The drinks weren't anywhere near "cold" but after a day of drinking luke-warm water, anything with a temperature even a few degrees lower, was "cold" and very welcome. This was a regular stop and the shopkeeper kept the "fridge" stocked accordingly. Our purchases on that one day alone, would probably keep her going for weeks. For me, as well as a drink, it became a regular place to buy a solid bar of chocolate, as opposed to one, which I could pour into my mouth.

We eventually reached Serondela Camp in Chobe National Park, about 10 to 12 exhausting hours after leaving the last camp, at North Gate on the River Xwai. Serondela was also right alongside a river, but this one was huge compared to the Xwai. It was the Chobe River and it forms part of the border between Botswana and Namibia. The area is fantastic for game-spotting, especially elephants. Herds of elephant in the Chobe National Park can number in their hundreds, and the total number in the area is thought to be around 12or 13 thousand.

Occasionally, one of the more inquisitive adults in the herd would wander over to our vehicle for an inspection. On one such occasion, a juvenile took exception to us being there and started to trumpet and shake his head. His ears were flapping wildly, a sure sign that he didn't like us. He then charged the vehicle. Press and I were sitting in the front, just watching his antics, knowing that this was just a mock charge, a warning to us not to come any closer, which we had no intention of doing. As the elephant charged towards us and suddenly stopped, I became aware of the truck suddenly sagging over to one side. When I looked around, all the clients had slid over to the far side of the truck, as far away from the elephant as was possible to get. Press just had this cheeky little grin on his face and the clients began to laugh in nervous outbursts.

In most of the camps we used in the parks, monkeys were a constant source of irritation, and the worst of them were the baboons. The troops had come to know that tourists meant food scraps and were constantly hanging around the camp, just waiting for an opportunity to raid us for anything they could get their nasty little paws on.

Over the years the tourists had been coming to the parks, the baboons had learned a few tricks, chief amongst which, was how to unzip a tent. At the start of the safari, the clients were all told that, when we were out on a drive, they should lock their tent flaps with a padlock to prevent nosey baboons getting in. Most of them took this advice, but some didn't. They generally had their tents raided by a troop looking for food and anything else that they may be able to eat. Having a baboon raid your tent is not a pleasant experience, everything will be turned out or ripped apart. On one occasion, some guy had failed to heed my warning and returned to camp to find all his belongings strewn over the entire camp and beyond and had even squeezed the toothpaste out of its tube in their hunt for food.

At Serondela Camp, I had a nasty little experience with a huge dog-baboon. It was late in the evening, just getting dark and the baboon troop were hanging around as usual, just outside the camp. They are generally fearful of humans, but some of the older males, the "dogs" are a little more brazen. I went around to the far side of the truck to get something, and came face to face with a large male, trying to get into one of the compartments. I immediately shouted at it and waved my arms around to scare it off, not thinking that I would need to do any more. The "dog" turned in my direction and "barked" at me, showing its canine teeth. A male baboon has larger canines than a lion and with hugely powerful limbs, can rip a human to shreds. It didn't scamper away as was usual, but started to come for me. Just at that point, Press came round the other side of the truck and distracted the baboon. Both of us were shouting and waving our arms at it. The baboon didn't move for a few seconds, but realising it was outnumbered, it scurried away back to the safety of its troop. It was a very scary moment. Having watched several terrible fights between baboons, where the weaker one either submits to the dominant male or gets killed, I had no illusions that that would have been the end of me.

We spent the next day, our last in the parks, game viewing and the following day, packed up the camp and headed slowly along the banks of the Chobe River, squeezing the maximum amount of time we could looking at animals, towards the town of Kasane. Here, we would buy some more cold drinks, before going on to the border crossing between Botswana and Zimbabawe at Kazangula.

Having negotiated the obsessively bureaucratic border guards at Kazangula, with their interminable forms and stamps, we arrived at Victoria Falls Camp-site. As we drove in, Ian directed me to the back-end of the camp and said I would see why later. The camp had all the usual facilities, toilets and showers etc. and was situated right in the heart of the town, so everything was within a short walk of the camp.

After setting out the tents and sending the clients off to explore, Ian and I walked into the town to make arrangements for the clients' activities. The previous evening, we had explained to them the various activities they could indulge in; white-water rafting of course, booze cruises on the Zambezi, bungee jumping from Victoria Falls Bridge, ranger-led, armed, walking safaris in a nearby game-park, sight-seeing at the Falls themselves and lots of others, but by far, the most popular activity was the rafting trip down the Zambezi. The following day, Ian sent me on the rafting trip whilst he "maintained the vehicle". In actual fact, he slept the day away as the Zambezi had another go at drowning me!

This was not a particularly good time of the year to see the Falls. There wasn't enough water flowing over the edge to make them truly spectacular, that would happen later in the year after the rains, but it was still a magnificent experience to see Devil's Cataract up close, getting drenched from the spray and witnessing the double rainbow.

The town itself was quite a different place to the one I had visited briefly in 1989, it had expanded beyond belief, mostly with clothes shops and activity centres. This was to be the hey-day of the town, as just a few short years later, the policies of Robert Mugabe would drive the companies and the tourists across the border into Zambia. But for now, it was a fantastic place to experience; people from all corners of the globe, travellers, traders, craftsmen, thieves, vagabonds and safari guides, all mixing together in one small town. There was never a dull moment, especially in the evenings when the bars and restaurants came to life.

This was when I realised why we camped where we had. As well as safari tours, groups of young people, most of them seemingly from England, Australia and New Zealand, travelled through Africa in large lorries. Their journeys were much longer than ours and they had gained the title of "Overlanders". In the Victoria Falls camp-site they generally tended to camp very close to the entry gate and consequently, very close to the town. As part of their adventure, "overlanders" seemed to conduct wild parties or get drunk most nights until well into the small hours. They seemed to think that because they wanted to party and get boozed up all night, everyone else should. Even if our clients were so inclined, the guides definitely weren't, and so we camped right down at the far end of the camp-site, as far away from them as possible. Good tip Ian, thanks!

I went rafting with the clients on a few of the subsequent trips I ran into the Falls, having a near-death experience from drowning each time. Eventually, I asked myself why did I do this, and from then on, remained safely on land, contenting myself with lazing around the town, bargaining with the marketeers and fixing the truck where necessary.

Neither did I have any inclination whatsoever to hurl myself off a perfectly sound and safe bridge, with a piece of elastic tied to my ankle. Heights and me have always been enemies, but in fairness to myself, I once did wander onto the Victoria Falls bridge where they did the bungee jumping into the Zambezi Gorge. I looked over the side to the river over 100 metres below and immediately felt nauseous and had to walk off the bridge smartly. From then on, I swore that I would only do a bungee jump when the fear was far outweighed by the desire for the exhilaration of falling through the air, which, with careful manipulation, would be never!

The souvenir market was always a favourite of mine. They had the most wonderful carvings of African heads, full of character and exquisitely carved from hard-wood, often ebony. The outside area was exclusively for the men selling carvings of just about anything that walked, flew or swam in Africa, and the women occupied an indoor shed with their baskets, crocheted dinner cloths and the like. Wherever you went, part of the experience of the market was the bartering for the items with the marketeers. One could be forgiven for thinking these men and women were the poorest of the poor, trying to sell articles in order just to buy a little food. In reality, they were quite well off compared to the real poor of Africa, and when it came to bartering, were as sharp as tacks. The marketeers gave the illusion of being dirt-poor to encourage tourists to buy out of sympathy, and it generally worked. However, whatever discount a buyer arranged, the vendor was still making a handsome profit on the deal.

One of my clients once asked me to help her buy a particular carving. She was German and a little shy when dealing with the local boys. I, on the other hand always enjoyed dealing with them. Whether they were rogues or crooks, I didn't really care, they were always polite, firm and sometimes a little rowdy in their dealings, but always polite. She had set her heart on this particular carving and it took me two hours to reach an accommodation with the seller. In the end, I even had to hand over my flip-flops, which was no problem as they were virtually dead anyway. Walking back to the camp-site was a bit painful though!

My mentor for this first trip, Ian Oberholzer was a man of the bush, he was born in the bush and spent most of his childhood there. To him, running a safari was a "walk in the park" (no pun intended). However, I think he recognised in me, someone who was from a completely alien culture, but who was able to interact with other people and who had a desire not only to experience another way of life, but also to enable others to enjoy the same experience. I had worked hard on our trip, doing all the cooking, driving and the various jobs around the camp, but I had also made copious notes to help me on future trips and I think Ian saw this as a commitment on my part to do the best job I could. I was never going to be as good as someone like Ian or Heiko, but at least I would try my hardest not to let them or the company down.

Just before we left Victoria Falls for the journey back to Nata, Ian phoned the Drifters base in Johannesburg and told Nigel that, in his opinion, I was capable of running my own trips and that I should be given the next Botswana safari as guide. He did this in front of me so that I could hear what he was saying about me, and very complimentary he was too! He explained how I treated the clients, cooked the food, bought the supplies, the efforts I was making to educate myself as to the African fauna and flora and the fact that I treated the safari vehicle, "BJ" with some respect and didn't thrash the gears out of it through the soft sand. After the phone call, he turned to me and told me that I was to lead the next Botswana trip as the guide.

It was a huge compliment to me! I had made it!

One of the schools I helped to build in Namibia.

Some of the school children in Mbambe village, Namibia.

Me, on a mokkorro in the Okavango Delta.

Sabine and myself after dunking her and me in the pool.

Myself and clients having fun in the river, somewhere in the Okavango Delta.

Heiko and his wife, Carina at the Bush Ways base in Maun.

This little girl stole all our hearts as she danced at a village on the Liuwa Plains.

About to cross a river in Zambia.

Chris and Karen and their youngest daughter, Samantha.

Chapter 24

On the fourth day at Victoria Falls, Saturday, we packed up the camp early and set out on the long drive back to Nata. Old "BJ" was incapable of going any faster than 50 or 60 k.p.h. and so the journey was long and laborious. We arrived back at Nata at about 6pm that evening to find the next trip to Botswana had already arrived from Johannesburg. Ordinarily, the finishing guide would take the clients back to Jo'burg in the people carrier and the starting guide would transfer to the safari truck for the new trip. On this particular occasion however, things would be slightly different.

The maximum number of clients that one safari truck could take was 12, and that was pretty rare because it would be such a squeeze. On this new trip however, there was around 14 clients. This meant that two separate safaris would run, but not in tandem. Part of the Drifters ethos was to get away from the crowds, to encourage the clients to believe they were completely alone in the vastness of the bush. To have two trucks running in the same direction on the same trip was against this ideal, and so, where more than one truck had to be used, one trip would go the "right" way around and the other would go the "wrong" way around. The "right" way was Nata, Maun, Okavango Delta, back to Maun the game parks, Victoria Falls and back to Nata, as I had just done. The "wrong" way was to go first to Victoria Falls, then through the parks to Maun, Okavango Delta, Maun and back to Nata.

The clients had been brought up from Jo'burg in two vehicles, but accompanied by only one other guide, who also happened to be named Neil. When Ian and Neil were explaining to me how the trip would work, I casually asked who the other guide was going to be and where was he. I was rather taken aback when they told me that I would be the other guide. Although I had enjoyed the experience with Ian and relished the thought of running my own safari, I had been looking forward to sleeping in a decent bed for a while and sorting out some clean clothes back at Bob and Helen's house before taking the next safari. Instead, I would be doing what they termed "a back-to-back", one safari straight after another without a break. Not only that, as I found out, I would be going the "wrong" way around. Neil couldn't take the "right way" safari as he had some relatives going with him on his trip and he needed to pick them up at Maun. Although the effort I had made on my training trip had made me pretty tired, I decided that this was a challenge; not only my first solo safari, but also to have to work backwards. Bed and laundry would have to wait!

I had made copious notes on when and where to buy food and for how long, where to buy enough diesel for the long hauls through the parks etc. Now, I had to sit down and work everything out backwards. The meals for each evening were all pre-determined, so that wherever you were on the trip, you would know what meal you were cooking that evening and the food buying reflected this. We had no freezer, only a cool box and so, the fresh meat and vegetables had to be carefully worked out so that produce didn't go off before I came to cook it. The clients weren't too bothered about some of them having to start at Victoria Falls, because they could finish on a high point in the Delta.

Neil and I sorted out which clients would go with which guide, and then set about having a serious drink in the bar, not really worrying about the early start the next day, Christmas Day 1994. Ian and Neil congratulated me on my success and insisted that we celebrate before we all parted company in the morning. It all got a bit serious, with Neil doing his world-famous Orang-u-Tang impression by hanging upside down from the rafters of the lodge. In a serious moment, I thanked Ian for all his help and guidance and promised not to let him down. I didn't get too much sleep that night, but awoke the following morning ready and raring to go.

With the safari truck loaded and the clients all on board, we set off. Drifters had supplied a couple of bottles of "champagne", (or should I say sparkling wine!) and so I spent Christmas morning driving clients on a safari through Botswana, and drinking "champagne" out of a tin mug at the side of the road. Even though I was trying to get everything about going the "wrong" way sorted in my head, I was absolutely delighted to be on my own, taking a group of clients on a trip around some very beautiful parts of Africa and knowing that the success of the safari rested fairly and squarely on my inexperienced shoulders. I was determined that each and every client would go home, the richer for the experience, but as hard as I might have tried, I was unable to disguise the fact that this was my first solo trip. However, I remember the clients were all very understanding and the trip went without a hitch. I think my police training helped me enormously in that I simply took the role of leader and made the clients aware that I was going to run the trip and I was going to give them the very best trip I could manage. The feedback forms to the Dott boys showed that my efforts had borne fruit in that they were all very positive and complimentary.

Including the safari with Ian, I ran six trips around Botswana. Although we followed exactly the same route each time, each one of the safaris was different, because the clients were different. Most of the clients were pretty regular people, keen to learn and help out. Sometimes, an odd-ball crept into the group, someone who just seemed beyond explanation. Eddie, the American was just such a person. He was a bachelor from Detroit, aged around 50 who constantly wore a grubby old fishing hat. When I say constantly, I mean constantly, he never once took it off. We all thought he slept with it as well.

One very early morning in Victoria Falls camp, I was sleeping outside and was awoken by someone passing by my sleeping bag, very hurriedly. I recognized the person as Eddie and just figured he was on his way to the toilet. Later that morning after breakfast, I was standing near to the fire when Eddie sidled up to me and announced in a very low voice, "I had to go to the toilet this morning Neil." I carried on gazing into the fire, stunned by his sparkling conversational skills and replied with something sarcastic like, "Really?" I probably couldn't hide the fact that I was completely at a loss as to why he would be telling me this. All was made clear however, with his next pronouncement, "Yeah, I didn't make it!" I carried on staring into the fire for a few seconds and then remembered seeing Eddie earlier that morning racing past my sleeping bag. He then proceeded to give me all the lurid details of how he had soiled himself, exactly where he was when it happened, the time it happened and what he was wearing. I listened intently to him, trying desperately to look concerned but really wanting to burst out laughing. I did however advise him not to repeat the story to the other clients, for the sake of his privacy. I did have some sympathy for him!

Later that morning, all the clients had gone into town, including myself. I returned to the camp a little later, before the clients and found certain items of clothing, washed and laid out on bushes to dry. On closer examination, they were a pair of jeans and a pair of underpants. On even closer examination, I saw horrible brown stains around the crotch area on both items but mainly on the underpants. I stood there in disbelief! "Don't tell anyone" I had said. So what does he do, he washes out the soiled garments and leaves them for the rest of the entire camp to see. And why was he washing them out anyway, why didn't he just dump them? And why, when it was obvious that his attempts at stain removal had failed spectacularly, was he trying to dry them out?? He was obviously intent on wearing them again! I immediately went and found a long stick from the bushes, very gingerly hooked both garments separately and dumped them in a bin far away from our camping place.

When Eddie returned, he was asking everyone if they had removed a pair of jeans and underpants from a particular bush, as if anyone would be crazy enough to even approach them let alone touch them! Eventually, I put him out of his misery by telling him that someone had told me they had seen baboons running off with his clothing and that he should say goodbye to them. He was crestfallen at the loss of his precious but seriously suspect underpants.

I thought this would be the end of the saga, but when we returned to the base in Johannesburg, Nigel took me aside and asked about "the American guy, Eddie" "Why do you ask?" I said, "Because" said Nigel, "he's just come up to me and said "I shit my pants in Victoria Falls!" "What did you say to that?" I asked. "Really, how interesting?!?" replied Nigel, the master of sarcasm!

On my fourth trip, one of my clients was a German lady named Sabine Haas, and she was gorgeous. She was tall, slim, good looking with fabulous red hair and an extraordinary sense of fun and humour, for a German! It was another "wrong-way" trip and by the time we reached the Delta, it was obvious that there was a strong attraction between the two of us, which had grown as the safari progressed. The day that we spent coming out of the delta, she engineered travelling with me in my mokkorro. We sat back-to-back, propping each other up, and just chatting between us. She had an excellent command of English, but still dipped into her English-German dictionary every now and then.

It was an unwritten rule of Drifters that guides were not to get romantically involved with clients whilst on a trip. Whatever happened after was fine, but not whilst the guide and client were on the same trip. I wholeheartedly agreed with this rule, but several guides didn't, and it invariably caused problems. I would be having enough problems of my own without having to deal with anything like this. I stuck rigidly to this rule, although, by the time we had reached even half-way, I think the other clients had begun to suspect something was happening, or at least, was going to happen between Sabine and I.

From the moment we left the last camp in the Delta, to when we reached Crocodile Camp later that afternoon, Sabine had been gently winding me up. Why didn't I do this, why didn't I do that? "Ach, you are English, how can you understand good German girl?" It was only good fun and I was giving as much as I was getting, but when I was setting up the camp at Crocodile, I pretended to get really fed up with her. I walked over to where she was standing, hands on hips, looking at me quizzically. She tried in vain to run off but I caught her, picked her up in a "fireman's lift", carried her kicking and struggling all the way down to the pool and dropped her in fully clothed. It would have been spectacular except for the fact that I lost my footing at the pool edge, and went in with her. One of the other clients, who came down to watch the fun, took a photo of us sitting at the side of the pool together. Looking at that photo, it was obvious we were getting very close.

A tragic and all too clear example of a client thinking he or she knows best happened to another guide, Vaughn. We regularly phoned the office from Victoria Falls, just to report any difficulties or problems. On this particular occasion, Vaughn was a week behind me on the following trip. When I spoke to Nigel at the office, he told me that Vaughn had "lost a client." Rather light-heartedly, I asked if he had found him, and Nigel replied, "No, no, he's lost him, he's dead!"

Apparently, it had happened at the first camp in the delta. Part of our briefing for the times we wild-camped, and something which had to be strictly adhered to, was to tell the clients that under no circumstances was any one of them ever to go out of sight or hearing of the camp, wherever we were at the time. Vaughn had told his clients this, but one of them, a German man, had decided to ignore him and go for a very early morning walk on his own away from the camp.

When he hadn't returned by mid-morning, Vaughn and a few others set out to look for him, including the polers, who tracked him in a certain direction. The client was found by the polers, accompanied unfortunately by his own son who was traveling with him, in a thicket, about half a mile from the camp. He had been gored and trampled by a buffalo, one of the most dangerous animals in the bush. Exactly what had happened, we will never know, but the theory was that the client had stumbled upon the buffalo in some way and it had attacked him out of fear and anger.

Many people think that the "Big Five", lion, leopard, buffalo, rhino and elephant, relate to the animals safari clients most want to see. In fact, they relate to the fact that they are the five most dangerous animals from a hunting perspective. Out of the five, the buffalo is probably the most dangerous, especially if wounded. The thinking on this occasion was that the buffalo had attacked the client as a "hunter", and nailed him.

Talking of rules, I broke one of my own once and nearly paid for it. The "rule" was that, if a client wished to go to the toilet in the night, he or she had to partially unzip their tent and before getting out fully, had to shine a torch around the camp to make sure nothing dangerous was lurking in the darkness. Only then should they emerge from the tent. One particular night, I had to pee and couldn't find my torch anywhere. It was absolutely pitch dark outside, but I thought there was very little risk of anything being in the camp, and so took the chance. I unzipped the tent fully and stepped outside. Just as I stood up straight, there was an almighty crash from the direction of the kitchen about 20 feet away. It sounded as though all the cooking pots and kitchen equipment had been knocked over. The crashing noise had split the African silence and I froze! Instantly, I knew that whatever it was, it could see me, but I had absolutely no idea what "it" was! And whatever "it" was, it was much bigger and more powerful than me!

Although the kitchen was only 20 feet away, I couldn't see a thing, not even a blurry outline. The noise had come straight out of the blackness, was really frightening, and then everything went deafeningly silent again. I could almost feel the invisible eyes watching me. Very slowly, without making any sudden movements, I bent down and crawled backwards into my tent and zipped it up, all the while waiting for, and praying against the sudden burst of noise and action signalling an attack.

When I was safely back inside, I unzipped again, just a little and shouted to Press on the other side of the camp, to ask if he could see it. When he shone his torch into the kitchen, there were two massive hyenas, both actually standing on the kitchen table, with all the equipment strewn about the floor. I knew there was no food available for them and that they were probably just curious. There was no point in trying to clear up in the dark, and so we left it till the morning, when we realised that the hyenas had made off with a whole 5 litre container of cooking oil, which they just love. We found the remains of the container just outside the camp.

Standing there alone and virtually blind in the dark, knowing that to a predator, I am a fully visible, potential threat, and that, should it attack, it could do so with impunity, brought home to me my own vulnerability and feebleness in an environment where I was only a tolerated guest.

Back to Sabine! We spent the last night camping on the salt-pans, and it was all Sabine and I could do to keep our hands off each other, especially me. However, I remember this particular camp for a different reason. It was the one time, I very nearly lost it with a client. Besides Sabine, there were other Germans on this trip, including a couple called Gerda and Richard. He was fine and I'm sure she didn't mean to be awkward, but Gerda spent practically the whole time moaning or whinging about something or other. It was as if she wasn't happy otherwise. For as long as she moaned, I tried my best to please her and make her happy.

When I had gone shopping in Maun before setting off for Nata, I had bought some speciality sausage, especially for her and Richard. I genuinely thought it was German sausage, and when Gerda asked me what they would be having for dinner that night, I proudly told her what I had bought, just for her. She became very excited and begged to smell it. When I opened the packet, she looked at it, stepped back and announced in a really imperious German accent, "Zis is not German sausage! Zis is Hungarian sausage!" She fixed me with a stare that made my blood go cold, then boil!

I got really angry, slammed the damned sausage back into the cool-box, picked up my personal bag and stormed off onto the pans. I walked for about half an hour, until I was very nearly out of sight of the camp. I sat down on a salty knoll, immediately regretting that I had left the clients alone and then imagined all sorts of horrible things happening at the camp, and most of them happening to Gerda!

All the way out, I had been muttering to myself, "German sausage, Hungarian sausage, what's the fucking difference? I hope it chokes you!" I didn't mean that last bit of course, but I was angry! When I figured I'd cooled down sufficiently, I walked back to the camp and calmly set about making dinner, which was a little late that evening. Nobody dared to speak to me all night!

The following night in Nata camp, with the trip virtually over, Sabine and I slept under the stars, and touched and kissed each other for the first time. When we got back to Johannesburg, we shared a room at the lodge attached to the office, covertly arranged for us by my friend who ran the place. When I finally left Africa to return to England, I went to stay with her in Germany for a couple of weeks.

At that time, Sabine lived in a fantastic flat in Koblenz, right alongside the River Mosel. If she wasn't at home, I used to spend hours watching the big cargo barges squeezing into, and occasionally crashing into the lock, which would take them on to the Rhine and the north of Germany. We spent the following two years, commuting either to Germany or England for week-ends and when we weren't together, we would be on the phone. She was gorgeous and in my own way, I loved and adored her, but there was always something in the background, niggling away at me. At the time, I couldn't figure it out. I was just aware that there was a part of me that I wasn't giving to her, and I think she realised it, but carried on regardless. I often wonder whether, had our relationship continued, she would have confronted me over this barrier of mine, and whether, with her help, I could have overcome it. Part of this barrier was of course, commitment. As if to demonstrate to myself that I was not capable of committing myself to one woman, I was unfaithful to Sabine, but only on one mindless and meaningless occasion, which I told her about.

I've had many relationships since the break-up of my marriage, all of them going the same way; ending because I simply couldn't commit myself. Sabine was no different, but I have to say that losing Sabine affected me very deeply.

That, however was not the reason I lost Sabine. Having had the benefit of a few more years in which to contemplate the issue, I have reached a sad and brutal conclusion. The "barrier" I have spoken of was not just my inability to commit myself. In a totally perverse way, I lost Sabine because I was determined to remain a victim. I saw myself very much as the victim of a broken relationship, that of myself and Susie, and nothing was going interfere with my status. Within coaching circles, there is such a thing called the "drama triangle". It consists of "persecutor", "victim" and "rescuer". When Sabine came along, I became more "persecutor" than "victim", sub-consciously exacting revenge for my failed marriage on the totally innocent Sabine. It would be easy to say now, "What on earth was I thinking?" but that's the point, I wasn't and didn't for a long time after. My head was still reeling from the loss of Susie

I was determined to show that even with a woman as beautiful as Sabine, I was goods damaged beyond repair. In effect, I persuaded myself out of a relationship I really wanted. I was so determined to punish Susie for what she had done to me, but in effect, succeeded only in punishing myself and other, absolutely innocent and loving people, mainly Sabine.

Amazingly though, Sabine and I are still good friends to this day, but if you ever get to read this Sabine, I am truly sorry.

In between running the six trips around Botswana, I also ran two safaris around South Africa. I think it will be very boring for the reader to have to plough through another description of a trip, so I will give a shortened version of our route.

As with the Botswana trip, we started from the base in Johannesburg, but this time, we stayed in the Toyota Hiace vans for the entire trip. They were very good vehicles, reliable and tough, but when everything was loaded, including the clients, they weren't the most comfortable of vehicles.

I did the first trip with Heiko to learn the route, and we each had a separate vehicle. From the base, we headed east immediately towards the Eastern Transvaal. Our route took us over Long Tom Pass, named for the "Long Tom" guns that the British used in the Boer War and on towards Pilgrims Rest, so called when a gold prospector settled in the area. This part of South Africa is particularly beautiful, with high peaks and grassy plains. It contains such sights as The Three Rondavels, a rock formation of 3 circular rocky outcrops, God's Window with its magnificent views across the land and the Blyde River Canyon, where the rivers Blyde and Treuer meet and cut sweeping channels through the limestone rock.

From Pilgrim's Rest, we continued east and entered Kruger National Park. This was a totally different park to those in Botswana. The roads, although gravel, were neatly laid out and well maintained. The accommodation comprised mostly Rondavels, fashioned after the Zulu huts of old, but there were some lodges available. In fact, the whole park just felt neater and less wild than Botswana. We drove south through the park, finally exiting through the Malelane Gate and drove on into Swaziland. We passed the wonderfully named Piggs Peak and spent the rest of the morning at the market in the capital Mbabane, the clients buying all sorts of colourful baskets and carvings and then Heiko and I trying desperately to find room on the vehicles for their purchases.

After Swaziland, it was south, through the Hluhluwe Game Reserve, (pronounced Shushluwee) and on to Durban, where Heiko and I told the clients to get lost for the morning on the beach, whilst we chilled out with a few beers and a couple of hours bouncing on the beach-front trampolines; good exercise after spending hours cramped at the wheel of a car.

From Durban, we headed northwest to the Drakensburg Mountains, where we hiked all day up the Tugela River Gorge to some fabulous swimming holes with ice-cold water, then on and around the top of Lesotho, taking in the Golden Gate National Park en route with its beautiful red/gold coloured rock formations. After this, we headed south again, down towards the coast, finally arriving at Grahamstown, which is more or less the start of the famous Garden Route.

After Grahamstown, we followed the coast road, visiting the Addo Elephant National Park where we saw not only elephant, but also the rarely seen white Rhinoceros, through Port Elizabeth and on to the beautiful Tsitsikamma Forest with its massive evergreen trees. We camped the night at one of the most spectacular camp-sites I have ever seen. It was at the mouth of the Storm River, right on the edge of a grassy promenade overlooking the Indian Ocean beyond. Before we left this camp-site the next morning, we took a walk along the coast for about 5 kilometres, to a beautiful waterfall, where Heiko demonstrated his manliness by climbing up the slippery sides and then practising Zen on a small plateau with the water cascading onto his head.

From Storm River, we journeyed on down the coast to Knysna, where we climbed "The Heads" marking the entrance to the lagoon of the Outenieka River and gazed out over the Indian Ocean. After Knysna, we took a short excursion inland, to Oudtshoorn and the recently explored Kango Caves. At Oudtshoorn, the clients could visit an ostrich farm, and if they wanted to, could actually ride one! Now, call me an old stick-in-the-mud if you like, but I steadfastly refused to ride on an ostrich and did my level best to persuade the clients not to either, without a great deal of success, unfortunately. I'm quite sure God didn't mean for us to ride ostriches when He created them! Horses are different, an ostrich is a bird!

After the fabulous limestone Kango Caves, we headed back along the Garden Route and camped at Stellenbosch, on the very edge of the wine growing region. The following day, we broke camp early and set off for the wineries. It was the last morning before we reached the final destination, Cape Town and we tried to visit as many vineyards as possible. Heiko's record was eight in five hours and it probably still stands today. There was the usual tour of the winery, which after the first three became very boring, followed by the obligatory free samples. South Africa makes some of the best wine in the world, and this was just when the news of the quality of their wines was spreading around the globe. Some of the clients bought several bottles, and some even had cases shipped back home. I bought my fair share too, although I have to say that as the guide, I was given most of it for nothing, as a sort of thank-you for bringing the clients in the first place.

And so, after 18 days on the road, we arrived at our final destination, The Breakwater Lodge Hotel, on Cape Town waterfront. After visiting this city, most people rave about just how beautiful the place is. I shan't be any different, although I won't rave about it. There is no doubt that Cape Town is a stunning place, but it contains its fair share of deprivation, crime and associated problems. Most people however, choose not to see this aspect. They see only the attractive old colonial houses set right back from the waterfront and nestling under Table Mountain, or the stunning coastline running down to Cape Point, where the Indian and Atlantic Oceans meet. And why shouldn't people see only these things? If everybody boycotted places simply because of the negative aspects, nobody would go anywhere. No, I only want to point out that as aesthetically stunning as Cape Town is, there is a dark side to her as well.

The clients were generally let loose in Cape Town for three days and they could wander wherever they wanted, although they were warned to stick to the tourist attractions. The only trips we organised for them were up onto Table Mountain and down to the Cape Point. Everyone who has been to Cape Town, will know that there is a cable-car up to the summit of Table Mountain. Fewer people know that you can actually walk up to the top, although the climb is a little arduous. I can't remember anyone saying they didn't want to get to the top somehow, so we gave them a choice. Those clients wishing to take the cable car were dropped off at the bottom, and those who wished to walk up, we took a little further along the road to where the path begins.

Looking at the mountain from ground level, you can't actually see the path, but it follows a cleft in the mountain side, and zig-zags along a practically vertical route. We had to be a bit careful whom we took on the climb, as only fit people should attempt it, and then it has to be done first thing in the morning when the air is cool. It took about two to three hours to climb, and by late morning, the heat was appalling. Still being half-way up by lunch-time was akin to suicide! And at the top, what a view you were greeted with! Sweeping views across the city below and far out across the ocean, with the ships at anchor in the approaches, waiting to dock in the harbour. To the left, views down the coastline towards Cape Point, and to the rear, views across the lush hinterland. Fabulous!

Cape Town was where the South Africa trip officially ended, but we, the guides, had to get back to Johannesburg, a 1400 Kilometre trip, which we had to make in one day. The clients generally all flew out from Cape Town, but for anyone wanting to come back to Johannesburg, we simply offered them a lift with us in the Toyotas, provided that they understood that we would leave at 4am sharp from the hotel and that we would not wait if they were not there. The journey back to Johannesburg was long and boring, and apart from fuel and toilet stops, we had no breaks. Breakfast and lunch were taken at the wheel and we eventually got back to Jo'burg around 6pm the same evening. The following day was clean-up day, repair equipment day and then, if we were lucky, we would get a day off. If not, it was almost straight back out onto another safari.

I remember feeling very good about myself on the second S.A. safari. It was my trip and Nigel, the financial director and Andy's brother, had taken me aside the day before we left and told me that he wasn't sure about the other guide he was sending with me to drive the other vehicle. He asked me to keep an eye on him and to report on him from somewhere on the trip.

I phoned Nigel from Grahamstown and told him I wasn't impressed with the other guide and said why. In my opinion, the guy was more interested in chatting with the female clients, rather than actually giving all of them an informative trip. I was the leader of the trip, but we should have shared the work between us. Instead, it seemed that I was doing most of it whilst he was off star-gazing with one of the clients. Not only this, he broke the cardinal rule and slept with this client whilst on the trip. I kept this bit back from Nigel.

I had completed five safaris around Botswana by this time, and I think at least Nigel, who was always more approachable than Andy or Ken, appreciated the efforts I had made to make a success of being a safari guide. I was never going to be as good as some of the more experienced guides, but just to have Nigel ask for my opinion on another guide, meant a lot to me and showed that maybe I did have something positive to contribute. In this instance however, it didn't matter a great deal as to what I had to say about the other guy, as he was kept on by Andy and given other trips. Maybe Andy thought that what I had to say was rubbish, which it wasn't, but at least someone had asked my opinion.

It was after this second South Africa trip that Andy and I had the row about the American woman. I did one more trip around Botswana, and at the end, made sure that Andy received all the feed-back forms from the clients, detailing their thoughts on the trip and my performance. They were highly complimentary, but still Andy couldn't find it in himself to say anything approaching "well done".

Bob used to be almost apoplectic with rage about the way I, and the other guides, was being treated. His most vehement criticism was that he thought I was being exploited. We had many a conversation on this subject, over a gin and tonic on his patio and on more than one occasion, I had to stop him from phoning the company and giving them a piece of his mind. I eventually managed to persuade Bob to my way of thinking. Yes, I told him, I was being exploited by Drifters, but I was also exploiting them. "Think about the opportunity for me here," I told him. I was a London policeman, running wild-camp safaris through Southern Africa. "How many people get to do that," I said. The opportunity was there and then, it was happening for me. The pittance they were paying me didn't matter one scrap, I had plenty of money. I was using Drifters to accomplish and experience something which would probably never come my way again. And to a large degree, I was successful at it. Despite the shortcomings of some of the Drifters' directors, I will always be grateful for the chance they gave me.

A couple of days after I got back from my sixth, and as it turned out, final trip around Botswana, Helen phoned the office and said that there was an urgent message waiting for me at Bob and Helen's house. I had to ring Ray Lowe, my friend back in Biggin Hill, as soon as I got the message. Ray and his lovely wife Sue, were looking after my affairs in Biggin Hill whilst I was away, and had "power of attorney" over my finances. I had also garaged my sports car with them for the year and arranged for Sue to drive it occasionally. Ray couldn't drive it as he was too short, bless him! When I got the message, my immediate thought was that either, I no longer owned a sports car, or was financially ruined in some way! Neither was the case. The message was that Chris, my friend from the mission station, had had a very serious accident and had been airlifted to Harare for specialist medical care. Apparently, he shouldn't even have been alive at that stage, and Karen was asking whether I could go back to the farm and manage it whilst they were in Zimbabwe. Ray was trying his best to explain what had happened, but he was being very vague. He said it had something to do with the Land-Rover but didn't know all the details. Karen was staying at someone's house in Harare and could I phone there to let her know whether I could go back.

When I eventually spoke to Karen, she was obviously very upset, but managed to give me an account of what had happened to Chris. The lake that was formed by the dam on the mission station is fed by a river, which flows from what was Zaire, (now the Democratic Republic of Congo). All the rivers in that part of Africa swell during the rainy season and diminish in the dry. About ten kilometers from the mission, this particular river broadened out somewhat, to form a roughly shaped circular pool, where it was safe to swim. There is no game in this part of Africa, and consequently, there are no crocodiles or other predators. The safety aspect was in regard to the depth of the river and the current.

Karen and Chris had decided to have the afternoon at the swimming spot. There was nothing to do at the house, all the children were at school, so the time was theirs to use. They both knew it well, as they had been there several times before with the children. This was about a month after the rains had finished and the river still looked swollen. Chris used to dive into the river from an overhanging tree branch. He was a good swimmer and had qualifications as a scuba-diver. On this day, he dived in as usual from the tree, but this time, Karen said, he came up screaming in agony. If Chris was screaming in agony, the pain must have been severe, he doesn't do "whimp".

Chris was obviously struggling and trying desperately to get back to the shore, so much so that Karen had to go into the river to help him. She still didn't know what had happened to him, she just knew she had to get him to the shore. Chris is a big man, and Karen really had to struggle to get him onto dry land, but when they got there, Chris told Karen that he had dived head-long onto a sand-bank, which had formed not far below the surface. He was sure it hadn't been there the year before, but as it turned out, the rains hadn't been that good that year and the river level had already begun to drop earlier than usual. When he dived in, thinking it was deeper than it was, he was already swinging his arms back to his sides to come to the surface. Instead, he crashed into the sandbank, head first.

Chris was in terrible agony. Every movement sent waves of pain down his spine and into his arms and legs. Karen knew that Chris was seriously hurt, but they were a long way from the farm and there was only her to get him into the Land-Rover and back to the mission. She knew that, somehow, she had to get him flat on his back and totally immobile. Goodness knows how, but she managed to man-handle Chris from the banks of the river, up into the back of the Land-Rover, where he could lie stretched out on the floor.

Karen had had some medical training, and knew very well that Chris' injury was to do with his spine and vertebrae. She also knew that in order to prevent more damage, it was imperative that Chris remained absolutely still, but the journey to the mission and safety involved some of the toughest roads in the region, where it was impossible to avoid rocks and pot-holes and sharp dips. Added to that, although the Land-Rover had come to their aid, it wasn't exactly the latest technology in suspension. It would rock from side to side over every bump and through every dip. But Karen did it! A journey that would ordinarily have taken them maybe an hour, took a tortuous five hours, with Chris screaming in agony with every movement of the vehicle. Poor Karen must have been beside herself with worry.

Karen had decided to take Chris back to the farm instead of down to the hospital at Mwinilunga, many more miles further away. I think she probably thought that, as hospitals go, Chris would have a better chance of recovery if she took him home and called for the doctors at the hospital to come up to the farm. Missionaries and doctors are fairly synonomous with each other, and being a fairly close-knit community,

Karen knew personally, the two Dutch doctors on secondment from their Holland based hospital.

They both came to the farm the following day, and after examining Chris, declared that he should fly immediately to Harare for specialist spinal treatment. In those days, Harare still had a strong and vibrant economy. Consequently, a lot of specialist surgeons and doctors still operated at the main hospital, and this was where Chris had been taken when I received the call from Karen.

When he was examined by surgeons at Harare, they were amazed he had survived such a traumatic collision. Colliding head first onto the sand-bank had caused severe damage to the vertebrae in his neck. They declared he was lucky to have survived, although I'm sure Chris, Karen or Ray would be able to explain it. To them, God works in wonderful, but mysterious ways!

Being asked to go back to the farm actually solved a dilemma I found myself in at Drifters. Call me padantic if you like, but if I was a tourist on safari, I would expect the "guide" to be able to guide the clients around on the trip. In other words, I would expect the guide to know where he was going. Steve had told me that my next trip would be to Zimbabwe, somewhere I had not been to on safari. When I asked who it was I would be learning the route from, he told me I was on my own. It was what they referred to as a "blind trip", and I would be supplied with maps and details of where to camp. It seemed ridiculous to me that, as the "guide", I would only have fractionally more idea of where I was going than the clients did. I suppose in some ways, I should have taken it as a compliment. At least they figured I could do it, but I wasn't happy about it at all and voiced my fears to Steve. He just said everything would be OK and that all guides did it at some time or other.

The phone call from Karen came just at the time I had been told I was going to Zimbabwe, so it solved the problem very neatly. I think, in truth, I was getting pretty tired anyway, and would have started to look forward to going back to England a few months hence. As it was, I went straight to Andy and told him what had happened to Chris and that I would be leaving as soon as I could for Zambia. Strangely enough, he wasn't at all happy that I was leaving. He told me that he had hoped to have me there for two years at least. Mind you, he never wished me luck, so it wasn't all good!

Just as I had bought all my equipment from Udo when I arrived at Drifters, so I sold it on to the next guide coming in. I left Drifters with regret, but at the same time, a lot of satisfaction. I had become a successful, efficient and knowledgeable guide, easily the equal of some and a damn sight better than others. However, my achievement meant more to me than that. It's probably a little arrogant, but it pleases me to think that, in all probability, I was the only Metropolitan police officer who had gone to Africa and become a safari guide. Too many of my colleagues are content to go to work, earn their money, go home and spend all night down the pub. I know the officers with families have no choice, but many other single officers are not prepared to see what is on the other side of the wall. They are too wrapped up in their own existences. I cannot be too critical, each person is an individual, and if they are happy doing that, then fine. I just think that there must come a time when they ask themselves if there is anything else, and if they, do, are they going to answer the question?

My immediate problem, was how do I get back to Mwinilunga as quickly as possible? I had a quiet word with the guide taking the next safari to Botswana and, as luck would have it, he was doing a wrong-way trip, going to Victoria Falls first. That meant I could then get the train to Livingstone and then the train to Lusaka, a train to Kitwe in the copper-belt and finally a bus to Mwinilunga. We arranged that Craig would pick me up on the highway behind Bob and Helen's house at six in the morning. He would tell the clients that I was another guide being taken up for another trip.

To get onto the highway, I had to climb over the 6 feet high back wall to Bob's house. It wasn't very safe at the best of times and I just prayed that it wouldn't choose that moment to collapse with me on top of it. The other thing I prayed for is that I wouldn't be spotted by some passing police patrol car. Climbing over a wall with a rucksack at 5-30 in the morning might just arouse suspicions. Luckily the wall didn't give way, and Craig arrived on the dot.

I was still travelling to Mwinilunga 3 days later. Bus and train services were appalling in those days. The train may or may not arrive. If it does, it may or may not leave that day, and when it does leave, you can probably walk faster than it travels!

The final stage is a 250 kilometre bus trip from Kitwe to Mwinilunga. These days, an express bus makes the trip, but then, it was an old brute of a bus, with awful plastic seats, actually made for two people but generally accommodating three. Having been on this bus before, I knew what to expect, chickens! and a lot of them, all in tiny little boxes stacked in the aisle, along with hundreds of other bags and assorted goods and livestock! Being nearly six feet tall and quite well-built, I unashamedly bullied my way onto the outside of the seat, where I could at least stretch my legs out on someone's chickens.

We hadn't been on the road long before a man approached my seat and asked if I was "Mr. Nil" from Sachibondu. When I said I was, at least half a dozen other people came back to where I was sitting to greet me. They were all from the town and the mission and seemed excited not only to see me, but also that I was going back to Sachibondu. They wanted to know everything I had been doing and how long I would be staying. I was very touched by their thoughts and didn't have the heart to tell them that it would only be for a matter of 3 or 4 weeks, until Chris and Karen came back. I simply told them I didn't know how long I would be staying. We chatted and laughed the whole way to Mwinilunga, even when the bus had the customary puncture and we had to unload all the luggage from the roof in order to get at the spare wheels.

We arrived at Mwinilunga very late in the evening and I went straight to Chris' friends, Andy and Charlotte. Although they had heard I might pitch up sometime, they weren't really expecting me. Nevertheless, I had a bed for the night and in the morning, I would catch the milk run from the farm and hitch a ride back to the mission station.

Karen had told me that at the time Chris had the accident, they had a young man from their church in Southampton staying with them. The timing was such that, they had no choice but to leave him in charge of running the farm. They didn't really want him to come out to Zambia in the first place, but apparently he had pestered them so much, they gave in eventually. His name was Steven and I met him the following morning. From that moment on, we didn't like each other, or should I say, I was completely ambivalent about him, but he really didn't like me. The fact is, we didn't get on.

Steven was one of the reasons why Chris had asked me to go back to the farm, he simply didn't trust him. He was young and very impressionable and very eager to prove something to himself and anybody else who took the slightest interest. Chris was worried that discipline on the farm would disappear under Steven's stewardship, and to some extent, he was right to be worried.

From the moment we met, Steven impressed on me that he was in charge, and obviously resented the fact that Chris had asked me to return. I realised I was in an awkward position. I didn't want to pull the rug from under his feet, but I told him that Chris had asked me to return, I couldn't alter that, and that I would simply make sure that things ticked over properly until they came back. I tried very hard to make him believe that he was running things, and in truth, he wasn't a bad lad.

I think we were both a bit overawed by the greeting I received as we drove onto the mission. Even without telephones, news travels fast and dozens of people ran from their homes, calling my name and running alongside the Toyota Land-cruiser Steven was using. When we got to the farmhouse, I greeted them all individually in the polite Lunda fashion, a slight curtsy, tapping my breast and gently clapping my hands together whilst saying "Mwane mwane", also calling them by name, if I could remember it.

With the greetings over, I went straight over to Gordon and Peggy. He was really happy to see me, and I him, but Peggy and I didn't have the same bond that Gordon and I seemed to have. He lost no time in telling me all that Steven had done wrong on the farm. The worst thing he'd done was to invite all the farm workers to the house one evening for a "drink". Apparently, Steven had brought some bottles of whisky with him from England and shared these with the boys on the farm. Oh dear! Africans love their alcohol, but they get it mainly from their own brew of beer or from the light beers sold in the towns. They are completely unprepared for the strength of Scotch whisky. As a result, he got them absolutely plastered. So much so, that many of them were quite ill over the following days. Gordon nearly sent him packing for that one!

As far as he and I were concerned, we dropped into a sort of routine. Steven would issue instructions to the boys on the farm and they would then come to me to ask if they should do it or not! I would tell them either that they should do as "Mr. Steven" asked, or would fine-tune the instruction somewhat before telling them to get on with it. I really don't know whether Steven knew this was going on, but it seemed to work and everybody was happy.

I think Chris, Karen, Gordon and Peggy, especially Peggy, were a little harsh on Steven. He was a young man, eager to please. Fair enough, he'd made mistakes, but whom amongst us doesn't do that? He had real energy and initiative. The reason that he was using the Land-cruiser when I got back was because he had done a deal with a guy in the town, for a new chassis for the old Land-Rover. Ruth's adopted son John, a qualified mechanic, (and apparently father to dozens!) was in the process of changing the old chassis for the new one. He had expressed doubts that the swap-over would be successful, and if it wasn't, then Steven would have been responsible for the farm having no means of transport of its own. But it was working, and Steven had persuaded John that it would work, and he was right! However, I think this was more to do with Steven's persuasion skills rather than his mechanical knowledge.

There was nothing nasty about Steven, at least that I experienced. He was just desperate to be liked and accepted. We tried to be sociable with each other and one day, we rode bicycles about 30 kilometres north of the mission, to the source of the Zambezi river, a little spurt of water coming out of the earth in deep undergrowth. How on earth anyone found it in the first place is a complete mystery to me!

On other occasions, we played board games in the afternoon, or rather, a board-game, which he was very good at and I was useless. But all the while, I was aware of a simmering resentment of me. On the day, the locals and I rebuilt the wooden bridge across the river, he was aware of what I was doing, but didn't once come to see what was happening. I put this down to the fact that, as it wasn't his idea, he wanted nothing to do with it.

I think Steven was eager to find his place in life. He'd gone to the farm to experience something different and had been placed in a position, not of his asking. I think he stepped up to the plate and all in all, I don't think he made a bad job of it. Over the following 3 or 4 weeks, the farm ticked over. We did the milk run to Mwinilunga every other day, made sure the cows got milked and ran the milling machine for the locals. Nothing went seriously wrong and the Land-Rover eventually got finished. When Chris arrived back from Harare, the farm was much as he had left it, not making a fortune, but providing a living for the workforce and produce for the mission and the wider local community.

I met Chris and Karen at Andy's house in the town. She looked very pale and drawn and he looked shorter by about an inch and a half. He'd lost a lot of weight but at least he was back with us, and we were all very grateful for that. Of course, all the Christians put it down to God's intervention but I think he was just plain lucky.

Steven and I decided independently to leave the farm at more or less the same time. He had been offered some job or other with a man called Malaplava down on the copper-belt, doing what, I can't remember, and left shortly before me. I learned later that on the way to the Copper-belt, Steven was driving Malaplava's new Toyota whilst he slept. Steven dozed off at the wheel and woke just yards away from a vital turn. He tried to slow the vehicle using the gears, but in his sleepy state shifted the four-wheel drive lever instead. There was an almighty crash followed by a tinkling sound as the Toyota's gears spewed out onto, and all over the road. Steven's employment with Malaplava was apparently quite short-lived!

I said another emotional farewell to Peggy and Gordon, waved everyone goodbye, again and finally took my leave of Sachibondu Mission.

Gordon died a few short years later and was buried on the mission, amongst the people he loved and who loved him back. I think of him often and remember him only with love and friendship. He could be a cantankerous old man at times, but there was always a twinkle in his eye and a laugh on his lips. I suppose I choose to forget the rows he had with Chris and the way he and Karen were treated by Gordon and the rest of the so-called missionaries, but I think to remember someone only for the negative aspects of their life tends to say more about the person remembering than the person being remembered.

My year away from the police was now very nearly up, and so I journeyed back to Victoria Falls in much the same way I had travelled to Mwinilunga. My eventual destination was Johannesburg but I didn't have the faintest idea how I would get from the Falls to South Africa. On an impulse, I went down to the camp-site at Victoria Falls and, as luck would have it, there was a Drifters truck there with two guides that I knew quite well. They were on their way back from the Johannesburg-Nairobi trip and were leaving for Jo'burg the following morning. They gladly gave me a lift, and I caught my flight back to the UK a couple of days later. It was July 1995 when I returned to the U.K..

I had had a phenomenal year away. I started this section of my story by saying that 1994/5 saw me succeed at something I could never have expected. However, it wasn't just the fact that I had been leading wild-camp safaris around Botswana and South Africa, or the fact that I had worked on the mission station farm with Chris and Karen, experiencing a side of African life not seen by that many people. Going away for this year made me realize that only a relatively few people are different enough to want to challenge themselves in this way. Many people that I know or am acquainted with often say, "I'd love to go there" or "I'd love to see that", but in fairness, family ties hold them back. On the other hand, I know many people with no such ties, who would never dream of stopping work and going abroad for a year with no fixed plan or schedule. Most people go on holiday to Spain or France, or to Florida and they never think about expanding their boundaries or experiencing something they thought they could only imagine. Even with no family ties to dictate where and when they might take their holidays, many people are generally afraid of taking that extra step out of their comfort zones. Don't misunderstand me, we all like what we know and are comfortable with and I'm no different. But every now and then, where circumstances allow us, I think we should all strive to experience something a little out of the ordinary, something which will set us apart from others. The fact that in reality we don't all seek to be a little different, only goes to help make those who do, more interesting. I would hope to fit into this latter category!

Chapter 25

I returned to England in July 1995, and was posted to Orpington police station, part of the London Borough of Bromley.

When I returned from travelling the world in 1989, I made the mistake of believing that other colleagues of mine would be interested in where I had been. As I was telling them about my travels, I could almost see them switching off, blank expressions coming over their faces. I was determined that this time, I would make no such mistake, even though I was bursting to tell them about my adventures.

I had been told to report to my new Inspector, a lady named Christine Pleece at 10pm on Monday evening, I don't remember the exact date, all ready for night duty. It seems that whenever I started at a new station, I always had to start with the night shift. We had a short chat before we went in to where the constables were waiting for "parade", and I was then introduced to them. I had asked Inspector Pleece not to mention where I had been or what I had done, and asked her simply to say that I was joining them following a career break, which was true. When the formalities were over, we all went to the canteen for the usual cup of tea, prior to going out on patrol. It would be at this point that any initial questions about my history would come. Nobody asked me anything, I was not exactly ignored, but not encouraged to join their conversations either.

Unlike today's modern police force, sorry "service", in those days, it was generally older officers with vast amounts of service, who were posted out to outlying stations and boroughs such as Bromley. I remember reading once in our in-house publication, "The Job" about an officer serving at Chislehurst station, also part of Bromley Division, who, because he only had 24 years service, was still the junior officer on the team and as such, had to make the tea for his colleagues!

There used to be a pecking order at stations, and officers with much more service than others, were treated deferentially, and officers with driving qualifications even had their own room. The officers with much lower amounts of service were not allowed into this room unless strictly invited by the drivers, and even then, it was usually only to deliver them their tea!

As a sergeant, I was not subject to this hierarchal system, we had our own. In the old days, sergeants and constables would never sit together at the same canteen table. It was all to do with the supervision aspect. As I explained earlier, constables nearly always tried to get away with things at work, and sergeants always tried to stop them. Hence, the constables never trusted a sergeant and would never have them sit with them in the canteen. Similarly, sergeants never trusted constables and wouldn't actually want to sit with them.

However, this culture had been under threat since before I joined the police, and slowly but surely, things were changing. The old ways were being swept aside by much younger constables and sergeants who believed that good policing could still be achieved by more cooperation and communication between the two groups. However, there was still a degree of separation between the two sides, and quite rightly so too. My view has always been that over-familiarisation would prevent or hinder a sergeant executing his or her duty when it came to discipline. I knew several young sergeants who insisted on mixing with the constables and joining them in whatever they were doing, but had come unstuck when a particular constable had had to be subjected to the discipline code. However, as wary as I was, I sometimes joined the constables and other sergeants on trips away, such as a day trip to France. It used to be that, as a group, constables were not actually allowed to take days away unless a supervising officer accompanied them, who was not always welcome. I remember one such trip to France with my team of officers from Carter Street police station when my drinks were spiked in France. I had a good working relationship with the officers, but this incident may highlight the attitude of constables towards sergeants. I have never drunk beer, generally only Gin and Tonic, and I know when I've had enough. On the drive back from Dover, I had to stop on the roadside to relieve myself and fell over probably three times before I got back to the mini-bus. The excess of alcohol was beginning to take effect and by the time, we got back to the meeting point, I was absolutely out of it. I hadn't had that much to drink but was not able to reconcile that with my condition. I was certainly in no fit state to drive my car home from the meeting point, but I did. How on earth I ever made it, I'll never know. When I got home, I was so drunk, I thought it would be a good idea to take a pee in the kitchen sink. Susie was not impressed!

It wasn't until the next day when I recalled falling over, driving and peeing in the sink that I knew my drinks were spiked. I had a good idea who it was, a useless police officer who liked to play practical jokes. Some joke! How on earth I didn't have a crash on the way home, I'll never know. Had I been a constable, the others wouldn't have let me drive, but I was a sergeant and as such, I was fair game to them. It was a learning curve for me and I never trusted any of them again.

It never ceased to amaze me just why a bunch of professional police officers always thought they had to act in an outrageous and thuggish manner whenever they went away together. I remember one occasion when around a dozen officers were arrested as their ferry from France docked. Apparently, they had all got very drunk and completely wrecked one of the lounges on board the ship. Goodness knows just what the public must have thought of them. And rugby tours, Christ, I avoided them like the plague. I had started playing with the local police team a few years earlier and had heard about the antics of some of the players. I'm as much in favour of a good, fun time as the next guy, but some of the players seemed to think that they had a duty to cause as much damage and general upset as they could. Amazing! I remember one rugby match I was watching between Carter Street and Peckham police stations. The referee abandoned the match half way through and walked off the pitch saying he was disgusted at all the foul play and fighting that was taking place on the pitch. Why did they have to fight, it was a rugby game for goodness sake!?

When I joined the relief at Orpington, three aspects influenced my arrival on the team, i.e. I was a sergeant, I was new to them and I had been away somewhere on a career break. 3 reasons why they shouldn't trust me! I would have to prove my worth, and as a long serving officer, I knew that and completely accepted the situation.

By this time in 1995, a lot of the old practices had all but disappeared. We no longer had drivers' rooms and we no longer hung cadets out of windows by their ankles until they agreed to make the tea, and we all sat at one big table in the canteen, all very cosy! I distinctly remember thinking to myself that if this was the way it was to be, then OK, but I wasn't all that happy with it.

Over the following weeks, I was still largely ignored, but gradually one or two of the more inquisitive officers asked me where I had been on career break. It was fairly obvious I hadn't been in the UK as I had a wonderful tan and spoke with a pronounced South African twang to my voice. I had found it was impossible to work with the guides at Drifters and not end up sounding like one of them. In answer to their questions, and still being reticent to tell them too much, I replied simply that I had been in Africa. Gradually however, I began to tell them more about what I had done and where I had been. Some were genuinely interested and asked a lot of questions. Others simply said that it must have been nice for me!

Having experienced the non-interest when I came back the first time from traveling, I was not surprised by the lack of interest from some officers. Understanding it was another matter. Here I was, a middle-aged London police officer, returning to policing for the second time in my career, having been in Africa working on a farm 30 kilometres into deep bush and running wild-camp safaris around the best game parks in southern Africa. To me, it was incredulous that some officers were not interested in the slightest. I appreciate that other people cannot always relate to what others do, but for goodness sake, these are intelligent men and women who would probably never have the opportunity that came my way. Even if they wouldn't have done for a pension, what I had done, they surely had to be a little inquisitive, to dismiss it out of hand was mystifying to me. I simply couldn't understand it.

After we had drunk the tea on that first night duty, Inspector Pleece and myself went to her office and she briefed me about the officers on my team, and more nearly, whom I should look out for. We went through the team one by one, and apart from the officers who were just awkward to deal with, I had to watch out for one officer who had been going through several traumatic experiences in his personal life, all at the same time and as a result, was dangerously close to a nervous breakdown, one officer who had been disqualified from driving his motor car and who had lied to the Superintendent about it and one officer, who according to Christine Pleece, was simply "waiting to play the race card". In addition to these, I found that one of my sergeant colleagues took an absolute delight in taking me to one side at least once in a shift, to tell me about some misdemeanour one of my officers had committed or something that one of them had said, and to tell me how, in his opinion, I should deal with it. I listened to this idiot a few times, completely ignored his "advice" all the time and eventually told him to mind his own business.

Inspector Pleece was a formidable woman, very competent as an Inspector, an excellent police officer with a great sense of humour, but a woman you didn't want to cross. Before I arrived at Orpington, outlying stations such as Biggin Hill and Chislehurst had been amalgamated into one area. Instead of having their own senior officers, these stations were now administered by the duty Inspector at Orpington, with one set of senior management operating from the divisional station at Bromley. Only constables remained at these outlying stations and they were supervised by sergeants from Orpington, who sometimes never got to visit the station during a shift. As a result, standards had begun to slip, and Inspector Pleece had heard some rumours she didn't like. On one occasion, she and a sergeant visited Biggin Hill station unexpectedly, at a time when the officers should all have been out on patrol. Instead she found most of the team sitting in their canteen, drinking tea and playing cards. The officers who were out on patrol, were allowed to remain at Biggin Hill, but those caught playing cards were all transferred immediately to either Bromley or Orpington, where they could be supervised much more closely, and more trustworthy constables were transferred out to Biggin Hill. Those officers who were transferred had made the mistake of thinking that Inspector Pleece was nothing more than a "plonk" with rank. They all had enough service to remember that women officers used to be treated appallingly, not thought capable of patrolling with male officers and used to deal mainly with children and menial tasks. They were known by the derogatory term, "plonks".

On another occasion, a constable apparently found out why one never wanted to cross swords with Inspector Pleece. I say "apparently" because it's a story that circulated the station at the time. If it's true, I can only imagine the officer didn't know who Inspector Pleece was. The constable entered the lift at Orpington police station, with Inspector Pleece in plain clothes. She was taking the lift from the second floor, and as there was no third floor, jokingly said to the constable, "Going down?" The constable replied, "shouldn't we kiss first?!" Apparently, after the verbal thrashing of the century, the constable suffered weeks of walking the beat instead of riding in a nice warm police car. Those officers in the cars had strict instructions that they were not to pick him up at any time, on pain of the same punishment, or worse! I don't know whether it's true or not, but it's a good story and would be very typical of her!

Not too long after returning to operational duty, I read that applications were being invited for sergeants to join the firearms department. The immediate vacancies were in the Armed Response Vehicles, which were able to respond to any emergency call involving firearms in the Metropolitan police area, and sometimes beyond. From the A.R.V.s, the selected sergeants could progress into the specialised departments dealing with situations such as hostage rescue, intelligence-led operations, snipers etc. At that stage, I had around nine years left before I retired from the police. I was still fit and healthy and I thought I had a reasonable chance of success. I discussed the idea at length with Christine Pleece and she saw no reason why I shouldn't apply either. The more I thought about it, the more I became excited by the prospect, and was determined to apply. The application form was much longer than I ever remembered them being. Only a few short years earlier, all that was required as an application was a short report, telling the recipient how good you were. And that was only if you *had* to "apply" for something, more often than not, it was a word of mouth recommendation or a bottle of good whisky to the right person. Political correctness was beginning to get a hold within the police service, the old, unfair and biased ways of doing things were fast disappearing. And good riddance to some of them as well, including "applications on a bottle please"!

Amongst other categories, this application form was asking for evidence of ability and one question read, "Give two examples of how you can react to a fast developing situation." The question said nothing about relating the incidents to police duty, only that they had to be recent. The second example I gave was the bull elephant which came into my camp in Botswana, and how I had to react quickly to safeguard the clients, equipment, food, tents and belongings.

Satisfied that my answers to all the other questions and the accompanying evidence was of the highest standard I could achieve, I got Christine Pleece to endorse the application, and sent it off. I confidently awaited a reply, inviting me to an interview, or a "board" as it's known in the police.

A few weeks later, Christine took me into her office and explained why my application for the firearms team had been rejected. She had had a long telephone conversation with a Chief Inspector from the firearms unit, who was one of the officers determining who should receive an interview board. He had asked her about the episode with the elephant as it had apparently caused huge mirth in the office. He actually thought I was joking and had sent in the application as a wind-up. When Christine told him I was serious, he asked how the elephant incident related to police work? Christine told him that it didn't, it simply demonstrated how I could react to a "fast developing situation". The Chief Inspector persisted in asking about the relevance of an elephant to police work, how does it fit in? Christine, bless her heart, tried her hardest to convince the idiot that being able to react to a "fast developing situation" could not be confined simply to police work. Could he not see that the relevance was in how I reacted to the incident, to get rid of the animal safely? Lives were at risk, holidays were in danger of being spoilt if I didn't react to this situation. "Yes, but what does that have to do with the police?" was his only answer. Christine had no choice eventually but to give in and say, "nothing". And that was it, application bounced!

It still rankles with me today that the Metropolitan police could not only employ senior officers incapable of thinking outside the box, but also promote them to ranks where they have a direct influence in the careers of others. I have no doubt that as administrators and policy makers, these men and women are excellent, but as judges of other's characters and abilities, I fear they are sadly lacking and whilst they continue to have such a narrow outlook, they will continue to overlook officers with obvious practical ability in favour of officers who are only capable of running with the "party line".

The following weeks and months, saw me working a fairly humdrum routine of shift work, earlies, lates and night duty. The men and women of my team, or "relief" as it was then, were all of the highest calibre, hard-working and by and large, a pleasure to work with. The warnings that Christine had given me about some members of the relief, whilst being founded on good reason, had turned out not to be as dire as I had been led to believe. There was only one occasion when I had to take disciplinary action against one of the afore-mentioned officers, and that was for a stupid procedural misdemeanour, about which he should have known better, but which might have had disastrous consequences. It remains the only time I ever had to report a constable for a discipline matter. I always preferred to sort out problems on a personal basis, rather than have to resort to formal proceedings. I saw this same officer from time to time and he went on to a good career within the Criminal Investigation Department at a very busy inner London station. He bears no grudges, in fact, he recalls the episode as a "wake-up call".

There isn't really a great deal I can say about this period except that, try as I might, I simply couldn't settle into a working life, which I found quite dull. In some respects, I would probably have been happier doing the constables' work of answering emergency calls, dealing with serious road traffic accidents, which happened quite often on the fast open roads around Orpington and the myriad of other duties assigned to constables. The one duty I did enjoy was attending scenes of crime, major incidents or accidents and taking charge, directing the constables in their duties, but even that was becoming dull. Having an experienced group of officers around me, I knew that they would do their jobs, but all the same, as the supervising officer, I had to ensure this was the case. The police force has always offered a very wide variety of career paths to choose from and it will always be a huge regret of mine that I didn't take more advantage of the opportunities on offer. To a large extent, the monotony that I was experiencing at this time was largely of my own making. It's not correct to describe the police force as monotonous, it's just that I felt there was no challenge to what I was doing. Having over 20 years experience at this stage, there weren't many incidents and calls that I couldn't deal with blindfold. It got to the stage, where I almost wished something major or disastrous would happen, just to give me something different to do.

Christine Pleece was excellent at allowing her sergeants to take charge at scenes of incidents. As Inspector, she was ultimately responsible, but she had the confidence in her sergeants to allow them to exercise their expertise and take any decisions necessary. If a particular decision was found later to be wrong under those particular conditions, Christine would still support that officer in his or her decision, provided that it had been made based on sound reasoning and judgement, and would discuss with that officer other options that may have been available. She had absolutely no qualms about taking one of her sergeants to task for a poor quality decision, and we all knew this. I have always employed the same work-ethic of supporting constables under my supervision, telling them and encouraging them to make decisions based on the same principles Christine used.

And so life trundled on. The months went by, summer came and went. There wasn't much happening in my private life, I had no girlfriend as such, although Sabine and I were still very much in touch. I had begun to play a lot more tennis with Ray, although he was still leagues ahead of me. One day, Ray said to me that he would give me £10 if I managed to take a set from him by September of the following year. As this was in April or May of that year, I don't remember precisely when, it meant that I had around 17 or 18 months in which to improve so much, I could take my first set from him. I was confident about accomplishing this, so confident in fact, I offered him odds of 10-1 that I would do it. This of course meant that if I did manage it, he would give me my £10 but if I lost, I would owe him £100. Needless to say, Ray's competitive edge kept him ahead all the time. Sometimes, I even got to within a couple of games of taking the set, but then he would switch on the afterburners and beat me to the line. September of the following year came, and I hadn't managed to take a set off him. I came close, but never quite managed it. Accordingly, I owed him £100 which he was determined to collect! I was disappointed, but was more angered by Ray's gloating, "I told you so" attitude. I now had to pay him £100, which rankled even more. Suddenly, an idea popped into my head! I would inscribe the cheque with copperplate writing and scroll-work. To explain, I need to take you back a few years.

When I was working for the National Coal Board as an apprentice mining surveyor, I was occasionally in the office of the colliery manager, a man named Douglas Dorn. He had a direct phone line to his deputies down the pit. Whomever he was talking to on the phone, he would be writing his name over and over on a sheet of paper, dozens of times. However, it was not just writing, Douglas Dorn was a calligrapher and he was writing the names in beautiful copperplate handwriting. I was fascinated by the art and immediately tried to emulate Mr. Dorn. Of course, I was rubbish at first, but Mr. Dorn gave me a lot of hints and showed me how to construct the letters in "copperplate" and "Old English". I had no pens or ink to start with, other than what Mr. Dorn had given me, but I just kept on practicing, and buying ever better equipment when I could afford it. However, even I don't think I had meant it to last for so long, but I continued to practice calligraphy for the next 25 years, improving all the time and experimenting with different aspects, such as delicate scroll-work around a word or heading, as one finds on a Bank of England currency note.

My colleagues at the various police stations I worked at often asked me to calligraph documents such as wedding cards or photo albums for them. On one occasion, I was walking home from Bow Street police station when I passed an exhibition to encourage children to take art seriously, in an old warehouse just off Covent Garden. The young lady persuaded me to go inside and take a look. I ended up staying for a couple of hours, writing out several alphabets in various calligraphic styles, and watching them being displayed around the walls. She took my address for administration purposes and a few days later, I received a letter from the organization with a newspaper clipping inside. Apparently, a journalist had written a piece in one of the good broadsheets, describing the exhibition and commenting that, " a local policeman, coaxed in on his way home, proved to be a talented calligrapher, preparing several beautiful alphabets for the exhibition." Understandably maybe, I still have the clipping.

I don't often blow my own trumpet, but I did get quite good at writing. I can't draw for a fortune, but I can write, or I could, until I managed to cut my calligraphy career short, the reasons for which are described later in this chapter.

Back to the bet! I devised a way that I could pay the debt but not necessarily lose £100. First, I wrote the cheque payable to Mr. R. Lowe in copperplate. I had a stock of good quality paper and so the next step was to write out, again in flowing copperplate, the following passage:-

"This £100 was received by the Rev. R. Lowe as settlement of a wager between himself and Mr. N. Robins. It indicates that the temporary superiority of the Rev. Lowe at the honourable game of tennis is hereby acknowledged by the aforementioned N. Robins, who nevertheless, vows to continue the struggle in order to curtail the abominable and insufferable gloating of the Rev. R. Lowe."

I then pasted the cheque onto the paper above the text and decorated the whole ensemble with delicate scroll work, or "illumination". Finally, I framed the cheque and passage and presented it to Ray, with the challenge to actually bank his winnings.

I had paid my debt. If he didn't want to recover the debt, that was up to him, but I had paid. Of course, he has never paid the cheque into his account and the presentation remains on his wall to this day.

It wasn't long after this little wager that I did actually take a set from Ray and have gone on to beat him regularly. He is very competitive at any sport and won't give an inch, especially where one of my tennis shots goes close to the line. We've had many a row over line calls, but it always ends with a hug and a handshake. To a large extent, tennis has been a great outlet for me and I'm grateful to Ray not only for getting me onto the court in the first place, but also for bullying me into improving my game to the extent that I am now one of the better players at my tennis club, Parklangley.

Around March 1996, I decided to take some holiday and go and visit my sister Lynne and her husband David in Perth, Australia. Their son, and my only nephew, Tom was about 7 or 8 years old at this time. Lynne and I have never been particularly close, but I was looking forward to seeing them, especially Tom, whom I hadn't seen since he was a baby. I flew first to Brisbane, where I visited an ex-client from the safaris. We had enjoyed a brief encounter in Africa and had stayed in touch since. Unfortunately, we had a very spectacular falling-out a few years later, and as a result, well, suffice to say we are no longer in touch.

I arrived in Perth early on a Saturday morning and after dropping my bags at the house, we all went for a walk in some gardens in Freemantle. I have to say that I can understand why so many people fall in love with Perth and Freemantle, they are both beautiful places. Perth sits astride the Swan river, (it sounds much better the way they say it, rather than how we in England would say The River Swan!) which winds its way gracefully through and around the city, and being a small city, the amount of greenery that surrounds it, enhances its looks no end. Freemantle sits on the edge of the Indian Ocean and doesn't look as though it has changed much since the days it was built, with wonderful old colonial style buildings, very reminiscent of some places in Africa.

Tom was obviously very excited at meeting his "Uncle Neil" and spent most of the walk through the gardens desperately trying to capture my entire attention. I was trying to chat with Lynne and Dave and be attentive to Tom all at the same time. It had rained very heavily the night before, leaving large pools of water all over the place. At one stage, Tom stamped into a shallow puddle and splashed water over my legs. I pretended to be angry with him, looking at him and then looking at my legs, then looking back at him and so on. He just stood there with a big grin on his face, so I said to him, "Tom, you do that again and I'll take you over to that very large and deep puddle over there, tip you upside down and put you in head-first!" Tom looked at me in that unique way that 7 or 8 year olds adopt when they are trying to work out whether you are serious or not, or whether they can push the boundary a little further away. I simply stared back at him, challenging him to make up his mind. He did; he splashed me again and ran off. "Right, that's it," I shouted and chased after him. It didn't take me long to catch him and I picked him up and tipped him upside down, holding him by his ankles. Now, I think Tom figured that even if he did splash me, and I did catch him and tip him upside down, the fact that, in order to carry out my threat of dipping his head in the muddy puddle, I would have to wade into the water ankle deep, thereby getting wet myself, would save him. I think even Lynne and Dave had their doubts that I would carry out my threat. No such luck for Tom. Together, with me holding this writhing, young boy upside down by his ankles, we marched over to the muddy puddle. As we got closer, Tom realised I was going to carry out the threat and began to struggle even more frantically. As I waded into the middle of the enormous puddle, he went silent. I stopped in the middle, grinned at him upside down and dipped his head into the muddy water, right up to his eye line. When I pulled him out and hoisted him over my shoulder, he was laughing and screaming with delight, begging me to do it again.

Over the following two weeks I was in Perth, Tom and I had a lot of fun together. We would go swimming at the local pool, where he proudly announced to his pals I was his "Uncle Neil" and we would spend practically the entire session with me launching him into the air from underwater, like a rocket. Then of course, I would have to do it to his pals as well. At breakfast, Tom would sit and wait patiently, until eventually the patience ran out and he would stand alongside me and beg, "Uncle Neil, chase me round the house, chase me round the house!" There had been one little episode where I chased Tom around the garden and into the house. Now it had grown into a daily chase around all the rooms, into the garden and back into the house. Sometimes, he would go one way, I would go the other and when he saw me coming, he would scream with delight and turn around and run back, away from me again. Sometimes, I would catch him, usually in the garden to spare Lynne the horror of thinking furniture and the like would get damaged and we would roll around on the grass. I would deliberately let him go, and the chase would start up again. I'm grinning to myself even as I write this, it was such a good time!

With my birthday on 9th March, I was obviously going to be with Lynne and Dave on the day. Lynne had told Tom that it was my birthday the following day and she told me that he wanted to bring me breakfast in bed as a treat. It was a school day for him, so I said to Tom that I would love to have breakfast with him in my room, but it would have to be at about 6-30am so that he could get ready for school.

I set my alarm for 6-30am, thinking that Tom would probably be just about up and around and Lynne would be preparing the breakfast tray. As soon as I was awake, I shouted at the top of my voice. "Tom, where's my breakfast?" No sooner had I stopped speaking, than there was a knock on the door and Tom walked in, struggling to hold a tray of breakfast goodies for him and I to have. I realised he must have been right outside at that moment and Lynne told me later that he had been up at 6am, helping to prepare the tray and had then stood outside my room, waiting for 6-30 to arrive. Both of us just sat on my bed, munching on a hearty breakfast and chatting like old pals. My heart just melted!

Not long after moving in to my present house in 1982, I decided to plant some quick-growing Leylandi trees around the front boundaries, to act as a sort of fence or a hedge. The plan was that they would grow quickly to a desired height, at which point, I would trim them back and shape them into a hedge. I chose the quick growing variety as I wanted the hedge as quickly as possible, which I got after a couple of years. Initially, I allowed them to grow quite high, well over 10 feet, which was a bit daft and brought well founded complaints from my neighbour about blocking out some of their light. Over the following years, I've gradually trimmed them down to a more manageable height of about 6 feet. Now, why, I hear you ask, am I prattling on about a bunch of trees? Those of you who know me will also know where this is going. For those who don't, I am about to reveal all!

In October 1996, I decided that they were once again a bit too high. It wasn't that they looked unsightly or even that my neighbour complained they blocked out her light, which they didn't, but they were just too awkward to trim back. As well as growing upwards, the damn things had of course, grown outwards, making the hedges really thick and wide, so wide in fact, it was impossible to reach from one side to the other. At this point, they were about 7 feet high and I wanted to bring them down to about 6 feet, or just under It's a very woody hedge and so I went to the local hire shop and hired myself a large, petrol-driven hedge trimmer, well capable of tackling the larger stems and boughs inside the hedge itself. Cutting the height out of the hedge was no problem, but trimming the inside growth would need an industrial sized trimmer. The hire shop showed me how it operated, how to start and stop it, and that was about it. There was no safety equipment supplied such as gloves or goggles and only a very cursory demonstration as to how to hold it or operate it safely. As the hirer, I was left very much to my own devices.

My house is on a steep hill and the pavement outside the hedge is very uneven and slopes away from the hedge towards the gutter. It was tough work, each main trunk had to be sawn through by hand and then the major inside boughs also had to be sawn out. The rest of it was taken out with the petrol trimmer.

In order to get to the top of the hedge, I used a step-ladder, which I had used for years, and still do to this day. On this occasion, I had reached a point where I would have to stand on the step-ladder and reach across to the far side of the hedge using the trimmer. This point was on the pavement side and so the step-ladder had to be placed on the tarmac. Initially, I put the step-ladder into an "A" formation, but with the slope of the pavement away from the hedge and towards the gutter, I didn't see this as being too safe. The pavement is very uneven at this point as well and the ladder was wobbling about all over the place.

Don't misunderstand me here about all this safety speak. I'm not part of the "nanny state" and do feel that as an intelligent and mature adult, I am capable of assessing for myself the degree of safety I need to employ in any particular sphere without having to be dictated to by Government. (I have currently refused to be dealt with by one particular dental hygienist, who insists on making me wear goggles in case the water splashes into my eyes, treating me like a child.)

As an alternative to the "A" formation, I put the step-ladder into the normal extendable mode and pushed the top of the ladder as hard as I could into the hedge, anchoring it against a substantial trunk. Throughout my life, I have been afraid of heights and coupled with that fear, has been a fear that, whilst up high, any ladder which I may be standing on, will slide away from under me, causing me to fall off, or I will overbalance and cause the ladder to slide across a wall, inexorably to the ground, with me on it. On this particular occasion, even though I wouldn't be more than a few feet off the ground, I made sure the top was right up against the trunk and couldn't push through the hedge with my weight on the ladder. It had rubber feet and so should have been OK on the tarmac surface of the pavement.

I started up the hedge-trimmer, which really was a massive tool, heavy and awkward to handle. The hire shop had given me basic handling instructions, which could really be reduced to three words, use both hands! It was a fairly old machine with no emergency cut-out safety features. The shop assistant did explain that I should be careful when stopping the machine temporarily as the blades tended to take a few seconds to stop their slicing action.

I had only climbed onto the third rung of the ladder and everything seemed to be going along swimmingly. There was one little clump of undergrowth, which annoyingly, was just out of reach to my right. I stood on tip-toe on the ladder and stretched myself across, scything away with the big, macho-trimmer. Suddenly, the ladder twisted! My weight being placed onto one side caused the top of the ladder to roll around the trunk. I was caught completely off-balance and immediately began to fall off, into the hedge. Falling off a ladder, my worst nightmare coming true! Instinctively, I let go of the machine and shot my right hand out in front of me to try and regain my balance. The machine fell into the hedge, with the blades still slicing away, followed by me. In that split-second, I had no idea where the machine was, but my right hand found it soon enough. To try and break my fall, I had stretched my arm to full length and my right hand fell into the blades of the machine. It's funny how certain memories stay clear and fresh in your mind, whilst others fade into the distance. The memory of feeling the blades slicing across my outstretched fingers is as fresh today as it was on that day. Many people ask if it was painful, it wasn't. It was more of a caress across my flesh, and this I have put down to the fact that the blades of the machine were so sharp, they cut through my fingers like a hot knife through butter. I remember the clatter of the ladder as it fell to the pavement and the staccato sound of the petrol-engine, still running somewhere. I then distinctly remember thinking to myself that the one thing I didn't want to do, was extract myself from the hedge and look at my hand. I knew straight away that I had done very serious damage to my hand and I didn't want to look at it and see fingers missing! A second later of course, I picked myself up and forced myself to look at the damage. Blood was pumping furiously out of massive lacerations across all four fingers on my right hand. Miraculously, all the fingers were still there, but this fact hardly registered. I stood there and stared at the blood pumping out of me for a second or two and then figured I needed some help. I ran down the path to my house and then clarity of thought began to return. I couldn't operate the fingers on my right hand, and my left was shaking with the shock, so how was I going to apply any form of dressing? I ran back up my path and round to my next-door neighbour, Barbara. I had no idea if she was in from work, I just knew I needed help. Barbara told me later, she knew I didn't just want a cup of tea by the way I kicked her door open, shouting her name!

She was an angel! Barbara readily confesses to being distressed by the sight of blood, and here she was, being confronted by masses of the stuff, shooting out all over the place. Being First-Aid trained at work, I knew that to help staunch the flow of blood, I had to elevate the hand. I sat on a stool in Barbara's kitchen, with my hand in the air, whilst she did her best to wrap pads around the injured fingers to stop the blood, which by now was very evident everywhere, all over me, over Barbara and her floor. She then went to phone for an ambulance and whilst she was away, I began to feel light-headed and faint. I knew this was due to the shock and immediately took myself off the stool and lay on the floor with my hand in the air. Barbara had succeeded in stemming the flow of blood but was alarmed to find me on the floor when she returned. I told her what was happening and that she should just stay with me. I immediately felt better for laying down and was then able to tell her just what had happened. Whilst chatting to her, I remembered that I was meeting David that evening in London for a drink and a film. I asked Barbara to ring Jane at home and tell her what had happened and that I probably wouldn't be able to meet David, sorry!

The ambulance arrived shortly after and I was whisked off to the accident and emergency department at Bromley hospital. The ambulance medics had placed a more professional dressing on my hand and after a few minutes at A.and E., I was seen by a young man wearing a short white coat. He removed the dressing and looked at my hand. He then directed the ambulance staff to take me into "minor injuries"! I saw both ambulance men look at each other and one of them protested that the injury was a little more serious than merely "minor" The young man insisted, and so I was escorted to a small cubicle, where the ambulance staff wished me luck, and then left. They were nice guys and had done their best for me. After another short wait, another man walked into the cubicle wearing a long white coat. I thought this was obviously the doctor as his coat was longer than the other guy's! He examined my hand and told me to waggle my fingers on my right hand. I tried to move all of them but could only manage the little finger. He repeated the instruction, telling me that he couldn't very well assess the damage if I didn't move my fingers! I tried once more, but again, only the little finger moved. I didn't know why and told him I was trying my best, but they simply wouldn't respond. He began to get a little angry with me, probably thinking I was being stupid or obstinate and in the end, stormed out of the cubicle. I sat there on the couch trying to move my fingers and wondering why they wouldn't, when yet another man walked in, again wearing a nice crisp, long white coat. He took one look at my hand and immediately shouted, "Why is this man in minor injuries? Get him on a trolley, get him an oxygen mask and get him into major injuries, NOW!" *He* was the doctor!! As if by magic, a bed with wheels instantly appeared at the cubicle. I remember saying to the doctor, "It's OK, I can walk from here." Having been in the accident and emergency department many times before to speak to victims of assault and the like, I knew where he meant me to go. The doctor looked back at me, and gave me a stern look and said, "get on the trolley!" I could tell he was having a bad day, and so, obediently, I heaved myself onto the trolley and had an oxygen mask slapped on straight away. I was then wheeled into another cubicle, all of about five yards away from the first, and abandoned.

I don't really remember how long I lay there. I had been given some mild sedatives and I think I was drifting in and out of a sort of sleepiness. The next thing I do remember, was hearing my name being called and recognising the voice of my good friend Ray Lowe. Apparently, Barbara had phoned Jane as I had asked, and then Jane had phoned Ray to let him know what had happened. Ray had dropped everything and rushed to the hospital to see me, bless him! He stayed with me the rest of the afternoon, and I will never be more grateful to have someone nearby than I was on that day.

I was taken into X-ray and examined by quite a number of doctors and nurses. Eventually, I was told that I had serious damage to all the fingers on my right hand, and would need micro-surgery to repair them, surgery that was not available at Bromley. I remember the doctor saying to me, "It's off to East Grinstead for you my lad." I had no idea what he was talking about or where he meant me to go when I got there. We had a discussion about how I was to get to East Grinstead and when the doctor said an ambulance wouldn't be available till much later that evening, Ray volunteered to take me in his car. During the discussion, the doctor outlined the damage which he could see. I had lacerated the top of my little finger, severed the arteries, nerves and tendons in my ring finger, middle finger and index finger and in addition, I had severed the bone in my index finger. (The severed tendons was the reason I couldn't move my fingers when told to do so by the first guy in the long white coat.) He told me East Grinstead was *the* centre of excellence for this type of surgery in the country. Actually called "Queen Victoria Hospital", it had gained a famous reputation during the Second World War, treating burned and mutilated soldiers and airmen and pioneering the use of skin-grafting and micro-surgery. All the patients undergoing this radical, new type of treatment were volunteers, earning the hospital the nickname of "The Guinea Pig" hospital. There is even a pub nearby called, "The Guinea Pig".

I arrived at the hospital late that evening and was booked into part of a ward known as the "Canadian Wing". I didn't sleep much that night, with my hand encased in the biggest bandage I had ever seen called a "boxing glove", for obvious reasons. When I did wake the following morning, I found myself in a four-bed side ward. During the morning, introductions were made. Alongside me was a guy named

Alan, who was due to have surgery to correct shortening tendons in his left hand. The effect of this condition, was to curl his fingers in towards the palm of his hand, giving it the appearance of a claw. Opposite, on the other side was a guy who was having his nose straightened after it was broken five years previously. I don't remember his name, but he was a nice guy. Directly opposite me, was Steve. Now, Steve told me that he was there to "have my head drained!" I just looked at him with a blank expression, but I did notice a tube running from his head into a bag containing what looked like blood, down at his side. He just laughed and explained that he had had cancer of the nose and the surgeons had grafted skin from his scalp to rebuild it after surgery. Unfortunately, from time to time fluid built up, he explained, necessitating him having to come into the hospital for it to be drained away. He had obviously been through a lot, but there wasn't a more cheerful and charismatic guy on the whole wing than Steve. He was often to be seen wandering around other beds, showing the patients his "bag of blood" and winding up the nurses, one of whom bore a striking resemblance to Bianca, a character in the soap-opera, "EastEnders". All four of us teased her mercilessly, but she took it in good heart.

Around mid-morning on that first day, the gang of doctors, nurses and consultants doing their rounds, descended on me. The obvious leader of the gang spoke to me and introduced himself as my consultant, Harry Belcher, what a fabulous name! He explained that I would be operated on later that afternoon and that, despite the fact I had very serious damage to my fingers, they would do their best to give me my hand back. I didn't have the slightest doubt that they would do their utmost.

I went down for surgery at about 3pm. It was the first time for many years, I had been in a general hospital ward for anything. (I had had an operation on my back a few years previously, but that was in a private hospital in London.) I found it an odd situation, being wheeled away in my bed, past other patients, all wishing me luck! Luck? Wasn't I in the hands of the top people in the country? What did luck have to do with it? I confidently expected to wake up in a few hours, with my hand all neatly repaired and sewn back together. But I appreciated their sentiments all the same!

My operation took 3 hours! When I eventually came out of the anaesthetic, I remember being extremely groggy and seeing four or five of everything. A few minutes later, one of the surgical team, (or was it all four?) spoke to me. I remember him saying the words "terminalise" and "finger", and thinking to myself, "what is he talking about?" He wasn't making any sense at all, in my drugged state. I then drifted off again, back into oblivion until I finally awoke back on the ward, with my right hand in an even bigger "boxing glove" than before.

It wasn't until the next morning, when Harry Belcher came round to see me that he explained that my right index finger had been so badly damaged by the machine, that the surgeons had had no alternative but to cut it off, or to put it their way, "terminalise" it. He explained that there was a possibility of a prosthetic finger being fitted, but the way he explained it, it would be so ridiculous as to be unworthy of consideration. The finger would be permanently straight, unbending and without feeling. In his opinion, I would be much better off simply having the stump. Experience has told me that he was absolutely right and I'm really glad I took his advice. He went on to explain that the next few weeks would be crucial in the healing process. As well as repairing all the tendons and sewing the blood vessels back together, the surgeons had actually sewn the nerves back together. Joining arteries and tendons was fairly routine, but nerves were a different subject. Yes, they could be joined, but the crucial part was whether the actual fibres within the nerves grew through each other, to form the complete nerve. If they didn't, I would have what Mr Belcher termed a "neuroma". This happens when the nerve fibres bunch up together instead of growing into the nerve itself. Imagine a train crashing into an immovable wall. The train can't go through the wall and so all the carriages crash into each other and form a huge pile of debris. With a neuroma, the nerve fibres all gather together into a lump that forms just under the flesh. It is apparently one of the most painful experiences known. The lump is formed of raw nerve-endings, and any slight touch sends agonising pain through the body. There are only two options in this case, live with the pain or have the nerve endings cauterised. The second option will involve a total loss of feeling, but would be infinitely preferable to the first. Any of the three fingers on my hand which had the nerves repaired, could have formed this "neuroma". Thankfully, none did, although the damage has caused a permanent loss of some feeling in the tips of my fingers. It's more of a sensation now than actual feeling, but most importantly, it isn't a problem.

That first day back in the ward after my operation, I saw Alan in the bed next to me with his boxing glove bandage, the same as mine, except his was on his left hand. He'd had his operation just before mine and the guy opposite had had his just after. Steve was still wandering around with his bag of blood, annoying the nurses and at one stage, came back with the menu for the evening. He read out what was on offer, amongst which were pork chops! "Oh great," I said, "pork chops. Tell you what Alan," I said, "you hold the knife, I'll hold the fork, then half way through, we'll swop over!" Steve then realised just how impossible it would be for either Alan or I to cut up and eat pork chops with one of our hands completely useless for the simple operation of eating. We all had a good laugh over that one!

The next stage for me was to report to the physiotherapy department. As I don't possess or wear pyjamas, the hospital had provided me with what they had, a bright yellow pair, that were at least two sizes too small. When I pulled on the trousers, it felt as though I was walking around with a thong. If I wanted to pull them up so that the waistband was where it should have been, around my waist, the crutch almost cut me in half. Alternatively, I could wear them with the waistband around my lower hips, just showing the very top of my pubic hair. So, the thong experience it was then!

When I walked into the physiotherapy department on that first day of many to come, a lovely girl named Louise took one look at my bright yellow pyjamas and called out to her colleagues, "Hey yup girls, it's the banana man!" (She was from the North!) We struck up an instant friendship with banter flying back and forth like crazy. I would have to challenge any person not to be completely possessed by Louise's personality and attitude to work and life.

I had treatment from Louise for the following year, and each time, she greeted me as "the banana man". She was completely irreverent, but she was very good at what she did and helped me enormously with regaining the use of my hand; just someone else from the hospital, to whom I will always be grateful.

The size of the boxing glove was reduced on the third day, in order that I could be fitted with a special type of splint, which held my hand in a position 90 degrees to my arm and which prevented me from bending my hand upwards. It looked a little like a ducks-head walking stick! I would have to wear this contraption for the next six weeks, sleeping with it, eating with it and travelling with it. When I slept, the splint would have to be supported so that my hand was elevated at all times, which meant my learning to sleep on my back, not natural for me.

Something that had troubled me for the immediate future, was how was I going to manage at home with my hand in this splint? I needn't have worried as Ray and Sue promptly insisted that I stay with them in their house for as long as it took. Ray had already screwed a hook into the ceiling of the bedroom so that the splint could be suspended in the upright position. When they told me this, I wondered if anyone had any better friends?

Before I left the hospital that day, Louise explained to me how I should strengthen and exercise the muscles in my remaining fingers on my right hand. Basically, it involved gently exerting pressure upwards, so that the fingers pushed against the roof of the splint. The repairs to the tendons had only taken place the previous day, and so, were very weak at that stage. Any undue strain was likely to snap the repair, so the exercises had to be done, gently.

Ray and Sue picked me up from the hospital late that afternoon and took me directly to their house in Biggin Hill, Having raised four daughters, who had all left home, there were plenty of bedrooms to go around. I sat in the lounge that evening, watching the television and gently exercising the fingers, just how I had been taught by Louise. Being a fairly positive sort of chap, I was determined that my fingers would reach full strength in as short a time as possible. To this end, I went into the exercise regime with gusto, so much gusto in fact, that after only five minutes of flexing them against the splint, I managed to snap the tendon repair to my middle finger! I shall never forget the sound the snap made. It was just like someone snapping their finger and thumb together, but it sounded like someone had banged a drum in my ear! Neither shall I forget the sick feeling that came over me immediately I realised that I could no longer move my middle finger. Ray and Sue were very sympathetic, but there was nothing they could do, I just had to wait till the next day, when I could phone the hospital and tell them what had happened.

They called me back to Queen Victoria immediately, and the surgeon who had performed the operation examined the finger. He confirmed that the tendon had indeed snapped, no big news there, but he also said another operation to re-repair the tendon again was out of the question at that stage. I didn't hear the last bit, I only heard, "out of the question!" However, he quickly explained his comments. Because of the trauma to my hand, it had swelled to almost twice its normal size. It was physically impossible to operate on the finger with all the swelling, I would have to wait for the hand to settle down. He went on to say this could be as long as a year down the line! A year!

He explained that in the interim, the broken ends of the tendon would shrink and retreat away from each other. I would have to undergo a three-stage operation when the time was right. The first stage would be to insert a silicon sheath inside my finger, extending from the middle of my palm to the end of the finger. The second stage would be to allow the sheath to become incorporated into the internal structure of my hand, which would take around three to four months.

The third stage would be the most fascinating. Everybody on Harry Belcher's team was brilliant at explaining things to me. Just after the initial operation, he had provided me with a very detailed diagram of the internal workings of a hand, and it was to this that the surgeon now referred. He showed me how each tendon was attached to each of the three sections of a finger and how each part was operated by different muscles. To my surprise, he told me that practically everyone has "spare" tendons somewhere in their body. Whilst inserting the tube into my hand, they would open my wrist and search for a "spare". Apparently, it goes back to our primate days. Because we no longer swing through trees, the particular tendons we used became defunct, but they're always still there. Other people have spare tendons in their ankles, used by primates for gripping with their feet. Wherever it was in my body, he explained, they would cut a length off and attach it to the end of the snapped tendon furthest from the end of my finger. They would then thread the tendon through the sheath, up to the end of my finger and bring it out through a small hole. The end of the new tendon would then be sewn to my fingernail. It was impossible to attach the tendon to the bone of the finger, as it occurs naturally, so the next best thing was to attach it to the flesh. The part of the tendon that was exposed would rot eventually and drop off, leaving the end neatly incorporated into the flesh. To this day, I have a tiny indentation on the end of my middle finger, where the tendon ends. I have no tendon attached to the middle part of the finger, but the new tendon would enable me to bend the finger and have some sort of grip. The surgeon would never be able to make the tendon exactly the right length, as it would occur naturally, so he would leave it slightly short. The effect of this would be to make the middle finger curl over slightly, giving it the appearance of a "crooked" finger. However, the alternative would be to leave the tendon too long, which would mean that I wouldn't be able to bend my finger fully into my palm, giving me no grip at all.

Over the following two years, I underwent two more major operations, a couple of minor procedures and intensive physiotherapy and recuperation before ending with what I now have, a working hand.

And so, thanks to all the surgeons and nursing staff and physiotherapists at the Queen Victoria Hospital in East Grinstead, I have a working right hand. Harry Belcher described the injury as very serious, leaving me with only 75% efficiency in that hand. When writing to the Occupational Health Department in the Metropolitan Police, he doubted that I would ever return to full operational duty. He was wrong on that score, but even if he was right, and I didn't ever return to full operational duty, I will be forever grateful for what he and his team gave me.

Chapter 26

After the initial operation, I spent a total of around six weeks with my right hand in what I had come to call, "the duck's head" plaster cast. As I mentioned before, I had to sleep with my hand elevated in a vertical position. This was to prevent too much blood being pumped into the hand. As it was, it was about twice its normal size, and almost twice as hairy. The trauma in the hand had stimulated the hair growth to such an extent, it was positively animal-like! I spent much of the six weeks, visiting and staying with friends and relatives. There must be at least half-a-dozen or so houses and flats dotted around the country with mysterious holes in bedroom ceilings and walls. When I first went down to my mother's flat in Weston-Super-Mare, she had had one of her neighbours in to fix a hook into the wall alongside the bed. When she met me off the train, she took one look at the plaster-cast and said, "Well, that was a bloody silly thing to do wasn't it!" Thanks, mum!

I eventually returned to work early in 1997, on what is known as "recuperative duties". Basically, it means I could perform certain functions at a desk etc, but could not perform operational duty. The first few weeks consisted of visits to occupational therapy, the Chief Medical Officer and physiotherapy. It also consisted of a lot of mickey-taking about my injury. The Metropolitan Police is an organisation which takes care of its injured officers and has a lot of support services to aid an officer to full recovery. The officers, however, have a different attitude. They will take every opportunity to take the piss out of an injured officer. Having been involved for over 20 years at that stage, I knew what to expect. Their sympathy is always tinged with humour and one of the funniest episodes was when I was sitting at a desk in the main office. One of my colleagues, Sergeant "Ken" Leverett came into the office. His name was actually Julian, but we called him "Ken" because of the nearness of his surname to Everett, Kenny Everett the comedian. And "Ken" was aptly named, he had a fantastic sense of humour. When he came into the office, he slammed his books down on the desk in a temper and shouted, "I'm fed up with this. My locker has been screwed again by some bastard and my flat hat's been nicked again". Everyone's locker got screwed from time to time by some unscrupulous officer wanting to "borrow" some item of equipment they had lost. There were two other officers sitting at the desk with me and by this time, we were beginning to think Ken was serious about this. He was obviously very ticked off, and went on shouting, "well I'm not putting up with it. I've put a crime report in and I've had the locker checked for prints! And I've got a suspect! The prints guy only found nine finger prints!!" The other two officers got it straight away and almost fell to the ground, they were laughing so much. I didn't get it for about 5 seconds and then fell in! The others found this almost as funny as what Ken had said!!

On another occasion much later, a load of us were sitting at a canteen table discussing organising a cricket match between supervising officers and constables. The question of food came up and Ken (again!) piped up with, "Well I think we should have a finger-buffet!" More laughs at my expense! Fortunately, I found all these jibes really funny, even when we actually played the cricket match and I dropped three catches in succession because I couldn't close my fingers around the ball. I'm sure the better batsmen amongst the constables even guided the ball down to me in the end just so that the spectators could whoop and shout in delight when I inevitably dropped the ball. When it was my turn to bowl, as we all had to have a go, the ball went everywhere apart from down the pitch. More laughs!

I got my own back the following year however when the match was replayed. I had got Hopper in America to send me a baseball glove and although my hand was much stronger, I still couldn't catch and hold the damn ball. I had again been placed in the field where it was likely that I would have to take a catch. That was when I whipped out the baseball glove, and waved it at the batsmen and the watching crowd. Funny, the batsmen didn't send the ball down to me then.

When it was my turn to bat in the second match, my good friend Karl was bowling. He was from Yorkshire and had played a good standard of cricket before joining the police, specialising in fast-bowling. He stared insolently at me as I walked to the crease. "Ah, the bearded wonder!!" he said as I arrived. He was tossing the ball in his hand casually, but menacingly and grinning at the same time. I got a little nervous when I saw the length of his run-up and then his contorted face as he launched his first ball at me. It was on me in a second and I managed to block it. The second ball whistled past me. I managed to stop the third ball with my groin, and later on another ball struck me fair and square in the ribs. But he didn't get me out!! I scored my maximum of thirty runs and retired undefeated, if a little battered. This time, it was my turn to grin at Karl! Apart from some outrageous decisions, such as L.B.W. when the ball hit the batsman in the chest, the matches were a huge success and everyone got into the spirit.

Cricket matches and mickey-taking notwithstanding, life was fairly dull at work by this stage. I was employed in the duties and events office, run by a patriarchal sergeant. He actually called me his assistant! I wasn't really enjoying it, but I was grateful to be back at work and at least doing something.

One bright spot in my life at this time however, came from a phone call from my good friends, Catherine and Lance. I had met both through Lance's sister Kim, where Susie had gone to live for a short while during one of her periods away. They asked me if I would consent to my being God-father to their second daughter, Helena. My mind immediately went back to the seventies, when my friends from Cardiff, Geof and Val had made me God-father to one of their daughters. I remembered I hadn't been too successful at that time, eventually losing touch with the family. This time however, I thought things would be different. I felt I had matured since then and attained some values which, it seemed others agreed with. I made it plain to Catherine and Lance that if I agreed, I would take it seriously and not be afraid to give Helena advice and guidance in their absence. That, Catherine told me, was exactly what they wanted. And so, I became a God-father for the second time, to a young lady whom I adore and love as my own. Her sister Caroline had been born two years earlier and she too is gorgeous.

Prior to my accident the previous year, I had applied to take part in an expedition run by a charitable organisation called Raleigh International. They organised several expeditions to various countries throughout the year for the benefit and development of young people aged between 17 and 23. The youngsters undertake various projects during the three months they are in situ and these can vary from building schools to irrigation projects, from bridge building to ditch clearing. Whatever it is they undertake, the local community benefit, so the projects are chosen very carefully.

I had longed to go back to Africa and consequently, had applied to be a project manager on the next expedition to Namibia, which was taking place in September 1996. I had been to a selection centre, deep in the Sussex countryside sometime in that same year and had been accepted. After my accident, I had to telephone them to tell them what had happened and that I would not be able to take up my position. Raleigh International were very understanding and promised to keep my application open for any new projects in the future. If the tendon repair hadn't snapped so early on, I would definitely have been in a position to go the following year, September of 1997. As it happened, the further surgery was completed earlier than expected and in August 1997, I contacted Raleigh to ask if any places were still available. As I expected, the answer was sorry, no. However, about a week later, I got a surprise phone call from the recruitment office at Raleigh headquarters in Parsons Green. The young lady explained that due to difficulties on the previous expedition, building schools in the Rundu area of northern Namibia, Raleigh had created a special role called the 'Northern Coordinator', and she was phoning to ask me specifically whether I was interested. She went to explain that this was a totally new role, never been tried before and that the recruiting staff thought I had the qualities to make a success of the first time that this particular role had been used.

The whole schools building project in Rundu had fallen so far behind as not to be anywhere near finished because of communication problems. What had happened on the previous expedition was this; imagine if you will, a triangle with the horizontal line at the top. The bottom point is "A" or base camp in Windhoek, the top left point is "B" the local suppliers in Rundu and the top right is "C" representing the schools building programme. The base camp in Windhoek was 700 kilometres from Rundu, and the schools were 120 kilometres further on from Rundu. "A" would radio up to the project manager at "C" and ask what building supplies were needed over the following two or three days. "C" would radio back to "A" with quantities and timetables. "A" would then telephone a local supplier, "B", in Rundu and give them the order. "A" would then radio back to "C" to confirm that the order had been placed and would be delivered. Sounds easy, but this is Africa! The problems arose after the order had been placed. Either the local supplier didn't actually have the supplies that had been ordered and so short-delivered to the schools site, or, having taken the order and promised delivery, the lorry used by the supplier broke down before delivery and the supplier didn't inform the base camp, "A", and all that was providing the telephones and radios were working! In either scenario, the school site was left short of materials and precious building days were lost by "C" having to wait for the scheduled radio times to inform "A" of the error and then "A" frantically phoning "B" to re-arrange the delivery or trying other suppliers to fulfill the materials order or "borrow" their lorries to make the delivery, and then "A" informing "C" what was happening, and so on!! The whole operation was a mess! In truth, I think the project managers were a little at fault for not ordering enough supplies to last them for longer than a few days at a time. As a consequence, the staff building the schools spent many days lying around and doing nothing for the lack of building materials. The end result was that out of the two schools scheduled to be completed, both were only half-way built and neither of them had a roof. In the case of one of the schools, called Cwa, the reason it didn't have a roof was partly because the staff building the school were so inexperienced, that the upper parts of the walls had detracted from the original oblong shape and were actually in the shape of a parallelogram. Cwa was abandoned before the three months building schedule had expired, and the other school site named Shambahey simply ran out of time, as well as materials! My job would be to fill this communication vacuum.

The notice of just a few weeks was a little short, but the senior police officers were very good about my going on what is known as "extended leave", without pay of course. I think the letter written on my behalf by the surgeon Harry Belcher, explaining how going to Namibia would aid the recovery of my hand, certainly helped.

I arrived in Windhoek on 18th September 1997 and ran into an immediate bureacratic problem. Going through immigration, when asked the purpose of my visit, I rather foolishly said, "well, I'm working with Raleigh International building schools in Rundu". Sounds innocent enough, and it was true of course, but the official only heard the word "working", which means a work permit. I was detained at the airport, interrogated by several officials, my passport was taken away (again!) and the deputy expedition leader was called to the immigration office. Copious phone calls were made to the Namibian Ministry of Home Affairs to confirm my story and they, of course, had never heard of Raleigh International. Eventually, after much persuasion, I was released on the promise of attending the Home Affairs office in town, which I did, and got everything sorted out. Phew!! won't make that mistake again in a hurry!

Base Camp, just outside Windhoek was pretty basic; long-drop toilets, poor sanitation, no beds and a damned dog that didn't stop howling all night! Most of the other project managers were already there when I arrived and I spent the first week getting to know them a little and being briefed on my duties and objectives. As well as finishing Cwa and Shambahey schools, there were two other school projects due to be undertaken, Mbambe and Likwatarera. Essentially, my brief was simple; I had to ensure that all four school sites received the right supplies at the right time, within budget and to ensure all four schools were ready for hand-over to Namibian authorities by a given date. To do this effectively, I would have to establish and develop contacts all over Rundu. This wouldn't only concern building supplies, I would also have to organise large food drops, once a week, to all four sites, have procedures in place to evacuate sick or injured "venturers", organise temporary accommodation prior to the youngsters getting out to the sites and many other minor little jobs. The expedition leader, Jon told me that he was giving me a "line authority" over the project managers, effectively making me third in line in the chain of command. I got the distinct impression that Raleigh International had been severely embarrassed by the failure to complete Cwa and Shambahey schools, especially as there were other charitable organisations operating out of Rundu doing the same thing, only more successfully. It was obvious to me that a lot was resting on my shoulders. I would be given a brand new Land Rover pick-up to use, the colour of which was to play a large part in an amusing little scenario later on in a supermarket in Rundu. To assist me, a Namibian guy called Viky, who, oddly enough was also a local police officer on leave, would come with me.

The first task for me was to reconnoitre all four sites to establish where exactly they were in the bush. I travelled north to Rundu with my deputy leader and the out-going deputy leader. As one might expect, there are no sign-posts in the bush and remembering which track to take to each village was quite difficult. Fortunately, I learned that even if I did take a different track on a visit to a particular site, they all generally ended up at the village anyway. Although I had run the safaris previously through Botswana, I wasn't prepared for what I encountered in the Namibian bush. The poverty was appalling; the adults and children alike were dressed in nothing more than rags, feral dogs and cats ran everywhere, defecating and urinating where they liked, the children were severely mal-nourished with typically distended stomachs and their huts made of mud and poles with thatched roofs, were just about falling down. These people were subsistence farmers, they grew only what they needed to eat and bartered any spare capacity for other goods such as clothing with other local villagers or with people who came to their village for whatever reason. They had no means of travelling to the main town of Rundu. However, in each of the four villages, the welcome we received from laughing and giggling children and smiling adults was overwhelming. They clearly appreciated what Raleigh was trying to do. Education was a big thing for these people, and the authorities in Rundu were keen to have a new school for the children. When I saw the old one, I realised why. It consisted only of a set of poles holding up an old thatched roof, which was falling apart. It was fine in the dry season, but when it rained, there was no shelter, the rain would come in from the top and sides. There were no black-boards or teaching aids, no desks, no chairs and each pupil had only one book and one pencil. It really opened my eyes and I was determined from the outset that not only would I do my utmost for these people, but also I would do my best to show the relatively affluent young Raleigh International "venturers", as they were known, how other, less fortunate people had to exist. For them, it shouldn't be just about building a school, they should interact with the villagers and take home a profound sense of reality and values.

Having completed my initial reconnaissance, I returned to base camp in Windhoek. The next step was to return to Rundu and take the new project managers to their respective sites, show them around and introduce them to the villagers, especially the Headman. We loaded all the baggage etc into a long-wheelbase Land Rover, which had been modified to take around 8 passengers seated in the back and headed off to Rundu. The journey was always the same, long and boring. We arrived in Rundu around 8pm that evening, having set out from Windhoek around 6am.

We went straight to a restcamp called Sarasungu, which was owned and run by a couple named Eduardo and Ines Raposo. I had been introduced to the camp by the out-going deputy manager and advised to use their camping facilities. I had met Eduardo and Ines when I was doing the first reconnaissance trip and liked them both immediately. Ines' sister, Ute also helped around the camp. Both Ines and Ute were from the south of Germany and Eduardo was Portugese. He had come over the border from Angola a few years earlier. I really liked Eduardo. He used to wear a bandana around his head, and with his dark, swarthy and handsome looks, always reminded me of a pirate. Later on, when I had been there a few weeks, he and I used to sit around the pool drinking gin and tonic till the early hours, 'putting the world to right'.

I spent the next few days doing introductions and driving through the bush to the school sites. Wherever we went, I was always greeted enthusiastically as "Mr Nil" and on one occasion, I had an experience, which was to remain with me and served to demonstrate to the others and me, just how easy it was to interact with the villagers. We had driven into one of the villages named Mbambe and I stopped the Land-Rover right in the middle of the village. I told the others to start walking around to get to know the villagers and I would unload the bags from the roof as we were going to camp that night at the village. I had used a long length of rope to tie down the baggage, and as I was standing on the roof, a large group of children of all ages stood around the vehicle, watching me. As I was coiling the length of rope, I suddenly turned to the group as if to frighten them. One or two of them gave a small scream and went to run away, but quickly realized I was only fooling around. I carried on with what I was doing and they carried on watching me. I suddenly turned to them again a few seconds later. This time they were waiting for me and all the group laughed and took a step back at the same time. The process repeated itself a few more times, and each time the laughter and screams became louder and louder. The adults in the village, including the project managers began to watch what was happening. I then began to tease the children even more by pretending to throw the rope at them and they screamed and laughed louder still. Then I actually did throw one end of the coil of rope at one of them, just touching him. That was it, the game was born! I pretended to ignore them whilst I recoiled the rope, but all the time, I had picked out another "victim" and was just waiting, biding my time, pretending to be looking towards another. The children were all shuffling forward, daring me to throw the rope and "get" one of them, each of them hoping it would be him or her, but at the same time, not getting too close, in case it was. The group had grown in number and they now completely surrounded the Land Rover, giving me even more "victims" The game continued for a few more minutes and then suddenly, I jumped down from the roof of the vehicle and chased my "victim" around until I got a clear shot, when I threw the rope. The screams and shouts of joy from the children were now at fever pitch and most of the adults in the village were watching the game and laughing along with the children. Time after time I recoiled the rope, looking as menacing as I could, sizing up my next victim and chasing them around the village.

Sometimes, I would let a victim go and suddenly start to chase after another. They enjoyed this even more, never knowing whether they would be the next "victim" but always hoping to be just that. I continued to chase them around for about half an hour, throwing the end of the rope dozens of times. They would have played on for hours, but I told myself I had work to do and so ended the game. In reality, I was knackered through all that running through soft sand. However, whenever I went back to Mbambe and the children were not in school, they would run to the Land Rover, laughing and screaming, waiting for the "game" to start again. I always obliged and played with them for even a little while, jumping from the open back of the pick-up.

It was a ridiculously simple game, played with just a length of rope and some enthusiasm, but it just demonstrated to me how the simplest of games can produce such joy and happiness. These kids didn't know anything about computers or play-stations etc, but their capacity for laughter and enjoying themselves was no less than their western counterparts. I couldn't imagine English or American kids getting so much enjoyment from being chased around by a mad, white man hurling the end of a rope at them. Everything is relative I suppose, but I do wonder why western parents feel the need to spend so much money on gadgetry and computer games etc, just to keep their children quiet.

Having completed the second reconnaissance trip, we returned to Windhoek, taking an extra day to visit a cheetah sanctuary. Over the following week, the various project managers made their plans and preparations. It was at this time I realized just how lucky I was to have landed the job of Northern Coordinator. Whereas they would be stuck on one site for the entire three month period, I would have a roving brief, visiting them whenever I felt like it, and then being able to drive away. Thinking back on it, I really wouldn't have enjoyed being in the one place for so long. However, they did have one distinct advantage over me. At the end of their particular projects, they could stand back and say, "I built that!" All I would be able to say would be, "and I helped." Now however, all these years later, I still reckon I had the best job going!

The youngsters arrived at the base-camp soon after we got back. They were from all walks of life, some from wealthy backgrounds, some from poor, a mixture of races and gender and most of them looking forward to their challenges. I say "most" as there were definitely one or two who were distinctly not up for the challenge. One couldn't help asking the question, why were they there in the first place? Whilst on the school site, one of them, a hulking and sulky youth later refused to help and simply sat down and watched his colleagues work. The project manager had tried everything to cajole him into working again, but apparently nothing had any effect. I was called to the site to speak with him and try and persuade him to continue. We had a long chat under a tree in the village and I eventually managed to get him back to work, appealing to his sense of personal fulfillment and macho image. If I had been unsuccessful, I would have had no choice but to send him back to base camp, where the expedition leader, Jon would have had no qualms about sending him home early.

The schools the kids were building, and they were just kids, mostly still in their teens, were all of one design. They were single storey, long oblong buildings with a steel roof and steel windows. They had two large classrooms with a storeroom in the middle. Initially, they were built of brick and then "washed" with a thin layer of cement to smooth out the brickwork. When I looked at the plans for the schools at Mbambe and Likwatarera at base camp, I made two suggestions. First, build them with blocks rather than bricks. This would cut down building time and expense, and secondly, rather than simply "wash" the bricks with cement, put on a full course of cement render to make the walls smooth. The first was a really good idea! The second, maybe not so! There is no doubt the schools looked really good, but rendering them was very time consuming. It probably completely negated all the time we had saved using blocks, and it was comparatively expensive. If truth be told, the schools on this project probably didn't come in on budget because of this. However, one of the reasons I suggested it was because Raleigh had to rescue their reputation after the fiasco of the non-finished schools at Cwa and Shambahey. Producing two absolutely beautifully finished schools at Mbambe and Likwaterera would go a long way to rescuing that tarnished reputation. And I was right! When they were completely finished, with the windows and walls painted, they were terrific, easily the equal of any other school being built by other charitable organisations in the area.

Part of the brief for the project managers was to look at the menus provided for each day and make any amendments they wished, providing they stayed within their budgets. They then gave these to me whilst I was still at Field Base. A few days later, I left the base camp in Windhoek and began the long drive back up to Rundu to prepare for the arrival of the "venturers".

When I arrived back in Rundu, I went straight to a large food wholesaler and discussed with the manager supplying the large list of food items on the menus. Having had experience of Africa before, I went to some lengths to ensure that the manager knew exactly what was required and when. The food drops to the school sites would be done on a Wednesday and I impressed on the manager the importance of having all the food ready for me to load onto the Land Rover that I was using, early Wednesday morning. This wasn't the people-carrier version, but a brand new Defender with an open back, green in colour. The manager assured me that all would be ready on the day. I even negotiated with him to supply me free of charge, a large consignment of soft drinks to give to the "venturers" when they arrived. I was spending so much money in the place, I figured it was the least he could do. He agreed, albeit reluctantly!

The equipment required for the building projects arrived a few days before the "venturers" and my assistant, Viky and I, spent the whole of that day and most of the next, getting a large lorry through soft sand into school sites to offload the equipment. It was tough going as the lorry got stuck several times and had to be dug out, but we managed it in the end. I made sure that someone from each village was made responsible by the Headman for looking after the equipment, pending the arrival of the youngsters.

They arrived in the late evening after an exhausting trip on a bus which never got above about 60k.p.h. I met them on the road into Rundu and handed out the cold drinks. I then took them to where they would camp the night, before going on to their respective school sites. The following day, Viky and I made arrangements to get them all to their sites and that night, I treated Viky and I to a steak and chips dinner at Sarasungu. The first part of the operation was completed on time, successfully getting everyone to where they were going with all their equipment. I slept well that night, under the stars in the camp at Sarasungu.

The next day, the work started in earnest. Raleigh had provided me with a line-of-sight radio link to each of the sites. The call-sign for the expedition leader was Bravo 1, the deputy Bravo 2 and I was Bravo 3. I had to sling a weight around the branch of a tree and then haul up the cable antenna roughly in the direction of the camp I wanted to speak to. I could do this wherever I was provided I had a high enough tree. I then had to run the cable back to the Land Rover and the radio, which was connected to the battery for power. I remember once setting up the radio on a flat piece of ground, little realising that I had parked the vehicle in the middle of the local football pitch. And of course, they arrived to play. They weren't very happy about my vehicle being in the middle of their pitch, but I was soon done and on my way! Using the radio would be the method by which the sites could tell me which supplies they needed and when. It would then be my responsibility to ensure the right supplies were transported out to them.

During my own reconnaisance trips, I went round to all the individual suppliers of building materials to introduce myself and get myself known. Chief amongst these suppliers was a firm called SAKKA. Other smaller suppliers had the same goods for sale, sand and cement and blocks for instance, but SAKKA had a six-wheel drive lorry which could get through the toughest bush and sand. Various other retailers supplied smaller stuff such as nails and tin sheeting.

Regular contact with all the building sites by radio and personal visits, ensured that I was aware of the progress of each of them and could anticipate when they might need supplies. Using the radio meant that each site manager could tell me what they needed and receive the supplies the same day, or at the latest, the following day. For instance, the manager of the Likwaterera site might tell me he needed 25 bags of cement, 3 cubic metres of sand and 3 cubic metres of "clip" (small stones). The manager of Mbambe might tell me that he needed blocks, tin sheeting and various smaller supplies such as a tool or nails. I would then go to SAKKA and order the goods and arrange for delivery that day. I would go to another supplier to buy the other goods and give them to SAKKA for delivery by the lorry. Sometimes, SAKKA would tell me their lorry was broken down and wouldn't be available till the next day, or even the day after. I then went off in search of a lorry from another supplier and negotiated the hire of their truck to transport SAKKA's goods. I would often have to promise the second supplier to buy my next consignment from them, a promise I always scrupulously honoured.

I spent most of my time hustling, arranging things and negotiating to get supplies out to the sites. This after all, was why I had been engaged by Raleigh. By the time I was finished, I knew exactly where to buy absolutely anything I needed, where to go for the best deals and how to deal with some fairly hard headed business-people.

I became particularly friendly with a local builder named Calvin Bezuidenhout. He often helped me out with supplying small amounts of goods or the loan of his truck. I would often stop at Calvin's on the way back from a day in the bush and arrange to meet him at Sarasungu, where he, Eduardo and I would drink cold beers and simply chill-out!

I had to sort out one little problem quite early on. The school sites of Mbambe and Likwaterera were fairly close to each other, so supplies for one would be on the same lorry as supplies for the other. The problem arose when the lorry went to Mbambe first to off-load. The manager there, an ex army officer named Malcolm seemed to think that he could help himself to anything that was on the lorry, even the goods intended for delivery to Likwaterera. Consequently, the site manager, Martin at Likwaterera was often short delivered. At first, I suspected that SAKKA hadn't put all the supplies on, but after questioning the lorry driver, he said that the manager at Mbambe had told him that most of it was for him. After a few choice words from me, the manager at Mbambe didn't do it again, except right at the end of the project. Not particularly trusting Malcolm, I left strict instructions that the lorry was always to call at Likwaterera first.

I arrived at the food wholesaler early on the first Wednesday morning to do the food drops. Despite promises and assurances from the manager, less than half of the items on the four lists had been prepared. He came up with all sorts of excuses but I just asked him to get everything ready as soon as he could, which took about another 2 hours. I had to deliver the food to all four sites that day, so 2 hours to me on that particular day was precious. Eventually it was all done and delivered and I finished another day, albeit very late, drinking a gin and tonic at Eduardo's.

The following day, I went straight to another supermarket. I had figured that I could get everything from this other shop myself, load it and deliver it in the same day, it wouldn't be any more expensive, and they were prepared to send Raleigh an invoice for payment. I would probably have to spend the night at the last school site, but that was no problem. I sourced all the items I needed, with a few substitutions and made my decision. I went back to the food wholesale supermarket and sacked him! He wasn't amused but I told him he had let me down and now he had to pay the price of failure. He probably thought I wasn't going to say anything as I hadn't balled him out that first day.

On the subject of the other supermarket, that was where the problem with the Land-Rover occurred. Viky was with me in the supermarket one Wednesday, about 7 or 8 weeks into the project time. We were doing our usual shopping when he came to me and told me that some men in suits wanted to talk with me. He signalled behind him and I saw four black guys in badly fitting suits approaching. The first one introduced himself as Captain someone-or-other from the Namibian Military Intelligence. He showed me an ID badge but I took scant notice, rather I carried on with my shopping, asking him what he wanted. Memories of the zealous Zambian security officers came immediately to mind. "We have had you and this man (indicating Viky) under surveillance for some time now. We think you are taking food to terrorists in the bush!" I almost burst out laughing, but I quickly realised the guy was serious, so I stopped what I was doing. I told him that I was with Raleigh International, and that the food I was taking into the bush was for the youngsters who were building the schools for "your" children, pointing at him and emphasising "your". I let the last bit sink in a bit, before showing him my Raleigh identity card. "And besides", I said, "I'm a British police officer and this man", indicating Viky, "is a Namibian police officer." "Yes," said the leader, "we know him, we know he's an officer"!! "So why the hell are you accusing me of taking food to terrorists if you know Viky is a police officer", I thundered.

It turned out that during the Angolan-South African bush war, South African troops used to use green, open-backed Land Rovers, just like the one I was using and apparently, some of the soldiers were none too careful about who they shot from the back of the vehicle. The security forces were consequently a little nervous at the sight of a white man driving a green Land Rover, from which so much death had been meted out, into the bush on a regular basis.

Although the war had been over for years by this stage, I found the explanation, sort of plausible as Angolan terrorists were once again becoming active and the local population obviously had long memories. I assured the military man that I was not taking food to terrorists and even invited him to accompany me on one of my trips to the bush, an offer he graciously declined. Satisfied, they went on their way. I somehow doubted they had had me under surveillance. The roads being very straight, I could see long distances behind me and I was very often the only vehicle on a particular stretch of road.

On my way from Windhoek to Rundu, I always had to pass through Grootfontein. I later learned that this was the site for a massive South African army base, from which they conducted the bush war around Rundu. It was probably where some of my Drifters colleagues had been based. The road from Grootfontein to Rundu was a smooth tarred road, absolutely dead straight for at least 200 kilometres and had been pushed through by the South Africans alongside the original dirt road with occasional, very wide stretches. These stretches were actually landing strips for the South African supply planes. Every so often, I could still see the old broadly painted white lines down the middle of the road, just as one would find on a modern runway.

There were still some remnants of the old South African colonial era around Rundu. I found one once in the form of a mechanic who fixed the brakes on my lorry. It was very late in the afternoon and the truck was due to take a new batch of "venturers" into the school sites at the monthly change-over when Viky told me the brakes weren't working. Cursing, I went off in search of a mechanic and found this guy just about to shut his garage for the evening. He very obligingly agreed to stay and fix them for me and at the end, I offered to pay him. He refused payment but asked me to join him in the office for a Rum and Coke. I duly accepted! Over the drink he told me how he had only recently come back to Rundu after an enforced absence of ten years. Intrigued, I asked why? Apparently, he had been a mechanic at a local garage, working alongside black mechanics. Everyone had their own bottles of water and guarded them jealously. One day, he found that some of his water had been drunk by someone else and thought it had obviously been taken by one of the black guys. To punish the thief, he emptied the water out of the bottle and replaced it with battery acid. He then left the bottle where it had been stood. Later on, sure enough, some of his water had been drunk and one of the black mechanics later became very ill, proving to the mechanic that he was right and that a thirsty man had stolen his water. As he was explaining this to me, I was becoming increasingly uncomfortable at his triumphant way of telling me the story. Unfortunately for the mechanic, the black guy took around a week to die, his interior organs being slowly burned away by the acid. Even then, he was delighted at the amount of pain he caused this "bleck", (S.A. accent!). When it was revealed how the man had died, the mechanic's boasting meant that if he had stayed in Rundu, he would have been killed by the dead man's family, so he ran away to another part of Namibia. Shame!! Sickened by the mechanic's attitude about how he had killed the black guy, I put my drink down, thanked him for it and walked out. I didn't see him again, thank goodness.

My days in Rundu were filled with continually solving little problems in order that the schools could progress. Every day I had to sort out crises such as a lack of transport, obtaining substitute supplies and problems with the local people in the villages. They had agreed to help the "venturers" with manual labour in return for supplies of food. Every so often, the head-man of the village would want to re-negotiate the "contract" and I would be called to the village to speak with the head-man. Sometimes the meetings would go on till late in the night, but I always managed to come up with some sort of agreement to keep the villagers happy.

A crisis of my own occurred one day as I was obtaining some goods from a hardware retailer. I had parked my Land Rover outside the shop as normal, but somehow, forgot to lock the vehicle. It didn't matter to the local population of Rundu that Raleigh was there to help them, given the opportunity, thieves outside the supermarkets and shops would steal anything they could. Someone had already stolen my camcorder. I knew all this and always locked the vehicle whenever I wasn't there. On this occasion, I simply forgot and paid the price. This particular day, thieves stole my small rucksack from inside the vehicle, along with my black leather hat. I'm not sure what I was more upset about, the hat being taken or the passport, police warrant card, cash and Raleigh receipts that were in the bag. The latter would certainly cause me more problems than the former, but I was very attached to my hat, it was like stealing part of me.

After berating myself, I went along to the local police station to report the theft. Anyone who has ever been to Africa and has had to confront the bureacracy there, will appreciate just how time consuming the whole process can be. It was at least a couple of hours before I managed to speak to anyone in authority. I was shown into the police Captain's office to find him on the phone. He was speaking Afrikaans to someone at the other end. Another officer entered the room and spoke to the captain. He replied in the local African dialect, and then immediately switched back to Afrikaans. When he had finished the call, he spoke to me in almost flawless English. I learned later that he also spoke Portugese and German, understandable I suppose, given Rundu's proximity to the former Portugese colony of Angola and the German links to Namibia. The local filling station manager's son was already speaking six languages at the age of around ten! It never ceases to amaze me that we here in the United Kingdom, a "first world" country never seem to be very keen on learning other languages, even though we are next door to a myriad different tongues in Europe. It's a little like unintentional arrogance and it's definitely laziness, given that most of the rest of the world speaks English. After finishing my statement to the captain, he politely showed me out of the station, with the promise that he and his men would do everything possible to find my missing articles, especially my passport. I had already begun to imagine the difficulties I was going to have when I came to leave the country without it. I also doubted the police captain's promise.

About a week later, I was driving through a road intersection, when I heard a shout, "Oi, chief!" I looked around and saw the police captain literally hanging out of the passenger side of a police car, waving at me. I drove over to him. He told me that some of his men had spent a couple of days following tracks through the bush and found the spot where my goods had been divided up amongst the thieves. Lo and behold, under a nearby bush, they found my passport and nearby, some of the Raleigh receipts that hadn't blown away in the wind. I was astounded! I tried to imagine British police officers spending so much time and energy on finding the possessions of a foreigner, but failed miserably. I knew that we would have a cursory look around, ask maybe one or two questions and give up. It would have been easy for them to do the same, but they didn't and I was immensely grateful to the captain and his men. In all fairness though, the Rundu police didn't have that much to do.

It wasn't all work in Rundu and Sundays were a day off for the school sites. Sometimes, I would drive the lorry into the bush and collect them from the villages and bring them to Sarasungu to enjoy a swim and a cold beer. One Saturday evening, I had arrived back at the rest camp and was setting up my tent, when I saw a couple of elderly ladies on the far side of the camp. I paid no attention to them at the time, but started chatting to them later in the restaurant. They were a couple of hardy travellers, intent on seeing as much of Africa as they could. One of them however, bemoaned the fact that all they ever seemed to be able to do was go where the local tour guides took them. This was usually to some souvenir shop or to some tourist-orientated village where the local men and women performed native dances for the tourists and then after, donned their "shades" and trainers and returned to their comfortable houses. "We would like to see a real village and interact with real villagers," one of them said. At that stage, I had not told them what I was doing in Rundu. "If you can be ready at 8am tomorrow morning, I'll take you to a village", I said. This particular Sunday, one group of "venturers" had already left to return to Windhoek, prior to going onto their next project. The new group hadn't arrived, so the village would be empty of white people.

At 8am prompt the next morning, we all climbed into the Land Rover and set off for Mbambe, the nearest of the villages. I've always had a bit of a thing about people going to see how other people, far less well off than themselves, live. It's always had a smack of, "Hey, lets see what the poor people are doing today!" I once got taken around Soweto, the black township in Johannesburg, by a senior Afrikaans police officer. As soon as I went in, I hated the fact that I was there. Even to a casual observer, I was obviously from a comparatively wealthy culture. Firstly, I was white, secondly, I was with a white police officer and thirdly, my clothes were clean! It's difficult to put my finger on the exact reasons, but it didn't feel right and I wanted nothing to do with the rich man/poor man thing.

These two women seemed different though. I think they genuinely wanted to interact with local village people. When we got to the village, I told the women to stay in the vehicle whilst I went to the headman and asked permission for them to visit. He readily agreed and the women started to wander about, looking at the school which was rapidly taking shape, chatting with the local women and playing with the children.

We stayed about an hour and afterwards, drove back to Sarasungu. Once back there, they thanked me profusely and then revealed that one of them was a writer for a travel magazine in Holland, and they were traveling around southern Africa looking for suitable subjects to write articles about. They said it was an experience they both valued and that their visit would be included in a forthcoming issue. They left that afternoon and I have no idea whether the article was actually written. It didn't really matter though, I thought they were genuine people and was happy to oblige them.

One Sunday, I was waiting for the new batch of "venturers" to arrive, when I decided to have a little fun with them when they got to the holding campsite before going into the bush. During my dealings around the town, I had met someone who had a microlight plane and who was always inviting me to take a flight with him. I went out to the airport and found him and told him about my little joke. He readily agreed. I knew roughly what time the new guys would arrive and so, arranged to come back to the airport later. I then went to the shop and bought a 1kg bag of mealie meal, a sort of flour, which is the staple diet of most people in Africa. I then wrapped the bag of mealimeal in a sheet of paper. It was much the same joke as I did on clients in South Africa when I dropped a water-bomb on them.

When I knew the "venturers" were all congregated in the camp, we took off. As the pilot flew towards the camp, he suddenly nose-dived down towards them. A few of them looked up as they heard the noise and then more of them looked up as the microlight got closer and closer. When we were only about 50 feet above them and with practically all of them looking up at this screaming engine diving towards them, the pilot suddenly pulled the plane up and I dropped the meali-bomb, not at them but in a clear space. It wouldn't look too good if I managed to kill one or two with a meali-bag bomb! On the sheet of paper wrapped around the bomb, I had written, "Violets are blue, Roses are ret (sic), times are hard, this is all you get!" I could see a lot of them were laughing as we flew off back to the airport, where I thanked the pilot with the promise of some beers later and then drove off to the camp. Everyone seemed to enjoy the joke and it probably set the right mood for them to go off into bush the next day.

A few weeks later, when all the projects were finished, I set off to return to field-base camp and detoured to Etosha to visit Sabine's friend Marion. Sabine had visited her and had come to Rundu to see me. She was working at an up-market, private lodge, which at that time, had virtually no clients. To save the reader all the boring details, we ended up in my room after dinner, both worse the wear for drink and had raw, unadulterated sex. I hesitate to use the phrase, "made love", as there was very little love involved on either side. I don't think either of us planned it, although to be fair, the thought had crossed my mind when she invited me. It was an odd sort of invite as we hardly knew each other. The next day, I left early and only saw Marion as I was walking to the Land Rover. We simply kissed on the cheek and said goodbye, and that was the last time I ever saw her.

Yet another episode I'm not particularly proud of. Sabine and I weren't in a relationship by that stage, so there wasn't the issue of being unfaithful to her, but on reflection, that is precisely what it was, except for "relationship", read "friendship". She had travelled all the way from Etosha to see me and I responded by shagging one of her friends. Good move! It hurt her deeply when she found out and for my part, I have regretted the incident ever since. I find it rather sad to say that the only thing I remember with any clarity about that night with Marion, is her fantastic breasts, but I wouldn't know her now if I tripped over them in the street.

As the days and weeks went by, the schools were slowly taking shape. The school at Cwa was especially important as that was the one with the wonky walls, which hadn't been finished by the previous expedition. It wasn't entirely the fault of the project manager, the lack of building supplies had meant that the "venturers" had spent days on end unable to do anything because they had nothing with which to work. However, when I first saw the site, I was appalled at the quality of the work that had actually been completed. If I was to criticise Raleigh for anything, it was that they expected men and women project managers to produce quality buildings when none of them had had any building experience. It would be a bit like asking a blacksmith to make a chair. Having said that, I was also amazed at the quality of the other schools being built at Shambahey, Mbambe and Likwatarera. Without any experience, the managers and "venturers" alike were producing superb results through sheer hard work, common sense and a strong desire to do a good job.

The school at Cwa had been completed up to the roof level, but there was no roof or even "A" frames for the roof, no windows, no doors, the brickwork hadn't been "washed" with a layer of cement and the surrounds of the site were littered with building detritus. In short, it was a mess. Not only that, the brickwork that had been completed had gone steadily wrong. As the walls went up vertically, the shape of the building changed from an oblong to a parallelogram. This meant that there was absolutely no way the roof trusses would fit where they were supposed to and consequently, nothing else could be done until the building had been rectified. To return the school to its original oblong shape, Raleigh brought out an expert builder named Richard. When I took him out to the site, he was absolutely aghast at what supposedly passed for brickwork, but was gracious enough to accept that the bricklayers themselves were a tad short of expertise. The school at Cwa would never have been finished without the expertise of this man.

Raleigh had previously set a date for the schools to be officially handed over to the local education authority. As the date got closer and closer, the days got busier and busier. All the major construction work had been completed, and now it was the small stuff, such as painting or puttying in the windows or making doors fit properly or nailing galvanised sheets to the "long-drop" toilets the "venturers" had constructed. These were essentially very deep holes in the ground with a small square building around them. They had a simple flue system, which took the foul odours up and out into the atmosphere. We had long-drop toilets back at the field-base in Windhoek, and one fine day, one of the female members of staff, Sally managed to drop her glasses right into the hole. I think most of us had a go at retrieving them with a hook wired onto a very long pole, but after gagging ourselves stupid, we all gave up. Sally, however, bravely fought on and she eventually got them out, only to run the gauntlet of the inevitable comments, such as, "shit glasses those, Sally!"

Although I wasn't racing around Rundu organising supplies, in many ways, I was busier than ever. The school sites at Cwa and Shambahey were fairly close together and as Cwa was already partially built, Raleigh had decided that the staff employed on finishing Cwa would then move to Shambahey to help those "venturers" building that school. As the date for the hand-over got ever closer, I was constantly out at one of the sites or another, doing anything that needed to be done. I remember borrowing a portable welder from a contact in Rundu and then using it to weld the roof trusses at Shambahey. I'd done very little welding at that stage, but by the time I had finished the roof, I could weld a neat and straight line. I think they call it, learning on the job!

Very close to the hand-over day, I sent some last minute supplies out to Likwaterera and Mbambe, including nails for fixing the galvanised sheets to the long-drop frames. The following morning, I got a radio call from the manager at Likwaterera, complaining that the manager at Mbambe had stolen his nails and he couldn't complete the long-drops. Apparently, the lorry driver forgot that he had to go to Likwaterera first. The handing-over ceremonies would be held the following day, so I had to drive back into Rundu, all the way to the hardware shop and then drive the thirty kilometres or so back into the bush just to deliver a bag of nails. It was too late to shout at the tosser of a manager at Mbambe, I just had to get on with it, as did the staff at the school site. When I did eventually speak to him, he simply said that he "thought he might need them!" I relayed this to Martin at Likwaterera and left it to him to speak to Malcolm!

The long-drops were finished that day, the flag poles had been erected and the national flag of Namibia had been delivered to each site. The formal hand-over took place at the local government offices, with the education minister and our expedition leader Jon, present. It went off without a hitch. I wasn't invited, but was told later by Jon, the local administration was over the moon with the work that the young "venturers" had accomplished, and quite rightly so too. They had worked very hard in difficult conditions, but then again, they were there to experience a different sort of life and to make a contribution to a society far less well off than their own. They were meant to suffer a little. Only in that way would they appreciate just how the rural communities in Rundu had to exist. By and large, they all gained personally from their experience and took something away with them, which hopefully, they will have used to their benefit back in the U.K.

During my never-ending travels around Rundu, I got to know and meet many people. Amongst these, was a man named Mr. Emangwene. He ran a local bus service but also sent buses down to Windhoek. I mentioned to the expedition leader at field-base that we might investigate the use of his buses to transport the youngsters back to Windhoek. He agreed and I eventually struck a deal with Mr Emangwene to transport everybody from Rundu back to Windhoek at the end of the expedition. The buses weren't "state of the art" superliners, equipped with toilets and refreshments etc, but I thought at the time that they would be more than adequate, and that at least, the youngsters and managers would be a little more comfortable than they were when they first came up from Windhoek. How wrong I was!

Two days before we were due to leave, SAKKA's lorry collected all the equipment from each site and brought it back to Rundu. When it had first arrived, I was appalled by the way it had been packed onto the back of the lorry and wondered just how some of it hadn't actually dropped off en route, or worse, the lorry hadn't tipped over. Everything had just been thrown on without any thought for stability, space or even safety.

When all the equipment had arrived from all the sites, Viky and I set to loading it onto the Raleigh lorry. When we finished, we had about 3 feet to spare at the back of the lorry, we had packed and tied it so well. "That'll show 'em how it's done at Field Base", I thought.

The following day, all the staff were collected from the sites. I remember the mood being ebullient, not only because of what they had achieved but also because they knew they would soon be on the plane home, back to their families and friends, fast-food and alcohol, movies and discos, mobile phones and computers, comfortable beds and dry houses, everything they had missed in Rundu. I often wonder if any of them ever spare a thought for the people they left behind in the villages; the adults who spent practically their entire lives simply growing enough maize to see them through the seasons or maybe, to swap for the odd item of fourth-hand clothing, or the children who took such pleasure from a white man throwing a rope at them and chasing them around the village.

And then the big day, setting off for home. The buses, two of them, arrived on time, clean but far from sparkly, at about 8am. All the kids piled quickly onto the buses, eager to be on their way, and then they were gone.

I set off about an hour later, after saying a few last minute goodbyes to friends such as Eduardo, Ines, Ute and Calvin with the usual promises to keep in touch. I never expected to catch the buses so quickly, but I passed them on the road, barely about 35 kilometres from Rundu. I remember wondering idly why they hadn't gone much farther but then dismissed the thought just as idly. I ploughed on to Etosha, and over dinner that evening, thought that the buses would have arrived at field base by that time. I figured, 700 kilometres at an average of about 80-90 k.p.h. should see them back at about 8pm. When I had spoken to Mr Emangwene, he'd told me that the journey would be long and tiring, but that they would get there in the same day. Wrong!

I spent a very comfortable, and I have to say, pleasurable night at Etosha and set off for Windhoek around 10am the following morning. I dawdled back to field-base, taking my time, stopping at a few markets to buy carvings and arrived around 4pm, expecting to see all the youngsters in the camp. There was nobody there. Jon, the expedition leader told me that the buses were so slow, they had had to spend the night at the roadside, under the stars.

When they did eventually get back, I learned that neither of the buses was capable of going faster than about 40 k.p.h. and for much of the time, were a good deal slower. They had to stop frequently for toilets and to buy food and water. What they had on board with them had been consumed. By the time I left Etosha, they hadn't even arrived at the road junction where I had diverted to the park. Consequently, I didn't pass them again on the road.

Boy, were they pissed off with me when they got back! All I could do was apologise and promise to take them swimming in the local pool the following day. That nearly turned into a nightmare as well. I had everyone loaded onto the back of the lorry and had to do a hill start at a set of traffic lights. As well as the brakes being a bit suspect, the clutch wasn't very good on the lorry and I had to slip it like crazy to get any forward momentum. It was jerking violently and just for a second, I thought I might snap a half-shaft or something, or even worse, lose all power and career backwards down the hill, smashing into cars and shop-fronts, oh, and killing everyone involved. Just a quick thought! She got going eventually, but it was a dodgy moment. I don't think anyone realised what was happening, judging by the noise and laughter coming from those on the back.

Everyone then spent the next three or four nights back at base-camp, clearing up the equipment and having parties, everyone that is, except me. When all my duties were completed, I headed into Windhoek and spent a couple of nights at the best hotel in town with a stunning girl named Merlen. She had been working at the Breakwater Lodge Hotel in Cape Town when I used to run safaris into there for Drifters. She was what was termed, "coloured", neither black nor white. She had black features but her skin was a gorgeous honey colour. In the bad days of apartheid, "coloureds" were treated even worse than black Africans, getting the roughest of deals with everything, including education. Merlen had apparently barely scraped through school, but she was intelligent and ambitious. She had fought her way into a receptionist's position at the hotel and was determined to go further. Her family was very poor, consequently, she had never traveled beyond Cape Town.

We had become friends and nothing more. I saw her every time I went to the Breakwater Hotel and we went out a few evenings for drinks. She was always very interested in my travels and we chatted the evenings away. When I was in Rundu, I invited her up to Windhoek for a couple of days. I remember she was very excited as this would be the first time she could use her new passport. We shared a room at the hotel, just as any two friends would. We had a pleasant couple of days wandering around Windhoek, drinking coffee, visiting the markets and generally enjoying a relaxing time.

We stayed in touch for a couple of years after that but I then made a conscious decision to finish the friendship. I had loaned her 3000 Rand, about £300 to finish a college course in hotel management. I had offered her the money and she of course, promised faithfully to repay it. After that, I seemed to be the one who made all the contact. She finished the course, graduated and got a good job in another hotel, but she never mentioned the money I had loaned her. I didn't really expect the money to come back but I was disappointed she made no effort. Eventually, I decided to let her keep the £300 or so but I never contacted her again and although I haven't heard from her to this day, I hope she is well and happy. I'm probably just a soft target!

And so, at the end of the expedition which had lasted three months, we all headed home. Raleigh International's reputation had been restored in Rundu with four fine schools built. In other parts of Namibia, shelters for park rangers had been built, the youngsters had worked at a cheetah sanctuary, done environmental research for various groups within Namibia and generally, went home with a powerful sense of having achieved something others only think about. That, however, was not quite the end for me.

One of my duties upon return to Windhoek, was to write an in-depth report on the position of Northern Coordinator in Namibia. In that report, I covered all the aspects I could think of from transport to money to equipment to public relations to local suppliers, everything. One of the more important aspects though, was my view on how the job would best be done in the future. As I had had the privilege of being the first Northern Coordinator, I think I was in a pretty good position to give an honest and intelligent critique. My conclusion though, was very simple, it should remain exactly as I had performed the role, i.e. one person for the duration of the expedition. The main reason for this was that it had taken me at least 3-4 weeks to ascertain where everything was in Rundu and to establish good working relationships with all the suppliers, big and small; in other words, continuity, and from that, efficiency. In my view, it simply wasn't practical to rotate the role.

It was all to no avail though, as I heard later through the grapevine that Raleigh had done just that with the next expedition to Namibia. The person performing the role of Northern Coordinator changed every three weeks. To be fair, I have no idea how it worked out, but knowing Raleigh senior personnel, it would have been made to "work". C'est la vie!

It was mystifying to me that Raleigh paid no attention to back-up visits. There were no plans for any senior Raleigh person to visit any of the project sites to ascertain how they were being used or to get any feedback as to how things might have been done differently or better. Raleigh went in, did the job and then left. It seemed to me that there should be something else, some form of return to the school sites.

Around 18 months after the expedition, I decided to make a private visit to Rundu and to return to at least some of the school sites to see how they were getting on. I wrote to Raleigh International personnel department at their head-office in Parsons Green, London and told them of my plans. I asked them if they had any problem with my returning on a private visit, (although I expected none) and, as I was going, was there anything I could take out with me to deliver to the field-base in Windhoek. I was thinking of administrative items or letters etc. I never received a reply.

I combined the trip with a visit to Bob and Helen in Johannesburg, and from there to Windhoek. I caught the night bus to Rundu from Windhoek, arriving around dawn. I had to wait a couple of hours at the petrol station, which doubled as the bus stop, before I made my way to Calvin's house. He had no idea I was arriving, so was rather shocked to see me standing in his doorway, pleased, but shocked. We hugged like long-lost brothers and then sat down to some welcome coffee. It was Calvin who told me of the way that the role of Northern Coordinator had changed. When I told him I wanted to go out to one of the schools, he immediately offered me the use of his quad-bike, which I was rather hoping he would. I told him I also planned to surprise Eduardo and Ines down at Sarasungu. He told me he would take me there in the evening as he was planning to go as well, Apparently, I had chosen to come back in time for Eduardo's birthday celebration that evening.

I set off for the school at Mbambe later that morning. I had no trouble finding the path, as I had travelled it so many times before, and arrived a couple of hours later. I arrived at a time when the children were not in school, they were all at their houses having lunch. Word soon spread though, that "Mr Nil" was back in the village, and soon, there was a throng of children and adults surrounding me, all talking at the same time and appearing to be very pleased to see me again. After spending time with them, I took a long look at the school and found it to be still in really good condition. However, I was very disappointed to see that the education authority had not kept their side of the bargain. The agreement was that Raleigh would build the school, but the authority had to put desks and chairs in the rooms, which in fairness they had, but they should also have put blackboards on the walls, along with shelves for books etc, which they hadn't. There was nothing on the walls, not even any pictures the kids had drawn and I noticed the blackboard was on the floor, propped up against the wall, in other words, lower than eye level. Whilst I was there, one of the adults complained to me that one of the windows didn't open. I got the distinct impression that this was a particularly big deal for this guy. I looked at the window and saw the problem immediately. I asked for a knife and went to work on the window. The only problem was that the paint hadn't quite dried when the window had been shut. Consequently, it had got stuck. All I had to do was cut away the paint from the frame and hey presto! it opened. I was a hero!

After spending a couple of hours at the two sites, Mbambe and Likwaterera, (Cwa and Shambahe were simply too far to go) I headed back into town on the quad bike. I have to say, it was enormous fun tearing up the bush tracks on a four-wheeled motorcycle, I wish I had done it when I was there before. I got back to Calvin's house, where we chatted until the early evening when I showered and we both headed off to the Sarasungu. It really was an idyllic setting for a "rest-camp" It was right alongside the Kavango River, surrounded by riverine forest. The camp itself comprised thatch-roofed chalets, a camping area, restaurant/bar and a swimming pool. Ines did most of the cooking, assisted by Ute and some domestic staff and Eduardo served at tables and acted as Maitre 'D.

Calvin and I pitched up at around 7pm, the time that Calvin had booked a table for him and a "friend". I walked to the restaurant door and saw Eduardo just walking away, back to the bar area. There were a few diners in, but not many. I threw open the door and shouted, "Gin and Tonic, Raposo and make it quick!" He of course, whirled round, as did all the other diners, at the disturbance in his restaurant. When he saw me, his face was initially one of shock, then a smile broke out, followed by a laugh. Ines came from the kitchen to see what all the fuss was about and we all had a good old hug in the middle of the restaurant. I wished Eduardo happy birthday and let him think I had come all that way to see him, just for that. It was coincidental of course, but I didn't see the harm.

The restaurant had been extended by Calvin in the interim, and was now a super place. I was treated like royalty and had a fabulous couple of days, just relaxing with Eduardo by the pool and canoeing down the river.

When I returned home, I set about dealing with Raleigh. It wasn't the fact that they didn't return to previous project sites, it was more about Raleigh not bothering to even reply to my letter. Few things annoy me more than being ignored.

I wrote another letter to Raleigh International, this time addressing it personally to the Chief Executive Officer, whom I had met when he paid a visit to the various projects, including mine at Rundu. He seemed like a smart and good man. In my letter, I mentioned the fact that nobody seemed bothered about making return visits to the schools. Mainly however, I bemoaned the fact that I, as a volunteer had returned to Rundu of my own volition and, having offered to help with taking anything I could manage to the base camp, I hadn't even received a reply from Raleigh. I laid it on fairly thick, asking just how an organisation like Raleigh International could be so cavalier about communicating with people. Having got everything off my chest, I posted the letter off, not really knowing whether I would receive a reply, but hoping so. I was not disappointed.

The Chief Executive Officer replied within a few days, sincerely apologising for the total lack of communication, something he said was fundamental to the ethos of Raleigh International. He thanked me for my efforts and promised that in future, letters like mine would not be ignored. I was satisfied with his response, but saddened that it had taken the C.E.O. to try and put right something, which even a minor member of Raleigh could have dealt with. In my mind, to ignore my letter, was not just unprofessional, it was discourteous. Raleigh International is all about teaching youngsters the value of communication and interaction with others. It seemed to me that some of their staff could have benefited themselves from a few weeks living in the bush and experiencing the way that other people, less fortunate than themselves had to survive.

Although this little episode with Raleigh had left a slightly bitter taste, I hoped my letter jolted at least one person out of his or her lethargy. Raleigh International remains a good organisation with high ideals, something which this world with its selfish, must-have-now-pay-later attitudes, could certainly do with more of.

I returned to the U.K. from the expedition to Namibia with Raleigh in December of 1997, having had a fantastic experience. Of course, I would rather not have cut my fingers off, but it has to be said that the accident enabled me to engage with Raleigh in a capacity, which suited my character and ability perfectly. To this day, I still reflect on my time in Rundu. I still smile at just how fortunate I was to have been offered the post and tearing around Rundu solving problem after problem. I still remember with fondness, my time with Ines, Eduardo, Ute and Calvin at the Sarasungu, sitting in the sunset, drinking gin and tonic. I still remember the villages and the people, especially the children and our little game with the rope. I often wonder whether they are all still there; probably, such is the way of their life out there. I would challenge anybody not to be totally captivated by the children

As I write this passage, I am sitting in an airport lounge in Nairobi on my way home from Zambia. I know that the vast majority of the village-people with whom I engaged in Rundu, will never experience the joy of travel, and I realise just how lucky I, and millions like me are that we are able to jet off anywhere in the world with scarcely a thought for those who cannot. It re-establishes some values for me.

Chapter 27

S itting on my patio one afternoon in February 1999, I was thinking to myself, "Should I do it, should I do it?" I knew there was a down-side to this plan, i.e. losing a lot of money but, if done right, the rewards could be substantial. I have always been cautious and careful with any spare money I have accrued, but at this stage, I had saved a few thousand pounds and I was now contemplating buying a flat for investment purposes. The Buy-to-Let market was apparently on the way up but was still not a popular investment choice for many. The Stock Market was still attracting the vast majority of investors. Being naturally cautious, I thought the vagaries of the market too much of a risk for me personally and my thoughts had turned to the property market. I remember dad saying to me once "bricks and mortar" was the best investment anyone could make, although he was talking purely about owning one's own home.

I decided to make some enquiries and went along to an agent specializing in the Buy-to-Let market. The upshot was that a few months later, I took the plunge and became the proud owner of a one bedroom flat in Beckenham, South London, an area reknowned for rental properties and its proximity to London bound trains. Contrary to what I thought would happen, I actually enjoyed the buying process, especially purchasing the furniture and other items to furnish the flat. I tried very hard to make sure that whatever I bought, whilst not being top of the range was functional, robust and at the same time, stylish.

I never consciously made the decision as to what type of landlord I would be, but having lived in some pretty horrible rented accommodation myself and done some research into unscrupulous landlords, I did know that I would never allow myself to be labelled a bad landlord. I simply ask myself the question, "Would I want to live with this?" and if the answer is "No" then I do something about it. It often costs me money, but I would rather that, than a bad reputation.

After a few nervous months following the purchase, always expecting the worse to happen, I settled into the role of landlord, knowing that the property was being well managed by the letting agent. This was a conscious decision. Working full time, I knew I would never have the time to attend to all the little problems that would inevitably arise. Turning the running of the flat over to the management company would release me from the day-to-day issues and give me peace of mind. They deal with everything to do with the administration of the flat and the well-being of the tenants.

The reader may remember that back in 1993, I had an operation on my back to correct a ruptured disc. As a result of that operation, I occasionally get a bad back due to the scar tissue becoming temporarily inflamed. The pain in my lower back becomes quite debilitating. I was suffering such an attack in the early part of 1999 and as a result, had been taken off operational duties for a short period whilst my back returned to normal and been placed in the Criminal Justice Unit at Bromley. The department dealt with the administration of the prosecution of cases at court. These cases, no matter how small, generate an enormous amount of paperwork, which has to be managed. I remember when I first joined the police, the "process department" as it was called then, dealt only with motoring offences and was operated by one or two constables, usually long-service officers with medical complaints keeping them off the streets. The administration of criminal cases was dealt with solely by the arresting officer, and in those days was much, much less that it had grown into in 1999.

The trend these days is for the police authorities in many areas to go into partnership with private organizations to provide modern, air-conditioned buildings housing police officers and the myriad of civilian staff departments. It's called Private Finance Initiative, or P.F.I. for short. It's a relatively new concept. The police don't actually own the buildings they occupy, they are leased from the P.F.I. company. Before this initiative, the police owned all their own buildings and were rightly called "police stations". Older officers often bemoan the fact that the old stations are fast disappearing in favour of the usually gigantic buildings of today. The officers say "ah, they haven't got the atmosphere of a proper police station" or maybe simply, "they're not the same as the old places". Well, I disagree! The "old places" were draughty, cold in winter, hot in summer, the rooms were cramped and dingy, the toilets smelt and there simply wasn't enough room for everyone connected with the modern police service. The new buildings are everything the old ones weren't. Personally, I would rather have comfortable surroundings than what some officers called an "atmosphere".

Just about the best place in the whole "nick" was the canteen, and that was probably one of the reasons why P.F.I. came about. The "canteen culture" of the 60's, 70's and 80's was something to be rid of, but at least the canteen was somewhere the officers could gather together and enjoy good, if not quite wholesome cooking. There was always lively and friendly banter between the officers and the canteen staff, who were often black.

Having the new buildings has helped to engender a huge change in attitudes. There is far more acceptance now of civilian staff than there ever used to be. The officers generally thought of the canteen as their place, but as more and more civilian staff joined the police service, it became obvious that they felt more and more uncomfortable in the presence of the officers. They rightly thought that they were just as much entitled to a relaxing meal break as the rather raucous and sometimes slovenly officers were. They didn't particularly want to be part of the "team" in this respect. The new buildings provide a much more congenial atmosphere. Officers and civilian staff get along much better as it has been drummed into officers that they have to accept that other people are just as much part of the police as they are and that their behaviour, not just in the canteen, has to be above reproach. The catering services for the police are now provided by outside companies and the food is generally much better and healthier, as is the behaviour and conversation.

In 1999, Bromley police station was an old Victorian building on the corner of two major roadways. To accommodate the ever growing army of civilian staff, the police authority had leased some offices above shops alongside the police station. The curious thing about these offices was that they were once private flats and had been converted to offices by the police, all except one. There was still a sitting tenant in one of the flats whilst the workings of the Metropolitan Police went on around him. Officers and staff who went down to the ground floor for a cigarette were often treated to his washing machine water or his dirty bath water overflowing the drain outside his block. Oddly enough, he never complained about the noise he must have endured day and night or the fact that he could never park his car behind the block because it was always full of police cars.

These offices were awful, in fact the entire police station was awful, just as I have described above. One of the offices in this converted block was treated to a fly infestation every year at about the same time. It seemed that nothing anybody could do would prevent it. The roof space was inspected for dead pigeons which might be attracting the flies, the windows had screens placed over them, special fly-zapping machines were suspended from the ceilings and still they buzzed continually around. And not just around the entire office. They seemed to concentrate over one particular desk, Alf's. Poor old Alf, the term "a buzzing in my ear" took on a whole meaning for him. In the end, we just accepted that the flies would be there and swatting them as we walked past Alf's desk became a casual sport.

There were a few police officers working within these largely civilian departments and I went to assist one such officer, a fellow sergeant named Tony, whose job it was to supervise completed case files before they were dispatched to the Crown Prosecution Service. He would look for obvious errors and where necessary, question the degree of evidence provided. I found the work particularly interesting and challenging, so interesting in fact, it later became my full time occupation.

In 1999, the Crown Prosecution Service had just begun to place solicitors within police stations. They only came in one or two days a week and their job was to examine the files for evidential content to ensure that the sufficiency of evidence was enough to obtain a conviction at court. Any case which they thought had little chance of succeeding at court was discontinued. As a dyed-in-the-wool police officer, this often went against the grain as I thought that cases were sometimes discontinued on the flimsiest excuse and later came to realize that the quality of some of the solicitors employed by the C.P.S. was far below that of the solicitors employed by the defence. It became obvious that C.P.S. solicitors were often afraid of going to court, standing up before the magistrates and actually arguing a case, in short, doing what they were employed to do, advocating.

One particular C.P.S. solicitor, who definitely did not fit the above profile, was Emma, (not her real name.) Dark haired and fiery, we often had good discussions about various cases, going over the intricacies of points of law. She had an extremely quick mind and a quicker tongue, and what's more, she was all for going to court and obtaining convictions, where she thought it necessary. The C.P.S. always had the last word as to whether a case would or should proceed to prosecution and with Emma, we always knew that if a case was discontinued, it was for sound evidential reasons, i.e. the lack of it.

Over the weeks that followed Emma's arrival at the station, she and I became good friends and eventually, began a relationship. We seemed to share many character traits such as a good, intelligent argument but Emma was rather more Bohemian than me. The relationship lasted several months, during which time we traveled to the States to visit Peg and Hopper at their Cape Cod holiday home and enjoyed several evenings out visiting various pubs and comedy venues around south London.

One fateful day, around October, we decided to go to Paris for the week-end. I had never been and so was looking forward immensely to visiting this romantic city. We set out early on a Friday morning and took the Eurostar train direct into the centre of Paris. Emma had booked us into a lovely, intimate little hotel, or "pension" just off one of the main roads leading away from the Arc de Triomph, I don't remember which one, or for that matter, the name of the hotel.

We spent the late Friday afternoon drinking coffee at one of the roadside cafes Paris is rightly famous for. Dinner that evening was at one of the many excellent restaurants in that part of the city.

Saturday morning saw me bright-eyed and bushy-tailed, eager to spend the day browsing around any part of the city that took our fancy. Emma was in the bathroom getting ready to go out. Now, I think I have a pretty good sense of humour, but I do know that I can sometimes say things which may appear to go over the top. I don't mean anything malicious by it, I just sometimes don't think about what I'm saying. On this particular occasion, I said to Emma in the bathroom, "are you going to be long?" She replied something along the lines of "Why?" I thought it was an odd reply, even a jokey sort of response. I shot back jokingly, with, "it's an easy question, how long?" Emma came out of the bathroom with all guns blazing!! She began to tongue lash me, saying that I had no right to speak to her like that. It took me completely by surprise. I tried to explain that I was only joking in my own stupid way, but nothing I said would mollify her. She kept on and on. In the end, I simply said, "Look, I was joking. I'm sorry if it offended you, I apologise," hoping that that would do the trick and we could move on. It didn't and neither did we! In fact, the whole relationship went down the pan at that precise moment. I was completely mystified by Emma's response, it almost seemed as though she was determined to keep the argument, no, row, alive at all costs. For my part, I had apologized if I had caused her offence, in fact, I kept trying to invent new ways to say sorry. It seemed reasonable to me for her to accept that I had said something stupid, accept that I had apologized for it and put the whole nasty business away. But she simply wouldn't let it rest.

We spent a very wary Saturday traipsing around some market or other and then around the Montmarte district, including the Sacre Couer church. Things were going from bad to worse. At the market, Emma suggested that we wander around in separate ways, she going one way and me the opposite way. Desperate to get everything back to normal, I agreed, but was extremely unhappy about the way it was going. The relationship seemed to be in freefall.

The evening found us around the Notre Dame cathedral area. For some reason, my right foot was becoming very painful to walk on. The ball of the foot was tender, and I had begun to limp. We had dinner somewhere, almost in silence and at the end, Emma said she wanted to walk back to the hotel, which I remembered was quite some distance. I explained to her that my foot was getting really painful and that I thought I shouldn't walk back, I would rather we took the Metro. She said, quite glibly that I could take the Metro if I liked, but she was going to walk, and that is exactly what we did. When I got back to the hotel, I sat up in bed reading until she arrived back a few hours later. She didn't speak to me at all.

The next morning, I was tongue lashed again for leaving her to walk back to the hotel alone! I thought this was a bit rich as she was the one who wanted to walk. If she didn't want to walk alone, she could have taken the Metro with me. I got the distinct impression that she was using this as a weapon to keep the row going even further.

We spent Sunday completely apart, she went her way and I took the Metro back down to the Notre Dame area. I wanted to see inside the cathedral and by this time, I was determined that whatever was happening between us, I was going to enjoy at least one aspect of Paris. I spent a miserable Sunday with a painful foot and a spinning head. The cathedral was wonderful, but I didn't really take much of it in as I was constantly thinking about what was going on between Emma and I. There were a number of occasions when I thought I might just quit and take an early train home. But that was defeatist and I knew that if I did that, the relationship would definitely be at an end. I was still hanging on to the thin hope that this was just a blip and that once back in England, everything would be forgotten, or at least dealt with, and we could move on.

The day dragged by and at last, it was time to head for the Eurostar station. I got there quite early and settled down to wait for the boarding time. I expected to see Emma come into the station, but by the time the boarding message came, there was no sign of her. I went to my seat, to find her already there. She had obviously entered the station, probably seen me sitting there and then ignored me. We said not one word to each other all the way back on the train, not one word on the bus back from Waterloo station to Norwood and then not one word on the short walk from the bus stop to where she lived. We said a very awkward goodbye at her house and I left without being invited in. And that was the end of that! The freefalling was over and I had crashed and burned! We didn't see each other again as partners. There were occasions that we bumped into each other at the station, said a polite hello, but that was all.

A few months later, we did see each other for a drink after work. The subject of Paris was raised, but to my mind, there was no real explanation of what had happened. She did say how disappointed she was, that she had wanted us to go to Paris so that she could find out more about me. Well, it turned out that she obviously didn't like what she saw. Me, I was just saddened that a seemingly minor little incident could have been blown up out of all proportion and that a relationship that had seemed to be going so well, had ended on such a sour note.

After the break-up of my marriage, the failed relationships with Jenny, Sabine and then Emma, I really began to think that permanent relationships were not for me. I have already discussed my marriage and do not intend to revisit it, but I began to ask why the others had folded. And I am still asking myself the question!

In early 2000, I bought my second property, a two bedroom, end-of-terrace house in Falmouth, Cornwall. I had not thought about buying a second property and even if I had, I would never have thought about buying it in Cornwall. It all came about because of a family member and her situation.

My aunty Rene, mother's sister had four daughters, Ginnie, Cathy, Julie and the youngest by several years, Jackie. By comparison to her three older sisters, Jackie was different altogether. She was a bit wild, completely non-conformist and disrespectful of anything that smacked of establishment or tradition, including as it turned out, family values. Of course, I had known her since she had been born and I only saw her on the annual Christmas trip my family made to Weston-super-Mare. She was too young at that stage to join in our fun with the tape-recordings, but even then, it was obvious she was different. She had a sullenness about her and the rest of us had very little to do with her. Later on, at family gatherings such as weddings, Jackie's rebellious nature took the form of sulkiness and stoney silence. I remember Auntie Rene being actually quite embarrassed by her behaviour at her older sister, Ginnie's wedding.

The years rolled by and there was the odd family contact with Jackie. She had married quite young and had two children. She divorced and remarried and eventually divorced again. In 2000, she had moved back to Weston from Scotland where her second marriage had ended. She was living in a little flat just along the road from where my mother lived. It was dingy and damp. I used to pop along for coffee with her when I went down to visit mum. Jackie had developed into a beautiful woman and having a coffee with her was a real pleasure.

She was at that time, in a relationship with her boss, a market owner. I got the impression that things weren't going too well for her and as I was leaving the flat one day after coffee, she looked at me and said, "you wouldn't fancy buying a flat in Falmouth would you?" She said it with a smile and in a jokey sort of way. At first, I thought she was poking fun at her capitalist, property owning cousin. I smiled back and said "No, not really!" On thinking about it later however, I wondered why she had specified Falmouth. When I got back to Biggin Hill, I phoned her and asked why. She explained that she had spent time in Cornwall, Falmouth in particular and felt that the place suited her character. Her boyfriend was not treating her well and she wanted to leave him but was afraid to because of his temper! To get away, she needed a completely different place to live and had chosen Falmouth. Her comment to me had been serious!

Despite saying "no" initially, I began to think about the benefits of buying a second investment property and obtained some house and flat prices from various estate agents in Falmouth. I was surprised at how relatively cheap they appeared to be. Additionally of course, I would have a ready-made tenant in Jackie with no management fees. I made the decision then to go to Falmouth to investigate further. I also decided to tell Jackie I was going and to ask if she wanted to come along. She jumped at the chance and we agreed to meet at the train station in Weston early one morning, giving us plenty of time to get to Falmouth and look at various properties which I had arranged. Buying a second investment property and having a relative live in it, seemed an ideal situation.

Despite living in Weston, Jackie was still regarded as the "black sheep" of the family, essentially because of her seeming contempt for her parents and sisters. Nobody could really work out Jackie and her attitudes, she was a bit of an enigma. A fierce critic of Jackie was my own mother, who rarely had a good word to say about her. For this reason, I made a third decision, not to tell her that I was going to Falmouth and taking Jackie with me. This decision was to cause a little difficulty a few weeks later.

We arrived in Cornwall later that morning and began to view the properties I thought might be suitable. Most were not and the first day was rather fruitless. I had arranged that we would spend that night in a bed and breakfast place recommended by one particular estate agent, with whom I had an appointment the following day to view a house in the centre of Falmouth. We had separate rooms.

The following day, we went to the property I had arranged to view just off one of the main roads into and out of Falmouth. As soon as we walked in, Jackie dug her elbow into my ribs and when I looked at her, she had a huge grin on her face. It was clear that she was thinking this would be the one. It was a two bedroom, end-of-terrace house with a huge basement area which served as a garage and utility area. I had to admit it was a lovely place. I think we viewed another property after that, but it was the first which really stayed in both our minds. I phoned the agent and arranged to meet him later in a local car park. We spoke a little longer about the property and eventually, I made the decision. I offered an amount just short of the asking price and the agent went off to speak privately with the vendor. Jackie and I wandered around the car park, hands in pockets, kicking stones around. He came back about five minutes later and announced that my offer had been accepted. We were standing alongside my car and I remember Jackie punching the air and hissing, "Yes!!" We then went back to the office with the agent and completed some rudimentary paperwork, after which, we set off back to Weston. Property number two was in the bag! All I had to do now was sort out the finances.

After days of doing my calculations as to how much I would need for deposits etc, I figured I was going to be about £3000 short! The actual deposit on the house was no problem, the shortfall was going to be for the conveyancing and legal fees etc. I could have gone to the bank and borrowed the money, but to me, the interest I would have had to pay would be disastrous. I thought about it long and hard and decided against the bank. At the same time, I decided that I would approach my mother and ask her for the loan. And this is where I start to feel slightly ashamed of myself. Knowing that she didn't approve of Jackie, I also decided that I wouldn't tell her immediately that it would be her living in the house. Big mistake, huge!! My mother loaned me the money without hesitation or question. For my part, it would have been repaid as soon as possible.

The purchase of the house ground along as slow as usual over the following months. Jackie and I had agreed that she would pay a certain amount in rent, which would cover the cost of the mortgage and insurances etc. but not much else. I went to great pains to ensure that she could actually pay the amount each month. She specifically asked for a rental agreement to be drawn up between us, which I had no problem with as this would give her legal rights as well as me. The only thing I didn't do which would have been normal, was to take a month's rent from her as deposit. Somehow, it didn't seem right as she was after all, family. Besides that, I didn't think she had the money anyway.

During one of our many conversations, she mentioned that she wanted to come up to London to visit her daughter, who was living with her boyfriend somewhere in the north of the city. Casually, I suggested she should come and stay at my house and I would take her to where her daughter lived and we could all go for dinner somewhere. Fine, that was arranged. The evening turned out to be not so successful however, as the boyfriend didn't actually pitch-up, making some sort of excuse. Jackie mentioned later that he had said he couldn't believe a Metropolitan police officer was in his flat, socially. The boyfriend apparently was black! I never met the guy and never have, but I suspect he stayed away simply because he didn't want to socialize with a police officer, even if he was family. And people accuse the police of stereotyping! In any event, the three of us had a lovely dinner and then Jackie and I made our way back on the train to Bromley, slightly the worse for drink. We drove back to my house, where we had a few more drinks and talked long into the night. Jackie also spent the following night at my house, although this was because she missed her train home.

Not long after this, the purchase was complete and Jackie was due to move into the house. Time to go and speak to mother! She didn't take the news well and without articulating the words, she made me feel underhanded and rather cheap, which is exactly what I was! Even before speaking to mum, I was regretting the decision not to tell her that Jackie would be living in the house. I should have told her! It's not that she would have refused the money, but she saw Jackie as rather manipulative. It was just simpler not to tell her initially, and when I did finally tell her about Jackie living in the house, it sort of cast me in the same mould that mum thought Jackie had come out of. Without doubt, it was one of my less well-judged decisions and I have deeply regretted it ever since.

If that was one of my worst decisions, as it turned out, actually allowing Jackie to live there, ran a close second! When she first moved in, things went well. She paid the rent on time and seemed to be looking after the house. I made a few trips down to Falmouth, ostensibly to check that everything was OK and by this time, Jackie's son Sam had moved down to Falmouth with her.

Over the course of the following two years, the usual little hiccups occurred that happen with any property, this item got broken or that needed replacing. We still had dialogue, we hadn't fallen out and so these things weren't a problem. On one occasion, Jackie contacted me and stated the hot-water tank needed fixing as it was leaking. I simply told her to go ahead and send me the invoice. When it hadn't arrived a few months later, I phoned Jackie and she told me she had sorted it out between herself and the plumber! OK, I thought.

Early in 2002, she started to fall behind with the rent. She had had problems with the rent for months prior to this and I had made alternative arrangements for her. She had met a man and in mid 2002, she asked permission for him to live at the house with her. I had no problem with this provided he signed a co-tenancy agreement, which he did. With their combined income, the rent should not have been a problem, but the arrears were not being cleared. I learned later that they had trolled off to South Africa and Egypt. In my view, the back-rent was the first thing that should have been paid, prior to any trip abroad. On another occasion I phoned the house and spoke to a complete stranger who stated he was staying temporarily, a man called Wiles.

In September 2002, Jackie missed the rent completely. Things were going from bad to worse. Had she been anyone else, she would have received "notice to quit" long before this, but she was family and I felt an obligation to keep trying to help. It was difficult though, it seemed that she simply didn't care about me, the house or the fact that I was trying to be patient and helpful. Apparently, this guy Wiles was a friend of Sam's and he was staying for a few weeks. Jackie assured me that was the position.

In October 2002, Jackie finally stated she wanted to leave. Having breathed a long and silent sigh of relief, I reminded her that I needed a month's notice, as per the rental agreement. She agreed to this. I never received any formal notice from Jackie and about a week later, I received a phone call from this guy Wiles, asking if he could take on the tenancy. When I asked if Jackie was there, or her partner, he said, "Oh no, they moved out last week!" When I asked Wiles who had the keys, he told me he had them as he and Sam were living at the house. Now I really did have alarm bells!! A total stranger was living in my house having been given the keys by someone who no longer lived there. Neither Sam nor this guy Wiles had any tenancy agreement and whilst I had no problem with him staying temporarily as a friend, Wiles certainly had no permission from me to live there. The consequences of Jackie's actions could be serious for me.

When I first bought the property, I remembered that it was let out through an agency called Homequest. I contacted this firm and the manager, Steven Fenton remembered the house well. I explained the position to him, promising that he could have the management of the house later and he volunteered to go round to the house to inspect it and tell Wiles and Sam that they should leave. I asked Steve if he would phone me before he entered and "walk" me through the house. When he did, the first thing he said to me was, "Neil, you don't want to see this!" Apparently, it was in an appalling condition. The carpets were stained with food, drink and other substances, the walls were grubby and stained, the hot-water tank that was supposedly fixed was not and had leaked water down the walls and into the woodwork which had rotted, the front door was broken, the kitchen was grease-stained, broken furniture was strewn about the garage floor, and the bathroom and toilet were disgusting. Mattresses lay all round the place, so goodness knows how many people were dossing there with this man Wiles, and Sam. On top of all that, Steve told me he didn't even need keys to get in, the patio doors had been left wide open. Steve was to have met Wiles at the property, but it seems that he had got the message early and bunked off along with Sam. There was nobody there. He did contact Steve later and ask about the tenancy. When Steve told him he would have to provide references and I would have to approve it, he rang off!

I received no word from Jackie for weeks. She had left no forwarding address and none of her family had heard from her. I was quite shocked to learn that she hadn't been in touch with any of her sisters or even her parents for several months. She never did have a good relationship with any of them especially her parents, but she did used to contact her older sister Julie by text message. Not even Julie had heard from her. Now, of course the story about the house was beginning to unfold, and with it came questions from my cousin Cathy. Somebody could be forgiven for thinking that I had purchased the house for Jackie to live there for all the wrong reasons. That was not the case. I did it for two reasons; one, because Jackie was in trouble and needed to get away from her relationship, and two, it was an investment for me. Helping Jackie get away from her boyfriend and start a new life did not however, apparently mean that much to Jackie. The house was repaired and redecorated over the following weeks, during which, I had an enquiry from a man at the Carrick District Council about the whereabouts of Jackie. I told him truthfully that I didn't know.

I now had to decide how much Jackie owed me. She had written to me at last, promising to pay what she owed, although she hadn't left an address. If I was to reply, it would have to go first to her ex-husband Keith, who would then forward it. I was getting really tired of Jackie's antics and so I wrote a five page letter detailing exactly how I felt and what I thought of her as a person and included just how much she owed me and for what. I told her I was happy to accept a certain amount each month, and for the first four months everything went according to plan. Then the payments began to shrink in size until they were about £20 or so. In the end, I realized that this situation would continue to deteriorate. I decided to call it quits with her and told her I would release her from the debt on her faithful promise to at least go and see her mother, who worried a lot about her and missed her. She promised she would, but for years, didn't bother. Such is Jackie, my cousin.

The last episode in this sad little saga occurred when, simply out of curiosity, I obtained my Credit Record. I was horrified to read that certain purchases had gone on with my name at the Falmouth address, but which were actually nothing to do with me. It took quite some time to convince the credit authority to remove the entries from my record.

I have not heard one word from Jackie since releasing her from the debt. Her father, my last remaining uncle, died a few years ago. She was informed of the death and the date of the funeral by text message from Julie. This is her only means of contact with Jackie. We all speculated as to whether Jackie would turn up to the funeral, and personally, I hoped not, as I had no wish to see her, but for her mother's sake, I hoped she did find the courage to attend and as it happened, the doubters were right. Apparently, there was not even a card of sympathy to her mother. Jackie's daughter Natalie did not attend and neither did her son Sam. Jackie's first husband Keith was there however. Maybe he was representing the whole, sad Jackie family!

(It would be fair to say that, since writing the above, Jackie moved back to Weston in 2009. She has re-established contact with her family, especially her mother. I have tried to repair damage between us by writing a Christmas card suggesting we put our past differences aside. I received no reply. Cathy tells me that she feels very bitter towards me, questioning the reasons for my buying the house in the first place. She casually forgets that when she began her relationship with her new boyfriend, I had no problem with him living there with her. Whenever she had money problems, which was often, I always made alternative arrangements for her so that she could remain in Falmouth. If what she says is true, I could have given her notice to quit and rented the house out for far more than the rent she was giving me. I nearly always lost out financially. I can't alter what happened, however my conscience is clear, but I often wonder if Jackie's is!)

I still own the property in Falmouth and it's now administered by the ever-efficient Steve and Homequest.

Later in 2000, there was an amusing incident which happened between myself and my then girlfriend, Ingrid. I was at Ingrid's house and we were expecting her sister and husband over for dinner. Ingrid and I were having a wonderfully active sex life, taking our opportunities whenever we wanted. She was an extremely sexy woman, to say the least. On this particular evening, I was in the shower and Ingrid was downstairs, preparing vegetables in the kitchen. I called down to Ingrid to "come and look what I've found!" She came up the stairs, giggling all the way, knowing exactly what I'd "found"! Ingrid came into the shower room and we immediately engaged in some heavy kissing and petting. After a minute or two, I began to feel a tingling sensation on my lips, quickly followed by a more extreme tingling on my scrotum sac. It got worse and worse and was definitely not normal. At about the same time, Ingrid suddenly shouted, "Oh my God, the chillies!!" She had been chopping chillies down in the kitchen. The burning became more and more extreme, especially down below! We both raced for taps, she to the sink and me to the bath. We were both laughing at our predicament, but mine was definitely worse than hers, she only had burning on her lips! Here's the science, chillie moisture on fingers, transfers to genitals, then transfers to Ingrid's lips, then to my lips! Imagine the scene, both of us scrubbing like mad to get the chillie juice off. After a few minutes of frantic scrubbing, we both managed to clear our respective lips, more or less, but my scrotum still felt like it was on fire! And Ingrid's sister and brother in law were expected any minute. I was hopping around the bedroom like a man possessed. I didn't dare touch my scrotum in case I transferred the juice once more to my hands but I couldn't stand the burning for much longer and I knew it was going to last much longer. Suddenly, I came up with an idea, although I wasn't quite sure how it would work in the presence of company. I pulled on a pair of trousers, no underpants and ran downstairs to the freezer, just as the doorbell rang. I whipped out a packet of frozen peas and shoved them down my trousers, just nestling into my crutch. I let out an involuntary yelp at the cold touch of the packet, but sat down at the table just as Ingrid's sister walked into the kitchen. Fortunately, she came over to me straight away and I only had to get halfway up to kiss her in greeting, the massive bulge from the pack of peas in my trousers thankfully still being hidden by the table top. Needless to say, I didn't stir from my allotted place all evening. Eventually, Ingrid ushered the other two into the lounge and I could retrieve the frozen peas, which by now of course were beginning to melt. So, not only did I have a nice flattering bulge in my trousers, but I also had a much less flattering wet patch all round the crutch, the sort of wet patch men get when the tap in the gents toilet is a bit fierce! Still, at least the burning had subsided! Praying that neither of our guests would walk into the kitchen just as I got up from the table, I shot upstairs and changed my trousers. I got a rather quizzical look from Ingrid's sister when I walked in to the lounge with different trousers on, but I just launched into conversation and didn't give her a chance to ask!

At around the same time, I was transferred back onto operational duty on my old team. The rest of 2000, passed off without incident.

Chapter 28

B y this time, still being operational, working on the streets, had begun to pall. There was no challenge anymore, incidents were becoming increasingly violent, shift work was sapping my energy but above all, I was seriously hacked off with my Inspector.

When I returned to the team, my old Inspector, a lovely man named Peter Laney had moved into an office job and a guy by the name of Stan Tullett had replaced him. As is normal with new people moving onto a team, his reputation preceeded him. To say that he sounded dodgy, was rather understating the situation. Apparently, he had been subject to a discipline procedure, which had culminated in his leaving the service. Rumours about Mr Tullett abounded, but I have absolutely no knowledge of the circumstances surrounding his leaving the police, and I wouldn't want to do him a dis-service. Whatever had happened, Stan Tullett somehow found himself back in the police force and eventually, re-promoted back as an Inspector. Every single officer with any amount of service above a couple of years had enough experience to know that it was highly likely that Stan's story would not be pretty and as a result, we were all just a little bit wary of him. I have to say though that Stan didn't do anybody any intentional harm or damage. It was his style that people objected to most! He was the sort of guy who would be talking on a mobile phone whilst driving and then, when he saw someone else, a member of the public doing the same thing, he would pull them over and give him or her a ticket. As a group, we sergeants tried to tell him that a lot of what he did was not conducive to good management, but he ignored us and carried on in his inimitable style.

Stan Tullett was a complete control freak; he would not allow any sergeant, much less an experienced constable to run any sort of incident without his direct control. As sergeants, we took him to task so many times about letting us run things on the streets and he always admitted that it was one of his faults to constantly want to control things. He always said that yes, we were right and he would stand back in future. For our part, we insisted that, as Inspector, he would always have overall responsibility but for goodness sake, let us do our jobs. He tended to treat us like children, always having to tell us what to do in any particular situation and never giving us the credit to run things efficiently and properly. I got really fed up with it in the end, and I had a blazing row with him in the yard at Bromley police station. He however, remained quite calm, smiling benevolently at his underling having a temper tantrum. The more I shouted at him and insulted his management style, the more he smiled and nodded agreement. I gave up and walked off, promising myself to do anything to get away from this control freak!

My second unsuccessful attempt at passing a board for Inspector occurred in early 2001. By this time, the system had changed dramatically and was known as

"The Structured Interview". Having passed the written exam in 1991, I did not have to re-sit that part. I would move directly to the second stage, where the candidate had to sit in front of two examiners, one a senior officer and the other a high ranking member of the police civilian staff. They would ask structured questions designed to test the candidate's knowledge and ability to interpret convoluted questions about subjects such as the Human Rights Act. They would often string two or three subjects together into one question and then ask for an example from your own experience. The whole interview lasted 40 minutes, four subjects, 10 minutes each, and it really was only 10 minutes. I was half way through one of my examples, when the examiner moved to the next subject and when I said I hadn't finished my example, he just looked up and said I was out of time. I felt like saying that if he'd asked me for the example earlier, I could have finished it, but that would have wasted valuable seconds, although I think had I said it, I would have felt better!

One of the examiners asked me such a complicated question, linking two or three sections of various pieces of legislation, I simply sat there and tried to work out some form of answer. It was so convoluted, it would probably never occur in real life. I was an operational, practical copper dealing with everyday problems with everyday solutions. Dealing with a ridiculously complicated, made-up scenario was something I hadn't considered. I sat there, and sat there, and sat there. Eventually, he looked up and kindly asked if I would like him to repeat the question. "Yes please" I said, not really expecting to have any better idea the second time around. I wasn't disappointed! I spluttered out an answer, which I realised later, probably had nothing whatsoever to do with the question. My only saving grace was that they didn't ask for an example; they probably thought there was little point! At that stage, I should have got my coat and left. The whole thing was quite awful for me and my feedback was dreadful. I vowed not to go through that again. Apart from anything else, I couldn't see how they could deduce someone would be a good leader from answering, (or not in my case!) complicated, theoretical questions. Yes, some candidates would answer their questions, and very well too, but could they lead a team of operational police officers?

An interesting footnote to this episode was that immediately after the interview, I went and had coffee with my friend Ian Blair, who by this time, was the Deputy Commissioner of the Metropolitan Police. He naturally asked how it went and I told him, especially about the example that was cut short and the convoluted questions. I bemoaned the fact that some people find that sort of board intimidating and wouldn't necessarily perform well on the day. (Was I trying to excuse myself, probably!)

I did however suggest that a more fair way of deciding on who to promote would be for a system of continual assessment. An officer who had been nominated, either by examination results or by Senior Management Team recommendation, could be continually assessed over a period of about 12 months on a range of competencies. Ian just nodded and smiled. A couple of years later, lo and behold, a new system of selecting officers for promotion was introduced called "Towbar". Essentially, officers are assessed continually for a year on various competencies! Now, I don't for one minute propose that it was my suggestion that prompted the change, these changes are often years in the planning but it does show that I was at least on the right wavelength.

A few weeks after the feedback on the ill-fated "structured interview" had arrived, I was walking along a corridor in Orpington police station, past the Chief Superintendent's office when suddenly the door opened and the "boss" came out. "Ah, Neil" he boomed, "just the man. Come into the office, I want to talk about your interview and manage your disappointment." The Chief Superintendent, Gerry Howlett was an absolute gentleman, a good copper but more importantly for a man in his position, a good manager. He was a big man with a big booming voice that one didn't ignore. Once inside his office, we talked about the interview and the feedback. I told him about the example which had been cut short and he also agreed that that was unfair, but all in all, we agreed that I hadn't performed well on the day and didn't deserve to pass. He didn't say that I didn't deserve to be an Inspector and encouraged me to carry on trying.

Whilst in with the boss, I took the opportunity to ask something which had been on my mind for a while. When officers get to a certain age and level of service, they can ask to come off working night duties. In my particular case, it wasn't the actual night-duties that were affecting me, it was the aftermath. Anyone who has worked shifts a lot will tell you that they completely muck up your body clock; you're awake when you should be asleep and asleep when you should be awake. I have never been able to sleep well during the day, three or four hours at most. We worked seven nights from 10pm till 6am. On the day we finished nights at 6am, we went home to sleep as much as possible but then had to be back on duty at 2pm the same day for a late shift. The reason for this was because if we started our days off immediately after finishing nights, our first day off would be spent sleeping, so we worked the extra shift on the last day. We would then have three days off and on the fourth day, we would be back to work for a week of early shifts, starting at 6am. This was what was killing me and had been for a number of years. I was really feeling the effects of these shifts, weak and always tired. I knew it wasn't doing me any good whatsoever, so, as I was old enough and had the requisite service, I decided to ask the boss to come off nights. "No," he said quite emphatically. He explained that he didn't have the manpower to let one person off nights as, if he gave it to me, others would ask and he would be obliged to give it to them. I argued that each case would have to be decided on its merits and it wouldn't necessarily mean giving it to everyone who asked, but he was adamant. "OK," I said, "how about I only do four nights a week?" "No, for the same reason." "OK," I said, "how about instead of doing normal nights at 10pm to 6am, I do a shift from 6pm till 2am. That way, I explained, I could get the right amount of sleep and be better prepared for the rigours of street work. He promised that he would look into this suggestion and I left the office quite hopeful. He had also asked me about how I would like to receive my "Long Service and Good Conduct" medal, which is awarded to officers with a clean disciplinary record and who had a total of 22 years service. I said I would like to receive it from him. I had always had a good relationship with Gerry Howlett and we were laughing together about just how late my medal was when I left the office. The cheery mood however was soon to disappear.

As I left the office, a colleague sergeant of mine was waiting for me outside. He pressed a note into my hand and told me that I had to ring my Auntie Rene, mother's sister in Weston-super-Mare, urgently! The laughter disappeared and a feeling of dread flooded in. The telephone number on the note was mum's. My Auntie had never contacted me before and deep down, I knew what the call was about; something had obviously happened to mum.

I wasn't wrong! I telephoned Rene from an empty office and through the tears and chokes, I learned that my mother had died the previous night. Rene was due to go around to meet mum and stroll into town that morning and when she couldn't get an answer at the door, she called the warden of the flats where she was living. Together, they went in and found mum sitting on the couch, semi-naked, but with some bed clothes on. She was either getting ready to go to bed, or had just risen for the morning. They called for a para-medic, who figured she had probably died the previous evening from heart failure. It would have been very quick, they explained. Heart failure is different from a heart attack. Put simply, the heart just gives up, stops working, and death occurs seconds after. She had always had heart problems, not big ones, just little murmurs now and again and when her doctor arrived at the flat, he concurred with the para-medics and wrote the death certificate accordingly.

The date was 8th March 2001, the day before my 50th birthday!

Fortunately, I had made no arrangements for a party etc but I didn't really figure on spending my birthday at the Registrar's office in Weston, registering mum's death.

As usual, the senior officers at the police station had been very decent and allowed me as much time as I needed to deal with everything including the funeral. Lynne had been informed by me before I left for Weston and I expected her a few days later.

When she arrived at Heathrow, I was there to meet her. We had never been a close family, mum and dad both found visiting Lynne and Dave in Australia a bit of a strain, purely because they weren't used to their ways. However, Lynne was visibly upset when she arrived. I think the realisation that both parents were now dead was hitting home, and that there was just her and me left. I don't know whether she felt a degree of loneliness, but I certainly felt that with Lynne in Australia, I was on my own. I know I have some relatives left here and I do have great feelings for them, but having no immediate family left anywhere near seemed to create a void in my life. I think, to a certain extent, we all take our parents and siblings for granted. We don't think they will be around forever, but then, neither do we think that at some stage, they won't. The gulf between Lynne and I was highlighted over breakfast one morning at the hotel we were staying at for the duration. Not having seen her for a few years, I was asking some questions about her and David and of course, Thomas. I didn't think they were particularly invasive, but Lynne suddenly turned on me, demanding to know why I was asking and what I really wanted to know. For my part, I reacted angrily towards her, telling her that I was her brother for goodness sake, not to treat me as a nosy stranger and that I merely wanted to know more about her life. She was slightly mollified afterwards, but thereafter, relations between us were strained. I think we both tried hard to get on with each other, but under the circumstances, it was an effort.

After registering mum's death and getting the certificates, we set about sorting out her effects at her flat. Of course, Auntie Rene and cousins Cathy and Julie, who all lived in Weston, were always on hand to give some help, although Rene's "help" resulted in the destruction of my old yellow mug which was given to me as a present, forty three years earlier. Apparently, because it was cracked and had been repaired, she thought the charity shop wouldn't accept it. True, tragic, but true! It ended its long life in the rubbish bin!

Mum's death hit Julie particularly hard. They were very close, always going on holiday together, and at one stage, they nearly bought a house together so that they could be close to each other. There were many occasions when Julie and mum would get a bus to one of the Kent ports and take a few days in France. When they returned, Mum would be loaded down with cheap cigarettes. This was in the days before the restrictions on duty-free goods were relaxed, and if she had ever been stopped by Customs, she would have had a hard time convincing the ever-suspicious officers that this mother-lode of fags was for her own consumption!

I'm sure mum saw Julie as a sort of surrogate daughter she very definitely connected with. As for Julie, I think she just enjoyed mum's company, her outlook on life and her infinite capacity for fun and laughter. I think in all fairness, Julie loved my mother in a way that her own daughter, being so far away, could not. I think mum craved that love and responded to Julie accordingly.

My own relationship with mum changed dramatically over the years following dad's death. I say "dramatically" because for me, it was totally unexpected. I had always been closer to dad in life than my mother. In my growing years and into my teens, it was dad who had had the most effect on me. It was dad's influence that gave me my values, such as they were. Of course, in my teens, whatever dad, or mum come to that, said to me about life and how I should live it, didn't mean that much to me at the time. But later on, in my twenties, thirties and later, I remembered what had been said and the example they had both tried to set for me. As I got older, these values became ever more important to me, but it was always the memories of what dad had said to me that remained with me the most, by far the most.

During the last years of his life, tragically, I came to realise that I hadn't spent anywhere near as much time with him as either he or I would have wanted. It's all very well saying that we weren't a close family, that's a fact, but it's no reason why a mother, father and son don't spend quality time together. Lynne was out of the equation, living in Australia. When dad passed away, my focus turned entirely towards my mother, not unnaturally I suppose. But I didn't expect it, never having had the same feelings towards her as I had had for dad.

I had begun to travel down to Wales where mum and dad were living far more frequently than I had before, to see both of them of course, but mainly, if I'm honest, to spend time with dad, pottering about with him in the garden, helping him with painting, playing bowls or even just taking him down to the pub for a drink. As I sit and write this now, the thought occurs to me, just how did mum feel about this? It was obvious that I was spending time with dad, did she feel left out at all, or was she just grateful that at least I was there visiting them both? I will never know, but suddenly, all the effort I had been putting in with dad, was transferred to mum. I'm quite certain it wasn't a case of feeling sorry for her now that she was on her own, I genuinely felt closer to her, and even more strangely, closer than I had felt to dad when he was alive. Does that happen to everyone who loses one or other parent? I don't know, but I began to see my mother in a totally different light. We had many a long chat over the following months and years and I learned a lot more about her and dad. For instance, she told me that she didn't actually want to move back to Wales when dad retired, she would rather have moved somewhere more central, somewhere in the countryside. She only went to Wales because dad persuaded her and he only wanted to go to Wales because he wanted to be nearer his best friend, Harold. Harold's wife Winnie and my mother were friends, but I don't think they were really close friends, like Harold and dad. On another occasion mum told me that she had tried to persuade dad to buy an open-top sports car, something they could both enjoy in their early retirement. Apparently, dad had poo-pooed the idea simply on the basis of the cost of insurance. The real reason was more likely to be that dad would have seen this as 'taking a chance'. He was always more reserved than mum and usually went for the safe option, in this case a Nissan Cherry!

She had no real love for the bungalow they were living in near Bridgend, it was right next to the main West Coast railway line where trains thundered past every 15 or 20 minutes or so, a real and actual conversation stopper, and it had a bloody great electricity pylon in the back garden, which crackled and fizzed alarmingly in bad weather. On top of that, the rear wall of the bungalow, which was painted white, was constantly bombarded with bird excrement in the summer. There were miles and miles of hedgerows around the bungalow, all with blackberry brambles and during the summer, the birds ate the blackberries and then as they flew around the bungalow, excreting as they went, they deposited dollops of reddish-purple crap all over the wall. It was as though they used it for target practice. Every summer, dad had to re-paint the entire wall. There was a small patio in front of the wall but you couldn't sit out on the patio in summer in case one of the birds' aims was slightly amiss! On reflection, I can see why mum didn't really go for the bungalow, but like a dutiful wife, she put up with it. However, as soon as dad died, the bungalow was up for sale and mum was determined then to go and live in Weston-super-Mare. It was now her turn to be nearer someone, her sister Rene.

She moved at first to a two-bedroomed flat on the second floor of a purpose-built block, on a hillside overlooking Weston bay. I say "overlooking", but you could just about see the pier in the distance, between the houses on the other side of the road, and the bay was only visible by tall people standing on tip-toe. Mum was only 5'6", so she had a problem with this. She was quite happy at first, spending about two years there, but she then had a problem with the fact that she couldn't look out of her lounge and watch the people walking by. It was "boring" she explained, and so that flat was sold, and she moved to a smaller, ground floor, one bedroomed warden controlled flat situated right on one of the main roads into Weston town, with her lounge facing the road. The whole of one wall was taken up with a patio-style window, so at last, she could sit in her lounge and watch all the characters passing in front of her little flat. Many is the time, we would be chatting in the lounge and she would break off the conversation to point out some person or other whom she had noted previously for some little oddity about them. When she wasn't watching them out of her window, she and Rene could often be found sitting on a bench on Weston seafront, just watching the world go by! She really loved her little flat, and this, of course is where she died.

One of the first things I did when I got down to Weston was to find out where the ambulance crew was based. Rene told me that when they arrived at the flat, they were comfort itself to her. They stayed with her for some time, during which, she told them that I would coming straight down to Weston from London. Passing away, half dressed, on the sofa, was not very dignified for mum. Despite the fact that mum was obviously dead, the ambulance crew picked her up and gently put her in her bed, covering her with her duvet. They did this for my benefit. When I arrived, the crew had gone but I found mum looking very peaceful in her bedroom, where I was able to spend a few minutes with her on my own, saying goodbye.

The actions of the crew touched me because I know that generally, when they attend an address where the person is dead, they don't tend to stay around. There's nothing they can do for the deceased, so once the death certificate is signed, they leave. This isn't from any lack of caring attitude, far from it. It's simply because they're so busy, they have to get on with answering other emergency calls. And they certainly don't pick up the bodies and put them to bed. This crew kindly stayed around, helped Rene and were sensitive enough to think that I might want to see mum in a more dignified pose.

After registering her death, I went in search of the ambulance crew. I had the address of the depot they were from, coincidentally only a few hundred yards from the house we used to live in before we moved out to Mark. At the depot, I spoke to a female ambulance person, who confirmed that she and her male colleague had attended mum's flat. She was looking at me rather suspiciously, possible expecting me to say something other than a sincere "thank you" for the way they treated mum and Rene. I got the impression they didn't get many people thanking them for their actions. In London, they seem to get more criticism for their attendance times and smacks from drunken louts than praise and thanks for the job they do.

The next days were taken up with arranging for the funeral and going through mum's belongings. I was joint executor for her will, but as nothing had been heard from the other executor for many years, I figured I'd be doing it on my own, which wasn't a bother to me. Lynne and I decided that we would donate any good clothes to the charity shops, and dump those clothes clearly too worn for resale. This included her underwear, a batch of which I discovered in a linen basket in the bathroom. I suggested that Lynne should sort out this as I felt it unseemly to be rifling through my mother's underwear! I concentrated on her bureau, where she kept all her papers including long-forgotten insurance policies. I discovered one that her mother had taken out for her when she was a toddler. Infant mortality was high in the early part of the 1900's and people often took out small insurance policies to cover the cost of unexpected child death funerals. This particular policy was 'fully paid up', which meant that although it was still valid, no contributions had been made for years. Later, when I contacted the insurance company to cash it in., I received the princely sum of £13!

I was still going through the bureau when Lynne suddenly called me into the bathroom to check out something she had found. She held up a plastic bag full of old Diazepan tablets in their bottles, which had been hidden right at the bottom of the basket and covered with layers of clothing. There must have been a couple of dozen bottles in there. "What on earth do you think she had all these for," Lynne asked, not unreasonably. As soon as I saw them, I knew exactly why mum had them.

I had forgotten all about what she had said to me a few years earlier, but seeing the tablets jolted my memory. I took Lynne by the hand and took her into the lounge where I sat down with her and explained mum's "plan". I remembered we had been chatting about her health during one of my visits to her. Mum was blessed, or cursed depending on your point of view, with a direct way of saying things. Although it hadn't ever crossed my mind what might happen to her if she ever became infirm, she was always in such rude health, she suddenly turned to me and said, "you won't ever have to worry about me Neil! I will never come to live with you, I will never go and live with Lynne, I will never go into hospital and I will never go and live in one of those awful homes where people sit out the rest of their lives in armchairs." I thought about this for a while and then said, "well, mum, that doesn't really leave an awful lot of choice left." "Ah," she said, "I've got a plan!" With all the possible places to live being ruled out, I realized what she was saying. She would have taken her own life. I looked at her, but she just smiled at me and squeezed my hand, "Don't worry," she repeated. I knew then that she was absolutely serious about what she had in mind. I had no idea how she would do it, but I did know that she would do exactly as she had said. My mother was nothing if not single-minded! Although I was fairly convinced that I had guessed the "plan", something inside me told me not to delve any deeper. I made a conscious decision to push the matter to the back of my mind and deal with it later, if it ever happened.

It still troubles me today that I never asked her any other questions about her "plan." Should I have tried to talk her out of it, should I have insisted she came to live with me if that time ever came, should I have spoken with Rene about it? All these questions have troubled me since her death. Did I do less than I should have as a human being, let alone her only son? I knew that she wouldn't have changed her plan, but it troubles me that I didn't at least try.

This big bag of pills then was the "plan." She would have taken her own life if she felt unable to cope with pain or with life itself. I suppose it sounds really quite sad, but mother was mother, pragmatic and dogged to the end. She was determined not to be a burden to anyone and absolutely hated the thought of someone having to care for her, wash her, help her with her toilet etc etc. Having set her mind on her course of action should it be necessary, she accumulated the pills over the years from various prescriptions from the doctor.

I explained all this to Lynne, who listened very intently to what I was saying. When I had finished, she sat staring straight ahead for about half a minute. I was afraid at one stage that she would break down, but she just turned to me and told me she understood. We talked about it for a little longer and all the while, Lynne was more and more accepting that if mum was so unselfish as to hatch her plan, then who were we to say anything detrimental about it or her? We decided to flush all the pills down the toilet and not to tell Rene about what we knew, that would have been terrible for Rene to accept. Do I think she had carried out her plan? No, definitely not, there was no need. She wasn't infirm or in pain, she was enjoying her life in the place she loved most. And the fact that the pills were still hidden when Lynne found them clinched it. Both Lynne and I knew that she had not taken her life.

We continued to sort through her belongings and paperwork over the next couple of days with me making the arrangements for her funeral and inviting family and friends. One day, a card arrived on the door-mat. There had been so many delivered over the previous days that I took scant notice of this one until I noticed that it was addressed to me personally with a London postmark. When I opened it, I was astonished to find that it was from the entire Senior Management Team at my police station in Bromley. Every member of the team had personally signed the card with a few words of sympathy from the "boss", Chief Superintendent Howlett. Lynne had been included in the interior address and we were both very touched by this simple act. When I returned to the station, the first thing I did was to go straight to Mr. Howlett and thank him on behalf of my family. I had no doubt that the card was instigated by the Chief Superintendent, showing that not only was he able to provide support for me but also that he had a very human side which he was not afraid to demonstrate. It was only a minor act I know, but knowing long-service police officers as I do, I know that showing a degree of care for another is not always something they are good at.

The choice of undertakers for the funeral was an easy one. Mum had chosen to live next-door to one! She used to joke that "when my time comes, don't bother with a coffin, just pass me over the wall!" The staff at the undertakers all knew mum, as they knew all the residents of the flats and they were kindness personified. As with dad's funeral arrangements, I had lots of help from them and everything went along very smoothly. However, the time eventually came around when Lynne, Rene and I had to discuss what would happen to mum's ashes. She had directed that she be cremated and so a burial was not an option. From the moment I knew we would have to discuss this, I knew what I wanted to do with her ashes. It seemed to me to be the perfect way to mark the end of "mum and dad". Neither Rene nor Lynne had given it much thought at that point, so I suggested that we, as a family including Rene, Uncle Frank, and cousins Ginnie, Catherine, Julie and Jackie scatter her ashes onto the waters of the River Severn, which forms the Weston bay area. The reader may remember that dad had been "buried at sea" in a Naval service and by scattering mum's ashes on the water, we would be symbolically joining them in a single grave. Thankfully, both Lynne and Rene thought it was a very fitting idea and Rene went further to suggest that we scatter the ashes, not from Weston pier as I had thought, but from Clevedon pier, a few miles up the coast from Weston. This was one of mum's favourite places and as an added bonus, we could contribute to the pier restoration fund by purchasing a small brass plaque in her memory and affixing it to one of the many pier seats. I thought this was a fine suggestion.

It would fall to me at the funeral, to deliver a eulogy for mum. I thought very carefully about what I would say and eventually had the basis of a short speech worked out. But I didn't want to leave it there! Mum had always had a zest for life, a zest somewhat dampened by the over-cautious attitude adopted by dad. However, one of her favourite pastimes was simply sitting down somewhere and watching the world go by. I wanted to pay homage to her attitude to life and began to search through a book of poems I had been given by a friend. I found the perfect one! It seemed so perfect, I could almost deliver the poem alone, without adding any words of my own. It seemed to sum up mum to a tee! However, I worked on adding a short eulogy, basing it on how mum liked to live her life.

The service was held in the local crematorium with lots of friends and relatives, some of whom I hadn't seen for years and some I didn't even know. For example, a woman approached me after the service and introduced herself as the daughter of one of mum's distant cousins who lived in Camarthen, west Wales. I had no idea who she was, mum had never mentioned she had family over there, but apparently, they exchanged letters every now and then. I remember there were some names in her address book that I didn't recognize, she was probably one of these. I had telephoned so many people over the previous days, I couldn't possibly remember them all.

The service was short and simple. I started my eulogy by reading the poem I had selected,

"Leisure"

"What is this life, if full of care,
We have no time to stand and stare?

No time to stand beneath the boughs,
And stare as long as sheep or cows.

No time to see, when woods we pass,
Where squirrels hide their nuts in grass.

No time to see, in broad daylight,
Streams full of stars, like skies at night.

No time to turn at beauty's glance,
And watch her feet, how they can dance.

No time to wait till her mouth can
Enrich that smile her eyes began.

A poor life this if, full of care,
We have no time to stand and stare.
                    W.H. Davies.

I could find no other poem which seemed to epitomize mum's attitude to life. She loved to sit and watch people passing by, she loved to watch the waves coming ashore, she loved to do the simple things in life such as rummaging through old boxes at boot fairs, looking for a bargain! If she found something, she liked nothing better than to argue the price with the vendor, smiling all the time.

She wasn't as academically gifted as dad was, but her other life-qualities set her apart from him. I loved them both, but I have to say that mum's take on life was far nearer to my own. I still miss them both, but I especially miss my mother!

Strangely enough, I wasn't anywhere near as nervous as I was when I had spoken at dad's funeral, the words seemed to flow out of me, crisp and clear. I seemed to be completely relaxed, as though mum's hand was on my shoulder, steadying me! I ended the eulogy by asking the congregation to remember mum with a smile, as that is how she would have remembered them!

Lynne and I had hired some rooms in a small local hotel on the seafront for the "wake". Most people came and chatted with Lynne and I. Jackie was there as well, which was slightly awkward, but nothing either of us couldn't handle. Thankfully, she went back to Cornwall as soon as she could manage. When it was all over, Lynne and I gratefully returned to our hotel, to our separate rooms and our separate thoughts.

The following day, the family re-gathered at mum's flat. I went next door to the undertakers to collect mum's ashes as arranged. On handing the urn over to me, the undertaker gave me a dire warning. I suppose that because we had chosen not to inter mum in the consecrated grounds of the crematorium, the undertaker, quite rightly assumed we had other plans. He warned me that to simply inter the ashes anywhere other than a place registered for such interment, a cemetery for example, was against the law. I took this to mean that if we did anything to do with disposal of the ashes apart from placing them in consecrated ground, we would be committing an offence. Not wishing to expose this kind and helpful man to something which now looked increasingly illegal, I simply looked back at him and told him we had made no plans at that stage for the urn. I'm not sure he believed me, but he appeared happy with this, we shook hands and he wished me luck.

I went back to the group in the flat and told them that what we were planning was possibly illegal. After discussing the issue for some time, we were all agreed that as the authorities were not likely to slap us in jail, we would plead ignorance if caught and take the consequences. We decided that as Lynne was due to return to Australia a few days hence, we would take the urn to Clevedon Pier the following day.

The entrance to the pier is through a small souvenir shop, which also houses the ticket desk. This is properly known as the Toll House. A building opposite the entrance used to house the Pier Master. The pier itself is a beautifully elegant construction of iron girders rising from the water level to hemi-spherical shaped supports under the wood planking. It stretches approximately 300 yards out into the Severn Estuary, ending in a pagoda-style building with a stairway leading down to the water's edge, from where paddle steamers used to embark and arrive from the Welsh coast. It is still possible today to take a pleasure-steamer from the pier to explore the Somerset coastline.

The pier was finished in 1869 and lasted over 100 years before, in 1970, two spans collapsed into the sea, effectively ending use of this superb piece of Victorian engineering. The local population however, had other ideas. If it wasn't for them, the pier would have decayed and rusted in the salt water, eventually being demolished and sold ignominiously for scrap. The decision was taken to try and save the pier, and through intense lobbying of influential persons, fundraising and sheer hard work, the pier was finally restored to its former glory in 1998.

Part of the fundraising campaign involved the sale of small commemorative brass plaques which could be let into the wooden planking of the walkway or set into one of the many benches along the sides of the pier. Walking along the pier, one can see the many thousands of brass plaques purchased to remember deceased relatives. In 2001, just before mum passed away, the pier was re-classified as a Grade 1 Listed Building, the only pier in the country to receive such a title. Seaside piers are a unique feature of British life and it is fitting that a beautiful and historic construction such as Clevedon Pier should receive this important accolade.

Our little group arrived at the Toll House around 2pm the following day. There was myself, Lynne, Auntie Rene and cousins Catherine and Julie. My other cousins Ginnie and Jackie had returned home and Rene's husband, Frank was ill in bed. I carried the urn in a supermarket bag so as not to attract any attention, but from our appearance, it was obvious we were a family group intent on doing something. I strode confidently over to the pay desk and asked for 5 adult entries. The lady behind the desk, eyed me suspiciously, looked at the others in the group and finally rested her eyes on my carrier bag. I probably began to sweat a little at that stage! She then fixed her eyes back on me and asked in a stern voice, "Are you here to do what I think you're here to do?" It was obvious then that we were undone, the master-plan shattered, so I simply blurted out, "It was our mother's last wish!" Not quite true I know, but it seemed appropriate. "Oh, that's OK then," she said smilingly, "we don't charge for these little occasions, go straight through!" The collective release of breath from all of us could probably have been detected down the coast in Weston! Although slightly puzzled, we thanked her profusely and as we passed through, she said, "Just ask the fishermen to move if they're in the way." What a helpful lady! We wandered down to the end of the pier where, sure enough, men were fishing in the estuary. I didn't even have to tell them what we were doing, they knew, and politely and unobtrusively, they withdrew to a respectful distance.

So this was it, the time had arrived. Lynne and I stood very close to each other whilst the others stood just a little apart from us. We looked over into the muddy waters of the Severn Estuary and I unscrewed the top of the urn. I said, "Well mum, this is goodbye, we love you and dad. Now go to join him." As I said these words, I tipped the ashes from the urn over the side of the pier. They were immediately caught by the wind and blown out over the estuary. I put my arm around Lynne and she inclined her head onto my shoulder as we watched the cloud of ashes disappearing into nothing. "It's just you and me now," I said, and she just nodded. I am quite a spiritual person, but I am more emotional. Tears were streaming down my face as I looked out into the estuary.

All five of us walked slowly back down the pier, taking in the rocky coastline of this part of Somerset. In the distance I could see the magnificent Second Severn Bridge. Finished in 1996, the second Severn crossing struck me as a complete contrast to the pier I was standing on; modern as opposed to old, vehicular not pedestrian, concrete as opposed to iron and wood, massive and robust rather than small and delicate. I think the only common feature between them is that they are both superb examples of elegant design and engineering.

When we finally reached the Toll House, I spoke again to the kind lady who showed us through. I asked about the fact that we were there to spread some ashes, which as far as I knew was against the law. She told me that she had come across this little problem many times before. She told me the law applied only to "interment" and not to disposing of ashes into the atmosphere or over water. I remembered that the undertaker had mentioned "interment" and realized that the law was aimed at burying the ashes in the ground or in a tomb, "interment"!

As we left, I took details of how to apply for a commemorative brass plaque. It cost £80, which I was happy to pay and the plaque to mum is now set into one of the benches along the side of the pier. Occasionally, Rene, Julie, Catherine and her husband Brian and myself have lunch in Clevedon and go for a wander along the pier to say hello to mum and sit on her bench.

Over the following months, I dealt with mum's estate. I found the whole process fairly straightforward and came across very few problems. I think this was because I adopted the attitude that I accepted the bureaucracy surrounding the world of probate and that I simply let it take its course. I was in no hurry to settle mum's estate, I had warned Lynne that it would take months before I sent her inheritance to her. Like me, she wasn't bothered how long it took. So I just sent off the paperwork as necessary and waited for the replies. Eventually, it all came together, probate was granted and I could tie up all the loose ends

It was towards the end of the year that the estate was settled, but 2001 had not finished with me.

Chapter 29

When I finally returned to work after mum's funeral, some wheels had obviously been grinding in my absence. I found that I had been taken off shift work and street duty and had been placed in a unit called at that time, the Custody and Arrest Support Team, CAST for short, at Bromley police station. The other bonus point about this move was that I was finally free of Inspector Stan Tullett and his controlling manner.

CAST was first pioneered in the Kent Constabulary and basically it is a system of prisoner handling. Over the previous 20 years or so, paperwork surrounding the processing of prisoners arrested for offences on the streets had increased to a burdensome degree. It could take a constable anything up to 6 or 7 hours to complete even the paperwork necessary for a rudimentary initial interview and charge. This of course, meant that the constable was not patrolling back out on the streets where he or she was supposed to be. The CAST took over the initial investigation from the arresting officer and completed the paperwork all the way up to presentation to the Crown Prosecution Service for consideration for placing the person before the courts. CAST took over the taking of statements from witnesses, interviewing the suspect(s), submission of articles to the Forensic Service, the writing of reports to the CPS, the charging of suspects, etc etc. Some cases could take months to come to fruition, time which the street constables could not afford.

The Kent prisoner handling model was brought to Bromley by a female Chief Inspector. This woman was the only senior officer I had ever sworn at in sheer anger and frustration. It was the first time I had used a new computer-based procedure for booking in prisoners. I was trying to process a prisoner arrested for burglary when she waltzed into the charge room and kept on interrupting, asking the arresting officer questions when he was supposed to be telling me what the evidence was against the suspect, a very important legal requirement. Eventually, I asked her to be quiet and let me do my job. I told her she could speak to the officer later. She wasn't amused by this and then told me off for not wearing my tie on duty in the station. Big deal!! I told her I would get it after I had completed the process. She was obviously very miffed that somebody actually had the effrontery to challenge her in public and seized on the chance to reprimand me, also in public, for not wearing my tie!

I was later summoned to her office and she had despatched my Inspector at that time, to escort me there! This really got me fired up! In her office, I refused point blank to sit down and discuss the issue of my tie, telling her that it was all "f…….. bollocks". I said a few other things which weren't complimentary about her competency as a senior officer and only obeyed my Inspector to remain in the room and listen to her trying to tell me how to behave. I only spoke once more after that, to

369

ask whether she had "finished?" I slammed the door on the way out and rarely spoke to the woman again.

Anyway, back to CAST! When I was transferred, I replaced one sergeant and joined another on the unit, and between the two of us, we supervised sixteen constables. They were mostly long serving and very capable officers who made the job of the sergeants, relatively easy. Our main task was to ensure that the case files prepared by the constables were complete with sufficient evidence to prove the case and with all the necessary forms present.

The unit was housed on the second floor of a building next-door to the police station, in some of the worst office accommodation I have ever seen. The space we had was nowhere large enough; the paint was peeling off the walls and one day, the stairs collapsed through dry-rot. This office was where we had the annual fly infestation I have previously described. The offices were far too hot in summer and not warm enough in winter. As if this wasn't enough, some busybody from Health and Safety decided that there was a danger that one of us might simply give up and hurl him or herself from one of the windows, down to the busy street below, making a terrible mess into the bargain!. A workman arrived one day and fixed bars to the windows so that they wouldn't open more than a few inches. A question about whether we would get ventilation from some air conditioning or perhaps a fan in summer, was met with a shrug and a simple stare of, "I don't give a toss, mate!"

A few months after joining CAST, the other sergeant on the unit left to go back to the CID. By this time, I had really begun to enjoy the work. I was getting involved in cases myself and thoroughly enjoyed the task of reading through the case files for the evidence. Occasionally, I would have a jousting session with one of the CPS lawyers on a point of evidence; sometimes I won, sometimes I lost but I always enjoyed the argument.

At this time, the unit was administered by the CID and when my colleague left, the Chief Inspector posted a female sergeant into the unit. She simply didn't want to be there and I didn't want to work with her. She was a dyed-in-the-wool CID officer, greatly experienced, but who thought the low-level crime CAST dealt with, was beneath her. The Chief Inspector spoke to me one day about general staffing problems in the main CID office. This was definitely a hint from him and I took the opportunity to suggest that my colleague was too qualified to work in my unit and that she would be better utilized in the main CID office. There wasn't a fight, and she was transferred the next day. It did mean however, that I would be the only supervising officer until a replacement for her was found.

I ran the unit myself for the next two years. The unit was set up under the supervision of a uniformed Chief Inspector, later changed to C.I.D. supervision, then changed back to uniform supervision. Later, the structure was changed yet again, back to the CID and three other newly promoted sergeants from the CID were drafted in. However, in that two years, I really feel I made a name for myself within Bromley and beyond. I received many requests for information on how the unit was run and for visits from other boroughs thinking about setting up prisoner handling units, to be allowed. On a relatively small scale, I became a bit of an expert on case files, prisoner handling and evidence. When I say "expert", I mean that my knowledge vastly outweighed that of other officers from the uniform side, including senior officers. I was often asked to look at cases which, for some reason had achieved notoriety in order that senior officers could speak from a position of strength to say, the press or to council officials, knowing that the case was evidentially sound.

Just after we moved to the new police station in Bromley high street, my unit, CAST was re-structured and given a new title, the Case Progression Unit. We did more or less the same work except that this time, the unit was totally under the control of the Detective Chief Inspector. The change was "met-wide" and came under the title of "Operation Emerald", designed to have closer links with the CPS, courts, witness liaison and various other bodies connected to the Criminal Justice System.

The sergeants were all meant to be detectives and detective constables were meant to have been incorporated in to the four CPU teams. There was absolutely no chance of the latter happening. The CPU teams were still made up of uniform constables and the detective constables objected so strongly to having to work with what they termed, "woodentops", that the Detective Chief Inspector shelved the idea at Bromley. I felt this was a real slap in the face for uniformed constables and demonstrated very weak leadership. Officers transferring to the CID from uniform are often persuaded by their new colleagues that the transfer is in fact, a step up the ladder, away from uniform duties. It isn't the case; the work is different, that's all. The sergeants, however had no option; they were newly promoted and easily saw that it was in their best interests to obey the Chief Inspector without a fight. Me, they left there because of my expertise, or so they told me and because I was getting close to retirement. I was perfectly happy with this arrangement. After so many years of not really enjoying my work, I had found something which suited me to a tee, interested me greatly and which I was good at.

In the latter half of 2001, I received a surprise phone call from an old colleague of mine from the 'Drifters' safari company in Johannesburg, Heiko Gelaitis, or as he announced himself at that time, Heiko Genzmer. He had decided to name himself after his mother rather than his father. I never asked!! I had seen Heiko on a few occasions when I went back to Drifters on various visits to South Africa, but we had lost touch for a number of years prior to this phone call. He told me he and another guide from the old firm, Marc Germiquet had formed their own safari company, Bush Ways, operating out of Maun in Botswana. Situated at the very edge of the Okavango Delta, what better place to start or finish a safari in Africa than Maun? In the space of about 25 years, Maun has exploded from being a run-down, frontier-type settlement to a rapidly expanding, modernizing and bustling town with good communications and hotels, which it owes in large part to the completion of the tar-road from Nata in the early 90's, not long before I took my first safari to Botswana. I used to cross the old dirt road from Nata to Maun to get on to the Makgadikgadi Salt Pan. The journey on that old road used to take at least two days, the road was so bad. These days however, on the modern tarred road, it takes around three hours.

Maun is the capitol town for the Batawana people of the region and the population is now around 30,000. It spreads itself along the Thamalakane River, where all manner of livestock wanders aimlessly around, in and out of the river. Although it is rapidly coming into the 21st century, there are still places where you can envisage how Maun used to be in the old days. 'Herero' women still walk the streets of Maun, dressed in the traditional huge, billowing, Victorian-style dresses with headgear shaped in the form of a cow's horns. Cows used to be the sole indicator of a man's wealth in many parts of Africa, including Botswana. The Herero people had come to Botswana from Namibia, then German South West Africa, following a war with the German colonial authority over cattle and land, and as a result of that war in 1904, the Herero people were "forbidden" to return to Namibia by a German governor, and so settled in Botswana. The cow-horn style of headdress and huge dresses worn by the women, are a living reminder of the fate of the Herero people. In Maun, it always seems odd to see a brand new BMW motor car passing a woman in the street, dressed as if she is living a century before.

During our conversation, Heiko mentioned that he and Marc now owned a lodge on the outskirts of Livingstone in Zambia, called Lost Horizons. He explained that they both thought that expanding into the lodge side of the safari experience would be a good thing for Bush Ways.

Since the time that I was running safaris into Victoria Falls for Drifters, the Mugabe regime in Zimbabwe had so decimated the leisure industry in that town, that practically all the companies offering extreme pursuits such as rafting, and bungee jumping from Victoria Falls, had transferred all their activities to Livingstone. The two towns, although in different countries, are only 10 kilometres apart, geographically. Demographically however, the towns couldn't be further apart. Whilst Victoria Falls has fallen into a steep and irrevocable decline, Livingstone has exploded. The new businesses that have started there over the last 10 years or so has meant that the population has expanded at a phenomenal rate. New housing has sprung up all over the town; new supermarkets, petrol filling stations, hotels, restaurants and most of all, new and relatively luxurious hotels and lodges have all demanded staff. People from all over Zambia gravitate to Livingstone, to find work in the ever burgeoning leisure industry.

Although I didn't know it at the time, the conversation I had with Heiko on this day was to mark my eventual return to the safari industry. More immediately however, as Heiko was describing the lodge at Lost Horizons, I began to think that I could take some holiday and go down to the lodge. He told me how the premises needed some work doing to it, small painting jobs here, a bit of brickwork there and maybe some carpentry somewhere. There was a group of workers already at the lodge, but as usual, Heiko wasn't confident they would be doing what they were supposed to be doing. Marc's sister Michelle was running the lodge at that time and I just mentioned to Heiko that maybe I could go down and help with the jobs. He agreed immediately. There was no way he intended for me to volunteer, but he sounded relieved when I asked him if I could go. Thinking about it later, I remember being slightly nervous about revisiting the place where I had had such a narrow escape from the Marxist officials in the town. I did however decide that things had probably changed by then, and I was right.

By this time, Chris and Karen, my two friends from the mission farm at Sachibondu, were living in a rented house just outside Lusaka, the capitol of Zambia. Chris was working as the manager of a slaughter house, where the hides of the slaughtered cows were sent off to another farm owned by the same man for tanning into workable leather. I stayed a few days with them before taking the bus down to Livingstone, where Michelle would pick me up and take me out to the lodge. The roads hadn't improved much by then and nor had the buses. I remember the 500 kilometre journey being very long and bumpy, and arriving in Livingstone around 8pm, not a good idea. There were plenty of unsavoury characters hanging around the bus terminus at that time of night, just looking for an innocent tourist to rip off. Being quite tall and well built, I don't think I was too much of a target but all the same, I was quite relieved when Michelle eventually pitched up and drove me out to the lodge. We drove quite far outside the town, towards the border with Zimbabwe and then along some sand tracks and eventually, into a gated compound. I must admit I was pretty tired by this time and simply went to bed in the chalet that had been prepared for me.

The next morning, I started to have a look around. The lodge was sited in a fabulous spot, on a hillside overlooking the Zambezi valley. The main building had a large open dining/lounge area with a small bar and terrace. Below this, was a large lawn area with a fire pit at the bottom. Either side of the main area, was where the chalets were sited, around 12 in all and each of them looked out over the valley. Oddly enough, the kitchen was in a separate part of the lodge, about 20-25 metres away from the dining area. All the cooked food had to be carried along little paths which weren't too well lit at night.

Just walking around, it was obvious to me that the whole place had been a bit neglected over the years, the bush especially. The view in front of most of the chalets was obscured to a great extent by overgrown bushes and small trees. I made a mental note that one of my jobs would be to clear all this overgrown bush away. The chalet that I had slept in was clean and tidy with fresh sheets on the bed, but it just had a very tired look about it. The bathroom had the basic amenities but the sink was coming away from the wall, the small bath was stained, the windows didn't quite fit properly, some of the mosquito mesh over the windows was missing. The chalet was constructed with poles and building blocks with a thatch roof, but some of the internal rendering was coming off the walls. It was comfortable but by no means up-market.

I found Michelle at work in her little office contained within an administration block set well away from the main lodge area, which also housed separate quarters for visiting tour guides and a maintenance room. Lost Horizons employed a team of workers who were currently trying to smarten the place up a bit, and we immediately set off to meet them. There were seven men in total, two of whom were security guards on the gate and around five or six women engaged in the laundry and other household tasks. The men's names were Daniel, Emmanuel, Andrew 1, Andrew 2, David, Godfrey and Levison. I don't remember the women's names except one,

Beauty. She was the overall supervisor of the entire workforce, something which I know the men were not too happy about. Their culture doesn't really accept that women can perform these roles. As we met each one individually, they greeted me formally and politely, but Daniel displayed open hostility towards me. It was the briefest and weakest of handshakes with no eye contact. I made a mental note of Daniel! Michelle and I spent the rest of the day chatting and walking around the compound.

The following morning, Beauty came to me at breakfast and told me Michelle wanted to see me in her office. When I got there, she wasted no time in telling me that she was off to Cape Town that afternoon and that I was in charge from that time on. She then proceeded to give me a lecture on how I should treat the staff, what food I should give them, what time they started and finished etc etc. As well as being taken rather aback by this sudden promotion, I was also quietly furious that she should be giving me a lecture about how to treat people. It had become obvious to me that Michelle and the staff did not get along. One aspect I do remember well was that she told me that I had to feed the staff on Kapenta and nshima, every day. Kapenta is a small fish, a little like whitebait and nshima is the staple dish of Africa made from ground "meali-meal", or corn. I was not to buy meat for them as it was too expensive. Chris and Karen used to feed kapenta to their dogs on the farm at Mwinilunga! I had no intentions of allowing the staff to become lazy or ill-disciplined but I also had no intentions of them disrespecting me, as they obviously did Michelle. I also decided that they would occasionally eat meat and would buy it for them with my own money.

After the 'lecture', she threw me the keys and asked me to drive her to the airport to catch her flight. If truth be told, I was actually rather relieved she had gone, I would not have been happy to listen to the way she spoke to the staff or treated them.

Over the next few days, I got to know all the staff and what they were currently working on. The various tasks they shared were gardening (Emmanuel), grass screens (Andrew 1) general odd-jobs (Andrew 2 and David) and repairs to the insides of the chalets, (Daniel). I went round each one and they explained to me what they were doing. I made some suggestions about what else we could do to the lodge and I immediately got to work making some wooden doors for an electricity cupboard which was just left open to the elements. I made sure I spent some time with each person for some part of the day. Daniel was still quite aloof and uncommunicative but one day, after I had visited him, I left the chalet singing that song "Oh Danny Boy". It wasn't an intentional stunt by me, the song just came into my head, but it seemed to work. The next day, Daniel smiled at me. I used to fetch the boys each day from the town in a pick-up truck and take them home in the evening. That evening, on the way to Livingstone, I heard Daniel singing "Oh Danny Boy" and from then on, he sang the first few lines every day, and he smiled at me every day.

During the following weeks, I just worked at the lodge, doing various tasks that needed doing and some that I invented, such as making a bird table for the lawn in front of the terrace. As usual, the problem was materials, but as I had learned on the farm with Chris and Karen, when you don't have something for a particular function, you find something else to do the job. I cleared the bush from in front of all the chalets to give them a panoramic view across the valley, I helped Andrew make grass screens to surround the hot water geysers for outside the chalets. I found this particularly fascinating as the screens were woven together in a traditional African way, which Andrew taught me. I think, out of all the boys at the lodge, this Andrew was the smartest. He was intelligent, articulate and a very good worker. I believe Heiko had used him in the past on at least one of the Bush Ways trips, as cook. I found a pile of paving tiles in a heap behind the office and used these to lay plinths at the entrances to all the chalets. I bought some cement and of course, sand wasn't a problem. I helped Daniel with his repair work and David with his carpentry. In the morning when I picked them all up in the town, there would be gales of laughter coming from the back as David regaled them with tales of his exploits in the shebeens of the compound where he lived. Apparently, he was also popular with the ladies!

One morning, Beauty came to find me to tell me that Emmanuel had received news by runner that his father had passed away in their village, several hours drive away in the bush. Emmanuel was one of the quietest and most pleasant of the bunch. He rarely spoke, but he had a ready smile and simply got on with his job. When I found him, he was distraught. He didn't speak much English, so Beauty had to interpret and it turned out, upset as he was about his father's death, he was more distraught at the cost implications of burying his father. As the eldest son, he was expected to buy a coffin, pay for the funeral expenses and also, cater for all the dozens of relatives who would descend on the village for the wake. He was in tears when I spoke to him. Unlike David, Emmanuel had a family and spent all his time at home with them. "Home" was a small hut in the village down the road from the lodge, Mukuni Village. (This incidentally, was where Beauty came from and also where the local chief lived. Known only as "Chief Mukuni", he and his family owned all the land the lodge was built on and most of the land surrounding the Victoria Falls. To say that he was a rich man, would be understating it somewhat. He visited the lodge occasionally, stepping out of a battered old Mercedes that might have passed as a local taxi!)

I spoke to Beauty alone and it was she, not Emmanuel who told me that, although it was expected of him, he simply couldn't afford to pay for it all. I had no doubt this was true knowing how much money he earned. She asked if I would be prepared to take him and his wife and child back to the village where his father had lived. I readily agreed to take him and also made up my mind to help him financially.

We left the lodge about an hour later, picked up his wife and child and eventually arrived at his father's village about two hours after that. I unloaded his small bundle of belongings and he came over to me. I remember he had very prominent teeth, which probably helped with the impression of always smiling, but he was smiling now as he thanked me for bringing him to the village. As he shook my hand, I pressed $50 worth of Zambian Kwacha into his hand. It was quite a pile and I told him to use it for his expenses. As he looked up at me, there was a tear in his eye, he held my gaze for a second or two, and then he simply put his head back down and turned away.

A cynic might say that Emmanuel and Beauty both connived to get me to give him money. I had only known both of them for a few short weeks, but I really don't think this was the case, especially not of Beauty. And anyway, it doesn't matter even if it was the case. In the absence of absolute proof to the contrary, I would still choose to believe Emmanuel's hardships and I would rather give the benefit of the doubt as opposed to believing in the cynical and negatively dogmatic views of a lot of white people about the integrity of black Africans. I may be wrong, but I would always rather take the chance that I'm right.

During the last days of my stay at the lodge, I had popped into town and was just about to walk into a shop when I heard a voice boom out from behind me, "Hey!" I turned around and found Heiko towering over me. I hadn't seen him for about 5 years and I would swear that he had got even bigger than when we were at Drifters together; typically South African, blonde hair, very tall and well muscled. He was on his way back to Maun after visiting some other lodges in the area.

We went out to Lost Horizons and spent the evening reminiscing, drinking beer and laughing. In the morning, as he was packing his Land Rover, he asked if I was interested in coming on a safari with him the following year in December. I didn't know it, but in December 2002 there was to be a total solar eclipse. Eclipses happen occasionally all over the world, but in December 2002, the total eclipse would be visible from the north of Botswana. In his usual fanatical style, Heiko had worked out the exact geographical position that the eclipse could best be viewed from and had begun to put together a particular safari to take people to that precise point, as well of course, as doing some game viewing. I was immediately excited at the prospect of going back on safari, but I told Heiko that I wouldn't go as a client. I would have to be part of the safari team. "Naturally", he said.

I carried on working at the lodge up to the day before I was due to leave and return to England via Lusaka. This was early in December 2001. I took the boys back into Livingstone for the last time and said goodbye to each of them. I had become quite fond of all of them and when I shook Daniel by the hand, he held on and said to me, "Why are you going Mr. Nil (sic), we need you here, we need you!" I just had to look at him and explain that I had to return to my job back here in the UK. Unfortunately, the old diesel pick-up I had been using, ran out of fuel on that Saturday afternoon as I was taking Beauty back to Mukuni village. Just as the truck stopped, a massive thunderstorm broke overhead. I hadn't driven more than about 200 metres from the lodge turn-off and just as the rain came down, a lorry appeared over the brow of a hill. I spent the next ten minutes negotiating with the driver of the truck to tow me back to the lodge. He was sitting in his cab and I was standing in just about the heaviest rain I could imagine. With my head and shoulders bowed under the torrential rain, we agreed a sum of money and I got the pick-up back to the lodge. I felt bad about leaving the vehicle, effectively useless but there was nothing I could do, and besides, there was no-one else at the lodge able to use it.

Sunday was a day off for all the workforce. I had arranged a taxi to take me into town to catch my bus in the morning and I would wait for the car at the end of the lodge driveway. I was just about to leave the lodge and walk to the end of the road to meet the taxi, when two of the workforce walked into the compound. Godfrey and

Levison were both security guards who patrolled the premises in shifts. Godfrey had hung around after his night-shift to say goodbye, but Levison, I knew lived in Livingstone town and wasn't supposed to be working that day. I had developed what I thought was a good working relationship with all the staff and I jokingly asked what Levison was doing at the lodge on his day off. It didn't matter to me what he did in his free time and he could come and go as he pleased. He told me however, that he had walked to the lodge, a distance of about 8 kilometres, especially to see me, to carry my bag for me to the end of the road and to escort me to the bus station where he would say goodbye. I was dumbfounded and simply stared at him. He picked up my bag, carried it to the end of the road, loaded it into the cab when it arrived, he paid for the cab at the bus station and then shook my hand warmly just before I boarded the bus for Lusaka. He told me I was to return some day and say "hello".

I thought about Levison and his actions all the way to Lusaka. I remember struggling to make sense of how I felt about this. On the one hand, I was very flattered that he would do that for me and very proud that I had made that sort of impression. On the other hand, I felt guilty that I was, or seemed to be, abandoning Levison and the others, although I couldn't finally determine just what fate I was abandoning them to! Why was I feeling guilty? I had done my best, I had treated them with respect and dignity, I had dirtied my hands so to speak, working with them. I had enjoyed my time working at the lodge, but I was equally looking forward to going home. Maybe that was it; going home to a life in England that I, as British, take for granted these days but which any one of the lodge workers would view as utter luxury; a decent standard of living, good housing, running water, plentiful food, a steady job, a car and all the amenities of modern life. Maybe I felt guilty because if I asked myself would I want to swap places with any one of them, the answer would be no, thanks! If I asked myself the question, would any one of them swap places with me, the answer would more likely be yes please, thank you very much! It really bugged me for a while

Should I have felt guilty about this? I don't think so! It's very easy to adopt a rather patronizing attitude, given the disparity in the relative wealth between someone who lives in a developed, industrialized and wealthy nation and someone who lives in a poor, under-developed nation. However, I choose to live where and how I do because it's my home, it's what I know. I'm not a rich man by any means and just because I might have more money at my disposal than someone who works at a lodge, doesn't mean that I should drag around a feeling of guilt. There are many other issues which could be discussed connected with this subject, not the least of which, is the endemic corruption associated with leaders of African countries. There are those who would blame colonial rule for their not being able to capitalize fully on their potential wealth, but many years on from colonial rule, corrupt leaders are still stripping assets from many countries rich in natural minerals. Countless billions of dollars have simply disappeared from national coffers, leaving the populations to struggle for survival on bad water, lack of food, sub-standard housing and virtually non-existent health facilities. One only has to look at Zimbabwe to see how far a country, rich in agriculture can fall victim to a despotic and corrupt regime.

No, I feel great sympathy for some people in Africa, but I don't feel guilt.

Chapter 30

The first half of 2002 was very much run-of-the-mill. I had returned to my duties in the Custody and Arrest Support Team and was really getting to like what I was doing. Examining evidence and case files seemed to suit my temperament, and as the months wore on, I began to achieve a certain reputation as someone who would examine a case fairly and then tell the officer just what else was needed to progress the case or just how quickly the case should be placed in the confidential shredder!

At the same time, tennis was continuing to go well and I was improving all the time. A couple of years earlier, I had joined a racquets club called Parklangley. I had no idea at that time of the prestigious nature of this club, I joined because my friend's wife recommended it to me. Looking back over my life, there are many things I regret, and not playing more sport when I was younger is definitely one of them.

At school, we only played football and cricket. I tried hard to like football because all my friends played, I just wasn't very good at it. I was much better at cricket, and I could sprint well, and that would be about the sum total of my sporting prowess at school. I wasn't particularly sporty anyway, and playing sport after leaving school never really occurred to me. Years later, I did play a little squash here and there but constant blisters, and big ones too, got the better of me and eventually, I put my racquet away. I also did a little running but soon got bored with that. It never ceases to amaze me how anybody, man or woman, young or old, summons the mental strength to pound their way along, mile after boring mile. I appreciate that there's an element of pushing and testing one's self but there are better ways of doing this than slogging your guts out on roads and pavements. And as for running on a treadmill in a gym, watching some inane video in front of you aimed at distracting you from the sheer mundanity of it all, well, it just beats me!

At the age of 35, I had decided that I would play rugby. 35, I ask you!!? Anybody who is any good at any sport usually starts around the age of 10! I decided to pitch up one day at a match my police division were playing against another division and said "I would like to play, please!" not really expecting to play but as it happened, they were short! "Ever played forward?" asked the captain, "Nope!", "Ever played in the centre?" "Nope!", "Ever played in the backs?", "Nope!" "Have you actually ever played anywhere before?" "Nope, first time!" I think my sheer audacity earned me a place on the wing, and the fact that I told them I could run quite fast, which was true. That first game earned me a very bloody and sore nose when I was unceremoniously "handed off" by a big, bruising centre on the opposition. I learned very quickly how to tackle properly and from then on, whatever I learned was entirely from mistakes or the frenzied shouting of instructions from my team-mates. I eventually joined a proper club, played in the bottom team (4ths) on a Saturday afternoon when I could, and really enjoyed it. I learned a few things like how to pass and receive the ball, side-step, tackling techniques. I was never afraid to get involved in a tackle but I never had the vision of younger, more accomplished players. Looking for gaps in the defence whilst at the same time, keeping one eye on the ball hurtling towards me, seemed beyond me, that is, if the centres actually bothered to pass it to me. There were several occasions when I was screaming for the ball on an overlap but it never got to me, because, I deduced, they didn't trust me. Although it was disappointing not to be trusted, I wasn't too bothered, it was their problem.

On one occasion I remember, I was playing full-back. At half-time all the team gathered in the middle for the usual pep talk from the captain, exorting us to even greater efforts with swear words never before heard, ending with asking if anyone has anything else to say. Playing behind everyone else at full-back gives one a pretty good idea of what happens in front of you and the weaknesses of the opposition. On this occasion, I saw that the other side were pretty weak on the outside centres and wings, unwilling to engage in tackles etc, so I quietly suggested that we pass the ball out to our wingers and let them run at the opposition, in all likelihood leaving them trailing in their wakes. Some of the more established players simply stared at me but everyone else ignored me. To me, it was so obvious, and it was frustrating to be so ignominiously ignored, as well as mis-trusted! That was the only occasion I spoke at half-time! However, if truth be told, I was pretty useless and probably only got picked for the team because I turned up, although I did once get picked to play in the 3rd team. I struggled on for about ten years, but eventually hung my boots up when I began to be regularly substituted after being told to feign an injury at half time. Let's face it, I was far too old for that sort of stuff, and anyway, tennis began to call much more loudly.

My good friend Ray and I had been playing tennis for around 8 years together. Ray had been a very good player in his youth, and still was. I gradually began to play a much better game and I have to say that I will always be grateful to Ray for his endurance. As a far better player than I, it would have been very easy for him not to play me, saying that I didn't give him anything like a challenging game. He's very, very competitive and at times, he must have been completely fed up with playing someone who could only just about hit the ball over the net, to begin with. As I got better, our games became more enjoyable, but the competitive nature within Ray always prevented him from allowing me to even get close to him. I like to think that this was a plan on his part to make me improve my game, infecting me with his competitive attitude, if you like. Whatever it was, it worked! I became more than a little fed up with constantly losing to him, even though I knew at that stage, I would never be able to beat him. Hence, the wager I mentioned a few chapters ago.

When I joined Parklangley, I very quickly decided that the way forward was with professional coaching. I booked a series of private lessons with one of the paid coaches at the club, a delightful and very capable player and coach, Suzanne. Over the next few years, I continued to have coaching, getting better and better all the time. Suzanne really opened my eyes to just how exciting and interesting the game of tennis can be, especially between players of equal ability. There are tactics to employ, shots to be chosen, techniques to use, senses of sight and hearing to pay attention to and all this within a split second. (The television pundits reckon that the time taken for a ball to leave a top-class server's racquet and arrive at the opponent's racquet is about half a second! That's half a second in which to pick up the flight of the ball, decide if it is coming on the forehand or the backhand, change the grip on the racquet, decide whether or not it has any spin, judge where it's going to bounce and then which direction it will spin off to, get your feet in the right position, prepare and then play a return shot good enough to put your opponent under pressure!) I fell in love with the game! I started to play at every opportunity, 2, 3, 4 times a week, more on the weekends during the club sessions and whenever anybody asked me to play, I would be there. Slowly, I began to be recognized as somebody with playing ability, not through some God-given talent but by sheer hard work and determination. I began to be asked to play in teams for Parklangley against other clubs. I began to be asked if I would join regular games between established players and all the time, I was improving and loving every minute of it. Why, oh why didn't I do this earlier in my life is a question I constantly ask myself. Just prior to retiring from the police, I became qualified as a coach. It was never intended by me to be a source of income, but other club members often seek me out to ask if I can help them sort out this problem or that problem, and generally speaking, I can!

Today, as I write this at the age of 58, despite some niggling injuries, I would regard myself as one of the better players at the club, certainly in the top 5 in the veteran's category, (45+) and definitely one of the best players for my age. I have been described as, "the man to beat!" and I regard this as the ultimate compliment.

Around the beginning of November 2002, I received a phone call from my good friend Annette. You may remember that Annette and I were at school together and to this day, we remain the closest of friends. Her phone call didn't come as too much of a surprise as we speak regularly, but what she said aroused my interest immediately. I had already purchased two properties for rental purposes, a flat in Beckenham and the house in Falmouth. I still had some spare cash in hand and had begun to think about buying a third property somewhere. I had mentioned my thoughts in a previous conversation with Annette, adding that I wouldn't mind looking for somewhere around the Stoke-on-Trent area. The reason for this was that Stoke was, and probably still is undergoing a huge redevelopment project over the whole area. Historically industrial, many of the towns and communities that made up Stoke-on-Trent were changing and fast becoming commuter areas, especially the more out-lying areas such as Biddulph, where I used to live. In fact Biddulph, is the nearest town to Cheshire, where houses and flats are much more expensive. Many people live in the Biddulph area but work around Cheshire and many more work around Stoke but live in Biddulph. Gone are the days when communities lived and worked in the same area. Annette's phone call was about a property that she knew about, but which wasn't at that time for sale. Her family friend Rita had lived in her 2-storey house all her life, about 60 years at that time but was now thinking about her future with regards to obtaining a bungalow from the council. As it happened, the house was in a road I knew very well, as I used to travel along it to and from the coal mine I worked at upon leaving school. It's officially in a village, or rather a suburb of Biddulph called Brownlees.

The problem was that the council would not entertain an application for such a bungalow from Rita as she was a home-owner. One possible solution would be for her to sell the house but carry on living there as a tenant. When Annette mentioned the idea to me, I could see very little downside. I would be able to invest in a new property and at the same time, have a tenant I could trust with no management fees to pay. The episode over Jackie and the house in Falmouth came immediately to mind, but I instinctively knew this scenario would be different.

Annette told me that she had talked the idea over with Rita and she was positive about the whole concept. I went to see Rita to talk it over with her and we soon agreed that the plan would go ahead. A price was agreed, Rita sold me her house and after all the formalities, she became my tenant. The fact that we know each other has made no difference to our landlord/tenant relationship. She has a tenancy agreement in place that protects her and me. Rita tells me what needs doing in the house and then gets on with making arrangements. She then sends me the bill and I pay. I don't know if Rita has ever made an application for a bungalow, our arrangement suits her too well. It's an ideal situation for me too! She still pays the same rent as when she became a tenant 7 years ago, any shortfall being swallowed up by the other properties and as far as I'm concerned, this is the way it will stay.

Property number 3 was in the bag!

At the same time as making arrangements to purchase Rita's house, I was preparing to go back on safari with Heiko for the "Eclipse" trip that he had organized. I was a little apprehensive as it had been several years since I had done a safari as a member of staff and with Heiko as the boss, I knew it wasn't going to be easy. He warned me that the one thing I had to do in preparation was to read and learn as much as I could about eclipses. Heiko is such a professional, he wasn't going to risk anyone criticizing Bush Ways' staff for lack of knowledge. I read up as much as I could and learned quite a bit about solar eclipses, why they occur, the different types, the explanations of terms such as "Umbra", "penumbra", "diamond ring", "first and second contact" etc etc. I was actually quite looking forward to someone on the trip asking a technical question on eclipses so that I could demonstrate my knowledge. It did occur to me that the clients would read as much as I did, but even so, I was ready for that one awkward question, known in the police as the "crippler"!

I arrived back in Zambia at the end of November 2002 and went straight to the Lost Horizons lodge, which at that time was still owned by Heiko and Marc's company Bush Ways. Beauty was still there, as was Godfrey, but the other workers had all disappeared to other places in their constant search for work. It was great to see Beauty again and she looked after me as though I was royalty.

Heiko arrived a few days later with the clients and another assistant called James. Later that evening, Heiko briefed me on the clients, all of whom were avid "eclipse chasers", people who travel all over the world, just watching eclipses. I immediately began to feel that my knowledge on eclipses was going to prove rather inadequate!

We then talked about the trip, where we were going, where we would be when the eclipse occurred, and the fact that I was to be the assistant, whilst James was being trained by Heiko as a guide. James was a terrific guy, young and keen, good-looking and although white, a true Motswana. His family had been in Botswana for a few generations. James was born in Maun and could obviously speak Tswana, and English along with a few other local dialects, a real bonus for a safari guide operating out of Botswana. Unfortunately, James was being trained by Heiko. He took James' language skills for granted, but there were other things for James to learn! Heiko's teaching philosophy was simple, do it my way! There was however, nothing simple about Heiko's zealousness in enforcing his will over James, and as it happened a few years later, me!! He was merciless and relentless in his quest to mould James. It seemed as though he was stripping him bare, in order to start from a blank canvas; not a bad idea, but Heiko had a habit of "stripping" James in public, in front of the clients. On a trip such as a safari, it's not always possible to take someone aside from the clients and point out a few things but Heiko seemed to actively pursue the public approach. For example, Heiko would tell James to lash the gear down on top of the trailer. To be fair, as he always did when teaching something new, he had shown James how he wanted it done but if he inspected it and found James hadn't used the knots he had shown him, he would demonstrate very publicly how the load would become insecure and fall off the trailer, perhaps being lost in the bush. James would then have to take all the lashings off and do it again, whilst the clients watched and waited. James was an intelligent man who had ideas of his own. The trouble began when his ideas conflicted with Heiko's. It got so bad at one stage, that I had a quiet word with Heiko to advise him to ease off a little, especially in front of the clients and to offer James a little praise every now and then. That didn't work, so then I had a quiet word with James, saying it was probably best just to do it Heiko's way and then when he had trips of his own, he could choose to use what he had learned or discard it. I inadvertently found myself in between two very stubborn personalities. Knowing Heiko for the perfectionist he is, I knew what he was doing and why, but found his methods a little extreme. Poor old James became a frazzled wreck by the end of it, but he survived and when I met him again a few years later, it had obviously had some effect on him as he was at that stage, a freelance safari-guide, in some demand, apparently! I will return to Heiko's teaching methods shortly.

We spent the first few days on game-viewing and then on the evening of 3rd December, arrived at our camp site nearest to the spot Heiko had chosen to view the eclipse. It occurred to me that there was a deal of pressure on this decision because, although an eclipse travels along a "path", it is relatively narrow and any slight miscalculation might mean an onlooker would only see a partial eclipse, or a "penumbral" eclipse. These dedicated eclipse chasers had paid good money to see a total eclipse and nothing else would do. Thank goodness for Global Positioning System technology, which Heiko had embraced with admirable gusto! The next morning, we arrived at the exact spot dictated by the G.P.S. coordinates at least an hour before the event. I was really quite excited as I had never witnessed an eclipse of any kind. Heiko had quietly assured me that it would be spectacular, the clients never knew this was my first time, not that it mattered a great deal.

As the time passed, I busied myself helping the clients set up all manner of equipment from cameras on tripods to small home-made "pin cameras". Whilst I was looking forward very much to seeing this, my first eclipse, I came nowhere near the level of excitement reached by the clients, one Scottish man in particular. As the seconds ticked away, he became more and more animated, scuttling around checking equipment and shouting to the rest of us to "be ready"! To be fair, it was quite infectious and I found myself checking my watch for the start time. Almost right on time, the Scot shouted "Here it comes"! I looked skyward through special sunglasses that Heiko had provided for everyone and saw the first hint of the moon moving between the sun and Earth. This is called "First contact" and then for the next few minutes, watched while the moon continued to move in front of the sun, darkening the atmosphere only a few scant hours after the sun had banished the darkness for this day. The birds and animals which had been gently going about their duties, suddenly, and I'm sure confusingly, found themselves preparing for another night. The birdsong disappeared, the rustling of antelope moving through the bush all but stopped, the temperature fell noticeably and an eerie silence fell over the whole area. Such a silence had fallen in the evenings for time immemorial, but watching the daylight slowly recede and listening to the silence at a few minutes after 7o'clock in the morning, could only be described as eerie. As the moon slowly obscured the sun, the light faded and it became darker and darker, until at last, the moon was directly in front of the sun, the period of total eclipse. Everyone in the group, including myself was very excited; cameras clicked away like crazy and everyone encouraged everyone else to gaze in wonder at the spectacle (as if anyone would be looking at anything else!!).

The "totality" lasted only a little over a minute and then the "Diamond Ring" appeared, for me the most stunning aspect of the whole spectacle. As the moon moves away from totally obscuring the sun's rays, a tiny pinpoint of light appears when the sun emerges. Depending on its astronomical position and because of the difference in size, the moon doesn't always fully obscure the sun, and when this is the case, there is a ring of sunlight, which appears to be around the circumference of the moon, called a "Corona". When the point of light appears, it and the "corona" give the appearance of a diamond ring! This lasts but a few, brief and beautiful seconds and I was thankful to have witnessed it.

Slowly, the sun re-appeared, brightness took over from the dark, the air warmed up and birds and animals started what they thought was another day, having had the shortest night's sleep in their histories! Their routine returned, birdsong started up again and animals resumed their never ending search for food in the bush. A large bull elephant appeared quite close to us, he must have approached whilst we were all so engrossed in the eclipse. The day returned to normality! We packed up all the photographic equipment, had a cup of tea, boarded the Land-Rover and headed off. We spent the next couple of days game viewing, Heiko was still riding roughshod over James who, unfortunately never seemed to get things right enough, but he still had a smile on his face at the end when we said goodbye to the clients. My flight home wasn't till a few days hence, so I spent the time helping out in the maintenance yard, under the ever watchful eyes of Heiko Genzmer.

When we had been at Drifters together, I knew that Heiko was a talented engineer. What I hadn't realized on this trip was that the Land Rover based vehicle we had used had been entirely designed and built by him. When he and Marc first set up Bush Ways, he had commissioned Land Rover Botswana to convert a vehicle into one capable of safari work. He wasn't satisfied with Land Rover's efforts, so re-designed the whole thing and built it himself, apart from having the chassis professionally stretched in South Africa. From a basic Land Rover 110 Defender, he produced a vehicle capable of carrying 16 clients on bench seats, 180 litres of fuel, 80 litres of water, all the necessary tools, much of the food and storage compartments for the clients' personal effects. He had incorporated a fridge unit under a bench seat and altered the front passenger seat area to accept a second 12 volt battery. From this, he was able to run lighting for the evenings and a freezer for the meat. He also cut up old Land Rovers and converted them into trailers capable of carrying all the luggage, tents, tarpaulins, mattresses, extra fuel jerry-cans, and crates of fruit. Fully loaded, these vehicles would weigh around 3 tons. As I write this, I know that Heiko has hand-built 9 of the 10 Land Rover Game-Drive vehicles in their fleet, an astonishing feat!! We are however, talking about a man who can strip, repair and replace a Land Rover gearbox in the bush, without power tools, hydraulic ramps or lifting gear!

Heiko Genzmer is a remarkable man!

Chapter 31

2003 was a pretty normal year. I continued to establish myself as the point of reference for officers seeking advice on cases, my tennis was improving all the time and I was happy!

Nothing particularly out of the ordinary happened until one evening, I received an email from Marc Germiquet, one of the co-owners of Bush Ways Safaris and Heiko's business partner. He had never contacted me before and I was immediately intrigued, and then having read the email, confused! Marc explained that Heiko was planning an expedition trip to somewhere called the Liuwa Plains in Zambia. When they want to start a new safari, or "trail" as they call it, they first of all run an "expedition" trip to see if the safari is feasible, spot any potential hazards and generally get a feel for the logistics. Marc asked me in the email if I wanted to go along. Heiko would be running it and with him would be several of his friends from Germany and Switzerland. This is where I got confused. Heiko would run the trip but Marc was asking if I wanted to go!! Why didn't Heiko ask me? I was immediately disappointed to think that Heiko couldn't have invited me himself and wondered, quite reasonably just what our "friendship" was. Did Heiko know that Marc had invited me? All sorts of questions popped into my head. I had already made up my mind not to go for this reason when another thought struck me. Heiko's friends would all be from Germany and Switzerland, where he had spent time before joining Marc at Bush Ways. There is little to do in camp at night except sit around the campfire and chat. I foresaw the situation where everyone else would be conversing in German and I, not being able to speak German at all well, would be marginalized. The rest of the camp would have to make the effort to speak English to include me, which I didn't want, it would make me feel like an outsider, which was probably not far from the truth. I emailed Marc and said, no thanks, and then lied, can't make it. I had always thought my connection with Heiko and Marc was tenuous at best and after turning down Marc's offer, I didn't think I would hear from either of them again.

During the rest of the year, I continued to cement my position within the prisoner handling unit. Following a short period under uniform supervision, the unit had once again, returned to the CID. Consequently, my boss changed from a uniformed Inspector to a Detective Inspector, a change neither my new boss nor I relished. His briefing to me about what he expected was, "It's your job to make me look good!" There was nothing about what I might expect from him.

From time immemorial, the uniform branch of the police has not got on with the detectives. Far from believing that we all do the same job, the detectives generally tend to think of themselves as above the uniformed branch, and the uniformed branch regard the detectives as arrogant and less brainy that they think. A cruel example of a detective's attitude is when I had a relationship with a female detective sergeant. When a male colleague of hers in the CID became aware of our relationship, he remarked to her "but he's uniformed!!"

There are occasions however, where uniformed officers do support CID, at major scenes of crime for instance. It's the job of the detectives to investigate at scenes of crime and they generally can't do this without the support of uniformed officers, particularly at major scenes where uniformed officers will secure the scene to allow forensic examination and photographic evidence to be collected. Patrolling officers will almost always be first on the scene when the phrase, "the golden hour" becomes critical. In that first hour, much of the vital evidence can be collected. Witnesses can be secured, scenes can be preserved, CCTV and photographic evidence can be obtained, the list is not exhaustive and all because the uniformed branch do their job. This first hour is crucial in an investigation and the uniformed officers are often not given enough credit for smart, intelligent work after arriving at a scene of crime. The credit for securing convictions against major criminals generally goes to the CID, who without doubt, will have done a superb job, but the work of the uniformed officers, without which the investigation could well falter, is all too often overlooked.

To be fair, the old differences are slowly disappearing with the retirement of older, cynical officers and the influx of younger, more aware officers who are less likely to be indoctrinated by the traditional dogma, even after joining the CID.

The year wore on, Christmas and New Year came and went. Early in 2004, I received an unexpected email from Heiko, the content of which took me very much by surprise. He explained that the expedition he undertook the previous year was to explore a new trip which they were going to call "The Hyena Trail". It was to be a 14 night wild-camp safari to an area of Zambia known as the Liuwa Plains National Park from mid-November to early December. The trip would officially end in Livingstone, Zambia but if any clients wanted to return to Maun with Bush Ways, there would be an additional four days when they would travel back to the base via the game parks Chobe and Moremi in Botswana for some extra game-viewing.

The Liuwa Plains is a wilderness area, seldom visited by tourists but which has an annual migration of wildebeest, zebra, and lots of other antelope from Angola in search of fresh grass. Packs of hyena follow them over and hunt the young wildebeest. The area actually comprises some 3600 square kilometers of virtually nothing but wide open, grassy plains, numerous waterholes and the ancient Lozi people living around the edges. There used to be far more species of game, including predators prior to the area becoming a National Park, but bad management and poaching took a disastrous toll. To get there, we would have to travel by Land-Rover and trailer for at least two to three days, driving through some of the toughest sand in southern Africa, across rivers and through villages that have not changed in appearance, location or culture for generations.

The purpose of Heiko's email was to ask me if I would like to run the trip for Bush Ways. To say I was flattered would be an understatement! Heiko had to know dozens of people in the safari industry who could have taken this trip, including the guys he already employed. I have never been under any illusion that what I learned about fauna and flora and actually running a trip while I was at Drifters, could compare in any way with what Heiko and his colleagues would know. Although he was confident with my knowledge, Heiko didn't want me for that reason, he wanted me because I could manage a group of disparate people, make them operate as a team, solve problems in situ without having to refer to the office, which apparently most of his other guides had a habit of doing, and most importantly, he knew I would do my utmost to make sure that every client had a positive experience of Bush Ways specifically, and of Africa in general. Even so, we would run my first trip together, naturally as he had to show me the route etc. When we were discussing this, I took the opportunity to insist that, as flattered as I was in his belief in me, he had to promise me that after running the trip together, he would tell me honestly whether he was still confident that I would do a good job for him. If he wasn't, he should find someone else. I didn't want him to feel committed to having me run the trip if he thought I wasn't up to it.

For the rest of the year, I swatted hard, again, on my birds, animals and trees. By the time I came to leave for the trip, I felt I was as ready as I could be, but I was still apprehensive. My previous experience at Drifters and the Eclipse Safari had taught me that no matter how well I could identify a bird or animal from a book, actually doing it for clients is far more difficult. On safari, there is nothing more embarrassing than mis-identifying a species and then have one of the clients correct you. And it's even worse when you know that one of the clients has a particular interest in say, birdlife. They will always be armed with the latest books, which they probably know back-to-front. In these cases, it's as well to acknowledge their expertise and use it to your advantage by asking their opinion. I always found that these people liked nothing better than to have their guide defer to them for their knowledge.

Experts notwithstanding, although I knew that Heiko would be with me, I still felt it was important for me to be able to identify various animals and birds and more than that, pass on information relevant to each, such as gender identification, family-group culture etc. Anyone could probably identify a wild-dog for instance, but to be able to explain the complicated family structure of such animals and the way they hunt, would certainly enhance my status as guide and at the same time, enhance the reputation of BushWays. Even at Drifters, it was never enough for me simply to take the clients to where the itinerary said we would go, the clients had to have an "experience" of Africa, which would remain with them forever. Part of this is imparting information and teaching them about the bush. If the clients realized that I knew what I was talking about, then my job would be that much easier and they would have the confidence to recommend BushWays to their friends and family.

The one part I was not apprehensive about however, was my ability to take charge of, and lead the group. Part of the art of leadership is the ability to make decisions, tough or simple and to be able to think ahead. Although I had given Heiko the opportunity not to hire me, I had no doubt that if he did reject me, it would not be for this reason.

For me, the trip was tough. Within a very short time of starting, I realised just what James must have felt under the harsh training by Heiko on the Eclipse Safari. I knew it was going to be tough, but I didn't think he would be quite so intense with me. The criticisms were non-stop, the rebukes for not getting something right, acerbic and I always knew that whatever I did, he would be watching. I knew from James, there was no way around it and so, it was just a matter of gritting teeth and getting on with it, riding the falls and bearing the embarrassment.

The driving was the biggest bug-bear. Although I had driven large trucks off-road with Drifters, driving these Land Rovers would be different. Heiko was justifiably proud of his Land Rovers and his skills in off-road driving were phenomenal. Everything he did was geared to getting the best out of the vehicle but also to ensure that something didn't break. He had just two weeks to pass on as many skills as he could and I really did try to see it that way but his constant haranguing was very wearing. One little habit I had always had, was to keep my left foot just resting on the clutch pedal. The pressure was very light but even so, the pedal was depressed just enough to cause wear on the clutch. Heiko's method of getting me out of this life-long habit was to tell me in the first instance and then to punch my left thigh whenever he saw my foot anywhere near the clutch when not using it to change gear. At the end of the trip, I actually had a large bruise on my leg from all his thumpings. Even to this day, I consciously keep my left foot away from the clutch unless I'm going to change gear.

I continued to stumble along with the driving and the trip generally, becoming more and more convinced that he wouldn't let me take the following year's trip. I remember one morning when we had arrived at our base in Livingstone, The Lost Horizon's Lodge. Heiko told me to strap some empty fuel gerry-cans under the chassis of the trailer. He had shown me how he wanted them done back in Maun before we set off, but for the life of me I couldn't remember what he'd said. Rather than go to him and risk yet another scolding, I did it how I thought it would be okay and tried to get away with it. He inspected it, naturally and declared my work, shall we say, unsuitable. They were quite secure, but another scolding came my way! At this one, I snapped. I rounded on Heiko and told him in no uncertain terms that his manner with people stank and that it was all very well driving someone on with a big stick but at some time, that stick will break, what then? I suggested that he might try and give a little praise every now and then, much as I'd said to him previously about James; he hadn't learnt. He just looked at me and told me to do it again but this time he relented and patiently explained how it should be done. I did it, he examined it again and then declared he was satisfied; a small victory for the small man!

We had picked up Heiko's wife, Carina in Livingstone and when we got back to Maun, we all went to dinner. The trauma of the trip was forgotten when Heiko declared that he was satisfied I could run the safari the following year. I knew I wasn't the best, but Heiko obviously saw that I could do it and not make a hash of the whole thing; I could bring back happy clients.

To date, 2009, I have run five successful safaris to The Liuwa Plains for Bush Ways.

(If anyone wishes to read a description of the trip, I have included a separate story, written through the eyes of an imaginary client, as an addendum. Everything described has actually happened on the Hyena Trail, but not necessarily on this one safari. The reader should bear in mind, the piece was written as promotional material for Bush Ways.)

Chapter 32

2005 also saw my third and last attempt to gain promotion. If I had any chance at all of succeeding, this would be the time. The system had changed yet again and was based this time on recommendation from a candidate's senior management team. For the previous four years, I had worked hard to raise the profile of the prisoner handling team, to a point where they had the respect and confidence of the rest of the station.

I thought I had a very good chance to get through this system, which my immediate boss agreed with. He was a hard man to please, and had already told me that if I got past him, it was more or less in the bag, so to speak!

Both he and I were wrong, yet again. The senior management decided that I hadn't done enough to convince them that I would make a good Inspector and failed me once more. In truth, I thought the decision was a little perverse and I did appeal to another board for a re-examination of my application but I had no doubt they would uphold the original decision. There would have to be something seriously wrong for one set of senior officers to counter the decision of others.

The only crumb of comfort for me was that I was hugely gratified and touched by the reaction of the officers on the ground, they were aghast at the decision. I had a steady stream of officers coming in to the office to say how sorry they were and how perverse they thought the decision was. However, that was my last chance, and so I would spend the last few years of my service, still enjoying my work, but feeling slightly unfulfilled, especially when I saw the quality of other officers selected for the rank of Inspector.

Although I was approaching retirement age, I would have stayed on for a few more years had I been successful in being promoted. As it was, things were happening within the Case Progression Unit which I found interesting, and not a little fun. I had been approached by training officers to help with teaching the young recruits, just out of Training School about case papers, interviews and most important, court appearances. I devised a 3 hour lecture on the preparation of a set of case papers for presentation to the Crown Prosecution Service and arranged training interviews. The recruit conducted a basic crime interview, with myself and a colleague acting as either awkward solicitors or even more awkward suspects.

The most fun however, was with the mock-court. The young probationer officers had to effect a mock arrest, prepare a set of case papers, present the papers to their instructing officers who would then pass a copy of the file to me, in preparation for appearing at a mock Magistrates court. The "Magistrate" would be a really crusty ex-police officer who was serving around the mid-sixties, other officers would act as clerk, usher, prosecutor and I would be the defence solicitor or barrister, depending on how I felt that day! The training room desks and tables would be configured exactly how a real court would appear and the whole exercise was treated with seriousness, especially by the "Magistrate"; God help any officer he caught smiling or smirking in his "court". The whole point of the exercise was to help familiarise the officers in court procedure, etiquette, how to address the Magistrate, how to present the evidence and then how to deal with cross-examination by me. It was my job not only to try and get the case dismissed, which wasn't usually difficult, but also to try and get the officers to feel uncomfortable in the witness box, to accuse them of lying, concocting evidence and always where possible, to lose their tempers with me. We had some spectacular successes with the latter exercise and when they had calmed down, the "court" would give them feedback about their performance. No matter what happened in the "court", all the participating recruits said they found the experience great fun and very useful, especially when they had to attend a real court.

Despite enjoying the work I was engaged on, the fun and laughs we, the officers had with the female office workers we shared our office with, fencing and jousting with my senior officers about results, I was very aware that retirement was looming. I was in a slightly awkward situation in my role as supervisor on the C.P.U. as my position should have been occupied by a detective sergeant. I had been retained in the department due to my experience and length of service. As a result, when I was approaching retirement age, 55 in 2006, I was told that I would have to retire or move to another department as the management could not justify keeping me on in that position. Although I was looking forward to retirement, I actually didn't want to at that stage for purely financial reasons. I needed to earn a decent salary to maintain some investments before they matured the following year. As it happened, the management suddenly changed their collective mind and I was told I could stay in my position until 2007.

The following year trundled by. I did my safari with Bush Ways in November and December of 2006, went skiing in early 2007 and then I read a letter in one of the local newspapers, berating the police for not having enough presence on the streets. The letter was supposedly written by a magistrate. I have always been very protective of the police as a workforce, knowing that if there is one thing almost every officer takes seriously, it's his or her service to the public. I decided to reply to the letter on the basis that the local Magistrates Court, Bromley, added to the police workload, keeping them off the streets because the justices too often released persistent thieves and drug addicts on bail, allowing them to steal more goods to pay for their drugs. The police officers found themselves arresting the same people for the same offences day after day. I thought I may as well have a pop at the C.P.S. at the same time, so I criticised them for keeping police officers at court all day and then releasing them without giving evidence.

I went to work a few days later and was immediately accosted by my boss, the Detective Chief Inspector. I had not seen it, but apparently, the local paper had printed my reply and made it the "star" letter complete with a nice photograph of the Magistrates Court. The headline read "More Efficiency From Magistrates Please" and the letter ended with "Neil Robins, Bromley Police." This was how I had signed my letter but I didn't think that the paper would interpret that as meaning I was a police spokesman. Unfortunately, the Magistrates Court and the Crown Prosecution

Service interpreted it exactly that way. Emails and telephone messages were flying around like exocet missiles, the court and C.P.S. demanding my head on a block and apologies from the police and more importantly, the borough commander, Chief Superintendent Charlie Griggs. Mr. Griggs was an old-style copper but his rank demanded that he played the political game with the various agencies and "partners".

I was whisked pretty smartly up to his office where we both had a good laugh at my letter. Privately he agreed absolutely with what I had written, but was however, serious when he told me he couldn't publicly support my protestations. He would have to reply to my letter in his official capacity, denying what I had contended and supporting his "partners". I argued that as my senior officer, he should support me and the officers who are affected most by the "revolving door" policy employed by the court. He didn't, and replied to my letter quite vociferously. I was in no mood to take this lying-down and I was able to re-reply, effectively winning the argument.

The most gratifying aspect was that dozens of officers who arrest these people and have to deal with them every day, came into the office and thanked me for making the point, even though it made not the slightest difference to the court. I viewed this very much as my "swansong."

I made up my mind that, even though I could have stayed on as a police officer working in another department, I was ready to retire. I had had enough and it was time to move on to the next stage of my life. I had no desire to return to the police in a civilian capacity, my retirement would signal the end of my association with the Metropolitan Police. I have known many officers who retire on a friday afternoon and then return to the same job as a civilian the following monday. Not for me, this would be the end.

I made arrangements to have some drinks with colleagues in a local bar. My Chief Superintendent, Charlie Griggs made a speech thanking me for my input over the many years we had known each other and I replied saying that I hoped that whatever younger officers had learned through me and my expertise, I hoped they would use it throughout their service and that they would remember me as having "made a difference" to their careers.

The following day was my birthday, 9th March 2007 and the day I would retire. Although a little groggy from singing songs in Bromley High Street after midnight, I was there to meet my friend The Commissioner of Police, Sir Ian Blair, who made a special trip down to Bromley to present me with my Certificate of Service of, "exemplary conduct." (Police officers usually translate this phrase as, "never been caught!") This was quite special as certificates are rarely presented by Commissioners, but there again, we are friends. I declined the offer to have lunch with him and the senior officers, suspecting that the latter would simply "button-hole" Ian to discuss policy etc. I returned to my office for the last time, and completed one last report my Inspector had asked me to write.

Officers had been coming in to the office to say their goodbyes and to wish me luck all through that morning. After finishing the report and sending it to the boss by email, I looked around the office. Constables were hunched over their computers, busy with cases and investigations, the ladies in the office were doing likewise and some were chatting amongst themselves, some were laughing. Various people popped into the office to drop off correspondence, the printers were humming and the keyboards, clacking. Everything was well in the office! I thought, "time to go!" I picked up my bag of personal belongings, walked to the door, turned round and said "Goodbye everyone, and thanks."

I walked out of the police station that day as plain old Neil Robins, an unremarkable man!

Postscript

Whilst writing this book, I decided to try and discover the reason why my dad was awarded the Distinguished Service Medal in WW2. Someone had previously researched it for me as a favour and had told me that dad's record had been destroyed in a fire. I decided to try and confirm this. After several weeks of writing letters and searching the internet, I received a letter from a Mr. Steven Spear in the Office of the Naval Secretary. He dealt with honours and awards and told me that, although his personal file no longer existed, the record of dad's award had been selected years earlier for permanent preservation and had been transferred to the National Archives at Kew, London. I spent a very pleasurable afternoon at the Archives reading through an enormous ledger entitled "Levant" where the citations and reasons for various awards were documented, brave men each and every one.

Eventually, I came to the entry for "Ivan (sic) Vivian Robins" Apparently, his ship H.M.S. Belvoir had been engaged in operations against German warships in the Aegean Sea and in maintaining supplies to the islands of Kos and Leros until they fell to the Germans, and all the while, being under almost constant bombardment and attack from German bombers and fighter aircraft. Under the heading of "Operations in the Aegean Sea October-November 1943", the citation for my dad read:-

"For cheerfulness and devotion to duty, above the average. This Petty Officer was a constant example to the ship's company."

Lt. Cmdr. John Bush

So there we have it, my dad was awarded a gallantry medal for being cheerful whilst having the crap bombed out of him by the Germans!

Did he save anyone's life directly, no! Was he instrumental in saving the lives of others, certainly! Did he perform his duty whilst under an almost constant threat of death, absolutely! Was he a hero, yes of course he was, he was my dad!

Addendum

FAINT HEARTED

"A one of a kind adventure", the internet web site said. "not for the faint hearted."

I had had a number of conversations with friends, all of whom had been "on safari" in Africa. Their descriptions varied between staying at luxury lodges with air conditioning and satellite television, and taking game-drives in the morning and evening to view African wild-life, to hiring their own vehicles and heading off to a fenced-in game park with well marked roads and rest lodges. All their descriptions seemed to have one thing in common, they all had sizeable chunks of luxury thrown in; a near-olympic size swimming pool or white-gloved African waiters serving a la carte food in the evening or maybe just decent toilet and washing facilities. "Is this really what a safari is all about," I wondered to myself. The dictionary defines "safari" as a Swahili word meaning "journey". It seemed to me that people had adapted the word to fit practically anything to do with African game-viewing. I decided to see if there was any company offering a safari which would be more in-keeping with the old fashioned view of a safari, perhaps a journey into the unknown.

After examining a number of web-sites thrown up by my Google search, I finally found a company in Botswana, which seemed to offer just what I was looking for. Bush Ways Safaris, based in Maun, were advertising a number of different trips, or "trails" as they call them, one of which was called "Hyena"; a 14 day, wild-camping safari starting in Botswana, crossing Namibia via the Caprivi Strip and then on into Zambia and to the Liuwa Plains National Park to see the annual migration of Wildebeest and Zebra from Angola to the lush grass-lands of the Zambian plains. The web-site promised adventure! The journey would take us along some of the worst tracks imaginable, through bush, along ancient sand roads, across rivers, past traditional African villages and finally, onto the Plains themselves, where 3660 sq. kms of grassy plains is home to thousands of game animals and members of the ancient Lozi tribe! We would make one stop en-route to take on supplies and diesel and from then on, we would be on our own! Fantastic, just what I was looking for, a true safari.

After an efficient booking service with the office in Maun, I flew from London, via Johannesburg and then on to Livingstone in Zambia, where I was met by a transfer company representative who would take me across the river border to Kasane in Botswana, where the safari would start. The border between Zambia and Botswana is actually at the point where two rivers, the Chobe and the Zambezi meet. At the crossing point, four countries converge, Zambia, Botswana, Namibia and Zimbabwe. As we drove along the approach road to the ferry, I couldn't help noticing the dozens and dozens of huge articulated lorries, lined up on both sides of the road. "They are waiting to cross", explained the driver. Owing to the size of the ferry, which can only take one lorry at a time plus a few cars and foot passengers, some of the drivers of these monster trucks have to wait maybe three days before they can get across. Tempers are often frayed by the heat and the seemingly endless wait, and fights are common.

The Kazangula border post is just a collection of ramshackle buildings where everybody crowds around any window which might be occupied by an official. Outside, the traffic is "controlled" by youths, all of whom seem to be able to whistle at the highest pitch imaginable and wave their arms constantly above their heads; lorries, vans, cars, safari trucks and foot passengers, all vying to get on the ferry first or indeed, to get out of the compound after leaving the ferry. Although the scene was absolutely chaotic, it was enjoyable to watch something which screamed out, "hey, this is Africa!" In total contrast, the border post on the Botswana side was a haven of tranquillity, no shouting, no whistling and everyone being polite to one another. I was met again by another transfer representative from the same company, but based in Botswana and taken to my lodge in Kasane, a four star hotel on the banks of the Chobe river. It was all very nice, but I couldn't wait to get on safari.

The following morning, as arranged by Bush Ways, I was picked up at the hotel, at exactly the arranged time by our safari guide. I say "our" because over the previous evening, I had met a charming couple in the hotel who would both be coming on the same trip, an American husband and wife from Georgia, Chris and Lynne. Our guide was named Neil, an Englishman with the sort of lived-in face that is somehow reassuring. He explained later that he and the owners of Bush Ways used to run safaris together for a safari company in South Africa. They started Bush Ways and invited him to come out every year to do this one trip. The vehicle we were in was a modified Land Rover 110 Defender, towing a massive trailer. Already on board the vehicle were two other clients, whom Neil introduced as Cathy from South Africa and Helmut from Germany, truly, an international trip! After the brief introductions and an assurance that we would be further briefed on the trip later that evening, we set off back into the town, back to a supermarket. Neil told us to stock up here with at least 5 litres of water per person per day, there would be no fresh water where we were going and we would have to take it all with us. At the supermarket, we met the last member of the trip, Neil's assistant, a Botswana man with the curious surname of Wireless but who liked to be called by his nickname, Aupo (pronounced ow-u-pa). He had been getting the last of the food supplies and when these were loaded into the trailer, Neil drove round to a nearby garage to fill up with diesel, something else he said was not available where we were going. This was sounding better and better; no popping down to the shops or to the bar for a casual drink, we take everything with us! Whilst Neil was filling the vehicle, Aupo was busy packing away all the 5 litre containers of water. It seemed that everywhere on the Land Rover had secret little storage places built in. This was when Aupo told me that the vehicle had been designed and built by one of the owners of Bush Ways, Heiko. The base was a Land Rover 110, but it had been fitted with a stretched chassis in Pretoria, South Africa and driven back to the Bush Ways base, where

Heiko had constructed the vehicle, which was actually called a "game-drive" and which, along with the trailer was capable of carrying 16 passengers, food, water, diesel in long-range tanks, camping equipment, spares and all luggage. Not only that, Aupo told me Heiko had built six other "game-drives" just like ours.

At last, we finished supplying and set off for the bush. My "adventure" had begun! Our first two nights would be in Chobe National Game Park, camping in a designated area but with no fences around, a totally wild area where animals could wander into the camp if they wished. When we got to the camp site, Neil and Aupo showed us how to erect our exterior-frame tents. They looked pretty substantial, but could they keep out something as big and nosy as say, a lion? In the late afternoon, we left the camp and went on a game-drive along the banks of the Chobe river. We saw elephant, in fact we saw a whole herd of elephant drinking and playing in the river. It was wonderful to watch the infants trying to emulate the adults but only succeeding in falling and sliding down the steep slopes to the water's edge, to be picked up gently by the ever-watchful females in the herd. There were antelope, zebra, monkeys galore.

During the evening, Neil gave us all a full briefing on the do's and don'ts of camping in the bush, including why lions etc do not enter tents unless invited by the occupants, and how to use the toilet tent (especially at night), erected a short distance from the camp, thank goodness! It consisted of a hole in the ground with a canvas sheet surround. It did however, have a collapsible seat and a peg for the loo paper! He explained what we could expect to see, what we could expect of him and Aupo and what he expected of us, namely our participation in the safari. He explained that the trip we were on was a proper "safari" in the true sense of the word, we had everything with us and if we ran out of something, tough; if the vehicle broke down in the bush, there would be no waiting for a passing vehicle to assist us, it would be fixed where we were or something made to work in its place. Dinner that night was cooked over the open fire by Aupo, barbecued chops and salad, fantastic! I felt sure that the standard of food on this trip was going to be excellent. I wasn't wrong!

The following morning and afternoon was taken up with a game-drive in the morning and a trip down the river on a boat in the afternoon. That was exciting as we managed to get really close to a pod of hippo and to crocodiles basking on the shoreline. As if that wasn't enough, during the drive back to camp, we came upon a small pride of lion, mostly female. They weren't doing anything, just lying in open grass on the river bank. Still, we watched them for about half an hour before they finally got up and wandered off into the bush where we couldn't follow. I know it sounds like a well used cliché, but it was a real privilege to see these magnificent animals in their own environment. Neil never ceased to stress upon us that we were visitors to their domain and that we should respect that.

After dinner, Neil briefed us on the following day. It was going to be tough, rising at around 5am (just about light!) and leaving camp by 0630. An hour and a half seemed a ridiculously short amount of time to get up, pack bags, wash, toilet, breakfast, fold away our tents, break camp and pack the vehicle. Impossible, I thought! However, Neil and Aupo worked quickly and diligently, continually chivvying us along, and lo and behold, the Landrover and trailer were all packed and the engine was warming up, just after 0635. "Not bad, for the first time", smiled Neil, "but don't worry, we'll get better at it!" We all groaned a little at the prospect! During those two nights, I had drifted off to sleep listening to the unique sounds of African wildlife; the dung-beetle scurrying around the bottom of my tent and the distant roar of a lion, somewhere out in the bush.

We left the camp as we had found it, completely devoid of evidence of human habitation and hit the road to take us across the Caprivi Strip in the north of Namibia and then on into Zambia. Having spent an interminable time at the border crossings, watching immigration officials idly caressing their stamps and finally stamping our passports in a blur of action and getting last minute supplies of diesel at Katima Mulilo in Namibia, we eventually took the road to our destination, the Liuwa Plains. The first few kilometres were tarred and I began to wonder if it would be like that all the way. However, the tar ended and the road became a smooth dirt road, then a slightly rougher dirt road, then an even rougher dirt road with potholes the size of a small family car. The Land Rover lurched from side to side as Neil negotiated the holes and plunged into deep depressions filled with water, which sometimes swept up over the bonnet. This was more like it!

Soon after midday, Neil stopped under a huge tree and he and Aupo took out the lunch they had prepared the previous evening, rice salad with cold meats and cheese. I then noticed a small group of African children watching us from about ten meters away. I could see a small village of thatched and mud huts in the distance and guessed this was where they had come from. They never approached any closer and didn't interfere with us at all. I was however, slightly concerned that we were eating enough food at that lunch to feed them for a week. Neil was obviously well used to seeing concern on clients' faces and quickly explained that, as unfortunate as the situation was, this would be the "the way of it." We had to eat and they lived where they lived, there wasn't anywhere we could stop where we wouldn't see local people. He explained that this would be part of our safari, this was Africa! It was clear however, that Neil and Aupo had prepared more than we needed for lunch and the left-overs were placed into a carrier bag and sealed. Neil then invited me to take the bag of food over to the children. He explained that this was what they had been waiting for; they weren't interested in us as "white people", they knew we would give them some of our food and were waiting for me to deliver it. He said that "this is how it works here!" He liked it even less than we did, but that is how it is there! Neil told me to make sure I gave it to the eldest child as there is a strict pecking order in African society. He or she would then distribute it. I gave the bag to a young girl, who gave me a delightful smile, a slight curtsy which is simply their way of being polite to everyone and what I presumed was "thank you" in her language. I still wasn't too sure about the whole thing, but it was obvious that it was entirely normal for the African people and the likes of Neil. Looking back on the incident, it was clear that we weren't flaunting our relative fiscal wealth in their faces, but it did serve to heighten my awareness of the differences between our circumstances.

After lunch, we pressed on along the steadily worsening road. We had to force our way up steep inclines, following ruts in the road about 2 feet deep and gingerly drop down the other side. At one stage, we had to stop while an old bull elephant idly crossed over the road. Neil explained that very little game still existed in a "wild" state in Zambia. Over the years, most animals have been hunted out or trapped for food by local people; there are some hunting concession areas where game is obviously more plentiful, but not many. The Liuwa Plains where we were going was also an exception but for different reasons, namely animal migration. The road ran alongside the Zambezi river for some way and at times, we were afforded the most beautiful views of the Zambezi valley and the mighty river meandering along in the distance.

On and on we drove, right through the afternoon. The heat was appalling, around 35C and the only respite was from the breeze allowed in through the open sides of the Land Rover, and there was an added bonus of being able to smell Africa. The road itself took on many different characteristics; deep, deep potholes, flooded potholes, rutted sand tracks, pleasantly wide dirt roads and very unpleasant, stony and bumpy tracks. "Puncture city!" Neil called the latter. We carried two spare wheels, a number of spare inner tubes and puncture repair materials. If there was such a thing as a world record puncture repair time, someone at Bush Ways probably held it!

On and on we drove, further north into Zambia. We passed through a small village called Sioma and then suddenly arrived in a larger town called Kalangola. Neil pointed out a ferry that took vehicles and passengers across the Zambezi. There were some tin shacks that passed as shops and one building, which from the look of the girls hanging themselves out of the window, was obviously the local brothel! Just outside the town, we came to a very old rusty looking bridge across a dry river-bed. Thankfully, Neil skirted round it, it didn't look as though it would take the weight of one human let alone a Land Rover and seven humans! After crossing a wide flood-plain, we found ourselves on a narrow sand road. Although the sand didn't appear to be deep, it seemed to grip the tyres as we passed and suck the vehicle down. Neil told us that this was by no means the worst we would encounter.

The sun was setting when we finally stopped on the track. Both Neil and Aupo were looking into the thick bush, which grew right to the edge of both sides of the track. Suddenly, the vehicle revved and we crashed over the edge of the track and began to force our way into the dense undergrowth. Neil ground our way in for about 200 meters and then stopped. "We make camp here", he announced. He had chosen a sandy spot relatively devoid of undergrowth away from prying eyes. I asked him how he knew it was there, he shrugged his shoulders and replied, "I could see it from the road." Experience tells, I suppose! We set about erecting our tents, Aupo made a fire and put a pot of water on a grill over the flames and prepared his kitchen. Neil took a shovel and began to dig our toilet hole. Very romantic! After the toilet, he took another roll of canvas and poles from the trailer and began to erect another screen. Aupo took a canvas bucket and poured some of the water from the pot into the bucket. "Shower time," he announced; a bush shower! After a 12 hour day in the heat and dust of Africa, nothing would feel so good as warm water on my body that evening?

Clean and dry, well fed and watered, we sat around the fire late into the evening chatting. Finally, Neil briefed us on the next day, which he said would be tougher than this and we went to our beds, happy and contented.

5am!!! Neil and Aupo were already up and preparing our breakfast. We were a little more leisurely that morning and left camp around 7am. The road was now getting very tough with soft sand. Neil had stopped to lessen the pressure in his tyres, standard practise apparently but still the Land Rover had to literally grind its way through the sand, often swinging wildly around the trunks of trees just on the edge of the road. We had to avoid the roots at all costs. A root could go through the side of the tyre like a knife through butter!

After a couple of hours, we crested a small hill and found ourselves in the middle of a village. Neil stopped the vehicle and began to change one of the wheels of the trailer which had a puncture. We clients took the opportunity to interact with the villagers who had all gathered around the vehicle to watch. We all took pictures of the children on digital cameras and then showed them on the screen. They absolutely loved it, all screaming with delight and laughter and vying with each for the best position. I think some of them had seen themselves before but it was still a pleasure for us to see them laughing.

From the vantage point of this hill, we could also see the route ahead of us stretching in a wide arc around a flood plain. On the left of the plain, we could see village after village perched on the side of what Neil explained were ancient sand dunes and along the edge of the plain, a continuous line of trees. This was the infamous "Mango Tree Road". Apparently, this was an old trading route where people would bring their goods to places like Kalangola, eating mangoes as they went. They threw the pips to the ground and from them, grew massive and innumerable mango trees. The distance to the next town, Kalabo was only about 70 kilometres but it would take us the rest of the day to reach it.

With the puncture repaired, we set off. At first, the road was easy but it soon turned into one of the toughest sand roads in Africa. Neil had to use all his considerable skill to keep the Land Rover going in some places and in others, it just ground to a halt, axle-deep in soft, fine sand almost the consistency of talcum powder. When that happened, we all had to get off and help to free the Landrover. Sometimes, all it took was for Neil to reverse a little and then power his way through. Other times though, we had to get off and physically push the vehicle to help it on its way. On a few occasions, we even had to dig channels in the sand in front of the wheels to provide a better track. We went round one bend and saw an incline ahead of us that seemed to go up forever. Neil revved the engine and powered his way up the first 50 metres or so but then simply bogged down. The Land Rover and trailer were just too heavy to take the sand. We all had to get off and push from the front as Neil tried to reverse down the slope. It seemed that there was only the one road, but after speaking to the local people, they showed Neil a little used track that skirted the hill and came out on the other side. The going was just as tough but at least we got through. Neil put that one into the memory banks for later on. As if that wasn't enough, often the sand road wound its way through a grove of trees. The over-hanging branches clattered against the vehicle roof and sides, sending a bombardment of green mangoes into where we were sitting. As we passed each of the villages, small children would race down to the road, waving and shouting "Makua, makua" which Neil told us meant "white people!" we spent most of our time waving back at the children, who seemed delighted to see us.

Close on the tails of the children, came the suicidal dogs. Mangy looking animals that seemed determined to die under the wheels of the Land Rover or trailer. They would race alongside the truck, barking and snarling, inches away from the tyres. We couldn't go that fast, so most of them were able to keep up with us quite well but they were so engrossed in chasing the truck, some of them didn't see the large bushes blocking their path. On a few occasions, Neil steered quite nicely towards the bush, only to hear the yelp of surprise from the dogs as they collided with a thick, impenetrable bush. One dog, obviously particularly thick, came racing down the slope toward the Land Rover, realised at the last second it was going too fast and tried to do a four-paw stop, sliding on its buttocks. It crashed quite spectacularly into the rear wheel of the trailer and bounced back a foot or two.

We stopped for lunch midway between two villages and instantly became surrounded by curious villagers. The same ritual with the leftover lunch was performed and the bag was very swiftly whisked away. Although dubious at first, I later came to accept this as just part of the adventure.

Later that afternoon, we saw a thin yellow line on the horizon, the new Mongu road connecting Mongu to Kalabo. A few minutes later, we drove up a steep incline and popped out onto a hard-sand road where the surface was still sand but had been compacted hard by other vehicles. It was now about 3-30 in the afternoon and Neil was against the clock for driving the remaining 15 kilometres to Kalabo and booking us into the national park. The office closed at 4pm, sharp! We just made it and whilst Neil was completing the bureaucratic nightmare of checking us into the park, we clients had a look around. It was another small town which had obviously grown from trading with African people living in and around the National park area. Some of the road was even tarred. There was a lovely river flowing through the town, the Luanginga, which Neil had already told us we would have to cross. It looked pretty deep to me! Once clear of the office booking-in procedure, we scrambled back onto the Land Rover and headed away from the river. Suddenly, we turned sharp right onto yet another sand road, albeit in amongst houses and buildings. We dropped down a pretty steep slope, crossed a small stream and stopped at the edge of the Luanginga. I could see lots of activity down by the river's edge, women washing clothes, men repairing fishing nets and whilst in the town, I had seen some men standing by a rather dodgy looking ferry. Neil later told us that the park officials always told him to cross the river via the ferry and he always said, yes of course he would. As soon as he left the office, he would drive quickly down to the river away from the office to where we now stood. He told us that he had once tried to obey the rules and use the ferry but the weight of the Land Rover and trailer caused the ferry to drift with only the front wheels of the vehicle on the ferry. He stopped trying to drive onto it, but because of the drift, the Land Rover and trailer began to "jack-knife". Somebody had to physically hold the ferry in place with ropes to stop it from pulling up its retaining stakes from the sandy banks. The Land Rover eventually had to be towed out by a tractor; not very elegant! We, on the other hand, were going to drive across the river! Right!

Neil and Aupo both stripped down to their shorts and waded across the river, first along the route the left wheels would take and then back across the river where the other wheels would go. This was just to check for any deep holes in the river bottom which the Land Rover might drop into. We stowed everything away off the floor and some of the others waded waist deep across the river to photograph and film Neil driving across. I personally thought the water was too deep. However, he dropped the front end into the water and then came at a steady pace across the current. The bow-wave was almost up to bonnet level and I couldn't see any of the wheels. When he climbed out on the other side, water streamed from the footwells and doors of the Land Rover. I stayed on the truck as we crossed because, in some perverse way, if anything happened to the Land Rover as it crossed, such as stalling or being swept away by the current, sceptical as I was, I wanted to be a part of it. When we got to the other side safely, I was elated and mildly disappointed at the same time! We stayed at the river for a little longer, replenishing our water tanks direct from the Luanginga. Neil had a rudimentary, but effective siphon system which had the job done in no time at all. He told us the water was not fit for us to drink direct from the river, but we could wash and cook with it. We left the river at about 5pm and drove a short distance to a small clearing in the trees on the edge of the National Park. We made camp here and after dinner and briefing, we all fell into our bedrolls and I for one, slept extremely well after an arduous day waving and pushing a three-ton Landrover.

The following morning, we had a leisurely breakfast around 7am and then packed up our camp. Today was the day we would enter the Liuwa Plains National Park and would signal the start of a four day wander across seemingly endless plains and horizons.

Neil had already informed us that we would be heading for a camp in the bush named Lyangu. When the park had first been established, it was possible to drive into the park and literally find a spot in the bush to set up camp, much as we had already done on the way up. Unfortunately, too many unscrupulous groups of campers had left these ad hoc camp sites too untidy, with old tin cans and beer cans much in evidence. They should have taken ALL rubbish out with them, but instead, had chosen simply to leave it in situ where it would not only look unsightly but could also damage wildlife and the environment. When Africa Parks took on the management of the park, they established three camps, Kwale, Katoyana and Lyangu. None of them has fences around and they are all secreted in the bush; they have rudimentary facilities such as toilets and dribbley showers, although later experience of the showers would show that our "bush-showers" were far more efficient and preferable. The camps all have local people to administer them, which brings much needed income to the communities.

For the first few kilometres, the landscape was forested in a sandy soil. At one stage, we passed a line of low, wicker fences set in a slight curve. Neil explained that these were fish traps. Although the area looked totally dry, in the wet season, the area was largely flooded and the local people used these traps to catch small fish in large numbers to sell in Kalabo market, which we would see later on our way back. As we were looking at the traps, Helmut suddenly cried "look" and pointed to the road ahead. A huge brown snake was sliding across the sand into the undergrowth. By the time we had driven the five metres or so to where it had been, it was gone.

The forested area gradually gave way to grassy plains and we saw our first wildebeest, properly named the Blue Wildebeest or Brindled Gnu. At this time of the year, October/November/December, they come east in their thousands from Angola in search of fresh grass made lush by the first rains of the season. With them, come zebra and a few other antelope. As we drove further and further onto the plains, the numbers of wildebeest increased dramatically. As the Land Rover approached, the wildebeest would take off in an odd springing gallop, its spindly legs seemingly too thin to support its weight. After a few shorts strides, the wildebeest would look back at us, snort and then continue its lazy gallop away. I noticed that there were a lot of calves with the various herds. Neil explained that wildebeest were one of several breeds of animal that drop their young more or less at the same time. This is the best way they have of protecting their young from predatory animals; strength in numbers, I suppose!

After stopping several times to watch the odd-looking wildebeest, we arrived at our camp, Lyangu. As we drove along the approach road, Neil dutifully stopped at a large sign with a large rudimentary "STOP" painted on it. Not blessed with the gift of patience, he sounded the horn and out from a crude shelter of branches, came a young African man. He welcomed us as best he could in faltering English, shook hands with Neil and pointed to where we were to camp. Neil however, had found out at the office that we were the only people booked into the camp for the entire four days and so just went off in search of the best place to set up camp. It wasn't where the young man had pointed but he didn't seem to mind. The entire camp was made up of separate and fairly small areas in which to camp. The toilets and showers were placed centrally and so Neil's choice was naturally the place nearest the amenities. Good old Neil!!

We had arrived around lunchtime and ate a leisurely meal, fiddled with our bags for a while, sat around chatting and drinking tea and coffee, and at around 4pm, we set off to explore the area. I don't propose to describe in detail every single day we spent on the plains, I think that would be rather boring for the reader. Instead, I will give a synopsis, highlighting the more memorable moments and sightings.

Our first day on the plains had been a real scorcher, piercing blue skies and not a cloud in sight. During the evening though, some cloud had built up but it still promised to be a memorable sunset. Neil told us we were heading for an area known as "Palm", so-called because of the one palm tree that grew there. Thousands of years ago, the entire area of the Liuwa Plains had been a vast desert, hence the sand and this remaining palm tree, where once there had been many. There were a few other palms dotted over the plains, but this was apparently the biggest. We drove by some waterholes on the way out to "Palm" hoping to catch some hyena lying on the grassy banks before going out to hunt for food. No luck on this occasion, but we did get to see a magnificent sunset behind the palm tree. The clouds turned a fiery red before finally getting duller and the light giving way to gloom and then darkness. When we got back to camp, Aupo had most of the dinner done. We opened some bottles of wine, ate a fabulous meal and chatted long into the night before finally going to bed. In the distance, I could hear the "laugh" of the hyena as they also chatted to each other.

The following morning, we set off early, around 0630 to explore the plains. We drove along tracks in the sand, sometimes no more than mere impressions in the grass, that didn't seem to lead anywhere, except to the horizon. We drove past thousands of wildebeest and zebra, often stopping to watch the wildebeest calves as they played and gamboled behind their mothers. The bird life on the plains was wonderful; the majestic Southern Crowned Cranes seemed to glide across the ground as they walked and as we got nearer, they took to the skies with a lazy beat of their wings; the haughty Secretary Bird strutting along and the myriad plover, ducks, rollers and many others with plumage of bright and vivid colours. On a seemingly empty plain, we found ourselves stopping every few kilometres to watch something new. It was always quite difficult for us to get close to the animals. Unlike the game of the parks in Botswana, these animals were not used to seeing humans or vehicles and would take off at a gallop at our approach. The little Oribi were especially nervous and they would exit the scene like express trains. As skilful as Neil clearly was, he could never get us really close; good job we all had decent lenses on our cameras then!

One day, as we were making our way to the north of the plains, Neil stopped the Land Rover and gazed ahead of us with a pair of field glasses. "Ah" he exclaimed, "homo sapiens!" On the far horizon, we could just about make out a line of four or five humans walking along. Although not really allowed to drive off the "roads", Neil immediately turned us off the track and headed for the little group. They were quite some way off in the distance and we had to get a bit of a wiggle on to catch them. Eventually, on the horizon, we saw a clump of trees and as we got nearer, it was obvious this was their temporary camp. There were crude shelters of grass and sticks, evidence of cooking fires and most importantly, racks of drying fish. I remembered that on our way onto the plains on that first day, we had passed a small group of people walking in the direction of Kalabo, about 40 kilometres distant, carrying bundles of dried fish to sell in the market. On closer inspection of the fish, I could see that they had obviously been there for some days, tiny little maggots were crawling all over the flesh. We all took some photos, well lots of photos actually and then set off to find the fishermen.

As we breasted a small hillock, we saw a large lake ahead of us and there were our fishermen, five men in total, in the middle of the lake, fishing in a way that had not changed in generation after generation. Before we all jumped off the Land Rover, Neil told us that we were about to watch something that very few white people ever get the privilege to watch; African men fishing in a traditional African way. He warned us not to encroach on their activities, remain a respectful distance from them and definitely not to take off shoes and socks and go paddling in the lake. There were plenty of little nasties lurking in the shallow water, just waiting for nice plump, white flesh to come along and provide them with munch material. The Africans were obviously immune.

Four of the men were in the middle of the lake, stretching a long net across the lake and gradually bringing it to one of the shallower ends, in effect, herding the fish into a smaller space. However, the one remaining fisherman was wading in the shallows along the edge of the lake. He was holding a bunch of three spears above his head as he carefully made his way along the edge. Suddenly, he loosed all three spears at the same time into the water. One of the spears had impaled a large catfish-type fish, and he brought it up wriggling and struggling to break free. He dropped into a basket he was carrying over his shoulder, retrieved his three spears and carried on. The purpose of having the three spears became obvious. If he only had one, he had just one chance of spearing the fish, but with three, they splayed out as they were thrown and so had a far greater chance of catching the prey. The spears themselves were simple lengths of wood with a crude metal point, just bound to the end. After herding what fish they could, the other four simply set about spearing them and throwing them into baskets. During the rainy season, these cat-fish are plentiful, but during the dry weather when the lakes dry up, they bury themselves into the mud and lie dormant till the next rains come along.

We watched these men fishing for about an hour and then set off back to camp for a brunch.

We spent the rest of the day lazing around the camp, some of us writing, some sleeping and Neil and Aupo busied themselves with maintenance on the Land Rover. We had taken a few punctures on the way up and these needed repairing before our return journey. We went back out onto the plains later in the afternoon and went to explore some other waterholes, looking for hyena. They love to lie on the soft grassy verges of the waterhole. We were rewarded by finding a group of four hyena, two actually lying in the shallow water and two just on the bank. They were pretty sleepy and only gave us a casual glance as we manouvered as close to them as we could. Over the next couple of days, we saw many more hyena out on the plains, some even coming close to the Land Rover to investigate us; curious looking creatures with huge shoulders and powerful jaws. They looked every inch, the survivors they are.

Although lacking the larger game animals such as giraffe and elephant, the wildlife we encountered on the plains was extensive and exciting. One early morning, we watched a Snouted Cobra snake hunting down a hole in the sandy track. It was continually burrowing into the hole, trying to locate and kill whatever it thought was down there. Suddenly, from another hole close by, we saw a huge toad emerge and hot-hop away from this powerful and deadly looking predator. The snake eventually gave up and slithered away into the long grass. On another occasion, I photographed a Green Mamba snake near my tent. I was actually taking a pee when I saw it hunting down small holes. By the time I had retrieved my camera, the snake had started to climb into a tree but I managed to take some pictures as it wound its way along a low branch. However, the highlight of our game hunting expeditions was when we saw and watched the only lion known to be on the plains. A huge female, dubbed the Matamanene Lion as this was the area she could be found in, we found her one morning striding majestically across the plain. As we watched her and as if by telepathic command, she lay down in a sandy spot, not too far from where we were. Once again, we disobeyed the park rules and drove as close to her as we could. She was magnificent, in superb condition and totally unphased by our presence. She had apparently been on the plains for some years, hunting small game such as Oribi antelope and taking wildebeest when she could.

Members of the Lozi tribe lived in small villages dotted around the edges of the plains. Our camp attendant belonged to one such village and he invited us to go to his village one afternoon to visit and watch his people dancing. We set off for the village just after lunch, with the attendant guiding Neil through the bush. The track soon disappeared and we were driving over very difficult terrain, very bumpy with long grass hiding the ground. It got more and more difficult and eventually Neil called a halt. He said he didn't want to risk going any further with the vehicle. The ground was quite soft and the grass very green, indicating that water was near. He decided to turn the vehicle around and return to firm ground where we could leave the Land Rover and walk the rest of the way. Apparently, the golden rule is that you always follow your own tracks out of an area and Neil was attempting to turn the vehicle around to pick up his tracks, when suddenly, the Land Rover lurched violently and alarmingly over to one side. Instinctively, I and the rest of the group lunged for the high side of the vehicle in case she toppled right over. Thankfully, she came to rest at an angle of about 30 degrees over to the driver's side. We were only allowed to get off the vehicle once Neil had decided that she was stable and not liable to tilt further without our weight. Unknown to Neil, he had attempted to turn the vehicle around right on the edge of a large marshy area. Just looking at the terrain, the marshy area looked no different to the solid ground we had been on. His instinct had proved correct. Had we driven any further, the front of the Land Rover would have gone over the edge into the swamp. However, we had come to rest with the two right side wheels just over the edge but sitting in soft swampy mud. Attempts to drive out proved unsuccessful as the mud simply filled in the tyre treads as the wheels spun, making it like trying to drive over ice. Within five minutes, all the villagers had come out to watch the spectacle and Neil soon had them organised into pulling and pushing parties, again without success. We dug long trenches into the mud away from the wheels to provide them with some sort of traction, but again the wheels simply span in the mud. Grasses and branches were put down without success, swearing in English didn't help, the dozens of ideas coming from the villagers didn't help, but we eventually got her out by placing some long poles which the villagers produced, into the trenches and thankfully the wheels just caught enough of the wood to get a grip and although the branches were sent spinning away, she came out onto the level. A grinning but very muddy Neil simply stated, "That's safari for you!"

Once we had stowed all the ropes and digging equipment back on the Landrover, we walked into the village and listened to the villagers making music from a xylophone type instrument. We talked with the villagers as best we could and had great fun joining in the dancing around the music makers. Eventually, it was time to leave and return to camp for a well earned rest and another delicious meal. It was Helmut's birthday that day and whilst we had been away, Aupo had baked a cake! Miles from anywhere, on an open fire with no oven, Aupo had baked a superb sponge cake! Fantastic!

We spent the last day much as we had spent the previous three, wandering over the plains. In all that time, we saw only one other vehicle and that was way in the distance on the horizon. To all intents and purposes, we were completely alone in that wilderness. We spent our last evening as we had spent the first, drinking wine at

Palm and watching the sunset; a perfect end to four wonderful days on the open African plains.

The following morning, we packed up our camp and began the return journey, heading first back towards the town of Kalabo. Neil drove back through the river, checked us out of the park and then drove us into the market on the outskirts of the town. Aupo stayed with the vehicle whilst Neil went off in search of some charcoal for the fire and some fresh tomatoes and rolls. He and Aupo had made bread for us in camp, but it was getting stale and hard. Fresh bread rolls would be a bonus. We could explore the market for an hour or so. It was a typical African market with tiny little stalls set off the main roadway, selling mainly colourful printed wraps, much like a sarong, called chitengis. I thought they would be the perfect gift to take home and at around the equivalent of £2 each, would not break my bank. At the far end of the market, there were dozens of women all squatting on the ground around small piles of mangos, tomatoes and eggs, each calling out to passers-by trying to sell their wares. I found I had to be quite firm in rejecting their efforts to sell me what I didn't actually want, they were very persuasive. It was yet another taste of rural African life.

Fully provisioned with charcoal and tomatoes, we set off to drive back along the Mango Tree road. It was as difficult going back as it was coming up with Neil having to grind our way through the sand. We got stuck again and again. Sometimes, it seemed almost impossible that we would get the Land Rover out of the sand, but Neil had lots of tricks and methods up his sleeve to get us going again. We finally drove into the little town of Sinongu at the end of the Mango Tree Road about five hours later and made a wild-camp in the bush shortly after. Aupo immediately got a fire going and put on a large pot of water to heat up. Within 30minutes, we had our first warm shower, in the bush for over four days. It was very nice to be able to stand in a proper shower cubicle in the camp on the plains, but the water was always cold and there is something magical about being able to stand naked under a warm shower and look out onto virgin African bush.

That night, we had a terrific thunderstorm. The clouds had been gathering all day and we had gone to bed with distant rumbles of thunder and flashes of lightning getting ever nearer. The storm broke right over our camp about 2 hours later. The rain came down in torrents. The tents we had were completely waterproof, so we all stayed nice and dry. The sound of the rain pounding down on the fabric was phenomenal but it paled compared to the sound of the thunder. The lightning strikes and thunder claps came as one and the thunder was so explosive and sudden, it made your eardrums hurt. The storm slowly built to a crescendo, so violent and continuous it made me shudder. And then, nothing! It was as if the tap had been switched off, no sound apart from the dripping of water off the leaves of the trees. It had lasted a little over 30 minutes but it seemed like hours.

The next day, the driving was easier as the rain had firmed up the sand. We had driven about 10 kilometres from the camp, when Neil stopped at a fork in the road. He turned round to us in the back and said, "We are at a fork. If we go to the right, we go back the same way as we came up, safe with no problems. If we go left, we will have to cross another river about 30 kilometres down the road. If the river is too swollen for the Land Rover to cross, I will not take us through and we will have to come back to this point and take the easy way back. We will hit the same road which ever way we go. Which way would you like to go, unanimous decision only!" As one, we all shouted, "The river!!" I think Neil was secretly pleased we made this decision, it would be another adventure for all of us.

We arrived at the river, The Lueti about 2 hours later and it was much wider than the one we crossed to get onto the plains. Neil did his usual trick of wading through the water along both tracks of the wheels. When he got back to our side, he had a long discussion with Aupo and it was clear that the water level was right on the cusp of what was safe for us and the vehicle. Just looking at his shorts, the water level was about waist deep. By this time, several local villagers had arrived to watch what we were doing and Neil then had a discussion with one of the elders who had asked him to take a young woman and her sick son across the river to the clinic on the other side. He made the decision to cross and we cleared everything valuable from the floor of the Land Rover, got our cameras ready and chatted animatedly about this crossing. Neil prepared the vehicle by placing a tent cover across the radiator grill to prevent too much water entering the engine space. He made sure everything was ready and finally drove in to the water. As he got to the centre of the river, the water was streaming over the bonnet and up the windscreen. It was pouring through the gaps in the door-flap and flooding the footwells. He drove across at a well rehearsed steady speed and finally emerged on the other side, stopping for a few minutes to allow all the water to drain away. We were all laughing and whooping excitedly like little children. In front of us, lay the wide flood plain of the Lueti with a barely discernible track to the other side. It was a bumpy ride across the plain but eventually, we climbed a small bank to regain the road. The lady was dropped at the clinic a few hundred metres away and we continued on to Kalangola where we stopped for a rest. There was the usual gaggle of ladies squatting by the roadside with small piles of vegetables they had grown in their gardens, waiting endlessly to make sales that would amount to just a few pence. A couple of us had a laugh and a joke with the ladies still hanging their wares out of the windows of the brothel and then we carried on. Lunch was taken under an enormous tree in the middle of a field and at around 4pm that afternoon, we arrived at a camp we had passed on the way up, Thebe River Safaris, used mainly by fishermen hunting the legendary tigerfish. Without doubt, this camp was sited in one of the most beautiful spots imaginable. The tent area was situated in amongst trees on a high bank overlooking the Zambezi. At this point the river snaked around bends created by the ancient, dark basalt rocks, formed eons earlier by cooling lava. The slow moving water had a deep blue hue and created swirling eddies at the edges of the river where the current tried to turn back on itself. There was a small drinks bar at the far end of the camp, where we took some beers and sat out on a balcony built right out over the river. At this time of the year, November, the water level is low, but in flood, the river level comes right up, almost touching the balcony. As I looked out over the river, I could see a small mokkorro, a dug-out canoe, with two people paddling lazily down the river. It was a scene of simple tranquillity.

After a late breakfast the next day, we packed up small rucksacks and headed the few kilometres back up the road to a point where we would cross the river and visit the magnificent Ngonye Falls, or Sioma Falls as they were sometimes known. Neil had described these falls as a little known jewel of this part of Africa, second in majesty only to the vast and thunderous Victoria Falls hundreds of kilometres to the south, and he promised us a surprise when we got to the falls. First, however, we had to cross the river. Our mode of transport for the crossing would be a mokkorro. The local people make them from a hard-wood tree trunk and literally hollow them out with axes to form a narrow, flat bottomed craft, capable of taking three or four passengers. Having no keel, they are highly unstable in inexperienced hands, but the local people handle them with great skill and dexterity. Neil had just one warning for us all, "Sit still! If you move around, you will tip over!" The action of the paddling caused the craft to rock from side to side, as I thought, quite alarmingly. The boatsman though, very skilfully countered these imbalances and very soon, we were all safely across. We walked a few hundred kilometres across the top of some flat rocks, clambered over some large boulders and arrived at the spectacular Ngonye Falls. Neil wasn't wrong, they are fantastic. Horseshoe in shape, the river bed drops from one level to another about 20 metres down. The volume of water cascading over the falls even at this low water period, was incredible. The sight and sound of the water crashing over the edge was mesmerising; I found myself staring for long periods at the top of the falls and letting my eyes follow the water down to the maelstrom that was the lower level. Spray was hanging permanently in the air, enough to give us a good soaking but not enough to obscure our view. I couldn't even begin to imagine the sight of these falls when the water level was high and in a way, I was glad to be seeing them at this time because at high water, the falls themselves would almost disappear from the sheer volume of water flowing over the edge.

Neil had brought our lunch along in his pack and we ate sitting on the rocks, looking at one of nature's marvels.

After lunch, Neil gathered us all together and told us to follow him. We walked over the flat rocks and came to an area of large, flat-faced rocks, below which, water emerged from under the rocks themselves. He explained that at this point, the Zambezi River actually flowed underground and emerged here, to form small pools and a fairly swift current that went down several levels. The 'surprise' was that we could actually go swimming in the Zambezi. All of us stripped down to underwear and gingerly stepped in to the flow. The water was surprisingly warm and crystal clear. I don't actually mean we could do breast-stroke in the river, but we could move around totally immersed or simply lie at the head of a small waterfall and let the lovely water flow over us. I found a terrific spot where I could sit on a submerged rock and lean backwards against the current. If I balanced correctly, the force of the water hitting my back was enough to prevent me from falling completely over. We stayed in the river till about 2pm, at which time, we left this beautiful spot and headed back to camp. Rain clouds had started to gather and we made it back to our tents just as a storm hit us. It only lasted a couple of minutes before the sun came back out and we could sit and discuss animatedly what we had done at the falls. Our last dinner in camp was a superbly cooked barbecue of boererwors sausage and chops with a pasta dish, followed by tinned fruit and custard.

The next day, we packed up our camp and set off on the 300 kilometre trip back to Livingstone, where our safari would finish. The road was just as bad and the almost daily rain, had filled the massive potholes to overflowing. We reached Sesheke, where we had crossed into Zambia from the Caprivi Strip in Nambia just before lunchtime and whilst Neil and Aupo re-inflated the tyres for tarmac driving, we had a rest and a leg-stretch. After lunch, we ploughed on towards Livingstone. As we passed the turnoff for the ferry across the Zambezi at Kazangula, I noticed that both sides of the road were still stacked with lorries waiting to cross into Botswana.

We finally drove into "The Waterfront" lodge where we would be staying at around 4pm. The drive had been long and hard. Neil must have been exhausted, but he still found the time to see that our rooms were as clean and tidy as they should be with sheets on the beds and towels in the bathroom; a proper bathroom! As the name suggests, the lodge is situated right on the water's edge of the Zambezi and our first evening was spent cruising the river at sunset. We saw some elephant and giraffe on the banks of the river, some hippopotamus and crocodile in the river and many species of birds over the river.

During the drive from Thebe camp to Livingstone, I had been thinking about what activities I would like to do in Livingstone, which shares the spectacle of the tremendous Victoria Falls with its neighbour of the same name in Zimbabwe. Livingstone has become an absolute mecca for thrill seekers from all over the world, white water rafting, flights over the falls in helicopters or microlights, bungee jumping off the famous Victoria Falls bridge, gorge-swinging, walking safaris in the Zambezi National Park, cycling, jet-boating and many more. Having been rafting before, I decided simply to take a microlight flight over the Falls. It was a stunning view, made all the more exciting by the open sided microlight. We flew across the entire 1700 metre length of the falls, from Devil's Cataract and then over Main Falls, Horseshoe Falls, Rainbow Falls and finally, Eastern Cataract. At this time of year, November, an average of 550 million litres of water flows over the falls every minute. Neil spent the day ferrying us to and from our activity choices. I suspect Aupo spent the day sleeping! Later that evening, we took our last dinner at a restaurant in Livingstone town.

My final morning was spent packing my now grubby clothes into my battered rucksack ready for the transfer to Livingstone airport, from where I would fly to Johannesburg in South Africa and then home to England. Before we left the lodge, my fellow travellers and I drank some wine and toasted each other, but mostly, we toasted Neil and Aupo. They had worked very hard to give us a wonderful trip and it was obvious that they did it because they enjoyed it. We shook hands and hugged each other warmly when it was time to go.

It had been a superb trip, well organised and lots of fun. I had seen things I would probably never see again and I had done things I would probably never do again. And it didn't matter if I didn't, the memories of this "safari" would not fade in a hurry.

The Hyena Trail, "Not for the faint-hearted" the internet website had stated, and I could now see why!

Lightning Source UK Ltd.
Milton Keynes UK
UKOW050357080312

188559UK00001B/109/P

9 781907 294952